GODDESS

The Secret Lives of
Marilyn Monroe

Anthony Summers

WEIDENFELD & NICOLSON

First published in Great Britain in 1985 by Victor Gollancz
First published in paperback by Indigo
This edition published in 2022 by Weidenfeld & Nicolson,
an imprint of The Orion Publishing Group Ltd
Carmelite House, 50 Victoria Embankment
London EC4Y 0DZ

An Hachette UK Company

3 5 7 9 10 8 6 4

A CIP catalogue record for this book is
available from the British Library.

ISBN (Mass Market Paperback) 978 1 4746 2594 4
ISBN (eBook) 978 1 7802 2707 8

Typeset by Input Data Services Ltd, Somerset

Printed and bound in Great Britain by Clays Ltd, Elcograf S.p.A.

www.weidenfeldandnicolson.co.uk
www.orionbooks.co.uk

for Olga and Ronan

'You're right about her not being easy to know. One sees her with intensity – sees her more than one sees almost anyone; but then one discovers that that isn't knowing her.'

HENRY JAMES
The Wings of the Dove

'She did originate something. She was the first person I know of who was truly unconventional. She was a nineteen-sixties person before it started – way before it started – like ten years.'

ARTHUR MILLER

'I can't tell the whole story . . . Talk to Robert Kennedy.'

Dr Ralph Greenson, Monroe's psychiatrist

Contents

Part One

INTO THE LAND OF THE SCORPIONS

'The Industry giveth, and the Industry taketh away. Hollywood, the dream factory, had created a dream girl. Could she awaken to reality? And what was the reality? Was there a life for her outside the dream?'

NORMAN ROSTEN,
Poet and Marilyn's longtime friend

'In Hollywood, "starlet" is the name for any woman under thirty not employed in a brothel.'

BEN HECHT,
with whom Marilyn did her first major interviews

1

The hour before midnight, Saturday, August 4, 1962, in Los Angeles. In the auditorium of the Hollywood Bowl, under a sickle moon, the crowd was listening to the bittersweet strains of the Henry Mancini orchestra.

Abruptly, unnoticed by most of the concertgoers, there was a minor disturbance. An attendant, whispering apologetically, passed an urgent message to a man seated in one of the higher-priced seats. The man rose, walked to a telephone, and listened. Then he spoke a few terse sentences, summoned his wife, and hurried to his car.

In the night hours that followed, as Los Angeles slept, there would be other little incidents, more comings and goings. Telephones would jangle at bedsides around the city, rousing doctors, a prominent lawyer, leading figures in show business, and private detectives. A famous actor, brother-in-law of the President of the United States, would place a call to Washington. Some of the actor's neighbors, in their fine houses on the beach, would be roused from sleep by the clatter of a helicopter. An ambulance would be summoned to an unpretentious house in the suburbs.

The public would learn nothing of these nocturnal events, nor, so far as we know, were they recorded by any official body. Yet the event that triggered them was the news story of the year, one that received more coverage than even the Missile Crisis, the near-nuclear confrontation that followed a few weeks later. Marilyn Monroe was dead.

Exactly twenty years later, in 1982, the Los Angeles District Attorney would reopen inquiries into a case that had never ceased to be the subject of rumor and controversy. His brief was limited. Was there sufficient evidence to open a criminal investigation? Could Monroe have been murdered? After four months, the DA was advised that the evidence failed 'to support any theory of criminal conduct.' This, though, had been only a 'threshold investigation.'

The DA's report would acknowledge that 'factual discrepancies' and 'unanswered questions' had surfaced during the Monroe inquiry. Privately, officials made it clear that they felt they had stumbled into a morass of untruth and obfuscation. Marilyn Monroe may, they surmised, have died by her own hand. Some felt, nevertheless, that something was covered up in 1962.

That something involved Monroe's relations with President John Kennedy and his brother Robert – and, in particular, Robert Kennedy's activities at the time Monroe died.

The DA's men would shrug ruefully when they discussed the Kennedy angle. 'We were not asked,' said one, 'to investigate a political cover-up.' With far less excuse, most of the press at the time preferred the easy wallow in pathos to serious reporting. Afterward, for all the profusion of writing about Marilyn Monroe, no author attempted a professional inquiry into the last days of the woman most firmly enthroned as the goddess of the American Century.

Who was the woman who turned herself into 'Marilyn Monroe'? She had a body, in truth, not so unlike other female bodies. How did she make us notice her more than any other woman, in her time and on into the end of the twentieth century? How much of this alchemy was achieved by talent, how much in the carefully chosen embraces of powerful males? What was at the hidden center of the phenomenon that was Marilyn Monroe?

Behind the hyperbole and the hysteria there was a child who grew to be a woman, who was a symbol of love yet essentially lonely, who died famously but in folly at the age of thirty-six. She postured as the world's mistress, yet yearned for monogamy and motherhood. The profile was crude while the pursuit was for culture. The brilliance of the actress masked a seriously disturbed psyche. The private person read philosophy and made a serious study of human anatomy, yet at times drowned herself in drugs and alcohol. Marilyn Monroe anticipated a decade that trumpeted fulfillment and achieved only confusion.

She told her last interviewer: 'When you're famous you kind of run into human nature in a raw kind of way . . . People you run into feel that, well, who is she – who does she think she is, Marilyn Monroe? It's nice to be included in people's fantasies but you also like to be accepted for your own sake.'

With another reporter, a few months earlier, she had mused, 'I wonder how I'll feel when I'm fifty?' Then, her mind turning to birthdays, she mentioned that she was born under the sign of Gemini.

'What kind of people are Geminis?' the reporter asked.

'Jekyll and Hyde. Two in one,' came the reply.

'And that's you?'

'More than two. I'm so many people. They shock me sometimes. I wish I was just *me*! I used to think I was going crazy, until I discovered some people I admired were like that, too.'

Marilyn – and we may call her Marilyn because that is how she is known from Connecticut to the Congo – never saw her fortieth birthday, let alone her half-century. Were she alive today, she would be in her mid-nineties. Yet her life long remained as unreliably reported as her death had been.

I thought it time to grant this goddess a measure of reality. Who do we think she was?

In 1983, unrecognized by passers-by, an elderly woman wearing a bucket hat regularly sallied forth into the streets of Gainesville, Florida, riding a tricycle with a red danger flag on the handle bars. The woman was a surprising survivor – Marilyn's octogenarian mother, living out her life in virtual anonymity.

Gladys Monroe – for Monroe was the name of Marilyn's maternal grandmother – was born in 1902, in Mexico, of American parents. By the age of twenty-four she had been married twice and borne two children, who were raised by relatives of her first husband. The second husband did not last long. He was gone by the time Marilyn was born on June 1, 1926, in Los Angeles General Hospital.

There was uncertainty about the identity of Marilyn's father. Her birth certificate identifies him as 'Edward Mortenson,' and her mother was married to a Martin E. Mortensen two years before Marilyn's birth. It appears he was a Norwegian immigrant, a baker who died in a motorcycle accident in 1929, but even that is disputed. At all events, although she used his name on official documents throughout her life, Marilyn later denied that Mortenson was her father.

Marilyn told one interviewer that her real father 'used to live in the same apartment building where my mother lived – he walked out and left her while I was getting born.' That scenario sits best with a man called Stanley Gifford. He worked for Consolidated Film Industries, where Marilyn's mother worked as a film cutter, and Gifford was apparently Gladys's lover about the time her marriage to Mortenson collapsed.

The infant Marilyn had to make do with an imagined father. Her mother once pointed to a photograph and said, 'That's your father.' She remembered the face of a man in a slouch hat – 'there was a lively smile in his eyes, and he had a thin moustache like Clark Gable.'

It was the beginning of a lifelong fantasy. As a child, Marilyn would recall, she told gullible friends that Clark Gable actually had been her father. In her last months, after she had acted with Gable in *The Misfits*, she fell back on the old fantasy. The widow of Marilyn's psychiatrist, Hildi Greenson, said, 'Marilyn had seen that photograph, and it looked like Gable, so sometimes she let herself believe her father was Gable.'

In 1962, the year of her death, Marilyn had to fill out an entry for 'Father's Name' on an official form. She wrote simply – and in her secretary's opinion savagely – 'Unknown.'

If mystery surrounds Marilyn's father, the facts about her mother's side of the family are painfully well documented. Knowing what she knew of that history, Marilyn feared she was genetically prone to insanity. The fear was understandable.

Her maternal great-grandfather, Tilford Hogan, hanged himself at the age of eighty-two. Suicide among the aged is not uncommon. It is certainly not necessarily a sign of madness, but mental illness did run in the family.

The maternal grandfather, Otis Monroe, died in an institution of general paresis, according to the death certificate. Paresis, and specifically paretic dementia, is recognized as a form of insanity provoked by syphilis in its final stage.

Marilyn ran no risk of inheriting syphilis, but her maternal grandmother, Delia, also died in an asylum, at age fifty-one, a year after Marilyn's birth. She had been something of a religious zealot. The cause of her death was given as heart disease, with 'manic-depressive psychosis' as a contributory factor.

The adult Marilyn would claim that she remembered her grandmother trying to smother her shortly before she was sent to the mental hospital. Since Marilyn was only thirteen months old at the time, it is highly unlikely she really remembered any such thing. Her little horror story almost certainly belongs in the ragbag of fantasies with which Marilyn embroidered her youth.

Family life was virtually nonexistent. After Marilyn's birth, apparently feeling unable to cope with full-time motherhood, Gladys went back to her work as a film cutter. She provided for her baby, but left her most of the time in the care of foster parents. Gladys's older children had long since been taken away by relatives of her first husband.

Catastrophe came when Marilyn was seven and living with her mother for a while. Gladys suffered a period of deep depression, then an explosion of rage and frustration. Some reports say she attacked a friend with a knife. She was promptly committed to the very hospital in which her own mother had died.

Except for brief periods, Gladys would remain confined until after Marilyn's death. Inez Melson, Marilyn's former business manager, was eventually appointed Gladys's guardian. She spent more time with her than anyone else, and considered her disturbed rather than insane.

'Marilyn's mother was overly taken up with her religion, Christian Science, and with evil,' Melson said. 'That was her area of disturbance. She figured she had done something wrong in her life, and was being punished for it.'

In that obsession Gladys was following the pattern set by her own mother. Religious fixation, and the notion of atoning for unspecified sin, is a feature found both in manic disorders and schizophrenia.

Marilyn had religious zeal thrust at her during childhood by Gladys and by one of the women who cared for her, and she remained a wobbly adherent of Christian Science into adulthood. With her, however, it was not a fixation. Marilyn would one day convert to the Jewish faith to marry the playwright Arthur Miller, and later cheerfully described herself as an 'atheist Jew.'

Marilyn was not definitely doomed to psychiatric illness, but she was born at serious risk. Psychiatrists consulted for this book point out that – as heavily documented in

8

Dear Board of Directors & all;
will you please pray &
help me, for I'm being used &
abused by *pugalush it*
works
My life as a Christian
Scientist and defrauded
me of the ~~living~~ goodness of the
dear mother Church." The
First Church of Christ
Scientist :" of which I'm a member
I helplessly pray for your
help! I shall alway be
your obedient servant
in spite of what apperances
seem to be. Always Love
Mrs Gladys P. Baker Eley

A letter from confinement of Marilyn's mother Gladys.
It is, typically, filled with religious references and signs of paranoia.

9

manuals used as guidelines by American doctors and the World Health Organization – manic and schizophrenic disorders frequently run in families.

This book will be an investigation of Marilyn's adult life, not of her childhood – that desolate, dislocated period has been well charted by earlier biographers. It was a time that the grown woman would never forget nor allow her public to ignore – ten foster homes, two years in the Los Angeles Orphans' Home, another foster home, and finally four years with the guardian appointed by county authorities after her mother's departure to an asylum.

This saga of deprivation made a classic launching pad for future psychiatric disorder. Dr Valérie Shikhverg, consultant psychiatrist at several New York hospitals, told me Marilyn was a prime candidate for what is today called a 'borderline' personality – someone who hovers 'on the border between psychotic and neurotic, with frequent fluctuations between the two.'

'The problems of such a person,' said Dr Shikhverg, 'originate very early in life. "Borderlines" tend to have had a mother who could not cope, or who suffered from overt psychosis. Their family histories typically feature separation or divorce, or the total absence of one or both parents during early childhood. Marilyn's background was tailor-made to make her "borderline."'

The 'borderline' person is likely to be emotionally unstable, excessively impulsive, and to show the world a mood that appears expansive and active. He or she is likely to be histrionic or seductive or overly concerned with good looks. A 'borderline' depends on constant external approval, loves applause, cannot bear to be alone, and suffers 'depressive, crashlike reactions' to rejection by others. A 'borderline' tends to abuse alcohol and drugs, and to make suicide threats as gestures to obtain help.

My Very Dear Mrs Melson:
I am so very thank-
full for all your many
kindness and good-
ness to me. May God
bless you & keep you.
give norma Jean my
Love and best wishes
also. I enjoyed the
Thanksgiving candy
you so kindly brought
me. I am very fond
of pepermint Christmas
candies —
with Love
and Gratitude
Mrs Gladys P. Eley.

A 1961 letter from Marilyn's mother to her guardian, Mrs Melson. In a copious correspondence, she only twice mentioned her famous daughter, 'Norma Jean'.

This personality profile, made on the basis of studies covering thousands of case histories, is chillingly recognizable in Marilyn Monroe. Marilyn's life was to be remorselessly faithful to the blueprint of her background, a scenario for brilliance and tragedy.

2

'My arrival in school, with painted lips and darkened brows, started everybody buzzing. Why I was a siren, I hadn't the faintest idea. I didn't want to be kissed, and I didn't dream of being seduced by a duke or a movie star. The truth was that with all my lipstick and mascara and precocious curves I was as unresponsive as a fossil. But I seemed to affect people quite otherwise.'

So spoke Marilyn Monroe in 1954, looking back on her teenage years. Thus at any rate, were her memories recorded by the writer Ben Hecht, to whom the newly successful star, at twenty-eight, told her 'life story' that year.

Hecht hoped to ghost the young Marilyn's autobiography, which had been commissioned by a major New York publisher. It is an important record, for Marilyn gave no other interviews of comparable scope. It is also controversial.

After a long series of talks with Hecht, Marilyn got him to read her the entire 160 pages of manuscript out loud. Then, according to Hecht's widow, she 'laughed and cried and expressed herself as "thrilled." She said she never imagined so wonderful a story could be written about her, and that Benny had captured every phase of her life.'

Marilyn even helped correct the manuscript, but then relations soured. Marilyn's husband at the time, Joe DiMaggio, reportedly objected to publication, and she backed out of the deal. When the material appeared anyway, in the *British Empire News,* Marilyn threatened to sue, alleging misquotation.

If the ghostwriter erred, so did Marilyn, for the truths in

her story were highly selective. Hecht reported to his editor during the interviews that he was sometimes sure Marilyn was fabricating. He explained, 'When I say lying, I mean she isn't telling the truth. I don't think so much that she is trying to deceive me as that she is a fantasizer.' Hecht found himself struggling to interpret Marilyn's 'odd little physical body language, to read when she was going into something fictional or when she was leveling.'

Many of Marilyn's statements on her early life, as reproduced in the Hecht manuscript, will be quoted in these pages. Where possible, they will be buttressed or countered by independent witnesses. We must treat what she tells us with informed skepticism, and that is no disadvantage. Marilyn, an international fantasy figure, constructed her image, both public and private, from a blend of fact and self-serving fantasy. She exercised to excess a common human license. Fantasy was part of this creature, and part of the challenge is to discover the woman who sheltered behind it.

What Marilyn did tell Ben Hecht was sad, strong stuff for the 1950s. What she did not tell might have finished her as an actress. At the time, indeed, it was nobody else's business.

At fifteen Marilyn was still 'Norma Jeane' (or Norma Jean, when she felt like spelling it that way), the name her mother had given her at birth. It was early that year, 1942, that her legal guardian, a middle-aged woman named Grace McKee, abruptly decided to thrust her charge into the adult world.

Norma Jeane's future triumphs and calamities would be defiantly of her own making. Her first marriage, however, was arranged. Grace McKee had decided to move East with her new husband, and they did not find it convenient to take Norma Jeane along. The answer was to find her a husband.

McKee saw a likely candidate in Jim Dougherty, the son of a neighbor she knew well. His family had seen the worst of the Great Depression – he was to recall living, at one stage, in a tent beside their battered car. At twenty-one he was tough and hardheaded, a gifted football player who had turned down college in favor of a job embalming corpses at a funeral home, then work as a night-shift fitter at Lockheed Aviation.

Jim Dougherty knew Norma Jeane. They had had a couple of dates, and he had enjoyed the discovery that, when dancing, she 'would lean extra close, eyes tight shut.' Norma Jeane 'laughed at the right moment and kept quiet when she was supposed to.' Even so, Dougherty was running around with a number of other girls.

It came as a total surprise to Jim Dougherty when Norma Jeane's guardian suggested he marry Norma Jeane. His mother passed on the message. It was a thought that had never even occurred to Dougherty, but he agreed when told the alternative would be to send Norma Jeane back to the orphanage. That, he said, was the way decisions were made in his family.

A wedding date was set for June, to give Norma Jeane time to turn sixteen. In the weeks that remained the couple belatedly started courting. Dougherty's pride and joy was his car, a 1940 Ford coupe, and he would whisk Norma Jeane to a trysting spot in the hills called Pop's Willow Lake. They would rent a canoe, paddle under the trees at the water's edge, and kiss.

They were duly married on June 19, 1942, when she was less than three weeks past her sixteenth birthday. There was no honeymoon. He went back to work at the aircraft factory on Monday morning.

Norma Jeane gave her account of the marriage in her first days of fame, in the interviews with Ben Hecht. Jim Dougherty finally told his full story in the seventies.

The couple seem to have been talking about entirely different relationships. She told Hecht, 'It was like being retired to a zoo. Actually our marriage was a sort of friendship with sexual privileges. I found out later that marriages are often no more than that. I was a peculiar wife. I disliked grown ups. . . . I liked boys and girls younger than me. I played games with them until my husband came out and started calling me to go to bed.'

Jim Dougherty seems not to have noticed such coolness. 'Our marriage,' he said, 'may have been made in some place short of heaven, like in the minds of two older ladies, but there was no pretense in how Norma Jeane and I felt about each other once we'd formed that partnership.'

At first the teenage wife was a hopeless housekeeper. She had no idea how to cook. Someone told her to put a pinch of salt in the coffee, so she made it a spoonful. Coffee came in handy to deal with a sparking short in the electrical wiring – she poured it over the carpet as well as the wiring, then locked herself in the bedroom. She served up raw fish.

Gradually, though, Norma Jeane learned. Dougherty said she prepared venison and rabbit really well, and cooked carrots and peas together 'because she liked the color.' All in all, the way Dougherty saw it, she had the makings of a good wife. Then, in the autumn of 1943, a year into their marriage, he joined the Merchant Marine.

The war was at first kind to Mr and Mrs Dougherty. He was merely posted to Catalina Island, just across the water from Los Angeles County, and Norma Jeane joined him there. The way it seemed to Dougherty, they spent an idyllic year together. They fished, swam, and got fit. She took weight-lifting lessons from a former Olympic champion. She showed herself off a little too much to the hordes of uniformed males on the island, but Dougherty was not a worrier. The couple went out a good deal, and one night

Norma Jeane spent most of the evening dancing with every man in the unit except Dougherty. When he said, 'Let's go home,' Norma Jeane wanted to dance some more. This caused their first real row, but still Dougherty felt secure.

He continued to feel secure in 1944, after the call came to go overseas. On arrival in New Guinea, he found a stack of letters waiting for him. Norma Jeane, now living with Dougherty's mother, had written nearly every day. The letters kept coming for months, while Dougherty sailed the Pacific and his teenage wife took a job at Radio Plane, a plant making aircraft used for target practice.

Norma Jeane inspected parachutes and sprayed fuselages. She would say later, 'I wore overalls in the factory. I was surprised that they insisted on this. Putting a girl in overalls is like having her work in tights, particularly if a girl knows how to wear them. The men buzzed around me just as the high-school boys had done. Maybe it was my fault that the men in the factory tried to date me and buy me drinks. I didn't feel like a married woman.'

In her letters, Norma Jeane told Jim how much she missed him. In one she quoted a song by Sammy Cahn and Jule Styne, whom she would one day know in the movie business. It was a song with a promise made by wartime sweethearts in Allied countries around the world. 'I'll walk alone,' she assured her sailor husband.

When Dougherty came home on his first leave after several months at sea, Norma Jeane was waiting at the railroad station. He recalled, 'We headed in my car for the most luxurious motor lodge on Ventura Boulevard, the La Fonda, and rarely left our room. Norma Jeane had bought a black net nightgown for the occasion and we had most of our meals brought to our room.' He did notice, that week, that his wife was drinking too much.

Shortly before he went back to sea, said Dougherty, 'a kind

of dread took hold of her. She didn't want to talk about or think of my leaving.' But Jim Dougherty had no choice about returning to the Pacific, and a few days later he did.

Norma Jeane went back to work at Radio Plane. At the end of 1944, with the war in its closing months, life changed. Or, more truthfully, Norma Jeane jumped at the chance to change it, when Private David Conover came to Radio Plane to take pictures of women doing war work.

Conover was an army photographer for an armed service motion picture unit. His commanding officer was Captain Ronald Reagan, the actor who was one day to become President of the United States. Conover's mission at Radio Plane was 'to take morale-boosting shots of pretty girls' for *Yank* magazine. He later said he noticed at once that the eighteen-year-old Norma Jeane was different, that 'her eyes held something that touched and intrigued me.' Conover photographed her on the assembly line and then – changed at his request into a clinging red sweater – during the lunchbreak. He told Norma Jeane she belonged on a magazine cover, not in a factory.

Conover's new discovery was making $20 a week working ten hours a day at Radio Plane. He offered her $5 an hour as a freelance model – unexpected pocket money which represented a bonanza to Norma Jeane. In the three weeks after meeting Conover there were several further picture sessions, and she joined him on a picture-taking safari through southern California. Some of the pictures ended up on the desk of the Blue Book Model Agency, and Norma Jeane was summoned for an interview. Her career as a cover girl had begun.

Success as a model came quickly. Soon photographs of Norma Jeane were appearing in girlie magazines with names like *Swank, Sir,* and *Peek.* Sometimes she would appear in a swimsuit, sometimes in shorts and halter top, but the pictures were perfectly respectable.

At nearly nineteen this model girl had a good figure – a thirty-five-inch bust which she used to the last centimeter* – and pale skin she liked to keep pale. She had shoulder-length California blond hair, really fair only in summer, when the sun bleached it. Norma Jeane had no trouble getting work as a model.

When Jim Dougherty next came home, after a voyage round the world, his wife was not waiting at the station. She arrived an hour late, blaming the delay on a modeling assignment. She seemed cool toward Dougherty, was no longer living with his mother, and had left her job at the factory.

Norma Jeane now only wanted to talk about her success as a pinup girl, and Dougherty could only make a pretense at being impressed. She had spent their savings on new clothes, and spent a good part of the precious leave going out on modeling jobs. In the coming months Dougherty tried to stay nearer home, making short hauls up and down the western seaboard of the United States.

At Christmas 1945, Norma Jeane found it impossible to be at home – another modeling assignment. There was a showdown when she returned. Dougherty said, 'I just told her she would have to choose between a modeling career and maybe the movies or a home life with me.'

Norma Jeane failed to respond, and Dougherty went back to sea. He was in China, halfway up the Yangtze River, buying bracelets and nail polish for Norma Jeane, when he next had news of her. It came in the form of a lawyer's letter, enclosing divorce papers for signature. Dougherty decided not to sign till he had seen his wife.

* Marilyn's studio liked to say it was larger – 37 inches was the official line in 1954. She herself once told a reporter she would like her epitaph to read 'Here lies Marilyn Monroe – 38-23-36.' Dress designer and sometime lover Billy Travilla, who should have known, said the true statistics – in Marilyn's prime – were 35-22-35. I have used his figure.

Early one morning, on his return to California, he took a taxi straight from the dock to the house where Norma Jeane was living. She came to the door pulling a wrap around her shoulders, exhausted. She was sorry, she said, but could they meet tomorrow? The next day, and at several subsequent meetings, Norma Jeane told him of her new resolve. She was going to become a movie actress.

Dougherty had once won first place at a high school Shakespeare festival, for his delivery of Shylock's 'revenge' speech in *The Merchant of Venice*. He said now, 'I always thought I was the ham around here. How come you want to perform all of a sudden?' Norma Jeane took his mockery, but insisted the marriage was over.

'There was this secret in me – acting,' she was to say years later. 'It was like being in jail and looking at a door that said "This Way Out."'

Norma Jeane had acted in school plays, usually playing male parts, but otherwise had no acting experience. Now, rattling in from the suburbs in the old car she had shared with Dougherty, she began exploring Hollywood.

'You sit alone,' she remembered later. 'It's night outside. Automobiles roll down Sunset Boulevard like an endless string of beetles. Their rubber tires make a purring high-class noise. You're hungry, and you say, "It's good for my waistline not to eat. There's nothing finer than a washboard belly."

'I used to think as I looked out on the Hollywood night, "There must be thousands of girls sitting alone like me, dreaming of becoming a movie star. But I'm not going to worry about them. I'm dreaming the hardest."'

3

'This is the end of my story of Norma Jeane. . . . I moved into a room in Hollywood to live by myself. I wanted to find out who I was. When I just wrote, "This is the end of Norma Jeane," I blushed as if I had been caught out in a lie. Because this sad, bitter child who grew up too fast is hardly ever out of my heart. With success all around me, I can still feel her frightened eyes looking out of mine. She keeps saying, "I never lived, I was never loved," and often I get confused and think it's I who am saying it.'

This was Marilyn, by then a household name, talking in 1954, and the confusion was real. As her actual psychiatrists would discover, and as armchair ones have insisted ever since, Norma Jeane did not cease to exist when Mrs Dougherty became an actress.

There was irony in the fact that the death certificate, in 1962, would refer only to the passing of a Hollywood invention called Marilyn Monroe. For it was Norma Jeane who died, a Norma Jeane who had spent most of her life presenting herself to the world and – most troubling of all – to herself, through a filter of untruth. Norma Jeane had begun weaving her web of delusion before the break with Jim Dougherty, and along with the fantasies there was some outright deceit. Only when that is dealt with can we move along to the actress called Marilyn Monroe.

The former Mrs Dougherty would tell Ben Hecht, 'I was completely faithful to my overseas husband.' Jim Dougherty could still maintain three decades later that 'it never entered my mind, and I don't believe to this day, that she was deceiving me. In all the years I was seeing her, I never knew Norma Jeane to lie. If she was having dates, she would have told me.'

A spouse often closes the shutters of the mind to the possibility of infidelity. In the lonely wartime sailor husband there was the need to close out pain. In ex-husband Dougherty, not least when the wife was Marilyn Monroe, there was the muffler of simple pride. The record, though, says Norma Jeane was unfaithful.

In late 1960, less than two years before her death, Marilyn herself told another interviewer, 'I didn't sleep around when I was married until my husband went into the service, and then it was just that I was so damn lonesome, and I had to have some kind of company, so once in a while I'd give in, mainly because I didn't want to be alone.'

By her own account, then, the teenage bride began deceiving her husband about halfway through their four-year marriage. There can be little doubt what she was up to over the bleak Christmas of 1945, when she left Dougherty alone at home while she stayed away on a modeling assignment.

Norma Jeane had told Jim in December that she had to go away for nearly a month, to work with a photographer named André de Dienes. He wanted to take her hundreds of miles north, to Washington State. The fee would be two hundred dollars, exactly the amount needed to pay for repairs to the Doughertys' old Ford. She said she did not really want to go, but felt she should, not only for the money, but because de Dienes was a prominent photographer who would be good for her career. So she went.

Norma Jeane called long-distance, in tears, while Jim Dougherty was eating his Christmas dinner. She said she wished she could be home but now felt obliged to stay with de Dienes. 'Most of his camera equipment was stolen because of me,' she explained. 'I left the car unlocked. . . .' When she did come home, said Dougherty, Norma Jeane refused to talk about the trip, except to say she never wanted to pose for de Dienes again.

André de Dienes, the immigrant son of a Hungarian banker, later told his side of what happened that Christmas. Aged thirty-two at the time, and a newcomer to California, he had been looking for a model who would pose outdoors in western settings, preferably nude. One day, in his bungalow at the Garden of Allah Hotel on Sunset Boulevard, the telephone rang. It was the Blue Book Agency, offering a new girl.

'There came this lovely little girl in a pink sweater and checkered slacks,' de Dienes was to recall. 'I fell right away in love with this young girl. In my subconscious I wanted to marry her. What was wrong with that? I was a nice young boy myself.'

That afternoon de Dienes, who was indeed to become a successful photographer, told Norma Jeane he wanted her to pose nude. She was unsure. As he recalled it, 'she told me she was married, but that her husband was at sea and she didn't love him.'

De Dienes began courting Norma Jeane in Dougherty's absence, sent flowers, came to dinner at her home. It was against this background that he and Norma Jeane set off on their Christmas trip.

Norma Jeane did not go to bed with de Dienes immediately. He said he tried to seduce her for days, until one happy night when they failed to find a hotel with two vacant rooms. Norma Jeane agreed to share a room – and her favors. 'She was lovely and very nice,' the Hungarian was to recall. 'But finally it was something she allowed me to do to her.' In bed, de Dienes recalled, nineteen-year-old Norma Jeane discovered variations on sex untried with Jim Dougherty.

While working outdoors in the snow with Norma Jeane, de Dienes was moved. 'She was sweet. Beautiful. Her smile. Her laughter. And she was frail – mentally and physically. As

23

soon as she finished her work she would hop back in the car and fall asleep. This girl had no business in show business. She was a sensitive, sweet little girl.'

Norma Jeane did leave the car unlocked, and de Dienes' equipment was stolen. He forgave her for that, and forgave her too when she still refused to pose in the nude. De Dienes was in love and soon, back in Los Angeles, he asked Norma Jeane to marry him. According to the photographer, she agreed. He then traveled on business to New York, where he papered his walls with her photographs.

Was de Dienes telling the truth? In this book there will be others, some more obscure than de Dienes, with claims to have bedded Marilyn. Were they her lovers, or were they braggarts and profiteers? The reader should know that those given this author's credence either convinced me in personal interviews, or were supported by other witnesses.

One man I did not believe was David Conover, the Army private who indeed took the photographs that led to her first modeling job – the pictures are there to prove it. He then went on to write a book claiming that he became Marilyn's lover and lifelong friend. A visit to Conover in Canada satisfied me that his 'documentation' was forged. He was either a confidence man or mentally ill, or both. Then there was Hans Jørgen Lembourn, a Dane who wrote a most literate account of what his publishers called 'a forty-night affair with Marilyn Monroe.' On analysis, his book has virtually no substance at all.

André de Dienes, on the other hand, had compelling backing. Jean-Louis, the fashion designer who served Marilyn in later years, knew de Dienes in the forties, and confirmed that 'he had a real relationship, a love affair, with Marilyn back then.' Was de Dienes a lone folly in the dying days of her marriage to Jim Dougherty, and how was he treated in the end?

Still the ardent suitor, still assuming himself engaged to

Norma Jeane, de Dienes sent her money to help pay for the divorce from Dougherty. 'But when it came to get married,' he was to recall wistfully, 'she cancelled it, on the phone, while I was driving to meet her in Vegas. Jealous, I drove to Los Angeles. And I surprised her, in her apartment, with a lover. . . . I knew then it was all over.'

De Dienes bore no grudge. Till his death in 1985, he treasured a copy of Mary Baker Eddy's book *Science and Health*, given to Norma Jeane by her last foster parent, a Christian Scientist. On the flyleaf is the inscription, in careful, childish handwriting:

Dearest André,
Lines 10 and 11 on page 494 of this book is my prayer for you always.
Love, Norma Jeane

Lines 10 and 11 read:

Divine love always has met and always will meet every human need . . . since to all mankind and in every hour, divine love supplies all good.

According to Norma Jeane herself, in her story of breaking into Hollywood, she firmly avoided giving herself to all mankind. Her sad tale went: 'Now I was a sort of "child widow." I looked at the streets with lonely eyes. I had no relatives to visit or chums to go places with. . . . There were always men willing to help a girl be less lonely. They said "Hi, baby," when you passed. When you didn't turn to look at them they sneered, "Stuck up, eh?" I never answered them.'

When she talked to Ben Hecht, Marilyn indicated that she lived a chaste life in 1946. She was broke that year, though, and there may have been some love that was less than divine. Later, while under the tutelage of drama teacher Lee

Strasberg, she offered the private admission that in the early days in Hollywood she had been a call girl. Strasberg, who often sought out frank verbal biographies from would-be pupils, said this emerged during their first serious discussion.

According to Strasberg, talking years later to his biographer, 'She told me she was the one summoned if anyone needed a beautiful girl for a convention.' He said that later she felt 'her call-girl background worked against her.' Strasberg's biographer, Cindy Adams, had no doubt of his meaning. 'He said it three times, on tape,' she recalled. 'And he meant exactly that – she was a call girl. It was exactly what he knew to be a fact from his pupil's own lips.'

Lena Pepitone, Marilyn's New York maid from 1957 till her death, claimed the actress confided in her on many matters. She said Marilyn told her how, as Norma Jeane, she had once literally sold herself to a man shortly before the end of her marriage to Dougherty. The man, middle-aged, had persuaded a tipsy Norma Jeane, for fifteen dollars, to go to his hotel room. At first he merely asked to see her naked, then demanded more. Norma Jeane wanted to run out, but changed her mind because, she supposedly told her maid, 'Then I thought about it. It didn't really bother me that much. So what was the difference?' She did insist that the man use a contraceptive. According to Pepitone, there would be other visits to the same bar, other men, and more pocket money for the drifting Norma Jeane.

The real-life sexuality of the world's sex symbol can be glimpsed through a mass of recollection, sometimes droll, more often sad.

Philippe Halsman, the distinguished *Life* photographer, took many pictures of Marilyn over the years. The first session was in 1949, when she was twenty-three. Marilyn was one of eight girls selected to act out four situations: a confrontation with a frightening monster, the taste of a delicious drink, the hilarity of a really good joke, and being in the embrace of a wonderful lover. Marilyn, he recalled later, performed well only the part of the girl in the lover's embrace.

Halsman would say years later, 'When she faced a man she didn't know, she felt safe and secure only when she knew the man desired her; so everything in her life was geared to provoke this feeling. Her talent in this respect was very great. I remember my experience in her tiny apartment with my assistant and the *Life* researcher. Each of us felt that if the other two would leave, something incredible would happen.'

On one occasion Halsman had Marilyn jump repeatedly into the air for his camera. He said later, 'I was greatly surprised to see the embodiment of sex appeal jump like a small, immature girl. I said to her, "Will you jump again? I'm not sure you expressed your character the first time." "You mean you can read my character from my jump?" she asked. "Of course," I replied. She then looked at me with big, frightened eyes and trembled and wouldn't jump any more.'

Halsman is the only man on record who asked Marilyn the question that may hold part of the explanation of Norma Jeane's perennial fear. 'Tell me,' he inquired, 'how old were you when you first had sex?'

'Seven,' Marilyn responded.

'*Mon Dieu!*' cried Halsman, lowering the camera. 'How old was the man?'

The reply came in the famous whisper, with a catch of breath: 'Younger.'

This was Marilyn's only jest about childhood sex. Normally her theme was different – and grim. She claimed early on that she had been sexually molested as a child, and it was a theme she would return to obsessively throughout her life. Was it a real event?

The first firmly recorded reference to the violation of Norma Jeane seems to have been in 1947, when she offered it to Lloyd Shearer, a journalist who interviewed her at the request of the Twentieth Century-Fox publicity office. He listened to a horrific package story, and his reaction was this: 'She confided to us over lunch that she had been assaulted by one of her guardians, raped by a policeman, and attacked by a sailor. She seemed to me then to live in a fantasy world, to be entangled in the process of invention, and to be completely absorbed in her own sexuality.' Shearer was so skeptical that he decided to write nothing about Marilyn.

The childhood assault, as she told it herself in 1954, took this form: 'I was almost nine, and I lived with a family that rented a room to a man named Kimmel. He was a stern-looking man, and everybody respected him and called him Mr Kimmel. I was passing his room when his door opened and he said quietly, 'Please come in here, Norma. ...' He smiled at me and turned the key in the lock. 'Now you can't get out,' he said, as if we were playing a game. I stood staring at him. I was frightened, but I didn't dare yell. ... When he put his arms around me I kicked and fought as hard as I could, but I didn't make any sound. He was stronger than I was and wouldn't let me go. He kept whispering to me to be a good girl. When he unlocked the door and let me out, I ran to tell my "aunt" what Mr Kimmel had done. "I want to tell you something," I stammered, "about Mr Kimmel. He – he—"'

By Norma Jeane's account her current foster parent told her, 'Don't you dare say anything against Mr Kimmel. Mr Kimmel's a fine man. He's my star boarder!' Kimmel later told Norma Jeane, she said, to go buy some ice cream.

Marilyn Monroe, the actress, would repeat this account of her girlhood nightmare over and over – to reporters, to lovers, to anyone who would listen. Peggy Feury, who ran the Loft acting studio in Los Angeles, recalled hearing about it when she and Marilyn were at a party shortly before her death in 1962.

The story may well have had a core of truth. Not long

before her death, during an interview with journalist Jaik Rosenstein, Marilyn said, 'It did happen. But I didn't run out of the room crying or screaming. . . . I knew it was wrong, but to tell the truth I think I was more curious than anything else. . . . Nobody ever told me about sex, and frankly, I never did think it was all that important or that it was wrong.'

Dr Ralph Greenson, the Hollywood psychiatrist who treated and befriended Marilyn in her last years, accepted the fact that she had a 'terrible, terrible background.' Marilyn may have used a core truth, however, as a model for later fabrications. Dr Greenson also referred to her 'mistreatment fantasy.' Delusions and hallucinations are a feature of schizophrenic disorders. Dr Ruth Bruun, a psychiatrist who considered Marilyn's family history for this book, perceived indications of schizophrenia in the surviving information about her mother and grandmother.

Dr Greenson was the only one of Marilyn's psychiatrists whose opinions have partially survived. In correspondence with a colleague, obtained exclusively for this book, he expressed his concern about Marilyn's 'tendency to paranoid reactions.' At first he thought perhaps that, rather than being schizophrenic, her paranoid tendencies were 'more masochistic, and an acting out of the orphan-girl rejections . . . the tendency towards severe depressive reactions, and the impulsive defenses against this, seem to me to be central.' In the end, after her death, Greenson would describe Marilyn as a woman with 'extremely weak psychological structures . . . ego weakness, and certain psychotic manifestations, including those of schizophrenia.'

The story of sexual assault in childhood is not the only episode hinting at fantasy, or at least self-serving exaggeration. First husband Jim Dougherty recalled a night when, after a minor tiff during the evening, Norma Jeane woke him in the middle of the night. She said she had been for a walk, wearing only a nightgown. Dougherty remembered: 'I felt her embracing me with tears streaming down her face as she cried, "There's a man after me! There's a man after me!" I held her a few moments and then told her, "Honey, you're having a nightmare." "No!" she insisted, "I'm awake. I was going to leave home. And I walked down the street and a man chased me home.'"

Professional controversy still whirls around Sigmund Freud's so-called seduction theory, which proposed that the sexual abuse of children by adults was a primary cause of neurosis. Freud himself is said to have abandoned the theory later, shifting to the view that most patients' claims of sexual abuse are fantasy rather than fact. He wrote in 1900: 'I must, after all, take an interest in *reality* in sexuality, which one learns about only with great difficulty.'

Real or imagined, Norma Jeane would never put her childhood horror story behind her. Back in the world of the flesh, what of the less violent side of Norma Jeane's sex life?

She told a story of a happier episode that supposedly occurred at the age of eight, the same year as Mr Kimmel's assault. 'I fell in love with a boy named George. . . . We used to hide in the grass together until he got frightened and jumped up and ran away. What we did in the grass never frightened me. I knew it was wrong or I wouldn't have hidden, but I didn't know *what* was wrong. At night I lay awake and tried to figure out what sex was and what love was. I wanted to ask a thousand questions but there was no one to ask.'

Norma Jeane said she fought off the boys till the age of sixteen and marriage to Jim Dougherty. 'There were,' she said for publication in 1954, 'no thoughts of sex in my head.' Within two years of that statement, in a long private talk with her New York hostess and close friend Amy Greene, Norma Jeane asserted that she had first slept with a boy while she was in high school. Norma Jeane had gone to Emerson Junior High School when she was eleven, and to

Van Nuys High School when she was just fifteen, dropping out in less than a year to marry Jim Dougherty. If Norma Jeane was telling the truth, she thus became one of the 3 per cent of American females of the forties who, as Kinsey would shortly reveal to a startled nation, lost their virginity before the age of sixteen, and one of the 50 per cent who did so before marriage.

All this would be new to Jim Dougherty, who asserted, 'She began our married life knowing nothing, but absolutely nothing about sex. But Mom had cautioned me before our wedding day and I knew I had to be careful that first night. ... That delicate threshold had never been crossed before ... not ever.'

Norma Jeane would say later, 'The first effect marriage had on me was to increase my lack of interest in sex. My husband either didn't mind this or wasn't aware of it. We were both too young to discuss such an embarrassing topic openly.'

Jim Dougherty's version? 'Norma Jeane loved sex. It was as natural to her as breakfast in the morning. There were never any problems with it.... Getting undressed unfailingly set us both a-tingle, and almost before the light was out we were locked together.... Sometimes she would tease me just a little, wearing only two small red bandannas when I got home from Lockheed....'

Dougherty also told an interviewer: 'She was something else. I couldn't even put my lunch box down when I came home from work before she'd drag me upstairs.' One might dismiss Dougherty's version as the predictable boast of Marilyn Monroe's first husband, but he has a supporting witness. Working beside Dougherty at the factory was the then unknown Robert Mitchum, who a few years later would play opposite a new star called Marilyn Monroe. He found Dougherty perennially cheerful, not least the morning he turned up with a photograph of his 'old lady.' It showed the teenage Norma Jeane standing by the garden gate in the nude. She was posed, Dougherty told Mitchum, as if waiting for him to come home.

Of the men who followed Dougherty in Marilyn's life, those who have talked paint a starkly different picture of her sexuality. They, and Marilyn herself in comments to psychiatrist Dr Greenson, suggest a woman who found little satisfaction in sex. The change may have been caused by the dismal personal experiences that followed the marriage to Dougherty. Somewhere in that same period also lies the genesis of perhaps the saddest preoccupation in the life of Marilyn Monroe – childbearing.

Year after year as the fifties unwound, a vast public would wait and watch as Marilyn tried to have babies. As marriage followed marriage the headlines would tell of repeated gyne-cological surgery or miscarriage after miscarriage. Time after time, Marilyn would speak of her longing for children, would make a point of favoring children's charities and funds for orphans. At her funeral, instead of flowers, donations were directed to children's hospitals. A children's clinic in London benefited from a bequest Marilyn made. Yet, in its origins, even this side of Marilyn was a sad confusion.

Looking back at the age of twenty-eight, the former Norma Jeane would say of her husband: 'He never hurt or upset me, except on one subject. He wanted a baby. The thought of having a baby stood my hair on end. I could see it only as myself, another Norma Jeane in an orphanage. Something would happen to me. I couldn't explain this to Jim. After he fell asleep, I would lie awake crying. I didn't quite know who it was that cried, Mrs Dougherty or the child she might have. It was neither. It was Norma Jeane, still alive, still alone, still wishing she were dead.'

Jim Dougherty again told a different tale. He said Norma Jeane was eager to have a baby as soon as they got married, and he talked her out of it. He also told a hilarious tale of Norma Jeane experimenting with a brand-new diaphragm purchased at his insistence. She got the device in, then had to summon her husband to help get it out.

Norma Jeane quickly demonstrated that she could cope with children, looking after Dougherty's nephews for weeks at a time. She reveled in doing so. When Dougherty joined the Merchant Marine, he said, his wife became frantic, 'begging me to make her pregnant so that she could have a piece of me, in case something happened.' Years later, as Marilyn, Norma Jeane would reportedly tell a friend, actress Jeanne Carmen, how much she had yearned for children by her first husband.*

Yet during their four-year marriage, things turned around. In the final months it was Dougherty who was begging Norma Jeane to have children. She now refused, declaring that she dreaded the possibility of losing her figure. There had been a drastic change in Norma Jeane's mind, and two fragments of information – both sourced to Norma Jeane – may account for the turmoil.

Marilyn Monroe died childless, by every public account. A 1979 book by her former maid, Lena Pepitone, contained an assertion that the teenage Norma Jeane had given birth to a child. Few noticed this claim and students of Marilyn suspected Pepitone was merely seeking headlines. Research for this book, however, turned up two other witnesses who said Marilyn spoke with them of having borne a child.

According to Pepitone, Marilyn told her story about being molested, but added that the man involved actually had intercourse with her. She became pregnant, but concealed the fact from her guardian for several months. When she did own up to the pregnancy, her guardian saw to it that she had medical attention and arranged for the child to be born in a

* Elements in Jeanne Carmen's background satisfied the author as to her credibility. A book written after her death by her son Brandon James, however, raises doubts. Items in that book have not been used in this text.

hospital. Pepitone quoted Marilyn as saying, 'I had the baby ... my baby. I was so scared, but it was wonderful. It was a little boy. I hugged him and kissed him. I just kept touching him. I couldn't believe this was my baby. ... But when it was time to leave, the doctor and a nurse came in with Grace [Grace McKee, her guardian]. They all looked real strange and said they'd be taking the baby. ... I begged them, "Don't take my baby. ..." They took my baby from me ... and I never saw him again.'

Pepitone said in an interview that Marilyn on one occasion said she never learned what happened to the child; on another, she said she did know and sent regular payments to the California couple who had reared the boy. Pepitone had the impression that the child had been born when Marilyn was about fourteen or fifteen.

Amy Greene, with whom Marilyn lived in 1955, also clearly recalled her saying she gave birth in her teens, let the baby go for adoption, and still felt guilty about it. Former actress Jeanne Carmen, who said she met Marilyn in the same period as Amy Greene, would recall a similar story with a variation – the baby was born, Marilyn told Carmen, after the marriage to Dougherty and before the real Hollywood breakthrough, when Marilyn was about twenty-one. Carmen said, 'Marilyn was enormously troubled over this. In one breath she would say, "There's no God"; then, "Am I going to be punished for giving the baby away?" Desperation was very near the surface.'

'Marilyn,' said Amy Greene, 'used to fabricate a great deal, especially when she wanted to shock, to get a reaction.' This may have been the fantasy of a woman who, by the time she was telling the story, feared she would never bear children.

Peter Leonardi, Marilyn's hairdresser and secretary in the mid-fifties, said she had a 'tube-tying' operation in her starlet days, on the advice of an agent who said pregnancy would spell professional failure. Robert Slatzer, who claimed he knew Marilyn for most of her adult life, said she later submitted to surgery to have the operation reversed. On top of that, persistent reports from friends suggest Marilyn had numerous abortions. Amy Greene, perhaps the most reliable of those sources, said Marilyn made the horrendous admission that she had had twelve abortions, some of them back-street butcheries dating back to her earliest days in Hollywood.

'And then,' said Amy Greene with a sigh, 'she was surprised when she had trouble having babies. . . .'

Marilyn's poor battlefield of a womb had been a torment since adolescence, even before those surgical invasions. First husband Dougherty said, 'Norma Jeane had so much trouble during her menstrual periods, the pain would just about knock her out.'

Sometimes, in her earliest starlet days, period pain would cause Marilyn to stop her car with a screech of brakes, jump out, and crouch on the ground in agony. Maurice Zolotow, her early biographer, once penetrated her studio dressing room and noted no less than fourteen boxes of pills. Almost all were painkillers prescribed for menstrual cramps.

Henry Rosenfeld, the wealthy New York dress manufacturer, knew Marilyn from early in her career till her death. 'She wanted a baby so much,' Rosenfeld remembered, 'that she'd convince herself of it every two or three months. She'd gain, maybe fourteen or fifteen pounds. She was forever having false pregnancies.'

Marilyn was to tell writer Ben Hecht of her dream of having a daughter. 'She won't be any Norma Jeane,' she enthused. And I know how I'll bring her up – without lies. No lies about there being a Santa Claus or about the world being full of noble and honorable people all eager to help each other and do good to each other.'

There was something else Marilyn told Ben Hecht about the world of Norma Jeane. Before she turned nineteen, Marilyn said, she had tried to commit suicide. She had done it twice – once by leaving the gas on, once by swallowing sleeping pills. When Ben Hecht came to write her story, he left out that detail.

On June 1, 1946, when she turned twenty, Norma Jeane had only her dreams. She spent her birthday in a rented room in Las Vegas, fulfilling residence qualifications for a quick divorce from Jim Dougherty. It was hot, and she was suffering from an unromantic case of trench mouth.

Two months later, in Los Angeles, Dougherty made one of his last visits to see Norma Jeane – to deliver his part of the divorce documentation. In their last conversation she had shown no sign of a longing for children. On the contrary, she talked only of her urgent desire to become an actress, and no studio, she said, would spend money training a married woman who might get pregnant.

Now, when Norma Jeane opened the door to Dougherty, she looked radiant, and not because he had finally agreed to go along with the divorce. Earlier that week, without the help of divorce papers, she had obtained what she wanted most, the promise of a contract as a stock player at Twentieth Century-Fox.

When Norma Jeane told Dougherty about the contract she added a detail. The studio had given her a new name. What did Jim think of it? 'Beautiful,' he replied politely, 'just beautiful.' Then he left.*

The name was Marilyn Monroe.

---

* Dougherty remarried and became a policeman. Years later he trained the police SWAT team, which made headlines in the fiery finale to the kidnapping of Patty Hearst. He later became a County Commissioner in Sabattus, Maine.

4

A month before Marilyn got her big break, Robert Slatzer, a budding magazine writer from Ohio with a passion for show business, had been cooling his heels in the lobby of the old Twentieth Century-Fox studios on Pico Boulevard. He was reading a book of poems, Walt Whitman's *Leaves of Grass*, and waiting to interview some minor star of the day. Slatzer, then nineteen, would remember that 'this girl came pushing herself in through the big doors, carrying a big scrapbook. She caught her heel or something and the pictures fell all over the floor. I went to her rescue, and I'm glad to say there was only one place for her to sit down and wait – next to me. She said her name was Norma Jeane Mortensen. She was really interested in my poetry, and I said I might be able to write a story about her. We ended up making a date for that same evening.'

That night Bob Slatzer borrowed a battered 1938 Studebaker and made his way to Nebraska Avenue to pick up Norma Jeane. They drove along the Pacific Coast Highway and ate dinner by the ocean. Malibu was still a lovely place in those days, not the clapboard and concrete jumble it was to become. Later they walked on the beach and paddled in the surf. Slatzer said he felt shy, shyer than Norma Jeane. He thought, though he could not swear to it, that they made love for the first time that very night. When they drove home, Norma Jeane asked him to leave her at the corner rather than take her to the front door.

'I think we had an instant affection towards each other,' said Slatzer, as though a man need apologize for having slept with Marilyn Monroe. 'For me there was something magic about her, different from the other girls the talent men at the studio would fix you up with. I don't know, I think I can say I loved her from the first time I saw her.'

As the years passed and Marilyn became the love of other men and an international byword, Robert Slatzer would stay in love with the girl who dropped her modeling portfolio in the lobby of Twentieth Century-Fox.* In the summer of 1946 he had frequent dates with her, and so did other young men.

One was Tommy Zahn, who was to become a legendary figure on the beaches of California. In 1946, it would be said, he looked like Tab Hunter after a weight-lifting course. He was a lifeguard in those days, and thought he might end up as an actor. The acting dream nearly came true, because he had met a teenager named Darrylin Zanuck on Muscle Beach. Darrylin fancied Tommy from afar, then introduced him to her father, Darryl Zanuck, chief of production at Twentieth Century-Fox. Zanuck signed Zahn as a contract player, and the beach boy went to the studio to learn to act, sing and dance. So it was, in the late summer of 1946, that Tommy Zahn met an aspiring actress who became one of his modest stable of girls for the next year. His memories of Norma Jeane were fond, and perhaps unique.

'She was in prime condition,' said Zahn,' tremendously fit. I used to take her surfing up at Malibu – tandem surfing, you know, two riders on the same surfboard. I'd take her later, in the dead of winter when it was cold, and it didn't faze her in

---

* Robert Slatzer was to become best known for a controversial book in which he claimed a relationship with Marilyn that lasted till she died, but which included as well the assertion that he briefly married her six years after they met – a madcap three-day folly celebrated on the Mexican border. That claim, which will be dealt with later, aroused skepticism. Slatzer's story, however, remained consistent throughout a series of intensive interviews, and a number of compelling witnesses corroborated the closeness of his relationship with Marilyn.

the least; she'd lay in the cold water, waiting for the waves. She was really good in the water, very robust, so healthy, a really fine attitude towards life. I was twenty-two when I met her, and I guess she was twenty. Gosh, I really liked her.'

While two men played on the beach with Norma Jeane, another lay injured in the hospital, ogling her photograph. Magazines like *Titter* and *Laff* were not the sort of thing you let your mother know you were reading, not that they showed much more than long legs in short shorts and pert breasts inside sweaters a size too small. By 1946 Howard Hughes, the actress collector, did not have to worry about his mother, and he was in the hospital following a serious flying accident. He sent out for girlie magazines by the score, partly because he enjoyed them and partly because he owned RKO Radio Pictures.

On July 29, 1946, the gossip column in the *Los Angeles Times* carried the following squib: 'Howard Hughes is on the mend. Picking up a magazine, he was attracted by the cover girl and promptly instructed an aide to sign her for pictures. She is Norma Jeane Dougherty, a model.' In those twelve months Norma Jeane had decorated the cover of *Laff* magazine no less than four times under three different names, two variations on her married name and as Jean Norman. It would have been hard for Hughes not to notice, but for once he was slow off the mark.*

A Hughes aide did indeed place a call to Norma Jeane's agent, who promptly used the opportunity to stoke up enthusiasm at another studio, Twentieth Century-Fox. Norma Jeane cut out the clipping from the *Los Angeles Times* and

* According to her acting coach, Natasha Lytess, Marilyn once mentioned that she was having a brief fling with Hughes. Actress Terry Moore, who married Hughes, said he gave Marilyn a piece of jewelry – a pin. Given that the donor was Howard Hughes, Marilyn was surprised to discover it was 'only' worth $500, 1950s' value.

excitedly showed it to friends. By that time, though, she had already made the vital connection.

The casting director at Fox was Ben Lyon, himself a star of the thirties, and in Britain celebrated for his radio series *Life with the Lyons*. Years earlier it had been Lyon who spotted the potential of Jean Harlow. Now it was he who agreed to see Norma Jeane. He recalled later that 'she had a good face. You can tell with some faces – the way the flesh sits on the bones, the planes and angles – that they'll photograph well. ... In addition, there was the way she moved.'

Two days later a movie camera turned its glass eye on Norma Jeane for the first time. Dressed in a sequined gown, teetering on high heels, she obeyed instructions to 'walk across the set. Sit down. Light a cigarette. Put it out. Go upstage. Cross. Look out of a window. Sit down. Come downstage and exit.'

The cameraman, Leon Shamroy, would one day photograph Marilyn in *There's No Business Like Show Business*. Now, as he looked at the rushes, he got a cold chill. 'This girl,' he was to say, 'had something I hadn't seen since silent pictures. She had a kind of fantastic beauty like Gloria Swanson ... she got sex on a piece of film like Jean Harlow. ... She was showing us she could sell emotions in pictures.'

Within a week Darryl Zanuck himself had seen the footage, enthused, and agreed that Norma Jeane Dougherty should be signed as a contract player, at $75 a week, to be reviewed in six months. Her weekly pay would then probably go up to $100. Norma Jeane rushed home with the news, announcing, 'It's the finest studio in the world. ... The people are wonderful, and I'm going to be in a movie. It'll be a small part. But once I'm on the screen. ...'

Now Norma Jeane could shed not only her previous life, but also her name. Tommy Zahn, the sometime lifeguard she joined in the ranks of Fox contract hopefuls, revealed that the studio christening got off to a false start. 'Ben Lyon,' said

Zahn, 'could not abide her real name, so he changed it to Carole Lind. They tried that for a while, but it didn't sound right; it was a rather obvious composite of an opera singer and a dead actress.'

Ben Lyon and his actress wife, Bebe Daniels, who quickly became fond of Norma Jeane, decided they could do better. They invited Norma Jeane to their Malibu beach house to swap ideas. Lyon recalled, 'I finally said to her, "I know who you are. You're Marilyn!" I told her that once there was a lovely actress named Marilyn Miller and that she reminded me of her. "But what about the last name?" Marilyn said, "My grandmother's name was Monroe and I'd like to keep that." I said, "Great! That's got a nice flow, and two M's should be lucky." That's how she got her name.' Marilyn was still doing modeling jobs, but her heart was at the studio. Tommy Zahn recalled that everyone worked hard, and nobody more so than her.

Zahn would pick up Marilyn early in the morning and the two of them would spend their weekdays learning to act, sing, and dance. The dancing did not come easy to either of them. On Saturdays all the stock players would meet at the studio. Some would do pantomime or charades, and others would guess exactly what they were portraying. Zahn would devise a pantomime, and he and a rather shy Marilyn would perform as a couple.

There were no real parts to play yet, but Marilyn busied herself paving the way. She made sure the publicity men knew who she was, and she courted the reporters permanently based at the studio. One of them, Ralph Casey Shawhan, remembered that often, when the artists' entrance was closed, Marilyn would whistle to the press men on the third floor to come down and let her in. Shawhan could still see her peering up at the window, dressed in 'cut-off jeans frayed at the bottom, before anyone else was wearing them.'

Marilyn, giggling in the cold, posed for still shots at the beach in mid-November. The journalists liked her, and the Press Club gave her a special award. None of this had anything to do with movies, but Marilyn understood early on the importance of a good press.

Sometime during that first year a diminutive figure, five feet tall, shoes scuffed and socks down round his ankles, was ambling through the Fox administration building. Sidney Skolsky, the legendary *New York Post* writer whose syndicated column on Hollywood could change careers, was headed for the water fountain. He was delayed, though less than irritated, by a shapely behind bent interminably over the fountain. He and the owner of the behind made jokes to each other about the capacity of camels, and ended up having a long conversation. Marilyn poured out the woeful tale of her childhood, and gained a new and influential friend. Except for an interruption during her New York years, Skolsky would remain Marilyn's confidant till she died.

He was to observe, 'It was clear that Marilyn was prepared to work hard to improve herself. She wanted to be an actress and a movie star. I knew nothing would stop her. The drive and determination and need inside Marilyn could not be halted.'

'My illusions didn't have anything to do with being a fine actress,' Marilyn would say a few years later. 'I knew how third-rate I was. I could actually feel my lack of talent, as if it were cheap clothes I was wearing inside. But, my God, how I wanted to learn! To change, to improve! I didn't want anything else. Not men, not money, not love, but the ability to act.'

In early 1947, at twenty-one, Marilyn moved across a sound stage at last, as one of a dozen extras in *Scudda Hoo! Scudda Hay!*, a movie about a farmer and his team of mules. Much of Marilyn's part ended up on the cutting-room floor, but one spoken line – fittingly, the one word 'Hello!' – survived, along with a brief long shot in which she was seen paddling a canoe.

Meanwhile the studio had been paying for Marilyn to attend classes at the Actors' Lab, a drama school off Sunset Boulevard in Hollywood. 'She came to classes on time and did all her assignments conscientiously,' said Mrs Morris Carnovsky, who ran the school with her husband, 'but I never would have predicted she would be a success.' To Mrs Carnovsky, Marilyn seemed very young, self-conscious, and shy. It was at this point that Marilyn suffered a massive setback. A year into her contract, Fox decided to drop her.

The firing of Marilyn has never been explained. Ben Lyon, her first studio benefactor, was dumbfounded. Marilyn desperately wandered the studio corridors till she found the office of the great man himself, Darryl Zanuck. Whenever she tried to see him, Zanuck was 'out of town.' Tommy Zahn, Marilyn's lifeguard boyfriend, thought he knew what happened, not least because he was fired at the same time. Zahn believed that he was only hired in the first place because Zanuck wished to groom him for marriage to one of his daughters. Zahn's dalliance with Marilyn was noted and disapproved of from on high, and both were fired. Zahn shipped out to Honolulu. Marilyn was adrift, professionally and emotionally.

She did not give up. Living now in a succession of furnished rooms, apparently alone or sharing with other girls, Marilyn continued at the Actors' Lab. She tried to pay her way with the proceeds from new modeling assignments, and perhaps with the call-girl sideline about which she would later tell Lee Strasberg.

One modeling job was arranged by Bill Burnside, a forty-three-year-old Scot who represented the J. Arthur Rank Organization in Hollywood. She was interested in him, not least because he knew her idol Clark Gable, whose photograph accompanied her everywhere. Now that Marilyn was out of work, Burnside tried to help. He took her to pose for Paul Hesse, a top commercial photographer. Hesse said simply, 'Darling, you're too fat,' and Marilyn burst into tears. Burnside salvaged the moment by taking pictures himself, and the two became close.

Burnside was to recall, 'She was very aware of how she affected men. If I took her to a restaurant, however elegant, the waiters were ready to jump at her bidding. She had it there all right, that star quality, at the age of twenty-one. . . . Physically, she was wary of me for the first months of our knowing each other.' In the end there was a sporadic affair, lasting for months. Burnside kept one of the photographs he took, inscribed, 'Anything worth having is worth waiting for. Love, Marilyn.'

'I think what she wanted from me was my education,' said Burnside. 'She was into Shelley and Keats, as well as some lighter stuff. She knew that she needed knowledge.' During this workless period, Marilyn plunged into the acquisition of 'Culture.' In school, which she had quit when she was fifteen, her work habits had been generally graded as only 'Acceptable'; but she had been rated 'Good' in her English classes. Now, seeking to broaden her mind – partly to help in her career, partly because she was thirsty for information – she began to build up a considerable library.

Marilyn had a lifetime interest in the occult, and she often visited astrologers and psychics. She retained a sense of proportion, however, and dismissed one famous astrologer, Carroll Righter, in a way that demonstrated her priorities. Righter asked her, 'Did you know you were born under the same sign [Gemini] as Rosalind Russell, Judy Garland, and Rosemary Clooney?' Marilyn looked him straight in the eye and replied, 'I know nothing of these people. I was born under the same sign as Ralph Waldo Emerson, Queen Victoria, and Walt Whitman.'

The sign of Gemini, Marilyn said, stood for intellect. Her search for knowledge was to become a lifetime preoccupation, one many would mock as pretentious posturing. It was not. Marilyn devoured Thomas Wolfe, James Joyce, poetry (mostly romantic), biographies, and history books.

Abraham Lincoln became Marilyn's special hero. (She would later strike up a friendship with Lincoln's biographer, Carl Sandburg.) Lincoln's portrait would follow her from home to home till the end of her life, and his Gettysburg Address usually hung nearby. It was her first love affair with a president of the United States.

From the Actors' Lab, Marilyn caught more than a whiff of left-wing politics; the Carnovskys, her teachers, would be labeled communists during congressional investigations into 'Un-American Activity' in the fifties. Marilyn never threw herself into political activity, but she thought of herself as working class and paid homage to the common man. In her last interview, in 1962, she would say, 'I want to say that the people – if I am a star – the people made me a star, no studio, no person, but the people did.'

Meanwhile, as she continued to pose for pinup pictures, Marilyn sought to elevate even that. As early as 1947 photographer Earl Theisen noticed she owned a book called *De Humani Corporis Fabrica*, a learned study of the human anatomy by the sixteenth-century scholar Andreas Vesalius. It was marked up in detail, and Marilyn explained that she was studying the bone structure of the body. Paintings from the book by Jan Stephan van Kalkar, of the Titian school, would long decorate the walls of her poorly furnished rooms, and even near the end of her life when she was in the grip of drugs, Marilyn would impress young friends with an encyclopedic knowledge of the human bone structure. The athletic Tommy Zahn had admired how she kept herself in shape, lifting weights and running in the mornings, thirty years before the jogging craze brought people out in the thousands to puff along the grass verges through the smog of Los Angeles.

Marilyn would never be poorer than she was at this time. She skimped on meals, when men were not buying them for her, to continue paying for acting lessons. She spent a good deal of time drinking coffee at Schwab's drugstore on Sunset Boulevard, the working headquarters of her journalist friend Sidney Skolsky. Skolsky helped Marilyn open a charge account at a bookshop, and that helped finance the culture binge.

The affair with Bill Burnside withered when he went on an extended trip to Latin America. On his return she would give him a poem:

> I could have loved you
> once and even said it
> But you went away,
> A long way away.
> When you came back it was too late
> And love was a forgotten word.
> Remember?

It may have been one of the young men Marilyn met at Schwab's who made it hard to wait for Bill Burnside. The drugstore was full of out-of-work actors, and one of them was called Charlie Chaplin. To him, too, Marilyn gave a little of herself – for a while.

5

In the twenties, *the* Charlie Chaplin had seduced and briefly married a fifteen-year-old girl named Lita Grey. She bore him two sons, a boy who was given no name for the first year of his life, and Sydney, born a year later. Lita, it is said, wanted to call her firstborn Charlie, but the great Charles was leery of having an actor son bearing the same name. After his parents' divorce, however, Charlie he became. In 1947 he was twenty-one, the same age as Marilyn. He was a would-be actor, just as his father had feared, struggling to make ends meet.

In spite of his father's immense wealth, young Charlie had been spurned, and he eked out a small allowance to keep himself and his grandmother while his mother toured the country as a nightclub singer. When she came home that year, Charlie brought his girl of the moment to lunch. It was Marilyn Monroe, whom Lita thought 'really naive, not at all sophisticated, like a little country girl. She was way heavier then; she hadn't been thinned down and glamorized yet. Charlie was smitten with her, though.'

Charlie stayed enamored for many months, and at Christmas he found the cash to buy Marilyn a number of stylish dresses. According to Arthur James, long a close friend of Chaplin, Marilyn would stay the night with Charlie. She would cram into a single bed with him, while brother Sydney slept in his bed in the same room. The romance ended one day when Charlie came home to find Marilyn in the wrong bunk – Sydney's. They remained good friends, though, and fifteen years later Marilyn would make some of her last despairing calls to Chaplin and James. Chaplin would not long survive her. He failed as an actor, was a lifelong heavy drinker, and was found dying in his bathroom in 1968.

There was a sad legacy of the affair with Chaplin. According to Arthur James, Marilyn became pregnant at some time in the winter of 1947 and had one of her many early abortions.

On and off, through this period of professional vacuum, Marilyn was still seeing Robert Slatzer, the young magazine writer from Ohio. Slatzer had a friend in town in Will Fowler, writer and newspaperman son of John Barrymore's biographer, Gene Fowler. Fowler's account of an evening at Marilyn's apartment suggests that, whatever her shyness in some situations, she now used her body to entertain male friends.

'She was stoned,' Fowler recalled. 'She just took off her clothes. She liked to show her body off to men. She used to do anything that men would ask her, really just as a favor. She just walked around stoned and naked. It was her suggestion as much as ours, not even a sexual thing as far as that evening was concerned.'

Compulsive nudity is too widely reported about Marilyn to be the boast of a chance acquaintance. Years later, in New York, she would give a naked interview to publicist Joe Wohlander. Mrs Ben Bodne, wife of the owner of the Algonquin Hotel, confirms that she once met Marilyn on Fifth Avenue wearing a new mink coat. When she asked what Marilyn was wearing with it the actress replied, 'Nothing,' and snapped the coat open to prove it. From husband Jim Dougherty onward, innumerable witnesses corroborated the legend that Marilyn disliked underwear and loathed wearing panties.

Speaking of her childhood, Marilyn herself told an interviewer: 'The wish for attention had something to do, I think, with my trouble in church on Sundays. No sooner was I in the pew with the organ playing and everybody singing a hymn than the impulse would come to me to take off all my clothes. I wanted desperately to stand up naked for God and everyone else to see. I had to clench my teeth and sit on my hands to keep myself from undressing. . . . I even had dreams about it. In the dreams I entered the church wearing a hooped skirt with nothing under it. The people would be lying on their backs in the church aisle, and I would step over them, and they would look up at me.'

By 1947, when she was parading naked in front of Robert Slatzer and Will Fowler, the twenty-one-year-old Marilyn had begun dabbling in the writings of Sigmund Freud. His *Interpretation of Dreams* suggested that the 'nakedness dream' is very common, and that the dream of being naked in public indicates a real-life fear of being unmasked. Perhaps, in Marilyn, life's irony was that the struggle to step away from her orphan childhood became a circular struggle, in which her most trusty weapon was to evoke sympathy for past mistreatment. In the summer of 1947 Marilyn added a fresh story to the catalogue of woes.

One midnight, while she was living at a house in Burbank, Marilyn rushed out into the street dressed in a skimpy nightgown and screaming blue murder. By her account, she had awakened to find a man clambering through her bedroom window. She challenged the man, then ran for her life. Neighbors were roused and the police called. According to Marilyn, the prowler reappeared while the police were at the scene, and turned out to be a policeman himself. Marilyn claimed that the police pressured her not to file charges against their colleague, so the matter was dropped.

The reader must decide what to make of Marilyn's multiple stories of sexual assault. There is the perennial account of childhood molestation or, if we accept her maid's account, full rape leading to pregnancy. There is a separate account by Marilyn of a violent embrace by her guardian's husband, one which made her feel 'violated.' And in 1947, at a time when few people who mattered were noticing Marilyn, she claimed the sexual assault by a policeman.

Was Marilyn a freak case in assault statistics? The key may be her first husband's account of the night, years earlier, when he was awakened by Marilyn screaming that she had been out in the street in her nightgown, running from a man. Jim Dougherty had no doubt this was a dream, and her loyal friend Sydney Skolsky never really believed her account of childhood rape.

The story served Marilyn well, however, as did the 1947 tale of the wicked policeman.

In late 1947 the actor John Carroll met Marilyn at a drive-in restaurant. She was carrying a bag containing a few belongings, and said she was about to hitchhike to San Francisco. She told Carroll she was depressed – sick of Hollywood and her failure to get proper work. Carroll said he would try to help. They met again when Marilyn made an appearance as a 'starlet caddy' at a golf tournament, and this time Marilyn also met Carroll's wife, Metro-Goldwyn-Mayer casting director, Lucille Ryman. Carroll, hearing the story of the midnight prowler, and not having failed to see the lusciousness of the victim, suggested to his wife that they help 'this little girl.'

Soon the Carrolls were paying Marilyn's rent and providing her with pocket money. Next she moved into an apartment the Carrolls owned but were not using, and there followed a now-familiar episode: Marilyn said she had seen a boy on a ladder peeping into her room. She then moved in with the Carrolls altogether.

Soon Carroll was giving Marilyn jewelry, which mysteriously vanished. For her part, Marilyn astounded Lucille one day by informing her, 'You don't love John. . . . I think I'm in love with him. . . . Would you divorce him so we can marry?' Astonishingly, there was no lasting acrimony. The relationship brought Marilyn a personal management contract with the Carrolls, and Lucille would one day be instrumental in Marilyn's most important breakthrough in movies, her part in John Huston's *The Asphalt Jungle*.

'Hollywood's a place where they'll pay you a thousand dollars for a kiss and fifty cents for your soul. I know, because I turned down the first offer often enough and my soul isn't for sale. Men who tried to proposition me made me sick. I didn't accept. . . .'

That was Marilyn's public line when she talked to writer Ben Hecht, in the first flush of success. She told a detailed story of how she foiled the advances of a casting-couch shark who lured her to his office at the Goldwyn studio. Tommy Zahn, Marilyn's old boyfriend, remembered that she could indeed be selective. Randolph Churchill, visiting California from England, had invited Marilyn to visit him in an otherwise empty beach house 'to discuss a deal.'

'I think she knew he had other things in mind,' says Zahn, 'and she asked me along as protection.'

Cynics, however, have suggested that a real chance of advancement in movies could on occasion buy Marilyn's body. The cynics, it seems, were right.

Two years before she died, in a conversation with writer Jaik Rosenstein, Marilyn said, 'When I started modeling, it was like part of the job. All the girls did. They weren't shooting all those sexy pictures just to sell peanut butter in an ad, or get a layout in some picture magazine. They wanted to sample the merchandise, and if you didn't go along, there were twenty-five girls who would. It wasn't any big dramatic tragedy. Nobody ever got cancer from sex.'

As for Hollywood, Marilyn told Rosenstein, 'You know that when a producer calls an actress into his office to discuss a script that isn't all he has in mind. And a part in a picture, or any kind of a little stock contract is the most important thing in the world to the girl, more than eating. She can go hungry, and she might have to sleep in her car, but she doesn't mind that a bit – if she can only get the part. I know, because I've done both, lots of times. And I've slept with producers. I'd be a liar if I said I didn't. . . . '

By the time she said that, Marilyn had known Rosenstein for years. She trusted him not to write about it at the time, and he did not. Today, however, it is clear that Marilyn made judicious use of her favors. A key beneficiary, reportedly, was the man who got Marilyn that vital first contract at Fox – Ben Lyon. According to writer Sheilah Graham, Lyon had been sleeping with Marilyn and promising to further her career. When nothing materialized, and Marilyn began badgering him, Lyon called the casting director who worked for Sol Wurtzel, a B-movie producer of the time. According to the casting director, Wurtzel obliged by giving Marilyn a small part in *Dangerous Years*, a 1947 movie about juvenile delinquents which he was producing. Marilyn, playing a waitress in a café used by a teenage gang, had a couple of lines.

There has long been speculation about Marilyn's relations with Joseph Schenck, the seventy-year-old potentate of Twentieth Century-Fox. He was one of the founding fathers of the studio, which had been formed a dozen years earlier in a merger between Fox and Twentieth Century Pictures, the company he owned with his brother and Darryl Zanuck. He was a weathered bear of a man, aging but active, a *bon viveur* who rightly saw himself as one of Hollywood's grand old men.

Schenck had a shrewd eye for potential stars and a vast appreciation of beautiful women. He gathered them around him, to quote one writer, 'the way certain men prize fine stallions.' By late 1947 the eye of this connoisseur had lit upon two such beauties, Marilyn Monroe and Marion Marshall, who would later become the wife of Robert Wagner.

Marion Wagner had met Marilyn when both were applying

for a job modeling bathing suits. She recalled, 'Marilyn was the most spectacular girl I ever met, not particularly beautiful, but she radiated a special dynamism. I remember, when I first saw her, she arrived late as usual, after all the other girls. I'm sitting with all these very sophisticated models, dressed in silks, with the gloves and the hat and all that, and Marilyn came in a little scoop-necked gingham sundress, her hair unbleached and unstraightened. When she walked in, it was like the room stopped, and everyone in the room knew she was going to get the job, and she did.'

Marion Wagner's is one of the best observed and most compassionate views of the early Marilyn, and she well remembered the evenings they shared at Joe Schenck's house off Sunset Boulevard. A limousine would bring the girls, together or separately, to the elegant Mediterranean-style mansion. There would be cocktails, dinner, then perhaps a private showing of a movie in the old man's personal projection room. Joe had a passion for cards, and Wagner recalled that 'he used to get a kick out of backing us when we played gin rummy against his male pals, and if we won it pleased him. He liked both of us very much. . . . He was like a father figure to me, a father confessor, a very wise, lovely old man. When the evening was over, I would simply be taken home in the limousine, and so far as I know it was the same for Marilyn.'

In March 1948 Marilyn was given a six-month contract at Columbia Pictures. As at Fox, she was to be paid $75 a week. There are varying accounts of how it came about, but Jonie Taps, then executive assistant to Harry Cohn, head of Columbia, offered this personal recollection.

'I got a call from Joe Schenck. He said, "I'm indebted to her, and if you can give her twenty-six weeks, I'd appreciate it." I went to see Harry Cohn, and he said, "Well, if he needs it that bad, give it to him. Put the girl on."'

Marion Wagner says, 'Whatever she did, I don't think it

was into bed every night. I think it was a tasteful relationship, that was my impression.' Marilyn herself, asked straight out by a writer, flatly denied ever having had sex with Joseph Schenck.

Veteran Hollywood columnist James Bacon, however, fueled the gossip in a highly specific way. He wrote, and repeated to me, an earthy account of the way he learned of services rendered to Schenck. Bacon said he met Marilyn in 1948, during her Columbia contract. They were introduced by press agent Milton Stein, and Bacon said his first thought was, 'Holy God! She's so exciting.' He went on: 'There was something about this girl. The moment you met her you knew she was going to make it.'

As a male, Bacon had other reactions, and he made sure he saw Marilyn again. After a third meeting Bacon offered to drive her home to the Studio Club, a hotel for aspiring young actresses, where she had been living. According to Bacon, Marilyn asked him to drive instead to Joe Schenck's property where, she explained, she was living in the guesthouse.

Bacon said Marilyn made it clear she was one of the girls who looked after Schenck's failing sexual needs. She had him in stitches, saying the old man could manage only an occasional brief erection, sometimes with medical assistance. By being in the guesthouse Marilyn was on hand should such a happy moment arise. She and Bacon merrily quaffed the great man's champagne, and ended up in bed themselves. Then, at 3:00 A.M., there came a knock at the door; it was Joe Schenck's butler, summoning Marilyn. She scrambled to oblige, only to return giggling that she had arrived 'too late.'

Bacon, as others confirmed, did know Marilyn well. He was a friend to many of the famous, and their press agents say he was an accurate reporter. He shrugged off criticism for having told his anecdote about Marilyn. He said, 'I know she was promiscuous in those early days. She admitted it helped, and I had no illusions that Marilyn Monroe was after me for me. She liked me, sure, but she was also after all the newspapers my syndicated column appeared in.'

Other stories seemed to support what James Bacon said about Marilyn and Schenck. Two reporters for national magazines recalled visiting Schenck at Palm Springs and becoming aware that Marilyn 'looked after' the old man. One remembered Schenck affably suggesting that Marilyn could look after the reporter too. Perhaps the most compelling verdict came from the venerable agent George Chasin. What was going on between Marilyn and Schenck was, he said, a 'physical thing.'

The relationship with Schenck, however, was more than a passing convenience. Actor Nico Minardos, who was close to Marilyn in late 1952, recalled visiting her in the hospital when she was having a gynecological operation. He blundered into her room to find her locked in the arms of the elderly Schenck.

Joe Schenck lived on to the age of eighty-two. In 1960, when a massive heart attack began his final decline, the star Marilyn was filming *Let's Make Love*. At a dinner party given by producer David O. Selznick, there was an angry scene when a guest accused her of heartlessness, of failing to visit the dying Schenck.

Rupert Allan, her aide and friend in later years, said the opposite was true. He accompanied Marilyn to see the old man as he lay helpless in his mansion. Other visitors were banished from the sickroom, and Allan, waiting below, still remembered Marilyn's peals of laughter from the sickroom upstairs. Schenck's nurse, astounded, said the old man had rallied as soon as he heard Marilyn was coming. On the way home, Marilyn wept. She never saw Joe Schenck again.

Amy Greene, Marilyn's close friend in the mid-fifties, said, 'She did give me the impression she slept her way to her start.' Marilyn talked of this time, said Greene, using an obvious allusion: 'I spent a great deal of time on my knees.'

By 1948, at twenty-two, Marilyn was being regularly squired around the fashionable Hollywood restaurants and nightclubs. A favourite was Romanoff's, where Marilyn became close to the owner, 'Prince' Mike Romanoff, and his wife Gloria.

Gloria Romanoff knew Marilyn from the late forties until her death, and held her in great affection. She offered this opinion on how much Marilyn used sex to advance her career: 'My view would not be a popular one. This was a girl who, early on, probably did whatever was necessary to get rolling in the business. As time passed, Marilyn, I think, became somewhat indifferent to sex. She didn't have any overwhelming need to be with men, and I think it had a lot to do with those early years.'

The final word on this subject should be Marilyn's. When British writer W. J. Weatherby asked her whether the stories about the casting couch were true, she responded, 'They can be. You can't sleep your way into being a star, though. It takes much, much more. But it helps. A lot of actresses get their first chance that way. Most of the men are such horrors, they deserve all they can get out of them!'

Marilyn would on occasion take younger lovers, but men who mattered to her would from now on almost always be older.

'Insecurity is what bugs me,' Marilyn was to say years later. 'I have always been attracted to older men, because the younger men don't have any brains, and all they do is try to make a pass, and it isn't even me they are thinking about. They are horny just because I'm a movie star. Older men are kinder, and they know more, and the ones I've known were important in the business, and have tried to help me.'

Marilyn told of having sat at the feet of Joe Schenck, 'hearing him talk. He was full of wisdom like some great explorer. I also liked to look at his face. It was as much the face of a town as of a man. The whole history of Hollywood was in it.' Now, in the real world of Hollywood, the men she seriously cultivated would be her seniors, and useful to her career.

Marilyn was looking for teachers. In 1948, when she was hired by Columbia, the first teacher to come her way happened to be a woman. Marilyn grasped the helping hand, and began an intense, strange relationship that would last seven years – longer than any liaison she would have with a man. That summer there was also a male teacher, and a passionate affair she was never able to forget.

6

'I have a new girl for you,' said the voice on the telephone, 'Her name is . . .'

Natasha Lytess, head drama coach at Columbia, waited as the studio's talent chief fumbled through his papers to find the unfamiliar name.

'Marilyn Monroe,' he said finally. 'See what you can do with her.'

It was spring 1948.

Natasha Lytess, herself a former actress, was a scraggy, graying woman of Russian and French ancestry. Many years older than Marilyn, highly strung and sensitive, she had come to the United States as an artistic refugee from Nazi Germany, where she had trained with the Max Reinhardt theater company and been married to the left-wing novelist, Bruno Frank. She now lived alone with her three-year-old daughter in Hollywood, where she had been teaching acting for seven years. She was used to starlets without experience or talent, and at first Marilyn seemed just one more.

'I was not impressed,' Lytess said years later. 'She was inhibited and cramped; she could not say a word freely. Her habit of speaking without using her lips was unnatural, obviously superimposed. Her voice was a piping sort of whimper.' Lytess, however, set to work on Marilyn, beginning a relationship that she would look back on with 'pride and frustration, love and fear.'

Marilyn came for her lessons regularly and fairly punctually, and worked with boundless enthusiasm. Lytess strove to get her 'to let go, to say things freely, to walk freely, to know that relaxation brings authority. These new sensations, to a girl suffering from acute insecurity, were the difference between existing underwater and coming alive.'

For a long time Marilyn told Lytess nothing about her background. Her teacher felt that 'she was accustomed to hiding everything,' and sometimes she did not know what to believe. One day, after coming to work for months in smart, expensive clothes, Marilyn arrived unkempt and in tears. She explained that her last and kindest foster parent, her dear friend Ana,* had died 'of malnutrition.' Lytess blinked, wondered, and decided it was none of her business. She was, by now, deeply attached to her young pupil.

There were those who would say that Natasha and Marilyn had a lesbian relationship. Marilyn's New York maid, Lena Pepitone, would report Marilyn as having said so herself. 'Any warmth shown to her, by any person, regardless of sex,' Pepitone wrote, 'was welcomed and cherished.' Marilyn needed to be loved – by anyone who was sincere. Florabel Muir, a veteran Hollywood reporter who knew Marilyn well, also said there was a sexual relationship with Lytess. Sidney Skolsky, a really close friend, thought the same.

Years later Marilyn herself told W. J. Weatherby, 'People tried to make me into a lesbian. I laughed. No sex is wrong if there's love in it.' Earlier, speaking of her life in 1948, she said the sexual side of relations with men had so far been a disappointment.

'Then it dawned on me,' she said, 'that other people – other women – were different than me. They could feel things I couldn't. And when I started reading books I ran into the words "frigid," "rejected," and "lesbian." I wondered if I was all three of them. ... There were times when I didn't feel human and times when all I could think of was dying. There

* Ana Lower.

was also the sinister fact that a well-made woman had always thrilled me to look at.'

Marilyn decided she was not a lesbian after all, she told writer Ben Hecht after several months of studying with Natasha Lytess. The moment came as Marilyn landed the first movie role that gave her a chance to talk, sing, and dance, in a low-budget picture called *Ladies of the Chorus*. Marilyn played the part of a poor girl who rises from poverty to become a star, the first of many roles that would strike an echo of her own real-life experience. She had two songs to sing, 'Every Baby Needs a Da Da Daddy' and 'Anyone Can See I Love You.'

It was while Marilyn was preparing to perform these songs, Lytess would recall, that 'she opened up, and leaned on me like a child for comfort and advice. One day she told me she was in love.' Marilyn did not at the time tell Lytess the name of her lover.

That summer of 1948 a young widow named Mary D'Aubrey, living with her mother on Harper Avenue in Hollywood, blundered into a bedroom to find her brother Fred in bed with his new girlfriend. 'Hi! Can I have some juice?' was Marilyn's cheery greeting. Fred Karger was then thirty-two, ten years older than Marilyn, and shakily married to another woman. He was director of music at Columbia Pictures, and an accomplished composer best remembered today for the theme of *From Here to Eternity*. He was the son of Maxwell Karger, one of the founders of M-G-M, and Anne, a Boston Irishwoman of great warmth and vivacity. Max had died long since, and Anne – universally known as Nana – ran a jolly household filled with children and grandchildren. Once, in her salad days, Nana had presided over a virtual *salon* of early Hollywood, and its gaiety still echoed through the life she lived, in reduced circumstances, at the house on Harper Avenue.

Marilyn had been sent to Fred for musical coaching by the

producer of *Ladies of the Chorus*. Karger recognized a voice that was reedy and untrained, and its owner as someone drowning in insecurity and stage fright. He also saw that she was resolved to drill herself into performing successfully. He took her to his friends' homes to get Marilyn to sing for an audience, however small. Director Richard Quine recalled Karger playing the piano as Marilyn, screwing up her courage, stood by the mantle to sing 'Baby Won't You Please Come Home.'

Lesson turned to love one day when Marilyn phoned to say she was sick. Karger dropped in to see her and found her, forlorn and hungry, in a cramped one-room apartment. He invited her home to the maternal ministrations of Nana, and an affair began.

Fred's niece and nephew, Anne and Bennett, still remembered their childhood awe at the strangely different creature their uncle had brought home. 'There was an old closet where I used to keep my toys,' said Bennett, 'and one morning, not knowing she was there, I burst into Fred's room and she was sitting in front of the mirror nude, putting on her makeup. I hastily went to back out again, but she said to come on in and get my baseball bat and glove.'

Bennett and his eight-year-old sister, Anne, shared a nearby room with bunk beds, and Anne recalled how one day 'this vision walked in, a beautiful blonde lady. She was very, very fond of children, and she just sort of became part of our group of little friends. She gave me a birthday party, and sat there on the floor and played party games with us. We came to love her very much.'

Marilyn, she of many names, took on a special one for her relationship with the Kargers. They always called her 'Marl,' and her generosity toward the children was boundless. At Christmas she arrived to find that Terry, Fred's daughter by a previous marriage, had more presents than Anne and Bennett. Marilyn quietly left, to return laden with extra gifts.

The orphan was doing something that became characteristic, finding a new family and eagerly trying to make it her own. After the affair with Charlie Chaplin, Jr. had ended, Marilyn stayed close to his grandmother. Now she put her trust in Fred's mother. Nana cooked for her, mended her clothes, and got her off to the studio in the mornings. In years to come, Marilyn would always remember Nana's birthday, and send her flowers on Mother's Day.

Marilyn had found a family, and for the first time she was dizzily in love. At Karger's urging she moved out of the depressing apartment to a better place just down the street from the Kargers. The lovers also took a place they could use together, near the studio. Marilyn later told Ben Hecht, 'A new life began for me ... I had always thought of myself as someone unloved. Now I know there had been something worse than that in my life. It had been my own unloving heart. ... I even forgot Norma Jeane. A new me appeared in my skin – not an actress, not somebody looking for a world of bright colors. When he said, "I love you" to me, it was better than a thousand critics calling me a great star.'

Marilyn worried about being an interloper in Karger's marriage, and wept when it finally broke up. At the same time she wanted him for herself, and the want went unfilled.

There was, as Marilyn put it, 'one cloud in my paradise. I knew he liked me and was happy to be with me. But his love didn't seem anything like mine. Most of his talk to me was a form of criticism. He criticized my mind. He kept pointing out how little I knew and how unaware of life I was. ... His cynicism hurt me, too ...'

Karger would ask, 'What's most important in life to you?'

'You are,' Marilyn would say.

'After I'm gone,' Karger would say with a smile.

When Marilyn wept he would tell her, 'You cry too easily. That's because your mind isn't developed. Compared to your figure, it's embryonic.'

Nana Karger hoped her son would marry Marilyn. He, meanwhile, was backing off. One night, according to Marilyn, he told her why. 'It would *be* all right for me, but I keep thinking of my son. If we were married and anything should happen to me – such as my dropping dead – it would be very bad for him.'

'Why?' Marilyn asked.

Karger's answer was hard. 'It wouldn't be right for him to be brought up by a woman like you. It would be unfair to him.'

Marilyn, wounded in the part of her that needed children, tried to leave Karger. For a while they rode that saddest of roller coasters, the breakup that is inevitable, yet seemingly impossible. Marilyn recalled, 'There was a third and fourth good-bye. But it was like rushing to the edge of a roof to jump off. I stopped each time and didn't jump, and turned to him and begged him to hold me. It's hard to do something that hurts your heart.'

Marilyn could not forget Karger. At Christmas 1948 she went to a fashionable jeweler, and bought Karger a $500 watch on the installment plan. She was broke at the time, and would spend two years paying it off. Throughout her life Marilyn reveled in giving engraved gifts and signed photographs, but the watch was marked merely '12.25.48.'

'You'll have some other girl to love,' she told Karger. 'You wouldn't be able to use my present if my name was on it.'

A year or so later, after fending off Marilyn for months, Karger would marry actress Jane Wyman, former wife of President-to-be Ronald Reagan. He would later divorce Wyman, then remarry her in 1961, a year before Marilyn's death. Even then, Marilyn had not let go of the memory. Her friend Sidney Skolsky recalled, 'The only bitchy thing I ever saw Marilyn do occurred one night at Chasen's restaurant. As we approached the checkroom, there was an event taking place in the large private party room. . . . Marilyn and I were told that the Fred Karger and Jane Wyman wedding party was in the room. Marilyn said she had to go in and congratulate Fred. She knew this would burn up Jane Wyman. She boldly crashed the reception and congratulated Fred. As Marilyn and Jane were pretending they didn't know the other was in the same room, the tension in the atmosphere would have been as easy to cut as the wedding cake.'

Perhaps the best estimate of Marilyn's feeling for Fred Karger comes from Patti, the wife he was married to at the time of his affair with Marilyn. She acknowledged without bitterness that, 'She deeply wanted him. I think her love was very profound.' Vi Russell, who was best friend to Karger's sister and virtually a member of the family, said, 'I don't think she ever got over Fred. After him, she could never believe a man could love her. But then she never believed in herself. How could anyone love her when she could not love herself?'

Fred Karger too, it seems, did not forget. In later years he was to call his former wife Patti, highly distraught, saying that Marilyn had just appeared to him in a dream. Karger would die, seventeen years after Marilyn, on the exact anniversary of her death.

In New York, in the mid-fifties, Marilyn would talk with remorse about her time with Fred Karger. The remorse was not least for the children she had not borne. In her months with Karger, Marilyn said, she had more than once made the now-familiar journey to the abortionist.

Natasha Lytess, the drama coach, told Marilyn that Karger was not worth her tears. She soon moved with her child into the apartment that Marilyn had taken to be near the Karger family. Neither of the women had much money, and the younger Kargers were bemused by the atmosphere of the place: two lonely women living in an apartment almost devoid of furniture, with Marilyn sleeping on a mattress on the floor. During the past months, Marilyn's acting hopes had collapsed again.

Jonie Taps, the executive assistant to Columbia Pictures chief Harry Cohn, took a call from Cohn the day his boss first saw rushes of Marilyn's scenes in *Ladies of the Chorus.* 'What did you put that fat pig in the picture for?' yelled Cohn. 'What're you doing, fucking her?' In September, when Marilyn's contract ended, Cohn failed to renew it. Old Joe Schenck again tried to come to the rescue, but this time he was unsuccessful.

According to Marilyn she lost favor with Harry Cohn because she rebuffed his sexual advances. She claimed that Cohn enticed her into his office, promised her a cruise on his yacht, then tried to have sex with her on the spot. She refused, she said. When Cohn threatened her, saying, 'This is your last chance,' she walked out.

Fred Karger recalled accompanying Marilyn to Cohn's office in a last-ditch attempt to persuade the studio chief to extend her contract. Marilyn, whose mother and last foster parent were ardent Christian Scientists, had recently been going to church a good deal with Fred Karger's daughter. Now, on the way to see Cohn, she telephoned her Christian Scientist practitioner for guidance.

The guidance did not help. Cohn stuck to his decision, and Marilyn had been fired again.

In October of that year, 1948, Marilyn had some consolation. The film she had made at Columbia, *Ladies of the Chorus,* made its undistinguished debut. It was terrible, but Karger had worked well, and Marilyn received her first review. 'One of the brightest spots is Miss Monroe's singing,' wrote Tibor Krekes of the *Motion Picture Herald.* 'She is pretty, and with her pleasing voice and style, shows promise.'

That month, with members of the Karger family, Marilyn went to see herself in a public showing for the first time. *Ladies of the Chorus* was playing at the Carmel Theater on Santa Monica Boulevard – which in later years was to show only pornographic movies. Fred Karger's niece, Anne, recalled that 'she was like a little child. She sat hunched in her seat so low that she could just see the screen. She came dressed in a big coat and wearing dark glasses.'

There was nobody to recognize Marilyn that night. However, at Columbia, which had just dropped her, a little fan mail trickled in.

7

'She is most definitely not a child,' an embittered Natasha Lytess would say in the future. 'A child is naive and open and trusting. But Marilyn is shrewd. I wish I had one tenth of her ability for business, of her clever knack of promoting what is right for her and discarding what is not.' In early 1949 Marilyn was again broke, jobless, and losing Fred Karger, the first man to whom she had really given her heart. She was a bruised twenty-three, and the bruises served her well in a way. She wanted to act, and she had learned how to hustle.

Jimmy Starr, former columnist on the *Los Angeles Herald-Express,* claimed to know the secret of the Marilyn Monroe walk. 'She learned a trick of cutting a quarter of an inch off one heel, so that when she walked, that little fanny would wiggle. It worked.'

It worked for Marilyn one spring day that year, when she was out of a job following abortive ventures as assistant to a magician and a trick golfer, and a session posing nude for a calendar series. By her own account, Marilyn was sitting in Schwab's drugstore when she heard that a sexy girl was needed for a walk-on part in a Marx Brothers film called *Love Happy.* Marilyn went to the set, met first the director, then Groucho and Harpo Marx. 'Can you walk?' asked the cigar-chomping Groucho. 'This role calls for a young lady who can walk by me in such a manner as to arouse my elderly libido and cause smoke to issue from my ears.'

Marilyn walked – presumably on one cutoff heel. When she turned, the smoke was positively billowing from Groucho Marx. He called Marilyn 'Mae West, Theda Bara, and Bo-peep all rolled into one,' and the scene was shot next morning.

The producer of *Love Happy* decided to use Marilyn to promote the movie. He pumped up some publicity, portraying her as Hollywood's very own 'orphan' trying to make good, and packed her off on a nationwide promotion tour. So it was that Marilyn made her first trip to New York. Fred Karger was not at the station to see her off.

A key assignment in New York State was an appearance in front of *Photoplay* magazine's 'Dream House,' a publicity caper that would simultaneously promote *Love Happy* and household products. Adele Fletcher, then editor of *Photoplay*, recalled a stuttering Marilyn asking her to accompany her to the 'p-p-powder room,' to help rinse a coffee stain out of her dress. There, as Fletcher worried about the time, her charge stripped off all her clothes (her underwear had also been stained). 'What's she so cross about?' asked the nude Marilyn as a shocked woman departed the restroom clucking in outrage. Marilyn then emerged, dress over damp panties, to push a vacuum cleaner around for the photographers.

New York had its consolations. Marilyn was interviewed by Earl Wilson, the show business columnist who would become her friend and a key East Coast press connection. At the urging of studio publicity men, he introduced her as the 'Mmmmmmm Girl.' Marilyn also met her old lover, photographer André de Dienes, who carried her off for modeling shots at the beach.

In Manhattan she was taken to El Morocco, then one of the most exclusive nightclubs in the country. Marilyn, who arrived as a humble 'tourist,' found herself invited to the 'right' side of the club by Henry Rosenfeld, the thirty-eight-year-old millionaire dress manufacturer.

Marilyn had made a long-term friend. She would join Rosenfeld at his home in Atlantic Beach for trips in his speedboat and for quiet evenings of talk and laughter. In years to come the millionaire would offer sympathy in her crises, find her doctors and psychiatrists, and sort out her finances. Years later, in his office in the Empire State Building, seventy-three-year-old Rosenfeld merely wrinkled a still-boyish face when asked whether he and Marilyn were lovers. He did confide that 'Marilyn thought sex got you closer, made you a closer friend. She told me she hardly ever had an orgasm, but she was very unselfish. She tried above all to please the opposite sex. Ah, but it wasn't just sex. She could be so happy and gay. How I remember that laughter!'

From New York, Marilyn was shunted off to the Midwest to pose as 'the hottest thing in bathing suits cooling off again.' Marilyn's enthusiasm for movie promotion also cooled. She returned to Los Angeles, to a bit part in a western obtained for her by the man who had christened her, Ben Lyon, and to the discovery that Fred Karger still did not want to marry her. It was now, at a house party in Palm Springs, that she met a man who did. He was also the man whose efforts assured the success of Marilyn Monroe.

Johnny Hyde, one of the most influential agents in the country, told Marilyn he could make her a star. He was fifty-three, thirty years older than she and very wealthy. He was also seriously ill with heart trouble, and had less than eighteen months to live. Hyde devoted these months almost wholly to Marilyn.

Previously, Fred Karger had found a dentist to fix her uneven teeth. Now Hyde arranged cosmetic surgery to erase two tiny unwanted blemishes on Marilyn's chin.* He hired hairdressers who would from now on regularly bleach her hair, and was reportedly the agent who, according to the story Marilyn later told, persuaded her to have an operation to prevent conception.

---

* Contrary to rumor, there is no evidence that Marilyn ever had the shape of her nose altered.

Most important of all, Hyde had access to every potentate in Hollywood. By day he praised Marilyn's talents; by night he escorted her to the homes of the famous and powerful. By the time he died Hyde had secured Marilyn her first part in a major film and a new contract with the studio that had once spurned her, Twentieth Century-Fox. It ensured a salary of $500 a week for the first movie, and would develop into a deal covering the next seven years, with an eventual salary ceiling of $1,500 a week.

The major film arranged by Hyde was *The Asphalt Jungle*, directed by John Huston. Three years earlier Huston had planned a screentest for Marilyn, then canceled it because he thought she was being set up, not for a role, but for sexual exploitation on the casting couch. Now she came to him, thanks to the machinations of three people – Johnny Hyde; her sometime lover Bill Burnside; and her forgiving former hostess, Lucille Ryman. Hyde brought her to a first meeting, then she went off to study a script.

Marilyn's coach, Natasha Lytess, said they worked together 'for the better part of three days and nights' to prepare for the reading. She came back, again escorted by Hyde, extremely shy – and anxious in an unnecessary way. She arrived with padding stuffed into her already ample bosom, which Huston unceremoniously removed. Her acting, however, easily carried the day. Huston said, 'Marilyn didn't get the part because of Johnny. She got it because she was damned good.'

Johnny Hyde now dismantled his marriage of twenty years and gave himself utterly to Marilyn. Accounts differ as to how she treated him. Scriptwriter Nunnally Johnson, who was close to Hyde, thought him 'a dear and gentle man more stirred by female beauty than almost anyone I have ever known.'

Johnson himself was unimpressed with Marilyn. 'When I saw her at that time,' he recalled, 'I took it for granted that she fell into that category of eager young hustlers. It was usually at lunch at Romanoff's, and when I sat with them from time to time she took little part in the conversation, though both Johnny and I did what we could to include her in what was generally no more than casual gossip. She listened intently, her eyes never left us, as the eyes of most lunchers at Romanoff's did to see who was coming in, who was with whom. But I'm afraid I can't remember her ever uttering one word.'

Gloria Romanoff, whose husband ran that restaurant and who knew Marilyn well, thought Marilyn somewhat indifferent to men. She said, though, that 'Johnny Hyde was very important to her. She was very touched by his genuine concern. He didn't exploit her in any way, and normally she was a bit of a target.'

When Hyde left his wife and bought a sumptuous new home, he had the dining room fitted with four white leather booths and a dance floor at the center. Marilyn called it 'My own private little Romanoff's.' Billy Wilder, who would one day direct her in two movies, recalled meeting Marilyn when he and Sam Spiegel would go to play cards with Johnny Hyde. 'She just sat in the back of the room and read a novel,' he remembered, 'waiting for Johnny to finish his gin rummy.'

Marilyn's silences may have been due to uncertainty about how to behave in exalted company, or just to the shrewd realization that she could trust Hyde to hustle for her. She told director Garson Kanin, 'Look, I had plenty of friends and acquaintances – you know what I mean, acquaintances? But not one of them, not one of those big shots, ever did a damn thing for me, not one, except Johnny. Because he believed in me. . . .'

There was mockery in Hollywood about the affair, not least about the sexual contradiction between Marilyn and the ailing Hyde. Writer James Bacon claimed his own liaison with Marilyn continued while she knew Hyde, and that, between the sheets, she mocked the sick man's sexual abilities. Then there was a weekend when Marilyn abandoned Hyde in Palm Springs to visit Karger in Los Angeles. Marilyn, talking with Karger himself, said of Hyde, 'He's so sweet. I love him dearly. But I don't feel the way he does.'

Marilyn would say later that Hyde implored her to marry him, but she told him, 'I don't love you Johnny.... It wouldn't be fair.' Characteristically, Marilyn seemed uninfluenced by the fact that by marrying Hyde she could have reaped a major share of his fortune. Meanwhile, Hyde went on working feverishly to further her career, then suffered the first of a fatal series of heart attacks.

Roy Craft, a Fox publicity agent who worked closely with Marilyn, recalled a rather pathetic occasion when an anxious Hyde called from his hospital bed. Craft had organized a magazine photo session in which Marilyn and a young actor, Dale Robertson, would act out the correct etiquette for behavior in a nightclub. Hyde pleaded that the assignment be canceled, for fear it would create the impression that Marilyn was actually involved with Robertson. In deference to Hyde, the studio obliged.

Marilyn was still living, on and off, with her coach Natasha Lytess. According to Lytess, Marilyn was dilatory in visiting this sick man who had given up everything for her. One night in December 1950, said Lytess, Hyde phoned to ask, 'Where is Marilyn, Natasha? I've been waiting, waiting. Natasha, never in all my life have I known such cruelty, such selfishness.'

A week later, after a deathwatch during which Marilyn was present, Johnny Hyde died in Cedars of Lebanon Hospital. In contrast to her earlier thoughtlessness, she now defied a Hyde family request that she stay away from the funeral, and threw herself sobbing on the coffin. Her New York friends, Amy Greene and Maureen Stapleton, said she was still mourning Johnny half a decade later, still miserable that his children had 'hated her as a homewrecker.'

Nunnally Johnson thought that 'Johnny was the first man who had ever treated her with almost deferential respect, and was also the only person in the world who was seriously concerned about her at all. When Johnny was buried she was again alone in the world.'

Days after the funeral, at Christmas 1950, Natasha Lytess drove home from work with the persistent feeling that something was wrong. She entered the apartment to find on her pillow a note from Marilyn reading: 'I leave my car and fur stole to Natasha.'

Another note, on Marilyn's bedroom door, asked the reader to make sure Lytess's daughter did not enter. Natasha burst in to find that 'the room looked like hell on earth. Marilyn was in bed, undressed, her cheeks puffed out like an adder's.'

Lytess said she shouted, 'Marilyn! What have you done?' When there was no reply, 'I jammed her mouth open and reached in and took out a handful of wet, greenish stuff she hadn't yet swallowed. On the night table was an empty bottle that had contained sleeping pills.'

Nearly twelve years later, the psychiatrists of the Los Angeles Suicide Prevention Center would say of the dead Marilyn: 'On several occasions in the past, when she was disappointed or depressed, she had taken overdoses of barbiturates and summoned help.'

If we accept her own account of two suicide incidents before she was nineteen, this was the third. Marilyn was still six months short of her twenty-fifth birthday.

8

'She was supposed to be at the studio by seven o'clock in the morning, and she never made it. I lived just across the street, and I had to go and bang on her door. She'd open the door looking a mess, wanting a cigarette,* and I'd say, "Come on, get your ass out of bed." Sometimes I literally had to push her into the shower.'

The man charged with getting Marilyn to work was French-born Alain Bernheim – the future producer – who had come to Hollywood in the forties. At the time, he was working with Charles Feldman and Hugh French, who had taken over as Marilyn's agents on the death of Johnny Hyde. As he and others discovered, Marilyn was a mass of contradictions and a mistress of transformation.

The German actress Hildegard Knef† first encountered Marilyn in a Twentieth Century-Fox dressing room, still only half-awake. She recalled this scene: 'The sleepy-looking girl with the transparent plastic shower cap over her white-blonde hair, and a thick layer of cream on her pale face, sits down beside me. She digs around in a faded beach bag and takes out a sandwich, a pillbox, a book. She smiles at my reflection in the mirror. "Hi, my name's Marilyn Monroe, what's yours?"'

Knef's first impression of Marilyn was of 'a child with short legs and a fat bottom, scuffing over to the makeup room in old sandals.' An hour and a half later, said Knef, 'only

* She had stopped smoking by the mid-fifties.
† Hollywood changed it to 'Neff.'

74

the eyes are still recognizable. She seems to have grown with the makeup, the legs seem longer, the body more willowy, the face glows as if lit by candles . . .'

The two appeared together the same evening at a dinner to announce awards and new discoveries. 'Now,' said Knef, 'she's wearing a red dress that's too tight for her; I've seen it before in the Fox wardrobe – although it's too tight, it looks like one of Mum's old ones dug out of the wardrobe. Eyes half-closed, mouth half-open, hands trembling a little. One glass too many, a child's first go at the punch. The photographers hold their cameras up high, flash into her cleavage. She leans and stretches, turns and smiles, is willing, offers herself to the lenses. Someone bends forward and whispers into her ear. "No, please," she says, "I can't." The trembling hand knocks over a glass. Finally she stands up, the people snigger, the tight skirt presses her knees together, she trips to the microphone. The walk is absurd and she's got miles to go; they stare at the dress, wait for it to burst and liberate the bosom, the belly, the bottom. The master of ceremonies roars: "Marilyn Monroe!" She steadies herself on the mike stand, closes her eyes, leaves a long pause in which one hears her amplified breathing – short, panting, obscene. "Hi," she whispers, and starts the trip back.'

The Asphalt Jungle, Marilyn's true break into pictures, appeared in June 1950. The tough story of a jewel robbery, of crime and punishment, and of what happens when thieves fall out, it still stands as one of the best of its kind ever made. Marilyn played the young mistress of an aging criminal, a relationship defined – to suit the morality of the day – as 'niece' and 'uncle.' She was noticed by the reviewers of the *New York Post* and the *Herald Tribune*, and *The Times* included Marilyn in its praise of 'an unimpeachable performance.'

In spite of that, Marilyn had little work that she wanted. Her previous year had otherwise been a series of bit parts for the Hollywood sausage machine. Johnny Hyde had arranged a seven-year contract with Fox, but Darryl Zanuck, the man who had once fired her, foisted her off with cameos in forgettable movies. Marilyn, in response, campaigned adroitly on two fronts – the flagrant advance of the sex symbol in public and the creation of the cultured actress in private.

In 1951, now twenty-five, Marilyn signed on for an adult extension course at the University of California at Los Angeles (UCLA). Her subject was literature and art appreciation, with a focus on the Renaissance. She appeared for classes quietly dressed, and hardly anyone knew she was a starlet. To her literature teacher she 'could have been some girl who had just come from a convent.'

When Marilyn had first met Hildegard Knef she had launched into a barrage of questions about German literature, and happened to be carrying a copy of Rainer Maria Rilke's poetry under one arm. Jack Paar, later to become host of the television show *Tonight*, acted with Marilyn that year in the film *Love Nest*. When he met Marilyn she was reading Marcel Proust, whom Paar has described as 'a rather exotic French author much in vogue among the intellectually pretentious of the time.' Paar called this Marilyn's 'act,' and commented, 'I fear that beneath the facade of Marilyn there was only a frightened waitress in a diner.' Paar, himself not best known for cultural devotion, was one of many who underestimated her.

Quietly, as superficial roles followed one on another, Marilyn worked away at her acting. She made sure that her acting coach, Natasha Lytess, followed her to Fox. Lytess would recall, 'Her habit of looking at me the second she finished a scene was to become a joke in projection rooms. . . . The film of the daily rushes was filled with scenes of Marilyn, finishing her dialogue and immediately shading her eyes to find me, to see if she had done well.'

Marilyn did not consult Lytess when she decided to take separate lessons from Michael Chekhov, nephew of the playwright, who had studied under Stanislavsky. She played Cordelia to his King Lear in private acting sessions, and became mesmerized by his talent. Shortly before her death, she was still talking of him in interviews as her acting idol, the man 'who showed me that I really had talent and that I needed to develop it.'

Once, in the middle of a scene from *The Cherry Orchard*, Chekhov stopped to ask Marilyn whether she had not been preoccupied with sex while playing her part. Marilyn said no. Chekhov shrewdly replied, 'I understand your problem with your studio now, Marilyn. You are a young woman who gives off sex vibrations, no matter what you are doing or thinking. And your studio bosses are only interested in your sex vibrations. I see now why they refuse to regard you as an actress. You are more valuable to them as a sex stimulant.'

Marilyn told an interviewer that her reply to Chekhov was: 'I want to be an artist, not an erotic freak. I don't want to be sold to the public as a celluloid aphrodisiac. It was all right for the first few years. But now it's different.'

Of course, Marilyn used the weapon of her sexuality when she chose, and not least to jolt studio chief Darryl Zanuck from his torpor. Writer Robert Cahn recorded the effect Marilyn achieved one night in 1951.

'The Café de Paris, more simply known as the Twentieth Century-Fox commissary, was crowded with a cheery assemblage of studio bigwigs and freshly manicured salesmen. The visitors were meeting, over highballs and hors d'oeuvres, such marquee names as Susan Hayward, Jeanne Crain, June Haver, Anne Baxter, Gregory Peck, and Tyrone Power. At the bar a weary press agent was asking for his fifth highball when he glanced toward the doorway where Marilyn Monroe, a recently acquired studio starlet, had just arrived. Amid a slowly gathering hush, she stood there, a blonde apparition in a strapless black cocktail gown, a little breathless as if she were Cinderella just stepped from the pumpkin coach.

While the long-established female stars silently measured her, young Marilyn Monroe, who has logged less than fifty minutes' screen time, stole the show. . . . Finally, as the guests sat down for dinner, the blonde was installed at the head of the No. 1 table, at the right hand of company president, Spyros Skouras.'

The public had already cast its verdict. Marilyn's minor screen appearances had brought a torrent of fan mail. Her pictures in pulp magazines had made her the nation's pinup – 'Miss Cheesecake of 1951' to the troops in Germany. Now, the morning after Marilyn took Spyros Skouras by storm, Darryl Zanuck bowed to the pressure. Marilyn's salary shot up to five hundred dollars a week, and Zanuck issued orders that Marilyn should be given more roles. Thanks to the intervention of her friend Sidney Skolsky, she was loaned to another studio to make *Clash by Night,* a sophisticated movie from a play by Clifford Odets. Soon the *New York World-Telegram* would acclaim her as 'a forceful actress, a gifted new star.'

Marilyn had never ceased to cultivate her friends in the publicity office, and now it paid off. That year her picture appeared, with those of other starlets, in *Life* magazine. In the fall, Roy Craft placed calls to Rupert Allan, the West Coast editor of *Look*, and to Ted Strauss, his counterpart at *Collier's.*

Rupert Allan, a cultured product of Oxford University, was quickly won over. He waited, as men would almost always wait, as Marilyn finished dressing in her tiny apartment. He watched quizzically as she did exercises for the camera and expounded on her studies of the human anatomy as taught by Florentine doctors. He observed with educated eyes the inexpensive reproductions taped to the wall of Dürer, Fra Angelico, and da Vinci.

Allan's interest grew when he espied, beside the bed, a picture of a woman in black, not Sarah Bernhardt or Garbo but the Italian actress Eleanora Duse. Within days Allan was Marilyn's counsel on art. He was to become her future press agent and a lifetime friend. In immediate terms, *Look* granted Marilyn its accolade: her first cover in a nationally respected magazine. It informed the world that this Hollywood actress wished to use her brains.

The studio told *Collier's* Ted Strauss that Marilyn was 'terrified' of being interviewed for a major article, and urged that he take her to dinner. Strauss made the pilgrimage to the same apartment, waited, then took her to Romanoff's. Now he experienced Marilyn's effect on a roomful of people.

'She was an apparition,' Strauss remembered. 'She was in something red, semi-dressed and semi-undressed, with cleavage almost to her navel. We came in down a sort of Ziegfeld Follies staircase, and everything stopped. Everyone there looked – I remember how the lighting made death's-head sockets of their eyes – like a party in a cemetery. That was not all. I had expected a clichéd little girl on the make. I came away from that dinner so impressed. She was doing what she thought people wanted her to do, but unsure – desperately trying to deal with where she came from. We talked about acting, but she talked as much about children, of having children who would be able to grow their own way.'

In this year of her film breakthrough, 1951, Marilyn turned twenty-five. She moved out of the apartment she shared with her acting coach, and returned to the secretive personal life she had lived before the very public affair with Johnny Hyde. She usually lived alone, but for some months she had for a roommate a young actress she had met at a charity baseball game a few years earlier. The new friend was Shelley Winters, who shared with Marilyn a history of broken romances, unborn children, and a healthy disrespect for the show business establishment.

Winters noticed Marilyn's extreme insecurity. She craved attention so much that she pursued her friend everywhere, even into the bathroom. 'When you went to the john,'

Winters had said, 'she'd think you'd disappeared and she'd been left alone. She'd open up the door to see if you were still there. She was a little child.'

On Sunday mornings the two young women would sit listening solemnly to classical music, then change over to Sinatra or Nat King Cole as soon as the clock struck noon. One day, as they perused the photographs of single actors in the *Academy Players' Directory*, they bemoaned the frustrations of love. Shelley Winters remembered Marilyn musing, 'Wouldn't it be nice to be like men and just get notches in your belt and sleep with the most attractive men and not get emotionally involved?'

The outcome was that each sat down to list the famous men they would like to have taken to bed. Marilyn's list, according to Winters, included Zero Mostel, Eli Wallach, Charles Boyer, Jean Renoir, Lee Strasberg, Nick Ray, John Huston, Elia Kazan, Harry Belafonte, Yves Montand, Charles Bickford, Ernest Hemingway, Charles Laughton, Clifford Odets, Dean Jagger, Arthur Miller, and Albert Einstein.

After Marilyn's death Shelley Winters would see among Marilyn's effects a framed photograph of Einstein inscribed: 'To Marilyn, with respect and love and thanks, Albert Einstein.' She drew what seemed the obvious conclusion. Another friend of Marilyn, a man who was on the original target list, put this little matter in perspective.

Actor Eli Wallach later worked with Marilyn, but denied that he was ever a lucky victim. He gleefully took responsibility, however, for the signed Einstein portrait. It was Wallach who gave it to Marilyn, as an 'in' joke, after Marilyn gave him a book of Einstein's letters. Wallach wishes future historians well when they come to analyze the handwriting on the photograph.

Of the seventeen men on Marilyn's list, she would know nine, and three would indeed be her lovers. One, almost certainly, enjoyed her favors the year she made the list.

On a warm day in 1951 photographer Jean Howard, the former wife of Marilyn's agent Charlie Feldman, came to Feldman's house in Coldwater Canyon. As she left, she recalled, 'I noticed this little blonde girl sitting by the pool. I didn't know who she was, but offered her some Coca-Cola, which she declined. Charlie was holding a meeting with Elia Kazan that day, and Marilyn was waiting for them.'

Elia Kazan – 'Gadge' to his friends – was already, at forty-one, a towering figure of the American stage and screen. He was both actor and director, and that year saw one of his great triumphs, *A Streetcar Named Desire.* Born in a suburb of the Turkish city of Istanbul, he was now an uncompromising New Yorker. He talked disparagingly of Hollywood, but had discovered it was a necessary evil for a leading film director. In 1951 he had long been married to playwright Molly Thatcher, and had four children. Kazan declined to discuss Marilyn Monroe for this book, but others support the longstanding rumor of their affair.

Photographer Milton Greene learned of the relationship direct from Marilyn, and actor Eli Wallach knew about it. Alain Bernheim, then working for Marilyn's agent, was drawn into its secrets. He recalled that '*Streetcar* had been nominated for several Academy awards, but Marilyn could not go to the ceremony with him because he was married. So he parked her with me, and said he'd join us later in some little club in Beverly Hills. So I found myself spending hours in the dark in a little piano bar with Marilyn Monroe, waiting till Gadge was free.'

Another agent, Milt Ebbins, remembered a hilarious event at another stage of the affair. He went to a business meeting with Kazan at his room in the Beverly Hills Hotel, and was astounded when Marilyn walked in wearing only half of Kazan's pyjamas – the top half.

As he sat with Marilyn on the night of the Academy Awards, Alain Bernheim was startled in a very different way.

'It was extraordinary,' he said. 'Marilyn was coming out with everything Kazan had told her as though the ideas were her own. I knew Kazan well, and I knew it all came from him. She had swallowed whole, virtually memorized, everything he had to say about love, acting, and politics.'

For Marilyn, the connection with Kazan no doubt meant a strong infusion of radical politics. Kazan had once been a member of the Communist Party. In 1952, within a year of meeting Marilyn, to the fury of friends and colleagues, he would testify about his past associates before Congress' Committee on Un-American Activities.

When Rupert Allan visited Marilyn at home for his *Look* article, he had noticed a photograph beside her bed. It showed two men, one of whom he recognized at once as Elia Kazan. Asked to identify the other one, a tall fellow, Marilyn replied, 'I'd rather not say, for the moment.'

Allan had failed to recognize Arthur Miller.

Marilyn had met Miller in December 1950, in the company of Elia Kazan, just a few days after her suicide gesture over the death of Johnny Hyde. She was working on her part as a secretary in *As Young as You Feel* and feeling very low indeed. She would appear for scenes, then wander off to some corner to be alone with her thoughts.

Arthur Miller was then thirty-five, ten years older than Marilyn, a rumpled man with dark hair, toweringly tall. Newspapermen usually labeled him 'gaunt,' though on occasion his bespectacled face could seem rounded and quite gentle. The son of a garment manufacturer, he had been born into a comfortable New York family living on 112th Street, in what was then a pleasant part of Harlem. Then the Depression turned the Millers' world upside-down. The family was forced to move to a small frame house in Flatbush, and Miller's father never did recover his former affluence. 'Art,' as the family called him, grew up doing odd jobs. He was a flop as a coat salesman, then did a brief stint as a crooner on a small Brooklyn radio station. The jobs helped pay for his education, which eventually took him to the University of Michigan. An old football injury kept him out of active service in World War II, though he spent a year as a fitter in the Brooklyn Navy Yard.

When Miller met Marilyn he was married, with two children, to a willowy brunette a year younger than himself. This was Mary Slattery, his girlfriend from college days. They had married in 1940, and Mary worked as a proofreader at a publishing house – *Harper's* – while Miller was trying to get his start as a freelance writer. During this period Miller espoused radical causes and included Communists among his friends, associations that would one day bring down on his head the wrath of a congressional committee.

It was a conversation with his mother-in-law, about a woman who had turned in her own father to the authorities for supplying faulty parts to the government in wartime, that gave Miller the spark for his first successful play. In 1947 *All My Sons* won the New York Drama Critics' Circle Award, and two years later *Death of a Salesman* brought him a Pulitzer Prize and lasting fame. By Christmas 1950, when he came to Hollywood with his friend, Elia Kazan, to discuss a movie about labor racketeering, Arthur Miller was America's most celebrated playwright.

From a variety of sources, including fragments provided by both of them, these were the beginnings of Miller's romance with Marilyn. According to Cameron Mitchell, a young actor who had appeared in the Broadway production of *Death of a Salesman*, he was walking to lunch with Marilyn one day when she suddenly stopped short. A few yards away, leaning against the wall of a sound stage, were two men – Kazan and Miller. Miller, a gangling giant of a man, had caught her eye, and she asked Mitchell who he was. Mitchell made perfunctory introductions.

The chance meeting, it seems, soon had Miller watching

Marilyn at work on the set of *As Young as You Feel*. Then, with Kazan in tow, he sought her out in her dressing room. She was not there, and the director of the movie, a friend of Kazan's, warned Miller that she had withdrawn into herself since the death of Johnny Hyde.

According to Miller, the two men eventually found Marilyn in a nearby studio warehouse. Marilyn later recalled that she was weeping when they found her.

Marilyn and Miller met again later the same week, at a party given by Charlie Feldman, Marilyn's agent and Kazan's neighbor. According to Natasha Lytess, Marilyn turned up afterward at 4:00 A.M., wanting to talk. 'I'd seldom seen her so contented,' Lytess recalled. 'She took off her shoe and wiggled her big toe. "I met a man, Natasha," she said. "It was Bam! You see my toe? This toe? He sat and held my toe. I mean I sat on the davenport, and he sat on it too, and he held my toe. It was like running into a tree! You know, like a cool drink when you've got a fever."'

Miller wrote to Marilyn within days, with a reading proposal. 'If you want someone to admire, why not Abraham Lincoln?' Marilyn, as the world could hardly fail to know, admired Lincoln already. Her idolatry had started, she said, in junior high school, when her essay on Lincoln was judged the best in the class. By happy coincidence, Arthur Miller had attended Abraham Lincoln High School. Five years later, before her marriage to Miller, Marilyn would enthuse to Joshua Logan, director of *Bus Stop*, 'Doesn't Arthur look wonderfully like Abraham Lincoln? I'm mad for him!'

'He attracted me because he is brilliant,' Marilyn would tell the then queen of columnists, Louella Parsons. 'His mind is better than that of any other man I've ever known. And he understands and approves my wanting to improve myself.'

Natasha Lytess recalled that immediately after the first meeting with Miller, 'I could tell Marilyn was in love with him. It wasn't anything big, but it showed in the way she acted.' A year later a friend spotted the picture of Miller beside Marilyn's bed, the same one *Look*'s Rupert Allan had seen. This visitor recognized the photograph and reported afterward that 'Marilyn squealed. She said other people who had been in the room had never recognized him. Marilyn gave the impression there was a great attraction between them. But she said he was married and she didn't think anything would come of it.' Later, when reporters came visiting, Marilyn would hide the picture by turning it face down. This, of course, merely aroused curiosity – and prompt recognition when the picture was examined.

The actress Maureen Stapleton, who worked with Marilyn in New York five years later, said, 'Marilyn told me she decided on Arthur long, long before they were married. She didn't come to New York and the Actors Studio just because she wanted to be a great artiste. That fellow didn't have a leg to stand on once she made up her mind. She'd decided on Arthur – and she got him.'

In 1951, however, Miller stayed with his wife and children in New York. Marilyn, in Hollywood, continued to face the challenges she had made for herself. In his long first letter to her, Miller had written: 'Bewitch them with this image they ask for, but I hope and almost pray you won't be hurt in this game, nor ever change. . . .'

On New Year's Eve, 1951, the telephone rang in the home of Associated Press writer Jim Bacon, who had now been seeing Marilyn sporadically for three years. She was calling with a plea: 'I don't want to stay at home alone on New Year's Eve, Jim. Can I go to a party with you?' Bacon, who was married, said his wife would not appreciate it.

At the other end of the line, the small voice of that year's Miss Cheesecake said, 'Oh, I understand,' and hung up.

There would be many lonely holidays for the girl who had dreamed the hardest.

9

'I want you to talk with this girl,' said Fox publicity director Harry Brand. 'We're grooming her – or maybe I should say she's grooming herself – to be the sexiest thing in pictures since Jean Harlow.' It was January 5, 1952, and Darryl Zanuck's fixer supreme was giving lunch to the columnist Hy Gardner.

Brand had a tip for Gardner, the careful seeding of a major coup in spoof publicity. 'There's only one thing we're a little worried about,' he confided. 'When things were real rough, Marilyn posed in the raw for a local photographer, and the pictures now adorn a calendar like *September Morn's* torso, only more so. I'd show you the shots but our legal department has them stashed away in the vault.'

On this tantalizing note Marilyn made her entrance, ready to hold court with the visiting columnist. Brand had laid the groundwork for the Calendar Caper, a story that would unfailingly win headlines for months, even years, to come.

The authorized version of the calendar story goes this way. In 1949, when she was twenty-three, Marilyn, broke and out of a job, had posed in the nude for photographer Tom Kelley. He eventually sold the pictures to the Western Lithograph Company for a calendar series, and three years later – to the supposed embarrassment of Marilyn, her studio, and the producer of the moment – someone happened to match the face of the new Fox star with the face and body hanging on garage and barbershop walls all over the United States.

In the early fifties nice girls did not pose nude, and soon

the press was howling at the doors of Twentieth Century-Fox. Studio fingers were supposedly on the panic button. There was talk of canceling Marilyn's contract and withdrawing her current movie, *Clash by Night*, and Marilyn herself was reportedly in tears. Then Marilyn suggested she should admit having posed nude, but emphasize that she had done so only out of dire need, when she had no money to pay the rent. This pitiful tale should arouse public sympathy and turn shameful scandal into triumphant publicity.

It worked, of course, and Marilyn's calendar shots would still be selling far into the future. The truth about the breaking of the story, though, has never been told in full. It is a droll tale, and one that reveals a good deal about Marilyn as mistress of her own propaganda.

With the collusion of her friend Sidney Skolsky, Marilyn stage-managed the newsbreak with a little trick of her own. She arranged to be interviewed by United Press International's female reporter, Aline Mosby. Mosby, whose agency serviced thousands of newspapers, magazines, and television and radio stations, was summoned to interview Marilyn and tipped off to ask her about the nude calendar. Sonia Wolfson and Johnny Campbell, studio publicity agents, sat in on the interview. They had been kept in the dark about the calendar ploy, and Marilyn found a way to give Mosby the impression she was truly getting a scoop.

'She asked Aline to follow her into the ladies' room,' Campbell recalled, 'making as though she was having some sort of menstrual mishap. I certainly could not follow them in there. Then, in the safety of the powder room, she proceeded to identify herself as the heroine of the calendar picture. We were all disturbed about it, but there was nothing we could do.'

Mosby's sympathetic story broke a few days later, and Marilyn was all amazement. 'I still don't know *how* I was recognized,' she protested. As Campbell admitted, 'Marilyn understood the temperament of the country better than all of us. She understood that the times had changed.'

The calendar story was one that would run and run. Soon the nude Marilyn Monroe was in living rooms across the nation, color-printed on cocktail trays and drinking glasses. Marilyn claimed that she did not want the picture to become 'a national institution,' but she said it very quietly.

Meanwhile, the defenders of American morals made certain the story did not die. In early 1953 a Los Angeles camera-shop owner was arrested after schoolboys had been observed peering at the calendar in his window display. The calendar was officially banned in Pennsylvania and Georgia. Marilyn graciously thanked the authorities, and the picture reappeared draped in black lace. The calendar was still selling a full three years later, after the U.S. Post Office ruled that the picture was obscene.

In December 1953 one of the nude calendar shots, purchased for $500 by a young unknown named Hugh Hefner, was to grace the pages of the first edition of a new magazine, *Playboy*. Marilyn also appeared, clothed, on the cover. *Playboy* would be able to boast that its first Playmate – or Sweetheart of the Month, as the spread was then called – was Marilyn Monroe.

Marilyn therefore played a key role in this early offensive in the American sexual revolution. Contrary to a highly commercialized fiction, however, there is no substance to the notion that she once paid the rent by making pornographic movies. Later years would see the exploitation of two old stag films, one a crude portrayal of the sex act, and one a striptease act, rejoicing in the title of *Apple Knockers and the Coke Bottle*. Both have been sold on the basis that the woman involved is Marilyn, but in each case research has identified the actress as someone else.

The closest Marilyn is known to have come to making pornographic movies was when she was twenty-one, five years before the calendar episode – and that was tame stuff. Steffi Skolsky, daughter of Marilyn's friend Sidney, once accompanied her father to the studio on a Saturday. While waiting for him, she wandered into a viewing room, where the contract players were running sequences they had made 'for fun and kicks, and because Zanuck liked to have something to run in the wee, small hours.' Young Steffi saw Marilyn, fully dressed, in a 'highly suggestive' embrace with the actor, Robert Karnes. The sequence has probably long since been junked.

The nude calendar story broke on March 13, 1952. Meanwhile, one of Marilyn's less successful press operations was quietly brewing. She had never tired of telling people of the saga of deprivation her childhood had been. It had become another tree of sympathy, one that she would feed on and feed to others till the end of her life. One of its main branches was the mystery of her parentage.

At the age of eighteen, while married to Dougherty, Marilyn had suddenly announced that she was going to call her 'father.' She said she had identified him through people who had once worked with her mother. In front of Dougherty, she dialed a number, then quickly hung up. Her 'father,' she said, had refused to talk to her.

Marilyn always called her first husband 'Daddy.' After she died Inez Melson, her executrix, found an attaché case containing letters from another husband, Joe DiMaggio. Melson noticed that DiMaggio signed himself 'Pa.'

This need for a father figure seems to have become part of Marilyn's tapestry of fantasies. In 1950, as a young starlet, she asked Sidney Skolsky to take a drive with her, to 'visit my father.' Next day she drove him in the direction of Palm Springs, claiming the father lived on a dairy farm in the area. At a chosen spot Marilyn parked the car, then walked up the drive of a house that lay hidden behind trees. Skolsky could not see what happened next.

When she returned, Marilyn told Skolsky that her 'father,' a 'sonofabitch,' had told her, 'Listen, Marilyn, I'm married, I have children. I don't want you to start any trouble for me.'

Skolsky did not write about the incident in his newspaper, though that may have been what Marilyn intended.

One wonders whether Marilyn really confronted anybody behind that screen of trees. Two weeks later, when Skolsky began telling the story to Natasha Lytess, she interrupted him. She explained, with most of the same details, that Marilyn had recently gone through the same performance with her.

Years later, again in two incidents separated by only a month or so, Marilyn rehearsed similar scenes with Ralph Roberts, her masseur and with her press aide, Pat Newcomb. They occurred in 1961, not long after Marilyn had emerged from a psychiatric hospital.

Were these genuine contacts with the father who had abandoned her? Or were they manifestations of a complex fantasy, a long-running screenplay on a theme of sympathy for Marilyn? Stanley Gifford, one of the men who may have been Marilyn's father, did own a dairy near Palm Springs after World War II. Perhaps he was indeed her father, and did reject her. What is certain is that after the odd double pilgrimage in 1950, Marilyn's mind became scrambled on the subject of paternity.

She was to tell her New York hostess, Amy Greene, that she had met her father. Yet Marilyn told Henry Rosenfeld, her longtime confidant, that she had discovered her father was 'a farmer in the Midwest,' and that she longed to meet him.

Once, at a New York party, Marilyn took part in a game in which she had to say what she wanted most in the world. Her reply, Rosenfeld said, was that she would like 'to put on her black wig, pick up her father in a bar, and have him make love to her. Then she'd say, "How do you feel now to have a daughter that you've made love to?"'

In early 1952, as the Marilyn legend began to take hold of the public imagination, she tried to capitalize on her family history. It happened when she went to meet reporter Jim Henaghan at his beachfront home in Malibu. Dusk fell and the drink flowed, Henaghan wrote later, and Marilyn began to expound. She said her father had been killed in a road accident, which had been the real fate of one of her putative fathers. Then she said, 'I never had a house or a home that was mine. Or anything that was really mine alone. My mother died when I was a baby. . . .'

Whatever the truth about her father, Marilyn's mother certainly was not dead. Marilyn knew full well that she was in a mental asylum not far away. However, she had long told her public relations people that both her parents were dead, and now she was happily exploiting the myth.

This time, events boomeranged. Henaghan filed a story depicting Marilyn the orphan as 'Hollywood's loneliest girl.' Then another journalist, Erskine Johnson, discovered that Marilyn's mother was alive. His newspaper ran the story.

Somewhat to her surprise, Marilyn's world did not collapse. The newspapers thought it was just one more good Monroe story. Why would they do otherwise? Marilyn had become a public property, a national entertainment that nobody wanted to lose. Her life henceforth was to seesaw between sensation and sadness, with all the world watching.

In spring 1952, in the wake of the calendar affair, Marilyn received massive publicity. *Life* magazine bestowed its prestigious benediction, proclaiming that 'the genuine article is here at last – a sensational glamor girl, guaranteed to entice people from all lands to the box office.' Then, while Marilyn was making *Monkey Business* with Cary Grant, the world had perhaps its surest sign that a star was born – the newspapers began reporting Marilyn's illnesses.

On April 28 production of the movie ground to a halt, as Marilyn lay abed waiting to have her appendix removed. The operation was performed at Cedars of Lebanon Hospital, where her lover Johnny Hyde had died just over a year earlier.

In the operating room, a nurse wondered aloud whether Marilyn really was 'blonde all over,' as she had once joked to the press. (She was not, and in later years pubic-hair peroxiding would become one of her hairdresser's chores.) The jokes stopped abruptly when a nurse found this note, scrawled in pencil, taped to the patient's stomach:

> <u>Most important</u> to Read Before operation.
> Dear Doctor,
> <u>Cut as little as possible</u> I know it seems vain but that doesn't really enter into it – the fact that I'm a woman is important and means much to me. Save please (can't ask you enough) what you can – I'm in your hands. You have children and you must know what it means – <u>please Doctor</u> – I know somehow you will! thank you – thank you – for Gods sakes Dear Doctor No <u>ovaries</u> removed – please again do whatever you can to prevent large <u>scars</u>. Thanking you with my all heart.
> Marilyn Monroe

The surgeon, Dr Marcus Rabwin, already knew of his patient's concern about being able to bear children. There was a small possibility of complications involving the pelvic area, and a gynecologist stood by. This was Dr Leon Krohn, who would henceforth serve Marilyn through most of her long quest to bear children.

The operation went smoothly, and the star awoke with only the routine scar. 'When I told Marilyn she could go home,' Dr Rabwin recalled, 'she looked tearful and said, "I

can't because I don't have the money to pay the hospital bill."
I told her to call the studio; they would do all that. She said,
"Do you think they would?" She did call, and of course they
had the bill paid and a limousine at the door within an hour.'

Insecurities and all, Marilyn could now live like a star. The
studio limousine swept her to the relatively modest Beverly
Carlton Hotel, where she had been staying before the operation. Soon, though, she was ensconced in the luxurious
privacy of a pool suite in the Bel-Air Hotel. She paid the
$750-a-month bill, and she could now afford it.

On June 1, 1952, her twenty-sixth birthday, Marilyn received mountains of gifts and telegrams from Hollywood's
elite. That night, it is said, the star dined alone; but she had a
long telephone conversation with a man in New York. It was
not Arthur Miller – he was not yet available. The man's name
was DiMaggio.

Part Two

THE DIMAGGIO DISASTER

'It's no fun being married to an electric light.'

JOE DIMAGGIO

10

The newspapers used to call him the Last Hero. Joe DiMaggio, who swung a bat in earnest for the last time in 1951, spent the half-century that followed listening to the applause. He played golf, made nostalgic appearances for the baseball faithful and, for those who watched television commercials, became 'Mr Coffee' and the Bowery Savings man. On thousands of sunny California mornings he held court in the taproom of the San Francisco restaurant that bore his name. Without doing very much anymore, his laurels remained evergreen.

Year after year, in the publishing mills of New York City, editors would realize that the Last Hero had never written his autobiography. They would offer contracts, and he would decline. It was not that DiMaggio was not prepared to talk about his long-ago heyday or the finer points of coffee commercials. 'People aren't fooling me,' he said in the early 1980s, 'they want to know about Marilyn, and that's something I'm not of a mind to talk about.'

On paper, what DiMaggio would not talk about was a nine-month wonder, an embryonic marriage that flared and popped as briefly as the flashbulbs of the press that made it a public circus. In fact, it was a full decade that DiMaggio could not bear to discuss, a time that began as glamor and ended in mystery and grief.

'There are two ways to look at it,' DiMaggio said. 'One is, stories should be told as a point of history. The other is, guys have the right to go to the end in privacy.' Without DiMaggio the story lacked a key witness. Research for this book, however, does provide a rounded picture of the saga – a sad saga in which the Last Hero often emerges as distinctly unheroic and Marilyn, for her part, as no romantic heroine.

Suitably – since that was the way she made sure it continued – Marilyn met Joe DiMaggio thanks to a publicity picture. In spring 1952, at the suggestion of press agent Roy Craft, Marilyn had posed at a training session with two players on the Chicago White Sox team. The picture had made the part of the newspaper that Joe DiMaggio read, and he studied it closely. Marilyn, looking refreshingly innocent in shorts and sweater, stood teetering on stilt heels wielding a baseball bat. DiMaggio, who made something of a hobby of meeting young actresses, checked with Gus Zernial, one of the ballplayers who had posed with Marilyn.

It happened that DiMaggio knew a business agent named David March, and March had a different sort of interest in Marilyn – he wanted her to retain his services. DiMaggio had a word with March, who promised he would try to arrange a blind date. When he telephoned Marilyn, she was unenthusiastic.

'I don't care to meet him,' Marilyn responded. 'I don't like men in loud clothes, with checked suits and big muscles and pink ties. I get nervous.'

Marilyn, who was vague as to the difference between baseball and football, admitted that she had heard the name DiMaggio. She ventured to say that he was, perhaps, an Italian actor. Finally, she agreed to make up a foursome for dinner with DiMaggio, March, and another young actress. The rendezvous was for 6:30 P.M. at an Italian restaurant – of course – called the Villa Nova.

Marilyn did not show up at the restaurant, and DiMaggio began to doubt whether his host really knew her at all. March telephoned Marilyn, who grumbled that she was too tired to come out. Finally, nearly two hours later, she floated into DiMaggio's vision for the first time. What Marilyn saw was a powerfully built, graying man, some twelve years her senior, wearing a conservative suit.

'He was different from what I'd expected,' she was to tell Sidney Skolsky, 'I'd visualized him as having slick black hair, wearing flashy sports clothes, and with a New York line of patter.' In fact, according to March, DiMaggio said hardly anything at all that evening.

The remainder of what took place at that first meeting is lost in a welter of imaginative reporting. By Marilyn's account, offered before the collapse of their marriage, she surprised herself by offering to drive DiMaggio home. Then, because there seemed to be a good deal to say after all, they drove around Beverly Hills for three hours. He ended up with her telephone number, and it dawned on Marilyn that DiMaggio was, as the rest of the nation already knew, a great celebrity in his world.

Next day at the studio, Marilyn promptly told her publicity man about the encounter. 'She was giggling like a school-girl,' recalled Roy Craft. 'She'd met this marvellous man. At first she made a secret of who it was. You'd think she was a fifteen-year-old on her first date.'

Craft's was the professional response – Marilyn must be photographed with America's favorite champion. When DiMaggio visited the set where Marilyn was making *Monkey Business,* he was persuaded to pose with Marilyn and Cary Grant. The photograph, with DiMaggio looking as if he wished he were somewhere else, was duly published around the country. Cary Grant's face had been carefully cropped out, and America had its new romance.

A few rumors aside, the love match would move from headline to inane headline for two years, and then to marriage. For Marilyn, and especially for DiMaggio, it was not so simple.

Joseph Paul DiMaggio was an Italian's Italian. He was the eighth of nine children born to a Sicilian couple who emigrated to the United States at the turn of the century. His father, Zio Pepe, was a fisherman, and after a false start in a fishing village to the north, he brought his children to San Francisco the year after Joseph was born. San Francisco was then an unspoiled place, but life in the port was tough. The business of catching fish aside, life on the piers was fiercely competitive and often dangerous. The brutal side of Sicilian custom had crossed the ocean with the immigrants, and violence was commonplace. Poverty, in those early days, was never far away.

Young DiMaggio was supposed to become a fisherman, but disappointed his father. He did not much like boats; he got seasick, and his father and brothers made him feel less than a man. He would sneak off and practice baseball in the sand, using a broken oar for a bat. That was considered childish, and for years DiMaggio lost that vital Italian possession, the respect of his brothers.

Pride returned when Joe DiMaggio was nineteen. Playing for the San Francisco Seals, the boy established a Pacific Coast record by hitting safely in 61 games. The talent scouts started watching, and in 1936, at twenty-two, DiMaggio was in Yankee Stadium playing baseball for New York. For the next fifteen years, with a break for Army Air Force service during the final phase of the war, his prowess mesmerized a vast public. In 1941, six months before Pearl Harbor, DiMaggio hit 56 runs in 56 consecutive games – one of them with a borrowed bat when his own had been stolen – and broke a record that has yet to be surpassed. The New York Yankees won the pennant, and the World Series, and the nation's jukeboxes blared out a song written specially for him:

> He'll live in baseball's Hall of Fame,
> He got there blow by blow.
> Our kids will tell their kids his name,
> Joltin' Joe DiMaggio

After the war DiMaggio continued to play and to fascinate, but was dogged by injury and illness. He had lived improbably hard through his years of glory, carousing more than his stomach ulcers allowed and smoking two or three packs of cigarettes a day. There had also been a marriage to a blonde would-be film star. Dorothy Arnold was a singer in a New York nightclub, and had a stock player's contract with Universal Studios. She and DiMaggio married in 1939, to joyous accolades from thousands of San Franciscans waving Italian flags. Four years later, after Dorothy sued him on the grounds of cruelty, they were divorced.

By 1951, when Joe DiMaggio retired, there had been many girls but none that anyone remembers. He was known for his male friends. There was Toots Shor, a Jewish entrepreneur who had come up through Prohibition days, and through friendship with racketeers, to running a celebrities' watering hole in New York. There was George Solotaire, a would-be songwriter who ended up as a wealthy ticket broker in New York. DiMaggio lived on the fringe of show business, and it was not unnatural. His own role had long been to entertain America.

Now, at thirty-seven, DiMaggio was rich, retired, and very obviously lonely. The king of the baseball field was out to pasture and looking for a queen. He thought he had found her in Marilyn Monroe. After the meeting at the Villa Nova, DiMaggio launched immediate pursuit. There were more rendezvous, and probably physical conquest. At first DiMaggio, not unaccustomed to horizontal triumph, was heard to brag a little. For publication, Marilyn would later say she 'had dinner with him the next night, and every night until he had to leave for New York.'

In less than two months the affair was more than just good copy for Marilyn's publicity office. Dr Rabwin, who performed Marilyn's appendectomy, remembered streams of calls from DiMaggio in New York. Roses arrived by the dozen. By her twenty-sixth birthday, on June 1, 1952, the newspapers were starting to chatter about possible marriage. Marilyn refused to comment on that, but vouchsafed, 'I want to love and be loved more than anything else in the world.' She also said, 'Men are like wine – they improve with age. But I have nothing against younger men.'

A year later columnist Dick Williams would quote Marilyn in these terms: '"There are always rumors about other men going around about me," she said, sipping a glass of water and watching me lazily with those bedroom eyes of hers. "I honestly don't know what they're talking about. Besides, it makes Joe very angry. He'd like to punch some of these people."'

Anger would have been a colossal understatement had DiMaggio known what was really going on. It appears that during their two-year courtship, and sometimes when DiMaggio was actually in Los Angeles, Marilyn had affairs with at least four other men. She seriously discussed marriage with one, and may even have been briefly – and secretly – married to another.

In spring 1952, on the set of her new movie *Monkey Business,* Marilyn noticed a fledgling actor of twenty, some six years younger than herself. Nico Minardos was a burly, darkly handsome Greek recently arrived from Athens. He was studying acting at UCLA, a course which included production classes at Twentieth Century-Fox. Marilyn asked another Greek, then working at Fox, to introduce her to Minardos, and an affair began.

Minardos, who went on to become a successful producer and veteran actor, never sought publicity in connection with Marilyn. He was interviewed for this book as the result of a chance remark by a doctor who also knew her. He said he had an affair with Marilyn from late spring 1952 for about seven months, and that they saw each other sporadically until her death ten years later. They were already involved when Marilyn met DiMaggio.

'I was a young buck,' Minardos remembered, 'and she was such a pretty girl. One of the most beautiful girls I've ever seen, waking up in the morning without makeup, absolutely gorgeous. She was bright – shrewd perhaps rather than profoundly intelligent – and such a sensitive kid. And yet she was a lousy lay. Oh, I used to love her. I was very young.'

'Lousy lay' notwithstanding, Minardos and Marilyn became close. They met either at her hotel or at his apartment on Wilshire Boulevard. Sometimes when she would arrive, driving her green Pontiac, he would be playing cards with a friend. The two young men would sit in their underwear in the summer heat, finishing the game, and Marilyn would have to wait. She did not seem to mind.

Clearly Marilyn was no longer the sexually fulfilled creature suggested by her first husband, Jim Dougherty. 'She could never have a climax,' Minardos said, 'though she would try so hard. She had such severe psychological problems. She was very, very unhappy.'

Marilyn told Minardos her story of childhood rape, and he was not sure what to believe. When she talked of wanting to have children, he somehow felt she was fantasizing. When she went to the hospital for an operation, which the surgeon later confirmed to me was a straightforward appendectomy, she told Minardos she was 'having an ovary removed.' Looking back, Minardos felt that 'the fascinating thing with Marilyn was that she was acting in her real life. She knew what the reality was, but she acted things out because she loved the drama. . . .'

Minardos ended up in no doubt that Marilyn had used sex, and was still using it, to get what she wanted. He named in particular Spyros Skouras, the Fox studio boss who had used his influence to advance Marilyn.

'One night at her hotel,' said Minardos, 'Marilyn said,

"Do you mind leaving for about an hour? I have a business appointment here between eight and nine." I thought there was something odd about the way she said it. I was young and jealous and sort of dragged things out. There was a knock at the door and a voice saying, "It's me, darling." There was no way to get out. I put on my pants and opened the door, and it was Skouras. He was so angry he barred me from the studio then. And later, when I knew him, he never called me by my name – he would always call me "Marilyn's boyfriend." I criticized Marilyn for what she was doing, then and later. She was achieving success partly in a dishonorable way, by using people.'

In November 1952, six months into the DiMaggio court-ship, Marilyn would take Minardos to his first Thanksgiving dinner – at the home of Fred Karger, the lover who had rejected her four years earlier. The Karger family, which Marilyn adopted more than any other as her own, welcomed the young Minardos. Months later, at Marilyn's request, Minardos would take her to observe Greek custom – an Easter service at the local Orthodox church. She was en-thralled by the interminable ceremony, and to Minardos' chagrin insisted on staying for the whole service.

By the fall of 1952, said Minardos, Marilyn was talking of marriage. Things went so far as placing a long-distance call to Athens to speak to his parents, whom Marilyn astonished by announcing theatrically, 'I want to have a child with your son.'

Young Minardos, however, had his own reasons for shying away from marriage. He said, 'I was never going to let myself become "Mr Monroe." If I married a woman she was going to be "Mrs Minardos."'

Minardos recalled with a shudder that a year or so later newspapers would be referring to Joe DiMaggio as 'Marilyn's mate.' Once while he was with Marilyn, Minardos caught her laboriously writing a love letter to DiMaggio, with a slim brown book open beside her. It turned out to be a volume of letters by an English romantic poet, and Marilyn was copying sections verbatim. In the end, the letter to DiMaggio was a joint production by Minardos and Marilyn together.

Early on, Minardos said, he realized that Joe DiMaggio was 'extremely jealous.' This was something that did not wholly escape mention even in the popular press, which carried no news of Marilyn's dalliances on the side. The newspapers had discovered that DiMaggio shunned publicity while Marilyn fed on it. At the Beverly Hills Hotel he would stalk upstairs to wait for Marilyn, knowing full well she was eating alone downstairs. The Italian from San Francisco was not amused by Marilyn's flaunting of her body. She said she was trying to moderate her style, but the exhibitionist in her was stronger.

Billy Travilla, the designer who was now dressing Marilyn for her films, tried in vain to stop her wearing overtight clothes. Once, when she had to wear a full skirt for the roller-skating scene in *Monkey Business,* Travilla thought he had her under control for once. He dressed her for the scene, then watched helplessly as 'she literally reached back, parted her buttocks, and stuck some of the pleats in the crack to hold them in place. "Fooled you, Billy, didn't I?" she said as she came off the set. "You and your big silly skirt."'

Marilyn had some trouble with nature when she tried another old trick. She told Travilla that Jean Harlow, one of her idols, deliberately made her nipples prominent by rubbing them with ice before going into a scene. 'Mine,' Marilyn complained, 'won't get hard. They're the wrong sort.' The problem was solved by artifice – a little round button inserted in the brassiere at the relevant places. The *New York Daily News* wrote of *Monkey Business:* 'Marilyn Monroe can look and act dumber than any of the screen's current blondes.' Marilyn reportedly took it as a compliment.

Offscreen, Marilyn's performance was guaranteed to upset Joe DiMaggio. On a visit to a U.S. Marine base, she teased ten thousand men with 'I don't know why you boys are always getting so excited about sweater girls. Take away their sweaters and what have they got?'

Later in the year, as Grand Marshal of the Miss America Beauty Parade Pageant, she wore a dress that was cut almost to the navel. DiMaggio was said to be hurt and embarrassed. If he knew what was going on behind the public cheesecake, the hurt must have become torment. Away from Los Angeles, on location, Marilyn had been toying with yet another man.

11

It was now six years since Marilyn had enjoyed a summer romance with Robert Slatzer, the young writer from Ohio who met her in the lobby of Twentieth Century-Fox. He had been dividing his time between his home in Columbus, where he had regular work on local newspapers, and visits to Hollywood, where he hoped to break into the film industry. Meanwhile, as he grew into his twenties, Slatzer remained mesmerized by the 'girl without guile' who had given herself to him on a California beach. Marilyn, for her part, encouraged him. He wrote letters from Ohio, and Marilyn responded with streams of long-distance calls, a habit that was to become a Monroe trademark. In the early days it resulted in unpaid bills and at least one lawsuit by the telephone company.

On and off, when Slatzer was in Hollywood, they shared furnished rooms. 'It was out of necessity sometimes,' said Slatzer. 'If you didn't pay the rent, they could lock up and take all your possessions. It had happened to us both a couple of times, so we shared a place from time to time, to split the cost. You could say we lived together, but just for two weeks here, a month there. We were occasional lovers, but I think I had become one of her few lasting friends.'

By the 1980s, when he was being interviewed for this book, Slatzer spent most of his time in his cramped crow's nest of a house high in the Hollywood hills. An American flag drooped at the door, and the guest was ushered into rooms piled high with books that had long since overflowed their shelves. In his middle age, Slatzer still enjoyed the regular company of young and pretty women. Conversation was interrupted repeatedly by the squawks of a cage bird and the jangling of the telephone – often heralding another inquiry about Marilyn Monroe.

Since Marilyn's death Slatzer had gained the dubious reputation of having become a Monroe obsessive. In 1974 his book, *The Life and Curious Death of Marilyn Monroe,* provided a platform for his persistent claim that Marilyn was murdered following an unhappy affair with Robert Kennedy. That, and Slatzer's rambling way of presenting his case, invited scorn and the suggestion that he was a charlatan. Some doubted whether he ever knew Marilyn at all. The criticism, verging on ridicule, came mostly from reporters and editors jumping at the chance to run a Monroe headline, yet recoiling from attempting serious research of their own.

Slatzer, to be sure, had none of the disciplines of the investigative reporter. His book on Marilyn, like his interviews, was muddled and virtually undocumented. In many ways I found it irritating and unconvincing. However, because of Slatzer's allegations about the last part of Marilyn's life – specifically, the very serious statements about President Kennedy and his brother Robert – it seemed essential to substantiate his claim to have known Marilyn or to knock it down. After intensive interviews with Slatzer himself covering a two-year period, and independent research, I came to accept that Slatzer had indeed been close to Marilyn for her entire adult life.

This conviction was based on interviews with numerous witnesses, most of them conducted without Slatzer's prior knowledge. They include Allan 'Whitey' Snyder, who made up Marilyn for her first screen test, became her regular makeup man, and finally prepared her, in death, for her funeral. Snyder, everywhere accepted as one of Marilyn's closest friends, said Slatzer indeed met Marilyn as early as 1946. Snyder wrote:

'Quite often while I was making her up she would tell

me that Bob sent me his best or mention that they had just talked on the phone or even tell me about a date she had with him that night. Bob Slatzer had the capacity for being a good listener which Marilyn so desperately needed through the years that they were friends. . . . Marilyn used to tell me how she could always call Bob in the middle of the night and he would talk with her for hours. . . . In my opinion, she always loved him very much.'

The early days of the Slatzer affair with Marilyn were remembered by Noble 'Kid' Chissell, a former navy boxing champion turned Hollywood stunt man and bit player. It was his car that Slatzer borrowed the night of his first date with Marilyn, and Chissell himself was with the couple when Slatzer took Marilyn home. He recalled that Marilyn cooked breakfast at Slatzer's home in those early days, and that their romance survived innumerable separations. One Christmas, late in the forties, Chissell accompanied Slatzer and Marilyn, laden with small presents, to the orphanage where she had once lived herself. It was Marilyn's idea to make a special delivery of gifts for the children.

Half a dozen other witnesses, all of whom had known Slatzer since the early fifties, confirmed his connection with Marilyn. They include Gordon Heaver, an Englishman who arrived in Hollywood in 1952 as a story editor for Paramount Studios. He met Marilyn in Slatzer's company that year. Others, from Slatzer's hometown of Columbus, Ohio, recall him talking about Marilyn as a close friend during the fifties. They included playwright and longtime correspondent for the *Columbus Star*, Doral Chenoweth; veteran *Scripps-Howard* writer Ron Pataki; wealthy restaurateur Lee Henry; and Slatzer's dentist, Dr Sanford Firestone.

By the late fifties Dr Firestone's interest was so piqued, after hearing Slatzer talking on the telephone to a woman identifying herself as Marilyn, that he went to great lengths to discover whether his friend was pulling some elaborate hoax. Using contacts of his own in Hollywood, Firestone managed to speak to Marilyn himself. She confirmed that it had indeed been her voice on the recent call, and Firestone eventually met Marilyn, thanks to the Slatzer connection.

Slatzer's account of events in 1952, when Marilyn was already firmly labeled as Joe DiMaggio's girl, is startling.

In early June that year, with *Monkey Business* completed, Marilyn flew East to play the part of an unfaithful wife in *Niagara*, a film that would succeed not least because of its dramatic setting in the shadow of the Falls. It became famous, however, for a sensual walking shot, then, and perhaps still, the longest walking shot in movie history.

While the cast and crew assembled at Buffalo, on the U.S. side of the Canadian border, Marilyn diverted to New York City for a brief interlude with DiMaggio. It was now, on a whirlwind round of Manhattan's night spots, that the champion showed off his prize to his friends.

The friends Marilyn met at Toots Shor's were men's men – boisterous sportsmen, gamblers, wrestlers, and habitual nightclubbers. A journalist who later interviewed her reported: 'To Marilyn, valiantly fighting the battle of the descending eyelids for Joe's sake, it was sheer garbage. She had other interests she had devoutly hoped to indulge during her New York stay – an afternoon at the theater, a visit to the museums and the like, but Joe, who succeeded in calling the shots, would have none of that.'

Meanwhile, presumably unbeknownst to DiMaggio, Marilyn was indulging yet another interest – a tryst with Robert Slatzer.

Slatzer said Marilyn called him in Ohio before she left Hollywood, suggesting he meet her at the *Niagara* location. Now twenty-five, bored with his work in newspapers and still fascinated by Marilyn, Slatzer jumped at the chance. At the General Brock Hotel, on the Canadian side of the falls, he made contact with Frank Neill, a studio publicist. Neill, who saw Slatzer as a newspaperman and occasional reviewer, found him the perfect accommodation – a room adjacent to Marilyn's.

Slatzer says Marilyn greeted him with enthusiasm. She was drinking heavily and flaunting her nudity more than Slatzer remembered from his visits to California, a point corroborated by one of her hairdressers, who told of Marilyn going naked to the window, then giggling when she saw a group of youths peering up at her.

Niagara Falls was a traditional honeymoon spot, and the woman the press was touting as Joe DiMaggio's bride-to-be now astonished Slatzer. 'Wouldn't this be a wonderful place to get married?' she said. 'We wouldn't have to go to Niagara Falls because we're already here.'

They had never considered marriage before, and Slatzer decided the drink was talking. Then, after another night of liquor and lovemaking, Slatzer found himself asking the question seriously. This time it was Marilyn who balked, saying she was not ready for marriage.

As shooting of *Niagara* continued, makeup man Whitey Snyder observed that Marilyn was again terrified of performing before the cameras. She was also extremely restless. The director appointed Snyder to the role that would soon become familiar, baby-sitting Marilyn. He spent hours gently talking her into appearing on the set, and escorted her to New York when she suddenly decided to visit DiMaggio again. Slatzer, meanwhile, had lost his job, as a result of dallying too long with Marilyn at Niagara. She called him, commiserated, and suggested he return to the location. Slatzer answered the summons and followed her to California when shooting ended.

Summer in Los Angeles appeared to be merely the next chapter in the DiMaggio romance. There were press reports about Marilyn with DiMaggio and his ten-year-old son, Joe, Jr, lounging beside a Hollywood swimming pool, and

DiMaggio's former wife noisily objected to her son being in such a place and in such company.

Then, curiously, the headlines began to fade. In early September 1952, Marilyn said she and DiMaggio had no wedding plans. On marriage in general, she ventured that a little male jealousy never hurt a wife. 'It would be pretty dull without that occasionally,' she said. 'But it's like salt on a steak. All you need is a bit of it.' DiMaggio, it seems, was certainly getting his share.

Robert Slatzer had come to California at Marilyn's bidding. For two months, he said, life was something of a French farce. 'I saw her as much as DiMaggio did,' Slatzer recalled. 'I don't know if she made up excuses when he called her and she wanted to go out with me, and vice versa. DiMaggio had some deal with the network to broadcast during the World Series, and when he was out of town I saw her practically every night. I was at the house when he would phone. Sometimes I would call at midnight and DiMaggio would be there; then she might call me back at three o'clock in the morning saying, "I can talk now."'

Slatzer had one classic encounter with DiMaggio when both men turned up for a date on the same night. 'I was there waiting for her,' said Slatzer, 'when DiMaggio drove up. We each knew who the other was, and there was a very quiet waiting period – there was not much we could say. Then Marilyn arrived and let us both into the house. He was a big guy, and I wasn't about to get into an argument. I poured myself a drink, and he was put out about the fact that I seemed to know the place pretty well. The two of them had an argument, and he asked me to leave. I wouldn't. And her temper just flared and she told us both to get out. About an hour later she called and apologized, and said she'd got her schedules mixed up.'

In late August, Dorothy Kilgallen's column carried a three-line teaser that broke the stream of gossip about DiMaggio.

It read: 'A dark horse in the Marilyn Monroe romance derby is Bob Slatzer, former Columbus, Ohio, literary critic. He's been wooing her by phone and mail, and improving Her Mind with gifts of the world's greatest books.'

Three weeks later Slatzer himself was in print, reporting that he had been supplying Marilyn with *The Rubáiyát of Omar Khayyám,* and the works of Edgar Allan Poe. She in turn, he said, had given him *The Prophet,* by Kahlil Gibran. This was not, one can assume, reading that Marilyn could share with Joe DiMaggio.

One night in early October Marilyn talked at length about DiMaggio. According to Slatzer, 'She told me she couldn't see any way she could be happy with him. Because he was so jealous, not only over me – he was jealous if they were sitting in a booth having dinner and somebody asked for an autograph. He'd be all knocked out of shape and start giving her hell. I would have bet at that time that she'd never marry DiMaggio, if she lived to be a hundred.' Instead, if Slatzer was to be believed, Marilyn now married him instead, in a civil ceremony on the Mexican border.

Slatzer's account of marrying Marilyn has understandably aroused skepticism. It has never been documented, and sensible people recoil from the notion that Marilyn could have done anything so significant without making headlines. The doubters point out that Slatzer said nothing publicly about such a marriage until years after Marilyn was dead. However, several people interviewed for this book supported the story.

Two sources seem especially significant, because they suggest Marilyn herself mentioned the episode. Dr Firestone, Slatzer's dentist, remembered Marilyn talking years later of her 'honeymoon in Mexico with Bob.' At the time Firestone had heard nothing of the marriage from Slatzer, and assumed Marilyn was speaking loosely about a romantic visit.

Actress Terry Moore, former wife of Howard Hughes, said she knew Marilyn from her earliest Hollywood days; they were both under contract to Fox, and later to Columbia, at the same time. Moore said, 'I remember very well her being excited about going out with Bob. She wanted so much to have culture, and she respected Bob because he was well-read. She did tell me she had married him, right after they did it. I remember, because I had been telling her about my own brief marriage to Glenn Davis.'

Will Fowler, Slatzer's writer friend in Hollywood, said, 'Bob told me he was going to slip away to Mexico and marry Marilyn. When they got back, I remember Bob showing me the marriage certificate. It looked like a fancy black-and-white high school diploma with a gold seal. . . .'

Slatzer said the marriage took place on October 4, 1952, after a long night of talk and alcohol, while DiMaggio was away in the East. They climbed into his prize possession, a 1948 Packard convertible, and headed for the Mexican border town of Tijuana. They had been to Mexico before on weekend trips, and Tijuana was famous for rubber-stamp marriages and divorces. A decade later, Marilyn would fly to another border town for her divorce from Arthur Miller.

'We weren't sure what the procedure was,' said Slatzer. 'I asked the assistant manager of the Foreign Club, whom I'd met before. He said to just go down the street to one of those real fast lawyers. Marilyn had been talking about a church, and she didn't think that was very romantic. Anyway, we found a lawyer behind a storefront right on the main street. I don't remember the name – it's going back so damn many years. He said he could take care of us in about an hour and we'd need two witnesses. His wife would be one, and we were going to find another one on the street.'

It was the second witness who provided Slatzer's only firsthand corroboration of events on the wedding day. Without forewarning Slatzer, I contacted Kid Chissell, the old actor who first met Marilyn with Slatzer in the forties. Of the alleged marriage Chissell said, 'It was pure chance. I was down in Tijuana looking up an old Navy buddy, and I suddenly saw Bob and Marilyn coming out of a shop. I gave him a shove and he swung round, looking mad. When they realized who I was, we all laughed, and they said, "Would I be their witness?" I said, "Yes." I thought it was about time. . . .' Then Marilyn said she'd feel better if she went into a church before she got married, and we went off to a Catholic church, which was the only sort they had there. Bob and I stayed near the door and Marilyn covered her head with her sweater and lit candles near the altar. When she was done we went to the lawyer, and his wife gave Marilyn a flower, and they filled out the forms, and he married them. Then we went to get Marilyn some Mexican sandals, because someone had taken the shoes she'd taken off at the lawyer's office. We did that, and then we went to the Foreign Club for a drink.'

If Chissell fabricated his story, he rehearsed it well. His account meshed with Slatzer's in all significant details. There was little likelihood that Marilyn would be recognized, said Slatzer. 'She was not looking like the raving beauty, Marilyn Monroe,' he explained. 'She had no makeup on, had her hair pulled back, looked just like any little girl going to Tijuana for the weekend.'

That night, said Slatzer, he and Marilyn consummated the marriage in the bedroom of the Rosarita Beach Hotel, then an isolated old-fashioned place about twenty miles from Tijuana. 'Next morning,' he said, 'I awoke to see her half sitting up in bed, kind of wiping her eyes. She was crying a little, but she wouldn't say why.'

The marriage lasted three days. 'We got back to Los Angeles wondering what we were going to do about DiMaggio,' said Slatzer, 'but Darryl Zanuck got to us first. Late on Monday afternoon Marilyn called and said there were problems at the studio. She had told a couple of people on the qt and word had gotten around quickly. I ended up in a confrontation with Zanuck, and he was firm. He said, "We've got a lot of money invested in this girl, and we're not going to be put on the hook with a marriage. Get it undone.'"

According to Slatzer, he and Marilyn both bowed to the studio's will. His friend, Will Fowler, said this is what Slatzer also told him at the time; and actress Terry Moore said, 'Marilyn told me the studio had put a stop on it in some way.'

Less readily, Slatzer admitted that Marilyn thought better of the marriage as soon as she returned to Hollywood. There were phone calls from DiMaggio, and Slatzer's brief wife seemed confused and disoriented. Next day the couple were back in Tijuana, bribing the lawyer to destroy the marriage certificate, which had not yet been officially filed. It was done.

In the sprawling mess that Tijuana became, the Slatzer claim of a brief marriage to Marilyn was beyond further investigation. The saddest comment on the matter came from Terry Moore. She said, 'Marilyn wanted to be free, and yet she was so afraid of loneliness. I think she was in a muddle over DiMaggio, and she liked Bob. She just ran into it and then ran out again.'

In the last weeks of 1952 Marilyn started shooting *Gentlemen Prefer Blondes,* one of the major musicals of the fifties. It was also a mighty success for Marilyn, who shared top billing with Jane Russell. The two had attended the same high school, and Russell had once met Marilyn at a dance with her first husband, Jim Dougherty. Now, to the frustration of the gossips, Jane Russell and Marilyn Monroe became good friends.

Russell was married to a retired football player, Bob Waterfield, and Marilyn asked her advice about marrying a famous sportsman. Russell said in an interview for this book, 'I told her she must find time to go off with her own friends to talk about books and poetry and the arts. But apparently she wasn't able to go off and do that. Marilyn felt part of her was dying because she wasn't getting it expressed.'

Joe DiMaggio showed no signs of going away. Marilyn's friend Sidney Skolsky told how 1952 ended. 'She had attended the studio's annual Christmas party, appearing gay, seeming to be enjoying herself. Then she left, with nothing to do but to return home – at that time a single room at the Beverly Hills Hotel – and wait for a phone call from Joe, who was visiting his family in San Francisco. When Marilyn entered her room she found a miniature Christmas tree standing on the table, a pasteboard sign on which was hand printed "Merry Christmas, Marilyn," and Joe sitting in a chair in the corner.'

Marilyn told Skolsky a few days later, 'It's the first time in my life anyone ever gave me a Christmas tree. I was so happy I cried.'

That same month, Marilyn's studio fed the press with stories that Marilyn Monroe was now officially a full-fledged star. According to the studio, she now had the curious double distinction of being 'more publicized' than either Rita Hayworth or the Queen of England. She was receiving more than five thousand fan letters a week, and was now to occupy a luxurious dressing room that had once been used by Marlene Dietrich. The studio began calling her '*Miss Monroe.*'

A few months earlier, a helicopter had clattered to earth beside the Hollywood swimming pool of bandleader Ray Anthony. The downdraft swept chairs and tables into the water, ruining the effect of thousands of floating gardenias. Marilyn descended from the helicopter in a flaming red dress that offended everyone except the photographers. She was there for a ceremony so tasteless that it appalled even the public relations man who had organized it – the unveiling of a song called 'Marilyn.' The words went:

> No gal, I believe,
> Beginning with Eve,
> Could weave a fascination like my MA-RI-LYN.

I planned everything,
The church and the ring,
The one I haven't told it yet is MA-RI-LYN.
She hasn't said yes,
I have to confess,
I haven't kissed or even met my MA-RI-LYN.
But if luck is with me,
She'll be my bride for evermore.

In fantasy, Marilyn was now wedded to all America. In the real world, she was a shipwreck in the arms of many, with a baseball champion for sheet anchor.

12

At midsummer 1953, shortly after her twenty-seventh birthday, Marilyn lay down on the sidewalk outside Grauman's Chinese Theater on Hollywood Boulevard. Beside her was Jane Russell, her co-star in *Gentlemen Prefer Blondes*. They placed their hands in wet cement, did the same with their feet, then scrawled their names alongside the prints. A crowd roared approval, and Marilyn came up with her customary quips. She mischievously suggested that Russell, for whom Howard Hughes had once designed a special brassiere, should bend over into the cement. As for herself, celebrated since *Niagara* as being the one actress who could make an entrance by walking away from the camera, Marilyn proposed sitting in it. Her ideas were turned down, along with the suggestion that the *i* in her signature be dotted with a diamond to commemorate her song 'Diamonds Are a Girl's Best Friend.' A rhinestone was used instead, and a thief stole it soon afterward.

The ceremony at Grauman's was corny but crucial, one more affirmation that Marilyn really was a star. Marilyn, said Jane Russell, was pleased and scared. Insecurity, those around her now saw, was ever-present in the world's most brazen actress.

On the day of the Grauman appearance, hairdresser Gladys Whitten, whom Marilyn called 'Gladness,' received a panic-stricken call from Marilyn. 'I need your help,' said the voice from miles across the city, 'please come, Gladness, and bring your mom.' It sounded like a real crisis, until Marilyn explained: 'I can't decide which dress to wear.'

Whitten obliged, as she always did. 'She was like a little girl,' said Whitten. 'I couldn't help it. I just wanted to help her.'

It was fortunate for Marilyn that her aides were long-suffering. 'Sometimes,' Whitten said, 'she'd come in; we'd get her hair all done, and her makeup on, and she'd start to get dressed, and then she'd say, "Oh, I forgot to take a shower." And she'd go ahead and take the shower – and then we'd start all over again. . . .'

Marilyn could be as funny as she was frustrating. Once the helpless little voice called from just outside the studio. 'Gladness,' it begged, 'would you come and pick me up? My car didn't arrive. I've had to walk all the way from Beverly Hills, and nobody would pick me up.'

A puzzled Whitten hastened to the rescue, to find Marilyn waiting, her face thickly coated in vaseline. It would, she insisted, keep her skin young, though others advised that it would simply encourage the growth of unwanted hair.* Drivers that morning had scorned to pick up the 'Fastest Rising Star of 1953', clad in jeans and sweater, her face smothered in grease.

The once-punctual Marilyn now began to enrage directors with the lateness that would become legendary. Jane Russell remembered that 'she would come in way before me, and she'd have rehearsed. She'd be all ready, but too nervous to go out on the set. So I'd arrange it with Whitey that when it was time to go I'd come and get her, and we'd walk out there together.' The insecurity was now chronic.

On the set Marilyn was easily wounded by any sort of criticism. Actor Tommy Noonan was heard to say, after a stage kiss with Marilyn, 'It was like being sucked into a vacuum.' Marilyn's response to Noonan's comment was tearful collapse.

---

* As photographs taken in her thirties show, Marilyn did later grow some facial hair on her cheeks.

'She was really distraught,' said Jane Russell. 'She said, "How can people be so cruel? Nobody can be so cruel and not pay for it one day."'

Behind the scenes Whitey Snyder had now become as much babysitter as makeup man. For some time now he had been assigned to sit with Marilyn in hotel or dressing room, quietly coaxing her into facing the cameras. Snyder, who married Marjorie Plecher, wardrobe assistant on several Monroe movies, said there never was a time when Marilyn did not feel 'terror, pure terror' about acting. Plecher said, 'She never felt secure in front of the cameras. She was so scared about looking right, acting right, that she was physically unable to leave the trailer. It was the ultimate stage fright. She had a great talent, but she never felt sure of herself, never could believe in herself.'

Snyder, hairdresser Whitten and a handful of others, were now to become Marilyn's loyal personal troops. These were the soldier ants of the industry, and Marilyn was more at ease with them than with most of the great and the famous. She knew their value and tried to let them know it with gifts. It might be a gold-plated money clip for Snyder, a silver-tagged decanter for Whitten, or a signed photograph reading, 'To Gladness, for making me look like this. I love you.'

After *Gentlemen Prefer Blondes* Marilyn gave her car, a Pontiac she had owned only a few months, to drama coach Natasha Lytess. It was followed by a vicuña coat. For Lytess, gratitude was tempered with the reflection that Marilyn gave material things because 'she was unable to give of herself.' It was a character judgment to be echoed, in the end, by the next in Marilyn's succession of men. This was Billy Travilla, dress designer on *Gentlemen Prefer Blondes* and several other movies.

Travilla had first met Marilyn in 1950. She was twenty-four, he twenty-five. 'My introduction,' he recalled, 'was the sight of her in a black bathing suit. She opened the sliding doors of my fitting room, and a strap fell off, and her breast was exposed. She had a delightful quality, being so beautiful, of wanting to show herself. Some people were offended by it – and of course she did it on purpose. She was so childlike she could do anything, and you would forgive her as you would forgive a seven-year-old. She was both a woman and a baby, and both men and women adored her. A man wouldn't know whether to sit her on his knee and pet her, or put his arms around her and get her in the sack. ... I've dressed many women in my life, but never one like this lady. She was for me a dual personality. She was not well educated, but an extremely bright woman, and she had the whims of a child. She had a wonderful ability to woo. She'd come in the office, as people would, to complain about something; but Marilyn would always have a little tear, a real tear, in one eye, and her lips would tremble. Those lips! And a man can't fight it. You don't want that baby to cry.'

'Billy Dear, Please Dress Me Forever. I love you, Marilyn,' reads the inscription on the nude calendar Billy Travilla was given. After three years of knowing each other professionally, said Travilla, there was a brief affair during *Gentlemen Prefer Blondes*, 'while my wife was in Florida and Joe DiMaggio was away.' The liaison lasted only weeks, but Travilla provides an intimate glimpse of the woman with the ways of a child.

It had been hard to resist a dalliance with Marilyn. Once the designer's secretary came in while Marilyn was sitting on his knee. Marilyn stood up while Travilla – in a condition that discouraged getting up till he could adjust himself – remained seated. Delightedly, and in front of his secretary, Marilyn giggled and asked, 'Billy, why can't you stand up?'

'I remember I was going to pick her up at seven-thirty,' said Travilla. 'I knocked at her hotel door, and she asked me to wait. Then came this handsome young actor, also carrying flowers. We knew each other casually, and we stood in line. He said he had a date, and I said I did. A good twenty minutes went by; then she opened the door. She took the flowers from the bellboy, told the other guy she had a date with me rather than him, and I went in. The place was obviously quickly made ready to receive a visitor, and done badly. Her barbells were sticking out from under the couch and she didn't know what to do with the flowers. I told her to call down to the office, and she said, "No, I've got a better idea," and put both the bouquets in the toilet. Then came the matter of whether she was too tall, in high heels, to go out with me. I had to prance to the mirror with her while we checked her height in high heels, and she was an inch taller than me. The high heels won anyway, after about twenty minutes.'

Another of Travilla's recollections was that 'one night we went to Tiffany's on Eighth Street. I went to the men's room, which was down past the club's office. I noticed Marilyn's nude calendar hanging in the office, and told Marilyn. She said, "Oh, Billy, where? I want to see it." We went back and the door was shut, so we knocked. A tall black man came and asked what we wanted, and Marilyn said she wanted to look at her calendar. As it turned out, Billie Holiday was using the office as a dressing room, and I guess she'd heard Marilyn Monroe was in the audience and thought Marilyn had come to say hello. When she learned different what we did see of Holiday was very fast – just a whirl of white sleeve with beads dangling from it, and a dark hand. She pulled the calendar off the wall, crumpled it, threw it in Marilyn's face, and called her a cunt. Dumbfounded, we went back to the table. The manager wanted us to stay and see the show, but we left.'

Looking back, Travilla tempered a lover's fondness with the keen perceptions of a lifetime spent working with female stars. 'I think she wanted to love, but could only love herself,' he said. 'She was totally narcissistic. She adored her own face, constantly wanted to make it better and different. Everything she did in that regard, by the way, was right at the time. She once told me, "I can make my face do anything, same as you can take a white board and build from that and make a painting." But the only way she was highly sexed was the charge she got out of looking in the mirror and seeing the beautiful mouth that she'd painted with about five shades of lipstick, to get the right curves, the right shadows to bring out the lips, because her lips were really very flat.'

'If ever there was a prick-teaser,' said Travilla, 'it was Marilyn, when she wanted to be. She did it for real and for show. We'd be doing a still picture in the gallery, and I'd be standing right next to her, and she'd whisper, "Say something dirty," and I would. And you could read it in the pictures, you could see it, that mouth was saying, "Fuck me" or "Suck me." It was a turn-on for her.'

'One time,' Travilla recalled, 'there was this little fuddy-duddy man from Eastman Kodak – we were using a new kind of film – and she comes out in this chiffon nightie, and she poses this way and that way, and the little guy gets uncomfortable. And she knew, and she came over and said, "Is this okay for you, Mr Eastman?" That was her sexual kick – to arouse.'

Like many others, colleagues as well as lovers, Travilla was amazed at his own tolerance of Marilyn. He said, 'There was something about the girl you had to love. She would be late for a morning appointment, call at three to say she was on the way, and you'd wait till seven. She was the one woman I've known who could make a man feel tall, handsome, fascinating, with that unblinking look of hers, dead in the eyes. You were the king of the evening, if she so decided. She made you feel like the only one, even when you were not.'

Travilla had no illusions about being the only one. Another lover that year, for a month or so, was Edward G. Robinson, Jr. Robinson, son of the famous actor, was a sad figure, the product of a broken home and a catastrophic relationship with his father. He never became more than an aspiring actor, and was to die an alcoholic at the age of forty, choking to death while watching one of his father's movies. In 1953 Robinson was nineteen, something of a hell-raiser, and chasing older women. Marilyn was one of them, according to Robinson's friend Arthur James and his last wife, Nan Morris.

James said Marilyn met Robinson through a mutual friendship with another son with a famous name – Charlie Chaplin, Jr., Marilyn's former lover. The acquaintance became an affair during *Gentlemen Prefer Blondes*. Robinson was looking for bit parts at Marilyn's studio, Twentieth Century-Fox, and Marilyn tried to help. He lived in an apartment in the same house as James's sister, and it was there that James would see them together.

Any passion in the Robinson affair was soon spent, and turned to friendship. James said, 'We three men were a sort of trio, and Marilyn saw us all occasionally, together or separately, for the rest of her life. They were all depressives, Marilyn, Charlie, and Eddie, and they would hunt each other down when things were bad. She was very dear to both of them, and they would try to help. But Charlie and Eddie were suicidal, more so than Marilyn. They couldn't make it on their own, and they couldn't deal with their famous names. Sometimes it was Marilyn who literally kept them alive.'

Arthur James, on the sidelines, became one of the many who put up with Marilyn's mindless late-night phone calls. 'She would call from somebody's place at three or four o'clock in the morning,' he remembered, 'asking me if I could come right over. I'd put something on over my pajamas, drive all the way there, and she'd be gone. . . .'

In Eddie Robinson, Marilyn had met not only a drinker, but a man experimenting with drugs, a 'pill freak,' as Arthur James put it. It was probably now and in these circles that Marilyn, the keep-fit girl with the barbells under the couch, crossed a grim new threshold into the Hollywood world of drugs.

Drug abuse had been the scourge of the movie colony since 1920. Only the fashions changed. The earliest stars of silent pictures fell for marijuana or, worse, heroin. Pills came into their own in the forties and fifties, with the growth of the pharmaceutical industry. The post-war years were the heyday of 'bennies,' the various derivatives of Benzedrine. Bennies kept you awake, kept you slim by suppressing the appetite, and provided a vague euphoria.

Next came Dexedrine, son of Benzedrine, and then, with amytal sodium thrown in, Dexamyl. Dexamyl, went the Hollywood talk in the early fifties, gave the perfect high. After the highs, and the metabolic chaos, came the craving for sleep. Stars and failures alike reached for the new wave of barbiturates – Seconal and Nembutal – little tickets to oblivion on the jagged sea of insomnia. Add alcohol, which had been there all along, and the cocktail of peril was complete. One day, Nembutal would kill Marilyn.

In Hollywood the steady trickle of deaths had done nothing to stop the torrent of lethal prescriptions. Dr Lee Siegel, a studio doctor for Twentieth Century-Fox, was physician to both Judy Garland, and for extended periods, to Marilyn Monroe. Still practicing on Wilshire Boulevard when interviewed for this book, Dr Siegel shook his head as he recalled how pill-taking was once positively encouraged by studio bosses. 'In those days,' he said, 'pills were seen as another tool to keep stars working. The doctors were caught in the middle. If one doctor would not prescribe, there was always another who would. When I first treated Marilyn, back in the early fifties, everyone was using pills.'

Since 1962, when Marilyn died of barbiturate poisoning, biographers have assumed she used only sleeping pills, and these only from the mid-fifties. Interviews with those who knew her suggest an earlier entrapment. Amy Greene, who lived with Marilyn in 1955, said, 'She told me she'd always used drugs. She was a baby when she started taking pills, just seventeen or eighteen years old.' Milton Greene, Marilyn's partner when she broke away from Fox, said she had long been using Dexamyl, the fashionable 'upper' of the period. This contained amphetamine, commonly known as 'speed.'

Bunny Gardel, who did Marilyn's body makeup on numerous pictures, knew her from her earliest days at Fox. By the early fifties, said Gardel, 'She used to come to the dressing room and put down a plastic bag, and you never saw so many pills in one bag. There would be uppers, downers, vitamins, and God knows what in the bag.'

In September 1953, Grace McKee, Marilyn's former guardian and the woman who had been the closest thing she ever had to a mother, committed suicide by taking an overdose of barbiturates. It may be that Marilyn never learned the precise cause, since the death certificate was only recently unearthed by a researcher, but she did know it was suicide. Meanwhile Marilyn herself careened onward into a life that would always, to varying degrees, be blurred by barbiturates.

In 1953 Marilyn's private confusions were matched by a growing professional dilemma. Encouraged by a gleeful studio, she was cementing her image as the national sex symbol. She caused an uproar by arriving at a *Photoplay* awards ceremony in a dress that designer Billy Travilla had to sew into position on every famous curve. 'When she wiggled through the audience to come up on the podium,' wrote her former journalist-lover James Bacon, 'her derrière looked like two puppies fighting under a silk sheet.'

Meanwhile, as the world sniggered, Marilyn was hanging on the words of director John Huston, who had once told her she could 'turn into a very good actress.' She now told the *New York Times,* 'That is really what I want to be. I want to grow and develop and play serious dramatic parts. My dramatic coach, Natasha Lytess, tells everybody that I have a great soul, but so far nobody's interested in it.'

Marilyn got her chance to act in *How to Marry a Million-aire*. She was to star with Betty Grable – the reigning queen of Hollywood – and Lauren Bacall, in a fairly sophisticated comedy about three New York models scheming to trap wealthy husbands. Brimming with doubts, Marilyn burst unannounced into the office of the director, Jean Negulesco. Her questions were self-conscious ones about 'characteriz-ation and motivation,' and an amused Negulesco soon learned that 'she was concerned about how her role would transmit the sex image, which is what she believed she had to represent.' He told her, 'Marilyn, don't try to sell this sex. You are sex. You are the institution of sex. The only motivation you need for this part is the fact that in the movie you are as blind as a bat without glasses.'

Marilyn understood, and plunged into her role. Nunnally Johnson, the producer and scriptwriter, believed that 'the first time anybody genuinely liked Marilyn for herself in a picture, was in *How to Marry a Millionaire*. She herself diagnosed the reason for that very shrewdly. She said that this was the only picture she'd been in in which she had a measure of modesty – not physical modesty, but modesty about her own attractiveness.'

Marilyn's producers and fellow actors saw a troubled woman and a struggling actress. In one scene, involving a telephone call during breakfast in bed, she became 'hope-lessly confused, answering the phone before it rang, drinking out of the coffee cup before she had filled it.' After an entire afternoon of stalled production, Marilyn was oblivious to the producer's concern.

Lauren Bacall recalled, 'Marilyn was frightened, insecure, trusted only her coach and was always late. During our scenes she'd look at my forehead instead of my eyes. ... Not easy, often irritating. And yet I couldn't dislike Marilyn. She had no meanness in her, no bitchery. She just had to concentrate on herself and the people who were there only for her.'

Soon scriptwriter Nunnally Johnson was writing to a friend, 'Monroe is something of a zombie. Talking to her is like talking to somebody underwater. . . .' Johnson never forgot the image. Years later he placed her 'ten feet under water. . . . You can't get through to her. She reminds me of a sloth. You stick a pin in a sloth's belly and eight days later it says, "Ouch."'

The sloth triumphed on the screen. Director Negulesco said, 'In the end I adored her, because she was a pure child who had this "something" that God had given her, that we still can't define or understand. It's the thing that made her a star. We did not know whether she'd been good or bad, and then when we put the picture together there was one person on that screen who was a *great* actress – Marilyn.' In the end, even Nunnally Johnson was pleased.

On the night of the premiere of *How to Marry a Millionaire,* Johnson and his wife included Marilyn in their party along with Humphrey Bogart and Betty Grable. The evening proved hilarious. 'Marilyn entered with a request for a drink, a stiff one, bourbon and soda,' Johnson recalled. 'Then, even though it was to be a quick and early dinner, she asked for another. She was on edge with excitement, nervous and frightened too, terrified about the evening. I had no idea how naive and youthful she was, how almost unbearably important the evening was for her. Then, as we're about to get in the car, a hired limousine with a driver, she asked for her third drink, a really stiff one this time. Gentlemen to the last, Bogey and I drank with her on the way to the theater. By the time we made our entrance you couldn't have found three more amiable people in the whole state of California.'

'In short,' said Johnson, 'she was tight when she had to go to the ladies' room as the picture began. Mrs Johnson, not tight, accompanied her, for clearly she needed company. She was tight in the ladies' room, and in a tight dress, for she had been sewn into it. . . . It was a wild and exhausting business (my wife told me afterward) getting Marilyn in condition for the john and then properly dressed again to return to her seat. Women who have been sewn into their clothes should never drink to excess. . . .'

The critics judged *How to Marry a Millionaire* an unqualified success. An actress was emerging from the chrysalis of flagrant sexuality. And now, behind the ballyhoo about celluloid husbands, Marilyn was on the brink of a new marriage of her own.

Lauren Bacall remembered how Marilyn 'came into my dressing room one day and said that what she really wanted was to be in San Francisco with Joe DiMaggio in some spaghetti joint. She wanted to know about my children, my home life – was I happy? She seemed envious of that aspect of my life, wistful, hoping to have it herself. . . .'

Marilyn had asked to join the Johnson party at the premiere because she did not want to be seen at the theater with any man other than Joe DiMaggio. The lover who had seemed dull a year ago was now her safe landfall. By November 1953, marriage to an American hero was only two months away. It had not been an easy passage.

13

There had come a moment, during the summer of 1953, when the trials of being Marilyn's suitor defeated even Joe DiMaggio. They had conducted a public courtship of more than a year, and the press was still parroting stories of the couple's devotion. Marilyn had taken an apartment on Doheny Drive, on the unfashionable side of Sunset Boulevard, a modest three-room place which Jane Russell helped her organize.

The apartment on Doheny would be a perennial retreat for years to come – and so far as the press was concerned, it was a love nest for Marilyn and DiMaggio. Marilyn made sure the public knew Joe had moved in some of his clothes. She would tell her reporter friend Sidney Skolsky that she was rushing home to cook dinner for her man. Skolsky dutifully regaled his readers with the details: Joe had taught Marilyn how to prepare Italian spaghetti, they drank Italian wine, and Marilyn had learned a few words of Italian. Joe liked to watch television, said Skolsky, breaking off occasionally to offer his actress lady a word of cultural advice such as 'Never mind the publicity, baby. Get the money.'

In late spring 1953 DiMaggio's brother Mike had been found dead in the water near his fishing boat in Bodega Bay, north of San Francisco. Marilyn traveled north with DiMaggio to the very Italian family gathering that followed. The word in Hollywood, when she came home, was that the sight of DiMaggio's grief had finally opened Marilyn's heart. She was ready to marry him – but not quite yet.

On the heels of the marriage rumor came conflicting news.

The couple were at odds, virtually splitting up. For the proud DiMaggio, Marilyn brought as much humiliation as bliss. He hated the foolish publicity, detested the way Marilyn flaunted her body in public. He had refused to attend the *Photoplay* awards ceremonies, where she made an exhibition of herself; it was not the way an Italian's woman behaved. Instead he was spotted lurking outside, waiting to whisk her away afterward. We now know that, worse than all this, these had been months in which Marilyn had a succession of lovers. If DiMaggio heard even a whisper of this, it was remarkable that he contained himself at all. He was possessive, and jealous of Marilyn's Hollywood intimates, regardless of sex.

Natasha Lytess, Marilyn's drama coach, was to say, 'I first met him when I went to her apartment on Doheny one evening. He opened the door, and I disliked him instinctively – a man with a closed, vapid look. She introduced us, and only two weeks later when I phoned her, he answered and said, "I think if you want to talk to Miss Monroe, you'd better call her agent. . . ." She hadn't the courage to stand up to him about it.'

There was more than a touch of jealousy on Lytess's part, too. George Masters, Marilyn's hairdresser in later years, knew both women well. Natasha, he said, once told Marilyn, 'You're wonderful. I love you.' To which Marilyn reportedly replied, 'Don't love me, Natasha. Just teach me.'

Henry Rosenfeld, Marilyn's New York confidant, suggested Natasha's love for her pupil was unrequited. He quoted Marilyn as saying harshly, 'God! If I had a cock, Natasha would never leave me.'

Natasha Lytess provides the first hint that the private DiMaggio could be different from the strong, silent hero of American imagination. Lytess was to say, 'All during those months of 1952 and 1953 she would phone me day and night, sometimes in tears, complaining about the way he misused her.'

In late summer 1953 Marilyn stepped off a train at Jasper, in the Canadian Rockies. She was arriving to make *River of No Return* with Robert Mitchum, a movie that overran its schedule so seriously that Mitchum dubbed it Picture of No Return. Marilyn, unhappy in love and resentful at being packed off to such a remote location, at first seemed a withdrawn, reclusive figure. Jim Bacon, sent to interview her before she left Los Angeles, had been shocked. 'Her hair was in tangles,' he wrote. 'She had cold cream all over her face, and her eyebrows were smeared. She was the same old Marilyn in spirit, but on the outside she was Dracula's daughter. I couldn't get out of there fast enough.'

Now, out in the wilderness, Marilyn hid behind the mask of grease, even on trips into the nearest town. Whitey Snyder, the trusty makeup man, finally told her, 'Get that crap off your face. You scare people.'

One person not scared was Robert Mitchum. He had first heard about Marilyn from Jim Dougherty, her first husband, on a factory line during World War II. On the set Mitchum was now playing the tough-guy lover to Marilyn's barroom singer. Off the set, Mitchum introduced her to his roistering hard-drinking style and brought her out of herself. The result was a string of bawdy anecdotes that were still current years later.

Mitchum recalled finding Marilyn poring over a dictionary of terms used in psychoanalysis, and asking for enlightenment. She listened wide-eyed, at the age of twenty-seven, as he attempted an explanation of 'anal eroticism.'

This was not the only hilarity over definitions. One day, said Mitchum, 'My stand-in went up to her and said, "Hey, blondie, let's have a round robin this afternoon." "What's that?" she says. "Well, what about my friend and me giving you a little bob?" She said, "Both at the same time?" He says, "Why not?" "Why," she said, "that would kill me." He said, "Well, I never heard of anybody dying of it yet." She said,

"Oh, but they do. Only that's not what they put in the papers; they call it natural causes.'" Mitchum, telling the story in 1982, added that Marilyn was joking. He was not so sure about his stand-in.

The shooting of *River of No Return* was a genuinely rugged affair. There were hair-raising scenes on a raft careering down a turbulent river, scenes that director Otto Preminger insisted could not be performed by stuntmen. The result was a chapter of accidents, both genuine and spurious.

First Marilyn slipped into the water while wearing high waders. The boots filled with water and she was hauled out by members of the crew, with Mitchum helping. Headlines across the country read: MARILYN MONROE NEARLY DROWNED. Another time, stuntman Norman Bishop recalled, 'Marilyn and Mitchum went out on a raft, and the goddam thing got stuck on a rock. It was bounding and setting to turn over any second.' Bishop and a colleague reached the raft with a lifeboat, and the day was saved once more.

A third incident, on August 20, would also make headlines, this time reading: MISS MONROE INJURES LEG IN CANADA. The report gave no details of any accident, because there were none. Marilyn had repeatedly clashed with director Otto Preminger, and it seems that she now took crafty revenge. Actress Shelley Winters, who had once shared an apartment with Marilyn, later recalled her deception.

Winters, who was working on another movie nearby, had come to visit Marilyn on the set. She watched, along with hundreds of tourists, as Marilyn stood on a raft tethered to a pier, making a scene that had taken all day. 'Marilyn,' Winters remembered, 'did what she always did when she was confused. She just opened her mouth and smiled at anything in sight. Preminger began to use dreadful language, implying that she was so untalented that she should stick to her original "profession." Marilyn never looked up; her smile just became more frozen.'

When shooting finished, Winters helped Marilyn come ashore and noticed that she slipped a little. 'Watch your step,' she warned her, 'you can break a leg on this slippery pier.' This inspired Marilyn. When the limousine reached the hotel she told Winters, 'I can't get out. I've broken my leg.' Strong men were summoned, doctors called. Winters fed Marilyn Percodan, a pain-reliever, and a double vodka, then listened as the star talked long-distance with studio chief Darryl Zanuck. She expected, she said generously, to be able to finish the film, in spite of 'considerable pain.'

Winters recalled, 'She didn't seem to be in any pain to me.' Marilyn, Mitchum, and Winters then enjoyed a vast lobster dinner, washed down with copious alcohol.

Next morning a posse of doctors arrived by private plane from Los Angeles. X-rays revealed no damage, and the experts politely suggested there was 'perhaps' a sprain. Marilyn insisted on being fitted with a plaster cast and crutches. Shooting resumed after an expensive delay, with Marilyn rigged out as a cripple, and Preminger oozing studied courtesy.

'Dumb? Like a fox, was my young friend Marilyn,' said Shelley Winters. 'That night we celebrated at a nightclub, and at one point she was sort of doing a rumba with Mitch. "For God's sake, Marilyn, sit down!" I told her. "You're supposed to be crippled!" "Oh, yes, I forgot," she said, giggling, and sat down on Mitch's lap.'

The caper not only tamed Otto Preminger but brought Joe DiMaggio running. According to Maurice Zolotow, who interviewed Marilyn a year or so later, he called her the night she began the injury charade. She wept, and DiMaggio arrived next day accompanied by yet another doctor. DiMaggio also brought along his habitual shadow, New York ticket broker George Solotaire. They made a curious pair in the Canadian wilderness: DiMaggio in sports clothes toting fishing gear; Solotaire tagging along behind in suit, dark glasses, and Homburg.

DiMaggio was more at home in the outdoors than he could ever be in the surreal atmosphere of Hollywood. He loped around, cigarette drooping, helping the crew and snapping pictures of Marilyn. The couple went fishing, taking with them ten-year-old Tommy Rettig, the child actor who played Mitchum's son in the movie. Earlier the boy had confided to Marilyn that, according to his priest, it was all right to work with 'a woman like you,' but not to see her socially. Shocked by the implication, Marilyn now tried hard to win his confidence. Children, it seems, were now increasingly on her mind.

One evening, on the train chartered to carry the cast, makeup man Whitey Snyder asked Marilyn, 'Why don't you marry that dago and raise a dozen kids?'

'Maybe I will,' she replied.

During the DiMaggio visit the couple vanished for a weekend, sparking rumors of a secret wedding. Soon there were visits to DiMaggio's home on Beach Street in San Francisco, the house he had bought for $14,000 in the early days of his success and where his sister Marie played hostess. Sometimes the couple would rise before dawn to go fishing, Marilyn bundled up in leather jacket, jeans, and scarf. They were rarely recognized, and the times when they were spotted DiMaggio angrily told reporters to 'beat it.' On his home turf, DiMaggio offered a tranquility rarely experienced by Marilyn.

On Halloween that year, the writer Lee Belser spent the evening with a new and calmer Marilyn. She lounged around the Doheny apartment, worried about a kitten crying outside, and took apples and cookies to young trick-or-treaters who came ringing the doorbell. The cookies had been made by Joe's sister, and Joe was the focus of conversation.

'The later it got,' Belser noticed, 'the older the guys got that came to the door. Marilyn asked me to start answering the bell, and it got really funny. There I was opening Marilyn

Monroe's door, turning away all these grown men in Halloween regalia.'

In the last weeks of 1953, Marilyn effectively vanished, beginning a new game with the press and her studio. She was due to start shooting a movie called *Pink Tights,* and Frank Sinatra was to be her co-star, a detail that was not enough to bring her back to work. After Christmas, when DiMaggio gave her a mink coat, Marilyn surfaced by telephone to say she had no plans to get married. A DiMaggio emissary arrived in Las Vegas, made plans for a marriage ceremony at a local hotel, then canceled.

The next day, in Los Angeles, Twentieth Century-Fox announced Marilyn's suspension for failing to appear for work. Marilyn, at last fully aware of her power, did nothing at all. She had decided that *Pink Tights* was not good enough for her.

A year later Marilyn was to offer a winningly prosaic scenario of what happened next: 'After much talk Joe and I decided that since we couldn't give each other up, marriage was the only solution. ... One day Joe said to me, "You're having all this trouble with the studio and not working, so why don't we get married now? I've got to go to Japan on some baseball business, and we could make a honeymoon out of the trip."

'And so we were married.'

14

On January 14, 1954, San Francisco Judge Charles Peery was disturbed at a Bar Association lunch by a phone call from Reno Barsochinni, manager of Joe DiMaggio's restaurant on Fisherman's Wharf, asking if the judge could perform a civil marriage ceremony at once. Peery arrived at City Hall just moments before DiMaggio and his bride. Marilyn was demurely dressed in a brown suit with an ermine collar. The bridegroom was accompanied by Barsochinni, his best man, and Frank 'Lefty' O'Doul, the old baseball star who had given DiMaggio his start in baseball before the war. No friends of Marilyn were at the wedding. Marilyn would say later that the decision to marry had been made only two days earlier.

The secrecy about the wedding had its drawbacks. There was an embarrassing delay on the third floor of City Hall when the Chief Clerk had to send out for a typewriter to fill out the marriage license. This was useful to Marilyn, who made a series of phone calls she considered vital.

Before leaving for the ceremony she had telephoned the publicity director at Fox, briskly announcing what she was about to do. Now, ignoring romance in her last unmarried minutes, she looked after her key press contacts. She tried to call Sidney Skolsky and got no reply. She was able to leave a message for the immensely powerful columnist Louella Parsons. Then she reached Los Angeles journalist Kendis Rochlen, couching her news in terms Rochlen never forgot.

There was hubbub around Marilyn in City Hall as Rochlen

asked Marilyn how she felt about getting married. 'Kendis,' she whispered, in the familiar fluttery voice, 'I have sucked my last cock. . . .'

Journalistic legend has Marilyn making this announcement on a number of occasions. Perhaps she did, but Rochlen, a veteran professional, insisted she did say it minutes before taking her vows with DiMaggio. At the time, as Marilyn well knew, the remark was unprintable.

By now five hundred people were gathered in the plaza outside City Hall. When the judge opened a window to let in the breeze, the baying of the crowd drowned out all conversation. Reporters peered over a partition. Finally DiMaggio cried, 'Okay, let's get this marriage going,' and the judge appealed to the crowd for quiet. An obedient 'sh-h-h' drifted up from the plaza.

Marilyn signed the marriage certificate as Norma Jeane Mortenson Dougherty, and falsely gave her age as twenty-five; she was nearly twenty-eight. DiMaggio produced the ring – white gold with a circle of diamonds.* The press observed that Marilyn pledged only to 'love, honor, and cherish' DiMaggio, and did not promise to obey him. This was already a fashionable omission by 1954, but it may not have sat easily with the son of a Sicilian immigrant. That afternoon a spokesman for the archbishop declared DiMaggio, whose previous marriage had been in the Catholic Church, 'automatically excommunicated' by his civil wedding to Monroe.

In the mêlée after the ceremony DiMaggio was asked what he and the bride were going to do next. 'What'cha think?' he replied with an emphatic wink. Asked whether they would have children, he said, 'We expect to have one.

---

* As her wedding gift, Marilyn gave DiMaggio nude photographs of herself, pictures from the famous calendar series that had been considered too suggestive for publication. This was not revealed until years later.

I can guarantee that.' Marilyn added, 'I'd like to have six.' Finally DiMaggio exploded. 'I've had enough of this mob. Let's call the reception off,' and the couple drove away.

Marilyn and DiMaggio sped south two hundred miles to the town of Paso Robles, where they ate steak by candlelight with the curious peering round the door. They then said they were leaving for Hollywood, but doubled back to the Clifton Motel. There, after DiMaggio had been assured there was a television set, the couple took a four-dollar room, hung out a Do Not Disturb sign, and stayed inside for fifteen hours. In days to come the room would be adorned with a brass plaque reading, 'Joe and Marilyn Slept Here'. After leaving the motel, Mr and Mrs DiMaggio vanished for more than two weeks, a rare event in the life of Marilyn Monroe.

In the last week of January, however, when DiMaggio flew to New York on business, Marilyn could not resist calling a journalist. Soon she was closeted with Sydney Skolsky in a car parked on a quiet street. Marilyn, who said she had been 'told she shouldn't be seen,' poured out the story of the honeymoon.

She and DiMaggio had holed up at a friend's cabin in the mountains near Palm Springs. 'There weren't any other guests,' she said. 'Joe and I took long walks in the snow. There wasn't a television set. We really got to know each other. And we played billiards. Joe taught me how to play.' Skolsky had a national exclusive and Marilyn prepared for the next stage of the honeymoon, which would be an international spectacle. The DiMaggios were to go to Japan.

For the baseball champion the trip to the Far East was routine business on familiar territory. Two years earlier in Tokyo, to shouts of 'Banzai DiMaggio!', Joe had played his last competitive game. General MacArthur and Joe DiMaggio were rated the two most popular Americans in Japan, and baseball was big business there. The DiMaggios' honeymoon was in fact a long-planned promotional trip, funded by the newspaper *Yomiuri Shimbun*, to launch the opening of the Japanese baseball season.

At San Francisco the couple were ushered aboard their Pan-American Clipper flight by Kay Patterson, the *Shimbun*'s representative in California. She said, 'Joe looked very comfortable – he was Mr Big in San Francisco – and Marilyn seemed charming, so in love, ogling him, playing the secondary role, of course.'

The airplane made a refueling stop at Hawaii, where the truly explosive nature of their union may have dawned on the couple for the first time. A crowd thousands strong swarmed on to the tarmac screaming Marilyn's name. Frenzied hands ripped out strands of Marilyn's hair on the way to the transit lounge. She recovered herself enough to murmur to the press, 'Marriage is my main career from now on.'

Hawaii was a foretaste of the utter hysteria that followed in Tokyo. The couple had to be smuggled out of the aircraft through a baggage hatch. The scream now was '*Mon-chan! Mon-chan*,' which means, roughly, 'sweet little girl.' Later, at the Imperial Hotel, two hundred police struggled with a throng that would not be satisfied until Marilyn appeared on the balcony. She thanked them for 'the wonderful reception,' but again she was frightened. 'I felt,' she told Sidney Skolsky later, 'like some dictator in a wartime newsreel.'

Marilyn tried to muzzle the monster of her own image. She emerged with dignity from a press conference at which two hundred Japanese reporters bombarded her with inanities. To the question, 'Do you wear underwear?' Marilyn replied, 'I'm buying a kimono.' Photographs reveal that she was, for once, wearing underwear on this occasion – DiMaggio's influence perhaps.

As the days passed the Japanese themselves calmed down a little. 'The Japanese will probably not discard their underwear as a result of the visit of the Honorable Buttocks-Swinging

Actress,' one pundit observed, 'because it is much too cold ... but I'm sure they will soon start swinging their buttocks.'

For ten days in Japan, and especially after they escaped from Tokyo, Marilyn did seem to play the 'secondary role' to DiMaggio's baseball hero. Modestly dressed, quietly made up, she traipsed behind as her husband played golf, sat unobtrusively in the car while DiMaggio held court for sports fans. In the evenings she watched as DiMaggio played snooker with his friend and colleague Lefty O'Doul. Then, after two weeks, Marilyn stepped back into her own myth. She went off to entertain American troops in Korea – without her husband.

Weeks earlier Marilyn had talked of 'a Marine who came to the door of my home after having been in Korea. He told me how much pictures had meant to the men in the service and while he talked he started to cry. . . .' Now, behind the canvas curtain of a makeshift dressing room, in freezing cold, she was changing into her Marilyn Monroe costume for the men of the First Marine Division. Thirteen thousand of them roared approval as she sang in a reedy voice unaided by amplifiers, 'Diamonds Are a Girl's Best Friend,' 'Bye, Bye Baby,' and 'Do It Again.'

Marilyn had trouble with 'Do It Again,' when an interfering officer claimed the song was too suggestive. She appealed in vain that it was written by the illustrious George Gershwin, then changed the chorus line to 'kiss me again.'

Marilyn did not allow censorship to percolate to the audience. In whirling snow, gowned in low-cut purple, she was the soldiers' angel of lust for three hectic days. Film of the concerts shows a Marilyn high on her own gyrations, visibly reveling in the excitement of the uniformed multitude.

Marilyn was later to tell her friend Amy Greene that, after that experience, crowds no longer scared her. She was to say, 'I never felt like a star before, in my heart. It was so wonderful to look down and see a fellow smiling at me.' Joe DiMaggio, waiting in Japan, had seen the newsreels and did not think them very wonderful.

There had been tense phone calls between the couple during her Korea trip; one of them, thanks to the expertise of the Signal Corps, broadcast over loudspeakers to a dinner party Marilyn was attending. The military audience had heard her ask, 'Do you still love me, Joe? Miss me?' DiMaggio's response had been distinctly muted.

A few weeks later, in front of Sidney Skolsky, Marilyn bubbled on for a while about her visit to sing for the troops, then turned to DiMaggio. 'Joe,' she said, 'do you have any idea what that's like? Did you ever have ten thousand people stand up and applaud you?'

Skolsky recalled later: 'Joe's voice was as unemotional as a pair of discarded spikes, underplaying his reply just as he had always underplayed his incredible feats in Yankee Stadium. "Seventy-five thousand," he answered quietly. Marilyn looked as embarrassed as a pinch runner picked off first base in the World Series.'

Marilyn came back to Tokyo to a mild case of pneumonia and an uneasy reunion with her husband. Accounts conflict as to how Marilyn originally decided to interrupt her honeymoon for the benefit of the U.S. Armed Forces. By her account an American general approached her with the idea during the flight from Hawaii to Tokyo. DiMaggio, she claimed, did not object. According to Sidney Skolsky, however, Marilyn planned the visit even before leaving the United States. Joe DiMaggio did not approve, but Marilyn went ahead against his wishes.

There had been one odd detail among the crass honeymoon headlines. The *Los Angeles Times* reported that Marilyn left for Tokyo 'with her right thumb in a splint, hidden most of the time under her mink coat. "I just bumped it," she said. "I have a witness. Joe was there. He heard it crack." She declined to go into details about the injured thumb.' The thumb was shown in its splint in an accompanying photograph.

Marilyn's story in private – and like all her stories it must be treated with great caution – was that the thumb was injured by Joe DiMaggio in a moment of irritation. She said this to several friends, including Amy Greene. As Greene recalled the story, 'Marilyn went to put her arms around him. He was talking to George Solotaire, and it annoyed him. Joe had such huge hands. All he did was fling her arms away, and the impact of the flinging of her arm injured her thumb in mid-air. . . .'

Amy Greene's account suggests the injury was the accidental result of DiMaggio not knowing his own strength. It prefaces, however, a series of reports that later in the brief marriage DiMaggio physically mistreated his wife.

Lois Weber, Marilyn's press agent in the mid-fifties, has said, 'I'm sure Marilyn was afraid of him, physically afraid. She said Joe had a bad temper. He was obviously rigid in his beliefs.' Sources agree that DiMaggio was possessive and jealous.

Henry Rosenfeld, Marilyn's New York confidant, quoted her as saying that even on the honeymoon 'he started accusing her of going to bed with everybody.' Marilyn told hairdresser Gladys Whitten, for whom she had brought a gift from the Far East, that DiMaggio was enraged by the hoopla over her visit to Korea. 'She went over so big,' said Whitten, 'that he got angry. Marilyn said, "He threatened to divorce me on our honeymoon!"'

After the marriage was over, Marilyn sat looking through old photographs with actress Maureen Stapleton. She held up a picture and said, 'Look, this was right after the wedding. And see my hands – I was really pushing him away. Really, deep down, I didn't want to marry him.'

Astonishingly, even when the ink on the marriage certificate was barely dry, Marilyn was already talking about marrying someone else. Immediately after the honeymoon, Sidney Skolsky was invited to visit the DiMaggios in their suite at the Beverly Hills Hotel. Joe DiMaggio left the room after a while and then, as Skolsky recalled years later, Marilyn 'dropped a bombshell.'

'Sidney?' she said.

'Yes.'

'Do you know who I'm going to marry?'

'Marry? What're you talking about?'

'I'm going to marry Arthur Miller,' Marilyn said.

Skolsky, dumbfounded, told Marilyn he did not understand.

'You wait,' said Marilyn. 'You'll see.'

Little more than a year after Marilyn's remarks to Skolsky, she and the playwright would begin courting in earnest. The year after that, she would fulfil her prophecy and marry Miller.

The marriage to Joe DiMaggio, launched in discord, would last less than nine months.

15

After the debacle in Asia, DiMaggio brought his wife home to his quiet house in San Francisco. There, for a month or so in early 1954, the couple were away from the intrusions of the press.

The world did get glimpses of them: Mr and Mrs DiMaggio boarding Joe's boat, the *Yankee Clipper*, with Marilyn, in jeans and moccasins, toting a paper bag containing the day's lunch. In San Francisco she could venture out more easily. She went shopping at Magnin's, and once startled bystanders by helping a brakeman turn one of the cable cars at the bottom of a hill.

The gossip columns burbled about a possible pregnancy, but neighbors and fishermen on the wharf saw more than any reporter. They wondered when they saw Marilyn standing alone on the back patio in the late evening, a coat thrown over her shoulders. One night she was seen running along the road away from the pier, weeping hysterically, with DiMaggio in pursuit. The fishermen looked away.

Hollywood was waiting. In March 1954 Marilyn was back in Los Angeles, signing in at her hotel with a wry joke about leaving blank the space in the register for children. She was in Hollywood to receive an award as 'Most Popular Actress,' a ceremony that turned into a tumultuous welcome home, one from which DiMaggio was absent. He said he would accompany Marilyn only when she won an Oscar – and that honor never would be hers.

Behind the scenes, and calling the contractual tune more than ever before, Marilyn now patched up her differences with Twentieth Century-Fox. She agreed to make *There's No Business Like Show Business*, a frothy musical tribute to composer Irving Berlin. For Marilyn the challenge was in the song-and-dance routines, one of them called, perhaps aptly, 'After You Get What You Want You Don't Want It.' DiMaggio, certainly, did not want the instant change caused by Marilyn's return to Hollywood.

Earlier in the year Marilyn had cooed, 'Joe's the head of our household, and I'll live wherever he decides.' Now DiMaggio was press-ganged into living for a while in Los Angeles, the town he most despised. The couple moved into a rented house on North Palm Drive in Beverly Hills. It had eight rooms – one for Joe's young son to use on visits – and a swimming pool. Twin black Cadillacs stood parked outside. It was also one of the least secluded houses in town, for its front door virtually opened on to the sidewalk.

Writer Sidney Skolsky, sitting in on one of Marilyn's music rehearsals at the studio, noticed phone calls coming in from Joe DiMaggio and assumed all was well. Marilyn seemed genuinely concerned that Joe, not she, was doing most of the moving in. She hurried home, with Skolsky in tow as the trusted chronicler, to observe the domestic scene.

Soon an avid public learned that Marilyn had the television set placed next to the fireplace so that her husband could watch sports events from his favorite armchair. She confided that he was addicted to baseball, big-time boxing, and sometimes Western movies, and that she served him his dinner in his chair.

'Joe doesn't have to move a muscle,' she told the press. 'Treat a husband this way and he'll enjoy you twice as much. I like to iron Joe's shirts, but often I haven't the time. I like to look at Joe in a shirt I ironed. A man should never have to think about his clothes. A wife should see to it that his shoes and suits are sent out to be cleaned.' All this, of course, was made easier by the trio of servants Marilyn had hired.

Sidney Skolsky duly published her cozy chatter, and allowed one fragment of reality to see the light of day. 'Joe and I have our quarrels,' he quoted Marilyn as saying. 'You can't outlaw human nature. Marriage is something you learn more about while you live it.' In fact the couple had quickly discovered they were hopeless at living together.

Marilyn's discourse on housekeeping was fantasy. Writer Sheilah Graham, who talked to Marilyn once the marriage was over, reported, 'They were equal in fame but not in habits. Joe was obsessively neat. Everything on his dressing table was arranged in alphabetical order: A, aspirin; B, brush; C, comb, etc. You could find Marilyn by following the trail of her stockings, her bra, her handkerchief, and her handbag, all dropped as she went. He was always trying to train her. And he could not. They reached a point where they could not speak without screaming.'

Sex was not the problem. By most accounts, including her own comments to friends and doctors, the world's sex symbol found little satisfaction in the many beds she shared. With her baseball champion, that at least was different. 'Joe's biggest bat,' Marilyn delighted in telling Jet Fore, a friend at the studio, 'is not the one he uses on the field.' She would later tell Truman Capote, 'If that's all it takes, we'd still be married.'

In a more serious vein, Marilyn had praise for DiMaggio's bedroom prowess when she went to live with her New York friend Amy Greene a few months later. 'She said nobody in her life was as good in bed as Joe,' Greene said, 'but at some point you had to get out of bed and start talking. And they couldn't do it.'

One night that year the phone rang in the home of Brad Dexter, an actor who had met Marilyn much earlier, during the shooting of *Asphalt Jungle*. They had not spoken since, and Dexter could hardly believe the caller was Marilyn Monroe. 'I'd like you to meet Joe,' she said. 'Can you come over to dinner? And come a little early, before Joe gets home, so we can talk.'

Dexter arrived at the appointed time, and Marilyn at once poured out her troubles. 'I have a very serious problem in my marriage,' she said. 'Joe has isolated me; he doesn't want me to associate with anybody in the movie industry. He has a terrible insecurity. He has estranged me even from my actress friends, and I don't know who to turn to. I thought maybe you could be a bridge between us. You're a tough guy, you play poker, and you like sports, and I thought you and Joe could become friends. Then, when we're together, you and I could talk about what we did at the studio all day.'

Somewhat apprehensively, Dexter said he would try to help. When DiMaggio arrived, though, the effort seemed pointless. 'Boy, was he stiff and unbending!' Dexter recalled. 'Joe just sat there and I could see all these things going through his mind – like, had I been to bed with her? Why was I there? We could all see it wasn't going to work. I pretended to have another appointment, and I didn't stay to dinner.'

When things finally fell apart, Marilyn was to tell the divorce judge: 'Your honor, my husband would get in moods where he wouldn't speak to me for five to seven days at a time. Sometimes longer. I would ask him what was wrong. He wouldn't answer. . . . I was permitted to have no visitors, no more than three times in the nine months we were married. . . . The relationship was mostly one of coldness and indifference.'

DiMaggio's duodenal ulcer, an old torment, started bleeding again. At the studio, still working on *There's No Business Like Show Business*, Marilyn began to break. Billy Travilla, her dress designer, remembered a day when, for technical reasons, it was essential to shoot three pages of script without cutting. 'Marilyn had just one line on the third page,' Travilla said, 'and she kept fluffing it. They told her they had to wrap the scene, and she started crying. She ran to her dressing room, then apologized like a little girl. Afterwards she told me, "You know, I'm losing a piece of my mind each day. My brains are leaving me. I think I'm going crazy, and I don't want to be seen this way. If I go crazy, please take me away and hide me.'"

'She was talking herself into the idea that she was going mad,' Travilla said. Marilyn's fear of inheriting mental illness, prompted by her family history, was now a perennial worry.

DiMaggio, the traditional Italian husband, was more than ever affronted by his wife's display of her body, not only in her work but – against his wishes – at home. Marriage had tempered Marilyn the exhibitionist to the extent that she wandered around the house nude only in front of females. One woman guest, sitting with DiMaggio on such an occasion, jokingly suggested that Marilyn was trying to lure him to the bedroom. DiMaggio was not amused.

When Marilyn had married DiMaggio, her bosses at Fox dreamed that their publicity cup would now overflow, with regular appearances by a tame baseball hero. One executive boasted, 'We haven't lost a star; we've gained a center fielder.' DiMaggio disappointed them. He showed up on the set only once during the filming of *There's No Business Like Show Business*, then objected to posing for pictures with his wife dressed in a revealing costume.

In August 1954, without even one day off, Marilyn moved from the *Show Business* set into production of *The Seven Year Itch*, directed by Billy Wilder. For her this movie was the payoff for having done *Show Business* at all, a chance to play a sustained role opposite one other lead actor. The distinction must have been lost on DiMaggio. *Itch* was the story of a fortyish married man, Tom Ewell, tempted by the girl upstairs, Marilyn, while his wife and children are away. It was an exercise in titillation and sexual double-entendre.

Wilder was still chuckling years later about the shooting of a scene in which Marilyn had to sneak down a back staircase to see the married man living below. 'She was wearing a nightdress,' he said, 'and I could see she was wearing a bra. "People don't wear bras under nightclothes," I told her, "and they will notice your breasts simply because you are wearing one." Marilyn replied "What bra?" and put my hand on her breast. She was not wearing a bra. Her bosom was a miracle of shape, density, and an apparent lack of gravity.'

Marilyn seemed to be nude in another scene, in which she was called upon to lean over a balcony, in the New York summer heat, to inform a male neighbor that she kept her underwear in the refrigerator. This was strong meat for the early fifties, but Wilder had to disabuse Marilyn of the idea that she could play one of her love scenes in the nude. No persuasion would be needed to get her to do the famous 'skirt' scene, which the press would call 'the most interesting dramatic display since *Lady Godiva*,' and which was to leave DiMaggio beside himself with rage.

Late that summer Marilyn visited Marlon Brando, then playing Napoleon on the set of *Désirée*. He noticed, as had others that day, that Marilyn's right arm was black and blue. When he asked why, Marilyn replied that she had bitten herself in her sleep. A few weeks later, after the skirt scene, friends would see other bruises, and she would claim DiMaggio had beaten her.

Marilyn flew into New York for the *Itch* location shooting on September 9, 1954. The scenes that followed were such that Roy Craft, Marilyn's publicity man, recalled, 'The Russians could have invaded Manhattan, and nobody would have taken any notice.' When Marilyn had left Hollywood, the town was awash with rumors that her marriage to DiMaggio was ending. She arrived in New York without him, but assured the press, 'Everything's fine with us. A happy marriage comes before anything.'

Five nights later, outside the Trans-Lux Theater, she arrived to shoot a sequence with her co-star Tom Ewell. The scene called for Marilyn to stand with a grinning Ewell as the draft from a subway grating blew her skirt high in the air.

Studio publicity men did not fail to inform the press exactly where the scene would be shot – at 52nd Street and Lexington Avenue – and that Marilyn's revealing costume would 'stop the traffic.' It was after midnight, but thousands of people stood ogling behind wooden police barriers as huge wind machines sent Marilyn's skirt billowing to her shoulders. Ironically, Wilder says, the shots of the lower half of Marilyn's body would eventually be shot in the studio – quite modestly. What New Yorkers saw that night, in take after take, was a bottom encased in panties thin enough to show a blur of pubic hair. Then Marilyn's husband arrived.

Joe DiMaggio, who had followed his wife to New York, had not intended to watch the filming. He remained a few blocks away, drinking with Broadway ticket broker George Solotaire. Then, persuaded by columnist Walter Winchell, an old acquaintance, he made his way through the police lines to watch the filming. DiMaggio stood briefly beside Camera 1, watching as his wife teetered on the grating, listening as the roar of the mob rose and fell in time with her skirt. Winchell heard him mutter, 'What the hell's going on here?' then, 'I told you I never did this. Let's get out of here.'

When filming was over Winchell went with DiMaggio to Marilyn's dressing room. He watched the forced gaiety of Marilyn's 'Hi, Giuseppe!' – one of her pet names for her husband – as she slumped exhausted in a chair. He listened as they quarreled about DiMaggio's baseball commitments and then bickered their way through dinner. Embarrassed, in spite of his profession, Winchell left them to it.

That night at the St Regis Hotel, crew members in rooms near the DiMaggio suite got little sleep. The cameraman on *Itch*, Milton Krasner, heard shouts of anger through the wall. Though one must ever be alert for fantasizing on Marilyn's part, the accounts that follow are hard to dismiss.

Hairdresser Gladys Whitten and the unit wardrobe mistress did not hear the rumpus during the night, but Marilyn came to them in the morning. 'She said she had screamed and yelled for us,' Whitten recalled. '... Her husband had got very, very mad with her, and he beat her up a little bit. ... It was on her shoulders, but we covered it up, you know ... a little makeup, and she went ahead and worked.'

Amy Greene, Marilyn's New York friend, also saw bruises. She was in the suite at the St Regis to fulfil the fantasy of trying on a mink coat. 'I was sitting on the bed with her mink around me,' Greene said, 'and Marilyn started to get undressed. She forgot I was sitting there and that she was taking off her blouse. ... Her back was black and blue – I couldn't believe it. ... She didn't know what to say, and she wasn't a liar, so she just said, "Yes. ..."'

Much later, talking with her longtime hairdresser Sydney Guilaroff, Marilyn would recall that, 'Joe slapped me around the hotel room until I screamed, "That's it!" The first time a man beats you up, it makes you angry. When it happens a second time, you'd have to be crazy to stay.'

Amy Greene added: 'Marilyn could be a smartass, and when she drank champagne she'd goad him. And they weren't intellectuals, they couldn't discuss their pain, so they lashed out at each other. ...' Greene saw only this one example of mistreatment.

Makeup man Whitey Snyder, one of the few Hollywood people who got on with DiMaggio, said, 'They loved one another, but they couldn't be married to one another. ... Sometimes he gave her a bad time – he'd hit her up a bit.'

In September 1954, after the skirt sensation in New York, Marilyn showed a brave face to the world. 'I'm just a pretty girl who's soon forgotten,' she told a group of sportswriters. 'But not Joe. He's an all-time great.'

In private the pretty girl was in pieces. Tom Ewell, her costar in *Itch*, noticed she was physically sick, 'shaking like hell' and guzzling medicine. Milton Greene, visiting her at the St Regis, found Marilyn in a haze of drugs – sedatives, he guessed – and incapable of sensible conversation.

Marilyn and DiMaggio flew back to California together and went to ground for ten days. Marilyn spent a good deal of time talking to Mary, Fred Karger's sister. Neighbors spotted her a couple of times walking the streets after midnight, apparently weeping. Within days she had taken to her bed, where she gave Sidney Skolsky an interview full of trivia about the visit to New York. Skolsky observed a quarrel between the couple, but published nothing.

On the morning of Monday, October 4, Marilyn telephoned Billy Wilder, director of *Itch*. Distraught and stammering, she said she would not be coming to work because 'J-Joe and I are going to get a d-d-divorce.'

The Twentieth Century-Fox publicity office promptly began a response masterminded by its director, Harry Brand. Everything was carefully stage-managed, and Brand conferred with Jerry Giesler, the colorful lawyer who habitually disentangled Hollywood follies. (It emerged later that Marilyn had been in touch with Giesler for the past ten days.) On Monday afternoon lawyer and publicity director emerged to say that 'conflict of careers' had caused the breakup. Giesler said he would file a divorce suit the next day on Marilyn's behalf; 'the usual mental cruelty,' he explained. He said the star herself was sick of an illness variously reported as a virus or a nervous disorder. One newspaper reported his only other comment – that Marilyn was not pregnant.

A horde of newsmen descended on the house on Palm Drive. Bus companies changed itineraries so that tourists could gawk at the DiMaggios under siege. Marilyn and DiMaggio stayed in the house for two days while the studio orchestrated a final spectacle. 'The Monroe divorce,' former Fox publicity officer Roy Craft recalled, 'was quite a production.'

Early on the morning of October 6, as the press gathered outside by appointment, Twentieth Century-Fox delivered Marilyn's usual team of beauticians. Hairdresser Gladys Whitten remembered, 'Somebody sneaked us in by the back alley. And all the time we were preparing Marilyn, she kept saying, "I don't want to do this," and holding her head and crying.'

Dress designer Billy Travilla was there, drinking wine with Marilyn in spite of the early hour. He said, 'She was crying, saying, "I wish I had been different. If only I could have given more love." She was cursing herself, without saying exactly why.' Their work done, the cosmetics crew were smuggled out again, and went round to the front of the house to watch.

Joe DiMaggio, offered the escape route through the alley, declined. At 10:00 A.M. he opened the door and ran the gauntlet of the reporters down the rose-lined walk to his car.

'Where are you going?' the newspapermen asked.

DiMaggio, briefly trapped in the crush, shouted above the din, 'I'm going to San Francisco.'

'Are you coming home again?'

'San Francisco's my home,' DiMaggio said, running for his car. 'It's always been my home. I'll never be coming back to this house.' The car, driven by his friend Reno Barsochinni, took off, and DiMaggio vanished with a perfunctory wave.

Gladys Whitten remembered what happened next as 'horrible.' *New York Herald Tribune* correspondent Joe Hyams said years later that he still could see 'as clearly as I had seen it then, her [Marilyn's] tear-stained face as she came out of the front door, the half-a-hundred newsmen crowded in on her like animals at the kill. Only little Sidney Skolsky tried to protect her. Something about the scene and my profession of journalism sickened me.'

The Associated Press correspondent had no such qualms. He merely wrote, 'Marilyn Monroe today made an exit worthy of an Academy Award. . . .'

She appeared fifty minutes after her husband had driven off. Though her face was caked with theatrical makeup, it was not enough to hide what appeared to be a bruise on her forehead. She was dressed in black, clinging to the arm of her lawyer and the Fox publicity boss. The reporters, promised a press conference, bombarded Marilyn with questions. She sobbed, 'There is nothing I can add,' and said repeatedly, 'I'm sorry. . . .' She started stuttering and rocking on her heels as though about to faint.

There was an immediate reason to sob. Billy Travilla said, 'On Marilyn's way to the car someone gave her an envelope with a piece of toilet paper inside. The word 'whore' was written on it in fecal matter. The public was so cruel with her. The ordinary people in front of the house were his fans, not hers.'

Early next morning Marilyn reported for work, confiding to her makeup man that she 'felt alive for the first time in days.' In San Francisco DiMaggio slept till noon, posed gamely for pictures, and then played golf. So far as the outside world was concerned the drama was over. The press had little left to do but wait for the formal divorce hearing, due in three weeks. Behind the scenes, the dirty business had hardly begun.

As his marriage was collapsing, an utterly frustrated Joe DiMaggio, jealous of shadows, tried to buy confidence. He turned to private detectives, those Raymond Chandler characters of the 1950s, gumshoes whose reports could bring a spouse comfort – or heartbreak.

Meanwhile, at Twentieth Century-Fox, other men had the same idea, but for different reasons. Uneasy Fox executives feared their investment in Marilyn could explode in scandal, a catastrophe they might be able to prevent. They too called out their retinue of paid investigators. Now, and not for the last time, Marilyn was being watched.

One night in that year of the DiMaggio marriage Marilyn

came, as she would till she died, to visit Anne, mother of the man she had once loved and lost, Fred Karger. She had known the family since she was dirt poor, and they gathered round delightedly to admire the clothes, the mink, and the Cadillac convertible. 'When she came to leave that night,' said Patti Karger, 'there were two guys out there, waiting to follow her. Everybody at the house picked up on it, and we tried to help her. Marilyn didn't know what to do.'

Marilyn had taken to phoning Sidney Skolsky at all hours. Once, his daughter Steffi recalled, she called again and again, starting in the early hours. 'I finally woke up my father,' the daughter remembered, 'and Marilyn came over at seven o'clock in the morning, with no makeup, her hair all over the place, and her fur coat just slung on. . . . My father said later Marilyn just had to get out, to get away. She thought "they" were trying to drug her.'

Within days of the DiMaggio separation, the actor Brad Dexter bumped into DiMaggio in Los Angeles at the Villa Capri restaurant. He was in a huddle with Frank Sinatra and a private detective named Barney Ruditsky.

Ruditsky was a former New York City detective who had emigrated to California and become part owner of Sherry's, on the Sunset Strip, then a known rendezvous for gangsters. As a sideline he ran the City Detective and Guard Service, which specialized in bodyguard work and the sleazier sort of divorce investigations.

Frank Sinatra, who listed his profession in *Who's Who* as 'baritone,' had at thirty-nine just struggled back from a slump in his fortunes. He had won an Academy Award for his role as Private Maggio in *From Here to Eternity*, and was established as 'the first great bedroom singer of modern times.' Within a few months *Time* magazine would be calling him, in a remarkable cover story, 'one of the most delightful, violent, dramatic, sad, and sometimes downright terrifying personalities now on public view.'

Time also said of Sinatra: 'The man looks, in fact, like the popular conception of a gangster, model 1929. He has bright, wild eyes, and his movements suggest spring steel; he talks out of the corner of his mouth. He dresses with a glaring, George Raft kind of snazziness – rich, dark shirts and white-figured ties . . . he had, at last count, roughly $30,000 worth of cuff links. . . . He hates to be photographed or seen in public without a hat or hairpiece to cover his retreating hairline.'

Sinatra had once written: 'If it hadn't been for my interest in music, I'd probably have ended in a life of crime.' *Time* noted: 'He is an admitted friend of Joe Fischetti, who is prominent in what is left of the Capone mob, and he once made himself a lot of trouble by buddying up to Lucky Luciano in Havana – all of which is not to say that he mixes his pleasure with their business; Frankie is too smart for that. . . .'

Frank Sinatra and Joe DiMaggio, both first-generation Americans, were the most celebrated Italian-Americans in the world. They patronized the same watering holes, such as Toots Shor's in New York City, and in 1954 it could be said they shared the same misfortune. Sinatra was having his own problems in the disastrous marriage with actress Ava Gardner. In Reno, even before they married, he had taken an overdose of sleeping pills. Two years into the marriage he was admitted to a New York hospital with 'several scratches on his lower arm.' At the time of DiMaggio's break with Marilyn Monroe, this tumultuous relationship with Ava Gardner remained unresolved.

So it was, in the fall of 1954, when Brad Dexter found the baritone, the baseball player, and the private detective huddled together in the Villa Capri. Dexter had seen neither Marilyn nor DiMaggio since the awkward encounter at North Palm Drive, when Marilyn had tried vainly to use him as a bridge to her husband. Now, in the shadows of the Villa Capri, DiMaggio vouchsafed, 'Jesus Christ, I'm sorry about the other night. I didn't know who you were, or what sort of guy you were. Can you help me now?'

According to Dexter, Marilyn was hiding out in her dressing room at Twentieth Century-Fox, refusing to see DiMaggio as the days ticked by to the divorce. DiMaggio was now desperate to get her back. Fox chief Darryl Zanuck had given orders that nothing should interfere with Marilyn's work, and had barred DiMaggio from the studio. The scheme now proposed was that Dexter, an actor known to the security guards, should smuggle DiMaggio into the studio in his car, hidden under a blanket.

'They tried to pressure me,' Dexter recalled, 'so I said, "I'll call Marilyn and ask if she wants to see you." I spoke to her, and she said, "Brad, please, I don't want to see Joe, I don't want to talk to him; it's over." So I went back, and I told them, and I refused to do it.'

On the morning of October 27, Marilyn appeared at the courthouse in Santa Monica. After a perfunctory hearing, she was granted a divorce on the grounds of 'mental cruelty.' Joe DiMaggio was not in court and did not contest the case. Formalities aside, however, he was still desperately trying to retrieve the situation. Seen in Los Angeles the day before the divorce, DiMaggio claimed he was only there 'to see my son.'

Then, on the day of the divorce itself, DiMaggio took the uncharacteristic step of contacting the press about his private life. He let it be known that he still hoped for a reconciliation. 'I hope she'll see the light,' he was quoted as saying.

Marilyn, meanwhile, was sending contradictory signals. On the eve of her court appearance she gave her first interview since the rift, to emphasize that there was no involvement with another man. Then, as she prepared to persuade a judge of DiMaggio's mental cruelty, she sought solace – with DiMaggio. She reportedly spent the night before the hearing, and the night of the divorce itself, closeted with her husband. Their hiding place was Frank Sinatra's apartment.

Skeptics in Los Angeles did not accept the reasons given publicly for the DiMaggio divorce. The courtroom script about DiMaggio's 'coldness and indifference' did not ring quite true. Nor did people accept that Marilyn's occupational displays of sexuality had triggered the separation. Fox spokesman Roy Craft bluntly rejected that explanation. 'Marilyn had a flamboyant reputation when they got married,' he said. 'If you build a home behind a slaughter house, you don't complain when you hear the pigs squealing.'

Eight years later, when Marilyn died, DiMaggio's friend Walter Winchell was to write: 'After the divorce Joe told me the "real" reason she filed. It has never been published and it won't be here. He wept telling it to me as the Cub Room crowd stared and wondered why he cried.'

With Marilyn dead and Joe DiMaggio silent, the smoke of mystery long eddied around the end of their marriage. New information, however, revealed a fresh scenario. It detailed an extraordinary pursuit of Marilyn, and the harassment of the man she was seeing.

Thirty years later, the man still recoiled at the very mention of the name DiMaggio.

16

A few days after the divorce hearing, in early November 1954, Joe DiMaggio telephoned Marilyn's journalist friend Sidney Skolsky asking for an urgent meeting. Skolsky suggested lunch, but DiMaggio insisted they talk in the privacy of his bedroom at the Hollywood Knickerbocker Hotel. What happened at the meeting made Skolsky squirm. He felt himself 'confronted by an idol on his knees, begging to have his clay feet examined.'

As Skolsky later recalled, DiMaggio 'pointed toward the bed and asked me to sit down on the edge of it. He drew his chair up close to me. "You know everything. There's one thing I must know," he said, as softly as a torch singer squeezing the pathos out of every note. "Is there another man? Why did Marilyn divorce me?"'

Skolsky, embarrassed, talked around the subject and ended the meeting as speedily as possible. He had been aware for some time of DiMaggio's obsessive jealousy. There had been Marilyn's frenzied calls, saying that she was being watched and trailed. In recent months, Skolsky believed, DiMaggio had picked up the widespread rumor that Marilyn was sexually involved with her drama coach, Natasha Lytess. The watching and the trailing, however, had been focused above all on a man – Marilyn's twenty-nine-year-old voice coach, Hal Schaefer.

Schaefer, a brilliant composer and pianist who had started as a protégé of Duke Ellington, would one day count among his pupils Peggy Lee, Judy Garland, and Barbra Streisand. He had won Marilyn's confidence the previous year during the shooting of *Gentlemen Prefer Blondes* and, two films later, they had become close friends. Marilyn had specifically requested his services, at the start of the marriage to DiMaggio, while she was doing *There's No Business Like Show Business,* and by April 1954 she and Schaefer were working flat out in Bungalow 4, at the back of the Fox lot.

The future heads of the music department did notice the mutual devotion of the star and the voice coach. They also noted gratefully that Marilyn's singing skills were improving by the day. Nobody made much of the fact that they worked till all hours of the night in Bungalow 4, or that they slipped out together for meals. As work progressed, though, Marilyn showed herself violently protective of Hal Schaefer.

The future head of the Fox Music Department, Lionel Newman, recalled an occasion on which Irving Berlin himself descended on the studio to hear some of the new arrangements of his songs. 'He raved about how good it was, and how well Marilyn was performing,' Newman remembered. 'Then next day Marilyn came to my office in a rage, asking why Hal was not getting the credit he deserved. She said that if Irving Berlin didn't go over and personally tell Hal how wonderful he was, she wasn't going to finish the picture. Eventually Berlin did sort it out, but she was ranting about it, screaming.'

Hal Schaefer kept silent about his relationship with Marilyn Monroe for thirty years, not least because of the appalling price he paid. Interviewed for this book at his home in another state, however, the musician talked quietly of a period that he recalled as the most painful year of his life. When he first met Marilyn, Schaefer said, 'She struck me as kind of fey, as not being altogether in this world, not all there. She was quiet, didn't open up much. At first she had no confidence, but she reacted to my teaching and she got better. I made her go out and buy a bunch of Ella Fitzgerald albums, and that was the strongest influence on her – she really became quite good. . . .' Professionally, she was fine to work with. There came a time when she started to show up late, but I told her it wouldn't work with me. . . . I had my reputation established. I told her she didn't impress me just because she was Marilyn Monroe, and she stopped being late.'

For many months, said Schaefer, the relationship with Marilyn remained strictly professional. 'It was during *No Business Like Show Business*,' he remembered, 'that I started to know her more personally. Marilyn seemed to feel that I was the kindest, most gentle man she'd been involved with. And she loved the way I played the piano, thought I ought to be world-famous. I wasn't the world's greatest lover, I wasn't Tyrone Power, but I did give what she needed most – help. I didn't use her. I was supportive – I cared about her.'

There came a time when Schaefer and Marilyn became lovers, though he made it clear that sex was not at the core of their affair. He echoed the irony other lovers report, that 'Marilyn must have been frustrated almost all of the time. I think she regarded it as her function, being this great attractive female, that she was *supposed* to have sex with a man, because that was something she could do, that she could give. She wasn't very successful at it, in terms of her own fulfillment.'

Schaefer insisted, 'I was not the cause of the breakup with DiMaggio. It was already broken up, and not because of me. She would have left him no matter what. It had nothing to do with me. It was not to do with anyone else. But DiMaggio couldn't believe that. His ego was such that he couldn't believe that.'

In midsummer of 1954 Marilyn had told Schaefer of her troubles with Joe DiMaggio. She was to claim to him, as she did to others, that her husband sometimes physically mistreated her, that he was hugely possessive. Quite soon, Schaefer said, he found that out for himself. He soon became convinced that DiMaggio's detectives had Marilyn's car wired for sound.

'She had this big, black, Cadillac convertible,' Schaefer remembered, 'and sometimes she'd say, "Let's just get in the car and go for a ride." I took her once to that Jewish section on Fairfax Avenue – it wasn't late – and she put on a black wig and no makeup. But finally somebody recognized her as we were leaving, and we got in the car and left. We were talking in the car, and talking about where we were going, and suddenly somebody shows up there. Either we were bugged or we had been followed. I told her I thought we were bugged.'

After a while Schaefer and Marilyn had no doubt they were under surveillance. 'The whole thing became a nightmare,' he said. 'She was terrified and also furious, because she felt she couldn't live her life. She was completely frustrated.'

After weeks of this, Schaefer said he decided to have it out with DiMaggio. He called the house on North Palm Drive and spoke to Marilyn's husband, who told him to come over in about an hour. At the last moment, Marilyn, fearing violence, persuaded Schaefer not to go.

On the night of July 27, 1954, three months before the divorce, Schaefer failed to turn up for an appointment with friends. They finally found him, at four o'clock in the morning, lying unconscious on the floor of his room at the studio. At the time it was said Schaefer had collapsed from overwork, but close friends knew he had tried to kill himself. Schaefer shuddered at the memory. 'I drank typewriter cleaning fluid, I drank carbon tetrachloride [a cleaning fluid], I drank about a quart of brandy, and I took about a hundred pills – anything that was there. . . .'

Schaefer barely survived. 'I just didn't want to go on any more,' he said. A great deal of the focus was on Marilyn, but it wasn't totally that. It was the way I was in my life. I was despondent, depressed, drinking too much.' Schaefer's liver and kidneys were seriously damaged, and he suffered several relapses. Once released from the hospital he hired two male nurses and took a house on the coast north of Los Angeles, there to begin a long and painful recovery.

Marilyn had visited Schaefer in the hospital immediately after his suicide attempt, and now she began visiting him at the beach. 'Marilyn came up there,' Schaefer said. 'I think she may have stayed on a Friday or Saturday night, but not all the time. I don't think Marilyn and I had any sex at that point. . . . I was still as sick as could be, and the male nurses were there.' Now, said Schaefer, the harassment began once more.

'Again, on one of the occasions Marilyn came,' Schaefer recalled, 'they followed her. I can't remember it well because I was so sick. I can only remember them screaming through the window, and the threatening. And they said they were going to come in. We said we'd call the police. They said they'd cut the phone lines. I remember one night it was about dawn. And neither of us had slept, and Marilyn was standing in the corner. And after the threats they'd said, "We'll come in, and we'll just take her out and we'll leave you alone. We won't harm you. We know she's there and we want to get her out." Marilyn was terrified. Eventually, she slipped out, reached her car, and got away. There never was any actual violence.'

The ordeal drew Schaefer and Marilyn closer to each other. 'Marilyn came up to help nurse me. She was very sweet, and quite practical. I got well there, and Marilyn enjoyed it. She looked well, went swimming, got some sun – it was a very isolated spot. We thought, we really did think, we could build something for the future.'

As summer turned to fall Schaefer recovered sufficiently to return to Los Angeles. He and Marilyn met rarely and in secret, hoping to avoid the publicity surrounding the DiMaggio divorce. They did not entirely succeed.

On the day of the separation one major newspaper carried reports that DiMaggio had 'disapproved' of Marilyn's visits to see Schaefer in the hospital the previous July. Columnist

Louella Parsons, who knew Marilyn well, used this as the basis for a powerful lead. She wrote: 'I believe that it was jealousy that reared its ugly head when Marilyn Monroe and Joe DiMaggio had their final battle. . . . Joe is Italian and of a jealous nature.'

After the divorce had been formalized, the press began blathering about a possible reconciliation. Marilyn and DiMaggio were indeed engaged in a series of meetings, but they did not end happily. Things came to a head on November 5, a day that neither of them would ever forget.

On the morning of that day Marilyn offered a firm comment for publication: 'There isn't a word of truth that we are reconciling.' DiMaggio, already divorced and therefore without conjugal rights of any kind, was now at his most desperate. Meanwhile, staked out on street corners and in parked cars, his private detectives were still on the prowl. That night, accompanied by his friend Frank Sinatra, DiMaggio set in motion a great folly.

What happened that Friday night was to boomerang on DiMaggio and Sinatra in an unpredictable way. Two years later a report in *Confidential*, a scandal magazine, would stir enough uproar to warrant probes by a California State Senate committee and a Los Angeles grand jury. The reconstruction that follows is drawn from evidence heard by those official bodies, a mass of conflicting eye-witness and press accounts, and new information gathered for this book.

On the evening of November 5, James Bacon, the ubiquitous journalist who had himself once enjoyed Marilyn's favors, took himself off to the Villa Capri restaurant. It was by no means the most star-studded watering hole in Los Angeles, more a cozy rendezvous serving spaghetti and meatballs. But it was patronized, even subsidized, by some famous Italians. They included Frank Sinatra and Joe DiMaggio, and both men were there when Bacon arrived.

'Over at a nearby table,' Bacon recalled later, 'it looked like a Sons of Italy meeting – Sinatra, DiMaggio, and a few other *paisanos*. Hank Sanicola, Sinatra's manager and a close friend in those days, was among the group. I didn't join the table, although I have always been a friend of Frank's, because I could see that DiMaggio was in a terrible mood.'

Meanwhile, across the city, a quiet evening was ending for the inhabitants of an apartment building on the corner of Kilkea Drive and Waring Avenue in West Hollywood. In her tiny downstairs apartment, fifty-year-old Florence Kotz was having an early night. Mrs Virginia Blasgen, the landlady, was preparing for bed, and her teenage son was already asleep. Upstairs, on the only other floor, an actress called Sheila Stewart was giving late dinner to Marilyn Monroe. Stewart, aged thirty-seven, had been friendly with Marilyn for some time, and they shared a common interest in singing. That evening, Marilyn was studying a movie script.

Out in the darkness a young private detective, twenty-four-year-old Philip Irwin, was cruising around in his car. He was employed by Barney Ruditsky, the detective hired by DiMaggio to watch Marilyn, and he had been involved in the surveillance for months.

Now, on a run past the Kilkea Drive apartment, Irwin spotted Marilyn's parked car. He hurriedly telephoned his boss. Ruditsky arrived, staked out the house for a while, then went off to call Frank Sinatra at the Villa Capri.

In the restaurant, reporter Jim Bacon watched as Sinatra and Joe DiMaggio first argued and then bustled out. DiMaggio was first to arrive at the apartment building. He circled the block twice, then parked behind his ex-wife's car.

'He was very upset. He was proceeding toward the apartment,' Irwin later testified. 'I stopped him and tried to calm him down.' Frank Sinatra drove up shortly afterward.

It was now that the landlady, Virginia Blasgen, looked out the window. She said she saw two men, 'a tall one and a short one ... the tall one was mad, and was walking up and down ... the little one was jumping up and down and grinning at me. ...' Mrs Blasgen recognized the large man as Joe DiMaggio, the small one as Frank Sinatra. About an hour later, at 11:15 P.M., mayhem came to Kilkea Drive.

The greatest shock was for Florence Kotz, asleep and oblivious to the strange comings and goings outside. She awoke to a crashing and splintering as men broke down her door, then to a glare of white light as the intruders began taking photographs. Mrs Kotz screamed. Then the men fled as quickly as they had come, tumbling over each other in their haste.

The DiMaggio war party, searching for Marilyn, had blundered into the wrong apartment. The idiotic adventure was to be known henceforth as the 'Wrong Door Raid.'

At the time, in 1954, the assault at Kilkea Drive was written off by the local police as attempted burglary. The frightened victim, Florence Kotz, was left with a broken door and a bad case of nerves. Not until 1957, when the California State Senate looked into the doings of unethical private detectives, was there a public accounting. The hearings then turned into a tussle for credibility between Philip Irwin, the detective who had spotted Monroe's car in the first place, and Frank Sinatra.

Ironically, it had been another dawn raid, with himself as the target, that forced Sinatra to answer the senators' questions: he had been served with a subpoena by two Los Angeles policemen who had marched into his Palm Springs bedroom at four o'clock in the morning. Then, under oath, Sinatra flatly denied that he was one of the men who broke into the Kotz apartment. He claimed he was sitting outside in his car when Joe DiMaggio, Barney Ruditsky, and Philip Irwin broke down the door. Irwin insisted that Sinatra had been one of the participants, and contested much of the detail in Sinatra's story. State Senator Edwin Regan, having listened to both statements, said drily, 'There is perjury apparent here.' The matter was referred to a grand jury.

Sinatra's lawyers, hunting for information to counter Irwin's claims, now hired another flamboyant Hollywood detective, Fred Otash. Otash sought to show that Irwin was a liar, that nobody could have recognized Sinatra on the dark night of November 5, 1954. The matter was never fully resolved. The Grand Jury proceedings fizzled out, with jurors referring the case to the Chief of Police for 'other possible testimony.'

Joe DiMaggio never gave his version of the 'Wrong Door Raid.' Two years later, when the California State Senate and the Grand Jury wanted to question him, he sent messages saying he was unable to attend. He did so from the safety of the East Coast, where he was beyond the reach of a California subpoena.

The official airing of the case did bring some small comfort to the aggrieved Florence Kotz. She sued Sinatra and DiMaggio, various friends and the detectives, and accepted an out-of-court settlement of $7,500.

In all the verbiage expended on the 'Wrong Door Raid,' one name is glaringly absent – that of the real intended target, Marilyn's lover, Hal Schaefer. Marilyn's hostess that night, Sheila Stewart, revealed in an interview for this book that 'Hal Schaefer was there with Marilyn that evening, and I made dinner for them. They were sitting in the dining room, and I had taken the dishes into the kitchen when we heard the crash.'

Schaefer, who admitted he was there, still recalled the shock. 'It was like somebody set off a bomb,' Schaefer recalled. 'The whole house shook. It was terrifying. . . .' Asked whether he and Marilyn were in bed at the time, Schaefer said, 'Not at that moment, no . . . but we were two grown, consenting adults, and she was already separated. . . .' He added, 'It was so lucky they got the wrong door. I think they would have done me terrible injury.'

Sheila Stewart said Marilyn understood at once what

was going on. She and Schaefer left the apartment in separate cars, and made their way to their separate homes. For Marilyn there was to be a confrontation with Joe DiMaggio that night. Yet another private detective, one of the large team assigned to the operation, was watching from the shadows two hours after the raid, when DiMaggio turned up on his ex-wife's doorstep. She let him in, and DiMaggio was still there when the detective finally left in the early hours of the morning.

Marilyn's avalanche of trouble was not yet over. She had been described at the time of her separation from DiMaggio as being 'emotionally and physically ill.' Her lawyer said she had a virus and denied she was pregnant. He did say, however, that she was being attended by Dr Leon Krohn.

Dr Krohn, 'Red' to his friends, was a prominent Hollywood gynecologist for several decades. His few male patients, whom he served as a general physician, included Frank Sinatra. Krohn mixed his profession with his social life, and played a special role following the collapse of the DiMaggio marriage. Joe DiMaggio became his house-guest, and he fielded dawn telephone calls from Marilyn, who checked regularly 'to see if Joe was okay.'

Dr Krohn had been looking after Marilyn for two years now, ever since her demand that a gynecologist be present at her appendix operation. On the morning after the 'Wrong Door Raid,' an event that would remain hidden from the press for a long time, it was announced that Marilyn would enter the hospital within twenty-four hours for 'an operation of a corrective nature,' to be performed by Dr Krohn.

Marilyn, feeling 'sick to the stomach,' appeared at the studio next day to pose for publicity photographs. Then, driven by Joe DiMaggio, she checked into the Cedars of Lebanon Hospital, by now a familiar port of call, for the operation. Dr Krohn told the press that the procedure was to correct a gynecological problem from which Marilyn had suffered 'for years.' Joe DiMaggio spent the night at the hospital, catnapping in the doctors' lounge or pacing the corridors outside Marilyn's room.

Marilyn left the hospital after four days, ungroomed and haggard and without speaking to reporters. That night she and DiMaggio were seen dining at the Villa Capri, the restaurant where he had embarked on the 'Wrong Door Raid' just a week earlier. There would be more such meetings in the next month, and the press would again prattle about reconciliation. Marilyn, however, had decided otherwise.

Within weeks Joe DiMaggio would find himself truly alone. Soon he would become a frequent visitor to the office of Marilyn's business manager on Sunset Boulevard, a sad hulking figure begging to know whether Marilyn had mentioned his name. He would see Marilyn many times in the future, would become famous as the man who carried a torch for her till her death and beyond. Marilyn would humor his obsession, be grateful for his help, but she would never give him her heart.

In December 1954, as the newspapers watched DiMaggio's struggle to turn back the clock, nobody paid attention to the other man who waited. Hal Schaefer, now deeply in love with Marilyn, was soon discarded. He received a phone call from her in which she said, 'Perhaps, one day, we'll meet again,' and he knew he had lost her.

In his interviews for this book, Schaefer still spoke of DiMaggio with a fear that the decades had done little to erase. He remembered Marilyn with sadness. 'She told me that she loved me,' he said quietly, 'but I don't think she really knew what that meant.'

Within twenty-four hours of the 'Wrong Door Raid,' and on the eve of her gynecological operation, Marilyn had danced till 3:00 A.M.. at a party in her honor at Romanoff's to celebrate the completion of *The Seven Year Itch*. She had looked in wonderment at the guests and whispered to Sidney

Skolsky, 'I feel like Cinderella. I didn't think they'd all show up. Honest.'

Marilyn had arrived an hour late because her car had run out of gas. Those lining up to sign a huge 'Marilyn' souvenir portrait included Humphrey Bogart and Lauren Bacall, Claudette Colbert, William Holden, Jimmy Stewart, Susan Hayward, Gary Cooper, and Doris Day. For the first time Marilyn met her childhood idol, Clark Gable, and they discussed making a movie together.

Also at the party, showering Marilyn with praise, were the moguls of Hollywood: Sam Goldwyn, Jack Warner, and Marilyn's old adversary, Darryl Zanuck. 'This party,' wrote Skolsky a few days later, 'was a big deal to Marilyn because it signified in its peculiar Hollywoodian manner that the elite of the town had finally accepted her.'

The elite of the town were about to get a nasty shock. While they were accepting her, at the age of twenty-eight, as a full-fledged star, Marilyn had already decided to reject them. She had resolved to turn her back on Hollywood – husband, lovers, moguls, and all. Just before Christmas 1954 Marilyn put on her black wig and dark glasses, and drove to the Los Angeles airport carrying a ticket in the name of Zelda Zonk.

Cinderella, alias Zonk, was about to disappear.

Part Three

BROKEN MARRIAGE – BROKEN MIND

'How can I capsulize Marilyn? The more you know about people the more complex they are to you. If she were simple, it would have been easy to help her.'

ARTHUR MILLER

17

In the frozen dark before dawn, as Marilyn's plane flew east, a diminutive young woman steered a station wagon along the wooded roads near Weston, Connecticut. Amy Greene was on her way to LaGuardia Airport to pick up Marilyn and her traveling companion. Amy's thirty-three-year-old husband, Milton, was Marilyn's accomplice in her flight from Hollywood. For the next two years he was to be her close friend and champion and her business partner.

Greene's wooing of Hollywood's most valued asset had not happened overnight. His meeting with Marilyn, eighteen months earlier, is recorded in Monroe lore rather like Stanley's with Livingstone. One look at the baby-faced Greene prompted her to say, 'Why, you're just a boy!' He replied, 'You're just a girl,' and they immediately took a liking to one another. Greene, a photographer of distinction, had been in Los Angeles to take pictures for *Look* magazine, and his approach had won over not only Marilyn but even Joe DiMaggio. He photographed her in bulky clothes and modest poses, depictions that departed from the sexpot cliché but kept all the Monroe allure.

The plan that would outrage Hollywood took its initial vague shape at their first dinner together. Over the wine Greene enthused about his personal dream of independent filmmaking. Marilyn said she would like to be in one of his future movies. She was unhappy at Fox for two reasons.

Marilyn felt that the studio was taking advantage of her. In spite of her huge success she was still tied to a contract that paid her a maximum of $1,500 a week. On that basis,

Gentlemen Prefer Blondes, five successful films ago, had brought her only $18,000. That did not amount to much, by Hollywood standards, after the payment of taxes, agents' fees, acting coach Natasha Lytess, and beauticians. Marilyn's co-star Jane Russell, not bound by a long-term contract, had by contrast been paid $100,000.

Milton Greene agreed with Marilyn that this was unfair. He assured her she could earn much more were she to break away from Fox.

Marilyn also complained about her studio's insistence on casting her in stultifying roles. That troubled her at least as much as the poor pay. For a long time now she had been telling reporters that she was 'really eager to do something else, roles such as Julie in *Bury the Dead,* Gretchen in *Faust,* and Teresa in *Cradle Song.*' She wanted to work opposite 'serious' actors like Marlon Brando and Richard Burton. She wanted to *act* – and no one at Fox was listening.

Greene could not help listening. 'I thought I'd seen them all,' he said. 'Being in the business I'd seen so many models and actresses. But I'd never seen anyone with that tone of voice, that kindness, that real softness. If she saw a dead dog in the road, she'd cry. She was so supersensitive you had to watch your tone of voice all the time. Later I was to find out that she was schizoid – that she could be absolutely brilliant or absolutely kind, then the total opposite.' In the early days, though, Marilyn seemed to Greene to be a prize without blemish.

The conspiracy began at once. Greene asked to see Marilyn's contract, got legal advice, and was soon telling her that her contract was void, that she could and should leave Twentieth Century-Fox. Marilyn was infected by the very heresy of the idea. When Greene left for New York she drove him to the airport, and surprised him with the fervor of her kiss.

In the months to come there were more meetings. They

talked at a cocktail party attended by the Bogarts, Frank Sinatra, and Judy Garland, and huddled together during an evening of charades at Gene Kelly's home, a regular haven for visitors from the East.

Greene and his wife, Amy, were on hand when Marilyn came to New York to shoot the skirt scene for *The Seven Year Itch*. Amy watched as an ashen-faced DiMaggio stalked away, and she was at the St Regis Hotel the next day to sympathize over the bruises. When Marilyn returned to Los Angeles, Milton stayed in touch by telephone, talking her through the fine details of her contractual commitments. In the coming weeks, miserable and confused during the collapse of her marriage, Marilyn simply did not know what to do about the contract. She was wooed, in the end, as much by the promise of tranquility as by the hope for a better professional future: Milton and Amy Greene were offering to take the famous foster child into their home.

So it was, in the dying days of 1954, that Marilyn came in secret to the Greene home in Connecticut. An old farm-house, dating from the early eighteenth century, it stood on twenty-five acres of woodland, with its own trout stream and a little lake. The living room was a cavernous place, the full two-story height of the old stable, warmed by an enormous log fire. Marilyn was given the studio, a home within a home, with its own balcony overlooking the water. For her, this house in the woods was wonderland.

Marilyn had rarely seen snow before or watched the seasons change. In the coming months, when spring came, she would greet it with the naive astonishment of a child. Here nobody bothered her. She could bundle up in Greene's warm clothes and go walking in the woods. She could wander off to lunch on sandwiches and homemade chocolate éclairs at The Little Corner, a nearby restaurant run by Greene's brother.

Amy recalled, 'She liked to drive. We'd take the convertible and go sailing along the highway with the top down. We both liked to feel the wind on our faces and the warmth of the heater on our legs.'

At home, Marilyn quickly became 'Auntie' to the Greene's year-old son, Josh. She helped feed and bathe him, and surprised the Greenes by staying home to baby-sit him, so that they could go out on New Year's Eve. Marilyn would tell an interviewer that year that the Greenes were 'the only real family I have ever known.'

That, of course, was untrue. Marilyn had said the same of the DiMaggio family in San Francisco and, years before, of Fred Karger's family. She made a habit of grafting herself onto other people. As Amy Greene noticed with prescience, though, Marilyn also had a way of 'shedding' people when they were no longer useful.

'Never forget,' said Amy Greene, 'that Marilyn wanted above all to become a *great* movie star. She would do anything, give up anyone, to move on up.'

Hal Schaefer, back in Los Angeles, was unceremoniously dumped with a single phone call. Marilyn's friend Sidney Skolsky who had loyally resisted the temptation to publish what he knew about the DiMaggio marriage, was put on ice until further required – several years hence. The curious intimacy with her dramatic coach, Natasha Lytess, now came to an end.

Lytess, realizing that her pupil was drawing away, pressured Marilyn for financial help. She later wrote: 'I had been her private director for long years, working with her day and night. Yet when she was asked to do something for me, she had the feeling that she was being used.' There were others, Marilyn aside, who felt Lytess did expect too much. At all events, she was soon to be discarded as redundant.

In her newfound world Marilyn needed new friends. The Greenes were soulmates who could show her Eastern sophistication and culture. Amy Greene, a former fashion model with looks that reflected her Latin ancestry, was lovely in her own right. She told Marilyn, six years her senior, that looking good in ordinary life did not demand the overtight skirts and sweaters that had made Marilyn's name on the screen.

'It dawned on me what pitiful clothes she had,' Amy recalled. 'She had to rummage through my drawers every time we wanted to go out. We brought Norman Norell to dinner, one of the top dress designers of the day, and had him design an elegant wardrobe for her.' Marilyn welcomed the change. She and Amy went off on shopping sprees in Manhattan at Milton Greene's expense.

Marilyn rarely had a close woman friend of her own age. In this sudden intimacy with Amy Greene she revealed a good deal of herself. Some of it was trivia. Amy learned, not least when Marilyn scandalized dressing-room attendants at Bonwit Teller on Fifth Avenue, the truth of the legend about Marilyn's reluctance to wear panties. She was, however, fanatical about wearing a brassiere. 'Somebody, somewhere, had told her that if she always wore a bra her boobs wouldn't sag,' Amy Greene said, 'and she insisted on it. She slept with a bra on. She told me she'd finish making love with someone and then, zoom, on with the bra.' At Bonwit Teller she wore the brassiere and a sanitary belt.

Much about Marilyn was irritating, certainly for the meticulously tidy Amy Greene. She observed that Marilyn lived in a chaos of clothes cascading from suitcase and closet, of cosmetics and toiletries scattered across her room. She was oblivious to the tedious responsibilities of her own life, such as a pending trial in Los Angeles for driving without a license. Her friends would sort it out.

The Greenes watched bemused as Marilyn plunged into their library. She started reading about Napoleon, discovered Josephine, and scooped up every book she could find about her. Supper conversation in the Greene household was dominated for a while by Marilyn enthusing about Josephine and her entourage.

'She was fascinated,' said Amy Greene, 'by women who had made it.' Marilyn especially enjoyed learning how Josephine's friend Juliette Récamier, who was renowned for her figure, had treated a specially commissioned nude statue of herself. As she aged, and her breasts started to droop, she had the marble breasts smashed.

Marilyn would sit on the stairs with Amy contemplating a cameo portrait of Emma, Lady Hamilton, Lord Nelson's mistress. She could hardly bring herself to believe that this imposing woman had begun life as a servant girl, and made a personal celebration of the way Emma improved herself. 'She was like a child about stories,' Amy Greene recalled. 'She said nobody had told her stories in her childhood, so when anybody told her a story, she was hooked.'

Milton Greene had a motorcycle with a sidecar and took Marilyn riding in it. One day, as they prepared to set off, Amy noticed Marilyn was wearing a long white scarf. She made a crack about Isadora Duncan, the eccentric American dance pioneer who died of strangulation when her scarf caught in the wheel spokes of a friend's sportscar. 'Who's Isadora Duncan?' Marilyn asked, and was enthralled by the explanation. 'It was,' Amy Greene recalled, 'Isadora Duncan Week in Connecticut.'

To record her new experiences Marilyn bought a small leather-covered diary, one with a clasp and tiny key. She would carry it around the house, making notes on conversations or magazine articles that caught her interest. At night the Greenes would hear the radio playing in Marilyn's room till all hours, as she fed her unquenchable appetite for reading. They became aware of the torment that would now never leave Marilyn – insomnia. Sleep, when it did come, was ushered in by barbiturates; the pills, Seconal in those days, were never far from Marilyn's bedside.

It was now that Marilyn told Amy of the misery in her past as a female, of the child she claimed to have had in her teenage years, of the endless string of abortions. Marilyn still suffered excruciating period pain. Amy would find her screaming in agony that no pills could quell, and took her to see a gynecologist friend.

Marilyn's longtime Los Angeles physician, Dr Lee Siegel, identified her ailment in an interview for this book as having been endometriosis, a condition in which womb-lining tissue forms in places other than the womb, such as the ovaries or Fallopian tubes. Extreme pain during menstruation, and pain in the reproductive organs, is a usual symptom. Women who have endometriosis and want to have children are urged not to wait too long before becoming pregnant, for the disease is progressive and worsens with time.

Marilyn was now nearly twenty-nine. With her history of myriad abortions, some of the early ones perhaps performed inefficiently, she had courted additional disaster. As Amy Greene put it, 'Her whole womb was weeping.' Marilyn now feared gynecologists, and insisted that Amy Greene stay in the room during the doctor's examination. The abortions had indeed caused damage, making it unlikely that Marilyn would ever bear children.

The doctor suggested that, with so much pain so often, Marilyn should consider a hysterectomy. She rejected the idea out of hand. 'Marilyn was emphatic,' said Amy Greene. 'She said, "I can't do that. I want to have a child. I'm going to have a son." She always talked of having a son.'

In the coming months Marilyn would hear from the actress Jane Russell, her friend from *Gentlemen Prefer Blondes*, asking her to help WAIF, an organization that found homes for unwanted children. This marked the beginning of Marilyn's active interest in children's causes, one she would maintain till she died. Soon the world's press would be chronicling her own frantic efforts to bear children.

During Christmas 1954, Marilyn and the Greens delighted in the sheer naughtiness of Marilyn's escape from Hollywood.

Amy answered the phone to a stream of famous callers. Frank Sinatra, still holding Joe DiMaggio's hand back in Los Angeles, was fobbed off with a tall story. So was Billy Wilder, Marilyn's director on *Itch*. Bob Hope, who wanted Marilyn for his Christmas show in Korea, called in person. With the others sitting around giggling, Amy Greene struggled to sound serious as she inquired, 'Tell me, Mr Hope, is Miss Monroe lost?' Afterward, she and Marilyn rolled about on the floor, hooting with laughter.

Marilyn did not remain wholly hidden for long. In early January 1955, Milton Greene called a press cocktail party in New York, limited to a select audience of eighty. Dripping ermine, Marilyn announced that she had formed her own corporation, Marilyn Monroe Productions, with herself as president, holding 51 per cent of the shares; and Milton Greene, as vice president, holding 49 per cent. She said she did not intend to renew her contract with Twentieth Century-Fox. It was all very startling for her Fox bosses, who were under the impression that her existing agreement had yet to expire.

Marilyn was, she said, 'a new woman.' She told the press she was making the break 'so I can play the better kind of roles I want to play. I didn't like a lot of my pictures. I'm tired of sex roles. I'm going to broaden my scope. People have scope, you know ... they really do.' Asked what sort of roles she now wished to play, Marilyn mentioned 'one of the parts in *The Brothers Karamazov*, by Dostoyevsky.' Asked by a tittering reporter how those names were spelled, Marilyn replied, 'Honey, I couldn't spell any of the names I told you.'

Milton Greene tried to explain his grand plan, which was to form a group of actors and directors who would conceive their own films freed from the production-line tyranny of the big studios. The press took little notice. For them the focus remained Marilyn, and Greene would soon discover that running Marilyn Monroe Productions was a full-time occupation – and a crushing financial burden.

Marilyn had told Greene she was underpaid – and that her only present asset was fame. She was broke, and – because her contract with Fox was still in force – could not legally take other paid work. Using his earnings as a photographer, Greene paid all her expenses during 1955.

For a year Greene was to gamble all on his conviction that, whatever the legal niceties, Hollywood could not afford to pass up the box-office bonanza that came with the name Monroe. Twentieth Century-Fox would have to come to terms, however much it objected to Marilyn going independent. Greene would be proved right, but meanwhile he mortgaged himself to the hilt to keep Marilyn in luxurious and visible limbo.

Greene believed Marilyn must maintain a star's standard of living, not slip into dowdy obscurity. Marilyn did not demur, and was soon installed in grand style at the Waldorf Astoria Towers. Her working base was now a vastly expensive three-room luxury apartment, her first home in Manhattan. Greene paid for everything – clothes, beautician expenses of $500 a week (at 1955 prices), and the cost of keeping Marilyn's mother in care. He also bought Marilyn a black Thunderbird sportscar; Marilyn had become a fast driver who fancied herself an expert behind the wheel.

Under the stipulations of the Fox contract, Marilyn could make unpaid public appearances. Greene saw to it that the public saw a nice mix of the new Marilyn and the old. First, he made sure that the rogue glamour girl did not disappear. In March 1955, scantily costumed, Marilyn rode a pink elephant into Madison Square Garden, as her contribution to an extravaganza in aid of the Arthritis and Rheumatism Foundation. She and the elephant made their entrance to the commands of a ringmaster in the person of comedian Milton Berle, who would later claim he and Marilyn had once been lovers.* Twenty-five thousand people roared approval at her entrance, and Marilyn stole the show.

At breakfast time on Good Friday, 1955, the Greene home in Connecticut was invaded by television crews. Milton Greene had arranged for an appearance on *Person to Person*, a live interview program conducted by Edward R. Murrow. The show was a supposedly 'informal' visit with Mr and Mrs Milton Greene and their celebrated houseguest. Marilyn, who had been dousing a worse menstrual period than usual with painkillers and sleeping pills, wished she had never agreed to take part. She was not used to television, was petrified at the idea of talking directly to fifty million viewers. Her voice quavering, the seasoned star seemed amateurish compared to her coolly articulate hostess, Amy Greene.

Murrow hastily started asking the Greenes about their guest. Did she cook? Did she help clean the house and make her own bed? The Greenes obligingly lied. Marilyn herself offered a few worthy thoughts about the importance of working with the right film director, then fell back on a trusty old theme. She had really enjoyed riding the pink elephant, she said, 'because I hadn't been to a circus as a kid.'

Away from the Greenes' country home, which she now used more as a weekend retreat, Marilyn spent most of her time in New York City. She was exploring, seeking the pulse of that seething town, avidly striving to become a New Yorker herself. In the process she made myriad acquaintances and a few real friends. One of them, improbably, turned out to be one of her own fans – a sixteen-year-old boy.

Late the previous year, when Marilyn was in New York to shoot the skirt-blowing scene for *Seven Year Itch*, a large crowd had gathered each night to see her emerge from the St

---

* In his memoirs, published in 1974, Berle claimed to have had an affair with Marilyn in 1948, during the making of *Ladies of the Chorus*.

Regis Hotel. One evening the crowd included Jim Haspiel, a youngster who had left home at the age of fifteen and was now living from hand to mouth, moving from furnished room to furnished room. He idled away a good deal of his time at the movies and, as he put it, he was expecting to see the Marilyn of the screen, 'the oversized, over-everything lady from *Niagara.*' When the flesh-and-blood Marilyn emerged, Haspiel was surprised that she seemed so small – she was five foot six according to her passport application – and by the fact that she had big ears. The youth knew at once that he wanted to meet her, and he was there when Marilyn returned two hours later.

When Marilyn emerged from her car she was surrounded by fans taking pictures or begging for her autograph. Then Haspiel, who had neither camera nor paper, asked for a kiss. 'The word "No" was all over her face,' Haspiel remembered, 'and I said, "C'mon, just here on the cheek," and a couple of people in the crowd went "Oh-h-h," and she gave in, and she did kiss me.' The next night Marilyn refused a kiss even to an eight-year-old boy, muttering that 'Joe' would not like it. For Haspiel it meant that something had drawn her to *him,* and events proved him right.

In those days Marilyn was followed everywhere in New York by a gaggle of persistent fans known as the Monroe Six, whose ages ranged from fourteen to thirty. They at first kept lonely, individual vigils outside apartments and office buildings, waiting for their heroine. Then, as they grew to know each other, they joined forces. Haspiel sometimes tagged along with the Six, but never became one of them. He was a loner, and came to believe Marilyn liked him for it.

After Marilyn's death a brown manila envelope would be found in her room, containing pictures of her 'children.' The photographs inside were those of Joe DiMaggio's son, Arthur Miller's children – and Jim Haspiel. In life, she had singled him out for a singular intimacy.

Marilyn quickly gave the sixteen-year-old her trust. He was welcomed to her New York apartment and accepted as a backseat companion as she zoomed around New York by cab. For many months, though, Marilyn did not even know his name. She never asked him, and he forgot to introduce himself until so long afterward that it seemed superfluous. It was not till a year later, in the middle of a conversation, that Marilyn suddenly called him 'Jimmy.' He concluded that she had finally asked members of the Monroe Six to brief her on the youngster who had never bothered to tell her his name. In hindsight, Haspiel came to think she liked him for his audacity, and because she saw in the solitary, obstinate adolescent the orphan that was her image of herself.

Haspiel's devotions to Marilyn were conducted on the run, and many of his anecdotes are based on taxi journeys. Marilyn, he discovered, was impatient with a certain kind of New York pushiness. When she waited after handing a cab driver the fare, he said, 'You're Marilyn Monroe, and you expect change?'; she made a point of extracting every last dime. Having made her point, she then gave a large tip.

Young Haspiel's feeling for Marilyn verged on infatuation. Once she rebuffed him as he started to follow her into a cab. She wanted to travel alone, and thrust a twenty-dollar bill at him to pay for his own taxi. He rejected the money and, in pique, slammed the door in her face.

'I was quite wrong, of course,' Haspiel says. 'But I think what separated me from the others for her was that, in her world of sycophants, I sometimes answered back.'

Marilyn's correspondence files, located in 1986, contain letters between the star and her young friend. Haspiel's story was undoubtedly truthful. By middle age, married and with two teenage sons, Haspiel would become probably the world's most erudite student of Marilyn, the owner of a massive collection of photographs, many of them taken with a five-dollar camera he had acquired thirty years earlier.

Even as Collier died, Marilyn was seeking a liberator for her talent. She found him in Lee Strasberg, founder of the Actors Studio, the New York theater workshop that had become the most influential institution of its kind in the world. Its alumni of the fifties included Marlon Brando, James Dean, Eli Wallach, Anne Jackson, Paul Newman, Montgomery Clift, Steve McQueen, Shelley Winters, Maureen Stapleton, and Tom Ewell, Marilyn's co-star in *Seven Year Itch*. Their teacher, a Strasberg biographer noted, was called rabbi by some, pope by others, guru, god or genius, fake, charlatan, or the Ultimate Shrink.

Strasberg, aged fifty-three when Marilyn came to New York, had been born into poverty in a Jewish ghetto in Poland. He came to America with his family as a boy and was involved in theater by the time he turned twenty-one. His revelation, and the guiding light he would show to generations of American actors, was the Stanislavsky Method, the science of acting that has been called the 'total immersion system.' It held that actors must break away from the banal through intense exploration of their scenes and themselves. They must seek motivation in every act and phrase, draw on their own personal experience, their own past pain and joy, to communicate with the audience. Self-analysis was thus obligatory, and Strasberg, an ardent student of psychology, encouraged his students to undergo psychoanalysis.

In the muddle that was Marilyn, Strasberg was to discover a creature of dangerous potency. She would find a teacher, a priest for her personality, and a new dependency.

Marilyn had met Strasberg's wife and daughter on a set in Hollywood, and had talked longingly of one day studying at the feet of the master. Now, in March 1955, Marilyn found herself seated opposite producer Cheryl Crawford, one of the co-founders of the Actors Studio. She talked of her interest in becoming a serious actress, and Crawford promised to help. The very next day Marilyn was sitting opposite Strasberg in his cluttered, book-lined apartment at Broadway and 86th Street. After a brief conversation he agreed to take her on as a private pupil; full membership in the Studio was reserved for those who already had stage experience. The first lessons would be at home because, as Strasberg saw at once, Marilyn was 'the kind who had emotional problems.'

As Marilyn described her past (it was now that she told Strasberg she had once been a call girl), he noticed that she was very nervous. In her fright, she was literally stammering. Nevertheless, the new teacher enthused.

Strasberg would recall, 'I saw that what she looked like was not what she really was, and what was going on inside was not what was going on outside, and that always means there may be something there to be worked with. It was almost as if she had been waiting for a button to be pushed, and when it was pushed a door opened and you saw a treasure of gold and jewels.'

In the end, no hyperbole was too much for Strasberg to use in describing Marilyn. He said of her presence: 'She was engulfed in a mystic-like flame, like when you see Jesus at the Last Supper and there's a halo around him. There was this great white light surrounding Marilyn.'

In 1955, however, Strasberg did not flatter Marilyn with overblown phrases. He offered instead months of grueling exercises and work. In the mecca of American acting, all were equal and none were stars. Marilyn would appear in baggy sweater and jeans, without makeup, and seek out the most obscure place in the room. Actor Kevin McCarthy hardly noticed her at first, as they sat side by side watching a badly acted scene from Chekhov's *Three Sisters*. When he did recognize her, he observed Marilyn's disconcerting ability to switch her Monroe persona from 'off' to 'on,' from obscurity to the white light of Strasberg's perception.

'This tousled piece of humanity was sitting on my right,' McCarthy remembered, 'looking like nothing. Then, fifteen minutes later, after I'd interrupted the scene with some fairly rude comments, I looked again. I realized that a breathing, palpitating Marilyn Monroe had developed out of that nothing ... I remember looking and thinking, "My God, it's her" – she'd just come to life.'

Marilyn was quickly befriended by Eli Wallach, then just back from London and acting in *Teahouse of the August Moon*. Wallach, who like McCarthy would one day act with her in *The Misfits*, was also struck by the phenomenon of Marilyn's instant metamorphosis. In the street heads would turn to stare or ogle whereas a moment before everyone had passed her by. 'I just felt like being Marilyn for a moment,' Marilyn would murmur.

Wallach was bemused by the contradictions in her. In the summer of 1955, when *Seven Year Itch* was about to open in New York, he sat watching with Marilyn as workmen erected a forty-foot-high poster of the famous skirt scene. Only the bottom half, showing her legs and upper thighs, was in place. As a huge crane lowered the cutout image of her torso into position, Marilyn mused, 'That's the way they think of me, with my skirt over my head.'

Wallach said, 'She didn't seem to mind. She accepted it.'

Sometimes the Strasberg acting sessions seemed intellectually beyond Marilyn. One of her colleagues, Frank Corsaro, came to call himself 'Marilyn's translator.' He said, 'She didn't know what Lee was talking about half the damn time.'

Acting coach Peggy Feury disagreed, saying, 'Marilyn was so bright about acting. Her trouble was only that she'd get so scared she wasn't going to be able to do it, and so tied up in knots, that then everyone thought she was dumb.'

Some work came more naturally to Marilyn than to others. Asked in improvisation class to make believe she was a kitten, she excelled. Marilyn had borrowed a kitten, watched it for hours, then undulated to perfection. The challenge for

Marilyn was to overcome the terror, the abject stage fright, that accompanied the speaking of dialogue in front of an audience.

Outside the Studio, Marilyn's thirst for security was now accommodated by Lee and Paula Strasberg. As she spent more and more time in the city, and less with the Greenes in Connecticut, the orphan by vocation allowed herself to be taken to the bosom of yet another family. She was permitted total freedom of access to the Strasberg home. In a bustling New York Jewish household, Marilyn became Paula Strasberg's third child. She spent holidays at the family's weekend place on Fire Island.

Strasberg's daughter Susan, herself an actress at the age of seventeen, sometimes shared a room with Marilyn. From her bed, Susan would watch in awe as the famous body, soon to be thirty years old, was prepared for the day. At night Susan would watch as Marilyn 'would kick off her shoes and dance in the middle of the room alone, if no one was willing to dance with her.'

Once, when the guest said she envied people who could draw, Susan lent her a sketchpad and pen. Marilyn's facility in drawing came as a surprise. 'I saved two of her sketches,' Susan said. 'In one, with quick, round lines depicting a feline sensual grace and movement, she had done a self-portrait. The other was of a little Negro girl in a sad-looking dress, one sock falling down around her ankles.' Marilyn called this drawing 'Lonely.' A number of her drawings have survived, amateurish in execution but showing wit and sensitivity. One of an elegant woman holding a glass of champagne, she called, 'Oh, What the Hell!'

Over the years, Marilyn would repay the Strasberg hospitality with her own whimsical generosity. She paid Lee Strasberg's traveling expenses for a trip to the Soviet Union. She gave her Thunderbird car to the Strasbergs' son, John, on his eighteenth birthday. At fund-raising events for the

Studio, Marilyn's very presence raised many thousands of dollars.

In her last will, Marilyn bequeathed all her personal effects to Strasberg. Dresses, furs, film awards, books, letters, even her underwear, would one day be delivered to the Strasberg home in New York. As an unexpected windfall, Strasberg was later to inherit the rights to one of Marilyn's films, *The Prince and the Showgirl*. Many of her personal belongings would remain, jealously guarded, in the care of Strasberg's second wife, Anna.

There is no doubt Marilyn brought greater renown to the Studio and greater wealth to Strasberg personally. His occasional habit of bringing to the Studio people who were famous personalities, qualified by fame as much as by acting skill, paid off handsomely. Critics have assailed Strasberg as an opportunist, and his own son said, 'The greatest tragedy was that people, even my father in a way, took advantage of her. They glommed on to her special sort of life, her special characteristics, when what she needed was love. My parents did give her some love, but it was inextricably linked with the acting.'

Also mentioned in Marilyn's will would be a New York couple who could never be accused of taking advantage of her. The poet Norman Rosten and his wife Hedda gave Marilyn uncomplicated privacy and companionship, and perhaps the longest association of pure friendship in her entire life. It began, utterly by chance, on a rainy day in the spring of 1955.

Norman Rosten was seated at his desk at home in Brooklyn Heights when a friend, the photographer Sam Shaw, called to ask if he could drop in. He and a companion had been caught in a downpour in nearby Prospect Park. Minutes later Rosten was watching Shaw tramp up the stairs followed by a drenched figure in a camel-hair coat. Shaw mumbled an introduction and Rosten thought he caught the name 'Marion.' The girl picked up a volume of poems Rosten had written for his daughter Patricia, and sat silently reading. It was later, when Hedda Rosten asked what she did for a living, that she timidly offered her name, Marilyn Monroe.

Rosten and his wife, almost alone among Marilyn's East Coast friends, had no concern with anyone but the private Marilyn. 'We really didn't give a damn who she was,' Rosten said, 'and she did step out of her stereotype in real life. With us she was thoroughly enchanting, such an odd human being....'

Throughout the summer of 1955, and sporadically for the next seven years, Marilyn enjoyed privacy with the Rostens. They kept a few of her notes and letters, rare windfalls, since they were from a woman who did not often correspond. After that first meeting Marilyn wrote from the Waldorf-Astoria:

Dear Norman,
It feels a little funny to be writing the name 'Norman' since my own name is Norma and it feels like I'm writing my own name almost, however—
First, thanks for letting Sam and me visit you and Hedda on Saturday – it was nice. I enjoyed meeting your wife she was very warm to me – However, again— Thanks the most for your book of poetry – which I spent all Sunday morning in bed with. It touched me very much – I used to think that if I had ever had a child I would have wanted only a son – but after 'Songs for Patricia' – I know I would have loved a little girl as much – but maybe the former feeling was only Freudian anyway or something—
I used to write poetry sometimes but usually I was depressed at those times. The few I showed it to – (in fact about two people) – said that it depressed them – one of them cried but it was an old friend I'd known for a long time.
I hope to see you again.

So anyway thanks
And my best to Hedda and Patricia and you—
Marilyn M.

'She liked poetry,' Rosten recalled. 'It was a shortcut for her. She understood, with the instinct of a poet, that it led directly into the heart of experience.'

In 1952, drunk on whisky with Robert Slatzer in the hotel at Niagara Falls, Marilyn had sat scribbling what Slatzer called 'herniated sonnets.' Now, in the upholstered hush of her room at the Waldorf-Astoria, she was trying her hand at poetry again.

The experiments grew from her evenings with the Rostens, who often held informal poetry readings. Two favorites were Walt Whitman, whose work Marilyn had long liked, and W. B. Yeats, a new discovery for her. At the Rosten readings, each person in turn would take a book of verse and read aloud the poem on whatever page fell open. Marilyn came to read, of all things, Yeats' 'Never Give All the Heart.' Rosten says, 'She read rather slowly, softly, as if in class, low but breathless':

> Never give all the heart, for love
> Will hardly seem worth thinking of
> To passionate women if it seem.
> Certain, and they never dream
> That it fades out from kiss to kiss;
> For everything that's lovely is
> But a brief, dreamy, kind delight.
> Oh, never give the heart outright,
> For they, for all smooth lips can say,
> Have given their hearts up to the play.
> And who could play it well enough
> If deaf and dumb and blind with love?
> He that made this knows all the cost,
> For he gave all his heart and lost.

There was a silence when Marilyn finished. Rosten said, 'She had thought poets were mystical, somehow separate and apart from ordinary people. I tried to disabuse her of that idea. ...' Soon, Marilyn was tentatively sending Rosten her own efforts, including these lines:

> Life—
> I am of both your directions
> Existing more with the cold frost
> Strong as a cobweb in the wind
> Hanging downward the most
> Somehow remaining
> those beaded rays have the colors
> I've seen in paintings – ah life
> they have cheated you. ...
> thinner than a cobweb's thread
> sheerer than any—
> but it did attach itself
> and held fast in strong winds
> and sin(d)ged by (?) leaping hot fires
> life – of which at singular times
> I am both of your directions
> somehow I remain hanging downward
> the most
> as both of your directions pull me.

For Marilyn 1955 was a year of exploration – of herself, of acting, and of arts she had never had time for in the past. Sometimes she would 'borrow' Rosten from his wife to escort her to a play or concert. Once, at Carnegie Hall, they were invited to meet the Russian pianist Emil Gilels. He kissed Marilyn's hand and said she should visit the Soviet Union. Marilyn told him, as she had been telling all and sundry for some time now, that she was currently reading Dostoyevsky.

(Better it done with an Sir. Olivian accent)

For Norman

From time to time
I make it ~~Ryme~~ me
but don't hold that kind
of thing
against
me.

Oh well what the hell
so it went sell
what I want to tell –
–is what's on my mind   →(intendandad to ryme with

taint Dishes
taint wishes
its Thoughts
flinging
by for I
die. (and to Think ! in ink

Scrawled lines given by Marilyn to poet Norman Rosten in the mid-fifties.
She was still capable of poking fun at herself.

When the press spotted Rosten as Marilyn's companion, gossip columns soon hinted at an affair. Rosten, who was happily married, said the idea never seriously occurred to him. 'With Marilyn, you're not talking about going to bed with a woman, you're talking about going to bed with an institution. Who can handle that? And how awful to be one!'

The Rostens saw a Marilyn who liked to be domestic, so long as household work was occasional entertainment rather than necessity. She would boast of her skill at doing the dishes, the legacy, she said, of childhood slavery in foster homes. Marilyn the cook used her new friends as guinea pigs. Rosten recalled good stews and bouillabaisse, and disastrous salads drowned in vinegar. He said 'her color schemes' (peas and carrots), if not striking, managed to be consistent. She once offered to 'tone down' a spicy dish by using a hairdryer!

The Rostens' daughter Patricia, who was then eight, had a child's-eye memory of a new acquaintance who 'was fun to be with because she broke the rules, and children love being around grown-ups who can get away with that. When Marilyn touched me or hugged me I felt a warmth and softness (dare I use the word "maternal" in relation to her?) that was very reassuring. It was not unlike falling into that champagne-colored quilt that graced her bed.'

Once Marilyn surprised Patricia in her bedroom, her nose in the enormous makeup box. 'She plunked me down at her vanity mirror,' Patricia remembered, 'and said she would show me how to do the job right. I watched her skilful hands transform my kid's face into something that even I might have called glamorous. She made my eyelids glimmer, my cheekbones appear accentuated, and my mouth rosy with color. She also arranged my hair, lifting it off my shoulders into an elegant French twist. "Why," I thought, "I could pass for seventeen." Then, proud of her handiwork, she happily took me by the hand back to the living room to show me off to the grown-ups.'

Sometimes the Rostens invited Marilyn to their rented summer place on Long Island. An excursion in her company could be anything but peaceful. Rosten told of a day when Marilyn spent a while sitting demurely on the beach, in bathing suit, straw hat and sunglasses, shaded by an umbrella.

'Slowly, imperceptibly,' said Rosten, 'as though the news had spread by some sort of telepathy, a group of young people appeared in swim attire and, before we were aware of it, closed us in a circle. They stared at Marilyn, unbelieving, as at a mirage. They came up to her uttering little cries of joy, reaching out to touch her. They began crowding, their enthusiasm getting out of control as she moved back, a reflex of fear now in her eyes.

'I was struck by this double effect: love of the crowd and the need of the adulation, and at the same time a nameless fear. She laughed nervously, abruptly broke from the circle, and ran toward the water about fifty yards away. The youthful admirers cheered and chased after her into the water. She began swimming out, calling for me to follow. I was a little scared, especially when the noisy kids surrounded her while I tried to push them away . . .'

Suddenly Marilyn began to splutter and swallow water. 'I'm not a good swimmer even when I'm good,' she gasped, her aquatic prowess with Tommy Zahn, the surfing champion of a decade earlier, apparently a thing of the past. She and Rosten were rescued by the crew of a passing speedboat. Its driver, a boy in his teens, then drove round and round in circles, staring transfixed at the exhausted female in his boat, until Rosten told him to snap out of it.

In other situations Marilyn had compassion for those who recognized her. Once, disguised in a bandanna and dark glasses, she and a male companion stopped at a gas station on the East Side Drive. The station attendant conferred with his mate, then announced, 'I just bet my friend here ten dollars that you're Marilyn Monroe.'

Marilyn's companion replied, 'No, she's not, though she's often mistaken for her.'

They were about to drive off when Marilyn cried, 'My God, he's paying his friend the ten dollars.' She called the attendants back, took off her glasses, and said, 'Give him back the money. I am Monroe.'

Jim Haspiel, the fan turned friend, went Christmas shopping at Saks Fifth Avenue with Marilyn at the end of that first year in New York. She had 'disguised' herself with a silk kerchief tied under the chin, an Ivy League cap, dark glasses, and hormone cream, instead of makeup, all over her face. It fooled no one, for when Haspiel left for a few minutes, after arranging with Marilyn to rejoin her at the men's tie counter, he returned to find that 'eight' salesmen were waiting on her, and 'about two hundred and fifty' customers were thronging around. The rest of the store was virtually empty.

Marilyn made her way through the crowd to Haspiel and whispered, 'Please don't say my name, I don't want anyone to know it's me.' Haspiel decided she had lived so long in the glare of fame that she no longer recognized it. Others might suspect Marilyn thrived on the attention – when it was convenient.

Norman Rosten concluded that Marilyn reveled in being female, accepted it for the power it gave her. 'She sensed the difference in sexual psychology between men and women,' Rosten believed, 'and would never censure a man for beating the woman to the draw, so to speak. We could lust after her, dream of possessing her, but no one would be hurt. She could be alluring and warm, and yet had the courage to battle alone against male-dominated Hollywood power – and win.'

Months after they first met, toward the end of 1955, Marilyn asked Rosten to take her to the Rodin exhibition at the Metropolitan Museum of Art. Two pieces fascinated her,' said Rosten, '*Pygmalion and Galatea* and *The Hand of God*.'

The Hand of God, in white marble, depicts a great curving

hand holding a man and a woman locked in passionate embrace. 'They are together and apart,' the poet remembered. 'The woman's hair streams from the stone. Marilyn walked around and around that small white miracle, her eyes wide as she removed her dark glasses.'

In her year of limbo in New York, Marilyn began telling friends that she had found her love. She was, certainly, close to achieving another ambition: she had America's foremost playwright on the hook, and soon it would be just a matter of reeling him in.

19

Arthur Miller rarely talked willingly about Marilyn Monroe during her lifetime, and in the years that followed declined interviews. He corresponded courteously during the writing of this book but said, 'When I have something to say about Marilyn I will do it on my own typewriter.'

His position was reasonable, given that he had lived in a glare of banal publicity for half a decade. However, thanks partly to his and Marilyn's own statements in 1956, when their romance was at full flood, we can reconstruct the courtship that led to one of the most ballyhooed marriages of its time.

When Marilyn settled in New York, Arthur Miller was about to turn forty. She was twenty-nine. He still lived in Brooklyn, where he had been raised, with Mary, his wife of fifteen years, and two children not yet into their teens.

Although America knew Miller only as a playwright, he believed fervently in the value of hard physical work, not least as vital grounding for his plays about the common man. At one point of his life Miller made a point of working a few weeks each year in a factory. He would say, 'Anyone who doesn't know what it means to stand in one place, eight hours a day, doesn't know what it's all about. It's the only way you can learn what makes men go into a gin mill after work and start fighting. You don't learn about those things in Sardi's.'

Miller had little time for such after-theater night spots or for the fashions of New York City. When he absolutely had to buy a new suit he delighted in announcing that he had found it on sale. He was partial to stout shoes with thick leather soles, and liked to say that he bought just one pair for each play he wrote. His favorite uniform, when not in town, was a windbreaker and khaki pants.

Not being in town was by 1955 becoming a preoccupation with him. After his first success with *All My Sons*, Miller had bought four acres, cheap, in Connecticut. He worked steadily for six weeks building himself a work shack, then sat in it during the next six weeks fashioning the play that won a Pulitzer Prize, *Death of a Salesman*.

Since 1950, when he had first met Marilyn in Hollywood, Miller had produced three more plays. *The Crucible*, based on the Salem witch trials of two hundred and fifty years ago, came in 1953, when Senator Joseph McCarthy's investigation of imagined communism was at its most pernicious. *A View from the Bridge*, about a man who betrays the illegal immigrant suitor of his daughter, appeared in 1955, the year Marilyn came East.

Arthur Miller was a man who for some time had been able to say, 'I have the name. They have to listen when I talk.' He was not enormously rich but he had money. He would say, 'You live fruitfully in tension. To create, and I don't only mean writing, is to be under tension. Paradise is a state of inertia where nothing happens. It is a form of death. The tension is necessary. Once it's over, you drop dead in six months.'

Marilyn arrived in New York when the vital tension had gone from Miller's personal life. His marriage was in the doldrums. The wife who had worked to keep him in the early days, who had borne his children and corrected his manuscripts, was no longer enough. They were headed for divorce, he was to say a year later, 'Marilyn or no.'

Miller told a *Time* reporter in 1956, 'I didn't know a thing about Marilyn coming to New York until I read about it in the papers.' There had been no contact between them since their encounter in late 1950, but neither had forgotten.

Miller's memory was of a young woman at a Hollywood

cocktail party, 'so terrified she couldn't speak a word, just stood there mute but refusing to engage in the vacuous small talk.' He said he had gained Marilyn's confidence, then seen her for about eight hours over three days. She had told him of her 'smothering feelings of inferiority, her inability to make any real friends, the fact that people thought of her only in terms of an inviting body and nothing else.'

Miller was struck by Marilyn's 'sensitivity and feeling and grasp of reality,' and he told her he thought she should come to New York and learn how to act. When he left California, she poured out her troubles in letters, and he responded – for a while. Then, as he plunged into writing his next play, the letters stopped.

Author and critic Maurice Zolotow, who knew both Miller and Marilyn, thought the encounter in Hollywood had haunted Miller and influenced his work from then on. In both *The Crucible* and *View from the Bridge*, Zolotow noted the themes of the eternal triangle, of infidelity in marriage, and of an older man's love for a young girl. Miller himself, though not till years later, would write that *View from the Bridge* 'was expressing a very personal preoccupation . . . not at all apart from my own psychological life. . . .'

Fellow playwright Clifford Odets said after reading *The Crucible*, which Miller wrote following his first meeting with Marilyn, 'No man would write this play unless his marriage was going to pieces.'

At all events, sometime in April 1955, when Marilyn had ridden her pink elephant, appeared on national television, and discovered Lee Strasberg, Miller reached out for the girl from Hollywood.

According to Marilyn the reunion occurred at another party, for theater people in New York. She was drinking vodka and orange, and Miller made the approach. They talked for a while and parted at the end of the evening. Miller held out for two weeks, then called Paula Strasberg of the Actors

Studio to ask for Marilyn's phone number. They met at the home of their mutual friend, poet Norman Rosten – who had been to the University of Michigan with Miller – and the affair began.

The couple managed a remarkable feat. They met for the best part of a year without being discovered by the press. Miller, who had been borrowing his son's bicycle for a long time, went out and bought a new one for himself. It was English, with gears, like Marilyn's, and the two of them would pedal unnoticed around Brooklyn's Sheepshead Bay or Coney Island, places where no gossip columnist lay in wait. They ate in corners of obscure restaurants.

Peter Leonardi, Marilyn's assistant that year, said later, 'I was with her morning, noon, and night for weeks, and I never even heard the name "Miller."'

In the summer of 1955 Marilyn gave a dinner party for friends who were in on the secret. Miller recalled that 'she did nothing else for two days. I never saw anyone so worried about a simple meal. Actually the whole thing was overdone, too formal, too meticulous, too manicured. She worked herself into a frazzle about the whole affair.'

On another occasion Marilyn was more true to her usual chaotic form. Maureen Stapleton, her colleague at the Actors Studio, remembered an evening when Marilyn, hurrying home from rehearsal, announced that she had to prepare a roast for Miller and some friends. Unfortunately, she had forgotten that the meat would take hours to cook, so dinner was served at an hour when most people were going to bed.

Miller, whose presence had long been nurtured, but only as a photograph at Marilyn's bedside, was now a day-to-day reality. He indeed looked, as journalists had long chorused, like a whiskerless version of the man in the other picture that accompanied her everywhere – Abraham Lincoln. Years later, asked what one thing she was most grateful to Miller for, Marilyn would say, 'He introduced me to the importance of political freedom in our society.' Miller was a man who liked to talk social theory for hours, a pipe gripped between his teeth or, when pipeless, swiveling a cigarette from tooth to tooth, like a gun. Marilyn listened.

A close friend of the couple said, 'Aside from personal attraction – and that's the biggest aside in history – a lot of what interested her in Arthur was this: here was a man with a whole structure of social ideas clarified by a great deal of reading.'

It was only twelve months since Marilyn had tried in vain to persuade Joe DiMaggio to read 'everything from Mickey Spillane to Jules Verne.' On DiMaggio's birthday Marilyn had given him a gold medal for his watch chain, inscribed with a quotation from *The Little Prince* by Antoine de Saint-Exupéry: 'True love is visible not to the eyes, but to the heart, for eyes may be deceived.' Perplexed, DiMaggio had asked, 'What the hell does that mean?' With Arthur Miller the roles were reversed. Marilyn was asking the questions.

She did admire Miller's intellect, as she had years earlier, but soon she would also insist that, 'I'm in love with the man, not his mind. The Arthur Miller who attracted me was a man of warmth and friendliness. Arthur has helped me adjust myself. I've always been unsure of myself. Arthur has helped me overcome this feeling.'

Marilyn, for her part, wrought a transformation in Arthur Miller. 'Miller was in love, completely, seriously,' Norman Rosten would say. 'It was wonderful to behold.'

Miller told *Time* reporter Robert Ajemian, 'She is the most womanly woman I can imagine. Being with her, people want to die. This girl sets up a challenge in every man. Most men become more of what they are natively when they are around her: a phoney becomes more phoney, a confused man becomes more confused, a retiring man more retiring. She's kind of a lodestone that draws out of the male animal his essential qualities.'

Miller was persuaded that Marilyn's reputation for promiscuity was vastly exaggerated. 'Sure, she had her men,' he said, 'but not from couch to couch, man to man. Any relation she ever had was meaningful to her, built on a thread of hope, however mistaken. I've known social workers who have had a more checkered history than she has.'

The playwright in Miller admired the honesty in Marilyn, thought her 'literally incapable of saying anything unless it was the truth.' He said that as an actress, 'she'll either do the truth or go on strike. There's something in her that's looking for the basic reality of a given situation. In acting, of course, this is a terrific thing. It enables you to get to the core.'

Miller talked of Marilyn's obsessive worry about her lack of education. 'She'll come to me and say, "I heard a new word the other day, what does it mean?" The other day she asked me about the word "impermeable." She often mispronounces a word – perhaps she will say "intraveniously" instead of "intravenously." But she wants to learn.'

Miller said Marilyn had recently been reading a book on the art of Goya. 'When I talked to her on the phone she said to me, "I haven't got to the good part yet." Next time I called her she said, "I'm two-thirds through and I still haven't hit the good part." The truth was, of course, that the book was mostly surmise, not positive fact. When Marilyn reached the end of the book she said to me, "Well, I finished it and there's still nothing. Why did they write it?" It was a good question. That's the way a book ought to be read.'

Miller told *Time*, 'Instead of becoming a disbeliever in life, which she had every reason to become, she kept her ability to feel and search for a genuine relationship. She has stopped wanting to throw herself away. She was preached to so much that she was a bad girl, not worth anything, that she developed an enormous self-destructiveness. She's coming out of it now.'

Miller was utterly smitten. So, thought their mutual friends, was Marilyn. She, however, was pursued by familiar ghosts – and new temptation.

In the early months of 1955 Joe DiMaggio had still not given up his pursuit of Marilyn, and she had not yet cut herself entirely free of him. Ironically, he reached her most through the family of the most important love in Marilyn's youth, Fred Karger. Fred's sister, Mary, had by now moved to New Jersey with her children, and Marilyn, sometimes accompanied by DiMaggio, visited often.

To the Kargers, Marilyn and DiMaggio now seemed to be on good terms. DiMaggio played golf with Mary, and Marilyn delighted the children with her eccentric diets and sense of fun.

Mary's daughter Anne recalled an afternoon when the neighbors, knowing Marilyn was next door, pulled an effective practical joke.

'Their son was in the Fire Department,' Anne recalled, 'and he called in a false fire alarm. Maybe ten trucks appeared in front of our house – someone told the firemen Marilyn was there, and they all insisted on meeting her. And she went out and talked to them; she was very sweet about it.'

In New York City, however, DiMaggio continued to show his jealous streak. He cast around pathetically, begging help and counsel from outsiders, even journalists. He asked columnist Earl Wilson and his wife for advice on how to get Marilyn back. Marilyn told her longtime New York friend Henry Rosenfeld that one night DiMaggio 'came into the Waldorf and almost broke the door down. Police had to be called to calm him down. He was very, very jealous.'

On June 1, 1955, Marilyn's twenty-ninth birthday, Marilyn arrived on DiMaggio's arm for the premiere of *Seven Year Itch*. He gave a party for her afterwards at Toots Shor's, but the mood quickly soured. The couple had a row at the supper table, and Marilyn left with her photographer friend, Sam Shaw.

Jim Haspiel told the saddest story of Joe DiMaggio's tormented persistence. Haspiel himself kept vigil for Marilyn at all hours of the day and night, and more than once spotted DiMaggio 'literally standing in a doorway near her apartment, in the late evening, just as any fan might stand on the street waiting to catch a glimpse of her. That was the extent of his need.'

The Seven Year Itch also gave Marilyn the opportunity to mount a somewhat devilish practical joke against the lover she had so much wanted to marry in 1948, Fred Karger. He was by now embroiled in marital problems with his second wife, the actress Jane Wyman, and Marilyn delighted in reminding Wyman that she too had once enjoyed Karger's love.

When *Seven Year Itch* was playing in Los Angeles Marilyn and two friends – one of them Karger's first wife, Patti – ventured out in the dead of night to Grauman's Theater to steal a cardboard blow-up of Marilyn in the famous skirt-blowing scene. They took the life-size likeness to Holmby Hills and planted it on Jane Wyman's lawn. She failed to see the joke.

In the summer of 1955 Fred Karger found himself staying at the Waldorf-Astoria in New York. Marilyn was living on one of the upper floors, and he called to invite her down for a drink. When she failed to appear, Karger called again, and this time Marilyn sounded drunk. Later, when he went up to her apartment, she was lost in a haze of alcohol and – an ominous new factor in her life – sleeping pills.

Marilyn did not see only Arthur Miller in the early months of their relationship. Dress manufacturer Henry Rosenfeld had been instrumental in arranging for her suite at the Waldorf, and loaned her a good deal of money. From then on, Marilyn consulted him about her financial affairs, and would one day propose that he take all the proceeds from one of her movies in exchange for paying her a guaranteed thousand dollars a week for life. Rosenfeld gently declined, explaining that he would make far more on the capital than was fair. He himself became deeply involved with Marilyn and, Marilyn told a close friend, even proposed marriage.

The year 1955 also saw an embryonic scheme to marry Marilyn off to the head of a European royal family – an idea supported by Aristotle Onassis. The millionaire was concerned because one of his favorite watering holes, the principality of Monaco, was going through a slump. The fashionable set had started going elsewhere. Onassis thought they might return if Prince Rainier married a suitably glamorous foreigner, and asked a friend, George Schlee, to cast around for brides in the United States. Schlee consulted Gardner Cowles, publisher of *Look* magazine, who happened to be a neighbor of Milton Greene in Connecticut.

'I suggested to Schlee that it might be a good thing to marry off Rainier to a movie actress,' Cowles said. 'He asked if I had anybody in particular in mind. I said, "Well, Marilyn Monroe is at the peak of her fame, and she's staying nearby. Let's put the idea to her."'

So it was that Marilyn and the Greenes were invited to meet Schlee at the Cowles' country home. Cowles said, 'We didn't beat about the bush. When I told Marilyn, she said the idea appealed to her, but she didn't even know where Monaco was. She said she'd be glad to meet the prince.'

Princess Marilyn of Monaco? That night, as the Greenes and Marilyn drove home, the atmosphere was one of huge hilarity tinged with the realization that the proposition was serious. For a while there was much chatter about Prince Rainier, who was quickly dubbed 'Reindeer.'

The idea fizzled altogether when Monaco's royal household announced that the prince was going to marry another actress, Grace Kelly. Marilyn added her own postscript. She telephoned Kelly with congratulations, adding, 'I'm so glad you've found a way out of this business.'

Arthur Miller may have thought Marilyn was not promiscuous, that she was now less insecure. However, just as she had been during the DiMaggio courtship, Marilyn was a less than constant lover. During 1955 she drew close to Marlon Brando.

Brando was Hollywood's most celebrated product of the Actors Studio, and Marilyn had long admired him. The previous year, after his triumph in *On the Waterfront*, she pressed Sam Goldwyn for a part in Brando's next film, *Guys and Dolls*. In New York, Marilyn hoped that one of her first independent projects would star Brando and Charlie Chaplin.

Asked to define sex appeal, Marilyn said, 'There are people to whom other people react and other people who do nothing for people. I react to men, too ... personally, I react to Marlon Brando.' Marilyn never did achieve her ambition to work with Brando, but in 1955 they had an affair.

Amy and Milton Greene, who still saw Marilyn regularly, became aware by the summer that she was involved with Brando. Other friends and colleagues confirmed that they had a relationship. Brando, famous on screen and off for arrogance and a tendency to violence, was also loved by intimates for his gentleness and loyalty. Marilyn spoke of him to Amy Greene as 'sweet, tender.' She referred to him by the codename 'Carlo,' and relished the fact that most people had no idea whom she was talking about. A photograph taken of them together in December 1955, at an actors' benefit, shows Marilyn and Brando looking dreamily happy together.*

The Brando affair, which had remained secret, faded as Marilyn prepared for a public involvement with Arthur Miller. The friendship, however, endured. In 1962, in the last

* Not the photograph shown in the picture section.

days before her death, Marilyn would spend hours talking on the telephone with Brando. Contacted in connection with this book, Brando responded with a rare personal call. Speaking with evident emotion, he said, 'I did know her, and out of that sentiment for her, I could never talk about her for publication. I think you can understand that.'

Throughout 1955 Marilyn contrived for once to keep her private life, if not entirely hidden from the press, at least indecipherable. Toward the end of the year, in a long interview with columnist Earl Wilson, she danced around cunningly baited questions. Asked who her favorite actor was, Marilyn named Brando – then quickly added a few others. Who was her favorite playwright? Marilyn said Arthur Miller – and Tennessee Williams. Asked if she had any love interests, her answer was classic Monroe: 'No serious interests, but I'm always interested.'

In January 1956, Earl Wilson broke the story that Arthur Miller and his wife were planning to divorce. In private, Miller and Marilyn were now talking about marriage. In public they stonewalled for five more months, but Marilyn had effectively fulfilled the wish she had callously expressed to Sidney Skolsky – just after her marriage to DiMaggios – to one day obtain the hand of Arthur Miller in marriage. The New Year, it seemed, was awash with success, and not only in love.

After nearly a year Lee Strasberg had decided Marilyn was ready to perform before an audience of her peers at the Actors Studio. She and Maureen Stapleton first worked for a while on a scene from Noël Coward's *Fallen Angels*, gave up, then settled on the opening scene from Eugene O'Neill's *Anna Christie*, which Marilyn had once done as an exercise with Natasha Lytess. Marilyn played Anna.

Maureen Stapleton recalled that 'she had terrible trouble remembering lines. I said, "Look, it's not as though it's some damn opening night. We'll just put the book in front of us on the table – lots of people do it." Marilyn refused to do that, and we never did get through it in rehearsal with her knowing the lines. Then when we did the scene she was fine, didn't forget a line in fifteen minutes. That exceedingly wispy voice of hers seemed to carry all right, for all her worrying about it. Afterwards we went out to a bar on Tenth Avenue, and celebrated having cheated death one more time.'

Some of the skeptics' voices were now stilled. 'She *was* wonderful,' said actress Kim Stanley. 'We were taught never to clap at the Actors Studio – it was like we were in church – and it was the first time I'd ever heard applause there.'

Others retained their doubts. The triumph, some felt, was that Marilyn had managed the scene at all. Lee Strasberg's success was that he had got her to do it competently, not that she had done it brilliantly. Marilyn herself sensed this reaction and played down the praise.

In early 1956, however, Lee Strasberg offered this accolade: 'I have worked with hundreds and hundreds of actors and actresses,' he told director Joshua Logan, 'and there are only two that stand out way above the rest. Number one is Marlon Brando, and the second is Marilyn Monroe. . . .'

Meanwhile, on top of such acclamation and her engagement to Arthur Miller, Marilyn had won her battle with Twentieth Century-Fox.

For a year now, ever since Marilyn's flight to New York, the studio had kept her Hollywood dressing room undisturbed. The cleaners still walked around a mountain of unanswered fan mail to dust the jumble of makeup, the false eyelashes, the bottles and boxes of pills, the discarded book of love poems – and a photograph of Joe DiMaggio. Now Milton Greene's gamble paid off. In the absence of any replacement for Marilyn, the studio struck a deal.

On New Year's Eve 1955 Marilyn signed a new contract with Fox that gave her uniquely favorable terms. She was required to make only four films for the studio over the next seven years, and would be free to make one film a year for a different studio. Marilyn Monroe Productions would receive $100,000 in salary for each film made for Fox, plus a percentage of the profits. It was an excellent deal by 1955 standards, and promised a potential income of some $8,000,000 over the full contract period.

A special clause, really important to Marilyn, gave her the right to reject any film she deemed not to be 'Class A,' and to reject directors or cameramen who did not meet with her approval. She submitted a list of sixteen directors, largely concocted for her by Milton and Amy Greene, with whom she was prepared to work. Twentieth Century-Fox did not argue.

In the flush of victory, Marilyn greeted 1956 with a barrage of plans. She would return to Hollywood to make *Bus Stop* with one of her chosen directors, Joshua Logan. She stood side by side with Sir Laurence Olivier to announce that they would soon work together on a film version of Terence Rattigan's play *The Sleeping Prince*.

The world's most distinguished actor pronounced a benediction. Marilyn was, Sir Laurence told the press, 'a brilliant comedienne and therefore an extremely good actress.' He watched in astonishment as 150 newsmen jostled for photographs, then became frenzied when the shoulder strap broke on Marilyn's dress.

Something about Marilyn bothered Sir Laurence. Away from the microphone, and in the limousine that bore him away, he said to producer Saul Colin, 'Saul, I wonder if I've made a mistake?' Later that year, Sir Laurence would find out.

Meeting Marilyn now was a confusing experience. The writer Dorothy Manning at first had the impression that 'gone was the shy, tense, little-girl voice, the slow groping for just the right word. . . . In its place was a poised woman. Gay, relaxed, less self-conscious, she came up in a few minutes with sprightlier conversation than most stars can manage in hours.'

The same day, meeting Marilyn a second time, Manning was startled by the abrupt change in her. She wrote: 'In the air was the feeling that Marilyn was again troubled, shrinking back into the shadows, anxious, still unsure. Now she was a strange, bewildering girl, one whose defenselessness caught at your heart.'

Manning was finding a kind way to express what Sir Laurence Olivier had glimpsed. Later, recalling their first meeting, Sir Laurence was to write, 'You would not be far out if you described her as schizoid.'

Even before she left Hollywood, Marilyn was no stranger to the psychiatrist's office. It was the heyday of the couch psychiatrist, especially in California. As one doctor who knew Marilyn put it: 'At that time out here, you could get psychoanalysis and a high colonic under the same neon sign. It was a time of fraudulence. A lot of questionable doctors had come here and succeeded just because they were glib and good at promoting themselves. They had a ready market – a lot of highly neurotic actors and actresses.'

The first record of Marilyn seeing a psychiatrist is in 1954, during her marriage to DiMaggio. She saw an analyst, identity unknown, for some six months.

Marilyn's medical doctors had no doubt she needed psychiatric help. Dr Milton Gottlieb, who gave Marilyn gynecological care, said, 'She was insecure, frightened of the reality of life. A very disturbed young woman.'

Dr Elliott Corday, Marilyn's physician from 1948 till the mid-fifties, says, 'I eventually withdrew from the case because she would not employ a decent psychiatrist. People would understand her death better had they been listening to her in my office back then. There had been many suicide attempts, more than were known. And by 1954 she was using drugs – I think the hard stuff as well as the sleeping pills. In the end I told her I was not going to be around to witness what was going to happen.'

Evidence of hard drug use by Marilyn is meager. Joe DiMaggio's detectives, appointed to investigate Marilyn's personal life, had reported finding 'hypodermic syringes, two or three vials containing some kind of powder, and other paraphernalia' in Marilyn's apartment. Whatever their significance, the woman who fled Hollywood for New York needed help.

Marilyn told Milton Greene she had stopped having psychiatric treatment. Greene said she should continue, and promised to find her a top-flight analyst. Greene, who himself gradually came to consider Marilyn 'schizo,' sent her to see Dr Hohenberg, a female psychiatrist practicing on New York's East Side. Marilyn saw this doctor five times a week during much of 1955.

At the Actors Studio, Lee Strasberg thought Marilyn's sessions with the psychiatrist 'freed' her for the rigors of his 'total immersion' acting technique. Arthur Miller would say, after she had undergone treatment for a year, that psychiatry had helped Marilyn a good deal. 'She is seeing the issues more clearly now,' he said, 'discovering that in so many situations in her life she was not the one who was wrong. She feels psychiatry has made a big difference to her.'

In time Miller was to wonder how much real use the analysis had been. Others were vocal in their scorn. Billy Wilder, Marilyn's director on *Seven Year Itch*, offered a coldly professional point of view: 'There are certain wonderful rascals in this world, like Monroe, and one day they lie down on an analyst's couch and out comes a clenched, dreary thing. It is better for Monroe not to be straightened out. The charm of her is her two left feet.'

By any normal standards Marilyn was still an emotional mess. Henry Rosenfeld saw a Marilyn who 'came out in red blotches at the idea of meeting a new acquaintance, such was her fear.'

Writer Adele Fletcher waited to have lunch with Marilyn one day in Elsa Maxwell's suite at the Waldorf Towers. 'She arrived at Elsa's suite three hours late, at precisely the hour when she was supposed to be at the Cecil Beaton studio. I later learned that she had had her hair shampooed and set three times before leaving. She was continually apprehensive that she would not look her best and people would start saying her looks were fading.'

Marilyn's aide in 1955, Peter Leonardi, said, 'She sits and sits and *projects* before every interview or public appearance. Sometimes she stares out of the window for hours, thinking and pulling at a lock of her hair. She often worries so much she becomes nauseated.'

While working, Marilyn often scribbled her thoughts and acting notes in a notebook. 'What am I afraid of?' one prying crew member read in the book. 'I know I can act. But I'm afraid. I am afraid and I should not be and I must not be. Shit!'

Milton Greene witnessed Marilyn gradually losing herself in addiction to barbiturates. She would take sleeping pills for insomnia at 3:00 A.M., knowing she had to be up to drive into the city at six. On the way to the appointment there would be more pills, often the stimulant Dexamyl, to shatter the stupor. Marilyn was drinking more, too, and in conjunction with the pills.

In 1955, Marilyn told Amy Greene and Henry Rosenfeld that she had had yet another abortion. It brought the total to thirteen at this point in her life – at twenty-nine years old – if Marilyn's own account to Amy Greene is correct, and it was surely yet another blow to her reeling psyche. Amy Greene did not know the father's identity, and Rosenfeld preferred not to identify him.

In spite of the security offered by the relationship with

Arthur Miller, Marilyn still acted as though she were desperately lonely. More than before, she indulged her habit of telephoning people in the early hours of the morning. Compliant friends would accept her suggestion that they go for a drive anywhere, around Manhattan or into the darkened suburbs, till dawn. Marilyn was now afraid to be alone at night.

Lee Strasberg tried to help by inviting her to sleep at his home. 'She was emotionally upset,' he recalled. 'She wanted a family. She wanted to be held. Not to be made love to but just to be supported, because when she'd taken the pills they'd somehow react on her so that she would want more. We wouldn't give them to her. That's why she got in the habit of coming over and staying over. I'd hold her a little and she'd go to sleep.'

In May 1956, *Time* magazine was to give Marilyn the accolade of a cover. Reporters worked for months on the research, doing interviews in places as far-flung as Tokyo, Paris, and London. Ezra Goodman, who had known Marilyn through Sidney Skolsky, spent weeks in Los Angeles unearthing facts about her. He sieved the myth she had spun about her past, talked to teachers from her schooldays, colleagues, doctors, and psychiatrists, and filed a massive report to *Time*.

Goodman concluded: 'It may be, as has been psychiatrically observed about her, that she has such contempt for herself that she is really trying to make peace with the world, not by adjusting to reality, but by reconstructing herself and the world around her ... there is in her some sort of enigmatic, almost magical, quotient, which no one has really been able to define, that has gotten her where she is today in spite of a background that might normally have found her ending up a schizophrenic in a state mental hospital or an alcoholic in the gutter. Perhaps the quality that many people find attractive in her is her very insecurity, her unhappiness, her sleepwalking through life. But the riddle that is Marilyn Monroe has not been solved. It is doubtful whether a year of ambulance chasing, flagpole climbing, and flatfooting would do the trick. That is probably one for the analyst's couch.'

According to Goodman, *Time* magazine ignored most of his report and printed a reassuring story about an actress on the road to an even more glorious future. Perhaps the public would not have had it otherwise.

Norman Rosten, possibly the most compassionate of Marilyn's New York friends, was not blind to her deep trouble. He hoped it could be balanced by the other side of her, the woman 'wise in the ways of the survivor.'

Surviving, for Marilyn, meant going on – and 'on' meant more films. There was no one, it seems, to tell her otherwise. Had there been, she would probably not have listened. Marilyn had made twenty-four films in the first seven years of her career. In the seven years from 1955 to her death she would complete only five. The very first of them, as she promised *Time* magazine, proved that she was indeed 'a real actress.'

20

In February 1956, ending a year of self-imposed exile, Marilyn flew back to Hollywood to a tumultuous reception. Hundreds of photographers mobbed the plane, and a crowd churned around for two hours before she could leave the airport.

Marilyn was back, on her own terms, to make the movie of the recent Broadway success *Bus Stop*, with a director tailor-made for the Monroe fresh from the Actors Studio. On Milton Greene's advice Marilyn had asked Fox for Joshua Logan, the only American director to have studied in the Soviet Union under Stanislavsky. Initially Logan balked at the notion of working with Marilyn, but Lee Strasberg's lavish praise of her persuaded him. Years later, more than any other director, he still bubbled with enthusiasm about Marilyn.

'I had no idea she had this incandescent talent,' Logan said. 'She made directing worthwhile. She had such fascinating things happen to her face and skin and hair and body as she read lines, that she was – it's a cliché, but she was inspiring. She got me all hot and bothered just with her acting. Sexually it went way beyond that, *ça va sans dire*. She was gorgeous to look at, to get close to, to smell, and feel – that, with her talent too. I was a goner for her. I still am.'

Bus Stop was the story of Cherie, a weary girl singer with too many men in her past, and Bo, the naive young cowboy who falls in love with her. Many in Hollywood sneered, saying the result would merely be a variation on the theme of Marilyn the sexpot. They were proved wrong, partly because of the disciplines she had learned from Strasberg, and thanks to Logan's infinite indulgence.

Milton Greene had warned the director, 'Watch the tone of your voice with Marilyn, because if you scare her, you'll lose her.' There were times Logan had to invoke patience worthy of the Buddha.

For the first time Marilyn was included in key script discussions. Logan appreciated Marilyn's contribution until she took exception to the way somebody *else's* role was being planned. She called Buddy Adler, the new chief at Fox, and Adler called Logan. As any director would be, Logan was furious that an actor had gone over his head to a studio executive.

Marilyn now had no further use for her original acting coach, Natasha Lytess. Lytess had gone to see Marilyn on her return to Hollywood, only to be turned away from the door by an aide. Her last sight of her most successful pupil was of a lone figure watching stonily through the window. The replacement for Lytess was Lee Strasberg's wife Paula, who now became indispensable.

Paula Strasberg was a lump of a woman in her mid-forties, described by her daughter Susan as 'a combination delicatessen, pharmacist, Jewish mother.' She dressed almost exclusively in flowing black robes, like a postcard Greek widow. She was never without a huge handbag crammed with food, medicines, flashlight, and magnifying glass. On hot locations, and many of Marilyn's locations were swelteringly hot, Paula was to be seen cooling herself with one of a vast selection of fans.

Although emotionally estranged from her husband, Paula had turned herself into the indispensable *doyenne* of the Strasberg household. She had long stage-managed life for Lee, promoting him as a genius, and she never tired of extolling the virtues of her children.

Now Marilyn had become virtually the third Strasberg

child, one who thought she needed the master's help on all her acting endeavors. Lee Strasberg was tied to his work at the Studio. So Paula, who herself had experience both as actress and teacher, was now appointed to hold Marilyn's hand. She offered genuine devotion to Marilyn, and vast irritation to film directors.

Joshua Logan was appalled when he heard Marilyn intended not only to use Paula as coach but to have her on the set during filming. He appealed to Milton Greene, who was now diplomat and troubleshooter. Greene negotiated with Lee Strasberg, and it was agreed that Paula could be present but only in the dressing room.

In many ways Paula Strasberg was beginning a thankless task. She received an excellent salary – as much as $2,000 a week – but was to become the butt of the derision and sometimes the hatred of film crews, and the target of Marilyn's increasingly arrogant whims. On *Bus Stop*, though, Greene's peace formula worked partly because the language of the Actors Studio was compatible with Logan's style of directing.

Logan was on the Studio wavelength when he advised Marilyn to slip into a coat 'as though you were slipping into a bubble bath.' On future films, though, the Strasberg system was ridiculed. On *Let's Make Love*, Paula exhorted Marilyn to kiss Yves Montand 'as if it were cold water going over an iron fence.' Script supervisor Rosie Steinberg never forgot that one.

On at least one occasion, Marilyn took method acting a step too far. A scene required her to slap co-star Don Murray with a piece of torn costume. Marilyn had not got on well with Murray, and now struck him viciously enough to slash his face. Marilyn may have been emulating her recent lover, Marlon Brando, who was known for carrying acted violence to extremes, but this incident caused a crisis. Despite Logan's pleas, Marilyn could not bring herself to apologize, and screamed at her colleagues in fury. The Miller relationship seemed to be supplying neither stability nor peace of mind. During *Bus Stop* Paula Strasberg made sure that Marilyn's friends in a bottle – her tranquilizers – were always within reach.

Marilyn was also to rely on Paula Strasberg for functions far removed from acting. On special occasions, it would be Paula who went in first to vet the other guests. If she disapproved of them, Marilyn would sit waiting in the limousine while Paula did the courtesies inside. Paula became a sounding board for Marilyn's problems in love, a nurse when she was sick. On *Bus Stop*, as almost always from then on, she was needed as a nurse.

In April 1956 came the now-familiar headline, MARILYN MONROE IN HOSPITAL. The doctor's diagnosis was 'virus infection, exhaustion, overwork, and acute bronchitis.' In a more relaxed comment the doctor said Marilyn was just 'tied in knots.'

Director Logan said his star was sick, 'but not two weeks' worth.' Since the company had to be paid anyway, Logan whiled away the time shooting and reshooting a scene that did not require Marilyn's presence. The company spent fifteen days, at $40,000 a day, filming a fight that lasted half a minute in the movie.

Once, when Marilyn was working, Logan realized she was going to be late for a key scene in which she had to run through the streets at sundown. She had had three hours to get ready. He ran to the dressing room and found 'the poor darling still looking at herself in the mirror.' Logan wasted no words. He physically lugged Marilyn to her camera position, shouting 'Run!' to her and 'Roll 'em!' to the cameraman.

Logan was able to forgive Marilyn for everything. He remembered with admiration her total involvement in her part, her ability to weep real tears when other actors would reach for the glycerine. He shared with her a determination to sneak risqué shots past the censor, a gleeful delight in sexual innuendo that was ahead of its time in the 1950s.

Logan indulged Marilyn's hesitant performances by letting her do a speech over and over while the camera consumed a vast amount of film. He tolerated her on the days when she failed to deliver one usable take and when, with Paula Strasberg's support, she walked wordlessly away 'to work out the motivation.' Others were not so patient.

The press, which Marilyn had courted to her advantage for so long, was kept away from her during *Bus Stop*. She was whisked to the door of her trailer in a limousine, then hustled in through specially constructed entranceways. No facilities were provided for the photographers, who were there in force. The press fell back on guerrilla tactics. They sat in ambush in neighboring hotel rooms, then lured Marilyn and her entourage to her balcony by abruptly switching on high-powered strobe lights.

Bill Woodfield, then a photographer for *This Week* magazine, found himself snatching pictures of Marilyn during the rodeo location in Arizona. Woodfield said, 'It got so bad that we were all hiding out and taking pictures under the stands at the stadium. I got some pictures of Marilyn throwing up under the bleachers, damn near on top of me. She'd be playing a scene and she'd lean over and throw up, or dry heave, and I was underneath. I had the pictures printed, threw them down in front of Milton Greene and said, "This is what we have to go with unless you give us some pictures." Finally he broke her loose and I got my shots.'

When *Time* magazine mounted its first cover story on Marilyn, during the shooting of *Bus Stop*, its researchers began uncovering a good deal about Marilyn's parentage. This was a vulnerable area because of her various deceptions. As a result, one of *Time*'s youngest reporters, Brad Darrach, was granted a personal interview in bizarre circumstances.

Darrach collected Marilyn at Fox at 11:00 A.M. and drove her to her hotel, the Chateau Marmont. Marilyn, herself a fast driver, asked the reporter to drive slowly. She seemed to him to be afraid, not of his driving but 'generally frightened.' Once in her suite Marilyn soon declared she was tired, and asked if they could do the interview in the bedroom.

So it was that Darrach ended up, he laughingly remembered, 'spending ten hours in bed with Marilyn Monroe.' She lay down with her head at one end of the bed. He settled at the foot, and there they talked until long after dark.

'She was Marilyn, and reasonably pretty,' Darrach said. 'And of course there were those extraordinary jutting breasts and jutting behind. I've never seen a behind like hers; it was really remarkable, it was a very subtly composed ass. Yet I never felt for a moment any sexual temptation. There was nothing about her skin that made me want to touch it. She looked strained and a little unhealthy, as though there was some nervous inner heat that dried the skin. But there was no sexual feeling emanating from her. I am sure that was something that she put on for the camera.'

For a while during *Bus Stop*, Marilyn's press was handled by Pat Newcomb, who worked for Arthur Jacobs, owner of one of Hollywood's top public relations firms. Newcomb, a very young woman from the East Coast, was new to the job. Her father was a judge, her mother a psychiatric social worker, and she herself had majored in psychology. Even this background, however, was insufficient for the handling of Marilyn Monroe.

'We had this terrible falling out almost immediately,' Newcomb said. 'I didn't know why for years, but it turned out to be over some guy that Marilyn thought I liked, someone I didn't have any interest in at all. I didn't know how to cope with it, and Arthur Jacobs told me I'd better get out of there at once.'

Newcomb had to leave the location. Ironically, years later she would become Marilyn's key press adviser and confidante, and was to be one of the last people to see Marilyn on the day she died. Even then, at the very end, they would be bickering.

Rivalry, or jealousy, was not limited to her press assistant. Marilyn had a tussle with her director over Hope Lange, who was playing the part of a young girl in *Bus Stop*. Lange's hair, Marilyn insisted, was too fair; she feared it would detract attention from herself. Logan had to surrender and have Lange's hair darkened. (In the last months of her life, during *Something's Got to Give*, Marilyn was to go into a similar irrational panic over her co-star Cyd Charisse.) On *Bus Stop*, for the first time, Marilyn's New York psychiatrist was flown to attend her at the location.

Out of the folly and misery came an excellent film and a brilliant performance by Marilyn. *New York Times* critic Bosley Crowther said flatly that Marilyn had 'finally proved herself an actress.' He went on: 'Fortunately for her and for the tradition of diligence leading to success, she gives a performance in this picture that marks her as a genuine acting star, not just a plushy personality and a sex symbol, as she has previously been.'

This was the accolade Marilyn had yearned for although, to her own dismay and that of many others, *Bus Stop* was not rewarded with an Oscar nomination. The tragedy, however, was that the woman was disintegrating even as the actress grasped her dream. In the midst of her success Joshua Logan sounded a warning. 'She can become one of the greatest stars we've ever had,' he said, 'if she can control her emotions and her health.'

Logan knew the depth of Marilyn's problems earlier than most. 'I almost choke up when I really think of her,' he told me. 'I don't think she ever really had two days of happiness, or contentment in her life, unless it was when she was working.'

As she approached her thirtieth birthday, Marilyn at last appeared to have found happiness in love.

21

Every day for eight weeks, in the spring of 1956, the telephone rang in the office of the Pyramid Lake Guest Ranch, fifty miles northeast of Reno, Nevada. The caller, who identified herself as a Mrs Leslie, would ask to speak to Mr Leslie. An employee would hasten to a cabin with the message, and Mr Leslie, pipe in hand, would hurry to take his call.

'Mrs Leslie' was Marilyn Monroe, busy making *Bus Stop*. 'Mr Leslie' was Arthur Miller, holed up in the desert waiting out his residency to qualify for a Nevada divorce. They had taken their code names from Vina Delmar's novel *About Mr Leslie*, the story of a nightclub singer and a married man who live together as man and wife for six weeks each year. In real life, Marilyn and Miller would soon be able to dispense with such deceptions.

Miller was cautious, as a man in the middle of a divorce was bound to be. When he talked to *Time* magazine, huddled with the reporter in a parked car, he avoided saying whether he wished to marry Marilyn. 'I can't afford to get married for a long time,' he said. 'Where will I get the money to support two families? My play *View from the Bridge* just closed on Broadway. I got $35,000, and that will have to last me for two years until I can write another one. And she is not ready to be married either. She's fanatic about the projects ahead of her.'

Marilyn, for her part, could not resist a few confidences. Just as she had done before marrying Joe DiMaggio, she made sure that her favorite reporters knew her plans. May

Mann, of the *New York Herald Tribune*, was surprised to receive a telegram from Marilyn, setting up a call for a specific hour. Marilyn phoned right on time, to confide that she and Miller would be married 'at midsummer – but don't print it yet.'

On June 2, with *Bus Stop* completed, Marilyn hurried back to New York. As Miller prepared to follow, disaster loomed. Still in Nevada, he was served with a subpoena by Congress' Committee on Un-American Activities. The congressmen intended to question the nation's leading playwright about his supposed Communist affiliations. As Miller well knew, this was an ordeal that in recent years had ruined dozens of his colleagues.

The House Un-American Activities Committee had leapt to prominence in 1947, when it gained access to the Attorney General's List, a catalogue of organizations that held allegedly totalitarian, Fascist, Communist, or 'any other subversive views.' Its function was to interrogate and expose, and its sights were leveled above all at Communists, real or imagined.

From 1950 on, the witch-hunters gained a figurehead in the shape of Senator Joseph McCarthy, the demagogue whose name has become synonymous with the repressive policies of the time. The Committee's friends had included two future presidents, Richard Nixon and the minor actor Ronald Reagan.

The Hollywood film community, which included many idealistic left-wingers of the 1930s and 1940s, was a prime target. Arthur Miller had watched appalled as the victimization of writers and directors took its toll. Some, their careers ended, committed suicide or became human flotsam. Screenwriter Alvah Bessie, whose career had held great promise, ended up as a technician in a nightclub. Mystery writer Dashiell Hammett went to prison rather than inform on left-wingers he had known. His career never recovered.

Until 1956 the Committee had never found a reason to call Arthur Miller, though he had long been assailed by the vocal right. A protest over his early play *All My Sons* led to it being banned in occupied Germany, because of its 'twisted' scenario of crooked military suppliers and lax military inspectors. In 1949 the film version of *Death of a Salesman* was picketed by right-wingers. It was at the height of the campaign, four years later, that Miller produced *The Crucible*, his powerful evocation of witch-hunting hysteria in the seventeenth century. Few missed the modern message in the play, yet Miller remained unscathed. On Broadway, the blacklist circulating in Hollywood – which prevented alleged left-wingers from working – had never taken hold. Now, in 1956, the House Un-American Activities Committee found an excuse to summon Miller.

It was quickly apparent that the decision had as much to do with Marilyn Monroe as it did with Miller. The press was alive with rumors of her impending marriage to Miller, and the Committee's Chairman, Congressman Francis Walter, saw an opportunity to get into the newspapers. The Committee had not been front-page news recently. Secretly, Miller was offered an easy ride if he would arrange for Marilyn to pose for photographs beside Congressman Walter. Miller refused.

His confrontation with the Committee came on June 21, 1956, in the Caucus Room of the Old House Office Building. Miller, in blue suit and horn-rimmed spectacles, admitted having 'signed some form or another' at a Marxist study course in about 1939. He said he had 'no knowledge' of having applied for Communist Party membership.

Miller's real clash with the Committee came when he refused, time and again, to name others he had met at Communist gatherings. 'I could not use the name of another person and bring trouble on him,' he told the congressmen. 'These were writers, poets, as far as I could see, and the life of a writer, despite what it sometimes seems, is pretty tough. I wouldn't make it any tougher on anybody. I ask you not to ask me that question.'

Miller's refusal to name names placed him in legal jeopardy. A month after his appearance the House of Representatives voted him in contempt of Congress, a charge which could have put the playwright in prison for a year. He was convicted, appealed, and was finally acquitted two years later. From the start, it was a fight conducted with the support of Marilyn Monroe.

Asked at the time to comment on Miller's congressional testimony, Marilyn played the good little woman. 'I don't know much about politics,' she said. 'I'll have to have a talk with him and I think he's very tired.' Two years later, when the case was finally resolved in Miller's favor, she said she never doubted the outcome, 'because I have been studying Thomas Jefferson for years and, according to Thomas Jefferson, this case had to turn out this way. . . .'

Marilyn played the ingénue, but she was fiercely loyal to Miller and learning to apply her shrewdness to political affairs. At press appearances during Miller's ordeal before the House Committee, she was a model of dignity and quiet support. The very aura of Marilyn protected Miller from adverse public opinion in a way that none of the committee's other victims enjoyed. Instead of being regarded as a left-wing writer under attack, Miller was transformed by the headlines into the harassed lover of the nation's sex symbol. Later Marilyn helped in a material way. It was her money, according to her financial adviser, Henry Rosenfeld, that eventually paid many of the legal fees.

Marilyn also proved, if it still needed proving, that she could be brave. In 1960 she told British writer W. J. Weatherby, 'Some of those bastards in Hollywood wanted me to drop Arthur, said it would ruin my career. They're born cowards and want you to be like them. One reason I want to

A model girl, aged about nineteen.
Hollywood was only a dream

Marilyn's mother, Gladys, in 1963, aged
sixty-two, and (below) as a young woman.
She survived her famous daughter
(PHOTO FILE)

A starlet with a library. Marilyn immersed herself in art and culture

The jogger. In about 1952, twenty years ahead of her time. Marilyn used to run through the Hollywood alleyways before breakfast

Some of the Lovers

Courtesy of André de Dienes

Courtesy of Tommy Zahn

above left: The photographer, André de Dienes, 1946. Marilyn took the picture
above right: The lifeguard, Tommy Zahn, 1946
below left: The voice coach, Fred Karger, to whom Marilyn gave her heart in 1948. He did not want to marry her
below right: Robert Slatzer at Niagara Falls with Marilyn in 1952

Courtesy of Anne Batté

Copyright © 1974 Robert F Slatzer

At home with 'Nana' Karger *(left)*, mother of a former lover, in 1960. They remained close for fourteen years. Marilyn reportedly called Mrs Karger the day before she died, talking of marrying Robert Kennedy

The courtship of the Last American Hero. With Joe DiMaggio, shortly before their 1954 marriage. The honeymoon was hardly over before she was talking of one day marrying Arthur Miller

Table companions. With another Hollywood personality, Ronald Reagan, in 1953

below left: The fan who became a friend. James Haspiel started by cadging a kiss from Marilyn at the age of sixteen and – in the New York period – became a regular companion

below right: A brief affair. With Marlon Brando, 1955

The Man who lasted longest. With playwright Arthur Miller in 1959.
Their marriage survived more than four years

The French lover. The 1960 affair with Yves Montand coincided with the
collapse of the Miller marriage but did not cause it. Marilyn's mental health
was deteriorating rapidly

The happy wife, 1957

see Kennedy win is that Nixon's associated with that whole scene.'

A year before her death, Danny Greenson, the student son of Marilyn's psychiatrist, would talk to her about the Committee hearings. 'The way Marilyn told it,' Greenson said, 'she would say to Miller, "You can't let those bastards push you around. You've got to stand up to them." She really was unsophisticated politically, but her instincts were always with the underdog and – to me – on the side of right. There was more to Marilyn than met the eye.'

Miller aside, some of Marilyn's closest associates were now, in 1950s terms, of the Far Left. The House Committee on Un-American Activities had records on both Lee and Paula Strasberg, linking them with what the Committee called 'Communist fronts.' Paula, a former member of the Communist Party, was now Marilyn's coach. The FBI had not failed to notice these associations.

Repeated applications under the Freedom of Information Act prised a clutch of documents on Marilyn out of the FBI. Some, relating to her new friendships in New York, were long almost entirely blanked out by the censor before release, under the B-1 national security exemption. (Readers scornful of the FBI's intense interest in the actress may be entertained by the fact that its Director J. Edgar Hoover, whose only intimate friend in forty years was a male colleague, proudly displayed in his home an original copy of Marilyn's nude calendar.)

On June 21, 1956, in the middle of his congressional testimony, Arthur Miller broke his own security. Asked why he currently wanted a passport to go to England, Miller replied, 'The objective is double. I have a production, which is in the talking stage in England, of *A View from the Bridge*, and I will be there with the woman who will then be my wife. That is my aim.' Afterward, talking to reporters in Washington, Miller ensured that any adverse publicity was totally defused.

He said flatly that he would marry Marilyn Monroe 'very shortly'.

That same day, at lunchtime in New York, Marilyn called Norman Rosten. She sounded almost hysterical. 'Have you heard?' she asked, 'He told the whole world he was marrying Marilyn Monroe. Me! Can you believe it? You know he never really asked me. You've got to come down right away. I need moral support. I mean, "Help!" I'm surrounded here, locked in my apartment. There are newspapermen trying to get in, crawling all over the place, in the foyer, in the halls.'

As the reporters milled around outside, Marilyn chatted with a repairman fixing the air-conditioner. It was he who finally emerged to announce triumphantly, 'She told me: "Sure I'm going to be married."' The journalists raced for their telephones, and the wedding circus began.

Soon the apartment building in New York's exclusive Sutton Place was besieged by a crowd three hundred strong. Marilyn and Miller climbed into an old station wagon and fled to the country retreat at Roxbury, Connecticut. The newsmen followed, and enraged Miller by camping on the doorstep. He finally persuaded them to go away by promising a press conference at the end of the week.

In their few days of relative peace, the couple juggled with wedding plans and waited to know whether Miller would be granted a passport to travel to England. With them at the house were Miller's seventy-two-year-old father Isadore and his mother Augusta. Marilyn had told them in tears: 'For the first time in my life, I have somebody I can call Father and Mother.' The Millers were Jews, devout though not overzealous, and Marilyn announced that she wished to marry in the Jewish faith.

For the past year Miller's bride had been surrounded by Jewish friends – the Rostens and the Strasbergs – and had latched on to their traditions. She had celebrated Passover with Milton Greene during *Bus Stop*, and had eaten bagels and gefilte fish with Eli Wallach. Friends had explained the *mezuzahs,* cylindrical containers bearing the Ten Commandments displayed on Jewish front doors.

Things reached the point where Marilyn was more enthusiastic about Jewish customs than Miller. At the Roxbury house, she bustled about learning Jewish recipes from Miller's mother. That week, at Marilyn's insistence, a phone call was placed to a rabbi of the Reformed branch of Judaism. He agreed to give Marilyn instruction and perform the marriage ceremony.

Arthur Miller was happy. Marilyn behaved as if she were happy, but there was something frenetic about her. She was, the press learned, 'under doctor's orders to rest.' Miller's father, who was to become one of Marilyn's loyal friends, wondered, 'Have they weighed this step carefully?'

The reporters, meanwhile, were never far away. They discovered the couple had taken blood tests, as required under local marriage laws, and Miller's cousin Morton had rushed the vials of blood to the laboratory. There were rumors the couple had obtained a wedding license, but the journalists checked fifty registry offices in vain.

The next day, June 29, was the day Miller had promised a press conference. The reporters returned in a horde, four hundred of them swarming around the intersection of Old Tophet and Goldmine roads. Soon they were wandering all over the Miller property, trampling the grass and dangling from the trees. There was no sign of the quarry.

At about one o'clock, from the near distance, came the sound of a crash and rending metal. Minutes later a car pulled up short of the crowd and disgorged Marilyn and Miller, who ran wordlessly for the house.

Minutes later, fighting back tears, Miller's cousin explained that there had been a tragedy. He had been taking Marilyn and Miller home, driving fast along the country road to evade a pursuing press car. The driver behind, who did not know the road, had lost control of the wheel and cannoned into a tree. His passenger Mara Scherbatoff, a White Russian aristocrat and the New York bureau chief of *Paris-Match*, had been hurled through the windshield. An artery in her neck had been severed, and she was to die later on the operating table.

Inside the Roxbury house, Marilyn alternated between hysteria over the accident and rage at an assistant because television cameras were being set up outside. Marilyn hated television. She finally appeared with Miller and his parents at a travesty of a press conference.

Milton Greene ran about issuing instructions and trying to keep the peace. The actress in Marilyn offered apparent serenity. Miller, a cigarette dangling unlit at the lip, almost snarled at the newsmen. He refused to say where or when they would be married.

That afternoon Marilyn called Milton Greene into the bedroom to ask for advice on a matter Greene thought long settled. 'Arthur wants me to marry him,' she said, 'now – tonight. Tell me if I'm making a mistake. What do you think?' Shaken, Greene walked to the window and back again. Then he said lamely, 'Marilyn, you must do what you think best.'

That evening, after a flurry of phone calls to lawyers and local authorities, Miller and Marilyn drove across the state line to White Plains, New York. For the second time in less than three years, a Marilyn Monroe wedding interrupted a judge's dinner appointment.

Judge Seymour Robinowitz postponed his own anniversary celebration, and hurried to the courthouse. Marilyn, in sweater and skirt, once again filled out a marriage license. She said her father had been Edward Mortenson, and this time told the truth about her age. Marilyn had turned thirty at the beginning of the month. Miller, nearly forty-one, wore a blue linen suit and no tie. He produced a borrowed ring.

The couple were married at 7:21 P.M., in the steamy heat of

a New York summer evening. The press knew nothing until afterward.

Two days later, again in secret, Marilyn got the Jewish wedding she wanted. She had taken brief instruction from Rabbi Robert Goldburg, who explained the basic tenets of Judaism. Marilyn satisfied him that any children of the marriage would be brought up in the Jewish faith.

This second ceremony took place in front of a marble mantlepiece at the home of Miller's literary agent, in Waccabuc, New York. This time Marilyn looked like a bride in gown and veil, and Miller managed a tie and a flower in his buttonhole. The couple drank wine, exchanged rings, and the bridegroom crushed a goblet in memory of the destruction of Jerusalem by its ancient foes.

Weeks of tension ended in a bucolic scene. Twenty-five wedding guests went outdoors to lunch on lobster, turkey, and champagne. Marilyn and her husband cut the wedding cake, made overnight by a New York baker after eight others had refused to bake one on twenty-four hours' notice. Bride and groom kissed and cuddled without restraint, with Miller exhibiting the physical abandon that had transformed him in recent months.

'It was a fairy tale come true,' Norman Rosten later recalled. 'The Prince had appeared, the Princess was saved.'

Miller had purchased a gold wedding band. It was inscribed 'A. to M., June 1956. Now Is Forever.' Marilyn, for her part, wrote three words on the back of a wedding photograph: 'Hope, Hope, Hope.'

22

Two weeks after their wedding, in an elegant English country house, Mr and Mrs Miller danced cheek to cheek to the tune of Gershwin's 'Embraceable You.' Miller's passport had been issued after all, and they had arrived in Britain to make *The Prince and the Showgirl* with Sir Laurence Olivier.

Terence Rattigan, author of the original stage play, had invited a glittering assemblage to welcome the honeymooners. Joining them on the dance floor were Sir John Gielgud, Douglas Fairbanks, Jr, Dame Sybil Thorndike and Sir Lewis Casson, Dames Peggy Ashcroft, Edith Evans and Margot Fonteyn, assorted dukes, duchesses, and knights, and the American ambassador.

At a more plebeian level, Britain had been excited about Marilyn for weeks. The national newspapers now rushed to outdo each other in fatuous headlines and overblown trivia about Marilyn. The story of her arrival dominated the front pages, eclipsing Prime Minister Anthony Eden's speech warning that the nation faced economic disaster. One newspaper presented Marilyn with a bicycle on which to ride around the English countryside, then complained when her servants were seen riding it instead. Little old ladies crocheted Marilyn's image in gold and silver thread. Marilyn was invited to attend cricket matches, shoot grouse in Scotland, and eat fish and chips with Teddy Boys. A band of students sang bawdy songs – and the 23rd Psalm – beneath the Millers' window.

None of the approaches, even more sensible ones, met with any response. Gone was the Marilyn who once courted and indulged the press. In her place was a withdrawn woman with a shy husband, hiding behind the gates of Parkside House, a country mansion rented from Lord Moore.

The staff had been warned in advance that 'Miss Monroe must have complete darkness when she sleeps,' and special window blinds had been installed. The bedroom had been fitted out in white – white bed, white curtains and furnishings, white carpet – to match Marilyn's Manhattan apartment. (The butler and cook, who dared mention such secrets to the press, were fired.) Marilyn was accompanied everywhere by a hulking ex-Scotland Yard police superintendent. She appeared, people noticed, to have lost her sense of humor. She was now a star in all the worst senses.

Months earlier, when he had heard of Olivier's plans, Noël Coward had written in his diary. 'Larry is going to make a movie of the Sleeping Prince with Marilyn Monroe, which might conceivably drive him round the bend.'

Marilyn had met Olivier a couple of times years before, when she was a nobody and he was already Sir Laurence, the leading actor of the English-speaking world. Now he was to be director and leading man to her leading lady, in a frothy tale about an American showgirl who falls in love with a reluctant Ruritanian prince.

Olivier had heard stories about the perils of working with Marilyn, but thought he could cope.

He had talked to three of her previous directors, John Huston, Billy Wilder, and Joshua Logan. Logan, who was emerging bloodied but triumphant from *Bus Stop*, wrote repeatedly, warning Olivier. 'Please, don't tell her what to do,' he told him. 'She probably knows more about acting in films than anyone in the world. Don't order her about, because it'll throw her and you won't get anything out of her.' That aside, Logan had said cheerily, 'It's the best combination since black and white.'

Olivier was irritated that Marilyn brought along her coach

Paula Strasberg. Then, remembering how 'schizoid' Marilyn had seemed to him in New York, he hoped Strasberg 'would bring out the better of those two halves.' When Marilyn proved disappointing at rehearsals, Olivier tried to get through by cultivating Strasberg instead. Soon he concluded that 'Paula knew nothing; she was no actress, no director, no teacher, no adviser, except in Marilyn's eyes. For she had one talent: she could butter Marilyn up.'

This realization came to Olivier one day as he, riding in the front of a limousine, listened to Marilyn and Strasberg talking in the back. 'My dear,' Paula Strasberg was saying, 'you haven't yet any idea of the importance of your position in the world. You are the greatest woman of your time, the greatest human being of your time, of any time – you name it. You can't think of anybody, I mean – no, not even Jesus – except you're more popular.'

Olivier swore his account was no exaggeration, that the flattery went on for a full hour, and that Marilyn lapped it up. Olivier exiled Paula Strasberg to New York for a while, but Marilyn made sure she came back again. Olivier was in for four months of professional hell.

Olivier tried to help Marilyn with her problems of drying up in front of the camera. He suggested she sit still, count up to three, then speak the line. When this failed, he burst out, 'Can't you count either?' Logan had warned that being authoritative, not to mention losing one's temper, was to lose Monroe, and Olivier swiftly lost touch with her altogether. He despaired even when Marilyn's system worked.

It was hard for Olivier to watch Marilyn capture a mood only after Paula Strasberg told her, 'Honey, just think of Coca-Cola and Frankie Sinatra!' He concluded she was a 'glorious amateur in show business, an untrained, probably untrainable, artist of instinct.'

'I saw the differences between Larry and Marilyn grow as they became more tired and tense,' cameraman Jack Cardiff recalled. 'She began asking herself whether he was really the genius she had at first imagined.' Marilyn herself said years later, 'Sir Olivier [sic] tried to be friendly, but he came on like someone slumming ... I started being bad with him, being late, and he hated it. But if you don't respect your artists, they can't work well. Respect is what you have to fight for.'

It was Marilyn who failed to give respect, to Olivier and everyone else, in big and little things. She failed to thank Olivier and his wife for their kindnesses, for the roses sent to welcome her, for the exquisite, engraved watch presented to her at the end of filming.

One day Marilyn broke even her record for unpunctuality, by arriving for an appointment more than nine hours late. She made Dame Sybil Thorndike, who was elderly and also acting in a stage play at night, wait all morning for her. Marilyn's columnist friend, Louella Parsons, visiting from the United States, thought she was 'testing to see if she was really the co-star. She behaved like a child asking to be spanked.'

Arthur Miller, too, bore the brunt of Marilyn the child. Two weeks into the filming, traveling under the name 'Mr Stevenson' to avoid reporters, he flew back to the United States. His purpose was to see his daughter by his previous marriage, who was sick, but Marilyn saw it as desertion. She stayed at home for a week, claiming a 'severe attack of colitis'. Production ground to a halt until Miller cut short his visit and returned.

The other partner in Marilyn Monroe Productions, photographer Milton Greene, who had bought an English Jaguar car, shuttled around from Marilyn's home to the studio, from the studio to London, trying to mend fences between Marilyn and Olivier and between both of them and the British press.

It was in part thanks to Greene that the film was finished at all, yet *The Prince and the Showgirl* was the beginning of the end of his connection with Marilyn. Word filtered back from England that Arthur Miller wanted Greene removed. Miller retorted, 'I have no more than the normal family interest in my wife's business affairs. Rumors of conflict between myself and Milton Greene are space fillers for unimaginative columnists.'

Greene said, 'Miller and I have had no trouble. Sell my stock in Marilyn Monroe Productions? Never.'

It was all a smokescreen. Miller, supposedly busy finishing his next play, was being drawn inexorably into his wife's professional life. Greene saw the writing on the wall when he found Miller selecting Marilyn's publicity photographs and organizing her scrapbook. Soon Miller was flying into rages over Greene's press releases. Greene told me, 'Miller would scream at me. He wanted her for himself, to do a movie and a play – for him.'

A year later, Greene would be driven out as vice-president of Marilyn Monroe Productions and paid off with $100,000. The new board of directors included Miller's brother-in-law and one of his friends. It was small thanks to Greene, who would wryly recall that the two films he was involved with, *Bus Stop* and *The Prince and the Showgirl*, were the only major Monroe films to finish within budget.

Against all odds *The Prince and the Showgirl* was not a disaster. When it appeared, most critics would be kinder than Noël Coward, and even he noted in his diary: 'Larry is superb. Marilyn Monroe looks very pretty and is charming at moments, but too much emphasis on tits and bottom. It is to me a charming picture.' The miracle Olivier had been promised by previous directors had occurred. In the finished product, Marilyn was magically effective. Olivier was to write wearily in his memoirs that people thought, 'I was as good as could be, and Marilyn! Marilyn was quite wonderful, the best of all. So. What do you know?'

Before leaving England, Marilyn managed a courteous

exchange with Queen Elizabeth at the Royal Command film performance. She had the guts to apologize, at Olivier's insistence, to the assembled company of *The Prince and the Showgirl.* She said, 'I hope you will all forgive me, as it wasn't altogether my fault. I have been ill.'

Marilyn would shortly be immortalized in wax at Madame Tussaud's in London. Her effigy stood, glamorously gowned, holding a glass of champagne. For Marilyn and her husband, however, after five months of marriage, there was little to celebrate.

A year before marrying Miller, Marilyn had been asked how she defined love. She replied that love was trust, that to love a man she had to trust him completely. Trust took a beating during the Miller honeymoon. The first blow came early on in the making of *The Prince and the Showgirl.*

It was an incident that Marilyn would refer to time and again in years to come, though not always with quite the same details. The core of the story is that, after a party, she happened upon some of Miller's notes lying on a table. They included comments about herself that Marilyn found deeply hurtful. Lee and Paula Strasberg, both in England at the time, were the first to hear what had happened.

'It was something about how disappointed he was in me,' Marilyn told the Strasbergs, 'how he thought I was some kind of angel but now he guessed he was wrong. That his first wife had let him down, but I had done something worse. Olivier was beginning to think I was a troublesome bitch and that he, Arthur, no longer had a decent answer to that one.'

Marilyn told Bob Josephy, a Connecticut friend of the Millers, that the sense of Miller's note was, 'My God, I've married the same woman' – meaning that he saw in Marilyn some flaw identical with a trait in his first wife, Mary Slattery. The discovery plunged Marilyn into misery because, she told Josephy, Miller had 'hated' his first wife. Years later, Marilyn was also to claim that Miller's note had described her as 'a whore.'

There seems no doubt that a note did exist; according to one source, it remained in the possession of Paula Strasberg for many years. Miller eventually acknowledged that he might have written such a note. Less than two years after Marilyn's death, moreover, his controversial play *After the Fall*, appeared, drawing heavily on the playwright's experiences with Marilyn. While it is dangerous to make too much of fiction, Miller did include a scene in which the female protagonist finds an upsetting note.

In *After the Fall* the Marilyn character, 'Maggie,' angrily tells her husband not to mix her up with his former wife. Her husband replies, 'That's just it. That I could have brought two women so different to the same accusation – it closed a circle for me. And I wanted to face the worst thing I could imagine – that I could not love. And I wrote it down, like a letter from hell.'

During *The Prince and the Showgirl* Miller may have realized, as he certainly would in the future, that he could not count on Marilyn's fidelity. There had long since been a public question mark over Marilyn's true relationship with her business partner Milton Greene. The rumors evaporated in the excitement over the marriage to Miller, but they may have been founded on truth.

In 1980, in his autobiography, entertainer Sammy Davis, Jr, wrote of Marilyn: 'While she was making *The Prince and the Showgirl* with Laurence Olivier, she was going through one of the most difficult periods of her life. She was having an affair with a close friend of mine. He was a photographer. . . . They met clandestinely, often at my house. She was always being followed there, and we had to get up all sorts of intrigues to keep the affair secret. I used to pretend we were having a party, and Marilyn would arrive and leave at different times from my pal.'

Milton Greene was of course a photographer, and he did count Sammy Davis among his friends. It was Greene, indeed, who introduced Davis to Marilyn. Asked about Davis's story, Greene laughed hugely and asked, 'Did he really say that? You may be right, but I'm not saying anything. I think the best way to keep it is that we were close friends and associates, and we loved each other. Period.'

In *After the Fall* the scene over the husband's note occurs as he struggles to prevent his wife from suicidally swallowing a combination of alcohol and sleeping pills. That, certainly, reflected a real situation during the making of *The Prince and the Showgirl*.

On Marilyn's arrival the press, all unknowing of the true situation, had asked fatuous questions about her sleeping habits. Marilyn replied, 'Well, let's say that now I am in England I like sleeping in just Yardley's Lavender.'

The truth was less romantic. Marilyn was sick from lack of sleep and from the remedies she used to try to induce it. Author Fred Guiles, who talked to Miller, wrote: 'Before, she had been troubled by insomnia partially relieved by pills. Now even they didn't work. As the night deepened, she became hysterical. He was unwilling to risk the amount of barbiturates that could drop her into a sodden slumber. Nightly vigils began.'

Milton Greene, who dealt with the wreckage of Marilyn in the mornings, added frightening detail. 'She wanted gin with her tea at 9:00 A.M. before going on the set. I would cut it and cut it again, to weaken it, and she would get angry. I would have to feed her the uppers she wanted. They came in a different color in London, and she'd think I was faking, changing the pills.'

On the set Paula Strasberg acted as keeper of the pills, and doled them out during breaks in filming. Greene put it bluntly: 'She was going out of her mind.' As on *Bus Stop*,

Marilyn's New York psychiatrist was flown to London to calm her down.

While in England Marilyn once again met the poetess Edith Sitwell, whom she had first encountered three years earlier in Hollywood. Sitwell declined to tell the press what they discussed, but she was to say when Marilyn died, 'If anyone had asked me to compile a list of people who I thought might commit suicide, I would have put her name on it.'

Arthur Miller and Sir Laurence Olivier found common ground in the ordeal of dealing with their women. Olivier's wife, Vivien Leigh, had long been subject to breakdowns and uncontrollable violent rages. During the shooting of *The Prince and the Showgirl*, Leigh suffered a miscarriage. Marilyn began vomiting, was attended by the Queen's obstetrician, and rumors flew around that she too was pregnant. Sources conflict as to whether she too lost a baby.

In the course of all the dramas, Olivier and Miller began to confide in each other. The British critic Kenneth Tynan learned something of what passed between them.

'Larry identified with Miller,' Tynan recalled. 'He saw the troubles Miller was going through in his marriage to Monroe, who was not far from being a madwoman with all her psychoneurotic idiosyncrasies – whereas Miller was a stable, sober character, much like Larry. He and Miller talked about it – about the trials of being married to huge stars who, in one way or another, were round the bend.

Miller was very defensive. He went on and on trying to justify his sufferance of Marilyn. But Larry soon came to re-alize that it was just rationalizing. He could see Miller being consumed by the relationship with Marilyn. Miller himself was confused, paralyzed, and he couldn't work, he couldn't do the things he needed to do, he couldn't concentrate.'

Miller had said he would be using the stay in England to finish his next play. Though the servants at Parkside House heard the clatter of the typewriter, there would be no major work from Miller till the screenplay of *The Misfits* four years later.

In mid-November 1956 a subdued Marilyn, wearing black under her mink, flew back to the United States with her husband. There would be no more filming for nearly two years. In that oasis of leisure, perhaps, the wounded marriage would have a chance to heal.

23

Marilyn's union with Arthur Miller was to last four and a half years, the longest full-time relationship of her life. She would one day say ruefully, 'I was never used to being happy, so that wasn't something I ever took for granted. I did sort of think you know, marriage did that.' If ever Marilyn hoped for happiness, and worked at it, it was now. As for Miller, he gave more of his life and love to Marilyn than did any other man.

After the false start in England the couple embarked on their first real honeymoon, in Jamaica. For a week or so, undisturbed by the press, they relaxed at Moot Point, the luxurious villa of a British aristocrat. Then it was back to New York and a new apartment at East 57th Street.

This was to be known as 'Marilyn's apartment,' just as the home in Connecticut would become 'Arthur's farm.' The phone number, curiously enough, was in the telephone directory for those who knew where to look. It was listed under 'Marilyn, Monroe' as opposed to 'Monroe, Marilyn.' Here, once again, the color scheme was white – white walls, white curtains, pale furniture, and white piano.

The piano, which had followed Marilyn from California, was virtually the only physical object to survive her childhood. It had once belonged to the actor Fredric March, and Marilyn's mother had bought it, 'a bit banged up,' when Marilyn was eight. She could pick out a few tunes on it, light classics such as 'To a Wild Rose,' 'The Spinning Wheel,' and 'Für Elise.'

The apartment overflowed with books and records, and

another familiar resident, Marilyn's lithograph of Abraham Lincoln, stared down from the wall. On a chess table in the library, ivory kings and queens usually stood suspended in mid-play. Beyond Marilyn's traditional Alaska of a living area was a well-appointed study for her husband.

That year, in two of the rare interviews she would now offer on her private life, Marilyn made her priorities clear. If ever it became an issue, she said, she would have no hesitation in giving up her career to preserve her marriage. 'Movies are my business,' she said, 'but Arthur is my life. Wherever he is, I want to be. When we're in New York Arthur is the boss.' Marilyn said later that at the start of their marriage she had a 'pupil-teacher relationship' with Miller.

Marilyn made other declarations of intent. She insisted, just as she had in the DiMaggio marriage, 'I need to be here to get my husband's breakfast and to make him a cheerful mid-morning cup of coffee occasionally. Writing's such a lonely kind of work.' Now, more than in the DiMaggio marriage, Marilyn actually did some of these things. 'Marriage,' she told one interviewer, makes me feel more womanly, more proud of myself. It also makes me feel less frantic. For the first time I have a feeling of being sheltered. It's as if I have come in out of the cold.'

Miller, whom Marilyn called 'Art,' 'Poppy,' or 'Pa,' called her 'Penny Dreadful,' 'Sugar Finney,' and 'Gramercy 5.' When his collected plays were published that year, he dedicated them to Marilyn. He said he had come to terms with being recognized wherever he went with Marilyn, and he vigorously defended her taste for revealing clothes. Miller's enthusiasm for Marilyn matched hers for him, in his serious way.

'Marilyn is a perfectionist,' he said, 'and she makes impossible demands of herself. I do, too. You can never reach what you're after. I try to help Marilyn accept this truth, and she helps me.'

On the wall of his study Miller kept a photograph of a blonde, the face almost lost in shadow, not instantly recognizable. 'That's Marilyn,' he would say. 'I like the tenderness in it, the dreaming quality, and I like it because she's relaxed. Not many people ever see her that way.' That year Miller would proclaim himself 'a new man at forty-one. I've learned about living from her.'

Jim Proctor, a close friend of Miller, said of that spring and summer, 'I don't think I ever saw two people so dizzy with love for each other. . . .' The ugly experience in England seemed to have been a false portent. Away from filming, Marilyn seemed to be getting herself under control.

Marilyn and her husband went rowing on the lake in Central Park. Disguised in Miller's horn-rimmed glasses, she walked Hugo, the basset hound. Marilyn sang what was by now her party piece, 'Diamonds Are a Girl's Best Friend,' at a Miller family gathering. She sat at the feet of Miller's father Isadore, and the old man pretended to be annoyed when she pampered him.

Marilyn entered eagerly into the role of stepmother to Jane, Miller's teenage daughter by his first marriage, and Robert, his nine-year-old son. Soon Marilyn would puzzle Hollywood visitors to the Manhattan apartment by abruptly vanishing during an important meeting. She would return to explain that she 'had to get the kids off to school.'

Years later she said of Miller's children and DiMaggio's son, 'I take a lot of pride in them, because they're from broken homes. I think I understand about them. I think I love them more than anyone. I wanted to be their friend. Only time could prove that to them and they had to give me time.' Marilyn kept in touch with 'her children' long after the Miller marriage was over, and their pictures would be found in her room after her death.

Marilyn, with the aid of a maid and a cook, achieved a degree of domesticity in the first year of the Miller marriage.

She could still be two and a half hours late for her own dinner party, but Miller would explain with a grimace, 'Ah, she's still in the tub.'

Actor Kevin McCarthy remembered Marilyn at the East 57th Street apartment, 'in high heels, without stockings, wobbling about in a short black dress. She had gashes in her legs because she'd made a mess of shaving them. She had a strange manner – sweet, poignant, a little distrait.'

Norman Rosten recalled happy champagne parties. 'Marilyn loved to dance,' he says, 'and Miller too – with a few drinks – would attempt an eerie, loping fox-trot, perilously off-balance.' Rosten, himself, dancing with Marilyn with more than a drink or two in him, promised to write a poem in praise of her breasts.

Miller had said, 'Life will go on the only way I know how to make it go – with a lot of work, a couple of laughs, and a lot of worry.' The spring of 1957 had its worries.

All was not joy when, in the first stage of the contempt-of-Congress case, Miller was found guilty. There was embarrassment when the 'Wrong Door Raid' inquiry brought national headlines, and the threat that Marilyn would have to testify. She begged off, claiming 'a virus infection.'

The collapse of Marilyn's partnership with Milton Greene brought heartache and divided loyalties. A scandal magazine raked up a story about Marilyn's infidelities to Joe DiMaggio in 1952, with Bob Slatzer. The article, complete with pictures of Marilyn and Slatzer together, had been leaked by Marilyn's former Hollywood maid. Marilyn placed panicky calls to Slatzer, reporting that her new husband was very annoyed.

These were mere irritations. 'It's no fun being married to an electric light,' Joe DiMaggio had once said. A columnist noted, 'Mr Miller seems to be faring better. But then he knows how to switch off.'

Switching off, for Arthur Miller, had always meant escaping to the countryside. In the summer of 1957 he and Marilyn spent little time in Manhattan. Norman Rosten, invited to use the apartment in their absence, would find a scrawled note of welcome from Marilyn. One read:

Dear Norman,
There is a homemade strawberry short cake in the Fridge, Also milk – help yourself. Also, however long you need to be here – 1 wk – 2 wks etc. feel free to come and go as you please ...
You are not imposing. We're glad you're aboard – even if we go down – sinking – the more the merrier!
I'm leaving you with this stanza (from an unchildlike childhood)—
Here goes—
Good nite
Sleep
and Sweet repose
Where ever you lay your Head—
I hope you find your nose—

                                                            Marilyn

In June 1957 the Millers climbed into a white Lincoln convertible and drove out of New York to the eastern tip of Long Island. Here, at Amagansett, they found their summer idyll. They rented a weatherbeaten wooden house, Stony Hill Farm, and dropped out of public view for several months. The locals saw Marilyn, dressed in tattered shorts and one of her husband's shirts, shopping at the village store. Posterity can record that the couple ate a great deal of angel food cake and ice cream, and that Arthur Miller liked his steaks thick.

Miller brought his typewriter to Amagansett and wrote in the mornings. He was still unable to finish his next stage play, but he did complete some short stories. They included *The Misfits*, which was to grow into a screenplay for the last film Marilyn would ever make.

At Amagansett, though, work took second place to wife. The couple were seen every day on the beach, walking or just quietly sitting. One photograph, taken by a friend, shows Marilyn clasping Miller adoringly around the waist as he fishes in the surf. Miller admitted to having gained twenty-five pounds since marrying Marilyn, and the picture shows it.

There were some excursions to the city. Miller was persuaded to get into a tuxedo, his wife into a gown, for the New York premiere of *The Prince and the Showgirl*. Marilyn, mysteriously, had agreed to open a Sidewalk Superintendents' Club at the site of the new Time and Life Building. Her husband declined to be dragged out for that one, and Marilyn agreed only if she could be whisked back and forth by helicopter. She arrived more than two hours late for a meeting with Laurance Rockefeller, and Rockefeller departed grumbling that he had 'never waited that long for anyone.'

For Marilyn-watchers these excursions offered related clues. The premiere was in aid of a children's charity, and Marilyn visited the Sidewalk Superintendents' Club feeling 'woozy in the stomach.'

Marilyn was pregnant. In June, in an interview suppressed in her lifetime because the publicity people judged it out of tune with her image, she had said, 'A man and a woman need something of their own. A baby makes a marriage perfect.' Within weeks of her thirty-first birthday, and on the eve of her first wedding anniversary, she conceived.

After all the talking about childbearing, Marilyn was delighted, awed, also confused. One evening, at a party on Long Island, Norman Rosten found her out on the porch alone, sobbing. Marilyn would keep a photograph of herself taken that month, and told a friend years later, that it had been 'the happiest point of my entire life.'

Miller was pleased too. 'To understand Marilyn best,' he

was to say, 'you have to see her around children. They love her; her whole approach to life has their kind of simplicity and directness.' Not entirely in jest, for Miller was a handsome fellow, a wit among their friends had reversed Shaw's famous reply to Isadora Duncan. 'How wonderful it would be,' he exclaimed, 'if their first child had his looks and her brains!'

The pregnancy did not last two months. On the first day of August, as Miller worked indoors at Amagansett, he heard Marilyn scream. She was in the garden, doubled up in pain. An ambulance rushed her to her gynecologist at Doctors Hospital in New York City. His efforts were in vain, for this was a tubular pregnancy. Marilyn awoke from surgery to learn that the embryo had been surgically removed.

Marilyn's friend Jim Haspiel visited her at the hospital. She was lying in near darkness, Miller at her side, with classical music playing on a bedside radio. She told Haspiel that, according to the doctors, the child she had lost would have been a son. Marilyn was to die, five years later, on the anniversary of this miscarriage.

At the time Marilyn seemed to rally well. She made a point of reviving an appointment for a champagne party that had been canceled on the day of the miscarriage. The doctors said she could yet bear a child, and Miller declared that she wanted 'as many babies as she can have, and I feel the same way. She has more courage than anyone I've met.'

Back at Amagansett, Marilyn rested and tried again. It was a sad ordeal. She would write to the Rostens:

I think I've been pregnant for about three weeks or may be two. My breasts(s) have been too sore to even touch – I've never had that in my life before also they ache – also I've been having cramps and slight staining since Monday – now the staining is increasing and pain is increasing by the minute. I did not eat all day yesterday – also last night I took 4 whole amutal sleeping pills – which was by actual count really 8 little amutal sleeping pills.

Could I have killed it by taking all the amutal on an empty stomach? (except I took some sherry wine also)

What shall I do? if it is still alive I want to keep it.

Marilyn was not pregnant that month, nor would she be for many months to come. In the last days of the summer of 1957 the couple returned to the Manhattan apartment.

A new personal maid hired that fall, Lena Pepitone, painted a picture of a disturbed Marilyn, unhealed by the quiet months in the sun. Her mistress, Pepitone said, lounged around in bed till all hours, and wandered around the apartment naked. She frequently called for a drink, usually vodka, as soon as she woke up. Miller seemed stoical, and kept mostly to himself. Fortunately for both of them, winter brought a new preoccupation: 'Arthur's farm.'

Miller, who was addicted to the country life, had been prospecting for some time for a new home in Connecticut. He had sold the house he had shared with his first wife, and in 1957 he and Marilyn searched for a new estate. Bob Josephy, their friend who lived in the area, recalled Marilyn arriving 'completely unequipped as far as clothing was concerned, tripping around a rough field in her high heels.' Late in the year, largely with Marilyn's funds, they bought a three-hundred-acre farm. It was near Miller's old property, not far from the colonial town of Roxbury.

As Marilyn described it, the eighteenth-century farmhouse was 'a kind of old saltbox with a kitchen extension.' Ignoring advice to tear it down and build anew, the couple started a refurbishing operation that Marilyn would never consider finished. Original beams and ceilings were left intact, and a writing studio was built for Miller's use. They also built a new wing, which Marilyn, in renewed hope, christened the

Nursery. Miller said, 'It's the place where we hope to live until we die.'

The Roxbury area of Connecticut was peopled by gentleman farmers and the descendants of families who had built their country retreats generations ago. There were some show business folk – including Richard Widmark, who had co-starred with Marilyn in *Don't Bother to Knock* – but no one pestered them here.

Marilyn assimilated easily, as a somewhat exotic addition to an established country clique. The immediate neighbors, the Diebolds, took a shine to her after meeting at a cocktail party. They treated her like one of their children, not as a movie actress, and Marilyn seemed happy.

To these American country squires, Marilyn seemed a Marie Antoinette figure playing at being a country girl. Here, more than ever, she could indulge her compulsive affection for all living things. Hugo the basset hound was admitted, rain-soaked and muddy, to the newly decorated living room. Marilyn adopted Cindy, a half-starved mongrel of uncertain breed who had stumbled into the backyard. She fixed a feeding station for birds in a maple tree, and worried about how birds eat during their migration. She acquired two talking parakeets, which were henceforth to make innumerable flights to and from Hollywood. Butch, her favorite, was smuggled aboard his first flight, only to awaken en route squawking his new chorus: 'I'm Marilyn's bird, Marilyn's bird.'

The concern for animals and nature was obsessive, and psychiatrists would make much of it. Inez Melson, Marilyn's former business manager in California, was once woken to take an urgent call from Connecticut. It was four o'clock in the morning on the East Coast, and Marilyn was calling to say that Butch the parakeet had been frightened by a thunderstorm.

Arthur Miller discovered how fraught life could be with a

mate who became frantic about the death of any living thing. He based a short story, 'Please Don't Kill Anything,' on what had happened the evening he and Marilyn watched fishermen hauling in their catch. Marilyn ran about throwing back the living rejects from the catch, worrying about their chances of survival.

'She looked up,' he wrote, 'like a little girl, with that naked wonder in her face, even as she was smiling in the way of a grown woman, and she said, "But some of them might live now till they're old . . . and see their children grow up!"'

In New York, on a walk to the little park at East 58th Street, Marilyn once came upon two boys trapping pigeons. When they explained the birds would fetch fifty cents each at the market, she paid the boys to release their catch. For a long time after that, she returned to the park each week to pay the ransom.

Another episode was truly pathetic. Once, arriving home at Roxbury, Marilyn noticed that the grass borders had been mown while she was out. The myriad nasturtiums that had covered the grass now lay in orange and yellow ruin. Marilyn, 'crying as if she were wounded,' made Miller stop the car. Then she rushed about picking up the fallen flowers, sticking the stalks back into the ground to see if they might recover.

Arthur Miller watched and listened and worried. In 'Please Don't Kill Anything' he wrote that 'while part of his heart worshipped her fierce tenderness toward all that lived, another part knew that she must come to understand that she did not die with the moths and the spiders and the fledgling birds.'

At Amagansett, after the loss of the baby, there had been an evening when Miller noticed his wife slumped in the chair, breathing stertorously. He counted her sleeping pills, or rather the absence of them, and realized Marilyn was going into a barbiturate coma. Her life was saved only because of the prompt action of an emergency medical crew from a nearby clinic.

One night at 3:00 A.M. in New York, Norman and Hedda Rosten were summoned urgently to the apartment on East 57th Street. There had been another overdose, and Marilyn's stomach had been pumped. When he arrived Marilyn was weeping quietly in her bed. It had been close; her fingers were still blue. Rosten leaned over in the half-light, and asked, 'How are you, dear?'

'Alive. Bad luck,' came the slurred reply. 'Cruel, all of them, all those bastards. Oh, Jesus. . . .'

At a party in Brooklyn Heights in 1958, Norman Rosten watched Marilyn sitting on a windowsill, glass in hand. She looked moody, 'in her personal daydream, gripped by thoughts that could not be pleasant.' Rosten walked to her and said, 'Hey, psst, come back.'

Marilyn talked of her sleepless nights, then pointed out the window. 'It's a quick way down from here. Who'd know the difference if I went?'

'I would,' said Rosten, 'and all the people in this room who care. They'd hear the crash.'

Marilyn laughed.

Jokingly, yet not entirely so, Rosten got Marilyn to agree to a pact. If either came close to committing suicide, he or she would call the other, to be talked out of it. Rosten thought then that, one day, Marilyn would call. He still keeps a fragment of a poem she wrote in 1958. It reads:

Help Help
Help I feel life coming closer
When all I want to do is to die.

In New York that year, in the divided self behind the famous eyes, Marilyn had begun to die.

24

'This, then,' mused British photographer Cecil Beaton, 'is the wonder of the age – a dreaming somnambule, a composite of Alice in Wonderland, Trilby, and a Minsky artist. Perhaps she was born the postwar day we had need of her. . . . Like Giraudoux's *Ondine,* she is only fifteen years old; but what will happen with the years, only time can tell.'

Of the millions of words disgorged on Marilyn, Beaton's three pages are among the most articulate and shrewd. He saw a creature 'as spectacular as the silvery shower of a Vesuvius fountain, an incredible display of inspired, narcissistic moods.' Marilyn's performance, for Beaton, was 'pure charade.'

In 1958 Marilyn posed for photographer Richard Avedon for a brilliant series of still pictures portraying film stars of the past. Across the pages of *Life* magazine Marilyn became Jean Harlow, Clara Bow, Lillian Russell, Theda Bara, and Marlene Dietrich. It was, as Arthur Miller commented, 'a kind of history of our mass fantasy, so far as seductresses are concerned.'

That year, as she performed fantasy to perfection, Marilyn really began her slide to defeat in the real world. The child was a woman of thirty-two, drinking real alcohol and too much of it, and she knew she was breaking apart. Marilyn now met one of her film idols – and a future co-star on *The Misfits* – Montgomery Clift. At their first encounter, a specially arranged dinner, both got drunk, he on Scotch and Marilyn on rum cocktails.

Later, during an evening with Marilyn and her husband, Clift disintegrated as he regularly did, falling about, failing to complete his sentences. Marilyn commented, 'He's the only person I know who's in worse shape than I am.'

Marilyn had arrived back in Los Angeles in early July, to make *Some Like It Hot.* She had not filmed in Hollywood since *Bus Stop*, and the press turned out in force at the airport. At first there was confusion as to whether she had arrived at all. Then, thirty minutes after the last passenger had left the aircraft, Marilyn appeared.

'An apparition in white materialized in the doorway,' wrote the *Los Angeles Times'* reporter, 'white hair aswirl in the propwash of another plane; white silk shirt open at the powdered white throat; white, tight, silk skirt; white shoes; white gloves. Marilyn Monroe blinked big, sleepy eyes at the world . . . began descending – slowly and wickedly – down the steps. "I'm so sorry," she cooed. "I was asleep."'

Reporters observed three books under Marilyn's arm: *The Importance of Living* by Lin Yutang, Shirley Jackson's *Life Among the Savages*, and *To the Actor* by Michael Chekhov. It was later reported that Marilyn's suite at the Bel-Air Hotel was decorated largely in white, to duplicate the New York apartment, and that she had purchased another parakeet because she was lonely for her dog, left on the East Coast.

Marilyn's behavior during the shooting of *Some Like It Hot* outdid all previous delinquencies. Director Billy Wilder, who four years earlier had survived *Seven Year Itch* with Marilyn, now began a five-month ordeal. Marilyn appeared for a lunchtime call at six in the evening. One day, while sitting in her dressing room reading Thomas Paine's *The Rights of Man*, she responded to an assistant director's call with 'Go fuck yourself.'

Marilyn, not generally known for foul language, apparently fell into it now. She responded to early rushes with 'I'm not going back into that fucking film until Wilder reshoots my opening. When Marilyn Monroe comes into a room, nobody's going to be looking at Tony Curtis playing Joan Crawford. They're going to be looking at Marilyn Monroe.'

Some Like It Hot is the comic tale of two men on the run from gangsters, who don female clothes to join a touring dance band made up entirely of women. One of them, played by Tony Curtis, falls for the girl played by Marilyn, a ukulele player with a taste for whisky and millionaires. Advertisements for the film would describe Curtis and his co-star, Jack Lemmon, as Marilyn's 'bosom companions.' On the set, things were otherwise.

The way Marilyn drove Curtis and Lemmon to distraction with her interminable delays – and an inability to remember even the simplest dialogue – became a movie business legend. Curtis, whom she once doused with a glass of champagne, was to speak later of Marilyn's 'vicious arrogance' and 'vindictive selfishness.' It was also Curtis, in an off-the-cuff remark while watching rushes, who inadvertently recorded for posterity his feelings about the world's sex symbol. Kissing Marilyn, he vouchsafed, was 'like kissing Hitler.'

Marilyn's preparations for performing astonished onlookers and infuriated colleagues. 'Before each take,' wrote Lloyd Shearer, 'Marilyn would close her eyes and enter a deep trance. She would pull down on her creeping-up bathing suit, style 1927, then suddenly start to flail her hands violently, up and down, up and down, as if she were desperately intent upon separating her hands from her wrists.' This was part of the technique Marilyn had picked up at the Actors Studio. Paula Strasberg, garbed in black robe, black hood, and dark glasses, was never far away.

Director Billy Wilder was ill during the making of *Some Like It Hot*. When it was over, he said, 'I am eating better. I have been able to sleep for the first time in months. I can look at my wife without wanting to hit her just because she's a woman.' Later, comparing the ordeal to a journey by air,

Wilder said, 'We were in mid-flight – and there was a nut on the plane.'

'When you are a director,' Wilder said in an interview for this book, 'you try to be a psychologist to some extent. You must establish communication with your people. Normally I learn quickly how to size them up. Marilyn was so difficult because she was totally unpredictable. I never knew what kind of a day we were going to have. I used to worry: What character is she going to be today? Will she be cooperative or obstructive? Will she explode, and we won't get one single shot? That was the problem. I can cope with anything, but I need to know what is in store. I never knew with Marilyn.'

In hindsight, like most other directors, Wilder had no regrets. In her uncanny way, Marilyn had once again worked celluloid sorcery. The film received a chorus of critical praise and made a fortune at the box office. It became the Monroe film shown most frequently on television.

Even before the film appeared, Wilder was saying, 'She has a certain indefinable magic that comes across which no actress in the business has. . . . I have an aunt in Vienna, also an actress. Her name, I think, is Mildred Lachenfarber. She always comes to the set on time. She knows her lines perfectly. She never gives anyone the slightest trouble. At the box office she is worth fourteen cents. Do you get my point?'

Marilyn, by contrast, Wilder said, was 'an absolute genius as a comic actress, with an extraordinary sense for comic dialogue. It was a God-given gift. Believe me, in the last fifteen years there were ten projects that came to me, and I'd start working on them and I'd think, "It's not going to work, it needs Marilyn Monroe." Nobody else is in that orbit; everyone else is earthbound by comparison.'

On September 11, 1958, Marilyn wrote to Norman Rosten from location at Coronado, California. The hotel notepaper was decorated with a beach scene, to which Marilyn added a little female stick figure in the water, waving its arms and shouting 'Help.' The letter read (see page 262):

> Dear Norman,
> Don't give up the ship while we're sinking. I have a feeling this boat is never going to dock. We are going through the Straits of Dire. It's rough and choppy but why should I worry I have no phallic symbol to lose.
>
> Marilyn
>
> P.S. 'Love me for my yellow hair alone'*
> I would have written this
> by hand but its trembling

Once again during this film Marilyn was attended by a psychiatrist and a medical doctor flown in from the East. Now, four days after writing to Rosten, she was admitted to Cedars of Lebanon Hospital suffering from 'nervous exhaustion.' This time there was reason for concern about Marilyn's physical health. She was pregnant again.

As the weeks slipped by Arthur Miller became increasingly worried. He asked Wilder to start letting Marilyn go home early in the afternoon.

Wilder retorted, 'But Arthur, I don't get my first shot until three o'clock. What does she do in the mornings?'

A puzzled Miller replied that, to his certain knowledge, Marilyn left their room for the set each morning at 7:00 a.m. The mystery of the lost mornings never was resolved.

On October 27, Marilyn wrote to Rosten:

---

* Marilyn was misquoting a Yeats poem in her postscript. The actual lines read:

> '. . . only God, my dear,
> Could love you for yourself alone
> And not your yellow hair.'

September 11,1958

Dear Norman,

Don't give up the ship while we're sinking. I have
a feeling this boat is never going to dock. We are going
through the Straits of Dire. It's rough and choppy but
why should I worry I have no phallic symbol to lose.

PS "Love me for my yellow hair alone"

i would have written this by hand but its trembling

Marilyn's note to Norman Rosten from the set of *Some Like It Hot*. Her stick figure shouting 'help' is at top right.

Dear Norman,

Thank you for your Halloween wishes. It's too bad we can't be together. I might scare you.

I haven't been writing anyone, let alone poems – it's so spooky here! Arthur looks well though weaker – from holding me up. . . . I need something to hold on to. . . .

Marilyn signed her note 'e.e.cummings,' – she had been reading Cummings' poetry.

The final scenes of *Some Like It Hot*, completed in early November, involved strenuous physical effort in high temperatures. Marilyn returned to the hospital, then took to her bed at her hotel, 'so as not to jar the baby.' She then traveled by ambulance to the airport, and flew back to New York. There, shortly before Christmas, she lost the baby.

Before she had started *Some Like It Hot* Marilyn had asked Rosten, 'Should I do my next picture or stay home and try to have a baby again? That's what I want most of all, the baby, I guess, but maybe God is trying to tell me something, I mean with my pregnancy. I'd probably make a kooky mother; I'd love my child to death. I want it, yet I'm scared. Arthur says he wants it, but he's losing his enthusiasm. He thinks I should do the picture. After all, I'm a movie star, right?'

The movie star had made her film and lost another baby. Marilyn submitted to more surgery to improve the chances of bearing a child, but 1959 brought no new pregnancy. Close friends now had the clear impression that the marriage to Miller was foundering. Rosten, watching the couple, thought they were playing out 'a facade of marital harmony.'

Susan Strasberg and her parents, visiting the couple at Roxbury, felt 'there was a heavy feeling in the house. We thought perhaps they were having a fight. We sat in the living room for well over an hour. Arthur neglected to offer us anything to eat or drink.'

The Strasbergs had been invited to lunch, yet when

Marilyn did appear, it turned out there was no food. Marilyn got drunk, Miller sat around moodily, and the guests ended up by going out to lunch.

Marilyn was continuing to attend the Actors Studio. In the summer of 1959, driving to the country with Susan Strasberg, Marilyn exclaimed, 'You know, if it weren't for the work [at the Actors Studio] I'd jump out of the car.' Miller, on the other hand, was increasingly disenchanted with the Strasbergs.

Actress Maureen Stapleton, Marilyn's friend from the Studio, was appalled by the imbalance she now saw in the couple. 'Arthur was becoming a lackey. He was carrying her makeup case and her purse, just doing too much for her, and I had the feeling things had gone hopelessly wrong.' The director Martin Ritt had the same feeling when he dined with the Millers. 'It was a disastrous evening,' said Ritt. 'He was at her beck and call, running around after her all evening, and it disturbed me.'

At the same time, as Norman Rosten saw it, Miller was drawing away from Marilyn emotionally, becoming an observer of his own marriage rather than a participant.

In his New York workroom Miller sat among a pile of scribbled notes, a new *Encyclopaedia Britannica* – a gift from Marilyn – at his elbow. Miller kept two photographs of her above the desk. Three years earlier he had been 'finishing' a new play, yet none had been forthcoming. None would be completed until after Marilyn's death. In the fall of 1959 *Esquire* published a profile of the playwright entitled 'The Creative Agony of Arthur Miller.'

For public consumption Marilyn continued to make cheerful statements, but they sounded more and more like rehashed versions of an analyst's advice. That summer she told a British interviewer, 'I've been scared all my life, really, until now. Scared about so many things, even picking up the phone to make a call. That is the sort of thing I'm getting over at last. My philosophy now is "Enjoy the day." I don't fear the future any more.'

The immediate future included a visit to Hollywood. In September 1959, Soviet leader Nikita Khrushchev came to Hollywood in the course of a visit to the United States. Various stars, including Marilyn, Elizabeth Taylor, and Debbie Reynolds, were asked to attend a welcome luncheon at Twentieth Century-Fox. Miller, wary after his battles with the House Un-American Activities Committee, did not go.

Marilyn flew to California alone, spent five hours beautifying herself, and actually arrived early for the lunch. Khrushchev stopped to speak to her, and she offered him greetings from Arthur Miller. Marilyn would later pound her chest with pride, recalling with delight how 'Khrushchev looked at me like a man looks at a woman.'

That episode probably added one more report to the FBI file on Marilyn.

There had reportedly been CIA interest in making use of Marilyn's acquaintance with another visiting political leader. During the shooting of *Bus Stop*, in 1956, Marilyn had met the Indonesian president, Achmed Sukarno. At first she had no idea who he was – she called him 'Prince' Sukarno – but she turned up for a diplomats' party at the Beverly Hills Hotel.

Marilyn and the Indonesian took a shine to one another. 'They kept disappearing to the edges of the party,' *Bus Stop* director Joshua Logan recalls. 'The atmosphere was all S-E-X. I think they made a date to meet afterwards.'

Years later Sukarno told his biographer that Marilyn, who was also staying at the Beverly Hills Hotel, telephoned to suggest a private meeting. A man who loved bragging about his conquests, he uncharacteristically failed to do so about Marilyn.

Marilyn, for her part, was to react with remarkable passion, a year or so after the Hollywood meeting, to news of an attempted coup against Sukarno. She amazed Arthur Miller by announcing her desire to 'rescue' the Indonesian by offering him a home in the United States. She would tell her friend Robert Slatzer that she and Sukarno had 'spent an evening together.'

Whatever occurred at the original meeting, it had not gone unnoticed at the Central Intelligence Agency. In those years Indonesia loomed as large as Vietnam in Washington's view of Asian priorities. In 1957 and 1958, the record shows, the CIA had engaged in all sorts of skullduggery aimed at dislodging Sukarno, who was seen as responsible for his country's drift toward communism.

Part of the CIA effort involved a scheme to produce a phoney pornographic film, supposedly showing a blonde Soviet agent in bed with Sukarno. The intention was to use the film to discredit the Indonesian president, but the project was aborted. Later, however, when the United States needed to curry favor with Sukarno, the CIA dreamed of using sex – in the shape of Marilyn Monroe – to make the dictator feel honored.

According to Joseph Smith, a former CIA career officer in Asia, 'There was an attempt to get Sukarno together with Monroe. In mid-1958 I heard of a plan to get them in bed together. I remember someone from Washington coming through and talking about "some crazy business with Marilyn Monroe that didn't work out right."'

There is no knowing how far the CIA went in its foolishness involving Marilyn. My applications for relevant documents were unsuccessful.

There was little secrecy, however, about the marital folly that Marilyn committed in 1960. At nearly thirty-four, after an unhappy idle year, she began to tear apart the faltering marriage to Arthur Miller. The final phase began when she returned to Hollywood for the filming of *Let's Make Love*, opposite the French actor Yves Montand.

25

In September 1959, Mr and Mrs Arthur Miller, M and Mme Montand, and Mr and Mrs Rosten stood in a Broadway dressing room, laughing uproariously about M Montand's fly buttons. It was the Frenchman's American debut, and his theater audience had been laughing at improbable moments. The guffaws, Montand learned from his New York friends, were because his fly buttons gleamed in the spotlight whenever he put his hands in his pockets. Thus began, in jollity, a relationship that would end in national scandal and private misery.

Improbable though it seemed at the time, Twentieth Century-Fox had to struggle to find a leading man for Marilyn's next film, *Let's Make Love*. For one reason or another Yul Brynner, Cary Grant, Rock Hudson, Charlton Heston, and Gregory Peck all sent regrets. In the moment of crisis, director George Cukor saw Yves Montand doing his song-and-dance routine on television and suggested his name to Marilyn. The call came just weeks after the meeting in New York. Marilyn's opinion, soon to be written in headlines, was that 'Next to my husband, and along with Brando, Yves is the most attractive man I've met.' Montand was hired.

Let's Make Love is the story of a billionaire (Yves Montand), the target of a satirical revue, who finds himself falling in love with one of its girl singers (Marilyn). The film was to prove disappointing, inane, an exception in the run of fine films that ended Marilyn's career. She distinguished herself, nevertheless, with her song-and-dance routines, not least in a sensual rendering of Cole Porter's 'My Heart Belongs to

Daddy.' Long before the film was finished, however, Marilyn's heart belonged to Yves Montand.

Arthur Miller knew and liked Montand. Montand had starred in the French production of *The Crucible,* and shared some of Miller's political convictions. With his wife, Simone Signoret, who had received an Oscar for her performance in *Room at the Top*, Montand had long avoided the United States rather than sign a declaration that he had never been a member of the Communist Party. He and Signoret regularly lent their names to liberal causes in France.

Montand was one inhabitant of the universe who had never seen a Monroe movie, and he spoke little English. Yet Miller's judgment was that 'He fits the role splendidly. He and Marilyn are both very vital people. They possess internal engines which emit indescribable rays of energy. Yves will be one of the big stars of the American screen.'

So it was in January 1960 that the Montands and the Millers moved into Bungalows 20 and 21 at the Beverly Hills Hotel. It was a cozy arrangement. The two couples joined each other for home-cooked meals, sat around talking into the night.

Simone Signoret befriended Marilyn and humored her eccentricities. She was amused by the ritual each Saturday, when a little old lady arrived to peroxide Marilyn's hair. The old lady had been Jean Harlow's hairdresser, and Marilyn had her specially flown to Los Angeles every weekend.

Signoret thought Marilyn looked like 'the most beautiful peasant girl imaginable from the Île-de-France, as the type has been celebrated for centuries.' Late at night Signoret told Marilyn acting anecdotes, and felt like a mother telling bedtime stories. As a woman, Marilyn did not seem to be any sort of threat.

As for Montand, he was soon bemoaning the irritations of working with Marilyn. Sometimes, without warning, she would leave the studio for an entire afternoon, and filming would grind to a halt. Montand would pace up and down mumbling, 'Where is she? I cannot wait and wait. I am not an automobile.'

Within weeks Miller had to go to Europe on business, and Marilyn promptly went into a decline. She told her doctors she could not continue working on the film because, according to her, one of the camera crew was homosexual.

One morning Montand telephoned his wife from the studio to say Marilyn had failed to arrive and did not answer her telephone. Simone Signoret hammered on Marilyn's door in vain. Then the switchboard operator revealed that, though Marilyn was failing to answer the phone, she had recently made an outgoing call. The actress was simply malingering.

A furious Montand came storming back to the hotel. He wrote a note reading, in essence:

> Next time you decide to hang around too late listening to my wife tell you stories instead of going to bed, because you've already decided not to get up the next morning and go to the studio, please tell me. I'm not the enemy. I'm your pal. And capricious little girls have never amused me.
> Best,
> Yves

Montand and his wife slipped the note under Marilyn's door, leaving one end protruding into the corridor, then watched as it was slowly pulled inside. Marilyn had the message, but still did nothing. Montand then shouted through the door that the day's work was canceled 'because of absentees,' and went out till evening.

At eleven that night there was still no word from Marilyn. Then Miller called the Montands long-distance from Europe to say Marilyn had telephoned him. He asked the Montands to go to her room.

'Suddenly,' Signoret recalled later, 'I had in my arms a weeping girl, who kept saying, "I'm bad, I'm bad, I'm bad. I won't do it again, I promise."' Montand patted her on the head, and told her to be on time the next day.

Let's Make Love was not all gloom and dissension, and Marilyn's sense of humor had not deserted her. She was told the censor would object to a kissing scene if it was performed lying down, on the grounds that she and Montand would appear to be actually making love. 'Well,' Marilyn responded, 'we could equally well do *that* standing up!'

Sometime that spring, for all their professional differences, Marilyn and the Frenchman began an affair. According to a close friend of the Millers who preferred not to be named, Marilyn had for some time ceased to be wholly faithful. 'She had this terrible neediness,' said the friend, 'she went with other men simply for something to hold on to, however short-lived.' One such brief infidelity had been with Nico Minardos, her lover of nearly a decade earlier. Now Marilyn turned to Yves Montand.

Marilyn had earmarked Montand long ago, when she and roommate Shelley Winters compiled lists of desirable lovers. Now she began telling friends, including her psychiatrist, that the Frenchman looked like Joe DiMaggio, that he excited her physically. On the set, it was obvious that they enjoyed playing at being in love. Not for the first time for a pair of screen lovers, the borderline between theater and reality became blurred.

Simone Signoret sensed danger, but had to leave to honor a contract in Europe. Arthur Miller was in and out of Los Angeles and, immediate peril aside, seemed increasingly resigned to the collapse of his marriage. Marilyn and Montand were now frequently alone in their adjoining bungalows.

One reporter, drawing on a later interview with Montand, said Marilyn, nude under her mink – an old Marilyn game

– simply knocked on the Frenchman's door one night and took him by storm.

Arthur Miller, by another account, once surprised the couple in bed together when he returned to the bungalow to fetch his pipe. Soon a room-service waiter was blabbing bedroom stories to a journalist patron. The affair, or the heavy hint of it, became public knowledge.

That summer, when filming finished, Montand flew back to Paris via New York. Marilyn, already on the East Coast, planned an elaborate interception. She reserved a room at a hotel and turned up at the airport laden with champagne. The short stopover turned into a five-hour delay, and Marilyn and Montand were observed huddled together in the back of her limousine. The Frenchman, vastly embarrassed, then departed for Paris – and a reunion with the long-suffering Simone Signoret.

More than a month later Marilyn, now working on *The Misfits* in Nevada, brought production to a halt with another of her breakdowns, and was flown to Los Angeles for detoxification. She was there when Montand made a brief return visit to California. Marilyn bombarded the Frenchman with telephone calls from her hospital bed, but he refused to speak to her.

Montand told columnist Hedda Hopper, who was with him when Marilyn called, 'I think she is an enchanting child, and I would like to see her to say good-bye, but I won't talk to her on the telephone; somebody might be listening. I've never met anyone quite like Marilyn Monroe, but she is still a child. I'm sorry, but nothing will break up my marriage.'

In the midst of denying there had been an affair, Montand was evidently a very confused man. 'The trouble was,' he told Art Buchwald, 'that Marilyn and I were a big contact together. ...' He told another reporter, 'If I were not married, and if Marilyn were not married, I would not object to marrying her.'

Marilyn, for her part, did not let go. For months to come, as her own marriage finally crumbled, she would fall back pathetically on the hope of luring Montand to her side. But they did not meet again.

Simone Signoret, though deeply upset, handled the matter impeccably. 'If Marilyn is in love with my husband,' she said in a rare comment, 'it proves she has good taste. For I am in love with him too.'

In a poignant passage of her biography, Montand's wife said of Marilyn: 'She never knew to what degree I never detested her, and how thoroughly I had understood. . . . She's gone without ever knowing that I never stopped wearing the champagne-colored silk scarf she'd lent me one day. It's a bit frayed now, but if I fold it carefully, the fray doesn't show.'

26

During one of Marilyn's 'collapses' while making *Let's Make Love*, a new doctor began attending her in Bungalow 21 at the Beverly Hills Hotel. Dr Ralph Greenson, a prominent California psychiatrist, had been asked by Marilyn's New York analyst to look after the actress while she was in California.

So began a most unusual relationship between doctor and patient. Ralph Greenson, with his wife and children, would in the end find themselves acting as yet another surrogate family for Marilyn. Two years later, Greenson would be one of the last people to speak to Marilyn alive, one of the first known to have seen her in death.

Marilyn's new psychiatrist was internationally respected. Of Russian extraction, trained in Vienna and Switzerland, he brought to his practice a firm grounding in the teachings of Freud. He was, indeed, close to Sigmund Freud's family and associates. During the war Greenson had been chief of the Combat Fatigue Section of the Army Air Corps. He was the author of dozens of learned publications, and by 1960 had long been Clinical Professor of Psychiatry at the University of California at Los Angeles. In the words of a colleague, the doctor was 'the backbone of psychoanalysis in the western United States.'

Greenson was no stranger to Hollywood; he had had numerous show business clients, among them Frank Sinatra. The psychiatrist was forty-nine when he first met Marilyn, an intense, slender man, known for his sensitivity and deep personal concern for his patients.

Quite properly, Dr Greenson generally refrained from

discussing his most famous client. After her death however, he briefed psychiatrists of the Los Angeles Suicide Prevention Center, who had been asked by the Coroner to look into the case. Greenson, now long dead, also gave guarded interviews to two writers, who kept their notes. Most importantly, the psychiatrist's widow Hildi Greenson – hoping to see her husband's work accurately reported at last – shared with me much of the doctor's professional correspondence about his patient. It is quoted exclusively in these pages.

The material throws a stark new light on the gravity of Marilyn's condition two years before her death. Marilyn's first visit to Dr Greenson had been after a day's work on the set of *Let's Make Love*. He noticed at once that she seemed heavily sedated, that she slurred her words, had poor reactions. She seemed remote, failed to understand simple conversational sallies, and rambled on incoherently. She wanted to go straight on to the couch for a session of Freudian therapy. Greenson, alarmed by her condition, decided instead on 'supportive therapy' rather than deep psychoanalysis. He explored first the facts of her day-to-day life.

Marilyn poured out a string of complaints. She said she disliked her part in the film, although she had earlier declared *Let's Make Love* the best screenplay she had ever read. She now said her acting coach, Paula Strasberg, was of little use, because she paid too much attention to her daughter Susan. Psychiatrist Greenson found himself taking on the role of 'supportive acting coach.'

Marilyn told of her chronic insomnia, and used that to justify a use of drugs that Greenson considered hugely excessive. The new patient moaned about her medical doctors, revealing in the process that she was flitting from doctor to doctor to obtain the drugs she wanted. As Greenson discovered, Marilyn would play one doctor off against another, secretly calling one behind another's back. She amazed Greenson with her knowledge of drugs, appalled him with the dangerous jumble of medicines she had been able to obtain.

Greenson discovered that Marilyn was accustomed to taking Demerol, a narcotic analgesic similar to morphine. She also used the barbiturate phenobarbital HMC; sodium pentothol, a depressant of the nervous system primarily used in anesthesia; and Amytal, another barbiturate. She habitually took several of these drugs intravenously.

Privately, an angry Greenson railed against the 'stupid doctors' who had caved in to Marilyn's past blandishments. He tried to make sure she henceforth used only one medical doctor, insisted on an end to drugs by injection, and especially objected to further use of Demerol, which can be highly dangerous if abused.

From doctors who had attended Marilyn, Greenson concluded that 'although she resembled an addict, she did not seem to be the usual addict.' She seemed able to give up her drugs on occasion, without withdrawal symptoms. Her doctors, however, feared she was on the way to becoming an addict.

As Greenson strove to wean Marilyn from drugs, he tried to teach her the art of sleeping. It was an uphill struggle. One day, called to her hotel room, he found Marilyn 'begging for intravenous sodium pentothol or Amytal – this despite some fourteen hours of sleep the day immediately preceding.'

'I told her,' the doctor wrote, 'that she'd already received so much medication that it would put five other people to sleep, but the reason she wasn't sleeping was because she was afraid of sleeping. I promised she would sleep with less medication if she would recognize she is fighting sleep as well as searching for some oblivion which is not sleep.'

Dr Greenson also listened to Marilyn's 'venomous resentment' toward Arthur Miller. She claimed her husband was 'cold and unresponsive' to her problems, attracted to other women, and dominated by his mother. She accused Miller of neglecting his father and not being 'nice' to his children. She said Miller would tell Greenson a different story, but not to believe him.

Greenson did meet Miller, and found him 'very interested in helping his wife and sincerely concerned about her, but from time to time gets angry and rejecting.' The psychiatrist felt Miller had 'the attitude of a father who had done more than most fathers would do, and is rapidly coming to the end of his rope.' He advised Miller that what Marilyn needed was love and devotion without conditions. Anything less was unbearable to her.

Much later, after Marilyn's death, Greenson would tell colleagues that he thought the Miller marriage had collapsed 'to a considerable degree' on sexual grounds. Marilyn, he observed, felt that she was frigid. She 'found it difficult to sustain a series of orgasms with the same individual.'

Greenson would also report that, pathetically, this sexually dissatisfied woman 'gloried and revelled in her personal appearance, feeling that she was an extremely beautiful woman, perhaps the most beautiful woman in the world. She always took great pains to be attractive and to give a very good appearance when she was out in public, although when she was at home and nobody could see her she might not be able to put herself together very well. She felt at times that she was unimportant and insignificant. The main mechanism she used to bring some feeling of stability and significance to her life was the attractiveness of her body.'

In 1960, as Greenson first listened to Marilyn's complaints about other people, he wrote, 'As she becomes more anxious, she begins to act like an orphan, a waif, and she masochistically provokes them to mistreat her and to take advantage of her. As fragments of her past history came out, she began to talk more and more about the traumatic experiences of an orphan child.' Dr Greenson thought that, at thirty-four, his patient still fed on the idea of herself as a 'fragile waif.'

Over the months, though he never voiced a firm diagnosis, Dr Greenson would move from noting symptoms of paranoia and 'depressive reaction' to observing signs of schizophrenia. He knew, above all, that he was dealing with a psyche so fragile that it could crumble into crisis at any time.

For the time being, in 1960, Greenson hoped mainly to bring a deteriorating situation under control, not least by enforcing a drastic cut in Marilyn's use of drugs. He told her flatly he 'would not help her kill herself, or spite her husband, or rush into oblivion . . .' A fine strategy but a vain hope.

'The most serious complication of a major depressive episode,' according to the *Manual of Mental Disorders*, the book used by psychiatrists in the United States for formal diagnosis, 'was suicide.'

27

Three years earlier in New York, as his wife lay recovering from one of her miscarriages, Arthur Miller had stepped out for a stroll in the little park in front of Doctors Hospital. He told a companion, photographer Sam Shaw, of a short story he had written called *The Misfits*.

The idea had come to Miller before marrying Marilyn – when he was living in a cabin in Nevada establishing residence for a divorce. There, at the Stix Ranch in Quail Canyon, Miller had met three cowboys who made their living hunting wild horses. They were wanderers, determinedly living their lives outside the conventional structure of American society, and they struck Miller as the last of a vanishing type of American. The horses they caught, which would be sold as dog food for six cents a pound, were also rarities, the harried survivors of a decimated breed. A story of the wilds could hardly be a play, Miller's usual medium, so he wrote it as a rather long short story for *Esquire* magazine.

Then, in the park outside Doctors Hospital, it occurred to Miller that he could expand 'The Misfits' into a screenplay, and it was, as a close friend put it, a valentine for Marilyn.

Miller's relationship with Marilyn had changed a great deal by July 1960, when a unique gathering of talent assembled at the Mapes Hotel in Reno, Nevada, to make what the producer described to *Time* magazine as 'an attempt at the ultimate motion picture.' It was to star Clark Gable and Marilyn Monroe, Montgomery Clift and Eli Wallach, and a number of noted actors playing minor roles just for the privilege of taking part. The director was to be John Huston, lured back to make a film on American soil for the first time in years.

Marilyn was to play Roslyn, a lonely, troubled woman from the East, who comes to Reno seeking a divorce. She falls in love with Gay, an older man and rugged individualist, portrayed by Clark Gable, who teams up with two other fellows to round up horses.

Roslyn, like Marilyn in real life, schemes and struggles to prevent the slaughter of the animals. Her fight for the horses becomes an epic struggle between man and woman, and from that – we are permitted to hope – love may survive.

Arthur Miller arrived in Nevada before Marilyn. He knew the marriage was disintegrating and was aware, though perhaps not fully, of his wife's treachery with Yves Montand. A few months earlier, when Miller was in Europe working on the *Misfits* script with John Huston, Huston had told a story about a couple who separated after each told the other of their infidelities. Miller had nodded and replied, 'Truth destroyed them.'

Brad Dexter, the actor whom Marilyn had asked to intervene when the DiMaggio marriage was crumbling, now found himself playing marriage counselor again. Marilyn said of Miller, 'He's accusing me of going to bed with every guy I ever met. It's terrible. Would you talk to him?' Dexter dined with Miller at La Scala restaurant in Beverly Hills, but got nowhere.

The Montand affair did not destroy Miller's marriage to Marilyn. It seems to have been at this time, though, that Miller ceased the endless effort to rescue his wife from her own turmoil. It was time to think of self-preservation.

On the set of *The Misfits*, shooting still photographs in company with Henri Cartier-Bresson, was the distinguished female photographer Inge Morath. Miller would eventually find in her his third wife, and make a lasting happy marriage.

The final painful act of marriage to Marilyn was to be played out during the making of *The Misfits*.

In New York, in the third week of July, Jim Haspiel went to the airport to see Marilyn off to the West Coast. He saw at once that she looked ravaged and unkempt, with 'bags under the eyes and a period stain across the back of her skirt. I didn't want to see her like that, and I turned away.'

When Marilyn arrived three days later at Reno, Nevada, she kept everyone waiting – as usual – while she changed in the airplane's restroom. Among those waiting was the wife of the governor of Nevada, who had been sent by her husband to welcome Marilyn with a bouquet.

Next day, as the desert heat crept up to over 100 degrees, Marilyn began filming. On the set, she could still look wonderful. Photographer Cartier-Bresson saw in her beauty and intelligence combining to make 'a certain myth of what we call in France la *femme éternelle*.'

Alice McIntyre of *Esquire* thought her 'like nothing human you have ever seen or dreamed. She is astonishingly white, so radically pale that in her presence you can look at others about as easily as you explore the darkness around the moon. Indeed, there seems the awful possibility in the various phases of her person that MM is a manifestation of the White Goddess herself: disdaining all lingerie and dressed in tight, white silk emblazoned with countless red cherries, she becomes at once the symbol of impartial and eternal availability, who yet remains forever pure – and a potentially terrible goddess whose instinct could also deal death and whose smile, when she directs it clearly at you, is exquisitely, heart-breakingly sweet.'

The White Goddess exulted that she was working with the King. Clark Gable was the idol who so resembled the picture her mother had once told her was a photograph of her father. He was the man who, in occasional fantasies, she had sometimes suggested really was her father.

'All these years,' she told an interviewer, 'and now, Rhett Butler! Doesn't he look marvelous? We were rehearsing a very long scene, and he started to tremble, just the slightest bit. I can't tell you how endearing that was to me. To find somebody – my idol – to be, well, *human*.'

Clark Gable himself, the quintessential professional, realized Marilyn's worth as an actress. He would live long enough to tell his agent, George Chasin, that working with Marilyn on *The Misfits* resulted in one of the very best of his seventy films. It was also Gable's turn to ask, 'What the hell is that girl's problem? Goddamn it, I like her, but she's so damn unprofessional. I damn near went nuts up there in Reno waiting for her to show.'

Soon the question each morning on the set of *The Misfits* was, 'Is Marilyn working today?' Away from the controlling influence of Dr Greenson, she was drowning once more in drink and pills. At one point John Huston reckoned she took up to twenty Nembutal sleeping pills a day, swilled down with vodka or champagne. Often, in the coma of the morning, her old friend Whitey Snyder made her up while she was still lying flat in bed.

'Marilyn would come to the set,' Huston recalled, 'and she'd be in her dressing room, and sometimes we'd wait the whole morning. Occasionally she'd be practically *non compos mentis*. I remember saying to Miller, "If she goes on at the rate she's going she'll be in an institution in two or three years or dead. Anyone who allows her to take narcotics ought to be shot." It was in the way of being an indictment against Miller, and then I discovered that he had no power whatever over her.'

On John Huston's birthday, August 5, Marilyn and Miller had a violent row in front of the *Misfits* company. It was even mentioned in the newspapers.

The immediate cause of the conflict was almost certainly guilt. Marilyn had been making weekend dashes to Los

Angeles to see – or try to see – Yves Montand, now back from Europe. On the set, she spread a false rumor that Miller was having an affair with John Huston's script assistant, Angela Allen. Her motive, Allen came to think, was to 'work out her own guilt over Montand. She could never allow herself to feel guilty, so attack became her means of defense.'

As Miller slaved away on the script, which required constant rewriting, Marilyn distanced herself from him in a physical way. One night she arrived in the makeup man's room and announced her intention of sleeping there to avoid being with Miller. Miller resolved the problem by lugging his typewriter off to another room. Paula Strasberg moved in with Marilyn.

'I found myself on Miller's side,' John Huston said. 'He had done everything in the world to make that marriage survive. During the picture she embarrassed him in front of people. One time she left him on the set, by which I mean in the middle of the fucking desert. We were riding away and I saw Miller standing there. There were no other cars, and she hadn't let him in her car. It was sheer malice, vindictiveness. It was shameful.'

Two weeks later a monstrous cloud of black smoke masked the sun over Reno as forest fires raged across the sierras. Electric power failed, and the only lights that night shone out from the casinos, the hospital, and one window on the ninth floor of the Mapes Hotel, where Arthur Miller toiled over the script, his desk lit by *The Misfits* company generator.

As Miller worked, Marilyn stood in the darkness with Rupert Allan, her press aide and friend, gazing out over the Truckee River. Allan told her about the life cycle of fish, how salmon go upriver to spawn, and how many thousands then die – or, as Allan put it, 'just give up the struggle, to be eaten by other fish or by the raccoons.'

'That's terrible,' said Marilyn. 'I can understand the salmon. I've felt like them.'

Marilyn told Allan of yet another occasion when she had considered suicide. In New York, she said, she had climbed out on to the ledge of her thirteenth-floor apartment in her nightgown, determined to jump. 'I saw a woman in a brown tweed suit,' said Marilyn, 'and I thought if I jumped I would do her in too. I waited out there for about five or ten minutes, but she didn't move and I got so cold, so I climbed back in. But I would've done it.'

Allan felt Marilyn was serious. He said he too had sometimes considered killing himself, and – like Norman Rosten before him – he suggested they made a pact. 'If you ever think of suicide again, and if I ever do,' he said, 'the one of us will call the other.' They agreed that if ever they had to make such a call, but had to leave a message, their code word would be 'Truckee River.'

Making suicide pacts, for Marilyn, was becoming a habit. After those with Norman Rosten and Rupert Allan, there would be one with Lee Strasberg, her acting teacher. Strasberg would recall that sometime in the next two years, 'I extracted a promise from her that if she got in that sort of mood she would call me first. . . .'

On August 26, 1960, seated with Marilyn in a station wagon, Gable had a speech that went: 'Honey, we all got to go sometime, reason or no reason. Dyin's as natural as livin'; man who's afraid to die is too afraid to live, far as I've ever seen. So there's nothing to do but forget it, that's all. Seems to me.'

The next day, amid reports that she had been saved from death only after having her stomach pumped, Marilyn was evacuated to Los Angeles. In the broiling heat, she was carried to a plane wrapped in a wet sheet. Behind her at the airport, as the rest of the company dispersed, girls waved placards reading 'Come Back Soon, Marilyn' and 'The Misfits Need You.'

Marilyn languished in Westside Hospital for ten days,

under the care of psychiatrist Ralph Greenson and an internist, Dr Hyman Engelberg. It was now that she tried desperately, and without success, to reach Yves Montand on the telephone. She did receive solicitous calls from her friend Marlon Brando and from Frank Sinatra.

By the time Marilyn returned to work, an air of unreality and restrained hysteria had taken over the company of *The Misfits*. During Marilyn's hospital stay, Louella Parsons had published a column saying flatly that Marilyn was 'a very sick girl, much sicker than at first believed,' and that she was under psychiatric care. The condition of the star on whom *The Misfits* depended was now public knowledge, and her colleagues persevered in a mood of fond hope fortified by black humor.

Once, at 4:30 A.M., a New York wire service telephoned to check a report that Marilyn had committed suicide. 'Why, that's impossible!' responded a *Misfits* press officer. 'She has to be on the set at seven-thirty! Besides, Paula Strasberg would never stand for it.'

In an early scene of *The Misfits*, Marilyn, as the woman in the throes of getting a divorce, is advised to toss her ring into the Truckee River. Local folklore, she learns, says this will keep her safe from divorce for the rest of her days. The scene left Marilyn morose, for her own next divorce was closer than anyone knew. During her stay in the hospital she had begged reporter Earl Wilson not to publish details of her drug-taking. There would soon be a bigger story, she said, about herself and Arthur Miller.

At the end of September, W. J. Weatherby, feature writer for England's *Manchester Guardian*, arrived on the set of *The Misfits*. His first impression 'was that it was like standing in a minefield among all those manic-depressive people.'

The reporter interviewed both Marilyn and Miller and found Miller protective and concerned about his wife. Perhaps, thought Weatherby, the rumors of a breakup were wrong?' Then, on October 10, after he and Miller had watched one of the Kennedy-Nixon debates on television, Marilyn came banging into the room. 'Thank goodness, you've brought someone home,' she said coldly to Miller. 'You never bring any company. It's so dull.' She then vanished into the bedroom. 'Miller,' Weatherby thought, 'looked as if he'd been struck.'

A week later the company celebrated Arthur Miller's forty-fifth birthday with a dinner at the Christmas Tree Inn. It was a rowdy affair, for the next day would see the end of the location shooting. Marilyn, for once, deigned to attend. In the midst of the merriment the unit's resident jester, cameraman Russell Metty, clambered to his feet. He aimed a few barbs at the famous males in the company, then turned to Marilyn. 'Marilyn, please do us a favor,' Metty said. 'Stand up and say Happy Birthday to Arthur.' There was a silence, and Marilyn shook her head.

The dinner broke up quickly, and Marilyn joined John Huston at one of the crap tables. She knew nothing about gambling, and asked Huston, 'What should I ask the dice for, John?' 'Don't think, honey, just throw,' Huston told her. 'That's the story of your life. Don't think, do it.' Huston recalled that, 'She had a lucky roll, but she didn't know what to do with it.'

When the shooting of *The Misfits* was finally over, Marilyn and Miller returned to New York on separate flights. On November 11, 1960, Marilyn kept her promise to give Earl Wilson an exclusive. 'The marriage of Marilyn Monroe and Arthur Miller is over,' Wilson wrote in his story, 'and there will soon be a friendly divorce.'

Marilyn, once again besieged by newsmen, emerged pale and tearful to confirm the truth of the story. In the melee, one reporter shoved his microphone right into her mouth, chipping a tooth.

Less than a week later, at four o'clock in the morning,

Marilyn was wakened to news that Clark Gable had died of a heart attack. Speaking on a house phone to a journalist in the lobby, Marilyn sobbed, 'Oh, God, what a tragedy! Knowing him and working with him was a great personal joy. I send all my love and my deepest sympathy to his wife, Kay.'

Kay Gable, then pregnant with a child her husband would never see, held equivocal feelings for Marilyn. She had privately suspected Marilyn of pursuing her husband. She certainly felt, Mrs Gable told her friend Kendis Rochlen, that 'the strain of working with Marilyn had contributed to Clark's death.' The following year, however, Marilyn was invited to the christening party, where she held the Gables' newborn son so long and so fervently that other guests felt uncomfortable.

Marilyn did indeed feel guilty about Gable's death. Admitting she had treated him shabbily during the making of *The Misfits*, she asked Sidney Skolsky, 'Was I punishing my father? Getting even for all the years *he's* kept me waiting?' She seemed to Skolsky to be 'in a dark pit of despair.'

John Huston and Arthur Miller had worked doggedly to complete *The Misfits*, yet the film was not received as 'the ultimate motion picture.' Few reviewers thought the movie worked, though many praised the acting by Gable and Marilyn.

John Huston was to reflect that Marilyn had not been acting at all, in the usual sense of the word. 'She went right down into her own personal experience for everything, reached down and pulled something out of herself that was unique and extraordinary. She had no techniques. It was all the truth, it was only Marilyn. But it was Marilyn, plus. She found things, found things about womankind in herself.'

Arthur Miller said years later, 'In *The Misfits*, her performance as a dramatic actress was extraordinary, but I'm not sure if all that torture was worth the result, all that agony. It's not worth anything.'

At the time, a week after the divorce announcement, Miller had sat in a viewing room stunned. 'I still don't understand it,' he said. 'We got through it. I made a present of this to her, and I left it without her.'

When *The Misfits* company disbanded, Marilyn sat on a desk drinking straight bourbon, and said, 'Mostly I am thinking ahead, hoping I will give a better performance next time.' Then she sighed. 'I am trying to find myself as a person. Millions of people live their entire lives without finding themselves. The best way for me to find myself as a person is to prove to myself that I'm an actress.'

For Marilyn the actress, the hope would not be realized. She would never complete another film. As a person, she was flailing around for solace. Weeks earlier, at her lowest ebb during the filming, she had renewed contact with her friend Robert Slatzer. She gave him a photograph inscribed:

To Bob, with many unforgettable memories of Reno –
and other places – from one 'Misfit' to another,
All my love,
<u>Always</u>
Marilyn
September 8, 1960

In November, from New York, Marilyn called Nico Minardos, another old lover. He was in Greece, filming with Jayne Mansfield, and Marilyn seemed pathetically concerned to know whether he and Mansfield were having an affair. Marilyn also tried to reach Milton Greene but, for reasons he cannot now recall, he did not call back. Above all, though, Marilyn still clung to a straw of hope that she could retrieve Yves Montand.

News of Marilyn's divorce plans had led to a new surge of speculation about the Frenchman. Reports from France suggested there was a real crisis between Montand and his wife, Simone Signoret. The rumors were apparently not unfounded. In the week before Christmas 1960, Pat Newcomb, the press aide who would henceforth be one of Marilyn's closest intimates, was present in Marilyn's apartment as the marital drama was being played out. Montand was due in New York any day, and Marilyn expected to see him again. Then Simone Signoret, swallowing her pride, telephoned Marilyn out of the blue. Marilyn asked Newcomb to listen in on the extension.

'Simone begged Marilyn not to see Montand, to please leave him alone,' Newcomb recalled. 'I felt so awful. Here was this wonderful woman, such a fine person, pleading with Marilyn.'

Montand did not come to New York. He canceled his trip at the last minute, and Marilyn, said Newcomb, was 'devastated.'

That Christmas, according to her maid, Lena Pepitone, Marilyn again came close to suicide. Pepitone found her standing by her bedroom window, 'clutching the outside molding.' When the maid grabbed her around the waist Marilyn cried, 'Lena, no. Let me die. I want to die. I deserve to die. What have I done with my life? Who do I have? It's Christmas.'

The rescuer at Christmas 1960 was Joe DiMaggio. He had always been available, and now, in the knowledge of the breakup with Miller, he came running. By one account, he arrived on Marilyn's doorstep on Christmas morning bearing a massive poinsettia plant.

Pepitone said DiMaggio began to appear regularly at dinner time, dressed in his sober city suit, entering discreetly by the service elevator. He would depart early in the morning, before other callers arrived.

In the first days of 1961 Marilyn's deterioration was evident. She had disturbed her lawyer over Christmas to ask about making a new will. She made no secret of her drug abuse. Friends watched her taking her barbiturates in the morning, like a ritual, pricking the capsules with a pin to speed the effect.

Some nights, during this desperate time, Marilyn sought comfort and shelter at the apartment of Paula and Lee Strasberg. She would use the bedroom of their son, John, and he would camp on the couch in the living room. John Strasberg vividly recalled the night he awoke to find Marilyn standing beside him dressed in a nightgown. John, then nineteen, did not know how to cope with a woman in her thirties, muttering vaguely about being 'kind of lonely . . . needing to talk. . . .'

John's sister Susan told of Marilyn, groggy on pills and alcohol, crawling 'on her hands and knees to my parents' doorway, scratching at it with her fingernails. . . .'

On January 20, 1961, at eight o'clock in the evening, a judge once again opened his office as a special favor to Marilyn Monroe. This time the scene was Ciudad Juarez, Mexico, the task the dissolution of the four-and-a-half year marriage between Marilyn and Arthur Miller. Marilyn, accompanied by Pat Newcomb and a Mexican lawyer, requested the divorce on the grounds of 'incompatibility of character.' A lawyer representing Miller said the desire to separate was mutual.

Dressed in black, Marilyn signed the papers without reading them, then fought her way out through the paparazzi. In an effort to dodge publicity, Marilyn had chosen the day of President Kennedy's inauguration to fly to Mexico. She was back in New York by lunchtime the next day.

In the loneliness after the divorce, Marilyn was again in touch with Jim Haspiel, by then a solid friend, who had been keeping his distance during the Miller years. She was to shock him with the gift of a photograph inscribed, 'For the one and only Jimmy, my friend. Love you, Marilyn.' 'Only Jimmy' was heavily underlined, and Haspiel, by that time a grown man, reflected sadly on Marilyn's implication that she had few real friends.

Early February saw the first reviews of *The Misfits,* many of them highly critical. One said of Marilyn's role, 'It really expresses no more than a neurotic individuality and symbolizes little.' Even Haspiel, who was always frank with Marilyn, phoned to say he disliked the film.

The next day John Huston's prediction came true earlier than he had foreseen. Marilyn entered a mental hospital.

28

The Payne Whitney Psychiatric Clinic lay at the heart of the New York Hospital – Cornell Medical Center, a white brick skyscraper overlooking Manhattan's East River. It had been recommended to Marilyn by her regular New York psychiatrist, Dr Marianne Kris. She had been visited by her patient no less than forty-seven times in the past two months. Now she persuaded Marilyn that she needed specialist treatment to arrest the slide into drugged oblivion.

Hospital, for Marilyn, had usually meant a pampered rest cure. In those terms, her reception at Payne Whitney came as a sharp shock.

Marilyn arrived at the Clinic enveloped in a huge fur coat. She registered as 'Faye Miller,' and was ushered to a room on a floor reserved for 'moderately disturbed' patients. By her own account, she at once felt more prisoner than patient. The door was locked from the outside, her clothes were taken away, there was no door on the bathroom, and phone calls were strictly limited.

Marilyn later told Susan Strasberg, 'I was always afraid I was crazy like my mother, but when I got in that psycho ward I realized *they* were really insane – I just had a lot of problems.'

A Payne Whitney nurse, interviewed years later by *Life* magazine, recalled how Marilyn stood behind her door shouting again and again, 'Open that door! I won't make any trouble, just let me out! Please! Open the door!' The door stayed closed.

What happened next, Marilyn would later insist, occurred

291

because she decided: 'Okay, if you're going to treat me like a nut, I'm going to act like one.'

According to another member of the staff, Marilyn stripped off her clothing and stood naked at the window. She was then taken to a security ward on the ninth floor, where she threw a chair through a glass door.

The hospital nurse told *Life*: 'We felt so protective toward her. She made us all feel like we wanted to hold her in our laps. We wanted to soothe her, wanted to say, "It's all right now." It was the feeling lonely, small children give you. You know, sort of dry their tears and pat them on the head and hold their hands.'

Months later, in California, Marilyn offered her lurid version of the experience to her friend Gloria Romanoff. 'It was like a nightmare,' she said. 'They had me in a restrainer. They had me sedated, but not so sedated that I didn't know what was going on. You'll find this hard to believe, but at night there was a steady procession of hospital personnel, doctors and nurses, coming to look at me. There I was, with my arms bound. I was not able to defend myself. I was a curiosity piece, with no one who had my interests at heart.'

The press soon discovered Marilyn had been admitted to the Clinic, but spokesmen would say only that she was suffering from 'an illness of undetermined origin.' One doctor denied the illness was schizophrenia, but said Marilyn was 'psychiatrically disconnected in an acute way because she works too hard.'

Marilyn, meanwhile, fought to be released. Here, complete with misspellings, is a note she dashed off to the Strasbergs:

Dear Lee and Paula,

Dr Kris has had me put into the New York Hospital – pstikiatric division under the care of two <u>idiot</u> doctors. they <u>both should not be my doctors.</u>

You haven't heard from me because I'm locked up with all these poor nutty people. I'm sure to end up a nut if I stay in this nightmare. please help me Lee, this is the last place I should be – maybe if you called Dr Kris and assured her of my sensitivity and that I must *get back to class* ... Lee, I try to remember what you said once in class 'that art goes far beyond science'

And the science memories around here I'd like to forget – like screaming women etc.

please help me – if Dr Kris assures you I am all right you can assure her I am not. I do not belong here!
I love you both
Marilyn

P.S. forgive the spelling – and theres nothing to write on here. I'm on the dangerous floor its like a cell. can you imagine – cement blocks they put me in her because they <u>lied</u> to me about calling my doctor and Joe and they had the bathroom door locked so I broke the glass and out side of that I havnt done anything that is uncooperative

It was Joe DiMaggio, not the Strasbergs, who arranged for Marilyn's discharge from the Clinic. She had used one of her ration of calls to telephone him in Florida, and he flew to New York at once. In the evening of her fourth day at the Clinic Marilyn was smuggled out through a basement passageway. She spent the next three weeks in the neurological department of Columbia-Presbyterian Medical Center. There were no more stories of hysteria and high drama.

Newsfilm of Marilyn's departure from this second hospital shows a mob of reporters disgracing themselves in a way unprecedented in all the years of covering her personal miseries. Marilyn was propelled into a waiting limousine by a flying wedge of sixteen policemen and hospital security staff.

The *New York Journal-American* outdid all rivals with an utterly tasteless story. The report quoted Marilyn as saying, 'I feel wonderful.' Then it added:

All's well with the world, men, so fear not, fear not. Marilyn's face still has the ethereal rose-petal texture, the smile's as delicately soft as ever, the figure – ah, yes, the figure – and best of all they've untied the knots in her nerves.

Norman Rosten, who visited Marilyn several times in the hospital, had a different verdict. 'She was ill,' he wrote later, 'not only of the body and mind, but of the soul, the innermost engine of desire. That light was missing from her eyes.'

For many weeks that spring Marilyn was propped up by Joe DiMaggio, the husband who had been unable to forget. No other woman had replaced Marilyn in his life and, when she permitted it, he offered some stability. Marilyn flew to see him in Florida, where he had been training the New York Yankees, his old team. Later, in New York, Marilyn's staff were again aware that DiMaggio sometimes stayed overnight. Rumors buzzed that they were thinking of remarrying. Marilyn, however, was in no condition to commit herself to anything at all.

Months earlier, plans had been made for Marilyn to play the part of Sadie Thompson in a television dramatization of *Rain,* the Somerset Maugham short story. The plans were shelved.

There had also been talk of her playing in *Freud,* which John Huston was about to make from a screenplay by philosopher Jean-Paul Sartre. Sartre thought Marilyn 'one of the greatest actresses alive,' and Marilyn was first choice to play the part of Cecily, one of Freud's psychotic patients. Dr Greenson, her California psychiatrist, advised against it – in part because Freud's daughter, whom Greenson knew, did not want the film made. Privately, Greenson must have balked at the upset that such a role would have meant for Marilyn.

Marilyn did not work at all in 1961. Twice that summer she found herself back in hospital beds, this time for physical ailments. In May, in Los Angeles, there was yet another gynecological operation. Doctors now determined that her Fallopian tubes were blocked, apparently the result of inept surgery following some earlier abortion.

A month later, in New York, Marilyn was carried on a stretcher into the Polyclinic Hospital, clutching a sheet over her face. The problem this time was an acutely inflamed gall bladder. Dr Richard Cottrell, who handled the case, was appalled to find that behind the glamorous exterior was a creature plagued with physical problems.

Gall bladder aside, Marilyn suffered frequent abnormal bleeding from the uterus, and also had an ulcerated colon. Dr Cottrell thought this last complaint was the result of 'a chronic fear neurosis,' and he found his patient 'highly nervous, frightened, and confused.' In pain after the operation, Marilyn once again had to be restrained.

The last scene of *The Misfits*, one of hope, had Gable and Marilyn driving into the night, following a star that would guide them home. Now, in the hospital, Marilyn stepped onto her balcony with Dr Cottrell and gazed up at the sky. 'Look at the stars,' she murmured. 'They are all up there shining so brightly, but each one must be so very much alone.' Later she muttered despondently, 'It's a make-believe world, isn't it?'

Dr Cottrell was not quite sure what to make of Marilyn. He did notice that, perhaps thinking of her origins, she had registered at the hospital under the name Norma Jean Baker.* It was a name she had not used for years.

---

* Baker was the name of Marilyn's mother's first husband, gone before she was born.

Reality, in 1961, was harsh. Her New York secretary Marjorie Stengel, whose employers would include Montgomery Clift and Faye Dunaway, was to remember Marilyn, at thirty-five, as 'the emptiest human being I have ever encountered.' Stengel told her hairdresser, who was pleading for insights into the life of the world's most celebrated star, 'My dear, in twenty-four hours your life is more busy and more glamorous than Marilyn Monroe's is in two weeks.'

Stengel found that Marilyn's apartment was now 'filthy dirty, and depressing, with dog stains all over the carpets.' She said, 'Really, her life was nothing. She did not see friends, she didn't go out, I never saw her really read anything – except once, Harold Robbins – she didn't do anything. There were phone calls, long secretive phone calls conducted in another room, often with her analyst in California. It was creepy.'

The Marilyn Stengel remembers had become habitually foul-mouthed, a woman who more and more talked in harsh tones, nothing like the breathless baby voice of legend.

For all the psychiatrists' efforts, drugs were still a permanent feature. Stengel said, 'Her apartment was littered with half-empty pill bottles, made out to my name, her name, friends' names. Some doctors will do that for you, if you're rich and famous.'

On her visits to California, a young hairdresser named George Masters had begun to work for Marilyn. He would recall seeing her soon after the gall bladder operation 'wearing a ripped terry-cloth robe. She said she was living on caviar, champagne, and hard-boiled eggs. She could let herself look like an old bag for two weeks. She'd smell sometimes and never comb her hair for weeks. That's why it would take nine hours to get her ready and recreate Marilyn Monroe.'

Marilyn once summoned Masters from California to New York to do her hair, then met him at the door to say she was sorry, she was too tired to see him. By way of consolation, she handed him a check for two thousand dollars.

Masters, too, observed Marilyn's drug-taking. 'I remember one time,' he said, 'when she offered me a pill, a Nembutal, like other people offer you a drink. I kept it under my lip, and spat it out afterwards. I think she popped the pills early in the morning. She'd keep me waiting for two hours while she was in the bathroom, supposedly washing her face. For two hours! I mean, that's very strange.'

'When I was working on her,' Masters said, 'she would start transforming, almost like a chameleon. Her voice would begin to change, and her actions. I would get goose bumps as she started changing into Marilyn Monroe.'

Masters had the impression that Marilyn had become 'asexual. I think if she had any drive at all by then it was to *conquer* men. That was the challenge, and I think that turned her on. I think she was two people, maybe even three – herself, Marilyn Monroe, and the asexual, calculating person only concerned with herself.'

In autumn 1961 a malodorous smell drifted into the Los Angeles apartment occupied by Jeanne Carmen – in a small building three blocks south of Sunset Strip. It came, Carmen said she discovered, from the garbage pail in which Marilyn Monroe was jettisoning used wound dressings, necessary for a while in the aftermath of her gall bladder operation.

Marilyn had returned to the same apartment on Doheny that she had used in the early fifties, and in Jeanne Carmen she rediscovered an old friend. The two had met years earlier at the Actors Studio in New York, and now, as neighbors, became close.

The place on Doheny was a low, nondescript corner building. Marilyn's mailbox bore not her name but that of her East Coast secretary, Marjorie Stengel. Marilyn's apartment was one of a number clustered around a courtyard. A dark hallway led into a large and even darker bedroom, a room of Stygian gloom thanks to heavy blackout curtains over the windows. Originally designed as the living room, it was now dominated by an enormous double bed. The apartment had become, as one friend put it, 'a shrine to sleeping.' It contained no pictures and few personal possessions.

Here at Doheny, Marilyn and Jeanne Carmen whiled away the time, and especially the night hours, talking and drinking. Carmen, at twenty-seven some eight years younger than Marilyn, was a would-be actress who sometimes used the name Saber Dareaux. She had begun her career like Marilyn, as a cover girl for girlie magazines, then graduated to parts in minor movies.

Carmen had a brilliant talent for golf, and worked it up into a trick golf act that brought her television appearances all over the country. She shared doctors with Marilyn – both visited Dr Lee Siegel and gynecologist Leon Krohn – and Carmen said, they held fervent discussions on injections to enlarge the bust, and surgery to narrow the vagina.

To Carmen, Marilyn's drinking capacity seemed 'Olympic standard.' On the subject of drugs, however, the two had much in common. 'I had gotten addicted to sleeping pills while I was living in Vegas,' said Carmen, 'and we became sleeping-pill buddies. We were both using Seconal and Nembutal, and we'd borrow each other's prescriptions. But I was knocked out on two or three a night; Marilyn was using a tremendous amount when I met her. . . .'

The two talked about men and sex. Marilyn talked about the baby she claimed she had had as a teenager, and of her fear that God would 'punish' her for not keeping it. 'From what she told me,' Carmen said, 'Marilyn got nothing out of sex at all. She'd never had an orgasm – she used to fake it.'

'She was so insecure,' Carmen recalled. 'She was sure that she'd lose even her best friends if she ever got old and ugly and down and out. . . .'

Marilyn was still talking about suicide. 'There's no way out for me except death,' she would say when in her cups. 'I'd want to go out in white, in a white satin nightgown and with white satin pillows. And I'd have someone come in and close my eyes and make me look beautiful. How about you doing it for me?'

In May that year, after her experience at the Payne Whitney Psychiatric Clinic, Marilyn had turned to Dr Ralph Greenson for her full-time psychiatric care. Greenson, distressed at Marilyn's 'terrible loneliness,' now made a decision – a highly unusual one in his tradition of psychiatry – to open his own home to Marilyn.

Greenson was to be criticized for this decision by some of his psychiatrist colleagues. At the time, said his widow, he felt he was providing a little of what Marilyn most lacked, security and a sense of family. He was also genuinely touched by this thirty-five-year-old waif. From now, until she died, Greenson's wife and two children acted as a virtual foster family for Marilyn.

The Greensons lived in a fine Mexican-style house at the summit of the only hill in Santa Monica, and to spare Marilyn needless exposure at his office, Dr Greenson usually received her there. Uncharacteristically, perhaps because Greenson said unpunctuality was a sign of disliking someone, Marilyn began arriving early. Greenson's daughter Joan, a twenty-one-year-old art student, would greet Marilyn when the doctor was not ready for her, and the two would amble along by the nearby reservoir, gazing out over the city and the Pacific Ocean.

For Joan Greenson the experience was unnerving but fascinating. Soon she was visiting the great star at her apartment, driving her around town, and beginning an unusual friendship. Marilyn offered advice about boyfriends, helped with makeup – she showed Joan how to bleach the hair shadowing her upper lip – and the two of them swapped clothes.

'The Twist craze was just starting,' Joan recalled, 'so she taught me her version of the Twist, and how to do a bump-and-grind – one you could see on TV, not anything lewd.

Marilyn treated me in a sense as a younger sister. She never let me see pictures of her nude, would never allude to the fact that she slept with anybody. She presented herself to me as a very virginal creature.'

Danny Greenson, Joan's twenty-four-year-old brother, had not expected to get on with Marilyn. He was a student, politically radical by contemporary standards, and he expected 'a rich Hollywood bitch.' Instead he found himself drawn to a woman who was 'in no way put on or artificial, with a real warmth.' Marilyn, in her black wig, went along with Danny when he was apartment hunting. They talked politics, and he found her sympathetic to his leftist opinions.

Marilyn was seeing Dr Greenson six, even seven, times a week. Because her appointments were at the doctor's home and he had to return from his office, she was usually the last patient of the day. She sat upright in a chair facing Greenson across his study, pouring out her troubles for the allotted hour. Then she and the psychiatrist would emerge to join the family, as often as not, for a drink. Marilyn's personal bottle of Dom Perignon champagne, sometimes a bit flat if it had been opened on a previous evening, would be produced from the refrigerator. Sometimes Marilyn would stay to dinner and join in the washing up, often throwing in the evergreen story of how she had once done kitchen chores at the orphanage.

Greenson wrote hopefully in May 1961, before Marilyn's gall bladder operation and the decline that followed, that she was 'doing quite well.' He added: 'I am appalled at the emptiness of her life in terms of object relations. Essentially, it is such a narcissistic way of life. . . . All in all, there's been some improvement, but I do not vouch for how deep it is, or how lasting.'

Three weeks later, on her thirty-fifth birthday, Marilyn sent Dr Greenson a telegram, reading:

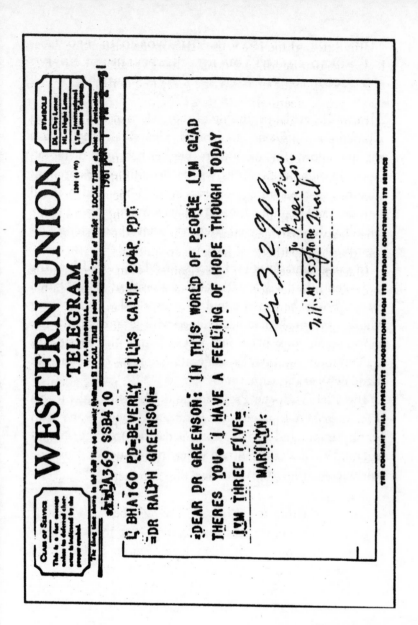

Marilyn's telegram to her psychiatrist on her thirty-fifth birthday, June 1, 1961.

DEAR DR GREEMSON IN THIS WORLD OF PEOPLE
I'M GLAD THERE'S YOU. I HAVE A FEELING OF HOPE
THOUGH TODAY I AM THREE FIVE. MARILYN

Meanwhile, at the beginning of 1961, Marilyn had uttered a momentous confidence to Gordon Heaver, an Englishman she had known for many years. Heaver had lived in Hollywood throughout the fifties, was a story editor at Paramount Pictures, worked on several Hitchcock films, and married into money. He prided himself on his recall of facts – Hitchcock had dubbed him 'Mr Memory,' after a character in *The Thirty-nine Steps*.

In early January 1961, Heaver said, Marilyn told him she had recently had 'a date with the next President of the United States.' From the way she said it, Heaver did not doubt that Marilyn meant she had been to bed with John Kennedy. The conversation took place just weeks before the President's inauguration. Kennedy's inauguration and Marilyn's divorce made news at the same time.

The affair with the President, and Marilyn's links to his brother Robert Kennedy, the Attorney General – and with Frank Sinatra and his associates – has become the stuff of legend. Within less than two years, in the aura of those involvements, Marilyn would die.

Part Four

MARILYN AND THE KENNEDY BROTHERS

'Marilyn Monroe never told anybody everything.'

PAT NEWCOMB,
Marilyn's press assistant and close friend of the Kennedys

'There is danger for the man who snatches a delusion from a woman.'

PERSIAN SAYING,
quoted by Sir Arthur Conan Doyle

29

On a warm summer night in the second week of July 1960, just before the filming of *The Misfits*, two men in a car had cruised along the Pacific shoreline north of Santa Monica, California. They drove past a group of grand beachfront homes, weaved around a muddle of double-parked cars, and quietly drew into the curb. Then they took off their shoes, padded down to the edge of the surf, and began walking back the way they had come.

The figures in the darkness were plainclothes officers of the Bureau of Investigation of the Los Angeles District Attorney's office. The mansion they were watching was the home of Peter Lawford, actor, and his wife Patricia Kennedy Lawford, sister of the Democratic presidential candidate. It was the week of Kennedy's nomination by the Democratic party convention, and – as the noise from the house made obvious – the Lawfords were throwing a party.

Frank Hronek, the senior of the two officers, had gone from a wartime career in intelligence to become a legendary figure in California law enforcement. A top investigator for the Los Angeles District Attorney, he was a walking encyclopedia on all matters that concerned his profession – and some that did not – from organized crime and political corruption to the seamier side of show business. Hronek had asked his superior for clearance to observe the Lawford party for the possible presence of guests linked to the mob. When his superior, a Democrat, told him to stay away, Hronek went along anyway.

That night, as the two officers drew closer to peer over the fence, they were intercepted by private security guards armed with shotguns. Hronek kept the guards talking for a while, then walked away. There had been time enough to observe a wild party going on around the Lawfords' pool, one that included a bevy of women, some familiar to the officers as call girls supplied by a known madame. Several of the girls were, as one of the officers put it, 'stark-ass naked.' Also present was John Kennedy.

The man soon to be President departed soon afterward, according to a spokesman, because 'the candidate needs some rest.' The rest, an informant told the DA's officers later, was in the company of Marilyn Monroe.

True or false? The revelry at the Lawford house was described to me by Investigator Hronek's colleague, and there is no good reason to doubt him. What, though, to make of the allegation about Kennedy and Marilyn? Was the informant in 1960 just passing on gossip, the sort to file and forget? Was there really a Kennedy in Marilyn's love life? Finding the answers, during research for this book, involved in-depth investigation.

Stories of an affair between Marilyn and President Kennedy, or with his brother Robert, or with both, circulated for years after her death. They were so numerous, so often the far-fetched fodder for supermarket scandal sheets, that thinking people may reasonably have written them off as legend. Research established that the stories have a basis in truth.

This book is not the place to rehearse the full sexual history of the Kennedys. Some attempts to do so have established a mythology that throws dust in the eyes of the public as much as on the legend of Marilyn herself. Nevertheless, there has been sufficient responsible reporting, and firsthand recollection by contemporaries, to allow a measure of balanced judgment.

It is evident that the Kennedys, from their fortress of a

family, with their vast wealth and power and with the arrogance that such a heritage endows, led sex lives that were, in ordinary mortals' terms, outside the ordinary. To comprehend the Kennedys' dealings with Marilyn we must glimpse, at least, the sexual tradition in which they thrived.

It began, for the children of John Kennedy's generation, in the attitudes of their father. Joseph Kennedy, a body of literature indicates, was a man who, like some feudal Lord of the Manor, pursued anything in skirts as though by right. He did this in front of his children, daughters as well as sons, and enlisted their help in arranging infidelities.

John Kennedy once confided to Clare Boothe Luce, a former United States Ambassador and wife of the publisher of *Time*, 'Dad told all the boys to get laid as often as possible.' John, as is now well documented, more than followed the paternal advice. From his days in the Navy, when he was known to his pals as 'Shafty,' to his years in the White House, the future President never ceased womanizing.

Nancy Dickerson, a reporter who dated Kennedy, said, 'You couldn't help but be swept over by him. But sex to Jack Kennedy was like another cup of coffee, or maybe dessert.' For this Kennedy, evidently, sex was not to be confused with love.

In contrast, the wheels of the rumor mill long remained virtually still when it came to Robert Kennedy – except where Marilyn is concerned. His brother John spoke of Robert's 'high moral standards . . . a puritan, absolutely incorruptible.' By 1960, when Robert turned thirty-five, he had been married for ten years and had seven children. He had just been named America's 'Father of the Year.'

All this is fact, but it need not force the conclusion that Robert Kennedy was a saint in sexual matters. Historian Arthur Schlesinger, his biographer and a Kennedy loyalist, gave me a frank answer when we lunched together. 'Bobby was human,' he said. 'He liked a drink and he liked young women. He indulged that liking when he traveled – and he had to travel a great deal.'

All the Kennedys were fascinated by the world of the movies. Joe, the father, had moved to California in the twenties to make films, and additional fortune, in Hollywood. Joe's most highly publicized affair was with the actress Gloria Swanson.

John Kennedy, on the West Coast in the forties and fifties, more than followed suit so far as Hollywood women were concerned. His targets over the years were names that now read like faded photographs: Gene Tierney, Sonja Henie, Angela Greene, Kim Novak, Janet Leigh, and Rhonda Fleming. During the presidency, Angie Dickinson was at least a close friend.

Film director Joshua Logan quoted Marlene Dietrich as having told him, 'Jack Kennedy got me to the White House and tried a little hanky-panky. Then, as I was getting into the elevator, he asked with great concern, "Just one thing – did you ever sleep with my Dad?"'

The Kennedy brothers needed a base of operations in California and by 1960 they had one – the beachfront home of their brother-in-law Peter Lawford. In most scenarios involving Marilyn and the Kennedys, Lawford is cast as the facilitator.

In the halcyon years of the Kennedy ascendancy, Peter and Pat Lawford lived the high life in the palatial mansion, complete with fifty-foot heated swimming pool and a movie projection room, that had originally been built for Louis B. Mayer, chief of Metro-Goldwyn-Mayer.

Lawford was thirty-seven in 1960, the British-born son of a World War I general who had fallen on hard times after emigrating to Florida in the thirties. Lawford had departed for Hollywood a few years later, and his good looks whisked him from a job as an usher in a movie theater to starring roles in B-movies.

By the mid-fifties, Lawford's acting career seemed to have peaked. His celebrity was based mostly on an incessant social whirl and an addiction to surfing. Then, in spring 1954, he married Patricia 'Pat' Kennedy, the sixth of Joseph Kennedy's brood and the loveliest of his daughters. By 1960, on the eve of the Kennedy presidency, they had settled at Santa Monica with their three children.

As a couple the Lawfords seemed a rare and enviable combination, one of California's Beautiful Beach People married into a great Eastern dynasty. One writer described Lawford as 'sun-tanned, unruffled, with that peculiar impersonal friendliness of the overprivileged.' Another wrote: 'The problem with the Lawfords is that they seem to have no problems.'

In private the Lawfords were on the way to problems aplenty. The marriage would not last, and both, according to neighbors, were heavy drinkers. Lawford, who was to die of liver disease in 1984, liked to drink till dawn in his own private bar. Friends and associates say he was an indiscriminate drug-user.

Lawford liked bizarre sex. His mother, Lady Lawford, once confided to the press somewhat opaquely that her son had been spanked a good deal in his youth. She said, 'I still insist, and Peter agrees, that the spankings did more than anything else to fit him for his present role.'

That curious judgment aside, two former female intimates said Lawford had outlandish tastes in sex. One recalled that, rather than making love, 'he wanted me to bite his nipples till they bled.' Another left him because he demanded that she take part in group sex.

This was the sad sybarite who played host to the Kennedy brothers when they sought relaxation in California. For a long time, few would discuss what went on during those visits. In 1984, however, I spoke at length with Jeanne Martin, former wife of singer Dean Martin. She and her husband were frequent guests at the Lawford home, and were there when both John and Robert Kennedy were present. Her memories were unromantic.

'I saw Peter in the role of pimp for Jack Kennedy,' said Jeanne Martin. 'It was a nasty business – they were just too gleeful about it, not discreet at all. Of course there was nothing discreet about either of the Kennedys, Bob or Jack. It was like high-school time, very sophomoric. The things that went on in that beach house were just mind-boggling.'

Martin continued, 'Ethel* could be in one room and Bobby could be in another with this or that woman. Yes, Bobby was a grabber, but not in the terms that Jack was. Jack really was instinctive, you know, straight for the jugular – "Come upstairs, come in the bathroom, anything." Bobby didn't have eyes for me, but I do know this. I have a friend that was in the library with him, and before she knew it the door was locked and he threw her on the couch – amazing . . .! It was so blatant.'

Jeanne Martin was sometimes present when Marilyn Monroe came to the Lawford beach house. She became 'quite sure' Marilyn was involved sexually with both Kennedy brothers but conceded, 'Unless you're in the bedroom, it's unfair to presume.'

The story of Marilyn's sexual connection with the Kennedys is covered by other witnesses. On the basis of the assembled information it must be considered beyond presumption.

* Wife of Robert Kennedy.

30

In the fall of 1954 John Kennedy, then a thirty-seven-year-old senator, had undergone major surgery in a New York hospital. He was suffering from spinal trouble complicated by Addison's disease, a progressive malfunction of the adrenal glands. As he recovered, he amused himself playing checkers and firing a popgun at floating balloons.

A reporter who visited Kennedy, Priscilla McMillan, thought the atmosphere was 'like that of a college dorm.' She noticed a tank of tropical fish, a Howdy Doody doll on the bed, and – on the wall – a poster of Marilyn Monroe. The picture showed Marilyn in blue shorts standing with her legs spread apart. It had been fixed upside down so that her feet stuck up in the air.

It was, by then, two years since Marilyn's nude calendar had become the talk of the nation, and thousands of males had her picture on the wall. The ailing Kennedy, though, may have gazed at his poster more knowingly than most. For nearly a decade his regular host on trips to Hollywood had been the prominent agent Charles Feldman. Feldman had represented Marilyn in the early fifties, and two witnesses have suggested that Kennedy met Marilyn through him as early as 1951.

Feldman's longtime secretary, Grace Dobish, believed there was such a meeting. Alain Bernheim, who worked with Feldman and knew Marilyn well, thought she was present at a dinner Feldman gave for Kennedy. Bernheim drove Kennedy home, however, and recalled that he left with another girl that night.

Two friends of Marilyn also referred to meetings with Kennedy in the fifties. Robert Slatzer, who knew her all her adult life, said she mentioned encountering Kennedy during the DiMaggio marriage – again at Charles Feldman's home – and later, during the Miller marriage, in New York. Arthur James, who knew Marilyn from her liaison with Charlie Chaplin, Jr., in the late forties, offered specific memories of the earliest phase of her relationship with the Kennedys.

In the mid-fifties James was a prosperous real-estate agent spending most of his time in Malibu, where he lived. He said an affair of sorts with John Kennedy occurred as early as 1954, in the declining months of the DiMaggio marriage. James said Marilyn told him she saw Kennedy when he visited California, and James himself once observed them together.

'Although Jack Kennedy was a Senator,' said James, 'he was unknown here, relatively speaking. He and Marilyn could get away with a great deal. They sometimes drank at the Malibu Cottage, which was the raunchiest place you've seen in your life. It was just a bar, with maybe eight stools and sawdust on the floor, but in those days it was a hangout for some of the most famous names in Hollywood.'

James, still bemused by the fact that it was 'all so damn open in a way,' said he saw John Kennedy walking on the shore with Marilyn near the Malibu pier. Marilyn told James that she and Kennedy had quietly used rooms at the Holiday House Motel in Malibu, and at another hotel located where Sunset Boulevard meets the Pacific Coast Highway – one regularly used for illicit lovers' rendezvous. (Its name subsequently changed.)

'I don't think it was ever really important to Jack Kennedy,' James said, 'but Marilyn never got over it, least of all when he became President. In the end, though, their headquarters was Peter Lawford's place, back at Santa Monica.'

Peter Lawford, whom I interviewed not long before his death in 1984, said he got to know Marilyn as early as 1950, when she was twenty-four. They met first at the William Morris agency, then at a party, and Lawford took a shine to her.

'I'll never forget going to pick her up on our first date,' Lawford said. 'When I walked into the apartment I had to step around the dogshit. Marilyn just looked and said, "Oh, he's done it again." She just clammed up over dinner, but I saw her some more. We went down to Malibu in the jeep, to go surfboarding. I remember her shielding her skin under a big sun hat. We had a couple of dates, I guess.'

Lawford glossed over the fact that he fell for Marilyn in a big way and she failed to respond. She complained about him to Anne, mother of her former lover, Fred Karger. 'Lawford was chasing her and calling her,' recalled Anne's close friend Vi Russell, 'and she'd come over to our house at three in the morning to get away from him and try to get some sleep. I don't think she had much love for Peter Lawford; she always talked about him giving her a hard time.'

Lawford and Marilyn continued to bump into each other as the years went by, though at a safe distance. Both were weekend guests at the home of Gene Kelly, who exhausted his famous friends with volleyball parties that tended to start *after* the party, when the sun was coming up. By that time Lawford was involved with Pat Kennedy, who became his wife.

Pat Lawford liked Marilyn and felt she needed help. It was her idea – according to Lawford – to start inviting Marilyn to the beach house in the months before John Kennedy's presidency.

Lawford, whose lasting devotion to Kennedy was little short of idolatry, flatly denied there was ever any affair between Marilyn and either Kennedy brother. He told a Los Angeles District Attorney's investigator, during a fresh inquiry into Marilyn's death in 1982, that Marilyn did not meet John Kennedy until 1961, when he was already President.

That occasion, said Lawford, was a party at which Marilyn happened to be a guest. 'The whole thing about an affair is balls,' Lawford told me. Research indicates otherwise.

In early 1960, as the Kennedy campaign went into high gear, the Lawford house at Santa Monica became a meeting place for the candidate's advisers. One was Pete Summers, a Kennedy political strategist with the key job of handling relations with the television networks. Summers met Marilyn in Kennedy's company several times, always at the Lawford house, and as one of a group of perhaps a dozen people.

'They were very close friends,' Summers recalled. 'I would say she was a very special guest – the President was really very, very fond of Marilyn. She was delightful, a little bit nervous perhaps, but I think the nervousness was because she was in a new territory with people who were political animals. She wasn't totally at ease. I did feel that she was so impressed by Kennedy's charm and charisma that she was almost starry-eyed. ... But she was totally able to hold her own conversationally; she was very bright.'

Given Marilyn's psychological problems and her abuse of alcohol and sleeping pills, one might wonder what attraction she held for a Kennedy. It is clear, however, that she never lost the ability to hide her miseries under a mask of dazzling beauty. That aside, she was by now more politically sophisticated than has ever been acknowledged.

For years, and especially during the Miller marriage, Marilyn had been mixing with people who talked politics a great deal. In New York she had cultivated a lasting friendship with the eminent journalist Lester Markel.

Markel had been Assistant Managing Editor of the *Herald Tribune* at the age of twenty-five, and was Sunday Editor of the *New York Times* for nearly half a century. Marilyn had written to him in the mid-fifties, in one of her bursts of eagerness to widen her intellectual horizon. They had lunched at Sardi's, and afterward the sixty-year-old Markel, himself a

The New York Times
Times Square
May 23, 1960

Dear (I think) Marilyn:

I write to the President of the United States and I get a prompt reply.

I write to the Vice President of the United States and I get a prompt reply.

I write to Sir Laurence Olivier and I get a prompt reply.

I write to Jayne Mansfield and I get a prompt reply.

I write to you and three weeks go by without even an acknowledgment of an important enclosure.

Who do you think you are -- Marilyn Monroe?

In any case, would you please return the script of that speech? I need it.

        Yours, in sorrow and bewilderment,

LM:ls

Mrs. Arthur Miller
Beverly Hills Hotel
Beverly Hills, California

A letter from Lester Markel, Sunday Editor of the *New York Times*. His worry was unfounded – correspondence shows that Marilyn stayed in touch with the legendary journalist.

star in his own professional world, amazed his colleagues by giving Marilyn a guided tour of the *Times* newsroom.

After Markel's death in the seventies, at the age of eighty-four, his daughter discovered – stuffed in the back of a desk drawer – a letter Markel had received from Marilyn in March 1960, while she was making *Let's Make Love*. It provides a remarkable insight into Marilyn's intelligence and political savvy. Marilyn wrote:

Lester dear,

Here I am still in bed. I've been lying here thinking – even of you. .... About our political conversation the other day: I take it back that there isn't *anybody*. What about Rockefeller? First of all he is a Republican like the *New York Times*, and secondly, and most interesting, he's more liberal than many of the Democrats. Maybe he could be developed? At this time, however, Humphrey might be the only one. But who knows since it's rather hard to find out anything about him. (I have no particular paper in mind!) Of course, Stevenson might have made it if he had been able to talk to people instead of professors. Of course, there hasn't been anyone like Nixon before because the rest of them at least had souls! Ideally, Justice William Douglas would be the best President, but he has been divorced so he couldn't make it – but I've got an idea – how about Douglas for President and Kennedy for Vice-President, then the Catholics who wouldn't have voted for Douglas would vote because of Kennedy so it wouldn't matter if he *is* so divorced! Then Stevenson could be Secretary of State! . . . It's true I am in your building quite frequently to see my wonderful doctor* as your spies have already reported. I didn't

* The Markels lived in the same building as the Strasbergs and Marilyn's then New York psychiatrist, Dr Marianne Kris.

want you to get a glimpse of me though until I was wearing my Somali leopard. I want you to think of me as a predatory animal.

Love and kisses,

Marilyn

P.S. Slogans for late '60:

'Nix on Nixon'

'Over the hump with Humphrey (?)'

'Stymied with Symington'

'Back to Boston by Xmas – Kennedy'

Obviously this was the letter of someone who either knew their politics, or – as was likely the case with Marilyn – someone who had been giving themselves a crash course in current affairs.

Marilyn by now talked regularly with the Greensons, whose politics were quietly liberal. They thought Marilyn quite radical. 'Marilyn was passionate about equal rights, rights for blacks, rights for the poor,' recalled Joan Greenson. 'She identified strongly with the workers, and she always felt they were her people.'

Years earlier, when she had first plunged into her self-education through reading, Marilyn expressed admiration for India's leader, Jawaharlal Nehru. Now, she felt Cuba's Fidel Castro should be given a chance to show whether he really intended to permit democracy.

In the spring of 1960, her name headed a list of Hollywood figures, including Marlon Brando, Gene Kelly, Shirley MacLaine, and Peter Lawford, sponsoring SANE, the National Committee for a Sane Nuclear Policy. Asked by an interviewer what dreams or nightmares she had, Marilyn responded, 'My nightmare is the H-bomb. What's yours?'

Marilyn had a healthy skepticism, which might not have seemed so healthy to right-wingers of the time, about U.S. foreign policy. In the summer of 1960 she telephoned long distance to Rupert Allan, one of her press aides, to discuss the morning's newspaper headlines. She was irritated that more prominence had not been given to a story about an American naval aircraft trespassing in Soviet airspace. Moscow claimed the plane was spying, while Washington said it was merely conducting an oceanic survey. This assertion of innocence came just weeks after a far greater furore, over the downing by the Russians of a CIA U-2 spy plane piloted by Gary Powers. The U.S. government had at first claimed, falsely, that the U-2 had only been engaged in weather research.

Marilyn wanted to know why this fresh story, about the naval aircraft, was being treated as minor news. Allan, a Navy veteran, replied that this time, perhaps, the U.S. government was telling the truth. 'I don't know, Rupert,' Marilyn said. 'I don't trust us.' On the other hand, said Allan, Marilyn 'loved being an American. She was very pro-America, naively sometimes.'

Marilyn was a registered Democrat. In April 1960, with the primaries under way, the Democratic town committee in Roxbury, Connecticut, where she and Arthur Miller were residents, suggested her as an alternate delegate.

'Wouldn't it be nice,' said a committee spokesman, 'if Marilyn could be a delegate to the convention?' The gesture was not entirely serious, but on the eve of the convention a Los Angeles newspaper reported that 'Marilyn Monroe's own Democratic friends are urging her to attend.'

31

In the second week of July 1960, meeting in Los Angeles for the first time in forty years, the Democrats gathered to choose their candidate. The Kennedys, of course, were there in force – brothers John and Robert, and their father, Joseph, the latter ensconced in the Beverly Hills mansion loaned to him by one of the great movie stars of his own era, Marion Davies.

Of Marilyn Monroe there was not a sign, nor was she mentioned, except behind the scenes at the Beverly Hilton Hotel. Fred Karger, the musician Marilyn had wanted to marry twelve years earlier, refused to play at a ball attended by John Kennedy. He withdrew his entire band, said Karger's first wife Patti, because he 'had heard of Kennedy's fooling with Marilyn, and it appalled him.' The Democrats made do with Frank Sinatra and Judy Garland instead.

Marilyn was not to be seen at that point for a good reason: she was in New York during the brief hiatus between finishing *Let's Make Love* and starting *The Misfits*. Ralph Roberts, the actor who at that time became her masseur and friend, was giving her a massage at the 57th Street apartment when news came through that Kennedy had won the nomination.

Two days later, as the sun began to set, a weary Kennedy stood in the Los Angeles Coliseum to declare: 'We stand today on the edge of a New Frontier – the frontier of the 1960s – a frontier of unknown opportunities and perils. ... I am asking each of you to be new pioneers on that New Frontier.'

By that time, testimony suggests, Marilyn had flown to Los Angeles and was with Kennedy on his night of triumph.

That night Peter Lawford threw a party for Kennedy, and borrowed the head bartender from Romanoff's, the Beverly Hills restaurant owned by one of Marilyn's oldest friends. The bartender, Ross Acuna, was a man used to watching the famous at play, and he had a long memory.

Acuna said of the party on the night of the Coliseum speech, 'I saw Sammy Davis coming in with Marilyn Monroe. I couldn't get the drift, but I was a bartender; you see a lot of things, you keep your mouth shut. But pretty soon here comes the Kennedy boy, from making that speech at the Coliseum. In fact when he ordered his drink he never told me what he wanted – he wrote it down because his voice was gone from making so many speeches. He used to drink daiquiris. Soon I saw that Monroe and the Kennedy boy were pretty close together. Sammy Davis? I think they just asked him to bring Monroe in.'

Jeanne Carmen, then Marilyn's neighbor – and, according to her, confidante – at the Doheny apartment, also said Marilyn met Kennedy that night. Her source was Marilyn, who mentioned it months later.

Pete Summers, the Kennedy campaign official who had seen Marilyn with Kennedy earlier in the year, now saw them again. Marilyn's lack of confidence around Kennedy had evaporated. It became clear to him that the pair were having a fling.

'There were a number of celebration parties going on,' said Summers. 'Marilyn was at one – at the Beverley Hilton, where there was a private celebration, with dancing. She was there, and I saw Jack, right after telephoning his wife on the East Coast, go out and start dancing with Marilyn.'

Summers said, 'We didn't know how serious this affair would be – platonic or otherwise.' On a visit to the Lawford beach house, he found out.

'I had to go and see Jack,' Summers recalled. 'He came out of the shower, putting on his tie, and started talking. And a few minutes later Marilyn came out of the shower, with just a towel around her. She had clearly been in there, in the shower, with him. It was obvious, but neither of them seemed worried about it.'

Peter Lawford's last wife Pat Seaton, interviewed following Lawford's death, offered corroboration of the sex activity in the bathroom. 'Peter told me there was an affair with JFK,' Seaton said. 'When we went through the house he showed me the onyx bathtub, and said "Jack and Marilyn fucked in here."'

Pete Summers and other Kennedy advisers were worried by the realization that the candidate had become involved with Marilyn. 'I had buddies in the media,' Summers recalled, who 'started asking me about it. I told the President, and I told Bobby, that we could have something very explosive here that could blow us out of the water. . . . Bobby made a real strong admonition to Jack on this. He was getting out of line. He was no longer, you know, just Senator Kennedy. He was more and more under the zoom. This was something that could destroy us.'

If Marilyn had a dalliance with Kennedy at the Convention, it occurred in the midst of her turmoil over Yves Montand and the collapse of her marriage to Miller.

Later, on the set of *The Misfits*, Marilyn asked British correspondent W. J. Weatherby what he thought of Kennedy. Weatherby replied cautiously that he preferred Kennedy to Nixon. Marilyn, who struck Weatherby as 'mischievous . . . excited,' said how fine it would be to have a President who was so young and good-looking.

'You mean he has a Hollywood image?' asked Weatherby.

'You must admit,' Marilyn replied, 'it's better than having old uglies who have no brains *or* beauty.'

Marilyn now told Weatherby she wanted Kennedy to

win in November. He did, of course, and just a day later Art Buchwald wrote:

Let's Be Firm on Monroe Doctrine
Who will be the next ambassador to Monroe? This is one of the many problems which President-elect Kennedy will have to work on in January. Obviously you can't leave Monroe adrift. There are too many greedy people eyeing her, and now that Ambassador Miller has left she could flounder around without any direction.

Few, except her psychiatrists and closest friends, knew how desperately Marilyn was floundering. She was now in that solitary three-month period before the ordeal at Payne Whitney Psychiatric Clinic. Miller was gone, Montand was finally rejecting her, and Marilyn was in a narcotic nose dive. She found some solace in occasional visits to the Actors Studio, and it was there she bumped into reporter W. J. Weatherby again. The Englishman suggested a drink, and thus began a series of conversations that any journalist would have envied.*

Weatherby and Marilyn met several times in the coming weeks at a nondescript, now defunct, bar on New York's Eighth Avenue. Over the first drink, Marilyn eyed Weatherby's notebook warily, then decided to trust him. 'Put me in the notebook if you like,' she said, 'but don't write about it now. Do it when I retire!' Weatherby duly scribbled a record of their conversations in two shorthand notebooks, and honored Marilyn's embargo until long after her death. In context, her comments on the Kennedys are revealing.

A month after the election Weatherby got a curt response from Marilyn when he ventured that even John Kennedy

* Weatherby's contact with Marilyn is corroborated by the discovery of his name in Marilyn's address book, located by the author.

did not talk sense all the time. 'Oh, he does,' came Marilyn's quick riposte.

Joan Greenson, daughter of Marilyn's psychiatrist, recalled that Marilyn 'liked to have everything black or white, right or wrong, good or bad. Her intensity of feelings made it, at times, difficult to have discussions.' This was something Weatherby also discovered.

In January 1961 Marilyn arrived for their meeting in a state that had Weatherby worried. She said she had been on pills, and her mood veered wildly from bright to irascible, from articulate to long, depressed silences. They talked of civil rights; Marilyn had mentioned once having had an affair with a young black man, and Weatherby himself was involved with a black woman. He now dared to suggest that Kennedy would give only limited help to the black cause. 'The President will go all the way . . .,' Marilyn insisted. 'The Kennedys know all about the situation already. . . . You just wait and see. You're in for some surprises.'

Two decades later, in his interview for this book, Weatherby still remembered vividly that 'Marilyn would not have me say a word against Kennedy. She talked in a knowing way, as though she had some sort of inside track.'

At their next rendezvous, the last in 1961, Marilyn was again dopey, fading in and out of the conversation. She enthused about establishing a memorial to her late drama teacher, Michael Chekhov, and seemed serious about the notion that the President might help. 'She seemed like a star-struck girl at the mention of the President's name,' Weatherby recalled. It struck him as odd, and he steered her away from the subject of the Kennedys.

When in New York, before and after the election, John Kennedy favored the Carlyle Hotel as his base. There he had a suite with spectacular views of Manhattan, a management who catered to his every whim, and total respect for his privacy. The press might be on watch downstairs, but during the presidency Secret Service men would accompany the President on his private escape route, a series of tunnels that connected the Carlyle with the nearby apartment houses and hotels. The hotel was eighteen blocks from Marilyn's apartment.

Reports that Marilyn visited Kennedy at the Carlyle were supported by Jane Shalam, a member of a New York family prominent in political circles. The windows of her apartment looked down on the side, or back, entrance of the Carlyle. 'I saw Marilyn coming and going at that time,' said Shalam, 'and she was certainly in and out enough to notice her. Most times people wouldn't know who she was – when she took her makeup off and had her hair back, you wouldn't know it was Marilyn Monroe. I saw her going there when the Kennedys were at the Carlyle. There seemed no other reason that she would be there.'

The President, like other mortals, once had to wait for Marilyn when he invited her to an intimate dinner at the Carlyle, according to reporter Earl Wilson, quoting the 'beard' of the evening – the front man used to escort Marilyn to the rendezvous. Wilson would not identify his source, but Peter Lawford's agent, Milt Ebbins, once played a similar role.

Ebbins, by then a man on friendly terms with the President, recalled Marilyn asking him to take her to a party on Park Avenue. He finally got her there two hours late; whisked her unrecognized past a group of newsmen in the lobby (Marilyn was wearing wig, bandanna, and dark glasses), and was then promptly abandoned. The President was at the party, and Marilyn was with him when Ebbins slipped away.

Marilyn herself told several people about her relationship with John Kennedy. Paula Strasberg, her acting coach, said privately that Marilyn told her about the affair. She added that she was in possession of related correspondence, which she had 'placed in a safe deposit box, to remain unopened for fifty years, so that people should not be hurt by it.'

Marilyn also talked about John Kennedy with Sidney Skolsky, the veteran Hollywood reporter who had advised her since the start of her career. Skolsky remembered, 'She told me she was having an affair with the President, and I did not doubt her.' Skolsky wrote nothing about Marilyn's confidence until years after her death, and, when he did refer to it, reflected, 'I confess I still find it grim to speculate on what might have happened to me if I had tried to write about this romance in my column when it first came to my attention.'

Skolsky said Marilyn always referred to Kennedy as 'the President,' never by his first name. 'She did complain to me,' Skolsky recalled, 'about the difficulties involved in being alone with the President. And even when Marilyn and the President were alone in Peter Lawford's beach house in Santa Monica, they had to leave a light on. If anything happened, if the light went out, the Secret Service would break down the door and burst in. I don't think that ever actually happened . . .'

Two other West Coast reporters claimed they learned from prime sources of Marilyn's affair with the President. James Bacon, who had known Marilyn for years, said, 'She was drinking heavily at the time – I think it was less than a year before her death – and she said she was sleeping with Jack Kennedy. She said he wouldn't indulge in foreplay, because he was on the run all the time.'

Jimmy Starr, also a Los Angeles columnist at the time, learned of Marilyn's involvement with Kennedy from actress Angie Dickinson, then a younger and less tight-lipped lady than she later became. Like Skolsky and Bacon, he published nothing at the time.

'When he became President,' Marilyn's New York confidant Henry Rosenfeld recalled, 'she became very excited. Her opinion was that this was the most important person in the world, and she was seeing him. She was so excited, you'd have thought she was a teenager.'

Rosenfeld, as did Skolsky, thought Marilyn gloried in the secrecy of the whole business, even as she was being indiscreet. Sometimes, on the telephone, she would refer to the President as 'You know who.'

As Rosenfeld understood it, 'In New York I believe they met occasionally at a place on Fifty-third Street, near Third Avenue. And Marilyn went to Washington to see him once or twice, though I'm almost sure she never went to the White House.'

In mid-November, ten months into his first year in office, the President returned to Los Angeles for the first time since his election. He had come to make speeches and to fire up the enthusiasm of key supporters on the West Coast. At the Beverly Hilton Hotel, where he stayed, there was a reception for about two hundred guests drawn from the ranks of local politics and administration.

One of the guests was Philip Watson, then beginning his campaign to become Los Angeles County Assessor, a post he would win and hold till 1977. Watson was a Republican, but the Assessor's office was a nonpartisan appointment. He was courting support from both parties. An introduction to the President could open many doors, and Mark Boyar, Kennedy's finance chief in California during the presidential campaign, fixed Watson's invitation. First, upstairs in the Hilton's Escoffier Room, Watson, one person in a long line, shook the President's hand. Later, to get him closer to Kennedy, Boyar took Watson to a smaller gathering in a suite on a lower floor. This time, he saw that the President was accompanied by Marilyn Monroe.

'She was there in the room with him,' Watson recalled, 'along with a couple of dozen other people. I had heard stories about them, and it came as no particular surprise. I was introduced to them both, I spoke to her too, and thought her a beauty – she was in a skin-tight white dress – but empty-headed was how I thought of her that evening. There was nothing obvious. They weren't holding hands or anything.'*

The date of that sighting of Marilyn with the President – in late fall 1961 – coincides, as best one can tell, with a new and troubling phase in her involvement with the Kennedys. The previous month, October, at a party at the Lawford beach house, she had encountered the President's brother Robert. 'She had too much to drink to drive home,' the Attorney General's press secretary Edwin Guthman remembered, 'and we both drove her to her place. Bob asked me to come along to. He didn't say why, but his reason was pretty obvious. He didn't want to be seen going off alone in a car at night with Marilyn Monroe. . . . We drove her home. We put her to bed, and we left. It was a two-person job. She wasn't "passed out," but she was pretty close.'

Around the same time, another contemporary saw Marilyn and Robert Kennedy together. Stanley Tretick, a *Look* magazine photographer who took some of the most memorable pictures of the First Family, remembered seeing them together at a social occasion, probably in San Francisco. 'They were dancing together. It was in a hotel, at a posh semi-private affair, a fund-raiser sort of thing. They were dancing very closely, with their bodies very close together, and it looked rather romantic. It just struck me at the time, "My, they really look like a nice couple together," but then I just dismissed it from my mind.'

Tretick did not take photographs. He recalled, 'There were certain times when you couldn't photograph . . . I am not even

---

* The day after the Hilton reception the President visited the Lawfords at Santa Monica. Whitey Snyder, Marilyn's makeup man, drove her to meet the President at the Lawfords' beach house, almost certainly on that day, November 19, 1961.

certain I had my cameras with me. The reason I remembered the incident is that they looked very good together, looked like they were very friendly. . . .'

Senator George Smathers of Florida had been a freshman Congressman with John Kennedy in 1947 and long remained a close friend. In an interview for this book, he said he heard about Marilyn's links to the brothers 'around the White House and in family circles'– and from the President himself.

Pat Newcomb, Marilyn's last press aide and the woman closest to her in the final months of her life, was also a Kennedy intimate. Asked about Marilyn and the President, Newcomb said, 'No comment.' Asked about Marilyn and Robert Kennedy, she replied, 'I did not know about it.'

Whatever the precise nature and timing of the Kennedy brothers' overlapping contacts with Marilyn, they were playing with fire. By the time Marilyn died, the danger would be extreme. Only years later did it become possible to piece together the extent to which the Kennedys' bitter enemies – the leaders of organized crime – penetrated the secrets of their personal lives.

Former FBI Assistant Director Courtney Evans, J. Edgar Hoover's liaison with Robert Kennedy, was famous among reporters for his elliptical way of parrying questions. In discussion of President Kennedy's vulnerability to sexual blackmail, however, Evans told me, 'There was, I know, an effort to bring pressure on the presidency – by organized crime. . . . That's my recollection.' He had said little, but more than any official source before him.

Pleading a poor memory, Evans would not be lured into providing detail, but pointed me towards two key Kennedy enemies – Sam Giancana, one of the most powerful Mafia bosses in history, and Jimmy Hoffa, criminal head of the Teamsters' Union. Long since, in the years before the presidency, Robert Kennedy's work on Senate committees had persuaded him that the Union, as run by Hoffa, was 'a conspiracy of evil.' He had linked Hoffa firmly to organized crime, and specifically to Giancana.

I asked the former Assistant Director whether at any stage he was aware of 'any sort of a flap about Monroe ... or of organized crime attempting to use involvement with Monroe as pressure on the President or his brother.'

Evans replied, 'I certainly heard such stories, because they were rampant both in Washington and Los Angeles, well before she died. Whether they were true or not I had no way of knowing. I had my own suspicions ...'

Evans pointed out, almost with relief, that his unenviable role as liaison between Director Hoover and Robert Kennedy, two men who deeply disliked each other, meant that neither necessarily gave him all the facts.

The researcher, driven back to the historical jigsaw, must take a hard look at yet another of Marilyn's lovers, one with whom she had an affair at the same time she was involved with the Kennedys – a singer named Frank Sinatra.

32

Shortly before her death a reporter asked Frank Sinatra how well he knew Marilyn Monroe.

'Who?' Sinatra replied sarcastically. 'Miss Monroe,' he observed, 'reminds me of a saintly young girl I went to high school with, who later became a nun. This is a recording.'

Marilyn, told of this exchange, responded tartly, 'Tell him to look in *Who's Who.*'

Marilyn had first met Sinatra, according to the photographer Milton Greene, at a dinner at Romanoff's in 1954, when the DiMaggio marriage was collapsing. The 'Wrong Door Raid,' in which Sinatra helped his friend DiMaggio in his pursuit of the unfaithful Marilyn, followed within weeks.

Six years later in 1960 – when the Miller marriage was falling apart and just after John Kennedy's nomination as President – Sinatra made contact with Marilyn again. In August that year he invited the entire company of *The Misfits* to see him perform at the Cal-Neva Lodge, not far from the Nevada location where the movie was being made. Marilyn went along, accompanied by an Arthur Miller who looked rather out of his element.

Sinatra was in the process of buying the Cal-Neva, a casino and resort complex on the wooded shores of Lake Tahoe. It sat on the heights overlooking the lake, with a swimming pool and a cluster of luxury bungalows. Advertisements called it 'Heaven in the High Sierras,' but it was a paradise custom-built for gangsters.

The Lodge's gimmick was that the state line dividing California and Nevada bisected its public rooms and swimming pool. Casino activity could take place only on the Nevada side of the line, because of the laws that banned gambling in California. Sinatra expanded the casino facilities, and brought in new managers. One was Paul 'Skinny' D'Amato of Atlantic City, one day to be described by Professor Robert Blakey, formerly a Special Attorney in the Organized Crimes Section of the Kennedy Justice Department, as 'a New Jersey gangster.' His role at the Lodge, according to the same source, was to protect the interests of Chicago Mafia chieftain Sam Giancana.

Giancana was 'boss of bosses' of the Chicago syndicate, the ruler on the throne once occupied by Al Capone. By 1960 he was master of an organized crime network reaching across huge swathes of the United States, including casinos and show-business rackets on the West Coast. With the advent of the Kennedy administration, Giancana became a prime target for prosecution. As Attorney General, Robert Kennedy took on no less a task than the destruction of the Mafia in the United States. Cornered, Giancana would be desperate.

In 1981, in sworn testimony to the Nevada Gaming Control Board, Sinatra was to say that as of 1960 he knew Giancana only slightly and had not realized he was a mobster. He said he never invited Giancana to the Cal-Neva Lodge, and – when he did learn he was there – issued instructions that he was to leave.

Giancana's daughter Antoinette, however, said she was present at several meetings between the two from as early as 1954, and that Sinatra always greeted Giancana 'with an embrace of respect and friendship.' Sinatra's daughter Tina recalled that her father 'openly cultivated a cozy acquaintanceship with "Momo" Giancana.' According to Peter Lawford, Sinatra 'almost took a pleasure in flaunting his friendship with Giancana,' and 'Giancana often stayed at Frank's house in Palm Springs.'

The Cal-Neva Lodge was to bring Sinatra his greatest public embarrassment, arising from the reported association with Giancana. The Mafia boss, overheard on FBI surveillance microphones, said he owned part of the Cal-Neva.

The official discovery of Giancana's presence at the Lodge would lead in 1963 to Sinatra's withdrawal from the business and a decision by the Gaming Board to revoke his gambling license.

The Kennedy family also had links with Cal-Neva. President Kennedy's father had often visited the place before the Sinatra takeover, and the Cal-Neva's maintenance manager shipped two ten-foot Tahoe Christmas trees to the Kennedy family each December.

The President's brother-in-law Peter Lawford was a regular, and was to accompany Marilyn to the Cal-Neva during the last weeks of her life. Marilyn's comings and goings at the Lodge would loom large in the mysteries that surround her final days.

At the end of 1960, as soon as Marilyn had separated permanently from Arthur Miller, Sinatra became solicitous. He presented her with a replacement for Hugo the basset hound, which stayed with Miller. The new dog was a white poodle, and Marilyn swiftly dreamed up a name for it. In light of the talk about Sinatra's friendships with mobsters, she christened it 'Maf' – for Mafia. She thought the idea hilarious.

In 1961, when Marilyn flew back to California after her spell in the Payne Whitney Psychiatric Clinic in New York, Sinatra, who was away at the time, let her have the use of his house. According to George Masters, one of Marilyn's hairdressers, Sinatra sometimes used an apartment in the Doheny building where Marilyn settled that year.

Masters said, 'I had never met Sinatra, though I felt as if I knew him intimately from my association with Marilyn. . . . Marilyn would take me with her to his home in the Bel-Air hills – when I was driven there, I never knew where I was going – it was a big secret – or to his openings in Las Vegas. So far as I was concerned he remained as invisible as Howard Hughes.'

In May, Marilyn's psychiatrist Dr Greenson wrote to a colleague: 'Above all, I try to help her not to be so lonely, and therefore to escape into the drugs or get involved with very destructive people, who will engage in some sort of sadomasochistic relationship with her. . . . This is the kind of planning you do with an adolescent girl who needs guidance, friendliness, and firmness, and she seems to take it very well. . . . She said, for the first time, she looked forward to coming to Los Angeles, because she could speak to me. Of course, this does not prevent her from canceling several hours [of therapy] to go to Palm Springs with Mr F. S. She is unfaithful to me as one is to a parent. . . .'

Early the next month, when Sinatra performed at the Sands Hotel, Las Vegas, Marilyn was there. Also present were two of President Kennedy's sisters, Pat Lawford and Jean, married to Stephen Smith.

Singer Eddie Fisher, who was there with his then wife Elizabeth Taylor, recalled, 'Elizabeth and I sat in the audience with Dean and Jeanne Martin and Marilyn Monroe, who was having an affair with Sinatra, to watch his act. But all eyes were on Marilyn as she swayed back and forth to the music and pounded her hands on the stage, her breasts falling out of her low-cut dress. She was so beautiful – and so drunk. She came to the party later that evening, but Sinatra made no secret of his displeasure at her behavior and she vanished almost immediately.'

In July, when Marilyn was back in Los Angeles after her gall bladder operation, Dr Greenson saw her constantly. He now thought, he later wrote to a colleague, that 'she was terribly, terribly lonely,' and expressing a 'feeling of mistreatment, which had paranoid undertones.' Greenson said he felt Marilyn was reacting to her current involvement with 'people who only hurt her.'

The next month, August 1961, Marilyn spent a weekend with Sinatra on his yacht. Dean Martin's wife, Jeanne, and Gloria Romanoff, who were also aboard, made it clear that Marilyn was present as Sinatra's woman of the moment – she shared his cabin.

Marilyn put up a show of socializing but seemed disorientated, was using drugs heavily. Jeanne Martin said, 'I remember going up to Frank's house before we got on the boat. And he said, "Will you please go in and get Marilyn dressed, so we can get in the limo and go." She couldn't get herself organized.'

'She was taking sleeping pills,' Gloria Romanoff recalled, 'so she'd disappear at ten o'clock at night and not be awake till eleven or twelve the next day. We kidded Frank, saying, "Some romance this is!"' Jeanne Martin remembered Marilyn 'wandering around the deck, pitifully trying to find more pills. She'd be unable to sleep, and go lurching about half-dressed, trying to find someone who could give her "reds" at three o'clock in the morning.'

At the end of the trip, as everyone else was planning a get-together ashore, Marilyn simply walked off and vanished without saying a word.

A month later Marilyn summoned her maid Lena Pepitone from New York, to bring out a dress she wanted for an evening with Sinatra. Pepitone was present when Sinatra came to pick up Marilyn. 'He pulled a box out of his pocket,' Pepitone said, 'and clipped two gorgeous emerald earrings on Marilyn's ears. They kissed so passionately that I was embarrassed to be standing by.'

Hairdresser George Masters, who also remembered the earrings, said Marilyn wore them only once. She then gave them away to her press aide Pat Newcomb.

In the summer of 1961, according to Pepitone, Marilyn

had started talking about marrying Sinatra. She became upset when he saw other women. In a few months, however, Sinatra would announce his brief engagement – it lasted only six weeks – to the actress Juliet Prowse. Though there is no evidence that he was ever really involved with Marilyn, he continued to see her until her death. By that time Marilyn had her reservations about Sinatra. As she glanced through photographs of the yacht cruise, she told a companion, 'I don't think I'll give him copies. I think I've already given him enough.'

The troubling question mark over Marilyn's relationship with Sinatra concerns not so much the singer himself as the potential opportunity it gave others to hurt the Kennedys. The Sinatra association brought Marilyn into a milieu peopled by some of the Kennedys' worst foes at a time when she was also seeing both Kennedy brothers. The question is – how much did the Mafia know?

33

Research reveals that mobsters in California had taken an interest in Marilyn Monroe some time before the Kennedy presidency. It had been a predatory interest, probably directed by Los Angeles gangster Mickey Cohen.

Cohen, a New Yorker by birth, cut a strange figure in the history of American organized crime. He was not a member of the Sicilian Mafia, and his proud boast was that he had triumphed in the gang warfare of the forties over who would run the Los Angeles rackets. Cohen, a survivor of innumerable assassination attempts, had murdered his way to an uneasy coexistence with the national crime families.

By 1959, after a spell in prison that weakened his power, Cohen was reasserting his strength. Publicly he was a flamboyant figure, a man who had made it his business to hobnob with big Hollywood names, including Sinatra and those around him. Cohen had put up the money for Dean Martin and Jerry Lewis to bring their show to California from the East Coast early in their careers. In 1951, asked by a Senate Committee on organized crime to explain how he came to have Sinatra's private telephone number, Cohen had replied, 'Why, he's a friend of mine.' With his pet bulldog – which had a penchant for lasagna – Cohen liked to patronize the Villa Capri restaurant, where Sinatra and DiMaggio had once discussed the 'Wrong Door Raid' against Marilyn Monroe.

In late 1959, as her marriage to Miller began to crumble, Marilyn had been in Hollywood more than she had been for years. These were the months of the protracted filming of *Let's Make Love*. It was also the time Marilyn featured, to the surprise of investigators, in the investigation of Mickey Cohen.

That year, the Bureau of Investigation of the Los Angeles District Attorney kept permanent surveillance on Cohen and the Italian mobsters who were his closest henchmen. Cohen was out of jail, and the intention was to put him inside again as soon as possible. The DA's men were taking a special interest in Cohen's involvement in narcotics and his efforts to compromise film stars sexually – for blackmail or commercial exploitation.

The method was old-fashioned and ruthless. One of Cohen's men would work calculatedly on the seduction of a female star, then arrange for them to be filmed and recorded having sex. This was reportedly done during the affair between Lana Turner and Cohen accomplice Johnny Stompanato, which had ended in Stompanato's killing at the hands of Turner's teenage daughter in 1958. Recordings of Turner and Stompanato making love had been peddled for hundreds of dollars each.

One night in late 1959, along with his colleague Frank Hronek, DA's investigator Gary Wean were observing a restaurant – Wean believed it was the Plymouth House – on Sunset Boulevard. They saw Marilyn Monroe enter the restaurant, accompanied by a female companion and two men. Her escort, said Wean, was one of Cohen's 'good-looking Italian boys,' twenty-eight-year-old George Piscitelle.

'We sat out there till about two o'clock in the morning,' Wean recalled, 'then Piscitelle came out with Monroe. We followed their car over Coldwater Canyon to a motel on Van Nuys Boulevard. We saw them go in, but Frank and I split soon afterwards. We didn't see them come out.'

According to Wean, Marilyn was trailed on other occasions, with less titillating results. Intelligence, however, revealed that Marilyn occasionally associated with both

Piscitelle and Sam LoCigno, another Cohen henchman. Wean said he heard a bedroom recording of Marilyn, and assumed the purpose was extortion.

Wean's account received some corroboration from Jack Tobin, former organized crime reporter for the *Los Angeles Times*. He recalled Hronek telling him about the episode. A senior law enforcement source, moreover, confirmed that the Cohen group had been investigated for a 'shakedown' operation against leading stars. Piscitelle was involved, and Marilyn Monroe was identified as one of the Mafia targets.*

The mobsters' purpose with Marilyn is heavy with potential significance. Long before the Kennedy era, Mickey Cohen had links to Sam Giancana. He also met with, and by 1960 probably toed the line for, Giancana's Hollywood representative, Johnny Roselli. Roselli, in turn, knew Marilyn.

Before Marilyn ever set foot in Hollywood, Roselli had been criminally close to two men who figured large in her career. Harry Cohn, who gave her one of her first contracts, had used mob money, procured by Roselli, to gain control of Columbia Pictures. He remained indebted, and he and Roselli were very close. They wore identical ruby rings, which Roselli said was the nearest a mafioso could come to making a non-Italian into a 'blood brother.'

Joe Schenck, the old Twentieth Century-Fox mogul, had served time in prison for perjury before the young Marilyn became his protégée and intimate guest at his dinner parties. He had been convicted because of his involvement in making payoffs to the Mafia – he had personally delivered the first cash payments, wrapped in brown paper. One of the

---

* Reports in the files of the Los Angeles DA's Bureau of Investigation, covering 1961, refer to Peter Lawford having raised funds to aid Cohen's associate, Candy Barr, then in jail on narcotics charges. Lawford was 'desperately attempting' to obtain compromising sound tapes of 'parties' he had attended in Barr's dressing room.

mobsters convicted in that extortion racket had been Johnny Roselli. Roselli may have met Marilyn when he emerged from prison after the Schenck affair. Patti Karger, first wife of Marilyn's lover Fred Karger, said Roselli was a familiar face at the Karger home. He used to come to pick up his girlfriend and her mother, who would come to the Kargers' to play poker.

Two other sources said Roselli knew Marilyn. Joseph Shimon, a former Washington, D.C. police inspector knowledgable about the Mob, said, 'Roselli met Monroe. He met her socially, he knew a lot of her friends, and he knew her close business associates.'

During the writing of this book, a senior former Treasury Department official recommended that I interview Harry Hall, who had long been a 'highly reliable' informant for law enforcement authorities on organized crime. He was also, incidentally, a trusted friend of Joe DiMaggio. Shortly after Marilyn's death, Hall bumped into Roselli in the drugstore of the Beverly Wilshire Hotel. The two men discussed Marilyn and, said Hall, 'Roselli made it clear that he knew Marilyn personally.'

As Giancana's man in California, Roselli had had considerable contact with another woman now known to have been the mistress of President Kennedy – Judith Campbell. Campbell, as the Senate Intelligence Committee was to reveal in the mid-1970s, had a sporadic affair with John Kennedy from early 1960 until at least spring 1962. Within about six weeks of beginning that relationship, Campbell met Mafia boss Sam Giancana. He stayed in close touch with her during the affair with the President.

There are striking points in common between Campbell's story and Marilyn's. Though insignificant compared to Marilyn, the twenty-six-year-old Campbell was a creature of Hollywood. She was a starlet who had contracts with Warner Brothers, M-G-M, and Universal. She too had an affair with Frank Sinatra, who subsequently introduced her to John Kennedy. In that context, she encountered others who were involved in Marilyn's life.

Campbell met Gloria Lovell, Sinatra's secretary, who became one of Marilyn's neighbors at the small Doheny apartment complex. Dr Red Krohn, a close friend of Sinatra, was to become Campbell's gynecologist. Marilyn had also long been his patient, and a frantic Marilyn would call him a few days before she died.

Giancana was murdered in 1975 before the Senate Intelligence Committee could question him about Campbell. Johnny Roselli was killed in 1976. The Committee failed to press Judith Campbell on detail, and did not call Frank Sinatra to testify.

William Safire, the *New York Times* political columnist, listed a number of questions Frank Sinatra should have been asked had he been summoned to testify. Did the mobsters discuss with Sinatra Judith Campbell's affair with the President? Were any recordings made, or pictures taken, of Kennedy with Campbell that could have been used by organized crime for blackmail purposes? Did the mobsters ask Sinatra to introduce her or anyone else to the Kennedys? Those same questions could have been asked of those who knew of Marilyn Monroe's relations with the Kennedys. The leaders of organized crime were indeed watching the Kennedy brothers with predatory interest.

In early 1961, the comedian Jerry Lewis was advised that he was going to be named as co-respondent in a divorce suit brought by the husband of a starlet named Judy Meredith. Lewis asked Judith Campbell, who was working for him at Paramount Studios, to get Mafia boss Giancana to intervene with the detective handling the divorce investigation. Giancana obliged, according to Campbell, and the evidence of adultery was destroyed.

The detective in the Meredith case had been the celebrated

Hollywood private eye Fred Otash. He confirmed the story, adding that a number of other men had been due to be named in the Meredith divorce. An FBI document, scrutinized by congressional investigators looking into another matter, noted that the men included 'Dean Martin, Jerry Lewis, Frank Sinatra, *etc., etc., etc.*'

One of the '*et ceteras,*' Otash said, was John Kennedy. According to the detective, Kennedy's name was removed from the divorce evidence thanks to intervention by the Mafia. It happened, according to Otash, in spring 1961. He received a call from Johnny Roselli, Giancana's lieutenant, requesting a meeting at the Brown Derby restaurant, 'at the request of the Attorney General.' Otash said Roselli virtually ordered him to remove the President's name from the divorce evidence. After a meeting attended by Giancana himself, Otash did as he was asked.

Judy Meredith, asked about this for this book, denied having slept with President Kennedy. The man who commissioned the divorce investigation on behalf of Meredith's husband, Peter Fairchild, maintained that it did produce evidence of her adultery with Kennedy.

The issue within this shabby subplot is Roselli's claim that he intervened in the Meredith case 'at the request of the Attorney General.' Nobody close to the President, of course, let alone Robert Kennedy, personally asked a top mobster to hush up a sexual indiscretion. The Kennedy administration, under Robert's impassioned leadership at the Justice Department, was committed as no other administration to fighting organized crime. Yet the Meredith case was fraught with the risks John Kennedy ran by associating with Sinatra and his friends.

If John Kennedy was about to be named in a divorce suit, along with Sinatra and friends, and if Sinatra and his group knew it, it could be that one of them mentioned the problem to Roselli. What Hollywood's top mafioso had done for

Jerry Lewis he would do for John F. Kennedy, in his own self-interest.

Sandy Smith, veteran investigative reporter for *Life* and the *Chicago Sun-Times,* was an authority on the Justice Department and organized crime during the Kennedy era. Referring to the Meredith case, he said of the Sinatra group, 'They were very close to Jack Kennedy at the time, and it would be very easy for them to do a favor for the President and whisper into Roselli's ear. And Roselli would be very eager to do a favor for the President.'

Sinatra was close to the President at this time. A man of catholic political tastes (he was to emerge as a staunch champion of Ronald Reagan), he and his 'Clan' had been a great boost to the Kennedy campaign. Sinatra's songs, 'All the Way' and 'High Hopes,' were rerecorded as campaign jingles. He helped catapult Kennedy into the presidency, masterminded the inaugural gala, and was publicly seen as the President's friend.

As for the mob, reporter Sandy Smith said, 'It's entirely in character for those guys to leap at the opportunity to do something for the government, or someone in a position in the government, just to have a marker or an IOU that they can call in at some future time. For Roselli it would be entirely in character.'

Thanks to the CIA, it was not surprising that Roselli saw himself as a man who could notch up an IOU with those in government. Just before Kennedy's election, over drinks in the same Brown Derby at which he would arrange the hushing up of the Judy Meredith divorce, Roselli had been recruited by the CIA for the infamous series of plots to assassinate Fidel Castro. The Agency would not break off contact with the Mafia, and with Roselli and Giancana in particular, until 1963.

Early in the evening of July 12, 1961, many months after the beginning of the Kennedy connection with Marilyn,

Giancana walked into a waiting room at Chicago's O'Hare Airport, on a routine stopover en route to New York. He was accompanied by Phyllis McGuire, the tallest and loveliest of the three McGuire Sisters, then one of the most popular female singing groups in the United States. The Mafia boss was head over heels in love with McGuire, who was by now his constant companion.

Waiting for the couple as they arrived at O'Hare was a team of FBI agents, acting on the orders of Robert Kennedy's Justice Department. They were working full-time on the pursuit of Giancana, and this was an opportunity to get at him through his lover Phyllis McGuire. Two of the agents offered McGuire the choice of accepting a subpoena or submitting to an interview then and there. She opted for the interview, and was whisked away from Giancana into a private room.

Giancana fumed impotently for a while, reboarded the plane, then walked back into the waiting room carrying McGuire's handbag and hat. The FBI men hooted with laughter at the sight of the mafioso toting a woman's handbag, and Giancana lost his temper. Today, knowing what we do about the President's sex life, the tirade that followed was fraught with danger for the Kennedys. According to the FBI report:

> Giancana then said he was aware that the Agents intended to report the results of this interview of him to their 'boss', who in turn would report the results to their 'super boss' and 'super super boss,' and he said, 'You know who I mean, I mean the Kennedys.' He then said, '*I know all about the Kennedys, and Phyllis knows a lot more about the Kennedys and one of these days we are going to tell all.* [author's italics]. . . . You lit a fire tonight that will never go out. You'll rue the day. . . .'

What was the 'all' that the mafioso knew about the Kennedys? When the agents asked what he meant, Giancana retreated into silence.

Did Giancana know only about the President's affair with Judith Campbell? Or only about the President and Judy Meredith? What was the 'lot more' that Phyllis McGuire knew?

In an interview with me, McGuire refused to discuss Sam Giancana. She was voluble, however – at first – about Marilyn Monroe. It turned out that McGuire knew Marilyn quite well. They had met in New York when Marilyn had been married to Arthur Miller, and McGuire had lived only four buildings away on East 57th Street. They did meet during the Kennedy presidency, though McGuire would not say exactly when or where.

Asked about Marilyn and the Kennedys, McGuire said at once, 'The initial relationship was with John. And there definitely was a relationship with Bob. . . . And, you know, that's very like the Kennedys, just to pass it down from one to the other – Joe Kennedy to John, Jack to Bobby, Bobby to Ted. That's just the way they did things.' What Phyllis McGuire learned, her lover Sam Giancana surely learned too.

'As in Greek tragedy,' wrote Robert Blakey, organized crime specialist and former Chief Counsel of the congressional committee that was to investigate John Kennedy's murder, 'there was in the President's character a fatal flaw, a *hamartia*, one that left him vulnerable to assassination by organized crime. . . .'

The fatal flaw in question was the President's womanizing. In 1961 and the following year, the year of Marilyn's death, womanizing – and their connection with Marilyn Monroe – left the Kennedys vulnerable to a different sort of assassination. They were wide open to pressure from the Mafia. The Kennedy brothers, it seems, did not take the threat seriously enough.

Taki Theodoracopulos, the Greek ship-owner's son and columnist for Britain's *Spectator* magazine, described a troubling encounter during the presidency with Kennedy brother-in-law Peter Lawford. Accompanying Lawford, Theodoracopulos recalled, was a man introduced as 'Sam Moody or Mooney'. Mooney had been one of Sam Giancana's nicknames since childhood, and this was indeed the Mafia leader.

It was evident that Giancana had personally met both Kennedy brothers. Theodoracopulos heard Lawford and Giancana 'talk fondly about past shenanigans with the First Family. . . . They talked about the girls Mooney used to produce for the Kennedys.'

Senator Smathers, John Kennedy's friend, did not think the President worried much about the risks that came with his voracious sexual appetite. 'He felt that he could walk on water so far as women were concerned,' the Senator said in an interview. 'He did not hold back.'

During the Kennedy presidency, former FBI supervisor William Kane was working on organized crime cases. He remembered Robert Kennedy with admiration, and treasured the cigarette case the Attorney General gave him. He still recalled, in a bemused sort of way, a remarkable episode that took place just before the Labor Day weekend in early September 1961.

The FBI, said Kane, had been told by informants that the Attorney General had spent an afternoon 'out in the desert near Las Vegas, with not one but two girls, on a blanket. Somebody – in organized crime – had taken telephoto pictures . . . and the word we got from our informants was that they were going to use them to blackmail the Attorney General of the United States. And this was confirmed several times over from several different sources. . . .'

According to Kane it fell to Courtney Evans, Hoover's liaison with the Justice Department, to warn Robert Kennedy.

The Attorney General, said Kane, listened in characteristic pose, sleeves rolled up and feet on the desk. Then he simply asked what Evans was doing for the holiday weekend and ended the meeting. 'He couldn't have given a shit less,' Kane thought. 'There was as much of a chance of shaking him down, or embarrassing him, as of flying to the moon.'

Former Assistant Director Evans did not recall this particular incident, but explained, 'It probably did happen as described. There were many times I had to go in with that sort of information. That was a typical Bobby Kennedy response.'

He added, 'When I would take an allegation to the Attorney General concerning the President, he never said yes or no. He was just non-committal. If it concerned himself he was inclined to say, "I can't be responsible for what other people say about me." I was there to give information, not to get it.'

The Kennedy brothers' insouciance was foolhardy, for little escaped the notice of their enemies.

34

Just before Christmas 1961, an FBI bug overheard a conversation between Johnny Roselli and Mafia boss Giancana. Roselli had just been at Romanoff's restaurant with Kennedy brother-in-law and Sinatra Clan member Peter Lawford, and the mafiosi were speaking of Sinatra with scorn. They had hoped the singer would be useful to them as a sort of hotline to the Kennedys, and been disappointed. Now, Roselli offered Giancana the politics of desperation. 'You've got the right idea, Mo, go the other way. Fuck everybody. . . . Let them see the other side of you.'

The same conversation, according to a congressional transcript, included discussion of bugging devices. It ended with what may have been a reference to eavesdropping on Robert Kennedy:

Giancana: 'What I want is something really small.'
Roselli: 'Alright, here's one you can put on a wall, I got a
    guy out there, this is what he brought me.'
Giancana: 'You can't take a big mike like that and put
    it in a flat . . .'
Roselli: 'The FBI out there . . . has got a portable, it takes
    conversations way out. . . . I told them, for Christ's
    sakes report on that thing . . . I got another kind you
    . . . A guy in LA who's got an electronic cap kind of a
    thing, and he showed me that . . . so I got to find out
    what the smallest thing is. If you put it in there, you
    got a receiver? And receive it when you are set up?'
Giancana: 'Maybe a block, two blocks, three blocks . . .'

Roselli: 'How big was your receiver?'

Giancana: 'Like a . . . the box was only this big, maybe three inches by three inches. We were talking "blah, blah, blah." It picked it up. Think about it.'

Roselli: 'Yeah. I'll work on it. Bobby is in Washington.'

Another Kennedy foe – and Giancana ally – had already been using electronic surveillance to entrap the Kennedys. Fred Otash, the go-to Hollywood private eye, had months earlier been summoned by Teamsters leader Jimmy Hoffa and the electronics expert that Hoffa used, Bernard Spindel. Spindel was a pioneer in the field, a veteran of war service with the U.S. Army Signal Corps who – after the War – had at first turned his skills to fraud and divorce cases. He had later been retained by Hoffa, both to bug fellow Teamsters and for defense against those snooping on the Teamsters.

'I got on a plane,' Otash recalled, 'and I met Hoffa and Spindel. What they wanted was for me to start developing a real, in-depth, derogatory report file on Jack and Bobby Kennedy.' Otash agreed. What followed draws on my interviews with Otash, interviews he later gave to the BBC and ABC network, and with interviews with others involved in the surveillance operation.

Spindel was East Coast-based, so Otash reached out for expert technical help in California. He found it in the person of Reed Wilson, an electronics expert who for years served politicians, Las Vegas casino operators, and government agencies. Wilson shunned publicity, and is named here – in the current edition of this book – only now that he has died.

To obtain information on the Kennedys in California, the obvious target was the place both brothers invariably visited, the grand Santa Monica home of Peter and Pat Lawford. Wilson personally installed eavesdropping devices there, he told me, during a social occasion – when the house was filled with visitors. There were four or five devices, and they were activated whenever Otash had information that one or other of the Kennedy brothers were coming to Los Angeles.

A former security man Otash employed, John Danoff – recommended to me by a Treasury Department official as being 'an honest informant' – said he had played a key part in the eavesdropping operation. The team, he said, succeeded in wiring rooms not only at the beach house but at Marilyn's apartment on Doheny and phone lines at both locations.

Danoff's job, stationed in a vehicle parked not far away from the Lawford mansion, was to monitor receiver equipment that picked up transmissions from the bugs planted there. 'Around Thanksgiving' 1961, he said, he 'located the strongest signal about 500 yards from the house', at first heard only desultory conversation, and then: 'To my amazement I started to recognize the voices – because of the President's distinct Bostonian accent, and Marilyn Monroe's voice … Then you heard them talking, and they were going about disrobing and going into the sex act on the bed. …'

As reported in an earlier chapter, the President was in Los Angeles that November, and did meet Marilyn. At some point in late 1961, recalled Reed Wilson, he and Otash reviewed a tape of the President having sex with Marilyn. Over time, Otash told me, some 'twenty-five or thirty' tapes were shipped East to Bernard Spindel.

In the hands of Spindel, with his connections to the Mob and to Mob associates – to Hoffa and on occasion Giancana – the recordings posed a tangible threat to the President. Kennedy's involvement with Marilyn, which had aways been folly, became more so as the months passed. For she was disintegrating emotionally.

35

For about a week in September 1961, the same female voice kept coming up on the call-in line of radio station KDAY in Los Angeles. Tom Clay, a well-known disc jockey, handled the calls. 'I asked for the woman's name,' Clay said, 'because that's the only way you put anyone on the air,' and she said she'd give it to me only if I promised *not* to say it on the air. She sounded really frightened, and I promised, and she said, "I'm Marilyn Monroe." I said, "Oh, okay, and I'm Frank Sinatra," and I hung up on her. She called back, really mad. And three or four days later she asked me if I'd ever like to come and have a cup of coffee with her.'

Tom Clay still did not really believe it, but went to the address the voice provided. He cannot recall the exact address, but the description fits that of the Doheny apartment. The woman he found there was indeed Marilyn.

She welcomed Clay to her home about 9:30 in the morning, dressed in a bathrobe and drinking champagne. There was no question, he says, of a seduction routine – only the outpourings of a lonely, disorientated woman.

'For about three weeks,' Clay recalled, 'I'd go over about every other day and stay about an hour. The thing she was most interested in was my family life, my wife, and my children. She wanted to hear just every word she could about my kids. She would ask me about my littlest baby, whom I called "Rebel" because she was such a devil. I asked her once, "How can you be so lonely?" Marilyn said, "Have you ever been in a house with forty rooms? Well, multiply my loneliness by forty."'

Marilyn's life in Los Angeles was now a dangerous vacuum. Gloria Romanoff, who saw a good deal of Marilyn during her Sinatra summer of 1961, said, 'There were several incidents when she had been mixing drink and sleeping pills, and had to be revived – very close calls.'

After one such scare, a sleeping-pill overdose, Twenti-eth Century-Fox chiefs hired security consultants to make sure the matter was hushed up. For the studio, Marilyn's self-destructive tendencies meant a risk of 'wrong' Monroe publicity and higher insurance when she came to make her next film.

In the same period, the consultants were also used to smooth over a bizarre matter involving a Hollywood woman who claimed to have had a lesbian encounter with Marilyn and seemed likely to brag about it. The woman was silenced with a cash payment, though the facts of the matter were never resolved.

Homosexuality was again a factor in Marilyn's psychiatric treatment that summer. Dr Greenson was seeing Marilyn seven days a week, 'mainly because she was lonely and had no one to see her, and nothing to do if I didn't see her.' He identified two clear problem areas: Marilyn's obsessive fear of homosexuality and her inability to cope with any sort of hurt.

'She couldn't bear the slightest hint of anything homo-sexual,' Dr Greenson wrote. 'She had an outright phobia of homosexuality, and yet unwillingly fell into situations which had homosexual coloring, which she then recognized and projected on to the other, who then became her enemy.' An example, Greenson said, was the occasion one of Marilyn's female friends dyed her hair with a streak roughly the same color as Marilyn's hair. 'Marilyn instantly jumped to the con-clusion that the girl was "trying to take possession of her, that identification means homosexual possessiveness." She turned with a fury against this girl.'

Dr Greenson identified the girl as 'Pat' in his correspondence. Pat Lawford aside, the 'Pat' Marilyn was close to in her last years was her press aide Pat Newcomb. She indeed remembered incidents like the pathetic fuss over hair coloring, and vividly recalled Marilyn's 'frequent rages.' It came as news to Newcomb, though, that Marilyn had any anxiety concerning homosexuality.

As for his patient's attitude toward men, Dr Greenson was to note Marilyn's increasing trend toward random promiscuity. In her last months she was to tell him she was having sex with one of the workmen remodeling her house. Once she invited in a taxi driver who brought her home late at night. An undercover investigator for the Los Angeles District Attorney, engaged on another case, told of stumbling on Marilyn having sex with a man in a darkened hallway during a Hollywood party.

For Dr Greenson, Marilyn was by late 1961 both patient and ever-present family friend. It was difficult to maintain the vital separation of the doctor-patient relationship. Marilyn, he found, took great offense at the slightest irritation on his part, could not abide the notion of any imperfection in 'certain ideal figures in her life.'

'Marilyn could not rest until peace had been reestablished,' Greenson wrote. But the psychiatrist feared that only one conclusion could bring the perfect peace Marilyn sought. Her inability to handle anything she perceived as hurtfulness, along with her abnormal fear of homosexuality – Greenson was to write – 'were ultimately the decisive factors that led to her death.'

In December 1961, Greenson wrote, 'She went through a severe depressive and paranoid reaction. She talked about retiring from the movie industry, killing herself, etc. I had to place nurses in her apartment day and night and keep strict control over the medication, since I felt she was potentially suicidal. Marilyn fought with these nurses, so that after a few weeks it was impossible to keep any of them.'

Marilyn's address book for this period, located during my research, lists no less than thirty-six doctors and several nurses. Few can have been necessary, and all – for Marilyn – represented optional sources of unnecessary drugs.

That last Christmas was not wholly desolate. Joe DiMaggio, who had made the holiday bearable the previous year, came to the rescue again – almost certainly in response to an initiative by Dr Greenson. Marilyn bought a tiny Christmas tree and lights and tried to make her apartment look cheerful. She and DiMaggio spent the afternoon of Christmas Day at the Greensons' home, where – to Marilyn's delight and everyone's amusement – DiMaggio the baseball hero was the center of attention.

On New Year's Eve, after midnight, Dr Greenson's daughter Joan and a boyfriend dropped in at the apartment to see Marilyn and DiMaggio. They drank champagne and roasted chestnuts on the open fire.

DiMaggio seemed 'doting, caring, like family,' Joan recalled. 'As for Marilyn, it seemed to please her to be doing things for him. It was like visiting an old married couple.'

Long after the holidays were over and DiMaggio gone, Marilyn kept the lights burning on the minuscule Christmas tree. It stayed until the decorations were drooping and the tree dead.

As 1962 began, at Dr Greenson's suggestion, Marilyn began to look for a house of her own. She had never owned her own home, and Greenson hoped it would give her security, encourage her to stop thinking of herself as a homeless orphan.

Marilyn began house-hunting helped by Eunice Murray, a sixty-year-old woman with some experience in looking after psychiatric patients. She had been brought in by Dr Greenson before Christmas, when trained nurses refused to tolerate Marilyn's behavior.

From now on, Mrs Murray was to act as general factotum and helpmate. She herself preferred the tag 'devoted assistant.'

House-hunting had its difficulties. At one potential house a woman shrilled, 'Get off my property!' when she realized the would-be purchaser was Marilyn Monroe. At the end of January, though, a house was found – a modest, singlestory home in the residential district of Brentwood. The style was Mexican, like Dr Greenson's house, with woodbeamed ceilings, a large, central living area, and small bedrooms.

The house was a far cry from the ostentatious homes expected of Hollywood stars, but it was what Marilyn wanted. It was at the closed end of a cul-de-sac, and therefore private. It was also close to homes where Marilyn sought a very different kind of solace. Dr Greenson lived a few minutes' drive away, and so did Kennedy brother-in-law Peter Lawford.

The house was purchased using the lawyer Marilyn shared with Frank Sinatra and some borrowed funds. She had not made a film for a year now, and her percentage of profits from previous movies would not come in for a long time. Much of that money, indeed, would come in only after Marilyn's death. She had little ready cash when she bought her new home and was to die with a mere $5,000 in her bank account.

Marilyn burst into tears when she signed the contract for the Brentwood house, explaining later, 'I felt badly because I was buying a home all alone.'

By early 1962, Dr Greenson felt the drug problem was under control, and hoped Marilyn was at last going to make real progress. Nobody, it seems, took note of the odd little coat of arms emblazoned on tiles outside the front door of the house. The motto read, in Latin, *Cursum Perficio*. This means, in English, 'I am finishing my journey.'

Marilyn was almost thirty-six. She had only six months to live.

36

'Goddammit,' Marilyn said, sitting with Dr Greenson's son Danny in the dining room of the Greensons' home, 'I'm going to dinner at the Lawfords' place, and Bobby's going to be there. Kim Novak will be talking about her new house near Big Sur, and I want to have something serious to talk to him about.'

It was late January 1962. Marilyn was indeed about to dine with Robert Kennedy – and it would be no secret. Marilyn was one of several guests invited to be at the Lawford home on February 1, when the Attorney General and his wife would pass through Los Angeles at the start of a world tour. That much was reported at the time in the newspapers.

In her talk with Danny Greenson, Marilyn was looking for political issues that would make talking points. 'She ended up writing them down,' recalled the younger Greenson. 'They were left-of-center criticisms – way back then I was worried about our support of the Diem regime in Vietnam – and there were questions about the House Un-American Activities Committee, and civil rights and so on. . . . She wanted to impress him. . . .'

During my research, I stayed in touch over many months with Marilyn's business manager Inez Melson. Aged and sick, she would often speak of a file cabinet in the garage that had been unopened since Marilyn's death. In 1985, after Melson in turn died, I at last examined its contents.

In a jumble of papers, I found two letters written by Marilyn the day after that encounter with Robert Kennedy. They were unsigned carbon copies but undoubtedly authentic.

On February 2, 1962, in a letter to her former father-in-law Isadore Miller, Marilyn wrote,

> Last night I attended a dinner in honor of the Attorney General, Robert Kennedy. He seems rather mature and brilliant for his 36 years, but what I liked best about him, besides his Civil Rights program, is he's got such a wonderful sense of humor.

On the same day Marilyn wrote to 'Bobbybones', Arthur Miller's fourteen-year-old son Robert. She thanked him for recommending a book. 'Is it *Lord of the Flies* or the *Fleas?*' Marilyn asked, 'I would love to read something really terrifying.'

Then Marilyn turned to her latest news:

> Oh Bobby, guess what. I had dinner last night with the Attorney General of the United States, Robert Kennedy, and I asked him what his department was going to do about Civil Rights and some other issues. He is very intelligent, and besides all that, he's got a terrific sense of humor. I think you would like him. Anyway, I had to go to this dinner last night as he was the guest of honor and when they asked him who he wanted to meet, he wanted to meet me.* So I went to the dinner and I sat next to him, and he isn't a bad dancer either. But I was mostly impressed about how serious he is about Civil Rights. He answered all of my questions and then he said he would write me a letter and put it

* The text of the letter would seem to suggest that Marilyn's February 1962 encounter with Robert Kennedy was their first – which runs counter to accounts (reported on earlier pages) that she had met him at least as early as the previous year. The possible contradiction cannot now be resolved.

on paper. So, I'll send you a copy of the letter when I get it because there will be some very interesting things in it, because I really asked many questions. First of all he asked if I had been attending some kind of meetings (ha ha!). I laughed and said 'No, but these are the kind of questions that the youth of America want answers to and want things done about.' Not that I'm so youthful, but I feel youthful. But he's an old 36 himself which astounded me because I'm 35. It was a pleasant evening, all in all.

When she talked with Danny Greenson after the dinner Marilyn said Robert Kennedy – for his part – had at first been quite impressed with the questions she had prepared. Until, that is, he caught Marilyn peering into her purse at her list of prepared questions. He was then much amused. The story has on occasion been used to mock Marilyn's intelligence. In fact, ever eager to make a good showing, Marilyn for years made a habit of planning dinner-table conversation in advance. In this case, her homework seems to have paid off.

Gloria Romanoff, one of the guests at the dinner, remembered Marilyn dancing with Kennedy that evening, in all propriety. She added a merry detail: 'Kennedy called his father long-distance to say he was seated with Marilyn Monroe, and would his father like to say hello to her?'

Six months later, after Marilyn had died, her business manager Inez Melson found a handwritten letter in a drawer. It had apparently been sent to Marilyn by Jean, one of the Kennedy sisters.

Under the letterhead bearing the address 'North Ocean Boulevard, Palm Beach, Florida' – the Kennedy vacation home – the note reads:

Dear Marilyn –

Mother asked me to write and thank you for your sweet note to Daddy— He really enjoyed it and you were very cute to send it—

Understand that you and Bobby are the new item! We all think you should come with him when he comes back East!

Again, thanks for the note—

Love, Jean Smith

The John F. Kennedy Library, the repository of vast quantities of family correspondence, claimed that it was 'unable' to find a specimen of Jean Kennedy's handwriting for the relevant period.

In 1984, I took the letter to Jean's husband, Stephen Smith, who managed the finances of the Kennedy family, to ask whether the letter seemed authentic. Smith said, 'It could be, could be, it's a possibility, let's say. The script is not entirely dissimilar. If Jean wrote the letter, she might or might not remember if she did. She would certainly remember her own hand. I'll have to ask Jean.'

The Kennedy brother-in-law became irritated as he reread the letter, but said he would indeed consult his wife. Smith later wrote to me to say that she 'has no recollection of ever writing such a letter and cannot identify the document....'

Assuming the note is genuine, what does it mean? It is undated, but there may be a clue in the reference to Marilyn's 'sweet note to Daddy.' 'Daddy,' seventy-three-year-old Joseph Kennedy, had suffered a serious stroke on December 19, 1961, at Palm Beach. He would remain chronically ill for many months, and incapacitated till the end of his life.

As for 'Bobby' returning to the East Coast, this could refer to Robert Kennedy's return from the global trip he was starting at the time of the Lawford dinner party.

NORTH OCEAN BOULEVARD
PALM BEACH, FLORIDA

Dear Marilyn —

Mother asked me to
write and thank you
for your sweet note
to Daddy — He really
enjoyed it and you
were very cute to send
it —

understand that you
and Bobby are the
new item! We all think
you should come with him
when he comes back
East!

Again thanks for
the note —

Love,
Jean Smith

The letter, from Jean Kennedy Smith to Marilyn, found after the actress's death. The reference to 'Bobby' has yet to be explained. Jean Kennedy's name, however, appears in Marilyn's address book. The two were undoubtedly in touch with each other.

359

On the other hand, the Attorney General's sister may have been replying to a note of sympathy sent to Joseph Kennedy anytime after Christmas, or – if Gloria Romanoff correctly recalls Marilyn speaking to the elderly Kennedy on the phone from the party – just after the dinner. Either way, that would place the date of the letter as January or February 1962.

Timing aside, what does one make of the provocative sentence, 'Understand that you and Bobby are the new item!'? Was this a wry jest, uttered in light of some public gossip linking Marilyn and Robert Kennedy? Hardly. It seems that there was no such gossip at this stage. Did this then mean exactly what it said, in the vernacular of the period? It is improbable, surely, that Jean Kennedy was cheerfully acknowledging a dalliance of some sort between Marilyn and her brother – and in writing.

Robert Kennedy's image as the faithful husband, the puritan of the three brothers, long went unquestioned. During the writing of *Goddess*, I looked no further than the relationship with Marilyn – the subject of my book. BBC and ABC television journalists following up on the information in this book, however, would conclude that the President's brother had extramarital affairs with at least four women. One was the wife of a key Kennedy aide. Robert Kennedy was apparently human. Allegations about Marilyn and Robert Kennedy have been made of fragile stuff, some of it malicious rumor-mongering. Both are dead and cannot defend themselves. Not least because Kennedy figures so prominently in the mysteries surrounding Marilyn's death, however, their relationship demands exhaustive investigation.

37

The former Attorney General's personal secretary at the Justice Department, Angie Novello, responded circumspectly but frankly to my questions about Marilyn and her former boss. She would remember meeting Marilyn at the Lawford house in spring 1962, when both Robert Kennedy and Pat Newcomb were present. Dating from about then, she recalled – and Marilyn's available phone records confirm – Marilyn made numerous calls to Kennedy at the Justice Department.

Angie Novello said Kennedy always accepted a call from Marilyn, or would return it soon afterward. 'He was such a sympathetic kind of person; he never turned away from anyone who needed help, and I'm sure he was well aware of her problems. He was a good listener and that, I think, is what she needed more than anything.' Novello pointed out that Kennedy was also a good friend to singer Judy Garland, and nobody has hinted at an affair with her.

Kennedy's press secretary, Ed Guthman, said carefully that the Attorney General 'may have met Marilyn a total of four or five times.' Courtney Evans, the FBI's liaison with Robert Kennedy, recalled that, 'The only place he ever went out alone at the end of the day was when we were in Los Angeles. I had my own suspicions at the time that he was seeing Marilyn Monroe.'

FBI Director Hoover's top aide Cartha DeLoach would recall a memo coming in from Los Angeles Agent-in-Charge William Simon. It reported that 'Bobby was borrowing his Cadillac convertible for the purpose of going to see Marilyn Monroe.'

Some Kennedy associates believed the couple indeed had a relationship. One, who preferred not to be named, told the *Manchester Guardian* reporter W. J. Weatherby that he 'accepted a Monroe affair as a fact . . .'

Tongues were apparently loosened much later, in 1968, on the night of Robert Kennedy's murder. Some of his friends, including writer John Marquand and Freddy Espy, then wife of the writer George Plimpton, sat reminiscing. The conversation, said a participant, included the matter-of-fact recollection that 'there was a good deal of flying about and flirtation, and that Miss Monroe was very much in love with Bob Kennedy.' This witness, a former member of Professionals for Kennedy, also preferred to remain anonymous.

The best evidence on Marilyn's relations with Robert Kennedy comes from firsthand contemporary witnesses. Joan Greenson, the daughter of Marilyn's psychiatrist, recalled sharing 'girlie talk' with Marilyn in her last months. Most of it concerned Joan's love life, but in early 1962 Marilyn was bubbling with excitement about a 'new man in her life.'

'She told me,' Joan Greenson said, 'that she was seeing somebody, but she didn't want to burden me with the responsibility of knowing who it was, because he was well known. So she said she was going to call him "the General." We both laughed. It wasn't so abstract that one couldn't figure it out or have a good idea what was happening.'

Joan Greenson knew nothing of the actual use of the title 'General,' and her guess was that Marilyn was referring to the President. A *Life* magazine profile, published at this exact period, shows that, in the Justice Department, Attorney General Robert Kennedy was addressed as just that – 'General.'

Dr Greenson himself struggled for years to stick to the letter of professional ethics regarding what he had learned of Marilyn's love life. The psychiatrist did so in the face of much scandalmongering, and usually fended off reporters altogether. Perhaps Greenson, a liberal who kept a Kennedy silver dollar on his desk, was simply trying to stop the rumor mill. In confidential interviews with psychiatrists of the Los Angeles Suicide Prevention Center, who were looking into the circumstances of Marilyn's death at the request of the Coroner, Dr Greenson was far more frank.

Dr Robert Litman, one of two Suicide Prevention Team members, recalled that Greenson was terribly upset, to the extent that Litman felt as much a bereavement counselor as a formal questioner. He had studied under Greenson, respected him greatly, and did not feel it right to discuss their interview until after Dr Greenson's death in 1979.

When approached by me in 1983, Dr Litman made available his reports and original notes. Referring to early 1962, he had written:

> Around this time, Marilyn started to date some 'very important men.' Greenson had very considerable concern that she was being used in these relationships ... However, it seemed so gratifying to her to be associated with such powerful and important men, that he could not declare himself to be against it ... He told her to be sure she was doing it for something that she felt was valuable and not just because she felt she had to do it.

Dr Litman said that Greenson spoke to him of 'close relationships with extremely important men in government,' that the relationships had been 'sexual,' and that the men concerned had been 'at the highest level.' Dr Litman said that while Dr Greenson did not actually name the Kennedys, he had 'no real doubt' whom he meant by 'important men in government.' Litman also felt Dr Greenson had not been 'totally candid,' even with him.

Greenson also told another member of the Suicide

Prevention Team, Dr Norman Tabachnick, about 'two important men' in Marilyn's life, and Tabachnick had no doubt the reference was to the Kennedy brothers. The head of the Suicide Prevention Team, Dr Norman Farberow, said that – nevertheless – the team did not ask for access to either of them. 'I'm sure,' he said, that 'discretion entered into it.'

Interviews conducted for this book with neighbors of Peter and Pat Lawford – and with their guests – suggest how Marilyn's affair with Robert Kennedy may have progressed. The Lawford mansion at Santa Monica was one of a string of beachfront houses owned by wealthy people.

The neighbors were fascinated by the comings and goings during the presidency, and some had special knowledge. Lynn Sherman, daughter of Harry, a maker of Western movies, lived next door to the Lawfords. She became aware that Marilyn was a regular visitor from watching volleyball games on the beach.

Sherman recalled, 'She would go out to join in, and just drop. It happened more than once. The combination of sun and pills was just too much, and they'd have to carry her into the house.' Lynn Sherman thought there was an affair with Robert Kennedy. 'Only fools draw conclusions when they don't really know what was going on,' she said, 'but there were many, many rendezvous there. The official car used to drive up, and you knew Robert Kennedy was in town, and then the help would come in and say, "Marilyn's arrived." She'd be wearing, maybe, a scarf over her head, and pants. Sometimes I'd notice Bobby and Marilyn go out through the patio to the beach to walk. From my balcony, it was pretty obvious they were there together on many occasions – there was no doubt in my mind.'

Sherman said her impression that there was an affair was to be confirmed months later – after Marilyn's death – by Robert's sister Pat, who used to drop in for a drink. 'She was complaining about Peter,' Sherman recalled, 'and said, "But we all go through it – look what Ethel's been going through."'

Another neighbor, Mrs Sherry James, talked to Peter Lawford after Marilyn's death. He led her to understand that 'Marilyn had been passed from him to Jack, and from Jack to Bobby.' Lawford was probably gilding the lily – the evidence is that, though he pursued Marilyn, she always turned *him* down.

The producer 'Bullets' Durgom, a Lawford friend, recalled an interruption while dining at the beach house in 1962. 'Suddenly, unexpectedly,' he remembered, 'Marilyn and Robert Kennedy came in. They took one look around them, saw there were several people there, and left. It was just "Hi!" and "Bye!". We looked at each other and said, "Well, okay . . ." I guess they felt it was the wrong place for them to be seen together. And they left.'

Of the people at the beach, the Lawfords were perhaps closest to Mr and Mrs Peter Dye. Marjorie Dye, an heiress to the Merriweather Post General Foods fortune, did not respond to interview requests. Her former husband, however, did talk to me.

Peter Dye met Marilyn at the beach, and remembered her as a sad figure, 'half-doped a lot of the time.' Once, as she lounged on the cushions at the beach house, Dye noticed blood spreading across Marilyn's white pants. As in the past, she seemed oblivious to it. One night at dinner, when a guest picked on Marilyn for some mistake in grammar, she left the table in tears.

Dye came to know the Kennedys well, and saw Marilyn with Robert Kennedy on several occasions at the Lawford house. His view was that 'there was certainly an affair. She was star-struck over him, staring at him half the time with her eyes fluttering. I hate the word "macho," but Kennedy was playing a sort of macho role. He was never animated, never cracked a smile. She was all over him. She told me she was nuts about him. I got the impression he felt the same way. But she was infatuated and scared of him at the same time. I think she was turned on by the idea of mental genius. She liked that type . . .'

Jeanne Carmen, who had been Marilyn's friend and neighbor at the old apartment on Doheny Drive, claimed she witnessed a couple of astonishing encounters involving Robert Kennedy. One evening when Marilyn was in the tub, she said, she answered the doorbell to find the Attorney General standing there. 'He had that expression of not knowing whether to run, or walk, or stay. Finally I got out of the way. Marilyn came flying out of the bathroom and jumped into his arms . . . She kissed him openly, which was out of character for her. . . .' Kennedy came in, and the three of them sat together talking and drinking wine.

There was a further encounter, Carmen said, one so extraordinary that she described it only with reluctance. The background was the friendship she and Marilyn shared with the comedian Jack Benny. (Others confirmed they were indeed friends, and Benny's phone number appears in one of Marilyn's address books.) Carmen and Marilyn delighted in shared pranks involving nudity and – Carmen said – the trio had more than once ventured out together to a 'nude beach.' There was such a beach in the early 1960s, not far from the present Pepperdine University. Marilyn and Benny, both of them usually so recognizable, had disguised themselves on such sorties – Marilyn in her black wig, Benny in a false beard acquired for the purpose.

At the time of the affair with Robert Kennedy, Carmen said, the beard was still lying around the Doheny apartment, 'I think he asked us what it was for,' Carmen said, 'and we told him about the Benny thing and he said, "You could recognize Benny if he had ten beards on." And Marilyn said, "Oh no you couldn't! Nobody'd recognize you if we fixed you up." And she put the beard on him. I put sunglasses on him, and we put a hat on him – a baseball cap kind of thing. And he looked in the mirror and said something like "I could probably get away with this." And we said, "Okay, we dare you! Let's go."'

Preposterous as the story sounds – and Carmen knew it sounded far-fetched – she said Robert Kennedy seemed unable to resist a dare. They went off to the nudist beach in Carmen's convertible, Kennedy in his getup and Marilyn in her wig. It was late, and not many people were around. 'We walked up and down,' Carmen said, 'and sat on a blanket we brought from the car. We just sort of lounged around. Here were two famous people that nobody recognized. On the way back, we really laughed a lot ...'

Checks of Carmen's background, and her own voluminous file on her show business career, indicate that Carmen was what she says she was and had many of the friends she claimed she had in that period, including Peter Lawford and Frank Sinatra. She correctly named the landlady of the Doheny apartments at the relevant time and was clearly familiar with the building when we visited it together. The events she described may indeed have occurred.

There can be do doubt, certainly, that Marilyn and Robert Kennedy were in close and frequent touch in 1962. Eunice Murray, who had become Marilyn's constant companion at the new house in Brentwood, eventually admitted to me that Robert – and on occasion his brother the President – phoned Marilyn in California.

Marilyn's studio maid, Hazel Washington, remembered calls from the Attorney General. So did the maid at the New York apartment, Lena Pepitone. 'I know Bobby used to phone her many times,' said Pepitone, 'but they were very secretive. He would only say, "May I speak to Marilyn?"; then she would close the bedroom door and speak for maybe one hour. I knew it was him because she told me once, and after that I knew the voice.'

Where did Bobby and Marilyn meet during the last months, other than at the Lawford house or at the Doheny apartment? Eunice Murray had previously spoken of only one Kennedy visit to Marilyn at home, a fleeting afternoon visit to 'see her kitchen.' Then, in another interview, Murray raised the figure to 'maybe two or three times,' but said – on that occasion – that there was nothing furtive about the visits. 'The Kennedys,' she said in a later interview, 'were a very important part of Marilyn's life.'

Murray's son-in-law, Norman Jeffries, was employed by Marilyn in 1962 to help with the remodeling of her house. Murray proved oddly reluctant to assist me in reaching Jeffries, but a researcher located him. There was indeed secrecy about the Robert Kennedy visit that he witnessed.

'It was funny,' said Norman Jeffries, 'because Eunice and I were there with Marilyn, and we were to leave. She and I were to clear out before he came ...' In the event, though, Jeffries was still outside the house when Robert Kennedy arrived alone, driving a convertible.

On the West Coast, Marilyn and Robert may sometimes have been prudent enough to meet at a separate, secret location. Police sources, and interviews with former security officers of General Telephone, suggest Marilyn used an apartment in Culver City, in the southwest section of Los Angeles. Three officers recalled investigations in the area after Marilyn's death.

In her last months Marilyn told Anne Karger, mother of Fred, Marilyn's great love of years earlier, that she was having an affair with Robert. Joe DiMaggio never talked publicly about Marilyn, but told his friend Harry Hall, who spent the days after Marilyn's death with DiMaggio, that he knew of an affair with Robert Kennedy. Hall said DiMaggio was 'angry about it, very angry.'

Henry Rosenfeld, Marilyn's longtime friend in New York, learned that she and Robert had become close, although he was convinced that, for Marilyn, the important affair was with President Kennedy. Ralph Roberts, Marilyn's masseur, had the same impression.

During his presidency John Kennedy on occasion used a house in Florida owned by Josephine Paul, celebrated as the first woman to head a member firm on the New York Stock Exchange and widow of a former Ambassador to Norway. Mrs Paul was 'scandalized' by the goings-on in her house on some of the President's visits. According to one of Mrs Paul's friends, who contacted me following first publication of *Goddess*, Mrs Paul had complained, 'They are flying Marilyn Monroe to my home for Bobby, and that is not why I let them have the place.'

It seems that the affairs with the Kennedy brothers overlapped at certain stages. A bewildering notion, but not incompatible with Kennedy legend. According to family lore, it was not unheard of for the males in the dynasty to compete for the same woman. In the case of Marilyn, it may have been not so much a matter of brothers competing as of a troubled woman imagining she could play one Kennedy off against another.

In early 1962, at a stage when she was apparently already involved with Robert Kennedy, Marilyn would still be telling her old friend, Hollywood correspondent Sidney Skolsky, about her link to John F. Kennedy. 'She talked about the President again,' Skolsky was to recall. 'She said she was going to dinner at the White House in March.'

Actress Terry Moore, a former wife of Howard Hughes, said Marilyn told her of her affairs with both Kennedys, and that her hopes knew no bounds. 'She even imagined herself as a future First Lady, with one or the other of them.'

Meetings with the brothers were less than secure. 'There was some sort of problem,' said the President's close friend Senator George Smathers. 'As I recall it, Marilyn got drunk on a plane, when she was going to meet Bobby. . . . They were trying to quiet her down, but she told them, "I'm going to meet Bobby. . . ."'

The President, said Smathers, 'expressed some concern to me, about his brother's relationship with Marilyn.' Here was an irony. The philandering President – who had been cautioned at the 1960 Convention by his younger brother about Marilyn – was now worrying about Robert's involvement.

Marilyn had not only discussed her involvement with Robert Kennedy with friends and associates she met socially in Los Angeles. She had also by that time blabbed about it to the singer Phyllis McGuire, whose lover was Mafia boss Sam Giancana. Marilyn was 'mysterious about it', McGuire told me, 'but when she had a few drinks, mainly when she was depressed, she would talk about it. At first it was really kept under the lid. Then she was pushing him to make a decision because she wanted to marry him. . . .'

At that point, in a telephone conversation with me, McGuire became nervous. Asked what Giancana for his part had said about the information coming to him about Marilyn, she replied nervously, 'I wouldn't want to want to say anything . . .' She did not respond to further calls and letters.

In the last months of her life, the Kennedys most dangerous enemies were only too well informed about Marilyn's involvements with the Kennedys.

38

In February 1962, on vacation in Florida, Arthur Miller's father Isadore received a telegram:

ARRIVING EASTERN AIRLINES FLIGHT 605 AT 9:05 TONIGHT. HAVE RESERVATIONS AT fontaine-BLEAU. LOVE YOU. MARILYN.

That night the old man and the actress dined at the Club Gigi, watched a bad floor show, and walked back to the hotel together. There Marilyn broke the news that Arthur was getting married again, to Inge Morath.

The playwright's father was taken aback. He said later, 'Marilyn wanted to make me feel right. She wanted me to protect her, but she also protected me.' Later that night Miller found $200 in his coat pocket. Marilyn, who had always tried to look after him, had been hiding her own pain.

In January she had been jolted by the news of Frank Sinatra's engagement to Juliet Prowse. Now Arthur Miller's impending remarriage reduced her to virtual collapse. She shut herself away from the world and refused to answer the telephone. Seven months later the new Mrs Miller would bear a child, a joy that had eluded Marilyn. Perhaps if she knew the birth was coming, she was all the more upset.

Marilyn was now involved in preparations for *Something's Got to Give*, the final film Twentieth Century-Fox was demanding under her contract, and one she would not complete. Henry Weinstein, producer of the film and a friend of the Greenson family, had a frightening glimpse into Marilyn's true condition.

One morning, about the time she learned of the new Miller marriage, Marilyn failed to turn up for an 8:00 A.M. costume conference. Weinstein telephoned her, heard a thick-tongued, rambling voice, and said he would come over at once. Marilyn had murmured vaguely, 'There's only one bed. Where will you sleep?' She was flat out in a barbiturate coma by the time Weinstein arrived. A doctor was called, the often-pumped stomach was pumped once more, and Marilyn recovered.

There was a conference at Twentieth Century-Fox. One executive said the film should be called off, because Marilyn was clearly in no condition to work. 'If she'd had a heart attack,' he said, 'we'd cancel. What's the difference if she's liable to kill herself any day with an overdose?'

'Ah,' a colleague replied, 'if she'd had a heart attack we'd never get insurance for the production. We don't have that problem. Medically, she's perfectly fit.'

This ruthless view prevailed. *Something's Got to Give,* aptly named, was to continue. First, however, on Dr Greenson's recommendation, Marilyn had time for a break. She went to Florida, saw Arthur Miller's father and Joe DiMaggio, and then, on February 20, sped off to Mexico.

Hairdresser George Masters found himself sitting in an airplane toilet with the world's most famous star on his knee. Marilyn had insisted on retreating there to have her hair and makeup fixed for the arrival in Mexico City. The trip had been intended as a private visit, but the secret was out.

At the Hilton Hotel, where Frank Sinatra had arranged accommodation, a quiet expedition turned into a state of siege. Armed guards prowled the corridors, and the press bayed for interviews. They got their way a couple of days later at a riotous press conference. Photographers fell over themselves for angles that would measure up to their readers' fantasies. One picture, not used at the time, came as close to pornography as any known photograph of Marilyn. It proved once and for all that Marilyn sometimes liked not to wear panties. Marilyn, looking gaunt, drank champagne throughout the press conference.

Tribute once paid, the reporters allowed Marilyn a few days of peace. She traveled outside Mexico City to the Toluca market and the mountain resort of Taxco. Accompanied by Eunice Murray, her Los Angeles companion, Marilyn bought things for her new house: a table, silver-framed mirrors, and paintings. She also made new friends.

Old Connecticut neighbors had given Marilyn an introduction to a couple who could show her around Mexico – Fred Vanderbilt Field and his Mexican wife. Field, born into the hugely wealthy Vanderbilt family, had been labeled 'America's foremost silver-spoon Communist.' He and his wife, part of a colony of left-wingers living in virtual exile in Mexico, took to Marilyn at once. They found her 'beautiful beyond measure – warm, attractive, bright and witty; curious about things, people, and ideas – also incredibly complicated.'

By Fred Field's lights, Marilyn's politics were 'excellent – she told us of her strong feelings about civil rights, for black equality, as well as her admiration for what was being done in China, her anger at redbaiting and McCarthyism and her hatred of J. Edgar Hoover.'

Over dinner with himself and his wife on several evenings, Field would remember, 'Marilyn talked of having met Robert Kennedy, of how – when she met him at the Lawford house – 'she and Kennedy retired to what she called the den. She said they had a very long talk, a very political talk. She told me she had asked Kennedy whether they were going to fire J. Edgar Hoover ... and Kennedy replied that he and President Kennedy didn't feel strong enough to do so, though they wanted to.'

Marilyn talked with Field, too 'of the things she'd lost, the marriage that had not worked, and the loss of her babies. She said she wanted to quit Hollywood and find some guy – a combination of Miller and Joe DiMaggio, as far as I could make out – someone who would be decent to her but also her intellectual leader and stimulant. She wanted to live in the country and change her life completely. She spoke a lot of her intellectual shortcomings, her inability to keep up with people she admired. She talked of her age, the fact that she would soon be thirty-six, and of the need to get going.'

Field saw that Marilyn drank heavily. He recalled, 'My impression was that, sexually, Marilyn did a fair amount of one-night stands, and apparently got some release from that sort of thing.' He noted with alarm Marilyn's speedy involvement with one man in particular. This was José Bolaños, a Mexican scriptwriter ten years her junior.

Bolaños, a slim young man with obvious good looks, a little too obvious, began a courtship that was more a bombardment. He started by sending flowers on a silver platter (he said it was the family plate) to Pat Newcomb, Marilyn's press assistant. Newcomb, mildly impressed, introduced Bolaños to Marilyn, so that she could 'go out and have a good time.'

Fred Field, arriving the next morning, saw at once that the Mexican had stayed the night. Later, when Marilyn travelled to Taxco, Bolaños followed. He arrived in the middle of the night, recruited not one but several mariachi bands, and mounted an almighty serenade outside Marilyn's hotel. In spite of being warned off by Field, Marilyn was to see more of him.

Bolaños, son of a middle-class family, was known in the film world. He counted himself a friend of the great director Luis Buñuel, and had written the script for the highly praised *La Cucaracha* when barely into his twenties. His career, though, was now in the doldrums.

Interviewed twenty years later, Bolaños was still rhapsodizing about Marilyn. He said he had an affair with her that lasted until her death, five months after their meeting, and that he gave her sexual satisfaction she had rarely known in previous relationships. He also claimed that at the time she died Marilyn was planning to marry him. His lawyer and friend Jorge Barragan had said as much in 1962 within days of Marilyn's death. Those close to Marilyn paint a contradictory picture.

According to the New York maid, Lena Pepitone, Marilyn talked about Bolaños and said that he did want to marry her. Photographs taken shortly after the Mexico visit show Bolaños dancing with Marilyn. She looks ecstatic, but witnesses said she was very drunk that night. Others, including Pat Newcomb, Eunice Murray, and hairdresser George Masters, confirmed that – as Bolaños himself said – he later followed up by traveling to Los Angeles.

Was the Bolaños relationship just Marilyn's sexual swan song? Whatever his motives, Marilyn's mind was now a jumble of confusion and regret.

Before leaving Mexico, Marilyn visited the National Institute for the Protection of Children, which provided for thousands of orphans and deprived youngsters. She had intended to make a donation of $1,000, but then, on impulse, tore up the check and wrote a new one for $10,000. Some reports indicate Marilyn made an application to adopt a Mexican child during her visit. Certainly she would now keep harking back to her own yearning for motherhood, a factor that will shortly take on a grim significance.

At mid-morning on March 2, when Marilyn was due to fly home, she could not be roused. Her hairdresser, George Masters, recalled, 'I had to carry her. I remember lifting her up out of the bed, and carrying her out of the room. I think she had taken too many pills again.' She appeared at the airport in dark glasses and with her hair awry, stumbling. One newspaper reported that her breath smelled of alcohol, that the visit to Mexico had been a drinking marathon.

Marilyn managed an '*Adios, muchachos*' for the newsmen, then walked unsteadily to the plane that would take her back to Los Angeles. She was now on the last lap.

39

It was March when Marilyn returned from Mexico, and it was in March that President Kennedy was to be confronted by FBI Director Hoover with the peril his womanizing had brought. The storm warnings had been sounding for months.

Nearly a year had passed since Mafia boss Giancana had threatened to '"tell all"' about the Kennedys. As Attorney General, Robert Kennedy should have been fully briefed on that outburst. If he was not – and that would have been a dire omission – he had certainly learned of ominous developments during 1961.

Giancana was only one of the Kennedys' dangerous foes. Like Giancana, Teamsters Union president Jimmy Hoffa was being remorselessly investigated. It would be Robert Kennedy's initiative that would eventually – years later – put him in jail. Meanwhile, during Marilyn's last year alive, Hoffa's battle against the Attorney General included bringing pressure on her studio, Twentieth Century-Fox.

During 1961, Fox had announced plans for a movie based on Robert Kennedy's book *The Enemy Within* – the exposé of Hoffa and the Mob that had been published in election year. The producer was Jerry Wald, who had produced two of Marilyn's earlier films.

Within days of the announcement Wald found himself listening to an anonymous caller asking, 'Are you the SOB who is going to photograph *The Enemy Within*?' It was the first of many calls and letters menacing Wald and the studio. The film project would founder in the end, after blatant intimidation by one of Hoffa's attorneys.

In 1962, though, the film was very much alive. Paul Newman was named as the male lead, and Robert Kennedy continued to attend script conferences. Meanwhile, Warner Brothers was pressing ahead with a movie about John Kennedy's war exploits while in command of PT 109. Like Wald, Jack Warner also received anonymous mail. It contained the assertion that the President was 'a sex pervert, with many mistresses,' and the promise that 'the scandals soon coming up for air will kill your picture and you.'

In November 1961 the FBI had received a letter offering proof that the President was an adulterer, 'including photographs.' It would not have been hard to obtain pictures that were at least embarrassing. It was within days of that letter being sent, that President Kennedy had allowed himself to be seen, with Marilyn at his side, at a reception in the Beverly Hilton Hotel.

Robert Kennedy also continued to take risks. Wald, the producer of *Enemy Within,* arrived to meet Kennedy at a house in Malibu and found him in Marilyn's company.

Then danger signals began literally pouring in. On December 11, 1961, J. Edgar Hoover had advised Robert Kennedy that FBI surveillance had picked up information that Sam Giancana hoped to use Frank Sinatra to intercede on his behalf with the Kennedys. According to the information, there had been contacts between Sinatra and the President's father. Justice Department lawyers were now complaining that they did not see how the administration could fight the Mafia while the Kennedys continued a friendship with Sinatra, a man who had criminal associates. On the initiative of a young lawyer, Dougald McMillan, department staff began preparing a series of reports on Sinatra.

In February 1962, while Marilyn was in Mexico, surveillance of Roselli had revealed the fact that another of the President's mistresses, Judith Campbell, was simultaneously in touch with both the President and Giancana. One of the time bombs ticking away under the presidency had been detected, and the Director of the FBI moved to defuse it.

Hoover had lunch with the President within weeks, and it is assumed they discussed Judith Campbell. According to the White House phone log, though, John Kennedy and Campbell would still be in touch as late as August. Kennedy did not take Hoover's warnings seriously enough. Kenneth O'Donnell, the Kennedy aide present when the FBI Director met the President, later quoted Kennedy as saying, 'Get rid of that bastard. He's the biggest bore.'

On March 23, the day after the Hoover lunch, both Kennedys were due to fly to California. John Kennedy had planned to stay with Frank Sinatra at Palm Springs, but switched at the last minute to Bing Crosby's home in the same area. Peter Lawford later said the President asked him to organize the change because, 'it was virtually a case of the President going to sleep in the same bed that Giancana, a man whom his brother is investigating, vacated only three weeks before. How could anyone blame the President?' Sinatra, mightily offended, expressed his wrath partly by breaking off relations with Peter Lawford.

Marilyn herself provided an insider's version of the worry over Sinatra. She told Sidney Skolsky that she had been present at a gathering in the Lawford house attended by at least one of the Kennedy brothers and Sinatra himself. Robert Kennedy, Marilyn said, had held forth on why the President could no longer be seen with Sinatra. According to Marilyn the Attorney General had spoken with great emphasis, had even talked of resigning if the President continued to see Sinatra. The gathering had ended in an icy silence.

Danger did not deter John Kennedy from seeing Marilyn again. They met within three days of the lunch with Hoover, during the presidential trip to California.

On Saturday, March 24, 1962, as Kennedy awoke in the Crosby home near Palm Springs, Marilyn – now in her new home – rose early. The plumbing was temporarily disconnected during the remodeling, so she sped over to Dr Greenson's house to wash her hair. Then she returned, had her hair done, and – according to Eunice Murray – was 'wearing a black wig over the new hairdo' when she emerged from her bedroom.

She left, accompanied by Peter Lawford, apparently on the first leg of a journey to join the presidential party at Palm Springs. Producer 'Bullets' Durgom recalled 'flying down to join the party in a private plane. On the way to the airport I was told there would be somebody else on board, but I was not supposed to recognize them. She was wearing a wig and all that, but of course I knew. It was Marilyn, and when we got there a car picked her up and took her off.'

Marilyn's friend and masseur Ralph Roberts provided detail. Marilyn often used a false name when traveling. On the Palm Springs trip, she called herself 'Toni Roberts', a mix of the masseur's name and that of another friend.

That weekend the President openly entertained famous show business guests, but Marilyn had a role not recorded in the newspapers. Two witnesses offered a glimpse of the weekend and an apparent presidential excursion from Bing Crosby's home, where he was officially staying.

Former Los Angeles County Assessor Philip Watson, who had seen Marilyn with the President at the Hilton four months earlier, was now astonished to meet them together again. At the Hilton there had been no overt intimacy, but Watson now had no doubts about the nature of the relationship.

'I was staying at a private home in Rancho Mirage,' said Watson, 'and I was invited to go to a party at a place that was represented to be the Sinatra compound. It was a cold desert evening, and there were, in a sense, two parties. There were a lot of people at the poolside, and some people were wandering in and out of a rambling Spanish-style house. I did not see Sinatra, but Marilyn was there and the President was there, and they were obviously together. There was no question in my mind that they were having a good time, doing what comes naturally.'

Watson said the President was with Marilyn at a cottage in the grounds, and was receiving a selected few guests. Watson was brought in, as he had been at the Hilton, by a friend keen to help his campaign to become Assessor. He spoke briefly to the President, who remembered him from their last meeting. 'There were only two or three other people present,' Watson said. 'The President was wearing a turtleneck sweater, and she was dressed in a kind of robe thing. She had obviously had a lot to drink. It was obvious they were intimate, that they were staying there together for the night.'

The second witness corroborates Watson's eyewitness impression of what was going on that weekend at Palm Springs. In her last months Marilyn often confided in Ralph Roberts, the actor and masseur she had first met at the Strasberg home in New York. In her darkened room, as Roberts tried to ease her insomnia with a long, relaxing massage, Marilyn would discuss the mechanics of the human anatomy, a subject on which she was herself well informed.

Marilyn had mentioned to Roberts that she expected to see the President shortly. She had asked him to explain how, as the old song has it, the thigh bone connects to the hip bone. During the Palm Springs weekend, Roberts received a call from Marilyn. She sounded mischievous.

'I've been arguing with my friend,' she said, knowing that Roberts would know who she was talking about, 'and he thinks I'm wrong about those muscles we discussed. I'm going to put him on the phone, and you can tell him.'

'A moment later,' Roberts recalled, 'I was listening to those familiar Boston accents. I told him about the muscles, and he thanked me. Of course, I didn't reveal that I knew who he was, and he didn't say.'

Marilyn later told Roberts that she and Kennedy had started discussing the muscle system while she was massaging the President's bad back. 'I told him he should get a massage from you, Ralph,' Marilyn said, 'but he said that wouldn't really be the same. I think I made his back feel better.'

Marilyn was dangerously talkative. The President and the Attorney General, for their part, behaved as though they were untouchable. And now, efforts to get compromising information on the brothers moved up a notch.

40

Shortly after Marilyn's return from Mexico, the phone had rung in the home of Art James, the real-estate agent who had known Marilyn for years – ever since her affairs with Charlie Chaplin, Jr., and Edward G. Robinson, Jr. James, Chaplin, and Robinson, long close friends, often saw Marilyn now that she was again living in Los Angeles. People knew about James's friendship with her, and that was why he received the troubling telephone call in March 1962.

The caller was a go-between, passing on a message from Carmine DeSapio, the corrupt Tammany Hall politician with links to the Mafia, and especially to Teamsters' boss Jimmy Hoffa. 'The request,' said James, 'was that I should get Marilyn away from her house for a while, perhaps for a weekend at my place in Laguna Beach. They wanted her place empty so they could install bugging equipment. I knew about Marilyn's relations with Robert Kennedy – she had told me – and that was evidently the reason for wanting to bug her.'

'I told them I wouldn't do it,' James said, 'and I didn't. To my great relief I never heard any more about it. But I did not warn Marilyn. I figured she worried about things enough, anyway. And if they wanted to bug the house, they would find a way.'

As explained in an earlier chapter, multiple sources – known practitioners of eavesdropping – told me that the Lawford mansion at the beach had been bugged. John Danoff, who vividly described overhearing a sexual encounter between Marilyn and the President there, said the eavesdroppers had also listened in to Marilyn's then apartment and phone. Now that she had moved to her new home in Brentwood, was that also targeted?

With extensive remodeling going on throughout 1962, workmen were constantly coming and going from the house. It was vulnerable for that reason alone. Whether it was bugged will be relevant – not only to what eavesdroppers may have learned of Marilyn's involvement with the Kennedys but to the events of the day – in late summer – when she was to die.

Fred Otash, who had organized the bugging at the Lawford beach house, responded carefully when asked whether the house at Brentwood had been penetrated. 'In the last months of Marilyn's life,' he said, 'Bernie Spindel came out to California and wanted me to engineer the wiring of her home, the placing of illicit devices in the bedroom, and wiretaps on the phone . . . and I said, "No." I didn't want to be any part of that.

'He said, "Well, can you give us some support, some personnel?" and I said, "Yes, I can". . . . Spindel did come out to the Coast and hit the phones. There was a room bug too – it wasn't just the phone . . ."' Otash, for his part, supplied facilities and field operatives and – he told me – continued to ensure that the 'take' reached Spindel.

Corroboration that Marilyn was bugged in her new house came in an interview I conducted – after the first publication of this book – with another Spindel associate. Paris Theodore, a weapons specialist who provided services to government agencies, recalled what Spindel told him later in the 1960s. The equipment installed in Marilyn's house, he confided, had included a minute 'grain of rice' microphone, almost invisible when installed in a wall or woodwork – in the actress' bedroom – and a bug on at least one of Marilyn's two telephones.

The devices transmitted to a 'tape bank' some distance away and below ground, perhaps in a basement. Spindel had developed a system for recording extremely slowly, so that one long reel could cover some fifteen hours of sound. Someone came in regularly to collect the 'take'.

Separately, I located the man who had been Spindel's assistant in 1962, Earl Jaycox. A plainspoken man who had been strictly a technician, Jaycox recalled: 'Some months before Marilyn Monroe died, Spindel showed me some tapes. I was in the dining room of his house at Holmes, New York. I remember he held up two tapes, and said, "I've got to give you copies of these, so you can keep a set." He said they were tapes of conversations between Marilyn Monroe and Bobby Kennedy. There were two seven-inch reels, fifteen hundred feet of tape, which could contain twelve hours of conversation. . . . He said the tapes included conversations with both Kennedys.'

'Spindel made it clear,' said Jaycox, 'that there had been a relationship with John Kennedy, and that there was a current one with Robert Kennedy.'

After Marilyn's death, said Jaycox, he was working in New York doing security inspections for Fabergé, the perfume company, which had premises not far from Marilyn's Manhattan apartment on East 57th Street. He said, 'Bernie made mention to me rather gleefully that he'd just received all the toll receipts for calls going from Marilyn's apartment . . .' Jaycox said Spindel had originals of the toll receipts, which showed calls to Robert Kennedy in Washington. Though the receipts involved only Bobby Kennedy, Spindel's tapes – as Jaycox understood it – covered conversations with the President as well.

According to Jaycox, Spindel even claimed that some of the information he got on Marilyn and Robert Kennedy came from a bug installed at the Justice Department in Washington. Spindel described the bug as transmitting through conductive paint from a device hidden in the baseboard of the Attorney General's office. The 'product' was collected by a Spindel contact working in the Justice Department.

Preposterous as this may sound, FBI documents show that, from summer 1961 till the spring of the year Marilyn died, there was serious concern that Teamsters boss Hoffa had 'two contacts in the Criminal Division of the Department.' While one Hoffa infiltrator was identified and investigated, the second source of the leaks remained a mystery. Was this Spindel's hidden bug, rather than a human being?

We know Marilyn did make frequent calls to the Justice Department, from interviews with Kennedy's secretary and from what remains of Marilyn's California telephone records. The most distinguished corroboration for Spindel's claims, however, came from a man who spent much of his career working for Robert Kennedy.

James Kelly, a former police detective, had worked closely with Robert Kennedy on Senator McClellan's Committee on Investigations, Kennedy's original forum for the pursuit of Hoffa. He went on to become chief investigator for another congressional committee and director of a law enforcement training project for the Justice Department. Kelly also worked for CBS News' Fact-finding Unit, and became director of a Boston television channel. He was universally respected for his integrity as a congressional investigator. His investigative skills had been praised by Kennedy himself, in *The Enemy Within.*

Kelly knew Spindel from 1955, when the electronics expert had been acting as a consultant to the New York City Anti-Crime Committee. Although on opposing sides of the law enforcement fence, the two men developed a professional respect for each other. Kelly was sometimes an overnight guest at Spindel's country home.

In 1979, shortly before his death, Kelly had lunch in Washington with Dan Moldea, the author of an investigative book on Jimmy Hoffa. One Kennedy loyalist was confiding in another, and Moldea was shocked to hear what Kelly said when the talk turned to wiretapping and Bernard Spindel. Kelly said Spindel had not only told him about his 'Monroe tapes,' but had allowed him to hear one of them. It was purportedly a record of 'pillow talk' between Marilyn and one of the Kennedys. The sound quality was poor and somewhat garbled, as surveillance tapes often are. Kelly, however, who knew both brothers' voices, believed the tape was genuine.

Joseph Shimon, the former Washington police inspector, knew both Spindel and Hoffa well. 'Jimmy Hoffa hired Spindel,' said Shimon. 'He was trying to get something on Bobby to blackmail him. . . . The rumor was that Bobby was playing around with Marilyn Monroe, and Spindel was to bug Marilyn – and I knew Bernie was out on the West Coast that year.'

Hoffa himself was asked directly, in the 1970s, what he had known about the Kennedy brothers' sex lives. He reacted with a series of violent denials when asked if he had Marilyn bugged, adding, 'I already had a tape on Bobby Kennedy and Jack Kennedy, which was so filthy and nasty – given to me by a girl – that though my people encouraged me to do it, I wouldn't do it. I put it away and said the hell with it. Forget about it. . . .' Asked whether he might have wanted to use such a tape against Robert Kennedy, Hoffa declared, 'I would not embarrass his wife and family.'

Few would believe that protestation. Two of those closest to Hoffa said he did obtain smear information on Robert Kennedy. Chuck O'Brien, Hoffa's foster son and once-trusted aide, said, 'Spindel told me he was in California working on this thing. He was working on the Monroe thing for the old man and for some political people. He did obtain tapes.'

Laurence Burns, who had been a Teamsters' attorney, said he was 'well aware' that Hoffa got compromising material on Kennedy, but he declined to discuss the matter further. 'It's a touchy subject,' Burns said. 'Hoffa was close-mouthed.'

As we shall see, it seems Hoffa did scheme to use the Monroe affair against Robert Kennedy, and would still be toying with the idea of using the information after her death.

If Marilyn had an inkling of what was going on in the spring and summer of 1962, she had good reason to be frightened. Some information suggests she was indeed nervous. According to her housekeeper/companion Eunice Murray, Marilyn 'had her neighbors checked out' and did not have her private number printed on her telephone. Mrs Murray interpreted that as a great star's natural concern to protect her privacy, and that may have been part of it. The worry, though, went deeper. In New York and California, Marilyn now took to making calls from public telephones. Two West Coast friends noticed this.

Robert Slatzer, who had known Marilyn since the forties, said, 'She said she thought her phone lines might be tapped, and she started carrying a heavy purse of coins around – she tried to go out to a public phone when she had to make a call of any importance. She seemed very paranoid.'

Arthur James, whom she saw a good deal in her last months, said, 'Marilyn would call up every few weeks from a booth in Barrington Park, and say "Please, can we meet?" She'd say she'd been standing in the booth watching the children play – it was very sad. She called from public phones, as I understood her, because she was obsessed with the idea that the secret life she was leading would leak. I couldn't blame her, when I myself had been asked a few months earlier to help bug her home. But I still didn't tell her that.'

Even if Marilyn had been warned of the dangers, it is doubtful if she would have been able to fully understand and assess them. She was now highly volatile, less in control of herself than ever before.

In the spring of 1962 another friend, poet Norman Rosten, was in Hollywood. He and his wife visited Marilyn at her new home in Brentwood. They listened to her eager chatter about the house, made appreciative noises about her tin masks from Mexico and her Aztec calendar. Yet standing there in the half-furnished rooms, their windows temporarily curtained with white sheets, Rosten felt a deep unease. Listening to Marilyn, he heard only 'controlled desperation.'

During his trip West, Rosten had chance meetings with both Joe DiMaggio and Frank Sinatra. 'DiMaggio,' Marilyn said, 'keeps an eye on me, sort of. If I have any trouble, I just call on Joe.' With Sinatra, who came to take her to dinner, Marilyn seemed 'giddy, a bit nervous.' Next morning she called Rosten at 7:30 A.M. to talk about Sinatra. 'He's nice, isn't he?' Marilyn asked hopefully. 'The tone in her voice,' Rosten thought later, 'was not eagerness, but panic.'

One evening Rosten sat with Marilyn as they listened to a tape of him reading his poetry. Saying she had 'taken a little pill' before he arrived, she got into bed. As she lay there drowsing, with the tape recorder still turning, Rosten left. He felt that she was drifting beyond the help of friends.

On Rosten's last day in California, he and Marilyn clambered into a limousine and went to look at art galleries. Marilyn's eye was caught by a Rodin, as it had been seven years earlier – also with Rosten – in New York's Metropolitan Museum of Art. This Rodin, one of a set of bronze copies, showed a man and woman embracing – the man predatory, the woman submitting. 'Look at them both,' said Marilyn, 'how beautiful. He's hurting her, but he wants to love her, too.' She promptly bought the statue – for more than a thousand 1962 dollars – and insisted on rushing off to show her purchase to Dr Greenson. What followed was troubling to both Rosten and the psychiatrist.

Greenson said he found the statue striking. Marilyn, not satisfied, kept touching it. 'What does it mean?' she wanted to know. 'Is he screwing her, or is it a fake? I'd like to know. What's this? It looks like a penis.' Her voice was oddly on edge. Examination suggested it was not a penis, but Marilyn kept asking, 'What do you think, Doctor? What does it *mean*?'

Rosten felt Marilyn wanted answers to the unanswerable – how could she feel, recognize, be protected against, love's tenderness or brutality? 'The truth was,' he decided, 'she was falling apart.'

Rosten knew nothing of Marilyn's tangled involvement with the Kennedy brothers, had no inkling of electronic eavesdroppers or of the sinister forces swirling around her. Sidney Skolsky, her reporter friend, did know by now – from Marilyn – about the connection with the President. She called Skolsky regularly each weekend, in an atmosphere of intrigue so palpable that Skolsky got his daughter to listen on an extension to witness what was said.

'She was lost,' Skolsky reflected later, 'a climber. A child of nature. The higher she climbed the more lost she became. Like Hemingway's leopard on Mount Kilimanjaro.'

41

In the midst of Marilyn's turmoil, there was a film to be made. A few months earlier, Marilyn had sat down in the Polo Lounge of the Beverly Hills Hotel and guzzled three bottles of champagne. She drank them with the paternal assistance of Nunnally Johnson, the scriptwriter of two previous Monroe screenplays. They were talking about *Something's Got to Give,* the film Twentieth Century-Fox insisted that Marilyn make. Dr Greenson hoped the work would get her out of herself.

Marilyn had little confidence in the movie, a rehash of a 1939 comedy called *My Favorite Wife* – the story of a woman, presumed dead for years, who comes home on the day that her husband remarries. The studio hoped to convince her, with the appointment of Henry Weinstein – a friend of Dr Greenson – as producer and with Johnson as scriptwriter, that it could be a success. Marilyn was agonizing over Arthur Miller's real-life remarriage but Johnson – and the champagne – won her over.

'She had slipped during the last two years,' Johnson recalled, 'and she was convinced that this was the one that would bring her back.' When he left California, the script complete, Marilyn rose uncharacteristically early to see him off. She got herself up to Johnson's hotel room by telling the desk she was a prostitute, then drove him to the airport 'soaring with happiness.' Once he was gone, things quickly fell apart.

Marilyn had confidence in her director, the great George Cukor, with whom she had made *Let's Make Love.* The trust, though, soon dissipated in arguments about the script. Cukor felt it was not right, and in early April, two weeks before shooting was due to start, a new scriptwriter was asked to produce a further rewrite. The changes threw Marilyn into panic, and her friend Nunnally Johnson was not there to hold her hand.

Something's Got to Give was doomed, caught up in a disaster greater than the fears and foibles of its star. Twentieth Century-Fox was being bled dry by the financial hemorrhage caused by another star and another movie half a world away, in Rome: Elizabeth Taylor and her *Cleopatra*. The studio had lost $22 million the previous year, and the new Monroe film was seen as a relatively low-budget money-maker. This star came cheap – she was to be paid a mere $100,000, under the old 1955 contract with Fox made by Milton Greene. For Marilyn it was a way to work out her commitment. Nobody got what they wanted.

Producer Weinstein had feared the worst weeks earlier, when he personally rescued Marilyn from a barbiturate overdose. Now he discovered that this was indeed 'one very ill, very paranoid lady.' Marilyn was sent script pages with the suggestion that she put one cross by a line she felt uncertain about, and a double cross – XX – by one she really disliked. To Weinstein's consternation, Marilyn read this as meaning that she was going to be double-crossed. Only Dr Greenson's intervention resolved the upset.

The new scriptwriter, Walter Bernstein, found Marilyn 'at once tentative, apologetic and intransigent.'

'Remember you've got Marilyn Monroe,' she told him once, when she insisted on wearing a bikini in a scene. 'You've got to use her.'

This Monroe, however, outdid her own legendary insecurity. She convinced herself that fellow actress Cyd Charisse wanted to have blonde hair like herself. Assured that Charisse's hair would be light brown, Marilyn replied knowingly, 'Her *unconscious* wants it blonde.'

Just to be on the safe side, the studio darkened the hair of even the fifty-year-old actress playing the part of a house-keeper. Scriptwriter Bernstein was ordered to remove any and all lines suggesting that Marilyn's screen husband, Dean Martin, could be attracted to any other woman.

The studio could fall over itself to please, but it had no way to counter Marilyn's absenteeism. In thirty-five days' shoot-ing, Marilyn graced the studio with her presence only twelve times. When she did appear, the guard at the studio gate would shout to subsequent arrivals, 'She's back! She's back!'

The excuse was illness. Marilyn had since the Mexico visit been suffering from a virus that gave her sinusitis and sporadic high temperatures. Her temperature now became everyone's daily preoccupation. It was agreed that the star would work unless the thermometer registered higher than 98.8 degrees, and executives hovered in the corridors as studio doctors made the crucial readings.

Marilyn was by now cooperative only when it suited her. Hairdresser George Masters, attending her at home, recalled maddening delaying tactics. 'She tried to keep me "acciden-tally on purpose," by smearing cream in her hair, just so I wouldn't make a plane. When I was getting her ready to go out she would take nine hours. Not that I worked on her all that time – she just wanted me to be there.'

At the studio, Marilyn was infuriating. One day she swept out on learning that Dean Martin had a cold, deaf to medi-cal assurances that he was no longer contagious. Virus or no virus, she procrastinated. Billy Travilla, her designer friend, was walking toward the studio exit one afternoon when a limousine stopped beside him. The window rolled down, and a figure in dark glasses called excitedly, 'Billy! Billy!' Then, after chatting normally for a minute, Marilyn clapped a hand to her mouth. 'Oh, Billy,' she whispered hoarsely, 'I forgot. I've lost my voice today.'

When she did arrive at the studio in the mornings, Marilyn was sometimes seen standing near the entrance gate retching. Producer Weinstein, a kind man, put it down to sheer dread of performing. 'Very few people experience terror,' he said. 'We all experience anxiety, unhappiness, heartbreaks, but that was sheer, primal terror.'

Marilyn's anchor, to the extent that she had one at all, was Dr Greenson. She saw him almost every day. As crisis followed crisis, and as Marilyn threatened to fall back wholly on drugs, his sessions with her would last four or five hours. 'I had become a prisoner of a form of treatment that I thought was correct for her but was almost impossible for me,' Greenson later wrote. 'At times I felt I couldn't go on with this.'

Greenson's wife was unwell, and the doctor had repeatedly postponed a vacation in order to see Marilyn through the movie. On May 10, leaving her in the care of a colleague, he departed with his wife for Europe. That very day, Marilyn's 'virus' stopped production. A week later she absconded to the East Coast to make her last memorable public appearance – for President Kennedy.

Earlier, in an atmosphere of great intrigue, Marilyn had summoned designer Jean-Louis to create a dress that was extraordinary even for her. He said, 'It was nude, very thin material, embroidered with rhinestones, so she would shine in the spotlight. She wore nothing, absolutely nothing, underneath. It cost about $5,000. It didn't look very pretty from the back, but . . .'

As Jean-Louis struggled with pins and zippers, a maid told Marilyn, 'You have a call from Hyannis Port.' Jean-Louis knew that was the Kennedy home in Massachusetts, and Marilyn's excitement told him what the dress was for. She started singing, 'Happy Birthday, Mr Presi—' and then said with a giggle, 'Oops, I'm not supposed to say that.'

The Birthday Salute at Madison Square Garden on May 19 had some of the flavor of a British Royal Birthday – it was not held on the President's actual birthdate. Fifteen thousand Democrats were gathering to cheer on their leader and pour a million dollars into party coffers. Jack Benny, Henry Fonda, Ella Fitzgerald, Peggy Lee, and Maria Callas were going to perform, and Peter Lawford said, 'Wouldn't it be fun if Marilyn Monroe could sing "Happy Birthday" to the President.'

The idea had been mentioned to the producers of *Something's Got to Give* before the production turned into a debacle. Though they protested vociferously, the then chairman of Fox's Executive Committee, Milton Gould, had received an imperious call from Robert Kennedy. 'I explained why we couldn't do it,' Gould recalled, but 'he got very angry and abusive and banged the phone down on me. He called me a "no good Jew bastard". . .'

Marilyn, for her part, pleaded a heavy period as a reason for missing yet more work. By the time Weinstein had asked himself, 'Why didn't she have a period *last* month?' it was too late. The producer waved good-bye as Peter Lawford whisked Marilyn away from the studio aboard Frank Sinatra's helicopter.

The terror was on Marilyn again. With Joan Greenson listening, she had sat in the bathtub to rehearse, turning 'Happy Birthday' into a seduction serenade. She would falter, muttering that she would never be able to pull it off. Joan Greenson had then lent her a children's book, *The Little Engine That Could,* about a broken-down train that tried and tried, and finally made it over the mountains. Marilyn took it with her to New York, for reassurance.

In her Manhattan apartment, Marilyn practiced her special lyrics hour upon hour, singing along to a rehearsal record. The gala organizers instructed her to drop in a couple of extra lines of her own, sly little political digs concocted with the help of Danny Greenson. She was still bungling even the well-known birthday refrain, and the President was forewarned by telephone. He laughed heartily. As the moment approached, heavy shots of liquor were added to the comfort of *The Little Engine That Could*. By the time Marilyn was waiting in the wings at the Garden, she was drunk. Literally sewn into her dress, she could hardly move.

Out in the vast auditorium sat the Kennedy brothers. Robert was with his wife, but the President had come alone. In spite of the glamour of the occasion, the First Lady was in Virginia – horseback riding.

John Kennedy sat in the presidential box, feet up on the rail, chomping contentedly on a cigar. With the show in full swing, Peter Lawford took the microphone to start a running gag.

'Mr President,' he announced, 'on this occasion of your birthday, this lovely lady is not only pulchritudinous but punctual. Mr President – Marilyn Monroe!' The audience cheered, but no Marilyn appeared.

Later, after acts by other stars, the brother-in-law coughed, looked over his shoulder, and again announced: 'A woman of whom it may truly be said – she needs no introduction.' On a drum roll, nothing happened.

Marilyn was to be the finale. At last Lawford said, 'Mr President, because, in the history of show business, perhaps there has been no one female who has meant so much, who has done more—' (here the audience tittered) 'Mr President—' (a heavy emphasis now) 'the *late* Marilyn Monroe!'

In the wings, Lawford's agent, Milt Ebbins, virtually propelled Marilyn onto the stage. For a long thirty seconds she collected herself. Then, soft and hesitant, she began:

Happy – birthday – to you,
Happy birthday to you,
Happy birthday Mr Pres – id – ent,
Happy birthday to you.

After applause, Marilyn went on – with no mistakes – into the special verse written by Richard Adler to the tune of 'Thanks for the Memory':

Thanks, Mr President,
For all the things you've done,
The battles that you've won,
The way you deal with U.S. Steel,
And our problems by the ton,
We thank you – so much.

Marilyn led the throng in a birthday chorus, and stepped away from the microphone. Then the President said, 'Thank you. I can now retire from politics after having had, ah, "Happy Birthday" sung to me in such a sweet, wholesome way.'

After the gala, at a backstage gathering, Marilyn introduced the President to her former father-in-law Isadore Miller, whom she had invited along that evening. Later she appeared at a smaller party given by Arthur Krim, the president of United Artists. Arthur Schlesinger, then Special Assistant at the White House, observed her there. He was 'enchanted by her manner and her wit, at once so masked, so ingenuous and so penetrating. But one felt a terrible unreality about her – as if talking to someone under water.'

Adlai Stevenson, then the American representative at the United Nations, recalled getting to Marilyn 'only after breaking through the strong defenses established by Robert Kennedy, who was dodging around her like a moth around the flame.'

Schlesinger, who included himself among the moths, wrote in his journal: 'Bobby and I engaged in mock competition for her; she was most agreeable to him and pleasant to me – but then she receded into her own glittering mist.'

Marilyn was back in Hollywood for work on Monday morning. The next day, a special hush descended over Stage 14 at Twentieth Century-Fox. Marilyn, back from the East Coast in apparently high spirits, was about to do a swimming scene for *Something's Got to Give*. It was scripted as a nude midnight dip, and she first entered the water in a flesh-colored bikini. The cameraman complained that it was obvious she was wearing a bathing suit. Marilyn consulted with director George Cukor, then vanished into her dressing room.

Minutes later she was back, as an electrician called to a colleague that one of the overhead lights was not bright enough. 'Bobby,' he called to the lighting operator, 'will you make 10-K a little hotter?'

Below, by the pool, Marilyn giggled. 'I hope Bobby is a girl,' she said. Then she shrugged off her blue robe and slipped naked into the water.

Cukor had cleared the set of all casual bystanders, but had not said why. So it was that three still photographers, on routine call for the studio, found themselves snapping away, oblivious at first to the fact that they were taking the first nude pictures of Marilyn Monroe since the famous calendar pictures of a dozen years earlier.

Bill Woodfield, who was one of the still photographers, recalled, 'We didn't have any idea what was going to happen. We couldn't really see much while she was in the water. Then, as she came out of the pool, it was suddenly very apparent that she was wearing nothing. The motor drives on our Nikons were whirring, we were taking pictures as fast as we could – and then she was gone.'

The fact that Marilyn had performed naked promptly made news. It brought welcome publicity for the studio, and generous comments about Marilyn's fine state of physical preservation. Her figure, the world was informed, was still a miraculous 37-22-35. The next month, *Life* magazine printed a series of pictures revealing just enough to show that Marilyn was naked.

As they rushed their own films to processing, Woodfield and his colleagues realized they were sitting on a gold mine. 'Some of the pictures showed nipples and her behind,' Woodfield remembered, 'and we couldn't release them without Marilyn's personal permission. So we went to see her. She said, in effect, "Look, fellas, what I want is to push Liz Taylor off the magazine covers around the world. Let me look through the photographs and take out what I want – and you get me on the covers."'

The photographers mounted a slick marketing operation. After Marilyn had checked the pictures (she deleted very few), they created an air of drama by placing the originals in a bank vault. Then they sent a set of copies to Hugh Hefner, publisher of *Playboy*, which in 1962 was the only possible American market for such pictures. Hefner made a deal for a record price of $25,000, and global sales brought the total to more than $150,000.

Woodfield said with feeling, 'It had been a good morning's work. . . .' In 1949, when Norma Jeane had posed for the nude calendar, she had been paid $50 and the photographer made $200. *Playboy*, as it turned out, published its pictures of the nude swim after a delay of more than a year, a decent interval after Marilyn's death.

On June 1, Marilyn was thirty-six. That evening, a mink beret perched on her head, she stood misty-eyed behind a cake adorned with crackling sparklers. It was her turn to listen to 'Happy Birthday,' raggedly sung by the crew of *Something's Got to Give*. Her stand-in, Evelyn Moriarty, had arranged for the cake, which was decorated with two replicas of Marilyn in scenes from the movie, one in a négligée and one in a bikini. The inscription on the cake read: 'Happy Birthday (Suit).'

Later that evening at Dodger Stadium, Marilyn threw out the first ball in a baseball game for the benefit of the Muscular Dystrophy Association. Studio executives, fearing more illness, had begged her not to go. She went anyway, partly because she had promised to take Dean Martin's young son with her. Then she dined with a friend, and went home to drink champagne with Danny and Joan Greenson, sitting on wooden boxes in the half-furnished house.

The Greensons gave her a champagne glass with her name engraved inside. 'Now,' Marilyn said, 'I'll know who I am when I'm drinking.'

Her birthday had been on a Friday. Within forty-eight hours Marilyn called Dr Greenson's son and daughter at home. She sounded heavily drugged, said she was unhappy, and they hurried over.

'She was in bed naked with just a sheet over her,' Danny Greenson remembered, 'and she was wearing a black sleeping mask, like the Lone Ranger wore. It was the least erotic sight you could imagine. This woman was desperate. She couldn't sleep – it was the middle of the afternoon – and she said how terrible she felt about herself, how worthless she felt. She talked about being a waif, that she was ugly, that people were only nice to her for what they could get from her. She said she had no one, that nobody loved her. She mentioned not having children. It was a whole litany of depressive thoughts. She said it wasn't worth living any more.'

Nothing the younger Greensons said could reassure Marilyn. With their father on vacation out of the country, they called in one of his psychiatrist colleagues. Seeing the array of pill bottles by the bed, he promptly swept them into his bag. There was nothing more the Greensons could do, so they left.

The crisis continued all the next week. Paula Strasberg, her acting coach, called the studio to say Marilyn was sick. The next day, unable to use the phone herself, Marilyn got

Eunice Murray to call Dr Greenson in Europe with a list of questions that seemed urgent to her. Mrs Murray said she could not remember what the questions were.

On Thursday that week, her black wig crammed on her head, Marilyn went for a nose X ray. She also consulted Dr Michael Gurdin, a plastic surgeon, complaining of a nose injury. Gurdin remembered being told she had 'slipped in the shower.' Mrs Murray said she could not remember either the injury or the medical visits.

Meanwhile, at Fox, the curtain was falling on the famous career. The producers, viewing the rushes of *Something's Got to Give*, saw a Marilyn who was acting 'in a kind of slow motion that was hypnotic.' Director George Cukor was shaken by what he saw, and top executives were talking about finding a replacement for her.

Dr Greenson called Henry Weinstein, the producer, to say he was on his way home. He would, he promised, have Marilyn back on the set by Monday. Greenson flew to Los Angeles at once, arriving late at night, and drove straight to his patient's house. He was too late. On Friday, Marilyn had been fired. Then the movie was canceled.

'The star system has got way out of hand,' said Fox Executive Vice-President Peter Levathes. 'We've let the inmates run the asylum and they've practically destroyed it.' He was speaking three days after Marilyn's dismissal, as *Something's Got to Give* collapsed in a tempest of recriminations and lawsuits. The studio sued Marilyn for half a million dollars. When Dean Martin refused to work with any other actress, they sued him too.

Marilyn, for her part, rushed off telegrams to all and sundry. Members of the *Give* crew had placed a sardonic announcement in *Variety*, 'thanking' her for putting them out of work. She responded with a message to each of them saying, 'Please believe me. It was not my doing. I so looked forward to working with you.' She reached Frank Sinatra, then in Monte Carlo, and he asked the attorney they shared, Milton Rudin, to intercede with the studio.

Less than two months later, on Marilyn's death, it would be said that she died in a state of depression following professional disgrace. Yet Marilyn did not weep long over the dismissal. Indeed, as the studio realized, nobody could replace Monroe, and negotiations soon began to reinstate her. Meanwhile, Marilyn embarked on a remarkable series of advertisements for herself.

Within two weeks of being fired, she was engaged in lengthy interviews and photographic sessions with three major magazines, *Life, Vogue,* and *Cosmopolitan.*

'Thirty-six,' Marilyn told one interviewer, 'is just great when kids twelve to seventeen still whistle.' Susan Strasberg, daughter of her coach, told her she was looking good. 'You know,' Marilyn responded, 'I am in better shape than I've ever been in. My body looks better now than when I was a young girl.' To prove it, she pulled up her blouse to show off her breasts.

In the few weeks that remained to her, Marilyn sought to show that her body could graduate through sixteen years, from *Laff* and *Peek* to the glossies of the sixties, without losing allure. For *Life,* she swung from the rafters in sweater and pants. At Peter Lawford's beach house, for *Cosmopolitan,* she posed with champagne glass in hand, and stood windswept, in a Mexican sweater, at the ocean's edge.

In extraordinary night sessions for *Vogue,* at the Bel-Air Hotel, Marilyn indulged her exhibitionism one last time. Alone with the photographer and bottles of champagne, she posed in furs then nude behind a diaphanous scarf. Finally she was photographed completely naked. The camera saw the weariness, the slash in the belly – a legacy of the gall bladder operation – but the cameraman saw some sort of immortality.

'Marilyn had the power,' photographer Bert Stern wrote

two decades later. 'She was the wind, that comet shape that Blake draws blowing around a sacred figure. She was the light, and the goddess, and the moon. The space and the dream, the mystery and the danger. But everything else all together too, including Hollywood, and the girl next door that every guy wants to marry. I could have hung up the camera, run off with her, lived happily ever after. . . .'

Another observer was not so overwhelmed. *Life*, which had been negotiating with Marilyn since the weekend of the President's birthday gala, sent reporter Richard Meryman to Los Angeles. He was thirty-six, Marilyn's own age, fresh from the position of Religion Editor in *Life*'s 'Manners and Morals' department. The magazine was preparing a series on Fame, and Marilyn's aide Pat Newcomb had suggested her client as a subject. Meryman rented a tape-recorder, which he did not know how to operate, and made his way to the house in Brentwood. His interview, which Marilyn saw in print a couple of days before she died, stands as her last public testament.

Meryman was sitting in the living room, tinkering with the recorder, when a voice said, 'Can I help?' The reporter's eye moved up a pair of bright yellow pants to the famous face.

'I was struck,' he recalled, 'by how pasty her skin was – pasty and lifeless-looking. There was not much health in that skin. It wasn't white and it wasn't gray. It was a little bit coarse, lifeless. It looked like skin that had had makeup on it for a long, long time. She looked terrific, but when you really studied that face, it was kind of cardboardy. Her hair was lifeless, had no body in it, like hair that had been primped and heated and blown a thousand times.'

Meryman and Marilyn got on well. He had been asked to supply questions in advance, and at their first encounter Marilyn offered rehearsed answers. After all the years in the business, she was still preparing, just as she had for the

Robert Kennedy dinner party. Gradually she relaxed, and Meryman listened as she chattered to a friend on the telephone, her high, squeaky laughter echoing through the bare rooms. The laughter was troubling, went on too long, did not seem normal.

Pat Newcomb was ever-present. Later, Meryman would remember her as 'obsessively loyal, totally devoted. She had made herself Marilyn's last friend.' Covertly, Marilyn apologized for Newcomb, shrugging her shoulders as if to say, 'What can I do?' Newcomb said she only attended the interview at Marilyn's insistence.

Marilyn told Meryman she wanted no pictures taken of her house. 'I don't want *everybody* to see exactly where I live,' she explained. She talked – eloquently but as she had always talked – of her deprived childhood. She talked of acting, of her allegiance to the ordinary people who made up her audiences rather than to the studio. 'An actor,' she said, 'is not a machine.'

'I've always felt,' said Marilyn, 'that the people ought to get their money's worth, and that this is an obligation. I do have feelings some days when there are some scenes with a lot of responsibility towards the meaning and I'll wish, gee, if only I could have been a cleaning woman. I think all actors go through this. We not only want to be good; we have to be. . . .'

'Fame has a special burden,' Marilyn told the *Life* reporter. 'I don't mind being burdened with being glamorous and sexual. We are all born sexual creatures, thank God, but it's a pity so many people despise and crush this natural gift. Art, real art, comes from it – everything.'

Marilyn talked with yearning of the stepchildren she had found and lost in the DiMaggio and Miller marriages. Again and again, she came back to 'kids, and older people, and workingmen,' the people who were no threat, who understood her. When Meryman left, late that first night, he said he would bring a transcript the next day. Marilyn was glad.

'I don't sleep very well,' she said. 'It'll give me something to read at night.'

Meryman went back to the Hilton thinking that he had interviewed a woman he liked, a woman who was 'very smart.' 'I felt very keenly,' he recalled, 'that Marilyn knew what she was doing every minute I was there. She was sculpting herself for me, for *Life*, for the situation, whatever it really was.'

He returned several times. Marilyn read his transcript carefully, tinkered with it little. She seemed particularly concerned to make sure she had said nothing that would hurt her stepchildren, and emended those paragraphs with skill and honesty. Once, when Meryman came by appointment, he rang the doorbell in vain, although it was obvious there were people in the house. Another time, when he did get in, Marilyn went out to the kitchen and returned holding up a little ampoule. 'No kidding,' she said, 'they're making me take liver shots.'

'The last time I came,' Meryman recalled, 'she came to the door and talked about the flowers in the garden. I walked down the drive and she stood at the door and watched me, and called to me, and said, "Hey, thanks!" I felt sad for her. It was very touching. That little girl thing was very strong.'

There was, too, another feeling. Meryman said, 'I was glad to leave. I didn't like the atmosphere in that house – there was something creepy, something sick about it. I felt that it was an island. There was a fortress feeling, a feeling of us against the world, of being embattled.'

Marilyn had given Meryman a line to fit *Life*'s theme. 'Fame will go by,' she had said into his microphone, 'and, so long, I've had you, Fame. If it goes by, I've always known it was fickle. So at least it's something I've experienced, but that's not where I live.'

They sounded like last lines, and have been treated so ever since, though Meryman had no such thought as he flew back to New York, the interview transcripts in a briefcase at his feet. At the same point on the tape, Marilyn had said something else: 'I now live in my work,' said the nervous, rapid-fire voice, 'and in a few relationships with the few people I can really count on.'

There was no more work, and Marilyn was left to agonize about her friends.

42

During the photo session for *Vogue,* the photographer had noticed Marilyn looking pensive when he wanted her laughing, alive. He asked Pat Newcomb to lighten her mood, and Newcomb said, 'What about those two loves in your life?' Marilyn giggled. Though the photographer had no idea who the lovers were, he got his shot.

Something's Got to Give had portrayed Marilyn as a shipwreck survivor who has been out of the world for years. She was to ask her rescuers, 'Who's President now?' Told it is Kennedy, she would respond, 'Which Kennedy?' In real life, Marilyn's friends could be forgiven for asking the same question, as they picked up stories linking her first to one brother, then to the other, and then again to the first.

New York had been abuzz with gossip when Marilyn sang at the President's birthday concert. Legend had since placed Marilyn in bed with one or the other brother that night. Susan Strasberg, who attended the party afterward, recalled that both the President and Marilyn left early – separately.

The *New York Times,* in its normal coverage, said the President returned to his hotel, the Carlyle, at 2:00 a.m. One biographer, Ralph Martin, later quoted an unnamed eyewitness as saying that Marilyn joined him there. If she did, she and the President had a fairly brief meeting.

Jim Haspiel, Marilyn's young friend, was waiting outside her apartment that night. He had been to Madison Square Garden earlier, and hoped to catch Marilyn for a word when she came home. She arrived alone soon after four o'clock, stepping out of a limousine carrying her shoes.

'Her hair,' said Haspiel, 'was no longer groomed as it had been for the show. It now looked like cotton candy, as though she had combed it out.'

Marilyn needed company and attention after she got home. Ralph Roberts, the masseur, remembers her calling him to request a massage. He shook himself awake, and hurried to her apartment to oblige.

Whatever occurred that night, the presidential follies were continuing. Once again they touch Marilyn's life, and there are allegations that add another factor to the dangerous scenario – drug-taking.

From early 1962 till his death, according to a number of sources, the President carried on a Washington liaison with a woman named Mary Meyer. Meyer, nearer to Kennedy's own age than his other mistresses, had known him since university days. In the late fifties, after a failed marriage to a senior CIA officer, she had moved to a home in Virginia, where she had Robert Kennedy and his family as next-door neighbors. During the presidency she pursued a somewhat dilettante life as a painter and friend of the famous. One friend was Jackie Kennedy, and Meyer on occasion visited the White House.

In the 1970s, during a welter of controversy about her relations with the President, one of the Meyer intimates made news with the allegation that she had introduced the President to marijuana. James Truitt, a friend and former *Washington Post* executive, said Meyer took six marijuana cigarettes to the White House on one of her trysts with Kennedy. They smoked together, and the President joked about a forthcoming conference on narcotics. He also showed an interest in drug use in general, according to Truitt, and mentioned that he was familiar with cocaine.

The President also discussed drug use with Marilyn, according to a statement made by Peter Lawford in 1982, when law-enforcement officials were reviewing the circumstances of Marilyn's death. Lawford said that when Kennedy and Marilyn met at his home in 1961 'they spent a portion of the evening discussing pills.'

Mary Meyer did not long survive Marilyn – she was shot dead in 1964 in circumstances that were never satisfactorily resolved. Her name would come up again twenty years later, with publication of an autobiography by Dr Timothy Leary, the psychologist best known for his experiments and advocacy of mind-altering drugs, LSD in particular.

Leary, who in 1962 was conducting research at Harvard University, said Meyer came to see him in the spring of that year. She talked of a mysterious lover, 'a very important man ... a public figure.' She said the lover was impressed by what he had heard of LSD and wanted to try it himself.

Meyer had come to Dr Leary, as a sort of academic fountainhead, to find out all she could about the drug. Intrigued, Leary obliged, and the two met several times in the coming months. Then, a few weeks later, Leary met Marilyn Monroe.

The encounter occurred in May, during Marilyn's hopeless weeks on *Something's Got to Give,* and probably just before she sang for the President. In California, just starting to take on its image as the fulcrum of the sixties' drug culture, Dr Leary was bemused to find himself feted as the guru of psychedelia, the role that would eventually make him a household name. On the East Coast his research had been largely academic; here he found a host of people, most of them in show business, who had already been experimenting with mind-altering drugs. Some of them were doing so with the support and approval of prominent psychiatrists.

The meeting with Marilyn came at the end of a party in the Hollywood Hills attended by a mix of doctors and celebrities, including Jennifer Jones and Dennis Hopper. 'I was exhausted,' Leary said. 'I had been rushed around town, taken to one of the big studios, and then bombarded all evening with questions about drugs. I went to a bedroom and lay down, and after a while Marilyn came in and roused me. I had not seen her earlier at the party, but guess she'd arrived after I'd gone to bed. She wanted to meet me, and she wanted me to introduce her to LSD.'

Leary tried to explain that LSD was not a drug one took nonchalantly. None was taken that night – indeed it was Marilyn who pressed a drug on Leary. She gave him two pills she called 'Randy-Mandys.' That was the street name for Mandrax, a sedative popular among drug users in the early sixties because it gives a sense of euphoria when combined with alcohol. Marilyn said she had got hers 'from a Mexican boyfriend,' and joked that they were aspirin. The pills sent Dr Leary off into a deep sleep.

Marilyn called Leary's hostess in the morning and they lunched at a restaurant on Sunset Boulevard. Leary, now awake and interested, found Marilyn 'full of contradictions. Funny and playful, but very shrewd. We talked about drugs, and I told Marilyn about a project I was setting up in Mexico that summer. She said she wanted to come on down and join us. But she also wanted to try LSD then and there.' Leary said Marilyn seemed 'wobbly,' but he had no idea that she was under constant psychiatric care, nor how disturbed she was.

That night Leary did introduce Marilyn to LSD – 'a very small dose.' They drove together to the wide beach at Venice, and walked by the sea in the dark. 'It was joyous,' said Leary.

Dr Oscar Janiger, who was to become Associate Clinical Professor of Psychology at the California School of Medicine, was a central figure in West Coast drug experimentation in the early sixties. He confirmed details of Leary's visit to Los Angeles that summer, and remembered that Leary's hostess, Virginia Dennison, gave Marilyn yoga lessons. Dr Janiger said, 'People I was working with knew Marilyn well.'

Leary's account indicates that two of the President's

women – Meyer and Marilyn – were seeking out LSD at the same period. The notion of Marilyn playing with LSD, in her mental condition and at that point in her life, is horrifying.

Early in the week after her dismissal by Twentieth Century-Fox, Marilyn flew to New York. Also that week or soon afterward, she met for the last time with W. J. Weatherby, the British reporter she had been seeing occasionally since *The Misfits*. They had not met since the previous year. 'I could see the change in her as I walked toward her,' Weatherby recalled. 'There was a delicate, worn air about her now. . . . I couldn't believe that the woman I saw had changed so much.'

Weatherby and Marilyn talked about Arthur Miller's re-marriage, and then Marilyn said mysteriously, 'Maybe I'll get married again myself.' She seemed serious, then vouchsafed, 'Only problem is, he's married right now. And he's famous; so we have to meet in secret.' She added that her lover was in politics in Washington. Then, minutes later, she was sing-ing the President's praises. She thought he was 'going to be another Lincoln.' Later, in Central Park, Weatherby dared to ask whether Marilyn knew the President personally. She did not reply, and went on throwing potato chips to the squirrels.

Henry Weinstein, producer of *Something's Got to Give*, dated the beginning of Marilyn's slide to death not to her firing on June 8 but to the previous weekend when – as we know from the Greenson children – she was plunged in black despair.

'Something happened that weekend,' Weinstein said, 'and what it was nobody really knows. I mean, people *do* know. I think the only one who really knew what happened is Pat Newcomb.'

Newcomb, the press aide, spent a great deal of time with Marilyn when she collapsed. According to Mrs Murray, she brought Marilyn sedatives to replace those taken by Dr

Greenson's stand-in. It even occurred to Norman Jeffries, Mrs Murray's son-in-law, that Marilyn 'seemed to be a prisoner in her bedroom.'

Pat Newcomb, for her part, vigorously denied ever having supplied medication, and rejected the notion that Marilyn was a 'prisoner'. Although a personal friend of the Kennedys since before her time with the actress, she threw no light on what caused the sudden crisis. Yet Marilyn's total collapses during her life can generally be linked to some specific disaster: the loss of a baby or the failure of a relationship. Had Marilyn's relationship with the Kennedy brothers started to collapse?

On June 13, Marilyn sent an odd, wordy telegram. It went to Robert Kennedy's home in Virginia, and read:

DEAR ATTORNEY GENERAL AND MRS ROBERT KEN-
NEDY: I WOULD HAVE BEEN DELIGHTED TO HAVE
ACCEPTED YOUR INVITATION HONORING PAT AND
PETER LAWFORD. UNFORTUNATELY I AM INVOLVED
IN A FREEDOM RIDE PROTESTING THE LOSS OF
THE MINORITY RIGHTS BELONGING TO THE FEW
REMAINING EARTHBOUND STARS. AFTER ALL, ALL
WE DEMANDED WAS OUR RIGHT TO TWINKLE.

MARILYN MONROE

Somewhat improbably, Marilyn was refusing a Kennedy invitation. Two weeks later, however, she did meet Robert Kennedy. He flew into Los Angeles on the evening of June 26, as part of a cross-country journey to discuss organized crime. FBI documents do not mention his wife, Ethel, as being with him.

Marilyn met the Attorney General over dinner at the Lawford house, arriving two and a half hours late. The next day, according to Mrs Murray and one of the neighbors, he visited Marilyn at home.

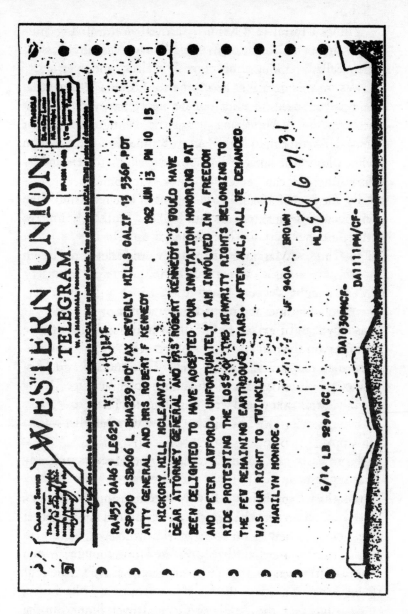

The rambling telegram to Robert and Ethel Kennedy, less than two months before Marilyn's death.

Eunice Murray said Kennedy arrived alone, driving himself in an open Cadillac convertible. 'He was casually dressed,' she recalled, 'looking almost boyish in slacks and open shirt.' It was on this occasion, according to Norman Jeffries, that he was supposed 'to clear out before Kennedy came.' But he happened to be leaving just as the distinguished visitor arrived. According to Mrs Murray, Kennedy stayed about an hour. She said Marilyn 'did not seem bubbly or excited by his visit.'

By most accounts, Marilyn seemed dejected from then on. According to Peter Lawford his wife, Pat, the Kennedys' sister, did her best to cheer Marilyn up. On several occasions the Lawfords invited her to stay overnight at the beach house, and once they were made acutely aware of her misery.

'I'm a light sleeper,' Lawford said in a brief interview for this book, 'and one night I woke up for some reason. It was dawn, and I looked out of the window and saw a figure standing on the balcony. It was Marilyn with a robe on, and it seemed like she was drunk, and I went out and said, "Are you okay?" There were tears streaming down her face. Pat by then had woken too, and we brought her in and talked to her.'

Peter Lawford said he did not know why Marilyn was so unhappy.

From early July, Marilyn turned to her doctors in a way that suggests desperation or hypochondria, or both. She saw psychiatrist Greenson on twenty-seven of thirty-five days, and her physician Dr Engelberg on thirteen. Assuming the doctors' records are correct, Marilyn was therefore in Los Angeles almost all that time. We know, though, from a number of witnesses, that she made at least three trips out of town – two of them to the Cal-Neva Lodge at Lake Tahoe, the casino resort reportedly owned jointly by Frank Sinatra and Mafia boss Sam Giancana.

Peter Lawford said he and his wife took Marilyn to the Cal-Neva three weeks before she died, when Sinatra was performing there. She stayed in Chalet 52, one of the cluster of cabins used by Sinatra and his guests. From the housekeeper to the bellboys, the staff remembered a sad, withdrawn figure.

Mae Shoopman, then a cashier at the Lodge, recalled, 'She wasn't well. She kept herself disguised pretty much, kept herself covered with a black scarf, and stayed in her room a good deal of the time. In fact, everyone became alarmed about it, because she would go to sleep with the telephone at her ear open to the switchboard. I think she was frightened, and it was a way of not being alone.'

It was thanks to the telephone operator, perhaps, that Marilyn did not die that weekend. Sitting up in the casino office, as the music blared and the late-shift croupiers hovered over the tables, the operator heard strange sounds and stertorous breathing on the line from Chalet 52. She called the manager, who raised the alarm, and Marilyn made it through another overdose.

Peter Lawford told me he knew nothing about the crisis until morning. In one statement to the police he said his wife Pat was in Marilyn's room that night, and realized the danger when Marilyn fell out of bed. Gloria Romanoff, who was also there that weekend, said, 'I think some of this gets a bit hazy because they were all drinking a good deal.'

As Romanoff recalled it, 'Marilyn drank champagne and some vodka, and would take sleeping pills. The Lawfords walked her about, after midnight, trying to keep her awake, and I think they called Frank in, too. I remember Marilyn telling me one of her problems was that she'd taken pills so long they didn't work for her the way they did for other people. So she'd begin about nine in the evening, and build up that lethal combination of booze and pills.'

In this pathetic state, Marilyn was whisked over the mountains to the airport at Reno, on to Frank Sinatra's private plane – which was making news that year as a sort of flying pleasure-dome – and back to the care of her doctors and her companion, Eunice Murray.

Murray said she recalled no trips to Tahoe. Nor did she have any recall at all on another vital issue – the possible real trigger for this week of Marilyn's despair. She may have been pregnant again.

'I'd like to be a complete woman, and have a child,' Marilyn had said early in the year during her trip to Mexico. She was still hoping, after all the miscarriages and all the damaging abortions. She went on talking about babies throughout her last months, and seemed to dwell on it in one of her last interviews.

In late June she told the photo-journalist George Barris, 'A woman must have to love a man with all her heart to have his child. I mean, especially when she's not married to him. And when a man leaves a woman when she tells him she's going to have his baby, when he doesn't marry her, that must hurt a woman very much, deep down inside.'

Marilyn was talking less than a month after her abrupt collapse into a haze of drugs. Several people, interviewed during research for this book, believed Marilyn had been pregnant a few weeks earlier.

Arthur James, mutual friend of Marilyn with Charlie Chaplin, Jr., and Edward G. Robinson, Jr., said Marilyn came to his house at Laguna Beach for a weekend 'about a month, maybe six weeks' before her death. Chaplin and Robinson were both present.

'It was obvious the poor girl was in trouble,' said James, 'even by her standards. She had told us about the Kennedy thing previously, and now she was sick. Marilyn said she had lost a baby, and I thought there had been a miscarriage.'

Word went around that Marilyn had had an abortion. Bill Woodfield, one of the photographers on call for *Something's Got to Give*, recalled one of Marilyn's dressing-room team

– he thought it was hairdresser Agnes Flanagan – telling him that Marilyn was 'looking so poorly' because she had just had an abortion. He was told it had been performed in Mexico.

The same suggestion was made by Fred Otash, the private investigator who was allegedly engaged in surveillance of Marilyn at this period. He said he learned from a police source that there had been an abortion. 'An American doctor went down to Tijuana to do it,' Otash asserted, 'which made Marilyn safe medically and made the doctor safe from U.S. law.'

Bordertown abortions were commonplace in 1962, when the operation was still illegal in the United States. Ironically, on the day Marilyn died, an American woman would make international news by traveling for an abortion to Sweden, where the operation was legal.

There is no medical evidence to support the theory that Marilyn had been pregnant. Her autopsy, on August 5, would offer no information one way or the other, but neither a recent miscarriage nor a properly performed abortion would necessarily leave traces. Marilyn's phone records do show that she was placing calls to Cedars-Sinai Hospital during June, which may or may not be significant.

The sources so far quoted on the alleged pregnancy all said they were told the father was one of the Kennedy brothers, but differed on whether he was John or Robert. Arthur James, who learned of a 'miscarriage' from Marilyn herself, understood that Robert was responsible.

Two other sources, well placed to know what was happening to Marilyn, become relevant here. In 1962, Michael Selsman worked for Arthur Jacobs, the close friend of Marilyn who ran her press relations. He was thus a colleague of Pat Newcomb, who personally handled Marilyn.

Selsman said he heard Newcomb and Jacobs discussing Marilyn's affairs with the President and – subsequently – with Robert. They were concerned, he said, that exposure of the relationships would damage the Kennedys politically. Selsman said he too heard that Marilyn had an abortion in her last months.

Arthur Jacobs, who was also a prominent Hollywood producer, was dead when this book was being prepared. His widow, Natalie, however, became a significant source on Marilyn's final year. 'Everyone that knew her,' said Natalie Jacobs, 'knew about her and the Kennedys. It was so pathetic in those last months. Sometimes Arthur and I would stay at her house till five or six in the morning talking to her, to try to stop her drinking or taking pills.'

According to Natalie Jacobs, 'Arthur absolutely knew about the affair with the President. She continued, 'Marilyn was madly pursuing the President. I think he was enamored of her, but it was a passing thing. There's a children's book called *A Wrinkle in Time,* and I think that's what she was for him, a wrinkle in time. I am not clear what the relationship was with Bobby, but he too came to see her here.'

Natalie Jacobs also heard about Marilyn's supposed pregnancy shortly before she died. 'Marilyn said she had had a miscarriage. Arthur did not know whether to believe her or whether she had fantasized it.'

Marilyn's friend Arthur James, the only person who claimed to have heard about the pregnancy direct from Marilyn, was still not sure what to make of it. He knew she had serious gynecological problems, and knew she would sometimes go for months without having a period.

Doctors consulted for this book said that people using drugs and alcohol lose touch with reality. Marilyn was on occasion prone to fantasizing, and – not least because she appears to have been its main source – the pregnancy story must be treated with caution. Truth or fantasy, it made the danger of potential scandal about Marilyn even greater. Now at last, almost certainly, the Kennedys tried to distance themselves from her.

Natalie Jacobs said that Marilyn desperately tried to get through to the brothers in her last weeks but was fobbed off. 'I believe that was the cause of her final despair,' said Mrs Jacobs, 'and so did my husband.'

During the weekend at Laguna, some six weeks before her death, Marilyn's friend Arthur James got the same impression. 'She spoke quite openly,' he said, 'with nothing but love and admiration for the Kennedys. But she was terribly hurt when she was told never to call or contact them – either John or Robert – again.'

Marilyn may now have seen a bitter irony in the fact that she had sung to President Kennedy, at his birthday gala, to the tune of 'Thanks for the Memory.' Because her link to the Kennedys, it appears, was now severed.

43

Marilyn had been calling Robert Kennedy at the Justice Department using an assumed name, according to the Attorney General's biographer, Arthur Schlesinger. Kennedy had given her a 'special number' to call, according to Marilyn's companion Eunice Murray.

The phone records for Marilyn's home numbers have long been missing, but research for this book recovered some of them, covering June to early August 1962. They consist of a list of calls, compiled by police during a visit to the General Telephone Company after Marilyn's death. They show that, as of June 25, Marilyn was no longer calling a special number but the main Washington switchboard number of the Justice Department – RE7-8200.

The call listed for June 25 lasted only a minute and presumably contained no significant conversation. As Marilyn was probably told, Robert Kennedy was already in the air headed for the West Coast by way of Chicago. She would see him the next night for dinner at the Lawford house, and the day after that, during the visit to Marilyn's home Eunice Murray and her son-in-law witnessed.

There were two more calls to the Justice Department, both very brief: on July 2, when Kennedy had just returned to Washington. Another occurred on July 16, when the Attorney General was about to leave for Las Vegas, and two more the following day.

During this month Marilyn was in repeated contact with Robert Slatzer, the lover of years earlier who had always kept

June 20	Brooklyn, N.Y.	875-1367
June 20	Brooklyn, N.Y.	Mrs. Rosten - Collect
June 25	Washington	RE 7-8200
July 2	Washington	RE 7-8200
July 2	Washington	RE 7-8200
July 6	San Diego	CR 6-1890
July 6	San Diego	DiMaggio - Collect
July 9	New York City	EL 5-2288
July 9	New York City	NU 3-6522
July 16	Washington	RE 7-8200
July 16	New York City	CR 3-7792
July 17	Fullerton	TR 1-3190
July 17	Washington	RE 7-8200
July 17	Washington	RE 7-8200

LONG DISTANCE

MUNROE PHONE CALLS — POB-16471
FROM TWO PHONES 6400 SUNSET
476-1890 & 472-4830 Hollywood

7/18	NYC	BR. 91175	3
7/23	WASH (DC)	RE. 78200	1
7/28	NYC	PL. 92497	10
7/30	NYC	LA. 41000	1
7/30	WASH. (DC)	RE. 78200	8
7/30	BKLN	TR. 51367	13
7/31	NYC.	TR. 72212	11
8/3	BKLN	TR. 51367	32
8/4	ANAHE	GR. 61890	5

Kennedy?

4830

Parts of Marilyn's phone records, long missing after her death, and retrieved by the author. The lists each cover one of the actress's two telephones. Note the eight calls to Washington RE7-8200, a 1962 number of the Justice Department. 'Kennedy?' (in the right-hand margin) has been written in by a detective.

421

in touch. As noted earlier,* I traced a number of witnesses who confirmed the Slatzer relationship existed, and who were on occasion present when Marilyn called him. In 1974, in his book about Marilyn, Slatzer said Marilyn told him in her last weeks about her affairs with the Kennedy brothers, and how the liaison with Robert was collapsing.[†]

Slatzer's book was received with skepticism, not least because he used the dubious technique of wholesale reconstructions of long conversations he could not possibly have remembered verbatim. In the context of the new information gathered for this book, his claims seem more credible.

Slatzer quoted Marilyn as saying of Robert Kennedy, 'He's been ignoring me. I've been trying to reach him on the telephone, and I just can't get to him.' Slatzer said Marilyn was cut off from Kennedy after he had the number of his private line changed. He said he heard this from Marilyn in the first two weeks of July 1962, the very period that the phone records show Marilyn started making repeated calls to the main Justice Department number. In judging Slatzer's veracity, it goes in his favor that he made his allegations years before the discovery of the telephone logs.

In the course of intensive interviews, Slatzer estimated

---

* See Chapter 11, p. 108.

† In 1972, when he was first ready to publish his Monroe book, which dealt at length with the Kennedy aspects of her story, Slatzer received a specific threat that his life would be in danger if publication went ahead. His then publisher, a minor California company, also received a frightening warning. Two men came to the home of Slatzer's editor, Thom Montgomery, and beat up the man who answered his door in the belief that they were attacking Montgomery. Montgomery, who confirmed to me that this incident and other threats occurred, said the company almost simultaneously went out of business, summarily bought out in a way that executives thought part of an operation to suppress the pending Monroe book. The book was published two years later by Pinnacle House, without incident.

dates of his contacts with Marilyn in a way that fits wholly with the phone records and other details, none of which Slatzer knew. Indeed, as this book went into its first edition, he was still unaware that the telephone logs existed.

In the summer of 1962, Slatzer produced a wildlife series for television, dividing his time between Hollywood and a cutting room in Columbus, Ohio. In mid-June, he said, he visited Marilyn at home. Like others, he had heard rumors about Marilyn and the Kennedys, and asked her about them.

Marilyn startled Slatzer by admitting that she was having an affair with the younger Kennedy, and even seemed to be deluding herself that she might one day marry him – shades of her hints to British reporter Weatherby. Slatzer was appalled. He told her it was ludicrous to imagine the Attorney General would wreck his political career and gravely endanger the President's, by doing any such thing. Monroe, however, was in no mood to listen to common sense. Slatzer said he simply warned her some more, and assumed the affair was headed for disaster.

Several weeks later – Slatzer reckoned it was about ten days after the Independence Day holiday, and thus just before or after her miseries at the Cal-Neva Lodge – Marilyn called him from a pay phone to arrange a meeting, around the corner from her house. That evening they drove up the coast to the beach at Point Dume, which they had visited in the past. Marilyn, said Slatzer, seemed weary and tense. When she blurted out that Robert Kennedy had been refusing to take her phone calls, Slatzer again advised her to put the whole thing behind her.

Marilyn alternated between tears and anger. According to Slatzer, she suddenly fished in an outsize shopping bag and produced – from a clutter of pill bottles and makeup paraphernalia – some papers held together with a rubber band. They were handwritten, on Justice Department stationery, and Marilyn said they were notes to her from Robert

Kennedy. She allowed Slatzer only a glimpse, but also showed him 'a small red book.'

Marilyn let Slatzer peruse the book, which she called her 'diary.' He said it contained notes of conversations with Kennedy and included references to Cuba, the Bay of Pigs invasion of the previous year, and to Kennedy's determination to put Teamsters' leader Jimmy Hoffa in jail.

Incredulous, Slatzer asked Marilyn why she had made the notes. 'Because,' Marilyn replied, 'Bobby liked to talk about political things. He got mad at me one day because he said I didn't remember anything he told me.'

Many scorned Slatzer's entire story because of his claim about the diary. Marilyn, they claimed, was not organized enough to keep any sort of record. They were wrong. For years Marilyn kept scribbled notes precisely because she was disorganized. Slatzer said the book he saw was 'not a day-to-day log but a record of highlights of Marilyn's activities,' – and that was in character.

Marilyn had bought herself a 'daily diary and memo book' as early as 1951, according to *Time* correspondent Ezra Goodman. Reporter James Bacon was amused to see her using it to write down something witty he had said. In 1955, Amy Greene noticed Marilyn carrying around 'a leather-covered diary with a little key,' and Susan Strasberg remembered her as 'a great note-taker.' As late as 1960, Richard Gehman observed her jotting in a notebook. Marilyn was still scribbling during her acquaintance with Robert Kennedy, and he may have known it.

According to Jeanne Carmen, Marilyn's neighbor at the Doheny apartment, 'She did keep some sort of diary. She would say, "Oh, wait, I want to write that down before I forget it," and she'd take it out and write a few lines. It could be trivial things. On one of the occasions I saw her with Bobby, he told some joke about the difference between a wife and a secretary. Marilyn reached for her book, and Bobby took a look at it and said, "Ah, get rid of that". At the time I thought it was purely dismissive. Now, I don't know, maybe he was really concerned.'

Less than a month before Marilyn's death, Marilyn's last agent George Chasin realized how close his client was to Robert Kennedy. On July 13 the government brought an anti-trust suit against his company, the Music Corporation of America, because of MCA's takeovers in the empire of show business. Chasin had been aware of a government investigation, but did not expect the suit. Six months earlier, over dinner in Romanoff's, Marilyn had warned him there would be one. When he failed to take her seriously, she hinted that her source was the Attorney General. That is not the way government is supposed to operate.

It may be that Kennedy did tell Marilyn more than jokes and, without giving away state secrets, said things that were better left unsaid. Slatzer and the diary references aside, two people Marilyn met in Mexico said she was full of her latest conversation with the Attorney General at the Lawford house. The man who introduced her to Mexico, Fred Vanderbilt Field, told of Kennedy's confidences about his attitude to J. Edgar Hoover. José Bolaños, her Mexican lover, quoted Marilyn as saying she and Kennedy discussed Castro's Cuba. As we shall see, Marilyn's loose lips may have caused her to be rated a security risk.

Harris Wofford, former Special Assistant to the President, wrote of Judith Campbell, Sam Giancana, and the long-secret CIA plots to kill Castro: 'Aside from moral issues, the morass of potential blackmail in which the Attorney General found himself must have appalled him. ... How could the CIA and John Kennedy have been so stupid? What could they or the Attorney General do to extricate themselves and minimize the risk of exposure?'

Perhaps, by July, the Kennedy brothers finally realized the folly of associating with Marilyn, not to mention the other women the President had been seeing. It was none too soon.

In May, after months of shilly-shallying, the CIA had told Robert Kennedy of its involvement with Mafia leaders – and with Sam Giancana and Johnny Roselli specifically – in plots to assassinate Castro. Only two months had passed since Kennedy had been told the FBI knew that the President was seeing Judith Campbell while she was also consorting with Giancana.

Also in May, the day before the President's birthday jamboree, Teamsters' leader Jimmy Hoffa had been indicted for extortion, the latest blow in a judicial assault that was now occupying all his time. In June, though investigators did not know it till later, Hoffa reportedly went so far as to discuss one solution to the problem – the desirability of Robert Kennedy being murdered. Sitting in his Washington office, Hoffa said of the Attorney General, 'Kennedy has got to go. . . . Somebody needs to bump that sonofabitch off. . . . You know I've got a rundown on him. He drives about in a convertible and swims by himself. I've got a .270 rifle with a high-power scope on it that shoots a long way without dropping any. It would be easy to get him with that. But I'm leery of it; it's too obvious. . . .'

Hoffa said this at the end of June or in the first days of July. It was on June 27, in exactly that period, that Kennedy had visited Marilyn at home, driving alone in a convertible. It seems that Hoffa, the man said to have been requesting surveillance of Kennedy and Marilyn, indeed had 'a rundown' on the Attorney General.

The same week, during an FBI wiretapping operation, the New York mobster Eddie McGrath was heard to say, 'Since when is fucking a federal offense?. . . . And if it is . . . I want the President of the United States indicted because I know he was whacking all those broads Sinatra brought him out. . . .'

Less than two weeks later, Justice Department attorneys produced the first of a series of reports on Frank Sinatra. Two more would follow that summer. They went into detail about the Cal-Neva Lodge and its criminal manager, Skinny D'Amato. They referred flatly to Sinatra's 'friendship' with Sam Giancana, the man who had threatened to 'tell all' about the Kennedys.

The man who compiled the Sinatra reports, Department lawyer Dougald McMillan, shied away when asked whether he knew at the time of Marilyn's simultaneous connection with the Kennedy brothers and Sinatra. 'You know,' he said, 'I don't think I should get into that.'

In May, in light of Giancana's involvement with the CIA, Robert Kennedy agreed not to prosecute the Mafia chieftain in a wiretapping case. He met FBI Director Hoover two days later, and Hoover noted that Kennedy 'well knew the "gutter gossip" was that the reason nothing had been done against Giancana was because of Giancana's close relationship with Frank Sinatra who, in turn, claimed to be a close friend of the Kennedy family. The Attorney General stated he realized this and it was for that reason he was quite concerned. . . .'

On June 27, the day Robert Kennedy visited Marilyn at home in Los Angeles, he showed uncharacteristic caution with regard to Jimmy Hoffa. An FBI report, partially censored for release to the public, shows that the Attorney General conferred that day with Jerry Wald, the would-be producer of Kennedy's own exposé of the Teamsters, *The Enemy Within.* 'There seems to be some question in the Attorney General's mind,' said the report, 'as to whether this picture should be produced until after prosecutions in which James Hoffa is involved are completed.' Robert Kennedy was apparently aware that this was a time of extraordinary peril.

On July 19, Joan Greenson's birthday, Marilyn put on a brave show. She helped arrange a surprise party, then did the Twist with a black girl who had no dancing partner. She and Joan were to talk on the telephone a few more times, but Marilyn's mind seemed elsewhere. Four days later, she tried calling the Justice Department again, but hung up within a minute.

Jeanne Carmen, who saw Marilyn briefly, thought 'she looked like death.' In the midsummer nights, sleep came harder than ever. She called on Ralph Roberts for late-night massages. Once she saw Dr Greenson twice in one day, as well as her internist, Dr Engelberg. She also telephoned Engelberg at two o'clock in the morning.

Marilyn now indulged a taste for intrigue and an ugly side to her temper. When studio bosses came to discuss a possible revival of *Something's Got to Give,* she had Pat Newcomb hide in the next-door room to witness what was said. Paula Strasberg, summoned back from Europe to help in the negotiations, found herself spurned. Marilyn abused her for doing nothing, and Strasberg flew back to New York.

Eunice Murray was not immune to Marilyn's rage. Her son-in-law Norman Jeffries arrived one day to find Murray had her bags packed ready to leave. Then, after all, she stayed on.

The nights began to merge with the days. While Strasberg had been there, she had awakened to see Marilyn pacing the hall in the small hours. In happier days, Marilyn had sometimes donned a wig and dark glasses to watch the merry-go-round on the Santa Monica pier. Now she was seen loitering on the pier, just a few hundred yards from the Lawford house, long after dark.

At the end of the week before her death, Marilyn returned to the most dangerous territory of all – the mob-infested Cal-Neva Lodge at Lake Tahoe. Eunice Murray said she could not remember the trip and Peter Lawford never mentioned it.

This was a trip shrouded in mystery, unmentioned in the

press except by Marilyn's friend, Sidney Skolsky. Members of the Cal-Neva staff, who remembered it well, told of another miserable episode.

Joe Langford, who worked under the Bell Captain, his brother Ray, recalled picking up Marilyn at the airport. 'I'd say it was a week before she died,' he said. 'She came on Sinatra's plane, and I remember the pilot saying, "God, am I glad to get rid of her." I guess she'd been drinking heavily; she drank a lot that weekend.'

Ray Langford, the Bell Captain, saw Marilyn in her chalet that weekend, after Sinatra called for room service. Marilyn had 'a kerchief round her face, and dark, dark glasses. She looked very sad.' Other employees told similar stories.

When Marilyn left, Joe Langford said, it was 'in an awful hurry. I think she was giving them some problems.' Two witnesses – the widow of Sinatra's pilot, and the co-pilot – told a haunting tale of the return to Los Angeles.*

Sinatra's aircraft, a twin-engined Martin named after the singer's daughter Christina, was a $6 million investment, a flying palace with wood paneling, wall-to-wall carpeting, bar, luxurious bathroom – and a piano. According to the pilot's widow, Barbara Lieto, her husband was ordered to Lake Tahoe on short notice. He came home in the early hours uncharacteristically furious.

According to Mrs Lieto, Marilyn boarded the plane drunk. It seems the flight first took Marilyn, Peter and Pat Lawford, and one of Marilyn's hairdressers, to San Francisco. The crew waited while the passengers went into the city, then Mrs Lawford took a commercial flight to the East Coast.

---

* Witnesses were somewhat confused about the timing of Marilyn's departure. At least two suggested it was the day before her death. The passing of time had presumably led them to concertina events in their minds, for other data placed Marilyn fairly firmly in Los Angeles in the very last days of her life.

It was late when the Sinatra plane left for Los Angeles and, according to Mrs Lieto, Peter Lawford, also now drunk, got into a violent argument with the pilot about where it should land. Lawford insisted they should land at Santa Monica, even when the pilot pointed out that the airport there was closed during the hours of darkness.

When the plane finally landed at Los Angeles, after midnight, Marilyn was 'out of it, a mess.' She emerged from the airplane barefoot, and the pilot had to help her put on her shoes. She then left for home in a limousine, while the crew gave Lawford a ride to Santa Monica in their car. The pilot became further angered when Lawford insisted on stopping a few blocks from his home to make a half-hour telephone call from a public booth. Why, they wondered, could he not wait a mere five minutes, till he got to the beach house and his own telephone?

Was Lawford, too, by that time worrying about security?

There had clearly been great tension during the visit to the Cal-Neva Lodge. One of Marilyn's East Coast friends, Dr Sandy Firestone, remembered a call from Marilyn in the weeks before she died, complaining that 'she was being pressured to go to parties, that she didn't particularly like Peter Lawford because he was having big orgies.'

Photographer Bill Woodfield, whom Sinatra often asked to process photographs he had taken, remembered how – after the final Cal-Neva visit – the singer asked him to print a roll of photographs taken at the Lodge. 'Some of the pictures, about nine frames,' Woodfield recalled, 'showed Marilyn on all fours. She looked sick. Astride, either riding her like a horse or trying to help her up – I couldn't make out which – was [Mafia boss] Sam Giancana.'

Marilyn appeared in the photographs to be in distress, and Sinatra asked Woodfield what he thought he should do with them. 'I suggested he burn them,' Woodfield said, 'and he did – in front of me.'

Though both Marilyn and Giancana had been fully clothed in the photographs, the mafioso told several people he had had sex with her. Marilyn said so, too, according to her friend Jeanne Carmen. Giancana mocked the actress's poor performance, while she spoke of the episode with disgust.

During the final nightmare Joe DiMaggio, still trying to help Marilyn, had come to Lake Tahoe. The Cal-Neva bell captain, Ray Langford, recalled getting him a room at the nearby Silver Crest Motel. DiMaggio wanted to know where Marilyn was, and Langford, not yet aware that she had arrived – said he did not know. Langford's brother Joe said DiMaggio wanted to get in touch, but did not actually enter the Cal-Neva 'because there was a feud between him and Sinatra at the time.'

Another witness, who arrived at the Cal-Neva within a week of Marilyn's death, was told an eerie story by an employee. He recalled having looked down from the casino, near dawn, to see Marilyn 'at the edge of the pool, barefoot, swaying back and forth. She was staring up the hill.' Concerned, the Cal-Neva man went up to Marilyn and found her still gazing upward. He followed her gaze, and there was DiMaggio standing in the driveway, 'staring back.'

Before she died, Marilyn talked about the Cal-Neva visit with her masseur Ralph Roberts. 'She told me it was a nightmare, a dreadful weekend,' Roberts recalled. 'She didn't want to go particularly, and when she got there she found Joe there. She couldn't go out of her room without the conflict of Sinatra. Joe was terribly jealous of Sinatra.'

Earlier in the year, when Marilyn had just moved into the new house, DiMaggio had gone to see her with Harry Hall, his old friend from sports-promotion days. 'He knocked at the door,' Hall recalled, 'and she opened it, saw Joe, and slammed the door. Joe said, "Well, one of these days."' They returned later, Hall said, and this time Marilyn let them in. He believed DiMaggio still had hopes of remarrying

Marilyn, and others said they met on friendly terms in the last months.

Even DiMaggio on occasion lost patience. During *Something's Got to Give*, scriptwriter Nunnally Johnson tried to get him to go to California to help Marilyn. 'He promised to call her on the phone,' Johnson recalled, 'but was adamant against trying anything further. . . . So far as he was concerned, she was a lost lady, and while there might be someone to save her, he wasn't the one.'

In the last weeks, nevertheless, DiMaggio returned to his obsession. The goings-on at Lake Tahoe enraged him. 'He was very upset,' said Harry Hall. 'She went up there, they gave her pills, they had sex parties, and Joe thought – because at that time he was a friend of Sinatra – it should never have happened. . . . He felt he should've had enough respect for Joe. He should've left her alone.'

By 1962, DiMaggio had a lucrative job, at a salary of $100,000 a year, as a representative of V. H. Monette, an East Coast company supplying American military post exchanges. He had told the company president, Valmore Monette, that he was 'still very much in love with Marilyn.' On August 1, 1962, the week Marilyn was to die, DiMaggio quit the company. According to Monette, 'He told me he had talked to Marilyn and thought she had finally agreed to leave the movies and remarry him.'

Marilyn wrote her former husband in the final months:

Dear Joe,
If I can only succeed in making you happy – I will have succeeded in the bigest [sic] and most difficult thing there is – that is to make *one person completely happy* [Marilyn's italics]. Your happiness means my happiness.

The letter, never sent, was found after Marilyn's death.

DiMaggio was furious not only with Sinatra but also the

Kennedys. In the spring of the year he had visited Marilyn along with his son Joe, Jr., and the son's fiancée, Pamela Ries. Ries remembered that Marilyn talked with DiMaggio about Robert Kennedy, and that a row ensued.

Marilyn was now twisting and turning in her bitterness over Kennedy. In late July, during a massage session with Ralph Roberts, she suddenly asked, 'Ralph, have you heard any stories about me and Bobby?'

Roberts replied, 'All Hollywood is talking about it!' To which Marilyn retorted, 'Well, it isn't true. He's not my sort. He's too puny.'

That same week, just before the last Cal-Neva visit, Robert Slatzer had been about to leave for the East Coast. During a farewell drive with Marilyn, she veered from enthusiasm to despondency, from talking about 'starting a whole new life' to complaining about Robert Kennedy. She wondered gloomily whether he had abandoned her because she was not sufficiently educated. She burst into tears, sobbing that men wanted her 'only as a plaything.' Kennedy, she supposed, 'had got what he wanted.'

Marilyn had said of Kennedy, as she and Slatzer looked at her diary together, 'Maybe his wife would like to know some of the things he told me. It's all in here, and I'm glad I made notes.'

Former private detective John Dolan, one of the sources on the wiretapping of Marilyn, says the wiretappers discovered she had once been desperate enough to call the Attorney General at home in Virginia. He had been enraged.

'Robert Kennedy became incommunicado,' Robert Slatzer said, 'and she wasn't going to settle for that.'

Paul D'Amato, the man said to have represented Giancana's interests at the Cal-Neva Lodge, confirmed to me that Marilyn had been there a week or so before she died. Chain-smoking Marlboros, while sitting in pyjamas on what would soon prove to be his deathbed, D'Amato spoke of the visit and the flight that took Marilyn away for the last time.

Then, pursing his thin lips, D'Amato murmured, 'Of course, I didn't say that.' He added, 'There was more to what happened than anyone has told. It would've been the big fall for Bobby Kennedy, wouldn't it?'

Marilyn was now thinking about death. She consulted the lawyer she shared with Sinatra, Milton Rudin, about making a new will. She reportedly wished to cut the Strasbergs out of it because they had 'taken advantage' of her. The will was not changed. Rudin, who thought 'she was obviously deeply ill,' kept putting Marilyn off.

Dr Greenson, the psychiatrist, had been seeing Marilyn almost every day, except when she went to Lake Tahoe. In other circumstances, he was to write to a friend within days of her death, 'I should have played it safe and put her in a sanitarium, but that would only have been safe for me and deadly for her. . . .'

Weeks earlier, talking about her career to *Life* magazine, Marilyn had said, 'It might be kind of a relief to be finished. It's sort of like I don't know what kind of a yard dash you're running, but then you're at the finish line and you sort of sigh – you've made it! But you never have, you have to start all over again.'

On July 26, Robert Kennedy came to Los Angeles once more, to address the National Insurance Association. At midday, as he was on his way to the engagement, the Los Angeles office of the FBI received an anonymous call warning of a plan to kill him. The caller said 'gangland characters' were plotting his murder.

On July 30, 1962, Marilyn made her final call to the Justice Department, as logged in the surviving telephone records. The call, which lasted eight minutes, was made on the Monday of her last week alive.

Part Five

THE CANDLE
BURNS DOWN

'Oh what a tangled web we weave . . .'

SIR WALTER SCOTT

44

'Do you know who I've always depended on?' Marilyn had asked reporter W. J. Weatherby. 'Not strangers, not friends. The telephone! That's my best friend. I love calling friends, especially late at night when I can't sleep.'

Marilyn worked her mechanical friend hard in her last days. Ensconced at home, she rattled off calls to contacts on the East Coast. She told Henry Rosenfeld, the fashion tycoon, that she would be coming East soon and wanted him to escort her to the first night of *Mr President*, a new show opening in Washington. She called Lena Pepitone, her New York maid, and talked about plans to give a party in September.

Marilyn was in a whirl of discussions about future projects. She talked to Gene Kelly about a musical with a World War I setting, to Sidney Skolsky about a film on Jean Harlow, with herself playing the lead. She made outings to a screening room to see the films of director Lee Thompson, who was keen to use her in the film that would later be made as *What a Way to Go*. She spoke to composer Jule Styne about plans for a musical version of *A Tree Grows in Brooklyn*, starring herself and Frank Sinatra.

The calls resulted in firm arrangements. On Sunday Marilyn was due to meet with Skolsky and Kelly, then dine with Sinatra and the Romanoffs. She was scheduled to see Lee Thompson on Monday, then fly to New York to meet with Styne.

None of the people Marilyn spoke with thought she sounded depressed that last week. Two old friends from the studio, makeup man Whitey Snyder and wardrobe assistant Marjorie Plecher, came round for drinks. They recalled, 'She never looked better; she was in great spirits.'

There were glimpses of another mood. Marilyn called the California psychic Kenny Kingston, whom she had consulted in the past. On this occasion her theme was love. Kingston quoted Marilyn as having said, 'Love is the one immortal thing about us. Without it, what can life mean?'

On Wednesday that week, gynecologist Dr Leon Krohn played a round of golf at the Hillcrest Golf Course. It was his day off, and he was irritated when summoned to the clubhouse for an urgent call. It came from Marilyn, whom he had last treated years earlier, shortly before her miscarriage at the end of *Some Like It Hot*.

Back then, Marilyn had stamped off in a temper over his warnings that she stay away from drugs and alcohol, and to take it easy if she wanted to have her baby. Now, calling out of the blue, Marilyn asked, 'Are you still angry with me – about the baby?' Nonplussed, the doctor assured her he was not.

Marilyn wanted to see Krohn as soon as possible. They agreed to have dinner, but Marilyn was to die before they could meet. Was Marilyn mourning her unborn children? That last week was the fifth anniversary of the loss of her first child by Arthur Miller. Or did she want to talk to Krohn about a more recent disaster, the reported abortion of a few weeks earlier?

Marilyn was reaching out to old friends. A day or two before she died, as masseur Ralph Roberts kneaded away the tension, she told him whom to accept calls from and whom to refuse. One caller she wanted to talk to was Marlon Brando, by now an intimate of seven years' standing. They chatted for a long time when he returned her messages. According to Roberts, Brando made her laugh a lot. The actor himself preferred not to comment on their last conversations.

Marilyn talked to at least three people about the Kennedys

Vodka at the casino. Carousing with friend and later brief lover Frank Sinatra, at the Cal-Neva Lodge, Lake Tahoe. Marilyn's visits to the lodge exposed her dangerously – it was a watering hole for the Mafia

The Attorney General and the singer. The man presumed to be Marilyn's last lover, Robert Kennedy, with Sinatra in 1961

Trysting place. Marilyn met both Kennedy brothers at Peter Lawford's California beach house. This rare photograph, showing the President (*seated centre*), was taken by a neighbour in 1962

The President returning to his New York base, the Carlyle Hotel. Marilyn, some suggested, was one of his female visitors there

Psychiatrist Dr Ralph Greenson, in whom Marilyn confided about her Kennedy affairs. He and his family befriended her in the final two years of her life

'Happy Birthday, Mr President.' Madison Square Garden, May, 1962

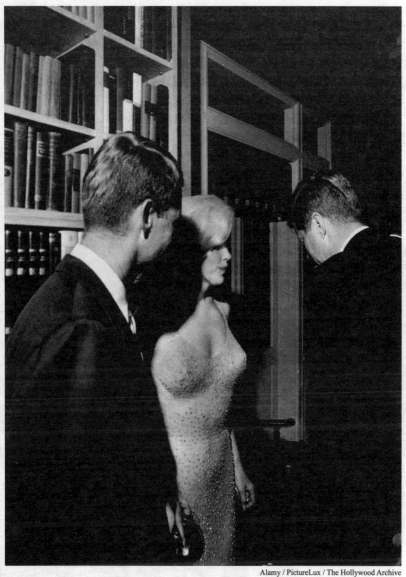

The only surviving photo of Marilyn with John and Robert Kennedy. Others once existed, but were seized from at least one agency – after Marilyn's death – by men claiming to be federal agents *below left*: Giancana, Mafia chieftain. 'I know all about the Kennedys . . . and one of these days we are going to tell all'

right: Jimmy Hoffa, Teamsters' leader. 'I already had a tape on Bobby Kennedy and Jack Kennedy . . .'

below right: The bugging expert Bernard Spindel, Hoffa's wireman

A place to die. The house in Brentwood, the morning of August 5, 1962. The room where Marilyn died lies obscured behind the tree on the left

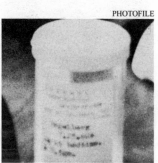

Death in a bottle. The Coroner's office never received some of the pills that littered Marilyn's room. The bottle above bears the name of her internist, Dr Hyman Engelberg, and is dated 25.7.62, eleven days before the end. It probably contained chloral hydrate, which helped to kill Marilyn. The floor is heaped with scripts and a Western Union telegram offering fresh work. The glass object on the right may or may not be a water container. In an incomplete investigation it was never properly identified

Showing the strain? Marilyn in spring 1962, during costume tests for her final, unfinished movie

– in a way that suggests great confusion. From the Barrington Park phone booth, where she stood watching children for the last time, she called Arthur James.

'What can I do about "He"?' she asked, apparently referring to the President. She went on to complain, as she had to Slatzer, that Robert Kennedy had 'cut her off cold,' but it was 'Jack' she could not get out of her mind.

Marilyn phoned James again on the final Wednesday, but reached only his answering service. She left word that she needed his help. 'I tried to call back,' James said, 'but another female answered the phone, and hung up.'

On Friday afternoon, August 3, according to the phone records, Marilyn telephoned Norman Rosten in New York. She wanted to know what he and his wife thought of her *Life* interview, and talked about new job offers and of coming East soon. 'We'll have a great time,' she said. 'Let's all start to live before we get old. . . .'

Marilyn's voice seemed to Rosten frenetic, racing on unnaturally from one thing to another. He was worried enough by the call to write a follow-up letter, but she was to die before it arrived.

Marilyn was flailing around for solace. On Friday she also called Anne Karger, mother of her long-ago lover Fred and a loyal friend. 'It was the day before she died,' said Elizabeth Karger, Fred's last wife. 'She said she was very much in love, and was going to marry Bobby Kennedy. But she sounded depressed.' Anne Karger, said her daughter-in-law, told Marilyn she was deluding herself. She replied, 'If he loves me, he will.'

That same day – Friday – Marilyn went to a phone booth to call Robert Slatzer in Columbus, Ohio. Four friends were with him at the time, and the three still alive when this book was being written all remembered the call. Two of them spoke with her themselves. Marilyn had been looking at a script by Doral Chenoweth, a writer friend of Slatzer, and she told him she liked it. He was impressed by the fact that she had clearly read his work carefully. The play, *This God Bu$ine$$*, was later successfully produced.

Slatzer's restaurateur friend Lee Henry also talked to Marilyn for a few moments. He recalled recognizing the famous voice but said, 'You could tell she was either on booze or drugs.'

Slatzer himself talked to Marilyn at length, not for the first time that week. The previous day, he said, he had called her to tell her Robert Kennedy was going to California that weekend and that – if Marilyn must – it would be a good chance to talk to him.

Now, on Friday, Marilyn was saying she had continued to try in vain to reach Kennedy in Washington. Was Slatzer sure Kennedy was coming to California? Slatzer told her to look in the papers. Marilyn said she would telephone Kennedy's sister Pat Lawford. Pat was at the Kennedy compound in Massachusetts, but Marilyn said she would call Peter Lawford to get the number. Pat Lawford, in turn, would tell her how to reach Robert Kennedy.

Peter Lawford later confirmed that Marilyn did call to ask for Pat's number. He gave it to her. We do not know whether Marilyn did then obtain a number for Robert Kennedy, and whether she reached him. We do know Robert Kennedy was in California that weekend.

Press coverage and FBI documents show that Kennedy flew into San Francisco on Friday afternoon accompanied by his wife and four of their children. The Attorney General was combining business with pleasure: an address to the American Bar Association would be followed by a vacation in the mountains of Washington State. The San Francisco *Chronicle* reported that he arrived 'without his usual flashing smile' and shook hands 'woodenly' with those who welcomed him.

A special FBI report, submitted to headquarters two weeks later, would note that the Attorney General and his family 'spent the weekend at the Bates ranch located about sixty miles south of San Francisco. This was strictly a personal affair.' The ranch was owned by John Bates, a wealthy lawyer who was acting as Kennedy's host on behalf of the Bar Association.

According to Bates, Marilyn did not call the ranch that weekend. One of the few contemporary reporters who was to do serious research after Marilyn's death, however, was to find traces of her despair. Florabel Muir, then Hollywood columnist for the *New York Daily News,* spent several weeks trying to reconstruct Marilyn's last days. Although Kennedy chose to spend the weekend at the Bates ranch, the Bar Association had provided accommodation in the city, at the St Francis Hotel. That is where Marilyn would have expected to find him.

According to her former assistant Elizabeth Fancher, reporter Muir paid a telephone operator at the St Francis for information about calls made that weekend. 'She discovered Marilyn had called the hotel several times, leaving messages for Kennedy,' Fancher said, 'and the calls were not returned.'

As Robert Kennedy flew West that day newspapers published a White House announcement that his brother the President would be going to California in two weeks' time. Marilyn had already advised reporter Sidney Skolsky, whom she had told only about her relationship with John Kennedy, that the President was coming. She said she expected to 'be with him' during the visit.

If either Kennedy brother read the *New York Journal-American* that Friday they saw all the more reason to avoid further contact with Marilyn. Columnist Dorothy Kilgallen wrote a teaser, saying that Marilyn had recently 'proved vastly alluring to a handsome gentleman who is a bigger name than Joe DiMaggio in his heyday. So don't write off Marilyn as finished.'

Friday, August 3, was the day before Marilyn was to die.

She spent part of it normally enough, visiting Frank's Nursery in Santa Monica, picking out plants for her garden. She also saw her doctor and her psychiatrist, which for her was routine. What she did that evening, however, presumably after the abortive effort to reach Robert Kennedy in San Francisco, would remain one of the many unknowns about the last weekend.

Some information, albeit vestigial, suggests she may have made a frantic flying visit northward, to seek out Robert Kennedy for herself. Pat Newcomb, Marilyn's press aide and a friend of the Kennedys, said she and Marilyn dined out that night at a Santa Monica restaurant. It was a favorite of theirs, she said, but she could no longer remember its name or where it was located.

The District Attorney's investigators, who talked to Newcomb during a review of the case in 1982, were not happy with Newcomb's account of the evening. There are some other, though inconclusive, clues. During the day Marilyn ordered food and liquor worth forty-nine dollars – quite a purchase when translated into today's prices – from Briggs Delicatessen. That night, according to Jean Leon of the fashionable La Scala restaurant, she ordered food to be brought to her home.

Leon, a Frenchman, had risen from being a waiter at the Villa Capri – an old haunt of Frank Sinatra and Joe DiMaggio – to becoming proprietor of La Scala. He had known Marilyn for years. Interviewed by me, he said he had taken food to Marilyn's house the night before she died, then stopped short. Somebody else had been at Marilyn's home that night, he said, but he refused to say who it was. 'I have a vivid memory,' said Leon, 'but you have to go into a lot of things, big personalities, and they are not here now.'

For reasons that remain mysterious, events that Friday evening demanded secrecy. For Marilyn, it was reportedly to be a sleepless night.

45

On Saturday, August 4, according to Jeanne Carmen, she was awakened by the telephone at first light. Still half-asleep, she listened as Marilyn poured out a story of a night disturbed by more than the usual demons.

Carmen recalled that 'she said some woman had been calling all night, harassing her and calling her names, then hanging up. Then she would call and not say anything, and hang up. Marilyn said the voice sounded familiar, but she couldn't put a name on it.'

In the first calls, according to Carmen, the anonymous woman said words to the effect, 'Leave Bobby alone, you tramp. Leave Bobby alone.' The calls had gone on till 5:30 A.M. and Marilyn was now exhausted. 'She wanted me to come over. She said, "Bring a bag of pills" – we were sleeping-pill buddies, and we always referred to them that way – "and we'll drink some wine."'

Carmen, who had appointments that day, said she could not come around. They agreed to talk again later. It was Carmen's birthday and, when she opened her mail, she found Marilyn had remembered to send her a card. As others confirmed, Marilyn was good about remembering birthdays.

At 3:00 A.M. that morning, presumably during the spate of anonymous calls, Marilyn had tried to reach Arthur James. He was out of town, and did not get the message until after her death.

It was going to be another hot day, with the temperature up in the eighties. Eunice Murray, who had stayed at her own apartment the previous night, came to work about eight o'clock. According to her, Marilyn wandered into the kitchen about an hour later, then chatted a little over a spartan breakfast of grapefruit juice. She said Pat Newcomb had stayed overnight and was still asleep. She was to stay asleep till noon, a state of bliss which irritated Marilyn.

Arthur Miller's father Isadore called that morning. He was told that Marilyn was dressing and would call back. She did not do so, which he found out of character. Marilyn usually interrupted even urgent business to return his calls.

During the morning Norman Jeffries, working on the kitchen floor, found himself looking at a pair of bare female feet. He looked up to see Marilyn wrapped in a huge bath towel, and was appalled.

'I will never forget the sight of her,' Jeffries said. 'She looked sick, desperately sick – not only in the physical sense – and I thought there must be something terribly wrong. She must have taken a lot of dope or something, or maybe she was scared out of her mind. I had never seen her look that way before.'

Marilyn had two telephones: one pink, with a number provided to ordinary callers; one white, with a number given only to the specially privileged. Both were on long extension leads, so Marilyn could wander about the house as she talked.

The surviving phone records, for reasons that will emerge later, throw no light on Marilyn's calls during her last twenty-four hours. However, closeted in her room – probably with the white phone – Marilyn had several conversations that last morning.

Ralph Roberts, the masseur, said Marilyn called to get him to do a chore: she wanted him to get hold of an unreleased record by a singer she hoped to help. She also talked of having dinner with Roberts that evening – a cookout on the patio – and they agreed to talk again later. By late afternoon, Marilyn said, she should know what she was doing.

From his home across the city, reporter Sidney Skolsky made his regular weekend call to Marilyn. He had been alarmed by her confidences about the Kennedy family and, as on other recent occasions, had his daughter Steffi listen in on an extension. He felt he wanted a witness.

'What are you doing tonight?' Skolsky asked cheerily. By now Marilyn appeared to have a plan for the evening. She replied, 'Maybe I'll go down to the beach. Everyone's going to be there.' As Skolsky's daughter remembered it, Marilyn said she expected to be seeing one of the Kennedys at the Lawford house.

That Saturday, probably in the late morning, Marilyn received a visit from Agnes Flanagan, one of her hairdressers and a longtime friend. Something odd occurred while Flanagan was at the house, one bizarre incident in a weekend of mystery.

Soon after she arrived, said Flanagan, a messenger arrived with a package. Marilyn opened it and walked out to the pool carrying its contents – a stuffed toy tiger. She then sat down by the pool, holding the tiger and saying nothing. Flanagan thought she was 'terribly, terribly depressed,' but did not say why. Flanagan, at a loss, got up and left.

Photographs of the back of Marilyn's house, taken the next day, show two stuffed animals lying by the pool. One of them could be a tiger. Had some devastating note arrived with the tiger or – curious thought – was the tiger itself the message? It may or may not be relevant that a real-life stuffed tiger had pride of place in Robert Kennedy's office at the Justice Department in Washington. Marilyn, at all events, now lost control.

The events of her remaining hours hang largely on the accounts of Peter Lawford, Pat Newcomb, Eunice Murray, and Dr Greenson. The first two witnesses are controversial, not least because of their close relations with the Kennedy brothers. Mrs Murray's statements about the evening hours, as will be seen, were unreliable.

Research for this book, including interviews with Dr Greenson's family and colleagues, and his contemporary correspondence, satisfied this author that Marilyn's psychiatrist was in general honest in his account of the events of that weekend. It is likely, though that, as he himself would on one occasion hint, that he did not tell the full truth about the way it ended. It is he who takes up the story of that Saturday, reliably – I believe – until the final phase.

'I received a call from Marilyn about 4:30 in the afternoon,' Greenson was to write to a friend. 'She seemed somewhat depressed and somewhat drugged. I went over to her place. She was still angry with her girlfriend who had slept fifteen hours that night, and Marilyn was furious because she had had such a poor sleep . . . but after I had spent about two and a half hours with her she seemed to quiet down.'

Dr Greenson's letters, and his statements to fellow psychiatrists on the Los Angeles Suicide Prevention Team, offer information on two key factors in Marilyn's last hours. They show that as early as Friday, when he had also seen her, Marilyn had been 'angry and resentful towards her friend Pat' – clearly, in this context – Pat Newcomb. On Friday night, according to Greenson, they continued bickering, and Marilyn was still in a rage with Newcomb as late as Saturday afternoon.

Why such rage against Pat Newcomb? The press aide agreed 'it made Marilyn crazy that she was not able to sleep. She was furious, it's true. But I think that she also was furious about something else, I think there was a lot more, not related to me, and that I don't even know about.'

Clearly referring to Newcomb, Susan Strasberg recalled that Marilyn nicknamed her publicity aide – as early as *The Misfits* – 'Sybil' for sibling rivalry. Steffi Skolsky said the same. Marilyn had been jealous of Newcomb in the past, as on *Bus Stop* years earlier, when she believed Newcomb – a woman a dozen years younger than herself – was pursuing a man Marilyn liked.

Now Steffi Skolsky, listening in on one of Marilyn's last conversations with her father, heard Marilyn say the tables were turned. 'Pat's jealous of me,' she said. Was Marilyn's quarrel with Newcomb, at the end, about Robert Kennedy?

Dean Martin's former wife, Jeanne, who would remain close to Newcomb, remembered how involved she got with her clients, how they became 'literally, her whole life. She always got overly involved.' Another deep commitment, apparently, was with Robert Kennedy.

Martin said, 'Pat got far too involved; she was deeply in love with Bobby Kennedy. She's only just got over that. If you want to know who knew more about Marilyn than anyone it's Pat Newcomb.' For years to come, however, Newcomb would clam up when asked about the Kennedys.

Of the squabbles with Marilyn that fatal Saturday, Newcomb would say only, 'Marilyn had calls that morning, and by the time I saw her she was in a rage.' Psychiatrist Dr Greenson, in his talks with the Suicide Prevention Team after Marilyn died, dropped heavy hints as to why she was so upset.

Along with saying that Marilyn had recently had sexual relationships with 'extremely important men in government ... at the highest level,' Dr Greenson revealed that on Saturday afternoon she 'expressed considerable dissatisfaction with the fact that here she was, the most beautiful woman in the world, and she did not have a date for Saturday night.'

According to one Suicide Team doctor, Norman Tabachnick, Greenson said Marilyn had been expecting to see one of the 'very important people' that night. She had called Greenson when she learned the meeting was off. Marilyn died, Greenson said, feeling 'rejected by some of the people she had been close to.'

Sometime before she called Greenson that day – over the telephone or conceivably in a message accompanying the mysterious tiger – Marilyn had learned she would not be seeing Robert Kennedy in the evening. That it was almost certainly Kennedy she had been expecting will become apparent as these final chapters unwind. On the evidence, the cancellation triggered her final despair.

After having seen Marilyn virtually every day for weeks, Greenson had hoped to keep that weekend free. He had a dinner appointment on Saturday night, and his afternoon visit to Marilyn seems to have been a holding operation.

Marilyn wanted Pat Newcomb to leave, and Greenson asked her to go. Newcomb said that she left of her own accord. Eunice Murray said Newcomb sprang up and left without saying good-bye.

At 6:30 P.M. Ralph Roberts called as planned, to ask Marilyn whether he was to come round to dinner. Greenson answered the phone and said Marilyn was out. Then, his dinner appointment in mind, the psychiatrist prepared to leave.

'Marilyn wanted to go for a walk on the pier at Santa Monica,' Dr Greenson recalled later, 'and I said she was too groggy for that, and if she drank a lot of fluid, I would allow the housekeeper to drive her to the beach.' Greenson thought, 'She seemed somewhat depressed, but I had seen her many, many times in a much worse condition.' As a precaution, he asked Eunice Murray to stay overnight. Then Greenson dashed home to dress for dinner. It was 7:15 P.M.

One of Marilyn's stepchildren, Joe DiMaggio, Jr., had twice tried to call her that afternoon. DiMaggio, a young marine serving at Camp Pendleton, California, telephoned collect, only to hear Mrs Murray say that Marilyn was out. Then, soon after Greenson had left, Joe Jr. did get through.

At 7:40 P.M. Marilyn called Dr Greenson, now busy shaving. He was glad to hear her sounding more cheerful: Joe Jr.'s news had been that he had broken off his engagement, and that pleased Marilyn. Dr Greenson told her to get a good night's sleep and to call in the morning.

According to Eunice Murray, Marilyn then announced that she would not be going for a drive after all. She went into her bedroom and closed the door. Mrs Murray heard the sound of music from the record player – Frank Sinatra songs.

According to Mrs Murray, she never saw Marilyn alive again. It was about eight o'clock, and dusk began to fall along the Pacific shore. In Marilyn's room, the music played on and on.

In her last call to Dr Greenson, Marilyn had asked, 'Did you take away my bottle of Nembutal?' He had not, and he was caught off-balance because he thought Marilyn had recently cut down on barbiturates. Nor was Greenson especially worried – if his patient had no sleeping pills.

The psychiatrist would have been more concerned had he known then what he learned later. An empty bottle, with a label indicating it had contained twenty-five Nembutal pills, would be among the medicines retrieved from Marilyn's room after her death. The label showed it had been prescribed the previous day, Friday. There would also be an almost empty bottle that had contained fifty capsules of chloral hydrate, a less dangerous sleeping aid, which had been prescribed on July 31.

Dr Hyman Engelberg, Marilyn's internist, rarely gave interviews. However, his contemporary bill showed that he visited Marilyn at home on Friday, the day of the Nembutal prescription, and a document in the Coroner's file says he prescribed Nembutal that day.

The Suicide Prevention Team would conclude that Marilyn had been receiving Nembutal prescriptions from both Dr Engelberg and from a Dr Lou Siegel, and that neither doctor knew of her visits to the other. Dr Lou Siegel, a gynecologist, vehemently denied in 1982 that he had ever treated Marilyn. Dr *Lee* Siegel, the studio doctor who did frequently treat Marilyn, said he did not see her for many weeks prior to her death.

Dr Greenson would later say he had brought in Dr Engelberg to try to wean Marilyn away from sleeping pills. The two doctors agreed to keep in touch concerning the drugs they prescribed for her, but the system may have broken down.

Marilyn had made an odd inquiry earlier that day, according to Eunice Murray. 'Mrs Murray,' she supposedly said, 'do we have any oxygen?' Marilyn let the subject drop, but Murray said it bothered her enough to telephone Dr Greenson. Greenson never mentioned such a call. Oxygen, of course, is used by medical teams as an aid to resuscitation.

Certainly Greenson knew nothing of Marilyn's dawn call to Jeanne Carmen, in which – Carmen said – she had asked her to come over with 'a bag of sleeping pills.' According to Carmen, she called again later, pressing the request. Carmen still pleaded other engagements.

Marilyn's wealthy New York friend Henry Rosenfeld telephoned her – probably between 8:00 and 9:00 P.M. California time – and she answered the phone herself. She sounded 'groggy,' he thought, but that was not unusual.

At about 9:30 P.M. Marilyn called Sydney Guilaroff, the prominent Hollywood hairdresser who styled her hair in eight of her movies and became a trusted confidant. He has featured little in these pages because – over many decades – he made it a rule never to discuss his clients. When I interviewed Guilaroff for the first edition of this book, it was clear that he was holding back something about the 9:30 P.M. call. He resisted attempts to persuade him to discuss the call – even off the record – confining himself to saying Marilyn told him that last night that she was 'very depressed.'

Only in 1996, when interviewed for his autobiography, did Guilaroff finally open up. What he had to say is remarkable, and indicates that Marilyn's involvement with the President and the Attorney General was uppermost in her mind in the final hours of her life.

'Marilyn telephoned me in despair,' Guilaroff said 'She rambled on about being surrounded by danger, about betrayals by "men in high places," about clandestine love affairs . . .' Sounding frantic, she then told Guilaroff that Robert Kennedy had been at the house, 'threatening me, yelling at me.' She said she was having an affair with Robert, that she had also had an affair with the President, and that – reneging on what she claimed was a promise to marry her – Robert was now saying their relationship was over.

According to Guilaroff, Marilyn said she had responded to being dumped by the President's brother with a threat of her own. She said she would 'go public,' hold a tell-all press conference. She then hung up without saying good-bye. Guilaroff, who was used to Marilyn, saw no cause for alarm.

There were three other reported phone calls that evening. José Bolaños, the lover who had followed Marilyn from Mexico, said he phoned Marilyn from the Ships Restaurant, not far from her home, between nine-thirty and ten o'clock. He would not reveal what they discussed. He did say Marilyn ended the conversation by simply laying down the phone – she did not hang up while he was on the line. Like Guilaroff, Bolaños thought it was typical Marilyn behavior. He thought he was the last person to speak to Marilyn – but perhaps not.

At about 10:00 p.m., according to Jeanne Carmen, Marilyn called her yet again. 'Are you sure you can't come over?' she said. Marilyn sounded nervous, and said she was afraid there would be a repetition of the previous night's calls telling her to leave Robert Kennedy alone. Later, when her phone rang again, Carmen did not answer it.

Also around 10:00 P.M., Ralph Roberts learned the next day, a woman with a 'slurred voice' called his answering service. Told Roberts was out, the caller hung up. Roberts, who was staying at a temporary address, had given his number to only two people apart from Marilyn, and they were business contacts. He believed the caller was Marilyn.

46

There were no more known calls. But there are two further, striking details – lingering puzzles – about the actress' conversations with her confidant Guilaroff and with her Mexican friend José Bolaños. 'You know, Sydney,' Guilaroff would recall her saying, 'I know a lot of secrets about what has gone on in Washington.' Asked what sort of secrets she was referring to, she had replied, 'Dangerous ones.'

Bolaños, for his part, said that – before ending her conversation with him that evening – Marilyn had told him 'something shocking, something that will one day shock the whole world.' This author pressed Bolaños to elaborate, time and again. But he would say no more.

What 'dangerous secrets' could Marilyn have known, or thought were dangerous secrets? The very concept seems overblown, over-dramatic. Perhaps, though, there was a core of truth to her belief that she was privy to secrets.

Los Angeles District Attorney's investigators, reviewing the circumstances of Marilyn's death in the 1980s, found themselves blocked when they asked to see certain material held by the FBI. The reason, they were told, was that it reflected monitoring of Marilyn's activity in Mexico during her 1962 visit there. Efforts by me and my lawyer using the Freedom of Information Act – to get at the same documents – elicited the fact that the Bureau had kept a '105' file on Marilyn.

The '105' designation technically applied to 'foreign counter-intelligence matters'. In practice, under J. Edgar Hoover, it provided a pretext to investigate anyone who did anything remotely political – for which read leftist. Parts of the 105 file on Marilyn were marked 'SM-C', for 'Security Matter – Communist'. They were withheld under category B1, used to cover foreign affairs matters and national security. Two documents 'released' to us in the 1980s were entirely blacked out – except for their heading – by the censor's pen. Since 2012, however, they have been released in full.

At the time of Marilyn's visit to Mexico City, FBI agents there were paying constant attention to a group of some several dozen expatriate Americans. They watched especially members of the Hollywood Ten, film-makers whose careers had been destroyed during the McCarthy Communist-hunting era of the 1950s, and other leftists. When Marilyn had been befriended during her stay by 'silver spoon Communist' Fred Vanderbilt Field, that had attracted intense FBI interest.

A four-page report filed to Director Hoover on March 6, 1962, a day after Marilyn left Mexico for home, makes it clear that she had been closely watched by the FBI during the trip and that compliant people – who had spent time with her – had been milked for information. The report did not fail to mention that – as reported in the previous chapter – the 'Subject' – Marilyn – had 'spent some time with ROBERT KENNEDY at the home of the PETER LAWFORDs in Hollywood. Subject reportedly challenged Mr. KENNEDY on some points. . . .'

Interviewed for this book, both Fred Field and José Bolaños, with whom she had a dalliance in Mexico, recalled that Marilyn had talked with them about her dinner meeting with Robert Kennedy months earlier. Bolaños, for his part, remembered that Marilyn talked of 'having had a blinding row with Kennedy on the Cuba matter. Bobby had called Marilyn "basically Communist" in her attitudes.'

So far so fairly innocuous, one could say. It is a second FBI report, dated July 13, 1962, less than a month before Marilyn's

UNITED STATES GOVERNMENT

M E M O R A N D U M

TO: DIRECTOR, FBI   DATE: 3/6/62

FROM: LEGAT, MEXICO (100-0)

SUBJECT: MARILYN MONROE
           SM - C

The following information was received from [____]
and [____] who have furnished reliable information in the
past, on 2/28/62. Extreme care should be used in reporting
any of this information to avoid disclosure of sources who
were associating closely with subject during her visit to
Mexico.

This source advised that MARILYN MONROE, the movie
actress, was recently in Mexico on vacation and while in
Mexico associated closely with certain members of the American
Communist Group in Mexico (ACGM). Source characterized the
ACGM as a loose association of a predominantly social nature
of present and/or past members of the Communist Party, USA,
and their friends and associates who share a common sympathy
for Communism and the Soviet Union.

According to CHURCHILL, the subject was much disturbed
by ARTHUR MILLER's marriage on 2/20/62 and feels like a "negated
sex symbol." CHURCHILL said that subject "has a lot of leftist
rubbed off from MILLER." Subject reportedly spent some time
with ROBERT KENNEDY at the home of the PETER LAWFORDs in
Hollywood. Subject reportedly challenged Mr. KENNEDY on some
points proposed to her by MILLER.

WORKING COPY

UNITED STATES GOVERNMENT

Memorandum

TO : Director, FBI   DATE: July 1962

CONFIDENTIAL

FROM : Legat, Mexico City (100-new) (RUC)

SUBJECT: MARILYN MONROE
SECURITY MATTER - C

and _____ who have furnished reliable
information in the past, _____
and were in contact with subject and her
entourage on several occasions. Subject said she had luncheon
at the PETER LAWFORDs with President KENNEDY just a few
days previously. She was very pleased, as she had asked the
President a lot of socially significant questions concerning
the morality of atomic testing and the future of the youth
of America. She already had been asked by LAWFORD to appear
at the President's birthday party.

She had just written FREDERICK VANDERBILT FIELD
(BuFile 100-2278) and offered him the use of her apartment
in New York. She said FIELD and his wife, [____] would be
in New York by June 1. (This information reported by
separate communication to New York.)

Subject's views are very positively and concisely
leftist; however, if she is being actively used by the Communist Party, it is not general knowledge among those working
with the movement in Los Angeles.

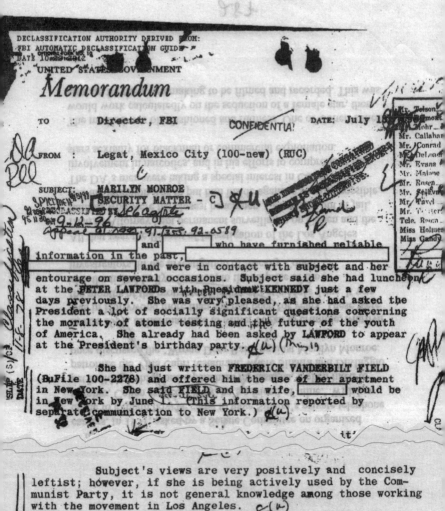

death, that is troubling. The report and an accompanying memo noted something the unnamed source had heard direct from Marilyn herself. She was quoted as saying she had 'lunched at the Peter Lawfords with President Kennedy just a few days previously. She was very pleased, as she had asked the President a lot of socially significant questions concerning the morality of atomic testing . . . Subject's views are very positively and concisely leftist; however, if she is being actively used by the Communist Party, it is not general knowledge among those working with the movement in Los Angeles.'

Detail in the report, and especially its date – July 13 – suggest it is inaccurate in one important respect. *President* Kennedy was not in California in July. It is entirely possible, though, that Marilyn had indeed lunched with *Robert* Kennedy.

The Attorney General was in Los Angeles from the afternoon of June 26 till the morning of June 28. He did indeed see Marilyn during that visit. He was to fly West again two weeks later, to Nevada, with the Chairman of the Joint Chiefs of Staff, General Maxwell Taylor. His specific purpose was to witness an atomic test.

The possibility of nuclear war – and extreme tension over Fidel Castro's Cuba and its Soviet ally – was the dominating issue in 1962. In late June and early July 1962, when – according to the FBI report one of the Kennedy brothers discussed nuclear matters with Marilyn – Castro, expecting a U.S. invasion, was making urgent appeals to the Soviet Union for help. As surveillance by U.S. aircraft would shortly discover, Nikita Khrushchev made the fateful decision to ship ballistic missiles to Cuba.

There is no suggestion in the released FBI documents that either Kennedy brother blurted out state secrets to Marilyn. The point, rather, is that any private conversation by the Attorney General or the President on the subject of nuclear weapons would have been of the utmost interest to

Soviet intelligence – at any time. U.S. intelligence doubted the loyalty of the left-wingers Marilyn had talked with during her recent Mexico trip – not least that of her host Fred Field. At Marilyn's invitation, Field would later stay in the actress' New York apartment and phone her from there. During the stay, *his* FBI file makes clear, he was under intense surveillance.

However innocuous comments either of the Kennedy brothers made to Marilyn on world affairs at any time – and in mid-1962 for sure – they would have been of intense interest to the enemies of the United States. The Kennedys' celebrity plaything was a volatile woman, running to her psychiatrist every day, chattering to all and sundry on the telephone – absolutely the wrong woman to be on intimate terms with the President and Attorney General.

This was how things were around 10.00 P.M. on the night of Saturday, August 4, when – in the wake of her troubling phone conversations with hairdresser Guilaroff and Bolaños – Marilyn began slurring her words.

47

Some five hours later – around 3:30 A.M. – Dr Greenson's daughter Joan woke to hear the phone ringing in her parents' bedroom. There were muffled voices, the sound of her parents going downstairs, then the car starting. Feeling hungry, Joan went to the kitchen to raid the refrigerator.

'I asked Mom what happened,' Joan recalled. 'She said there was a problem over at Marilyn's, and I said, "Oh" – and went back to bed.'

It was just a mile and a half from the Greenson house to Marilyn's home. As he drove, the psychiatrist was to say, he already feared the worst. The caller had been house-keeper Eunice Murray, saying that she had noticed a light in Marilyn's room at midnight. Then, after three, she had wakened to see the light still on. Afraid to anger Marilyn by waking her unnecessarily, Murray said, she had called Dr Greenson instead.

'I told her to bang on the door,' Greenson wrote to a friend shortly afterward. 'She did, and there was no answer. And she went to the front of the house and looked into the window and could see Marilyn lying very quietly on the bed. I told her I was coming right over, and for her to call Dr Engelberg.'

Greenson reached Marilyn's house in five minutes. He too, he was to say, found the bedroom door locked. He in turn went outside to peer through a window. An examination of contemporary photographs, and of the window as it was when the first edition of this book was written, showed it was possible to reach in, part the drapes, and look straight at Marilyn's bed.

There was no way, however, of getting into the room, because that window was barred. Greenson said he took a poker, broke an unbarred window at the side of the house – the smashed pane appeared later in press photographs – and then reached in to turn the handle. It was easy, then, to climb over the low sill.

'I could see from many feet away,' Greenson was to write, 'that Marilyn was no longer living. There she was, lying face down on the bed, bare shoulders exposed, and as I got closer I could see the phone clutched fiercely in her right hand. I suppose she was trying to make a phone call before she was overwhelmed. It was just unbelievable, so simple and final and over.'

Police pictures, taken a few hours later, show Marilyn stretched out, more or less covered with rumpled bedclothes. Her head lies on the pillow, right cheek down, eyes closed and face in repose as though serenely asleep.

Dr Greenson opened the door and told Eunice Murray, 'We've lost her.' Dr Engelberg arrived fifteen minutes later and agreed, in Greenson's words, that 'she was hopelessly gone.'

At 4:25 A.M., less than an hour after Eunice Murray had raised the alarm, the Central Los Angeles police switchboard took a call from Dr Engelberg. It was transferred to the West Los Angeles desk, which covered Marilyn's neighborhood. The watch commander, Sergeant Jack Clemmons, picked up the phone himself. When the doctor said, 'I am calling from the home of Marilyn Monroe. She's dead,' Clemmons suspected a practical joke. He decided to go to the scene himself.

At the house, now alive with light, Eunice Murray showed the sergeant straight into Marilyn's room, where the two doctors were sitting with the body.

Dr Greenson, who did most of the talking, pointed out one pill bottle among the many that littered the bedside table. It seemed to tell its own story: the bottle was empty, and the label read 'Nembutal.' There was no sign of a suicide note. The telephone was back on its rest, having apparently been replaced by Dr Greenson.

The tragedy of Marilyn's death aside, everything seemed to Sergeant Clemmons to be normal enough in the house. Mrs Murray was tidying up in the kitchen, even doing the laundry.

The truth of some of the details covered in the last few pages, notably the timeframe, and what had led the housekeeper to call in Dr Greenson when she did, is highly questionable.

48

At about five o'clock in the morning that Sunday, August 5, a young Los Angeles reporter named Joe Ramirez got a world scoop. The great actor Charles Laughton was known to be dying, and Ramirez had asked a contact in the Coroner's office to call him as soon as it happened. The contact called instead to say Marilyn Monroe was dead. Ramirez, who worked for a minor agency called City News, rushed to his office and put the news on the wire.

The story broke too late for the Sunday newspapers but flashed around the world, startling early-morning radio listeners and sending news editors scrambling for the telephones.

Over in Studio City, photographer Bill Woodfield was rousted out of bed by reporter Joe Hyams. Both men knew Marilyn – Woodfield was still in the midst of negotiations over the nude swim pictures. Hyams, a respected correspondent for the *New York Herald Tribune*, had written a story on her only weeks earlier. In the first thin light of dawn, Hyams and Woodfield piled into Hyams' black Mercedes – it had once belonged to Humphrey Bogart – and headed for Marilyn's house.

Associated Press columnist James Bacon, a sometime lover from Marilyn's starlet days, was tipped off about the death by a friend with a radio tuned to the police network. He too drove to the scene. There were a couple of police cars there when he arrived, and a small cluster of neighbors standing in the street in their dressing gowns. 'I pulled an old trick,' Bacon said. 'I went up to a cop and said I was from the Coroner's office, and got into the house. I didn't stay long, just long enough to see her lying there on the bed. . . . I noticed that her fingernails were unkempt. The Coroner's staff did arrive a few minutes later, and I got out of there right away.'

The Coroner's man Guy Hockett saw at once, as Dr Greenson had observed earlier, that Marilyn had been dead for 'several hours.' Rigor mortis was advanced, and 'it took about five minutes to straighten her out. . . . She was not lying quite straight, sort of in a semifetal position. Her hair was all burnt up, in terrible condition from all those treatments, you know. She didn't look good, not like Marilyn Monroe. She looked just like a poor little girl that had died, no makeup, fuzzy unmade hair, a tired body. To some degree or other, we all come to that. . . .'

The Coroner's men wheeled out Marilyn's body, covered in a blue blanket, and loaded it into a battered station wagon. They took their burden first to Westwood Village Mortuary, next to the cemetery where her maternal grandmother was buried. The remains of the most famous star on earth were lodged for a while in a broom closet cluttered with brushes, coats, and specimen bottles.

A couple of hours later the body was moved to Crypt 33 at the County Morgue, in the Los Angeles Hall of Justice. Marilyn had become a statistic – Coroner's Case No. 81128.

Two photographers got into the morgue that day. One, Bud Gray of the *Herald-Examiner,* snatched a picture of the shrouded corpse while a colleague covered the click of his camera shutter by flicking his cigarette lighter. Leigh Wiener, a freelance photographer who sent his pictures to *Life* magazine, arrived carrying a camera case in one hand and bottles of whiskey in the other. Offered a drink, one of the attendants opened a stainless-steel door and pulled out the sliding shelf that bore Marilyn's remains. Wiener took pictures of the body covered and uncovered. One, which has been published, shows a toe sticking out of the crypt, with an identification tag attached. The press had photographed the famous body for the last time.

Across the country, the living were asked for their reactions. The former husbands said little. Reached on the beat by police radio, James Dougherty managed only, 'I'm sorry.' Arthur Miller, for all his skill as a wordsmith, could hardly speak at all. Through a family member, he was quoted as saying, 'It had to happen. I don't know when or how, but it was inevitable.' Miller said he would not be going to the funeral, because 'she's not really there any more.'

The day before, in San Francisco, Joe DiMaggio had played in an exhibition game, then met friends at Bimbo's club. When he heard the news, early the following morning, he took the first available flight to Los Angeles. He contacted his son Joe Jr. at Camp Pendleton, then retreated with two close friends behind the door of Suite 1035 at the Miramar Hotel, not far from Marilyn's house.

DiMaggio quietly did what somebody had to do. Marilyn's body was at first unclaimed. Her mother was mentally incompetent, in a home, and Marilyn's half-sister agreed that DiMaggio should arrange the funeral. He insisted it was to be a small, restrained affair. DiMaggio said nothing at all to the press. In private, his friend Harry Hall remembered, he sat in his room weeping, unopened telegrams scattered on a table beside him. When he did talk, he fulminated about Sinatra, those in his circle, and about the Kennedys. 'He held Bobby Kennedy responsible for her death,' Hall remembered. 'He said that right there in the Miramar.'

Between fits of weeping, Paula Strasberg said Marilyn had 'a quality second to no actress in the world.' She added fatuously that 'Marilyn had no worries at all.' Her daughter Susan later offered the compassionate reflection, 'An iron butterfly, some people had called her. Butterflies are very beautiful, give great pleasure, and have very short life-spans.'

Milton and Amy Greene heard the news over the telephone in their hotel bedroom in Paris. They were especially shaken because Amy had had a premonition that Marilyn was in serious trouble, and had made Milton call her before leaving New York. She had said she was fine, and everyone had laughed.

Hollywood bosses, directors, and stars were badgered for opinions. Billy Wilder, getting off a plane in Paris without knowing the news, was asked what he thought of Marilyn. 'I said whatever I said, probably not all that kind,' Wilder recalls ruefully. 'Then in the cab on the way to the hotel I suddenly saw the placards through the cab window. They never told me, those SOB's. . . .'

Wilder later paid tribute to Marilyn's acting ability, as did John Huston. During *The Misfits*, Huston recalled, he had feared 'it would only be a few short years before she died or went into an institution.' Joshua Logan declared Marilyn 'one of the most unappreciated people in the world.'

Darryl Zanuck, president of Twentieth Century-Fox and a man who had taken a long time to appreciate Marilyn, was generous. 'Nobody discovered her,' he said, 'she earned her own way to stardom.'

Sir Laurence Olivier thought, 'Popular opinion is a horribly unsteady conveyance for life, and she was exploited beyond anyone's means.'

'I heard the flash over the radio at seven a.m.,' said Clark Gable's widow, Kay, whose husband had died after working with Marilyn on *The Misfits*, 'and I went to Mass and prayed for her.'

The Greenson family was grief-stricken. Dr Greenson had telephoned the news from Marilyn's home during the night, then come home exhausted. He was sure, he kept repeating, that it had been an accident. Long afterward, still punishing himself, he would say, 'She was a poor creature whom I tried to help and ended up hurting.' In the immediate aftermath, when he met Joe DiMaggio, each found himself consoling the other.

Frank Sinatra said he was 'deeply saddened ... I'll miss her very much.' His valet George Jacobs recalled, 'It was a bad time, that August. Strange things had been happening. Frank was in shock for weeks after Marilyn died, distraught. He called me and said, "Let's get out of here," and we went down to Palm Springs.'

Pat Newcomb, who had reached Marilyn's home very early that morning, caused a scene as she left. 'Keep shooting, vultures!' the press aide shrieked at the photographers. She was quoted as saying – though she denied it in an interview for this book – 'When your best friend kills herself, how do you feel?' In contradiction of all we now know, Newcomb said Marilyn had been 'feeling great,' had been in high spirits the previous evening.

In public, Peter Lawford said 'Pat [Kennedy] and I loved her dearly. She was probably one of the most marvelous and warm human beings I have ever met. Anything else I could say would be superfluous.'

On the telephone to a friend that morning, Lawford had been incoherent. He had found a pair of Marilyn's sandals at the beach house and ordered his butler to have them bronzed. He wandered into the home of a neighbor, Sherry Houser, 'in a complete state of shock, devastated, weeping. He kept saying he had been the last person to talk to her.' That detail was far from superfluous. It lies at the core of the puzzles surrounding Marilyn's death.

In New York that day, Marilyn's then biographer Maurice Zolotow found himself at a party crowded with people in politics, some of them close to the Kennedys. Already, Zolotow would recall, Robert Kennedy's name was being woven into conversations about Marilyn's tragedy.

In the afternoon East Coast time, at the Kennedy compound at Hyannis Port, the elderly Joseph Kennedy, still recovering from his stroke, was doing convalescent exercises in the swimming pool. Relatives and members of the entourage were close by. The patriarch's chauffeur and Man Friday, Frank Saunders, was in the water with him. 'His niece Ann Gargan came up and said Marilyn Monroe was dead,' Saunders recalled. 'The old man began saying, "No ... No ...," and we left the pool. A strange silence came over everybody there. It was such a curious reaction, I thought, and it stuck in my mind. Years later, when the rumors came out about Marilyn Monroe and John Kennedy and then Robert Kennedy, I remembered the silence that August afternoon. It was like attending a wake, but there wasn't one. ...'

In California, at the Bates ranch south of San Francisco, Robert Kennedy went to church that Sunday morning. Then he relaxed with his hosts, went horseback riding and played touch football. His host John Bates said Marilyn's name had come up several times since the Attorney General's arrival on Friday, but only in the general context of her problems. 'We were all aware,' he added, 'that she had some acquaintance with Jack.'

According to Bates, the fact that Marilyn had died came up only in the evening of the day the news broke, when the party returned to San Francisco. Asked whether Kennedy showed any reaction, Bates said, 'No. It was really taken rather lightly. ...' As if it was just another Hollywood tragedy? 'That's right. It was discussed,' said Bates, 'in sort of an amusing way.'

On the Monday, Robert Kennedy addressed a meeting of the American Bar Association. Then he dined privately with the Director of the CIA, before setting off on vacation with his family.

In Washington, President Kennedy made a scheduled announcement. He called on Congress for laws to enforce stricter control over the use of dangerous drugs.

*

Early on the Sunday morning, in Los Angeles, a young Deputy Medical Examiner, Dr Thomas Noguchi, had reported for the weekend shift. He found a note on his desk from his chief, Coroner Theodore Curphey, asking him to perform the autopsy on Marilyn Monroe. A Deputy District Attorney with forensic experience, John Miner, would attend as observer for the DA.

The Los Angeles Chief of Detectives, Deputy Police Chief Thad Brown, was a legendary figure, a man given to working around the clock. When he did relax he would escape to a hideaway at Malibu, a trailer with no telephone. That Sunday morning, a police dispatch rider arrived with an urgent message. Marilyn Monroe had died, and there was a problem. Would the Chief of Detectives please come to headquarters at once?

The man with ultimate responsibility for the inquiry into Marilyn's death would be Police Chief William Parker, a nationally respected officer. He shared a good deal of his worries with his wife, Helen, and she remembered that 'he wanted special attention paid to this particular case by the investigators, and he tried to send the best men out there, including detectives from the downtown office, because there was so much talk that she was very close to John or Robert Kennedy. And Mr Parker was very fond of Robert, thought he was very intelligent, thought he would've been a better President than John.'

'Robert and John Kennedy were supposed to be Catholics, I think,' said the Chief's widow, 'and Mr Parker was a Catholic. And maybe he thought undue pressure would be brought, that possibly the Republicans would jump on it. And so he said, "The thing has to be straightened out in more ways than one." Mr Parker was very, very strict, and he would lay the law down to get to the bottom of this. He would say, "Save no one."'

Chief Parker was indeed to be remembered as a man

of integrity. Yet weeks later, when his wife asked how the Monroe case was going, Parker was uncharacteristically vague. 'It seemed to be a big question mark,' Helen Parker recalled. 'I remember him just doing this' – and she drew a big question mark in the air.

There was a Coroner's investigation, and it was flawed. There was a police investigation, and there was a cover-up.

49

By 10:30 A.M. on August 5, within six hours of the first official knowledge that Marilyn was dead, the most highly advertised, overpromoted body on earth lay, covered by a plastic sheet, in a long, windowless room under the Hall of Justice. Eddy Day, the autopsy assistant, had prepared Marilyn on Table 1, a stainless-steel slab equipped with a water hose and drainage system and a scale for weighing human organs.

The autopsy surgeon, Dr Noguchi, would become a controversial figure in later years. Having risen to the post of Chief Medical Examiner, he would be demoted for allegedly mismanaging his office and sensationalizing celebrity deaths – a charge he fought. In the storm of controversy that followed, his colleagues elected him Chairman of the Board of the National Association of Medical Examiners.

Noguchi's subjects were to include the bodies of Sharon Tate, William Holden, Natalie Wood, and John Belushi. In 1968 he would probe the ruined head of Senator Robert Kennedy.

Noguchi and John Miner, the observer from the District Attorney's office, were profoundly affected when the sheet that covered Marilyn was drawn back. Miner said, 'Tom and I had looked at thousands of bodies, but we were both very touched. We had a sense of real sadness, and the feeling that this young, young woman could stand up and get off the table any minute.'

Noguchi labored over Marilyn for hours, his scalpel slicing into the body that had graced so many pinups, his surgeon's saw carving a way to remove the brain that had made millions lust and laugh. We learn from his notes that Marilyn was a '36-year-old, well-developed, well-nourished Caucasian female weighing 117 pounds and measuring 65½ inches in length. The scalp is covered with bleached blonde hair. The eyes are blue.' We are told that 'distribution of the pubic hair is of female pattern. The uterus is of usual size.' We learn of the scars the photographer's airbrush had hidden so efficiently, of the appendectomy, of the gall-bladder removal. We learn that, for all the storied excess, the living Monroe had been in fairly good shape.

When Marilyn was wheeled away, the beauty was gone. A picture retrieved from police files – the only known surviving postmortem photograph – shows a sagging, bloated face, hair hanging limp and straight over the edge of the table. The facial muscles had been severed during the removal of the brain, the remains sluiced with water once the doctor's work was done.

The surgical part of the autopsy, Noguchi knew by now, did not hold the medical explanation of Marilyn's death. Apart from a couple of bruises, which could have been caused by blundering into furniture, there was no evidence of physical violence. Knowing that pill bottles had been found on the bedside table, Noguchi said, he guessed already that the vital answers would come from the toxicologist – the poisons specialist.

Early on Monday morning, while Los Angeles commuters were still on their way to work, head toxicologist Ralph Abernethy considered a range of specimens waiting in his laboratory. They included eight pill containers – one of them the empty Nembutal bottle – vials of blood and urine, and specimens from Marilyn's stomach, intestines, liver, and kidneys. Dr Noguchi was requesting a test for alcohol and for barbiturates.

Within hours Noguchi knew that Marilyn's blood contained 4.5 milligrams per cent barbiturates, and no alcohol at all; she had not drunk any quantity of her favorite tipple, champagne, for several hours before expiring. Contrary to repeated assumptions over the years, Marilyn did not die from the classic combination of alcohol and pills.

The drugs, however, were the key. Further tests showed 13 milligrams per cent pentobarbital in the liver, and 8 milligrams per cent chloral hydrate in the blood. Pentobarbital is the chemical identified in the sleeping pill Nembutal, and chloral hydrate was one of the less dangerous sedatives found at Marilyn's house.

A pathologist at St Bartholomew's Hospital in London, Dr Christopher Foster – consulted for this book – pointed out that it is notoriously difficult to say precisely how much of a drug has been consumed by a deceased person. He calculated, however, that Marilyn's Nembutal intake was some ten times the normal therapeutic dose. The chloral hydrate level itself, he said, indicated 'a fairly stunning intake,' up to twenty times the amount usually recommended for sleep. Either of the drugs, taken in such quantities, could individually have proved fatal. Taken together, they were even more likely to kill.

Noguchi's internal examination had shown congestion and hemorrhaging of the stomach lining, a typical result of the irritation caused by barbiturates taken in excess. Together with the laboratory analysis and the bottles found in Marilyn's room, this was all too familiar to men who saw overdose victims every day.

On August 10, five days after the death, Dr Noguchi submitted his final autopsy report, giving the cause of death as 'acute barbiturate poisoning due to ingestion of overdose.' Under the heading 'Mode of Death,' he circled 'Suicide,' adding the word 'probable' in his own hand. This was the verdict the Coroner would announce to the press a week later.

The suicide finding did not satisfy a number of critics, who would dispute, above all, Noguchi's conclusion that Marilyn had swallowed the overdose, or – in Coroner Curphey's phrase – that it was 'self-administered.'

The critics raised several objections. They said it was usual to find traces of pills in the stomach – fragments of gelatin capsules and sometimes intact undigested pills. They claimed barbiturate capsules would have left a telltale trail of colored dye in the system. They suggested that barbiturate victims usually vomit before expiring.

Skeptics have also noted that no drinking glass was apparently found in Marilyn's bedroom, and no water – she would surely have needed water to wash down all those pills. In short, their suspicion has been that somebody else administered Marilyn's fatal dose – that she may have been murdered.

The absence of a drinking glass is curious. A District Attorney's review in 1982 tried to resolve the problem by referring to a published photograph of the death scene, which 'appears to show a drinking vessel.' The relevant picture shows an object by the bedside table that could conceivably be a flask.

Marilyn's bathroom, which opened off her bedroom, had no functioning plumbing that night because of remodeling operations. If she went to another room for water, Mrs Murray did not notice.

Good police work at the start should have documented the presence or absence of a glass. Yet none of three relevant police reports mention the subject. The meagre record only creates further confusion. The Death Report states that fifteen medicine bottles were found on the bedside table. Only eight are listed in the toxicology reports.

Press reports noted that Marilyn's house was formally sealed by 8:30 A.M.. on the morning of her death. Inez Melson, as her mother's guardian, was authorized to deal with Marilyn's effects. She was allowed in with her husband a day later, and recalled having noticed that the bedside table was still littered with pill bottles. 'We found bottle after bottle after bottle,' Melson said in an interview. 'There were sleeping pills, including Nembutal and Seconal. Whoever had been there before us did not take them away.'

Mrs Melson, thinking impetuously of Marilyn's reputation, destroyed the drugs. 'We threw them all down the toilet, and I think I took the bottles away and put them in the garbage,' she recalled. 'There've been many times since that I've wished I'd saved them.' Melson cannot be blamed; it was immensely inefficient that each and all of the bottles had not been delivered to the Coroner at the outset.*

Inefficiencies aside, the critics' further objections have been rebuffed by leading forensic pathologists. Medical Examiners from six American cities, two British pathologists, two toxicologists, and a gastroenterologist were consulted during research for this book, in some cases without knowing that the subject was Marilyn Monroe.

On the minor issues raised, the doctors agreed with the opinions offered to the Los Angeles District Attorney, during his 1982 review, by Dr Boyd Stephens, Chief Medical Examiner for San Francisco.

As to the absence of vomit, the pathologists unanimously rejected the notion that most barbiturate victims throw up before dying. Sometimes they do; more often, especially when Nembutal is taken over several hours, they simply go peacefully to sleep.

Nembutal capsules do contain a coloring agent, but it rarely leaves a trail, unlike Seconal, which often does. The coloring, when it is found, comes from the capsule rather

---

* Press coverage shows that, ludicrously, photographers were able to trample through the house before it was sealed. I traced one previously unpublished picture that clearly shows a bottle bearing the words: 'Engelberg ... 7.25.62 ... 0.5 gm ... at bedtime.' The name of the drug is indecipherable, but this was probably the chloral hydrate, which did reach the Coroner's office.

than the Nembutal itself. There would be no stain if the capsules had been broken open and swallowed as liquid, and that is something Marilyn sometimes did do.

These details dealt with, there is a considerable difference of opinion over the matter on which the critics were most vociferous – the fact that no residue of the capsules was discovered in Marilyn's stomach. This indicates, some critics suggested, that she did not swallow the fatal dose, that it was administered some other way – perhaps by injection. This, they said, would point to murder.

Dr Stephens, reporting to the Los Angeles DA in 1982, was not troubled by the absence of capsule residue. It was, he pointed out, again a question of 'sometimes, and sometimes not.' Remnants of capsules are often found in the stomach, but whether they are found depends on several factors: when the victim last ate, or drank liquid, and how much; the victim's individual metabolism; whether the victim was a habitual drug user with a high tolerance; and whether the drug was taken in one dose or over a period of several hours.

In Marilyn's case there was conflicting evidence on food intake. Eunice Murray said Marilyn did not eat all day, while Pat Newcomb recalled having eaten a hamburger lunch with her. By evening, in either case, her stomach would have been virtually empty and prone to rapid absorption of barbiturates. After years of drug abuse, Marilyn almost certainly had a high tolerance for barbiturates; friends recalled her having taken astonishingly high dosages without serious effect.

None of the doctors consulted were prepared to commit themselves on the number of capsules consumed. Dr Noguchi ventured a figure of between thirty and forty, and other doctors' estimates hovered between fifteen and forty.

In 1962, at his press conference, Los Angeles Coroner Curphey expressed the opinion that Marilyn ingested a large amount of the drugs 'within a short period of time.' He was quoted as estimating that she swallowed the pills in 'one gulp within – let's say – a period of seconds.'

None of the doctors commenting later, including Dr Noguchi, agreed with this notion. Absorption of a drug by the liver, as in Marilyn's case, means the digestive process has been underway for some time. The liver evidence suggests that Marilyn had taken some drugs several hours before dying.

It is here that the experts start to differ. Dr Stephens, of San Francisco, reporting to the Los Angeles District Attorney in 1982, said that, on the basis of the autopsy record, he too would have concluded that Marilyn died 'of acute barbiturate poisoning from the ingestion of an overdose.' Other eminent doctors found that conclusion too sweeping, and it was the empty stomach that bothered them.

Dr Keith Simpson was Emeritus Professor in Forensic Medicine at London University and senior pathologist to the Home Office, the top government forensic expert in Britain. He studied all the available information on Marilyn's death, at my request, and commented: 'Had I been doing that autopsy I would not have been happy to write it off promptly as suicide due to ingestion. The barbiturate levels in the blood and liver are high enough, in my experience, to make it likely that you would find a residue of the capsules in the stomach. Yet nothing was found.'

Professor Simpson said, 'It should have been routine to look further on in the digestive process, in the duodenum and the rest of the small bowel. An examination of those organs would probably have located at least some small residue if the overdose was indeed a result of swallowing Nembutal capsules.'

In Los Angeles, Dr Noguchi admitted ruefully that no such examination was ever made. He sent specimens of the relevant organs to the laboratory, but they were not tested. The tests were not done, Noguchi assumed, because the toxicologist felt the evidence in blood and liver was sufficient proof of the cause of death.

Noguchi said he did in fact try belatedly to have the specimens tested. 'For some reason I felt uncomfortable,' he said, 'and shortly after the case was formally closed I called Toxicology and requested the check. . . . Abernethy told me the organ specimens had been destroyed.'

Toxicologist Abernethy refused to comment on the destruction of the medical evidence. Later efforts to find the slides from the specimens, which are listed in the official record, turned up nothing. Nor do any medical photographs survive, though many were taken.

Dr Noguchi said he wished he had demanded checks on the intestines in the first place. 'I should have insisted that all the organs be analyzed,' he said. 'But I didn't follow through as I should have. As a junior member of the staff, I didn't feel I could challenge the department heads on procedures. . . .'

A fuller examination of the small intestine might have revealed the capsule residue that was absent in the stomach, and a great deal of controversy would have been avoided. As it was, the field was left clear for murder theories.

Could it be that Marilyn was given the fatal barbiturate dose by injection? All the doctors interviewed say this method – by introducing the drug straight into the bloodstream through a vein, into a muscle, or subcutaneously – would cause very rapid death, and that goes against the fact that a large quantity of barbiturates had been in the system long enough to be absorbed by the liver. All three people present at the autopsy said that Dr Noguchi used a magnifying glass to look for injection marks, not omitting to study the vagina and under the tongue. He found nothing.

There is one other way the fatal dose could have been administered. It is possible to insert drugs colonically – in layman's terms, by enema. Amy Greene, Marilyn's friend in New York, said Marilyn took frequent enemas, as early as the mid-fifties. Marilyn's former Los Angeles neighbor, Jeanne Carmen, remembered her complaining about chronic constipation. Enemas are used to relieve that complaint. Their use was also a common fad, particularly among show business people in those days, as an aid to instant weight loss.

'The colon shows marked congestion and purplish discoloration,' says the autopsy record. This could have been a clue, except that it does not say where on the colon the damage was.

Professor Simpson summed up: 'The absence of capsule residue, somewhat surprising in view of the barbiturate level in the blood and liver, would suggest to me one of three things. The first possibility is that Marilyn Monroe took a gradual intake of barbiturates during the course of the day – and Dr Greenson did think she was somewhat drugged when he visited her in the afternoon. This earlier Nembutal intake would have stayed in the blood for up to eight or twelve hours. She may then have taken a sudden dose of perhaps fifteen pills together – not necessarily more – and this, coupled with the previous doses, may have proved fatal. Monroe is known to have abused sleeping pills, and may have survived such a dose in the past. She may have believed she could do so again, not realizing the cumulative effect of the pills taken earlier. In that case, her death may have been not suicide but a tragic mistake.'

Before addressing Professor Simpson's second possibility, it is important to reconsider the series of telephone calls Marilyn had allegedly made to her friend Jeanne Carmen that fatal Saturday. She had, Carmen said, called early in the morning, asking her to bring over some sleeping pills. She had made the same request later, and then called again about 10:00 P.M. – though Carmen could not remember whether she was still asking for pills.

If Marilyn was begging for pills, what might that mean? Did she want to be sure of having enough drugs to commit suicide? Had she already consumed the bulk of the twenty-five capsules prescribed on the previous day? Was that why, as Eunice Murray's son-in-law observed, she looked so ravaged on Saturday morning? The questions are unanswerable, but they bring us to Professor Simpson's next option. It is as sad to contemplate as the first.

'I would also want to know,' said the Professor, 'whether, on top of the pills taken during the day, there was a separate dose administered by another route. On the evidence, the possibility of another mode of entry should be seriously considered. The fatal dose – the one that pushed her over the edge – could have been administered rectally. It could easily have been put in along with a washout.'

Such a final dose, Professor Simpson pointed out, could have been given by somebody who was unaware of the dangerously high drug level that had accumulated in Marilyn's system during the preceding hours. Again, her death would have been an accident, caused inadvertently by a second person.

The third possibility, and it is just that – a possibility – is that the fatal dose, by 'another mode of entry,' was delivered with malice aforethought. That, of course, would have been murder.

Evidence aside, what reason was there to kill Marilyn? Did anyone have a motive? Three main theories have been offered.

Some hinted darkly that Marilyn knew too much, that she and her diary had become too explosive, that the Kennedys – or some shadowy agency on their behalf – did away with her. Others speculated that Marilyn, already linked to the Kennedys by gossip, was killed by the brothers' enemies to ensure an explosion of scandal that would destroy the presidency. Which enemies?

One right-wing tract, noting that many of those around

Marilyn had leftist connections, suggested a Communist murder plot designed to protect Robert Kennedy – portrayed by the Right as a rabid left-winger – from scandal.

Norman Mailer, in his 1973 book on Marilyn, took the murder possibility seriously. He considered 'there was much motive for the right wing of the FBI or the CIA to implicate Bobby Kennedy in a scandal.'

Hank Messick was an award-winning writer on organized crime and a former consultant to New York's Joint Legislative Committee on Crime. He speculated that the Mafia – aware of the Kennedy affairs, and inspired by Marilyn's recent close call with death at Lake Tahoe – manipulated a drugged Marilyn, calling out for help, to lure Robert Kennedy into a trap.

Only the previous year, Messick pointed out, mobsters had used chloral hydrate, one of the drugs found in Marilyn's system, in a scheme to discredit a man running for local office by drugging him, putting him in bed with a young woman, then having photographs taken. In Marilyn's case, Messick suggested, the plan would have been to have Robert Kennedy come to Marilyn's rescue. Then, compromised by being at Marilyn's home in the dead of night, he would be forced to ease up on organized crime or be destroyed by exposure.

The plot failed, Messick said, when Kennedy hardened his heart and failed to rise to the bait. He refused to respond to Marilyn's pleas, and she died. Messick said his thesis was based on unattributable interviews with sources at the Justice Department and in organized crime.

Those who scorned murder theories pointed to the fact that Marilyn had tried suicide before, that she was plainly on the way to destroying herself. Her life story certainly demonstrates that. Still, murder theorists would retort, what safer way to murder a test pilot than by sabotaging his aircraft? What easier way to murder Marilyn than by simulating suicide?

Norman Mailer wrote: 'For anyone who wished to embarrass the Kennedys profoundly, and begin perhaps a whispering campaign which would destroy them by '64, how perfect a move to kill Marilyn in just such a way as to make it look like suicide in the first reports. As a suicide, however, it is so clumsily staged that by the second week every newspaper would be hinting at murder. That could do the Kennedys an unholy damage. Given the force of underground gossip … who would believe they had nothing to do with it? Even loyal Democrats might begin to wonder.'

In a sense, outside the requirements of justice, it does not matter whether Marilyn was murdered, whether she died by her own hand, or – as is possible – overestimated her capacity for Nembutal. The key to the events surrounding her end lies in the word 'scandal.' In the summer of 1962 womanizing – and the loving and leaving of Marilyn – left the Kennedy brothers open to a different sort of assassination.

The information in this book leaves no doubt that the Kennedys took a perilously cavalier attitude toward sex, perilous because the evidence shows that their enemies knew, watched, listened, and waited for an opportunity to expose them. Murder or not, Marilyn's death was such an opportunity.

It was wonderfully lucky for the Kennedys that the press failed to investigate Marilyn's passing thoroughly in 1962, that the job was left to right-wing scandalmongers with a limited audience. Luck, though, is perhaps an ill-chosen word. The circumstances of Marilyn's death, which very much involved the Kennedys, were deliberately covered up.

50

In the weeks after Marilyn's death, autopsy surgeon Thomas Noguchi was troubled by things other than forensic detail. At his office in the Hall of Justice, he said, he 'had the strong feeling that the case was being delayed, and that the scene of death had been disturbed.'

In 1962, before Coroners' investigators were introduced, a forensic pathologist had to rely on law-enforcement sources for relevant evidence other than the dead body itself. Noguchi said, 'It seemed to me, from all I observed, that it's very likely the Police Department did close things down. I've encountered this often in my experience, in deaths involving important people. . . .'The facts support his hunch.

On the morning Marilyn died, and before her house was sealed, experienced reporters saw the familiar beginnings of a police inquiry into an unnatural death. 'It was a typical police scene,' recalled James Bacon of the Associated Press, 'with the cops checking things, making chalk marks, measuring, and so on.' Many photographs were taken, the Los Angeles District Attorney determined during his 1982 review. According to a retired police officer, who asked not to be named, fingerprints were lifted. Joe Hyams, for the *New York Herald Tribune,* saw detectives covering Marilyn's bedroom 'with large canvas evidence-preserving cloth.'

At this early stage it seems, the inquiry was being conducted by detectives of the West Los Angeles Division, because the death occurred in their jurisdiction. Meanwhile, just as Police Chief Parker had told his wife he intended, headquarters began its own investigation. Although never publicly revealed, it lasted for weeks.

Thad Brown, the Chief of Detectives summoned from his weekend retreat when Marilyn died, was a man who insisted on staying in personal touch with his men and the cases they were investigating. 'Thad involved himself personally in the Monroe case,' recalled one of Brown's senior staff, former Inspector Kenneth McCauley. 'He was particularly interested in it. The boys did their homework.' Brown's brother and son, both former policemen themselves, confirmed this.

Brown's adjutant, 'Pete' Stenderup, handled the Chief of Detectives' paperwork. 'Thad followed through considerably on that one,' he remembered. 'If any guys that were working on it wanted to see him, I was to make sure they got in to see him. If anything written came in, I made sure he got it. I remember anything from three to eight pages a day for weeks and weeks. These were notes, what we called "fifteen/sevens," officers' memoranda. They were confidential, not part of the package that can be subpoenaed into court – the informal suspicions as to what might have happened. Robert Kennedy was mentioned frequently in those reports. . . .'

Brown was not personally running the Monroe inquiry. His responsibility was Homicide, and – perhaps thanks to the early forensic indications – his men never got the case. It was sent instead to another legendary figure, Captain James Hamilton, head of the Intelligence Division. He handled the matter in an atmosphere of secrecy that cut off his most trusted employees.

Hamilton's top aide, Lieutenant Marion Phillips, said, 'We knew about the inquiry, but we didn't get in on it at all. It was too damned hot. Captain Hamilton and Chief Parker were conferring on it. It went on and on, and weeks later the file went to the Chief.'

At the time this book was being researched, it appeared that little remained of the blizzard of paperwork that had gone across police desks. In 1974, after a new surge of public interest, Kenneth McCauley, by then Commander, had requested a search for the Monroe records. Homicide Special Section informed him that:

RHD [Robbery and Homicide Division] has no such records. Investigators contacted West Los Angeles Division and were informed that they had no crime reports in their files pertaining to Miss Monroe's death.

The report concluded that the vacuum was the innocent result of routine file destruction every ten years. A year later, after press allegations that Chief Parker had blocked the Monroe inquiry to curry favor with the Kennedys, the then Police Chief asked OCID – the Organized Crime Intelligence Division – to make a fresh search. They reported that even the routine Death Report, the most basic record of an unnatural death, was missing from the files. Officers began a somewhat humiliating paper chase across the city.

The Death Report, along with a handful of other documents, was finally located in a suburban garage. Chief of Detectives Thad Brown, never satisfied with the outcome of the case, had squirreled away a few documents from the early stages of the investigation. His son now handed them back to the Intelligence team, who duly collated them and reported to the Office of Operations.

In 1979, in an apparent follow-up to the 1975 inquiry, a note went to Captain Finck of OCID. It read:

The case folder ... is on file in OSS; the case folder in OSS contains all the reports in this folder, plus additional information and photographs.

OSS (Office of Special Service) was used for oddball jobs that did not fit normal categories. Since the Police Department found it so hard to keep track of things, it seems sensible to record where the surviving Monroe file was last sighted. It would, of course, be interesting to examine the full file, along with its 'additional information and photographs,' but the Police Department has not welcomed research on Monroe.

The man who supervised the 1975 review of the case was Daryl Gates, then Director of Operations. In 1984, as Police Chief, he refused to release the force's file on Marilyn's death. That, he said, was 'retained in a confidential file', but he did release what appeared to be part of the original dossier.

In 1986 former Police Chief Tom Reddin told me that there had indeed been a major report in the 1960s by the force's Organized Crime Intelligence Division and that it would 'be kept in perpetuity.' The report had not surfaced, he said, because 'There was not only a major embarrassment for the Kennedys but also apparently a national security implication.'

Lieutenant Marion Phillips, the former senior desk man in Police Intelligence, did not know what happened to the original files. He was told in 1962 that Chief Parker 'had taken the file to show someone in Washington. That was the last we heard of it.'

After Parker's death, in 1966, the Republican Mayor of Los Angeles, Sam Yorty, asked the Police Department to send over the Monroe file; he had heard the Kennedy rumors and was curious. The police told him simply, 'It isn't here. . . .'

It would be wrong to imply that Chief Parker broke his tradition of iron integrity over the Monroe case. On the evidence, it seems however possible that – presumably satisfied that murder was not involved – he passed the file on to a higher authority, thus washing his hands of the matter. That would account for the Chief's weary gesture to his wife weeks later, when he simply drew a question mark in the air.

The Police Department was not the only authority to investigate Marilyn's death. In 1982, after a fresh burst of public controversy, the Los Angeles Board of Supervisors asked the District Attorney's office to review the case.

The trigger for this review had been a public statement by a former Coroner's aide, Lionel Grandison. He had claimed publicly that he had been pressured into signing Marilyn's death certificate when he worked in the Coroner's office in 1962. Because he had been a County employee, the Board of Supervisors felt his allegations should be examined.

Assistant District Attorney Ronald Carroll investigated Grandison's claims and some other aspects of the case. He did not find Grandison credible, and disposed of some red herrings that had been raised over the years. He concluded – and was at pains to point out his careful qualification – that 'based on the information available, no further criminal investigation appears required into Miss Monroe's death.'

The Carroll enquiry, however, did discover that the District Attorney's office had been actively involved after Marilyn died. During research for this book, the Deputy DA assigned to the case at the time, John Dickey, steadfastly avoided discussing the matter. Specifically, he would not say whether he tried to interview Peter Lawford or Robert Kennedy. No trace of his inquiry could be located in existing files.

Research, however, revealed that a number of reports were made in 1962 by the DA's Investigator, Frank Hronek, who – as we noted earlier – had earlier observed both Marilyn's contacts with mobsters and nocturnal goings-on at the Lawford house. Supposedly, however, there is no trace of Hronek's reports in the DA's files.

According to his family, Hronek died suspecting that organized criminals were involved in the events surrounding Marilyn's death, and that there was indeed linkage to the Kennedy affairs. He specifically mentioned mobsters Sam

Giancana and Johnny Roselli, and said the Central Intelligence Agency intervened at some stage.

In 1962, within thirty-six hours of Marilyn's death, Coroner Curphey asked that 'all available information' be passed to the Los Angeles Suicide Prevention Center. Next day the Center's founder, Dr Norman Farberow, said, 'We are interviewing anybody and everybody. We will go as far back as is necessary.' Two days later, as he was saying that his inquiries had no limitations, the *Los Angeles Times* reported: INQUEST POSSIBILITY LOOMS. The following day the *New York Herald Tribune* headline was WHAT KILLED MARILYN? PROBE WIDENS.

Quite suddenly, however, that investigation died. On August 12, exactly a week after Marilyn's death, the headline in the San Francisco and New York press – but not in Los Angeles – read BARE MYSTERY 'PRESSURES' IN MARILYN PROBE. Florabel Muir, a veteran police reporter, wrote that 'strange pressures are being put on Los Angeles police ... sources close to the probers said tonight. ... The purported pressures are mysterious. They apparently are coming from persons who had been closely in touch with Marilyn the past few weeks.'

Five days later the case was closed down. Seventy newsmen were summoned to hear Coroner Curphey and the Suicide Prevention Team announce the verdict of 'probable suicide.' There was plenty to say about pills, Marilyn's past history, and probable time of death. Newsmen went away satisfied, and that was that.

Dr Greenson was left struggling with his ethical conscience. Over the years, as it became evident that the story the public had been given was full of holes, he became the subject of malicious gossip. After his death, when I talked with his widow and children, it was clear that this was a sensitive subject.

Her husband, Hildi Greenson indicated, had not shared the whole truth even with her. He 'wouldn't,' she said, 'want to burden me with a knowledge that I would then have had to hide.' Dr Greenson did share what he knew with his son Danny, who like him went on to become a noted psychiatrist on the West Coast. Even years later, though, Danny did not feel at liberty to share what his father had told him. Though in general very open with me, he said, 'I just don't feel comfortable telling you what he told me.'

In fact, Marilyn's psychiatrist had himself come close to revealing what he knew. Two years after Marilyn's death, caught on the run by a reporter, Greenson had said, 'I can't explain or defend myself without revealing things that I don't want to reveal. It's a terrible position to be in, to say I can't talk about it. I just can't tell the whole story.'

Pressed to say more, the psychiatrist ended the conversation with an abrupt: 'Listen . . . Talk to Bobby Kennedy.'

The exchange was preserved on audiotape.

51

The key to the 'whole story' may have been the silent witness grasped in Marilyn's stiff fingers when Dr Greenson stepped in to find her dead – the telephone. It was a dramatic angle, and the press pounced on it. So, before the abrupt end to their investigation, did the Suicide Team.

The Team's chief, Dr Farberow, wanted to ask Greenson whether, before he hung up the phone, he had heard a dial tone or silence, indicating a broken connection. Had Marilyn died while talking with someone, and if so with whom? By the second day there were banner headlines about the 'Mystery Phone Call,' and the star of the show – for a while – was Eunice Murray.

Murray said in a press interview that she 'thought Marilyn might have been phoning someone when she saw that the light was on in Marilyn's bedroom as she went to bed at midnight.' On radio broadcasts, Mrs Murray was quoted as saying that she 'saw a light shining under Miss Monroe's door.'

How Murray knew the light was on, since she agreed later that the pile of the new carpet allowed no light to shine through, would become a bone of contention. Separately, Murray was to maintain that it was not the light but the sight of the telephone extension cord, snaking across the hall and under the door, that alerted her.

Virtually none of the detail that Mrs Murray provided on the events of Marilyn's last hours and death can be taken as fact. This is clear from her contacts with two independent researchers years later. At a meeting with one of them,

Justin Clayton, she said she had 'found Marilyn's door ajar' at about midnight. Murray then 'stopped dead, suddenly raised her hand to her mouth and said, "I mean, I found the door locked . . ."' When another researcher, Roy Turner, sent her a list of questions, she responded that the door had *not* been locked.

A memoir ghosted by a relative, Rose Shade, avoided the issue by stating merely that 'some sixth sense warned Eunice of danger.' That is clearly nonsense.

Whether or not the door was locked is of course a crucial issue – relevant to the whole story about first her and then psychiatrist Dr Greenson having had to go outside and peer through a window to get a glimpse of Marilyn in her bed.

The inconsistencies in Mrs Murray's accounts cannot be attributed to failing memory or old age. As will become evident in these pages, they were almost certainly deliberate. Anything Mrs Murray said about the night of Marilyn's death must be regarded as tainted. Bear in mind, meanwhile, hairdresser Guilaroff's account of Marilyn's telephone rant to him about the Kennedys. Against that background, consider the speculation about the mystery phone call, which became a major news item.

Murray was quoted as saying of the call, 'I don't remember what time it was and I don't know who called her, but Marilyn seemed disturbed about it. . . .' How Murray knew the call *disturbed* Marilyn, when she said she last saw her around 8:00 p.m., is another moot point. She told me she could not remember the call at all.

As the banner newspaper headline became HUNT MYSTERY friend, one of Marilyn's friends came out of the woodwork. Kennedy brother-in-law Peter Lawford issued a statement through his agent, Milt Ebbins. 'At approximately 7:00 P.M.,' said Ebbins, Lawford 'called to invite her and her friend, Pat Newcomb, to attend a small dinner party at his home.' He says Miss Monroe told him she would like to come but that she was tired and was going to bed early. In an interview, Lawford himself said, 'There didn't seem to be anything at all wrong with Marilyn. She sounded fine.'

Whatever the truth of the Lawford tale – and he was to change it as time went by – it was certainly not, as one newspaper claimed, 'the end of the mystery.' If he called at seven, whose call 'disturbed' Marilyn much later that evening?

In 1962 the authorities snuffed out further speculation. 'There was no mystery call,' said a member of the Suicide Team at Coroner Curphey's final press conference. The police, for their part, had blandly announced that Marilyn 'received no telephone calls at a time which might have been related to her death.' Sergeant Byron, the detective called in to make inquiries at Marilyn's house – after the initial response by Sergeant Clemmons – reported as though it were fact that Lawford's call was the last Marilyn received.

This conclusion, reportedly made 'after an extensive investigation,' suggests supernatural sleuthing ability. There was no way to determine what calls had been *received* at a number. Only *outgoing* calls were registered at the telephone company, for billing purposes. Marilyn's outgoing calls were potentially vital information. The police did check them, on the very first morning, but thereby hangs a troubling tale.

One of the surviving fragments of the police file is a report written in the late afternoon of the day after Marilyn's death. Inspired by information given to Sergeant Byron by his boss, Lieutenant Armstrong, it states:

> Miss Monroe's phone, GR6-1890, has been checked and no toll calls were made during the hours of this occurrence. Phone number 472-4830 is being checked at the present time.

Exhaustive interviews with employees of General Telephone (GTE), the company that supplied Marilyn's service, suggest this report was nonsense. In 1962 toll calls were recorded by hand, on cardboard slips, by the operator handling the call at the local traffic center. They were filed in boxes, which were then picked up at about midnight, seven days a week, and taken to company headquarters. Calls that could be dialed, Measured Message Unit calls, were recorded on a yellow tape roll that also ended up at headquarters. The toll calls were sorted first thing in the morning, then vanished into the accounting system for at least a week, usually longer.

'There was just that brief time in limbo, in the very early morning, when you could theoretically get to them,' said a former company security officer. 'After that, they were irretrievable for days, even if J. Edgar Hoover himself wanted them. With the formalities we had then, no ordinary cop could have got to Marilyn's records till nearly two weeks after her death.'

Sergeant Byron himself long refused to comment on the Monroe case, but GTE officials assumed his 'check' on one of Marilyn's lines added up to no more than a comment from the security department that the only record immediately available had been that of Marilyn's collated bill, which was probably made up until the end of July, four days before the crucial night.

Routine practice, if a police check was required, was for the Police Chief personally to sign a request to the telephone company. Then, when the call slips came back to roost, an officer would go in person to General Telephone and make handwritten notes. Marilyn's surviving phone records reflect exactly this procedure – done some two weeks after her death. They, in turn, offer up remarkable information of their own.

The records for Marilyn's two phones, as processed for billing up to late July, show a stream of toll calls, including the ones to the Justice Department. The police list of calls covering her last days, August 1 to 4, show only three calls. One, on Friday, was to Norman Rosten in New York, and the other two were to places near Los Angeles. This is odd indeed, for testimony indicates that Marilyn spent a good deal of time talking long distance in her last two days. What happened, in the ten days before the police made their notes, to the missing calls?

On August 12, in her article reporting 'strange pressures' on the police inquiry, reporter Florabel Muir wrote of Marilyn's phone records that: 'The police have impounded the telephone company's taped record of those outgoing calls.' Muir was an old hand on the police beat, with excellent contacts.

Joe Hyams of the *Herald Tribune,* meanwhile, who with Muir was one of the very few reporters who did serious digging, was also quizzing his contacts. He stumbled on something sensational.

'The morning after her death,' said Hyams, 'I contacted a telephone company employee and asked him to copy for me the list of numbers on her tape – a service he was willing to provide for a fee. Within the hour my contact called me back from a pay phone. "All hell has broken loose down here," he told me. "Apparently you're not the only one interested in Marilyn's calls. But the tape's disappeared. I'm told it was impounded by the Secret Service – I've never before heard of the government getting in on the act. Obviously somebody high up ordered it."'

Checks on how Hyams and Muir got their information supported their stories, and indicated that the phone records had already been removed by mid-morning on Sunday, within hours of Marilyn's death being known publicly. It seems, moreover, that it was in fact the FBI that took the records, rather than the Secret Service.

It is significant that the records had been removed by early Sunday morning, because that was the one time they could be scooped up before vanishing for weeks in the accounting system. Such prompt and sweeping action required the intervention of someone with great authority and clout, someone who could roust a top General Telephone executive from his bed early on a Sunday and pressure him into immediate action.

Dean Funk, former publisher of the Santa Monica *Evening Outlook,* was a close friend of the Division Manager for General Telephone, Robert Tiarks. Funk clearly recalled sitting with Tiarks before a board meeting, not long after Marilyn's death, discussing the affair. Tiarks told him, he recalled, that 'the FBI came in and got the records, the next day . . .'

In a partially censored FBI document, written in 1973, a former senior FBI Los Angeles agent noted that he had responded to a press inquiry on the subject by saying he 'had no recollection of any such event.' 'No recollection' is a time-honored official formula for providing a negative while reserving the right to 'remember' later if facts are subsequently exposed.

The truth emerged after this book was first published. A former senior FBI agent, James Doyle, revealed to me that the FBI had indeed intervened to ensure that the records of Marilyn's final phone calls remained beyond the reach of other investigators. His knowledge was first hand.

'I was on a visit to California when Monroe died,' Doyle said, 'We were on the scene immediately, before anyone realized what had happened.' As the former agent understood it, the orders to remove the records had come from 'either the Attorney General or the President. I know that from my knowledge of the structure of the FBI, the way things were handled in those days. I knew this had come from someone via telephone and not through any trackable communication.' So that it would not appear on the record? 'That's right,' Doyle replied.

The FBI Director's close aide Cartha DeLoach said that, though he personally had not known about the FBI's seizure of the phone records, he 'did not doubt that it happened.

It would have happened because RFK asked the Old Man [J. Edgar Hoover] to have it done. And it would be another way for the Old Man to have RFK tied to his apron strings.'

Dean Funk, the Santa Monica newspaper publisher, remembered one final detail from his conversations with former telephone company executive Tiarks. 'He was hesitant in talking about it,' Funk recalled, 'but he said he knew there had been a call to Washington on the night Monroe died.'

Before his enquiry was closed down, Dr Litman of the Los Angeles Suicide Prevention Team also learned that Marilyn had called the East Coast at about 9:00 P.M. on the night of her death.

The most significant testimony on the removal of the phone records is clearly that of retired FBI agent Doyle. His certainty that the orders came from Robert Kennedy or the President himself suggests that the brothers knew the incalculable damage they could suffer were the phone records made public. To contain the damage, they were forced to turn for help to FBI Director Hoover. The brothers would forever be indebted to him.

Robert Kennedy, meanwhile, was still threatened by the record of earlier calls which – by the night of Marilyn's death – had progressed so far into the accounting system that they could not be removed by FBI intervention. The string of calls Marilyn had made to the Justice Department in June and July, obtained by this author from Los Angeles police records, could only be obtained in the formal way, by a police visit to General Telephone's office a couple of weeks after the actress' death. Once again, somebody saw to it that normal routine was bypassed.

In 1962 one police secretary, Shirley Brough, was responsible for typing all applications to see telephone records. She specifically recalled that, quite exceptionally, she was not given the Monroe paperwork. Brough, who worked in the Intelligence Division, remembered that 'it was all handled by the Captain's secretary. This was done for confidentiality. This was something very extraordinary, because of the people Marilyn Monroe was known to have associated with. So they figured they would not take any chances at all.'

The Captain, and head of the Intelligence Division, was James Hamilton, who directed the Monroe work for Chief Parker. Some time after the event he lunched with a crime reporter he had come to know and trust, Jack Tobin of the *Los Angeles Times*. Tobin said, 'Hamilton told me he had the telephone history of the last day or two of Marilyn Monroe's life. When I expressed interest, he said, "I will tell you nothing more." But it was obvious he knew much more.'

Robert Kennedy knew Captain Hamilton very well indeed. He mentioned him in his book, *The Enemy Within*, and referred to him in the foreword as 'my friend.' Kennedy admired Hamilton's intelligence-gathering system, had turned to him for advice during his work in the Senate and at the Justice Department. A year after Marilyn's death, on his retirement from the police force, Hamilton became Chief Security Officer for the National Football League. Robert Kennedy was one of those who recommended him for the job. Hamilton's son said, 'He had a relationship with the Kennedys independent of his professional function.'

On the morning of Marilyn's death, when Chief of Detectives Thad Brown had been summoned to head-quarters because of a 'problem,' he had been about to spend the day with the Assistant Chief of the regional Intelligence Division of the Treasury Department, Virgil Crabtree. The problem, Brown told Crabtree, was that a piece of crumpled paper had been found in Marilyn's bedclothes. It bore a telephone number at the White House.

Former FBI Assistant Director Cartha DeLoach had a similar recollection, with a different detail. The Bureau in Los

Angeles, he said, reported that 'Bobby Kennedy's telephone number was on the nightstand by her bed.'

Police Chief Parker's successor was Tom Reddin, who in 1962 was a Deputy Chief. He told me, 'Where Hamilton and his Intelligence Division were concerned, nobody knew a bloody thing about what was going on. Hamilton talked to only two people, God and Chief Parker. I was aware of the fact that there was a Hamilton investigation on the Monroe case, but I never knew what it was. I was also aware that there was supposed to be an internal document that never became public.'

Former Chief Reddin added: 'The Kennedy connection was a matter of common knowledge at the Police Department level I was at. The Kennedy – I should say Kennedys – relationship with Marilyn Monroe was pretty generally accepted. We heard that one of her last calls was to Bobby.'

Lawrence Schiller, one of the photographers who had covered the nude swim in *Something's Got to Give*, was out of town when he heard the news of Marilyn's death. He hurried back to Los Angeles, and that evening found himself sitting in the office of Arthur Jacobs, Marilyn's public relations consultant.

As he sat in the office, Schiller said, he overheard Jacobs talking with Pat Newcomb. Their great concern at the time, he said, was 'what would be revealed by the telephone records.'

They need not have worried. That embarrassment had been looked after.

52

What really happened the night Marilyn died? Who did what in the vital hours? The answers are there, but they are elusive. Witnesses talked only with reluctance.

In 1983, when I interviewed him in a fashionable Los Angeles restaurant, Peter Lawford looked like a frail old man. Though only sixty years old, he was worn out by a lifetime of excess. As our conversation turned to the fatal night, the slouched figure stiffened and a shaking hand crawled across the table to the ashtray. The drawling voice started to tell the story. Then Lawford said, half-sobbing, 'To this day I cannot forgive myself; there is no excuse for the fact I did not go. ...' Then, when he burst into tears, the subject had to be dropped. Lawford died as this book was going to press.

Also in 1983, Eunice Murray, to all appearances as sharp as a pin at eighty-two, sat in a rundown house in Santa Monica, taking questions and giving careful answers. A memory that seemed clear on irrelevant minutiae would suddenly became foggy on key issues concerning the night of the tragedy. I departed feeling that Murray had, very courteously, been playing with me.

Though Lawford and Murray had been prime witnesses to Marilyn's last hours, neither was ever heard under oath. Police questioned Murray within hours of Marilyn's death, then again a few days later. The second time, Lieutenant Armstrong, Commander of the West Los Angeles Detective Division, and Sergeant Robert Byron, were present. Their report of the interview read:

Los Angeles Police Department

EMPLOYEE'S REPORT

RE-INTERVIEW OF PERSONS KNOWN TO MARILYN MONROE

August 6, 1962 | Various |

G. H. ARMSTRONG, COMMANDER, WEST L. A. DETECTIVE DIVISION | 8-10-62 8:30A

The following is a resume of the interview conducted in an effort to obtain the times of various phone calls received by Miss Monroe on the evening of her death. All of the below times are estimations of the persons interviewed. None are able to state definite times as none checked the time of these calls.

MRS. EUNICE MURRAY -

Mrs. Murray stated that she had worked for Marilyn Monroe since November, 1961, that on the evening of 8-4-62 Miss Monroe had received a collect call from a Joe DiMaggio, Jr. at about 7:30P. Mrs. Murray said that at the time of this call coming in, Miss Monroe was in bed and possibly had been asleep. She took the call and after talking to Joe DiMaggio, Jr., she then made a call to Dr. Greenson and Mrs. Murray overheard her say, "Joe Jr. is not getting married, I'm so happy about this." Mrs. Murray states that from the tone of Miss Monroe's voice, she believed her to be in very good spirits. At about 9P, Mrs. Murray received a call from Mr. Rudin who inquired about Miss Monroe. Mr. Rudin did not talk to Miss Monroe. Mrs. Murray states that these are the only phone calls that she recalls receiving on this date. Note: It is officers opinion that Mrs. Murray was vague and possibly evasive in answering questions pertaining to the activities of Miss Monroe during this time. It is not known whether this is, or is not intentional. During the interrogation of Joe DiMaggio, Jr., he indicated he had made three phone calls to the Monroe home, only one of which Mrs. Murray mentioned.

JOE DiMAGGIO - Miramar Hotel, Room 1035, Santa Monica

Mr. DiMaggio was informed of the rumor which quoted him as saying that

8-10-62 9A | WLA | | R. E. BYRNE | 2730
| | | LT. J. H. A. 2030, OCRB 59

Part of the police file on Marilyn's death, released in 1985, only after it had been obtained privately by the author. It shows that investigating officers were less than satisfied with the evidence of housekeeper Mrs Murray, a key witness.

It is officers opinion that Mrs Murray was vague and possibly evasive in answering questions pertaining to the activities of Miss Monroe during this time. It is not known whether this is, or is not, intentional.

When I interviewed him – following first publication of this book – Sergeant Byron said his feeling had been that Mrs Murray 'had been told what to say, that it had all been rehearsed beforehand. She had her story and that was it.'

As for Dr Engelberg and Marilyn's attorney Milton Rudin, Byron felt, 'They were telling me what they wanted me to know. I was thrown by their attitude ... I got some wild answers. There was a lot more they could have told us ... I didn't feel they were telling us the correct time or the situation, but we did not do what we'd normally do, and drag them into the station.'

If investigating police doubted Mrs Murray, Dr Engelberg and lawyer Rudin, Peter Lawford initially left them totally frustrated. A 1962 police report reads: 'An attempt was made to contact Mr Lawford, but officers were informed by his secretary that Mr Lawford had taken an airplane at 1:00 P.M.' It was August 8, three days after Marilyn's death, and Lawford had sought refuge at the Kennedy compound in Massachusetts.

He was joined there, at the invitation of the Kennedy family, by Pat Newcomb. According to Dr Farberow, chief of the Suicide Prevention Team, Newcomb had declined to be interviewed before leaving. 'She stonewalled me,' Farberow recalled, 'was uncommunicative.'

It was thirteen years before Peter Lawford was finally interviewed by the police, during the police review of the case in 1975. He also talked to the District Attorney in 1982. Investigators found it hard to evaluate Lawford's statements. 'He was intense,' said one interrogator. 'He was not iffy about it, he was real sure about what he was saying.'

Lawford's story changed as the years passed, and from one police interview to another. Comparing the key players' statements with those of others, however, we can make a stab at reconstructing the last hours.

Several people were invited to Lawford's home on the fateful Saturday evening. They included a television producer, Joe Naar, and his wife Dolores. The Naars lived two miles from the Lawford beach house and just four blocks away from Marilyn. They were friendly with the Lawfords and had met both Marilyn and Robert Kennedy at their home. According to the Naars, Peter Lawford telephoned sometime on Saturday to ask them over for supper. Since Marilyn was also invited, Lawford asked if they would bring her in their car.

Later, before they set out that evening, Joe Naar remembered, 'Peter called to say Marilyn would not be coming after all. She was tired and felt like staying at home.'

It may be, however, that Marilyn did make a brief appearance at the Lawford house, early in the evening – perhaps going ahead with her intention, as expressed to Dr Greenson in the afternoon, of driving to the beach.

In 1979, in a conversation after Darryl Zanuck's funeral, actress Natalie Wood, who had been a friend of Marilyn for years, said she and actor Warren Beatty had been at the Lawford house a few hours before Marilyn died.

Following up on this, I contacted Beatty in 1983. He said, very hesitantly, 'I, ah, I did see her the night before she died. But, ah, I don't think I would see any particular thing to be gained by expounding on it, er ... I don't really want to be quoted. I don't think I'll speak about it. . . .'

By 'the night before she died,' was Beatty referring to the Friday or the Saturday? Beatty refused to say more on the subject. Years later, though – in a late-night conversation with producer Jørn Winther – Peter Lawford was more loose-lipped. He said he had told Marilyn that, 'Bobby Kennedy was going to be there and Warren Beatty and Natalie Wood would maybe be dropping in. Marilyn had said, "Who else?" and Lawford mentioned some ladies whose names she said she recognized as high-priced call girls. She got very upset about that and asked how he dared invite her when those women were going to be there. And she hung up. . . . Lawford talked to her once more, after she had taken the pills, and he phoned the lawyer, Milton Rudin.'

If Marilyn did go to the Lawford house on Saturday evening – or indeed if Beatty and Wood were there – it was an extremely brief visit that occurred before the other supper guests arrived. None of them were there when Joe and Dolores Naar arrived at around eight-thirty.

With the Naars at the supper party was producer George 'Bullets' Durgom. He had been at the Lawford house in the past, he said, when Marilyn 'would come in with Bobby and then leave.' That night, Durgom recalled, Lawford had ordered a Chinese dinner to be sent in, and there was talk of Marilyn being invited. She did not show up that night but he recalled that Pat Newcomb had come in 'at maybe 9.00. She stood on the step and said, "Peter, Marilyn's not coming. She's not feeling well."'

The stories remain a jumble. Lawford, in his original statement to the press, spoke of only one call to Marilyn, at 7:00 P.M., during which she begged off claiming weariness. This meshes with the Naars' version, which has Marilyn canceling before they arrived at the party. When finally interviewed by the police in 1975, however, Lawford introduced a whole new series of phone calls to Marilyn – and an ensuing drama.

Lawford told the police he had first telephoned Marilyn about 5:00 P.M., around the time a distraught Marilyn had called in Dr Greenson. Lawford said she 'sounded despondent' over the dismissal from *Something's Got to Give* and about 'some other personal matters.' He urged her to come over for the evening, and she said she would think about it.

At 7:30 P.M. or a little later, according to this Lawford version, he called Marilyn again because she had failed to turn up. She still sounded depressed, and 'her manner of speech was slurred. She stated she was tired and would not be coming. Her voice became less and less audible and Lawford began to yell at her in an attempt to revive her. [He described it as a verbal slap in the face.] Then she stated, "Say good-bye to Jack [John Kennedy], and say good-bye to yourself, because you're a nice guy."'

The phone then went dead, Lawford told the police in 1975. He assumed Marilyn had hung up, tried several times to call her back but found the number continually busy.

In 1982 Lawford told a similar story to the District Attorney's investigators, with variations. He now said there had been no second conversation, that the number was busy when he tried to call back. When it stayed busy for half an hour, he called the operator. Told the phone was off the hook, he became seriously concerned. By that time, according to one of his servants, Lawford was also very drunk.

A member of the Suicide Prevention Team, Dr Litman, said he learned that, after the last call from Marilyn, Lawford placed a call to Washington.

Lawford said he wanted to go to check on Marilyn himself, but first turned for advice to his agent, Milton Ebbins. Ebbins confirmed that this conversation occurred, though accounts differ as to whether Ebbins was present at the beach house or whether Lawford called him at home. He said he told Lawford it would be a mistake to go, and promised instead to call the attorney Marilyn shared with Frank Sinatra, Milton Rudin, who also happened to be Dr Greenson's brother-in-law.

Ebbins said he reached Rudin at another party, and Rudin – interviewed by police in 1962 – said he received the call at about 8:45 P.M. Ebbins told him of the cause for concern and he agreed to call Marilyn's house. When he did call, perhaps fifteen minutes later, the phone was answered by Mrs Murray.

Rudin turned down an interview request during research for this book, so we must make do with what he told the police three days after Marilyn died. According to the police report, he said he had asked Mrs Murray 'as to the physical well-being of Miss Monroe, and was assured by Mrs Murray that Miss Monroe was alright. Believing that Miss Monroe was suffering from one of her despondent moments, Mr Rudin dismissed the possibility of anything further being wrong.'

Eunice Murray agreed that Rudin called, but insisted the lawyer said nothing about the troubling call Marilyn had supposedly had with Lawford. She assumed it was merely a casual inquiry and, without checking on Marilyn, said all was well. By her early account, Mrs Murray would then doze until about 3.30 A.M., find the door locked, and call Dr Greenson in alarm. As we have seen, though, she was later to say the door was in fact <u>not</u> locked. What did motivate her to phone Greenson?

A pivotal question remains, too, as to Peter Lawford's behavior. Why, after his worrying telephone conversation with Marilyn, did he not simply get in his car and make the short trip to her house?

Lawford's answer was that his agent Ebbins said, 'You can't go over there! You're the brother-in-law of the President of the United States. Your wife's away. Let me get in touch with her lawyer or doctor. They should be the ones to go over.'

Though Ebbins backed up the gist of this story, does it ring true? If, as Lawford always maintained, there was no Marilyn involvement with the Kennedys, why did he feel it necessary to start a complicated chain of phone calls? Why did Ebbins, for his part, feel the matter was so sensitive? There really was no reason not to respond naturally and go to check on Marilyn.

The next snag is the problem of timing – both of Mrs

Murray's actions and of the activity at the Lawford house. Here the stories collapse in a mess of inconsistencies, which, unraveled, help resolve the bigger questions.

Mr and Mrs Naar, who offered the most cogent account of the evening, said they left the Lawfords' supper party fairly early, 'well before eleven.' They were home, getting undressed for bed, when they got an unexpected call from Lawford. He said he was worried because 'Marilyn had called to say she had taken pills, perhaps too many. She herself had expressed concern that perhaps she had overdone it.'

Lawford asked Joe Naar to stand by to go to check on Marilyn, and Naar agreed. Then, said the Naars, Lawford called again to say there was, after all, no cause for alarm. The Naars went to bed.

The Naars' evidence is vital, because it shifts the whole drama to a much later point in the evening. Both Mr and Mrs Naar are adamant that, during the supper party, between eight and soon after ten, there was no talk of concern for Marilyn, not a word about 'good-bye' phone calls. Had this drama started already, they insist, they could not have failed to hear about it. It was an intimate gathering, and they knew Lawford and Marilyn well. Yet, until the Naars left the Lawford house, all was calm.

The evidence of Bullets Durgom, the other known guest, is consistent with the Naars over the vital question of timing. He said it was late that evening, when he and Lawford were sitting around drinking, that Lawford declared his serious concern about Marilyn. It was then, Durgom said, that inquiries were started.

Here we must turn back to Mrs Murray. Immediately after the death, Dr Greenson wrote to friends saying Mrs Murray had first noticed a light on in Marilyn's room at *midnight*. She had then, as Greenson understood her, dozed off again till her 'sixth sense' woke her again about 3:30 a.m.

In the very first press quotation attributed to her, Murray

spoke of first seeing the light on 'at midnight.' The first officer on the scene, Sergeant Clemmons, said Murray told him she had first become alarmed 'at midnight.'

In a long initial interview with me, Murray also said – three times – that she had wakened to discover the body 'about midnight.' Pressed on the point however, Murray backtracked, saying the events of that unhappy night could have become jumbled in her mind.

Mrs Murray agreed there was a lengthy delay in calling the police, but laid that delay at the doctors' door. 'They had much to talk about,' she said, 'on how it could have happened, no doubt having to do with how many tablets they had prescribed for her.' Yet Dr Greenson's earliest statements to the police, and his correspondence, say flatly that the first he knew of a crisis was the call from Mrs Murray at *3:30 A.M.*

There is a great difference, actually and in the ordinary perception of a witness, between midnight and half past three. If Mrs Murray did realize Marilyn was dead or in serious trouble at midnight, and if she did not call Dr Greenson then, what did occur between the late evening and the early hours of the morning?

That mystery has almost certainly been resolved, thanks to the discovery of new witnesses and startling revelations.

53

Arthur Jacobs, head of the company that handled Marilyn's public relations, was never questioned about events on the night of her death. He died before work on this book began. His widow, Natalie, however, offered a firsthand account that completely changes the story.

As we have seen, the Jacobses were close to Marilyn. They spent a great deal of time with her in the last months, nursing her through her troubles and listening to her stories of affairs with the President and with Bobby Kennedy.

Natalie Jacobs would never forget the night of Saturday, August 4, 1962. It was the eve of her birthday, and she and Arthur went to a concert at the Hollywood Bowl. They sat under the stars listening to Henry Mancini's orchestra and piano duets by Ferrante and Teicher.

It was a fine night, and Natalie was in love. She and Arthur were not yet married, and this was a rare peaceful evening undisturbed by the demands of Hollywood clients. Then, toward the end of the concert, the peace was interrupted. Someone – she thought one of the Hollywood Bowl staff – brought Jacobs a message. It was from Pat Newcomb, Natalie believed, and the news was that Marilyn was dead.

'We got the news long before it broke,' said Natalie. 'We left the concert at once and Arthur left me at our house. He went to Marilyn's house, and I don't think I saw him for two days. He had to fudge the press.'

Natalie Jacobs was absolutely certain that the news of Marilyn's death reached them before the concert ended. A check in the *Los Angeles Times* for that day shows that the concert had begun at 8:30 p.m.; it certainly ended well before midnight. Natalie Jacobs believed they had the news by 11:00 p.m.

Reminded that, according to the version given to the police and for public consumption, Marilyn's body was not discovered till 3:40 A.M. the next morning, Natalie replied, 'Allow me to tell you why. My husband fudged everything – I cannot tell you why. I was not there. I was at home. That was his business.'

Natalie Jacobs' memory that Marilyn was known to be seriously ill or dead well before midnight, does not stand alone. Juliet Roswell, one of her husband's employees, corroborated what she said. Her boss Arthur Jacobs told her, she remembered, that he 'went out there' – to Marilyn's house – 'at eleven o'clock'.

With this testimony, a great deal falls into place. It is now apparent why the various guests at the Lawford house heard nothing about alarming phone calls with Marilyn during the early evening. We can now see why Lawford called two of his guests, the Naars, only after they had returned home, to ask them to stand by to go and check on Marilyn. And if the truth was now to be 'fudged,' we can see exactly why he called back to tell them not to bother.

It is time, too, to turn for a moment to the medical evidence. Professor Keith Simpson was keenly interested to learn that Marilyn's body was already stiff, in rigor mortis, when Dr Greenson entered the actress' room at about 3:40 A.M. Professor Simpson said, 'Rigor mortis only shows after four to six hours, *which places her death well before midnight.*'

Marilyn sounded befuddled when she spoke to various friends between eight and ten o'clock that Saturday night. It seems probable that it was not long after 10:00 P.M. that she slipped into a terminal coma. It is highly unlikely, though, that she simply lay dead in her bed until Mrs Murray's call to Dr Greenson in the early hours.

Another piece of evidence strongly suggests that this timing is correct, that the true drama began long before Greenson was alerted. That others were present at the house long before Marilyn's psychiatrist, and that, for a while, they hoped she might survive.

In 1982, during the District Attorney's review of the case, investigators received the fresh information – never even hinted at before – that an ambulance was called to Marilyn's home that night.

The DA's staff talked to a former ambulance driver called Ken Hunter, who in 1962 worked for Schaefer Ambulance, the biggest private ambulance company in the Los Angeles area. He said he attended Marilyn's home with an assistant, 'in the early morning hours.' In his account to DA's staff, he said Marilyn was already dead when the ambulance arrived. Later, however, he would be quoted as saying she had been not dead but 'in a comatose state'.

Hunter told me he saw no doctors or police. He seemed evasive and refused further contact. He had told the District Attorney that he thought his assistant that night had been an employee named Murray Liebowitz. So I traced Liebowitz, who had changed his name to Leib.

The telephone interview with Leib began with a series of silences on his part. When I explained my interest, he burst out, 'I don't want to be involved in this. . . . I wasn't on duty that night. I heard about it when I came to work next morning. . . . I'm not worried about anything, there's nothing to worry about. Don't bother to call me anymore.'

The late Walt Schaefer, then still running the ambulance company he had founded, gave several interviews for this book. He confirmed with absolute certainty that a Schaefer ambulance had indeed been called to Marilyn's home. Asked whether Murray Liebowitz had been one of the crew, he said, 'I know he was.'

Schaefer said he learned of the Monroe call the next

morning, and that the bill was subsequently paid by her estate. 'We'd hauled her before,' he recalled, 'because of the barbiturates. We'd hauled her when she comatosed.'

No less than seven former Schaefer employees recalled having heard about the call at the time, back in 1962. Further significant corroboration came from a former reporter named John Sherlock, who brought up the subject of Marilyn's death with psychiatrist Dr Greenson. Greenson, whom Sherlock met while covering a medical convention, also said Marilyn had been removed from her home by ambulance on the night she died.

Ambulance company chief Schaefer, for his part, added the most remarkable detail of all on the events of the fatal night. He said the ambulance 'took her to Santa Monica Hospital. She passed away at the hospital. She did not die at home.'

Schaefer's memory was foggy, he said, as to who summoned the ambulance or whether anyone accompanied Marilyn to the hospital. As his company kept records for only five years, there was no way of documenting the episode. Initial research at Santa Monica Hospital bore no fruit. The staff had changed many times since 1962, and it may be that the emergency room personnel never knew who they were treating – if indeed Marilyn ever reached the hospital.

That an ambulance did come to Marilyn's house – and hours before the story fed to the public as to when she was found dead – now seems confirmed. After initial publication of this book, Marilyn's next-door neighbor – a businessman named Abe Landau – told what he and his wife witnessed when they returned home at about 1:00 A.M. 'We had been out to a party and we came home and the place was like Grand Central Station,' he said in television interviews, 'Cars were all the way up the alley ... There was quite a few cars and an ambulance.'

*

The questions remain. Who called the ambulance? Who was able to accomplish the quiet return of a dead Marilyn to her home – before Mrs Murray sounded the alarm at 3:30 A.M.? If this was done, how to explain the telephone found in Marilyn's dead hand?

Testimony suggests that several people may have been at Marilyn's home well before that hour. Natalie Jacobs said Arthur Jacobs was there within an hour of leaving the Hollywood Bowl, probably by 11:30 P.M. Several people placed Milton Rudin, the lawyer, at Marilyn's house in the middle of the night.

Lawford's agent, Ebbins, who said he called Rudin earlier in the evening to raise the first alarm, said the lawyer called him at four in the morning – before the police were called.

"'I'm at Marilyn's house now,'" Ebbins quoted Rudin as saying, "'and she's dead.'" And do you know, no one has ever mentioned Rudin being at her house? He was *there.*'

Interviewed in 1973, Pat Newcomb also said she heard news of Marilyn's death 'around four,' from Rudin, calling – she thought – from Marilyn's home. Reinterviewed in 2021, she said she may in fact have been called even earlier.

In 1982, in a statement to the District Attorney's staff, Peter Lawford for the first time injected into his story the precise time at which he heard the death news, and how. He said he was wakened at 1:30 A.M. by a phone call from Ebbins, passing on news from Rudin that Marilyn was dead. Lawford said he was 'sure he received the verification at 1:30 A.M. because he looked at the bedside clock at the time of Ebbins' call.'

Ebbins, for his part, said he indeed tried to pass on the news to Lawford – but not till 4:00 A.M., and *he* said he got no response from Lawford's phone. 'I called but I couldn't get anyone,' Ebbins said. 'The phone didn't answer. . . .' Had Peter Lawford gone out? Gone where? And if so, what was his purpose?

At 6:04 A.M. that Sunday morning, West Coast time, Lawford and President Kennedy spoke on the telephone. The President was spending the weekend in Massachusetts, and – as the White House log (below) shows – it was his first call of the day. One is left to imagine what they said to each other – and what the President's reaction was when Lawford briefed him on the events of the night.

Damage control was already under way.

54

At perhaps 5:00 A.M., that Sunday morning, the radio had crackled into life at a Hollywood apartment used by Reed Wilson, the security man who had earlier been used to plant electronic devices at the Lawford beach house.

The radio call, Wilson told me, was a summons from Fred Otash, the Hollywood private detective whose name has also been linked – earlier in these pages – with hostile surveillance of Marilyn and the Kennedy brothers. Otash, Wilson, and other associates were specialists for hire. There were only a handful of them in Los Angeles in 1962 and on this occasion – great historical irony – the new mission called for a cover-up *on behalf of* the Kennedys.

At Otash's office, Wilson said, he found his colleague closeted with Peter Lawford, who was 'squirming like a worm in a frying pan.' The briefing was intense and to the point. Marilyn Monroe was dead, Wilson was told. She had tried the previous night to get through to the President – and had been greatly upset about his brother Robert.

According to Wilson, 'Lawford said Monroe had been in a rage about being used and then rejected. She felt she had been treated as a piece of meat.' Marilyn had left some sort of compromising note, but that had already been removed. Wilson's job, he was told, was to go to her house and check for anything else, papers, letters – anything – that might give away her affairs with the Kennedys.

Faced with what Wilson had told me, Fred Otash admitted that he had indeed had a dawn meeting with Lawford and Wilson, but would say no more.

Wilson said he judged the assignment to clear up at Marilyn's house impracticable, but he was to be well paid – thousands of dollars were involved. He had excellent police contacts, and by about nine o'clock he was able to walk into Marilyn's house accompanied by a police officer. The policeman, though, had no proper business at the house and was nervous. The two men spent only twenty minutes on the scene. With no chance of carrying out his mission properly, Wilson left empty-handed. Before leaving, however, he noted one important detail – a filing cabinet in the garden room had been forced open.

Bills submitted to Marilyn's estate by the A-1 Lock and Safe Company show that during the summer she had the lock changed on a filing cabinet at her home. Joe DiMaggio's friend Harry Hall, who accompanied him to the house after Marilyn died, said DiMaggio 'looked for what he referred to as a book, and it was gone. Her personal notes were gone.'

At the meeting with Lawford that morning, Reed Wilson had been told that 'Bobby Kennedy had been at Marilyn's house sometime Saturday, and was at Lawford's house sometime in the evening. They had tried to talk her into coming to the beach house. I understood Bobby had been in town and had then got out by what Lawford referred to as "the Air Force." I think he left soon after Marilyn's last call.'

Robert Kennedy, as is well documented, was indeed in California that weekend. But did he stay in the San Francisco area? Or did he go to see Marilyn in Los Angeles?

'Even Peter Pan would have had a hard time doing that,' scoffed John Bates, who had been Kennedy's host that weekend. 'It's mind-boggling.' During their weekend on the Bates ranch, Robert and Ethel Kennedy and their children spent much of their time with the Bates family. Although they used a separate guest cottage, most meals were eaten communally.

Bates thought everyone went horseback riding together

sometime on Saturday, Marilyn's last day alive. He said he would have known if Kennedy had left for long enough to reach Los Angeles and return by the early hours of Sunday.

The ranch is at Gilroy, three hundred miles northwest of Los Angeles. Kennedy, the parish priest confirmed, had been at Gilroy by 9:30 A.M. on Sunday, attending Mass at the church of St Mary.

Questioning of the Bateses aside, further checks on Kennedy's time at the ranch proved difficult. The weekend arrangements were private. The Kennedys were assisted at various stages by the San Francisco office of the FBI, but the Special Agent in Charge at the time, Frank Price, refused to comment on the Attorney General's movements.

If Robert Kennedy did make the trip to Los Angeles that Saturday, he must have made it by air. There are airstrips in the vicinity capable of taking private aircraft. And according to a number of people in Los Angeles, Kennedy did make the journey.

Ironically, information on this seems to have come from Peter Lawford, who in public was adamant that Robert Kennedy was nowhere near Los Angeles that weekend.

Marilyn's former business partner, Milton Greene, told me the matter came up when he lunched with Lawford after Marilyn's death. Lawford, Greene said, told him that Kennedy 'was in town. He saw her. He left, and went to the beach, and Marilyn got on the telephone to Lawford.'

Two senior policemen were quoted as saying that Kennedy did indeed come to Los Angeles. According to former Mayor Sam Yorty, Chief Parker told him the President's brother had been 'seen at the Beverly Hilton Hotel the night she died.'

Chief of Detectives Thad Brown told several people he believed Kennedy was in Los Angeles. Brown's brother Finis, himself a former detective, did some work on the case. He said he talked to contacts who 'said they had seen Kennedy and Lawford at a hotel the night she took the overdose. I went to Thad with the information, and he said he had been informed of the fact. He did believe Kennedy was in Los Angeles that night.'

Hugh McDonald, who was in charge of Homicide at the Sheriff's Department in 1962, quoted Thad Brown as saying, 'Bobby was indeed at the Lawford house that night, but failed to keep a dinner engagement' with Marilyn.

During the District Attorney's review in the 1980s, former Deputy DA John Dickey told investigators that he received information in 1962 that Kennedy had been in Los Angeles, and believed it.

'The truth is,' former Police Chief Daryl Gates wrote in 1992, 'we knew Robert Kennedy was in town on August 4. We always knew when he was here. ... While we knew Robert Kennedy was in town that day, we paid no attention to where he went or what he did.'

Two fragmentary reports, one from a police source, one from a former member of the Twentieth Century-Fox staff, Frank Neill, suggest Kennedy arrived in the city by helicopter, putting down near the studio's Stage 18, in an open space then used by helicopters serving the area near the Beverly Hilton. According to these sources, the President's brother arrived in the early afternoon.

In 1982, the District Attorney gave cursory attention to a report that Kennedy was seen arriving at Marilyn's home during the afternoon. I tracked that story to its source, a woman called Betty Pollard. She said her mother had been playing bridge at a neighbor's home that day, when her hostess drew the players' attention to a car parking outside. Robert Kennedy, immediately recognizable, had emerged from the car and entered Marilyn's house. The hostess mentioned that she had seen him visiting on previous occasions.

If this happened as described, it must have been before 5:00 P.M., when Dr Greenson arrived. Eunice Murray denied having seen Kennedy that day, but said that she went out shopping between two and four o'clock, leaving Pat New-comb and Marilyn in the house.*

In 1985, while being interviewed by me for the BBC, Mrs Murray at first delivered herself of the version she had usu-ally offered for public consumption. Then, as the camera crew were starting to clear up, she suddenly said, 'Why, at my age, do I still have to cover this thing? It became so sticky that the protectors of Robert Kennedy, you know, had to step in to protect him.'

Mrs Murray then astonished me by saying Robert Ken-nedy had indeed visited Marilyn on the day she died, and that a doctor and an ambulance had come while she was still alive. She said much the same in a later interview for the ABC network.

Pat Newcomb, for her part, acknowledged in a new, 2021 interview with me that, 'Something tells me that RFK might've been there on Saturday. I wouldn't have been sur-prised . . . They were friends . . .'

It was, of course, at 4:30 that Saturday afternoon that Dr Greenson, who the previous day had thought Marilyn in fairly good spirits, received an unexpected call from her. She sounded depressed.

One of the things she was distressed about, according to a Suicide Prevention Team doctor who interviewed Greenson, was that 'Marilyn had been expecting to see one of the "very important people" that evening, but the arrangement was canceled. Something had happened.'

One witness I interviewed said he sighted Kennedy at the beach that day. A check of former beach residents located

---

* Shortly before Murray went out, a mechanic, Henry D'Antonio, returned her car from the garage. Approached by me, he contradicted himself on whether or not he entered the house or not, and became highly defensive when asked what he observed that afternoon. He referred all questions back to Mrs Murray.

Ward Wood, who lived next door to the Lawford house. He had happened to be outside his house in the late afternoon or early evening, and saw Kennedy arrive. Kennedy was not in an official car. Wood, who had been in the automobile trade, thought the vehicle had been a Mercedes.

If Robert Kennedy did come to Los Angeles to see Marilyn, how and when did he leave?

Former *Herald Tribune* Bureau Chief Joe Hyams and photographer Bill Woodfield teamed up after Marilyn's death to dig into the events of the fatal night. They hired a former policeman, Bob Phillips, to help with the research. Hyams and Phillips were both told that a helicopter had touched down on the beach, close to the Lawford house, late that night. They learned this in separate interviews with Lawford's neighbors.

There is nothing inherently improbable about a helicopter being used to move people to or from the Lawford beach house. Checks with neighbors and in old press clippings revealed that Peter Lawford was infatuated with this then relatively new form of transport.

Lawford himself, in his interview with me, cheerfully admitted that he was 'chopper-happy' in those days. Neighbors at the beach regularly complained during the Kennedy presidency that helicopters landing at the beach blew sand into their swimming pools.

Reporter Joe Hyams tried to track down the helicopter said to have landed at the beach on the night of the tragedy. At an aircraft rental company, he established that 'a small helicopter had been rented on the night of Marilyn's death. But the company was not willing to allow me access to the records and flatly refused to tell me the name of the passenger. I was, in fact, warned off the premises.'

Hyams' colleague, photographer Woodfield, had better luck. He had recently used a helicopter for air-to-ground shooting when preparing an article on Frank Sinatra's luxurious private plane. The helicopter in question was one Frank Sinatra and Lawford regularly chartered. Within three days of Marilyn's death, Woodfield said, he revisited the pilot, who had flown him before, at Clover Field, Santa Monica. That was the nearest airfield to the Lawford beach house.

Woodfield said he went to the pilot on the pretext of preparing a follow-up article on the use of helicopters by celebrities, an idea he had discussed when they previously met. Because it promised welcome publicity, the pilot proved agreeable. When Woodfield asked to leaf through the helicopter's logbook, supposedly in search of famous customers who had recently used the service, he raised no objection.

Seated quietly with the log, Woodfield turned back a few days to the page covering the night of August 4–5, 1962 – and found what he had hardly dared hope for. An entry for the night of Marilyn's death showed that a helicopter had been rented to pick up a passenger at the Lawford beach house and deposit him at the main Los Angeles airport.

'The time in the log,' Woodfield recalled, 'was sometime after midnight – I think between midnight and two in the morning. It showed clearly that a helicopter had picked up Robert Kennedy at the Santa Monica Beach.'

Following up the lead that Kennedy had left by helicopter, I interviewed the family of the late Hal Conners, who frequently flew to the beach for Peter Lawford. Conners' daughter Patricia remembered her father staying out late the night Marilyn died. 'Next morning,' she said, 'I remember saying, "Did you hear Marilyn Monroe died?", and he didn't really answer at all.'

Conners' chief pilot, and Vice-President of the Los Angeles Air Taxi Service, was James Zonlick. Zonlick, traced in Florida, recalled an occasion in the second half of 1962 when Conners had picked up Robert Kennedy at the beach, and in unusual circumstances.

'Hal told me about it about three days later,' Zonlick remembered. 'We got a call from the police department because there had been complaints from the neighbors about the late hour. This was the only night trip we made in there. I got the impression it was around 9:30, or perhaps as late as 11:00 P.M. Hal had picked Robert Kennedy up at the beach house and left him at Los Angeles International Airport. . . . He was a little pleased that we'd handled that VIP sort of person.'

Ed Connelly, who also flew for Conners, had a similar memory. 'He had landed on the Santa Monica Beach without lights,' said Connelly. 'It was mysterious . . . uncharacteristic for Hal to do that sort of thing. He was almost giggly about it.'

Back in 1962, just after Marilyn's death, reporters Hyams and Woodfield realized they had the makings of a remarkable story. Huddled in the little office behind Hyams' house, they placed a call to Robert Kennedy's office in Washington. They told an aide what they had learned, and asked if Kennedy would comment, 'to put the story to rest.' The reply came quickly. They were told, Woodfield recalled, that 'the Attorney General would appreciate it if you would not do the story.'

Hyams phoned the story in to the *Herald Tribune* desk in New York anyway. An hour later he received a call from a senior editor, congratulating him on his research. 'But although we're a Republican paper and it's an election year,' said the editor, 'the story would be a gratuitous slap at the President. He'd be guilty by association. So we're killing it.'

Marilyn's adult life had been one long newspaper event, yet the only serious press effort to report a key aspect of her death had been scuttled.

55

Close associates of wiretapper Bernard Spindel, whom Teamsters' boss Hoffa reportedly hired to get information on Marilyn and the Kennedy brothers, offered a troubling account of Marilyn's final hours.

According to Spindel's associate Paris Theodore,* the wiretapper later played him some forty minutes of tape recording covering activity at Marilyn's home on the day she died.

The recording reflected two visits to Marilyn's house by Robert Kennedy. 'First,' Theodore said, 'you could hear Marilyn and Kennedy talking. It was kind of echoey and at a distance, as though the sound was in a room next to the site of the transmitter, perhaps in some sort of hallway.' Marilyn's bedroom was, in fact, around a corner from a large vestibule opening off the front door. According to Theodore, both Marilyn's and Kennedy's voices were easily recognizable.

There had been a heated argument. 'Their voices grew louder and louder,' Theodore said. 'They were arguing about something that had been promised by Robert Kennedy. Marilyn was demanding an explanation as to why Kennedy was not going to marry her. As they argued, the voices got shriller. If I had not recognized RFK's voice already, I am not sure that I would have known it was him at this point. He was screeching, high-pitched like an old lady. . . .' Kennedy, Theodore said, asked her again and again, 'Where is it? Where the fuck is it?' Marilyn did not answer, and that part of the recording ended with the sound of a door slamming.

* See Chapter 40.

The tape resumed – Theodore had no way of knowing whether Spindel had edited the recording – with Kennedy's apparent return accompanied by Peter Lawford. Alhough not familiar with Lawford's voice, Theodore relied on Spindel's identification. 'There were these three distinct voices,' he said, 'at first echoey again. RFK was saying words to the effect, "We have to know. It's important to the family. We can make any arrangements you want, but we must find it."'

'There was a clack, clack, clack on the tape,' Theodore recalled, 'which Bernie says he thought was hangers being pushed along a rail. They were still searching for whatever they were after. And there was a flopping sound – maybe books being turned over. Sometimes the tape was clear, sometimes not so clear. Kennedy was again screeching and Lawford was saying, "Calm down, calm down. . . ." Monroe was screaming at them, ordering them out of the house.'

Theodore said the next part of the recording contained 'thumping, bumping, noises, then muffled, calming sounds. It sounded as though she was being put on the bed.' The final portion of the recording included discussion between Kennedy and Lawford about Kennedy's return to the San Francisco area. It was arranged that a call would be made to Marilyn's number once Kennedy had left the area. The last sound on the tape was that of a telephone ringing, and being picked up. The person who did so, however, said nothing at all.

Does the above go any way to explaining the fact that, according to Dr Greenson, Marilyn had a phone 'clutched fiercely' in her hand when he discovered her dead? The matter of the telephone remains troubling. Two pathologists, consulted on this point, felt that a person dying of a barbiturate overdose would be 'far more likely' to relax and *let go* of the telephone as they drifted into terminal sleep. One pathologist said he found it more likely that the phone had been placed in the hand after death. After death, with the onset of rigor mortis, the muscles of the hand would naturally contract around the instrument.

Paris Theodore was the only person I interviewed who claimed to have actually heard the alleged final-hours tape in its entirety. Two other men offered partial corroboration that it existed. One, Bill Holt, was an explosives and electronics expert who worked for Spindel's company after his death in 1971. Holt, who had gone on to become a security consultant, said he knew Paris Theodore had indeed associated with Spindel. He said, too, that he was told about the tape by yet another Spindel employee, Michael Morrissey.*

Holt quoted Morrissey as having said Spindel had also played him the tape, and that it indeed reflected a visit to Marilyn's house by Kennedy and Lawford. There had been an argument, and sounds that indicated Marilyn might have fallen down.

Morrissey, who by the time of my interview had become a Washington attorney, admitted that Spindel played him a tape – but only for a few seconds. He also remembered hearing a bang or thump, as though someone had fallen heavily.

Other Spindel associates quoted the wiretapper as having discussed the Marilyn tapes. Richard Butterfield, who had become an executive for Fabergé – and his wife – said Spindel told them that Robert Kennedy was 'with her when she died'. Spindel's doctor and friend, Dr Henry Kamin, said Spindel told him of the tapes and insisted there had been some sort of incident. Earl Jaycox, the technician who had worked for Spindel in 1962, said the same. Jaycox said his employer was 'very nervous' about it.

---

* In 1975, during a Senate inquiry into CIA involvement with other Government agencies, Morrissey admitted briefing a federal official on what was described as electronic assassination equipment.

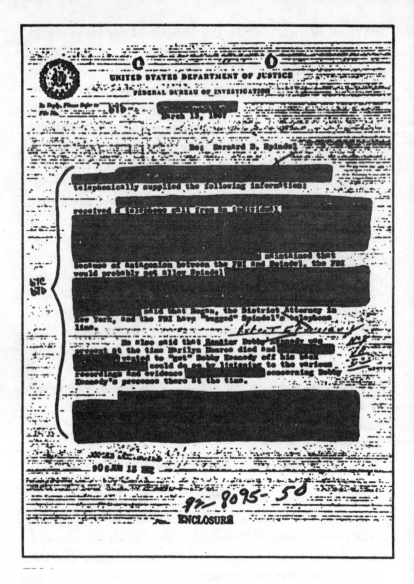

FBI document on wiretapper Bernard Spindel. Both the FBI and the CIA have released part of their heavily censored files referring to Spindel and his allegations about Marilyn and Robert Kennedy.

Whatever their exact content, what became of the tapes? At dawn on December 15, 1966 – four years after Marilyn's death – a posse of police and District Attorney's investigators descended on Spindel's home in New York State armed with a search warrant. They confiscated a great deal of material, mostly electronic equipment, and Spindel formally claimed that one purpose of the raid had been to remove evidence on Marilyn and Kennedy.

In 1985, a Freedom of Information suit resulted in obtaining heavily censored CIA and FBI reports dated soon after the raid. They show that both agencies had received information on Spindel and his alleged Monroe information (see previous page).

Spindel's lawyers sued to recover the items seized from the wiretapper's home – specifically Spindel's 'confidential file containing tapes and evidence concerning circumstances surrounding and causes of death of Marilyn Monroe, which strongly suggests that the official reported circumstances of her death are erroneous.'

Spindel told John Neary, a *Life* reporter: 'Hogan (the then New York District Attorney) really did Kennedy a favor by pulling the raid. They stole my tapes on Marilyn Monroe and my complete file.'

During the raid, court records show, Spindel had objected to the removal of certain files. They were sealed before being handed over, and appear on a signed inventory as '2 Sealed Folders – Confidential Communications.'

Research for this book did not establish what became of the material seized. A suit by Spindel's widow, which included a demand for its return, did not succeed. According to the FBI, its New York investigative file on Spindel was destroyed as a matter of 'routine.'

A lawyer who dealt with the Spindel suit, Arnold Stream, told me, 'I cannot reveal what my client told me regarding the tapes. It is still privileged information even though he is dead. I believe he told me the truth, in general and on this specific matter. . . . I am satisfied the tapes did exist, and that copies were in the possession of the District Attorney.'

56

This has above all been a book that attempts to tell a story, to report known facts and the recollections of credible witnesses. It seems justifiable however – taking the mass of information into account – to suggest a hypothesis, a possible scenario, for the last days and hours of Marilyn's life. For months, it appears, she had engaged in intermittent intimate encounters with both the President and Robert Kennedy. There had been the initial mutual attraction between stars, each of them glittering prizes in the interlocking galaxies of politics and show business. The brothers, bred to the notion that they could have any woman they desired, at first failed to perceive that in Marilyn they were dealing with a female who was doubly dangerous.

She was dangerous in a way that less celebrated mistresses – like Judith Campbell – were not. Unless literally caught in the act, perhaps by the lens of a prying camera, allegations of an affair could easily be shrugged off. In those pre-Watergate days of assumed trust in public figures, sex allegations hardly needed dignifying with a denial. Marilyn Monroe was another matter altogether. Her name was as potent as that of the Kennedys themselves.

Unstable as she was, Marilyn posed additional danger. Neither Kennedy, almost certainly, at first saw past the beauty and the intelligence to the shattered nature of her personality. It was one that – had her name not been Marilyn Monroe – as psychiatrist Dr Greenson later admitted, would have made her a candidate for an institution.

For her part, Marilyn – her grip on reality failing – may

have dreamed that something permanent could come of a Kennedy relationship. Reading between the lines of some of her comments to friends, it seems she may even have deluded herself – after marriages to great American stars of sport and culture – that she could eventually obtain the ultimate prize, the hand of a Kennedy in marriage.

In more lucid moments, the improbability of such a notion surely dawned on Marilyn. Meetings with the President were always sporadic; by the summer of 1962 it must have been apparent that his interest was little more than his habitual, cavalier self-indulgence. Meanwhile, there was Robert Kennedy.

The Attorney General, never the philanderer that his brother was, may have begun his relationship with Marilyn as a rescue mission, an attempt to steer her into comparative emotional calm. Soon enough though, perhaps at first tempted to follow his brother merely in grasping the sexual prize, Robert perhaps fell for the flickering light of Marilyn's fragile spirit. Their affair lasted for several months. Then, alarmed not least by reports that criminals were hoping to take advantage of the Kennedys' follies, the Attorney General tried to sever the connection.

That was not easily done. Nose-diving into her last despair, Marilyn proved hard to discard. She became a pest, demanded constant attention, may have tried to hold him by threatening exposure.

Kennedy brother-in-law Peter Lawford seems to have been assigned to contain the danger. But he was a weak creature, a man seduced by turns both by his White House connections and by his association with criminals like Sam Giancana. To calm Marilyn, he chose more than once to take her to the Cal-Neva Lodge, a place infested with the Kennedys' enemies. It was there that she spent her last full weekend alive, floundering in drink and drugs, beyond the help of the one man who could perhaps have brought her back from the brink, Joe DiMaggio.

On the final Friday, when Robert Kennedy arrived in San Francisco, Marilyn's pleas seem to have reached a peak. Imagining perhaps that he could reason with her, the Attorney General made a hurried visit to Los Angeles, arriving soon after midday on the Saturday. He saw her briefly at her home in Brentwood, reiterated that the Kennedy affairs could not continue, then retreated – to spend the evening either at Lawford's house, or somewhere nearby.

Unable to smother her anguish with a steady intake of sedatives, Marilyn now called in her psychiatrist, Dr Greenson. She told him that she had expected to see Robert Kennedy that night, said she was being rejected. Greenson tried to talk her down, as one would a person teetering atop some high building. He left believing he had succeeded.

Alone with her telephone and her drugs, Marilyn then made a series of calls for help. Ordinary friends were either not home or failed to understand that this moment of despair was different. Repeated calls to Robert Kennedy, or frantic messages to him through Peter Lawford, failed to bring Kennedy running. Like many a man or woman attempting to shed a lover, he may have believed that the kindest course was to take a hard stance, hang tough, keep his distance. And, too, that it was safer not to risk a further visit to Marilyn's home, in light of the danger of further exposing himself to perceived enemies.

Today it is impossible to say whether Kennedy's enemies – the agents of Sam Giancana and Jimmy Hoffa – played a role in Marilyn's last hours. The medical evidence, as we have seen, does leave open the possibility that someone other than Marilyn administered the fatal barbiturate dose. More probably, she simply underestimated the effects of a sudden large dose taken on top of a steady intake during the day. Alternatively, she deliberately took her own life.

Late that Saturday night, probably soon after 10:00 P.M., Marilyn made her final call to the Lawford home. She was rambling, confused, and it was suddenly evident that she was slipping into unconsciousness. It is fair to conjecture – and one would like to believe – that word of this jolted Robert Kennedy into a decent, humane action. It may have been he, perhaps accompanied by or followed by Peter Lawford, who now hastened the short distance to Marilyn's home. There they found her comatose, but not yet dead.

The testimony that an ambulance was called becomes pivotal. If the information from the director of the ambulance company is correct, Marilyn was taken from the house comatose but alive. She may have died on arrival at a hospital where, without makeup and swathed in blankets, no one recognized her. This author thinks it more likely that Marilyn died *before* arriving at the hospital, that someone accompanying her – Robert Kennedy himself? – was faced with an awful dilemma.

Marilyn was dead under circumstances that could spell ruin for the Attorney General. Even had he never had an affair with Marilyn – and all the evidence suggests the contrary – for a Kennedy to be found with a dead Marilyn Monroe, even on a legitimate mission of mercy, would have meant certain political disaster.

The solution was to return the body to the house in Brentwood and to the bed from which she had made her last frantic calls. Time was needed, time to get Robert Kennedy out of town. Only when that had been accomplished did a call go out to Dr Greenson, who duly came to 'discover' the body sometime between 3:30 and 4:00 A.M.

As the trail followed by reporters Hyams and Woodfield indicates, the Attorney General returned to northern California by air. His brother-in-law Peter Lawford commissioned private detective Fred Otash to try to obliterate whatever telltale tracks might remain. In the event, Otash and his associates achieved little. By early on Sunday morning however, when they were activated, more powerful wheels had been set in motion.

Summoned from the concert at the Hollywood Bowl, some time before midnight, Marilyn's public relations consultant Arthur Jacobs, a man with considerable influence in Los Angeles, had rushed to her home. He may not have known the full story of the night's events, of the aborted ambulance journey, of Robert Kennedy's nocturnal movements. But he was the right man, as his widow put it, to 'fudge everything.' Meanwhile someone with real power – perhaps Robert Kennedy himself – roused FBI director J. Edgar Hoover. Orders went out from Washington to remove the telephone records covering Marilyn's last hours, at that time still retrievable from the telephone company.

This scenario may be wrong in certain details, but it is a fair construction from the information now available. For Robert Kennedy, those night hours and the days that followed were likely some of the most harrowing of his life. If my reconstruction is essentially correct, the death of Marilyn Monroe had been his Chappaquiddick. Unlike his less fortunate brother Edward, he escaped public exposure by a hair's breadth.

57

The cover-up, and the threat of exposure, continued for years. It is not mere chance that photo agency files contain no photographs of Marilyn with either Kennedy brother, not even of the very public meeting with the President on the night she sang 'Happy Birthday' at Madison Square Garden.

Globe Photos once had at least two pictures of Marilyn with the President that night. 'In one of them,' a former senior executive said, 'he was looking up at her. You could see the admiration in his eyes – it was a great picture. . . .'

About a fortnight after Marilyn's death, however, two men flashing FBI badges visited Globe's offices. 'They said they were collecting material for the presidential library,' the former executive recalled. 'They asked to see everything we had on Monroe. I had a stock girl look after them and then – afterwards – we found that everything was gone, even the negatives. Over the years that loss must have cost us thousands of dollars. They took the lot.'

The danger was greatest for Robert Kennedy, would dog him for years. Two weeks after Marilyn died, FBI Assistant Director Courtney Evans briefed the Attorney General on information received 'that he was having an affair with a girl in El Paso.' On its face, that made little sense, and Kennedy brushed it off by saying he had never been to El Paso, Texas.

Long afterwards however, I obtained the text of the original FBI surveillance information that sparked the alert. On August 1st, Mafia 'finance minister' Meyer Lansky had been overheard by FBI surveillance microphones talking with his wife Teddy about:

> Bobby Kennedy who has seven kids and is carrying on an affair with a girl in ??? (*possibly El Paso*) [author's italics]. Teddy says it's all Frank Sinatra's fault and he is nothing but a procurer of women for those guys ... Meyer says it's not Sinatra's fault and it starts with the President and goes right down the line.

The placename had been unclear to FBI analysts transcribing the fuzzy recording about the woman allegedly linked to Robert Kennedy. Given what we know today, however, it is reasonable to guess that what the analysts heard as 'El Paso' was in fact 'Lake Tahoe' on the California-Nevada border. Robert Kennedy had been visiting the West Coast in the final days of July, and the available record does not say where he spent the weekend. Marilyn, however, was reportedly at Lake Tahoe.

In his report to J. Edgar Hoover on Kennedy's response to the Lansky wiretap, Evans wrote that: 'He said he appreciated our informing him of it, that being in public life the gossipmongers just had to talk. He said he was aware there had been several allegations concerning his possibly being involved with Marilyn Monroe. He said he had at least met Marilyn Monroe, since she was a good friend of his sister, Pat Lawford, but these allegations just had a way of growing beyond any semblance of the truth.'

On the day the Assistant Director wrote this memorandum, August 20, FBI surveillance microphones picked up an ominous conversation between three syndicate figures. They were discussing what one of them called 'a dangerous situation', in which he and his associates were likely to be prosecuted. He feared this was inevitable, but spoke of one tactic that might force the administration to hold off. It involved

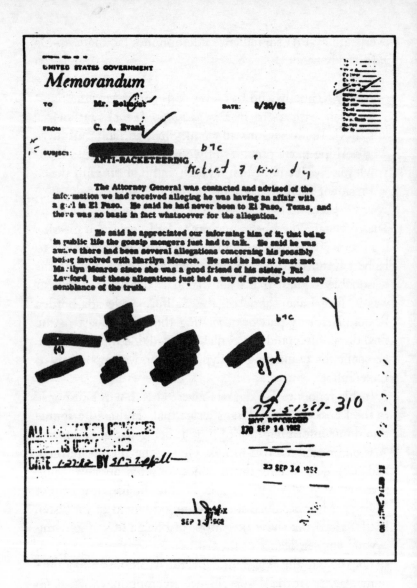

A fortnight after Marilyn's death, a dry report by FBI Assistant Director
Courtney Evans, after briefing Robert Kennedy on Mafia interest in the
Kennedy's womanizing. The latest intelligence, picked up by FBI surveillance
microphones, had come from underworld 'finance minister' Meyer Lansky –
just days before Marilyn's death.

pressure on the Kennedy brothers – and specifically on Robert Kennedy. The weapon to be used was scandal over Marilyn Monroe.

'They will go for every name,' the syndicate figure said. 'Unless the brother – it's big enough to cause a scandal against them. Would he like to see a headline about Marilyn Monroe come out? And him? How would he like it? Don't you know? . . . he has been in there plenty of times. It's been a hard affair – and this – – – – – – – – – – [female associate of Marilyn] used to be in all the time with him – do you think it's a secret?'

Robert Kennedy's assault on the Mafia continued as long as he remained in office, until 1964. That year, though, the mystery surrounding his activity at the time of Marilyn's death became dangerously public.

On July 8, 1964, J. Edgar Hoover wrote to Kennedy to warn him of pending publication of a booklet by a right-wing activist named Frank Capell. This book, Hoover wrote, 'would make reference to your alleged friendship with the late Miss Marilyn Monroe. Mr Capell stated that he will indicate in his book that you and Miss Monroe were intimate, and that you were in Miss Monroe's home at the time of her death.'

Capell had been digging into the Marilyn case since the moment of the actress' death. His book offers an insight into the dirty side of American politics of the 1960s.

Sergeant Jack Clemmons, the policeman who had been first to respond to Marilyn's house on the night she died, was no ordinary policeman. He had been a sometime Director of Fi-Po, the Fire and Police Research Association, an organization with the stated aim of spreading information on 'the subversive activities which threaten our American way of life'. Subversive activity, in 1962, referred to communism, the Red Menace. Clemmons and Capell had met shortly before Marilyn's death. Capell, himself a former sheriff's investigator, had founded the *Herald of Freedom*, a propaganda pamphlet that was to attack American liberals, and especially Robert Kennedy, for years to come.

A month after Marilyn's death, Clemmons and Capell went together to see Maurice Ries, an anthropologist who had earlier worked for the State Department. He was now associated with a Hollywood group called the Motion Picture Alliance for the Preservation of American Ideals. Its founders included John Wayne, the writer Borden Chase, and Ginger Rogers's mother. The Alliance had actively persecuted Hollywood's left-wingers.

Working together, the three men gathered as much dirt as was then possible on the Kennedy-Marilyn affair and on Marilyn's death. Then in September 1964, when Robert Kennedy was running for election as Senator for New York, Capell published a poisonous little book entitled *The Strange Death of Marilyn Monroe*. It 'identified' Marilyn's medical doctor, Hyman Engelberg, as a former Communist and pinned similar labels on others who had been close to her, acting coach Paula Strasberg and her poet friend Norman Rosten. It portrayed Robert Kennedy as an Attorney General who had let communism run rampant in the United States. And it alleged, virtually in as many words, that Robert Kennedy had murdered Marilyn – with the help of the 'Communist Conspiracy' – to protect his reputation.

Though the book failed to hurt Kennedy, efforts to smear him continued. Teamsters' leader Hoffa reached out to Fred Otash, one of the detectives who had been hired to bug Marilyn and the Kennedy brothers, in hopes of mounting a public exposé.

The specter of scandal over Marilyn was to pose a threat to Robert Kennedy almost to the end of his life. In the spring of 1968, when he was running for President, Washington reporter and Kennedy critic Ralph de Toledano was approached by a senior executive of a major corporation who was gathering information for a 'bipartisan group determined to stop Kennedy'.

If copies of the Monroe/Kennedy tapes had survived, the executive told de Toledano, the group was ready to purchase them. A retired Army Colonel, E. Dennis Harris, hired to locate the tapes, reported that authentic copies did indeed still exist and could be purchased for the right price. The plan was that 'the tapes were to be transcribed and mailed to the editors of every newspaper in the country.' Negotiations were at an advanced stage in June that year, when – six years after Marilyn's death – Robert Kennedy was assassinated.

Malign political efforts to expose their connection with Marilyn aside, the Kennedy family has also had to confront the peril posed by legitimate journalism. In 1985, ABC TV's news magazine *20/20* assigned a team of distinguished journalists to follow up the leads in this book. For award-winning *20/20* producer Stanhope Gould, the story – if it could be corroborated – was that 'the President and Attorney General of the United States had put themselves in a position to have the nation's most powerful criminals eavesdrop on their affairs with the nation's most famous actress and were exposed to blackmail . . . That's one hell of a story.'

The team asked three questions. Did the affairs really happen? Did the Mob obtain compromising bedroom tape recordings? By visiting Marilyn in Los Angeles just hours before she died, did Robert Kennedy become even more seriously compromised? Four months and a quarter of a million dollars later – a huge outlay in those days – the team had confirmed the reporting in this book and taken it further.

On the day of transmission, however, the *20/20* program on Marilyn and the Kennedys was axed and replaced by a stand-by item about guide dogs. The production team were devastated. *20/20*'s illustrious presenters, Barbara Walters and Hugh Downs, went public in their support for the production team. Downs, at the time one of the most respected figures on American television, considered the canceled program had been 'more carefully documented than anything any network did during Watergate'.

ABC News' President Roone Arledge, who had killed the program, was a longtime close friend of Robert Kennedy's widow Ethel. His Senior Assistant David Burke was a former Kennedy strategist. Arledge aide Jeff Ruhe had married one of Robert Kennedy's children. Two political operatives close to the Kennedys, Dick Tuck and William Haddad, tried to discredit the information developed for the *20/20* report and for this book.

The man who had directed two of Marilyn's movies, *Let's Make Love* and *Something's Got to Give*, George Cukor, held a firm view on the circumstances of his former star's death. 'It was a nasty business,' he told a companion, 'her worst rejection. Power and money. In the end she was too innocent.'

Part Six

EPILOGUE

'I never wanted to be Marilyn – it just happened. Marilyn's like a veil I wear over Norma Jeane.'

58

'If anything happens to me,' Marilyn had once said to Whitey Snyder, 'promise me you'll make me up.' She had been only twenty-seven at the time, busy making *Gentlemen Prefer Blondes* but already thinking of death. To ensure he remembered, she gave her makeup man a gold clip inscribed, 'While I'm Still Warm, Marilyn.'

Snyder had the clip in his pocket in August 1962, two days after the actress' death, when he made his way to the Westwood Memorial Park mortuary. He also took a bottle of gin with him. For it fell to Snyder and his future wife, Marilyn's longtime wardrobe assistant Marjorie Plecher, to restore the embalmed ruin that had been Marilyn's body.

The hair, hanging straight and limp, was covered with a wig she had worn in *The Misfits*. A chiffon scarf was wound around the neck. Below it, the famous figure was no more. After the surgeon's assault, the swelling breasts were gone.

'Oh my God,' thought Plecher, 'Marilyn without a bosom! She'd die.' She and Snyder tore up a cushion for stuffing, found plastic bags, and made their friend a false bosom. The corpse was then dressed in a simple Pucci dress that had been Marilyn's recent favorite. 'She looked beautiful,' a mourner was to say after the funeral, 'like a beautiful doll.'

With the permission of her half-sister Bernice Miracle, the funeral arrangements were made by Joe DiMaggio and Marilyn's former business manager Inez Melson. They knew she had not liked the idea of being buried, so a wall crypt was chosen. DiMaggio paid for the crypt, which cost $800, and for a bronze casket. The public was told donations should be sent to organizations that helped needy children.

DiMaggio and Melson issued a prepared statement, letting it be known that this was to be a small funeral, 'so that she can go to her final resting place in the quiet she has always sought.' Only twenty-four people were invited, including the Greensons, members of the Karger family, Lee and Paula Strasberg, veteran members of Marilyn's dressing-room team including hairdresser Guilaroff, masseur Ralph Roberts, lawyer Milton Rudin, and Pat Newcomb.

One of those not invited was Frank Sinatra. 'Sinatra and Ella Fitzgerald, and Sammy Davis, Jr,' Mrs Melson recalled, 'were determined to come. They had the audacity to bring security men and try to say they had permission to go to the chapel.' Sinatra was not allowed in, but the poodle he had given Marilyn, the dog called Maf, spent a while at Sinatra's kennel.

Peter and Pat Lawford were not included. Lawford ful-minated publicly about the fact that his wife, the President's sister, had flown from the East Coast in vain. 'It seems to be a concerted effort,' Lawford said, 'to keep some of Marilyn's old friends from attending.'

In the mortuary, Joe DiMaggio was overheard giving in-structions to one of the funeral directors. 'Be sure,' he said, 'that none of those damned Kennedys come to the funeral.'

DiMaggio spent a solitary night, before the funeral, beside Marilyn's remains. He was on his knees for much of the time.

While the ex-husband mourned inside, some devoted followers kept vigil through the night outside the gates. Next day a crowd about a thousand strong gathered to watch the ceremonies.

'There were hundreds of reporters and photographers,' Joan Greenson recalled. 'The noise of the shutters and the motor drives on the cameras drowned out any normal con-versation. At first we were not permitted to enter the chapel, the mortician informed us, because the family was with the body. I thought to myself, What family? If she'd had a family to be with, we probably wouldn't have to be here.'

The chosen guests gathered in the chapel facing a coffin that looked much too large. The eulogy was given by Marilyn's acting teacher Lee Strasberg, who said she had 'a luminous quality, a combination of wistfulness, radiance, yearning, that set her apart and yet made everyone wish to be part of it.'

A nondenominational pastor made a brief address, drawing on a verse from the Book of Psalms: 'How fearfully and wonderfully she was made by the Creator!'

The music of 'Over the Rainbow' was piped into the chapel – Marilyn had been a fan of Judy Garland. Attendants then slid a mass of flowers toward the foot of the coffin, and lifted the lid. As they did so, Joan Greenson remembered, 'a shock of yellow hair popped out. I couldn't bear to look.'

Of those who did look, DiMaggio was last. Marilyn was lying, cushioned in what the press called 'champagne-colored' velvet, a posy of DiMaggio's roses in her dead hands. Her former husband, who had wept throughout the ceremony, was heard to say 'I love you' again and again. Then he bent to give Marilyn a final kiss.

Held back by more police than were needed, the crowd watched as the coffin was borne to the Mausoleum of Memories. The hearse moved slowly, incongruously flanked by security guards from Pinkerton's, in powder-blue uniforms and white gloves.

The pastor said, 'Ashes to ashes,' and the coffin was wheeled to a hole in the wall covered by a brown curtain. Sweating in the heat, four men in black shoved the coffin into a waist-high vault.

Wreaths from the famous included those from Sinatra, Jack Benny, and Spyros Skouras. There were flowers marked simply 'Arthur,' and more from Miller's children.

One anonymous wreath bore the text of the Elizabeth Barrett Browning sonnet that goes:

How do I love thee? Let me count the ways.
 . . . I love thee with the breath,
Smiles, tears, of all my life! – and, if God choose,
I shall but love thee better after death.

Three times a week, for twenty years, Joe DiMaggio had a pair of red roses delivered to Marilyn's crypt. In 1982, without explanation, the order was canceled.

Marilyn's friend Robert Slatzer filled the gap. He sent white roses, under a covenant that would ensure delivery until long after his own death.

'Do you know where the poor darling is buried?' George Cukor said. 'You go into this cemetery past an automobile dealer and past a bank building, and there she lies, right between Wilshire Boulevard and Westwood Boulevard, with the traffic moving past.'

Gowned in green, the goddess lies behind a marble plaque reading simply: 'Marilyn Monroe 1926–1962.'

A number of other celebrities would become her neighbors in death. Peter Lawford's ashes lie fifty feet from Marilyn's crypt. Sometimes in later years, when the flowers in Marilyn's urn seemed too fresh to throw out, an attendant would move them to Natalie Wood's grave a few paces away.

One tier above Marilyn, in the same wall, lies the body of an obscure teenager called Darbi Winters. She was murdered in 1962, just after Marilyn's death. She had only recently told her mother that, one day in the distant future, she wanted to be buried near Marilyn Monroe.

Beside her, since his death in 2017, lies Hugh Hefner, the man made rich and famous by *Playboy* magazine – which had featured a nude photograph of Marilyn as its very first centerfold. Hefner had reportedly paid $75,000 to purchase the vault. 'Spending eternity next to Marilyn,' he had said, 'is too sweet to pass up.'

The Monroe faithful and the idle curious still come to

peer at the crypt. The facing stone was replaced once, after it had been chipped by souvenir hunters and marked with the lipstick smears of female kisses.

In 1965, Joe DiMaggio stood in a ceremonial lineup for baseball hero Mickey Mantle at New York's Yankee Stadium. Robert Kennedy came along the line, smiling and shaking hands. Rather than shake Kennedy's hand, Di-Maggio quickly backed away.

Three weeks after Marilyn's death, her mother Gladys had written a sad but unusually lucid little letter from the Rock Haven Sanitarium, where she was still confined. In a note to her guardian, Inez Melson, she said of 'dear Norma Jeane':

> She is at peace and at rest now and May Our God bless her and help her always ... Wanted Her to be happy and joyous. God Bless you all for Your Goodness. Loving Gratitude.

On a dark night a few months later, Marilyn's mother escaped from the Sanitarium. Clutching a Bible and a Christian Science manual, she climbed down a rope of knotted sheets and wandered off across suburban Los Angeles.

She was found in a Baptist church, and a clergyman talked to her before she was returned to confinement. 'People ought to know,' the mother said of her famous offspring, 'that I never did want her to become an actress in the first place. Her career never did her any good.'

A month before she died, sitting with the head of the studio at Twentieth Century-Fox, Peter Levathes, Marilyn had offered a sad commentary on herself.

'I'm a failure as a woman,' she said. 'My men expect so much of me, because of the image they've made of me and that I've made of myself, as a sex symbol. Men expect so much, and I can't live up to it. They expect bells to ring and

My Dear Friend Mrs Milson.
I am very Greatfull
for your kind and
gracious help
toward Berniece and
my self and to dear
Norma Jeane. She is
at peace and at rest
now and May Our
God bless her & help
theis always. Wanted
Her to be happy &
Joyous. God Bless you
all for your goodness.
    Loving
    Gratitude
    Mrs Gladys P. Eley.

whistles to whistle, but my anatomy is the same as any other woman's. I can't live up to it.'

Within days of that conversation Marilyn had asked *Life* reporter Richard Meryman, 'Do you know the book *Everyman?*' Meryman replied that he did. 'Well,' Marilyn told him, 'I want to stay just in the fantasy of Everyman.'

Dean Martin's former wife Jeanne offered this view on Marilyn and other idols of our time. 'I call them the Poster People. They're the most durably famous, yet in many cases they have nothing to them. You find them only through the roles they played in their films. I am not an uncompassionate person, but look at the way they were. The Montgomery Clifts and the Marilyn Monroes, Elizabeth Taylor. . . . In life they attract each other. They meet socially, they rush straight at each other, but they have nothing that means anything to mortals. History jettisons them forward into time, and I find their portraits on my son's bedroom wall, pale and beautiful but lost to reality.'

Marilyn Monroe was more than a Poster Person – although she had once been just that on the wall of John Kennedy's hospital room. She was a mass of paradoxes, a sex symbol who found no happiness in love, an actress who was terrified each time she stepped on to a sound stage. She was an ardent pursuer of learning who never learned to live with herself, who toppled in the end into something very close to madness.

Marilyn's legacy, for all that, is made of more solid stuff than fantasy. 'Everyman,' to whom – in the *Life* interview – she had offered her last public aspiration, remains bewitched. A fugitive from a deprived childhood, she had battled her way to world prominence with more than sex. She did it with sheer hard work, and an innate brilliance that shines out of even the inane movies with which Hollywood chose to launch her. Her presence on and off the screen made millions laugh and cry, and – even now – they show little sign of forgetting.

In the fickle century that invented 'stardom,' only Charlie Chaplin was memorialized and chronicled more than Marilyn Monroe, a fact that would probably amaze and amuse her. Marilyn's brittle, too-long laughter follows us down the decades of an era that some call the Age of Anxiety.

In that odd telegram to Robert Kennedy, weeks before she died, she described herself as one of the few remaining earthbound stars. 'All we demanded,' Marilyn said in the telegram, 'was our right to twinkle.' She more than earned that right, and Everyman has made her a goddess.

Bibliography

On Marilyn Monroe

Agan, Patrick. *The Decline and Fall of the Love Goddesses*. New York: Pinnacle, 1979.

Anderson, Janice. *Marilyn Monroe*. New York: Hamlyn, 1983.

Capell, Frank A. *The Strange Death of Marilyn Monroe*. Herald of Freedom, 1966.

Carpozi, George, Jr. *The Agony of Marilyn Monroe*. London: World Distributors, 1962.

Conover, David. *Finding Marilyn: A Romance*. New York: Grosset & Dunlap, 1981.

Conway, Michael, and Mark Ricci. *The Films of Marilyn Monroe*. Secaucus, N.J.: Citadel, 1973.

Dougherty, James E. *The Secret Happiness of Marilyn Monroe*. Chicago: Playboy, 1976.

Franklin, Joe, and Laurie Palmer. *The Marilyn Monroe Story*. New York: Rudolph Field, 1953.

Goode, James. *The Story of the Misfits*. New York: Bobbs-Merrill, 1963.

Greenson, Joan. Unpublished manuscript by the daughter of Marilyn Monroe's last psychiatrist.

Guilaroff, Sydney. *Crowning Glory*, LA: General Publishing, 1996.

Guiles, Fred Lawrence. *Norma Jean: The Life of Marilyn Monroe*. London: W. H. Allen, 1969.

—. *Legend: The Life and Death of Marilyn Monroe*. London: Granada Publishing, 1985.

Hoyt, Edwin P. *Marilyn: The Tragic Venus*. London: Robert Hale, 1967.

Hudson, James A. *The Mysterious Death of Marilyn Monroe*. New York: Volitant, 1968.

Hutchinson, Tom. *The Screen Greats: Marilyn Monroe*. New York: Exeter, 1982.

Kobal, John, ed. *Marilyn Monroe: A Life on Film*. London: Hamlyn, 1974.

Lembourn, Hans Jørgen. *Forty Days with Marilyn Monroe*. London: Arrow, Hutchinson, 1979.

Lytess, Natasha, with Jane Wilkie. *My Years with Marilyn*. Unpublished manuscript (Zolotow Collection, University of Texas, Austin).

Mailer, Norman. *Marilyn*. London: Hodder & Stoughton, 1974.

—. *Of Women and Their Elegance*. London: Hodder & Stoughton, 1980.

Martin, Pete. *Will Acting Spoil Marilyn Monroe?* New York: Doubleday, 1956.

Mellen, Joan. *Marilyn Monroe*. London: Star Books, W. H. Allen, 1974.

Monroe, Marilyn. *My Story*. London: W. H. Allen, 1974.

Moore, Robin, and Gene Schoor. *Marilyn & Joe DiMaggio*. New York: Manor, 1977.

Murray, Eunice, with Rose Shade. *Marilyn: The Last Months*. New York: Pyramid, 1975.

Pepitone, Lena, and William Stadiem. *Marilyn Monroe Confidential*. London: Sidgwick & Jackson, 1979.

Robinson, David, and John Kobal. *Marilyn Monroe: A Life on Film*. New York: Hamlyn, 1974.

Rosten, Norman. *Marilyn: An Untold Story*. London, Millington Ltd, 1974.

Sciacca, Tony *Who Killed Marilyn?* New York: Manor, 1976.

Shaw, Sam. *Marilyn Monroe as the Girl: The Making of 'The Seven Year Itch' in Pictures*. New York: Ballantine, 1955.

Skolsky, Sidney. *The Story of Marilyn Monroe*. New York: Dell, 1954.

Slatzer, Robert. *The Life and Curious Death of Marilyn Monroe*. London: W. H. Allen, 1975.

—. *The Marilyn Files*. NY: SPI, 1992.

Smith, Milburn. *Marilyn*. New York: Barven, 1971.

Spada, James, with George Zeno. *Monroe: Her Life in Pictures*. London: Sidgwick & Jackson, 1982.

Sperigilo, Milo. *Marilyn Monroe: Murder Cover-Up.* Van Nuys, Calif.: Seville, 1982.

—. *The Marilyn Conspiracy.* New York: Pocket, 1986.

Spoto, Donald. *Marilyn Monroe: The Biography.* London: Chatto & Windus, 1993.

Stern, Bert. *The Last Sitting.* London: Orbis, 1982.

Wagenknecht, Edward, ed. *Marilyn Monroe: A Composite View.* New York: Chilton, 1969.

Weatherby, W. J. *Conversations with Marilyn.* London: Robson Books, 1976.

Wolfe, Donald. *The Assassination of Marilyn Monroe.* London: Little, Brown, 1998.

Zolotow, Maurice. *Marilyn Monroe.* London: W. H. Allen, 1961.

General

Adams, Cindy. *My Friend the Dictator.* New York: Bobbs-Merrill, 1967.

—. *The Imperfect Genius.* New York: Doubleday, 1980.

Alleged Assassination Plots Involving Foreign Leaders. Interim Report of the Select Committee to Study Governmental Operations, with Respect to Intelligence Activities. U.S. Senate. Washington, D.C.: U.S. Government Printing Office, 1975.

Allen, Maury. *Where Have You Gone, Joe DiMaggio? The Story of America's Last Hero.* New York: Dutton, 1975.

Arnold, William. *Frances Farmer, Shadowland.* New York: Berkley, 1978.

Bacall, Lauren. *By Myself.* London: Jonathan Cape, 1978.

Bacon, James. *Hollywood Is a Four-Letter Town.* New York: Avon, 1976.

—. *Made in Hollywood.* Chicago: Contemporary, 1977.

Bentley, Eric, ed. *Thirty Years of Treason: Excerpts from Hearings before the House Committee on Un-American Activities, 1938–1968.* New York: Viking, 1971.

Berle, Milton. *An Autobiography.* New York: Delacorte, 1974.

Bigsby, Christopher. *Arthur Miller: 1915–1962.* London: Weidenfeld & Nicolson, 2008.

Blair, Clay, Jr, and Joan. *The Search for J. F. K.* New York: Putnam, 1976.

Blakey, Robert G., and Richard N. Billings. *The Plot to Kill the President.* New York: Times Books, 1981.

Bonanno, Joseph, with Sergio Lalli. *A Man of Honor: The Autobiography of Joseph Bonanno.* New York: Simon & Schuster, 1983.

Bosworth, Patricia. *Montgomery Clift.* London: Sidgwick & Jackson, 1979.

Brashler, William. *The Don: The Life and Death of Sam Giancana.* New York: Ballantine, 1977.

Bryant, Traphes, and Frances Spatz Leighton. *Dog Days at the White House.* London: Collier Macmillan, 1975.

Capote, Truman. *Music for Chameleons, New Writing.* London: Hamish Hamilton, 1981.

—. *The Dogs Bark, Public People and Private Places.* London: Weidenfeld & Nicolson, 1981.

Chapman, Gil and Ann. *Who's Listening Now?* San Diego: Publishers Export, 1967.

Clinch, Nancy Gager. *The Kennedy Neurosis.* New York: Grosset & Dunlap, 1973.

Cogley, John. *Blacklisting: (Movies, Vol. I,* and *Radio & Television, Vol. II).* Fund for the Republic, 1956.

Cohen, Mickey, as told to John Peer Nugent. *In My Own Words: The Underworld Autobiography of Michael 'Mickey' Cohen.* Englewood Cliffs, N.J.: Prentice-Hall, 1975.

Collier, Peter, and David Horowitz. *The Kennedys.* London: Secker & Warburg, 1984.

Corrigan, Robert W., ed. *Arthur Miller: A Collection of Critical Essays.* London: Prentice Hall, 1969.

Dallas, Rita, with Jeanira Ratcliffe. *The Kennedy Case.* New York: Popular Library, 1973.

Davis, Deborah. *Katharine the Great: Katharine Graham and The Washington Post.* New York: Harcourt Brace Jovanovich, 1979.

Davis, Sammy, Jr. *Yes, I Can.* London: Cassell, 1965.

—. *Hollywood in a Suitcase.* London: Granada Publishing, 1980.

De Gregorio, George. *Joe DiMaggio: An Informal Biography.* New York: Stein & Day, 1981.

Demaris, Ovid. *The Last Mafioso.* New York: Times Books, 1981.

De Toledano, Ralph. *R.F.K.: The Man Who Would Be President.* New York: Putnam, 1967.

—. *J. Edgar Hoover: The Man in His Time.* New Rochelle, N.Y.: Arlington, 1973.

Dick, Bernard F. *Billy Wilder.* Boston: Twayne, 1980.

Dunleavy, Stephen, and Peter Brennan. *Those Wild, Wild Kennedy Boys!* New York: Pinnacle, 1976.

Easty, Edward Dwight. *On Method Acting.* Orlando, Fla.: The House of Collectibles, 1981.

Epstein, Edward Z., and Joe Morella. *Lana.* New York: Dell, 1971, 1982.

Exner, Judith, as told to Ovid Demaris. *My Story.* New York: Grove, 1977.

Farberow, Norman L., and Edwin S. Schneidman, eds. *The Cry for Help.* New York: McGraw-Hill, 1961.

Feinman, Jeffrey. *Hollywood Confidential.* Chicago: Playboy, 1976.

Field, Frederick Vanderbilt. *From Left to Right: An Autobiography.* Westport, Conn.: Lawrence Hill & Co., 1983.

Fisher, Eddie. *Eddie: My Life, My Loves.* London: W. H. Allen, 1982.

Frank, Gerold. *Judy.* London: W. H. Allen, 1975.

Gage, Nicholas. *The Mafia Is Not an Equal Opportunity Employer.* New York: McGraw-Hill, 1971.

Gehman, Richard. *Sinatra and His Rat Pack.* New York: Belmont, 1961.

Giancana, Antoinette, and Thomas C. Renner. *Mafia Princess.* London: Allen & Unwin, 1984.

Goodman, Ezra. *The Fifty-Year Decline and Fall of Hollywood.* New York: MacFadden, 1962.

Graham, Sheilah. *Scratch an Actor.* London: W. H. Allen, 1969.

—. *My Hollywood.* London: Michael Joseph, 1984.

Guiles, Fred Lawrence. *Marion Davies.* London: W. H. Allen, 1973.

Gussow, Mel. *Darryl F. Zanuck: Don't Say Yes Until I've Finished Talking.* London: W. H. Allen, 1972.

Hamblett, Charles. *Who Killed Marilyn Monroe?* London: Leslie Frewin, 1966.

Harris, Radie. *Radie's World.* London: W. H. Allen, 1975.

Head, Edith, and Paddy Calistro. *Edith Head's Hollywood.* New York: Dutton, 1983.

Hougan, Jim. *Spooks: The Haunting of America: The Private Use of Secret Agents.* London: W. H. Allen, 1979.

Hunt, Irma. *The President's Mistresses.* New York: McGraw-Hill, 1978.

Huston, John. *An Open Book.* London: Macmillan, 1981.

Hyams, Joe. *Mislaid in Hollywood.* New York: Wyden, 1973.

Israel, Lee. *Kilgallen.* New York: Dell, 1979.

Johnson, Dorris, and Ellen Leventhal, eds. *The Letters of Nunnally Johnson.* New York: Knopf, 1981.

Kanin, Garson. *Hollywood.* London: Hart-Davis MacGibbon, 1975.

Kennedy, Robert F. *The Enemy Within.* New York: Harper & Row, 1960.

Kiernan, Thomas. *Olivier.* London: Sidgwick & Jackson, 1981.

Klurfeld, Herman. *Winchell: His Life and Times.* New York: Praeger, 1976.

Knef, Hildegard. *The Gift Horse.* London: André Deutsch, 1971.

LaGuardia, Robert. *Montgomery Clift.* London: W. H. Allen, 1973.

Lambert, Gavin. *On Cukor.* London: W. H. Allen, 1973.

Lasky, Victor. *It Didn't Start with Watergate.* New York: Dial, 1977.

Leary, Timothy. *Flashbacks: An Autobiography.* Los Angeles: Tarcher, 1984.

—. *Life Goes to the Movies.* New York: Time-Life Books, 1975.

Logan, Joshua. *Movie Stars, Real People, and Me.* New York: Delacorte, 1978.

Madsen, Axel. *Billy Wilder.* London: Secker & Warburg, 1968.

Manchester, William. *The Glory and the Dream: A Narrative History of America.* London: Michael Joseph, 1975.

Martin, Ralph G. *A Hero for Our Time.* New York: Macmillan, 1983.

Martin, Robert A., ed. *Theater Essays of Arthur Miller.* London: Penguin, 1978.

Marvin, Susan. *The Women Around R.F.K.* New York: Lancer, 1967.

Masters, George, and Norma Lee Browning. *The Masters Way to Beauty.* New York: Dutton, 1977.

Mazzola, Reparata, and Sonny Gibson. *Mafia Kingpin*. New York: Grosset & Dunlap, 1981.

Meaker, M. J. *Sudden Endings*. New York: Doubleday, 1964.

Mellen, Joan. *Pyramid Illustrated History of the Movies*. New York: Pyramid, 1973.

Messick, Hank. *The Mob in Show Business*. New York: Pyramid, 1973.

Michaelis, David. *The Best of Friends: Profiles of Extraordinary Friendships*. New York: Morrow, 1983.

Miller, Arthur. *The Misfits*. London: Secker & Warburg, 1961.

—. *Death of a Salesman*. London: Heinemann Educational, 1968.

—. *I Don't Need You Any More* (stories). London: Secker & Warburg, 1967.

—. *After the Fall*. London: Secker & Warburg, 1965.

—. *Collected Plays, Vol. II*. London: Secker & Warburg, 1981.

Miller, William. 'Fishbait,' as told to Frances Spatz Leighton. *The Memoirs of the Congressional Doorkeeper*. Englewood Cliffs, N.J.: Prentice-Hall, 1977.

Moldea, Dan E. *The Hoffa Wars*. London: Paddington Press, 1979.

Mordden, Ethan. *Movie Star: A Look at the Women Who Made Hollywood*. New York: St. Martin's, 1983.

Morella, Joe and Edward Z. Epstein. *Lana: The Public and Private Lives of Miss Turner*. London: W. H. Allen, 1983.

Muir, Florabel. *Headline Happy*. New York: Holt, 1950.

Navasky, Victor. *Kennedy Justice*. New York: Atheneum, 1971.

Negulesco, Jean. *Things I Did and Things I Think I Did: A Hollywood Memoir*. New York: Linden, 1984.

Newfield, Jack. *Robert F. Kennedy: A Memoir*. London: Jonathan Cape, 1970.

Noguchi, Thomas T., with Joseph DiMona. *Coroner to the Stars*. London: Corgi, 1984.

O'Grady, John, and Nolan Davis. *O'Grady*. Los Angeles: Tarcher, 1974.

Olivier, Laurence. *Confessions of an Actor*. London: Weidenfeld & Nicolson, 1982.

Otash, Fred. *Investigation Hollywood*. Chicago: Regnery, 1976.

Paar, Jack. *P.S. Jack Paar*. New York: Doubleday, 1983.

Parish, James Robert. *The Fox Girls*. New York: Arlington House, 1971.

Parks, Lillian Rogers, with Frances Spatz Leighton. *My Thirty Years Backstairs at the White House*. New York: Avon, 1961.

Parmet, Herbert S. Jack, *The Struggles of John F. Kennedy*. New York: Dial, 1980.

—. *JFK: The Presidency of John F. Kennedy*. London: Penguin, 1984.

Parsons, Louella. *Tell It to Louella*. New York: Putnam, 1961.

Payn, Graham, and Sheridan Morley, eds. *The Noel Coward Diaries*. London: Weidenfeld & Nicolson, 1982.

Peary, Danny. *Close-Ups*. New York: Galahad, 1981.

Powers, Thomas. *The Man Who Kept the Secrets: Richard Helms and the CIA*. London: Weidenfeld & Nicolson, 1980.

Reid, Ed. *The Grim Reapers*. Chicago: Regnery, 1969.

—. *Mickey Cohen: Mobster*. New York: Pinnacle, 1973.

Report of the Select Committee on Assassinations. U.S. House of Representatives, Ninety-fifth Congress. Washington, D.C.: U.S. Government Printing Office, 1979.

Rivkin, Allen, and Laura Kerr. *Hello, Hollywood*. New York: Doubleday, 1962.

Robinson, Edward G. *All My Yesterdays*. London: W. H. Allen, 1974.

Rosten, Leo. *Captain Newman, M.D.* New York: Harper & Row, 1961.

Saunders, Frank, with James Southwood. *Torn Lace Curtain*. London: Sidgwick & Jackson, 1983.

Scheim, David E. *Contract on America: The Mafia Murders of John and Robert Kennedy*. Silver Spring, Md.: Argyle, 1983.

Schickel, Richard. *The Stars*. New York: Dial, 1962.

Schlesinger, Arthur M., Jr. *John F. Kennedy in the White House*. London: Andre Deutsch, 1965.

—. *Robert Kennedy and His Times*. London: André Deutsch, 1978.

Sciacca, Tony. *Kennedy and His Women*. New York: Manor, 1976.

—. *Sinatra*. New York: Pinnacle, 1976.

—. *Screen Greats Vol. II*. New York: Starlog Press, 1980.

Selznick, Irene Mayer. *A Private View*. London: Weidenfeld & Nicolson, 1983.

Shaw, Arnold. *Sinatra: Twentieth-Century Romantic.* New York: Pocket Books, 1969.

Sheridan, Walter. *The Fall and Rise of Jimmy Hoffa.* New York: Saturday Review Press, 1972.

Signoret, Simone. *Nostalgia Isn't What It Used to Be.* London: Weidenfeld & Nicolson, 1978.

Skolsky, Sidney. *Don't Get Me Wrong, I Love Hollywood.* New York: Putnam, 1975.

Smith, Joseph Burkholder. *Portrait of a Cold Warrior.* New York: Putnam, 1976.

Spindel, Bernard B. *The Ominous Ear.* New York: Award House, 1968.

Stempel, Tom. *Screenwriter: The Life and Times of Nunnally Johnson.* London: Tantivy Press, 1980.

Strasberg, Susan. *Bitter Sweet.* New York: Putnam, 1980.

Sullivan, William C., with Bill Brown. *The Bureau: My Thirty Years in Hoover's F.B.I.* New York: Norton, 1979.

Summers, Anthony. *Not in Your Lifetime.* New York: Open Road, 2013.

Talese, Gay. *Thy Neighbor's Wife.* London: William Collins, 1980.

Teresa, Vincent. *My Life in the Mafia.* London: Hart-Davis MacGibbon, 1973.

Thomas, Bob. *Winchell.* New York: Doubleday, 1971.

Thompson, Nelson. *The Dark Side of Camelot.* Chicago: Playboy, 1976.

Tierney, Gene, with Mickey Herskowitz. *Self Portrait.* New York: Wyden, 1979.

Ungar, Sanford J. *F.B.I.* Boston: Little, Brown, 1976.

Wagenknecht, Edward. *As Far as Yesterday: Memories and Recollections.* Norman: University of Oklahoma Press, 1968.

—. *Seven Daughters of the Theater.* Norman: University of Oklahoma Press, 1964.

Walker, Alexander. *The Celluloid Sacrifice.* London: Michael Joseph, 1966.

Wallace, Irving; Amy Wallace; David Wallechinsky; and Sylvia Wallace. *The Intimate Sex Lives of Famous People.* London: Arrow Books, Hutchinson, 1982.

Warner, R. H., Chief Special Agent, General Telephone Co. *Wireless Electronic Surveillance: Handbook for Investigators.*

Wilkie, Jane. *Confessions of an Ex-Fan Magazine Writer.* New York: Doubleday, 1981.

Wills, Garry. *The Kennedy Imprisonment.* New York: Pocket Books, 1981, 1982.

Wilson, Earl. *The Show Business Nobody Knows.* London: W. H. Allen, 1972.

—. *Show Business Laid Bare.* New York: Putnam, 1975.

—. *Sinatra.* London: W. H. Allen, 1976.

—. *Hot Times: True Tales of Hollywood and Broadway.* New York: Contemporary Books, 1984.

Winters, Shelley. *Shelley.* London: Granada Publishing, 1981.

Wofford, Harris. *Of Kennedys and Kings.* New York: Farrar, Straus & Giroux, 1980.

Yeats, W. B. *Selected Poetry.* London: Pan Books, 1974.

Zolotow, Maurice. *Billy Wilder in Hollywood.* London: W. H. Allen, 1977.

Since publication of *Goddess*, there has been a continuing stream of books about Marilyn Monroe. The following merit mention:

Banner, Lois. *The Passion and the Paradox.* London: Bloomsbury, 2012.

Casillo, Charles. *Marilyn Monroe: The Private Life of a Public Icon.* New York: St. Martin's Press, 2018.

Gates, Daryl, with Diane Shah. *Chief: My Life in the LAPD.* New York: Bantam, 1992.

Guilaroff, Sydney, with Cathy Griffin. *Crowning Glory: Reflections of Hollywood's Favorite Confidant.* Los Angeles: General Publishing, 1996.

Marshall, David. *The DD Group: An Online Investigation into the Death of Marilyn Monroe.* New York: iUniverse, 2005.

McGovern, Donald. *Murder Orthodoxies: A Non-Conspiracist's View of Marilyn Monroe's Death.* Morrisville, NC: Lulu Publishing, 2018.

Spoto, Donald. *Marilyn Monroe: The Biography*. London: Chatto & Windus, 1993.

Vitacco-Robles, Gary. *Cursum Perficio: Marilyn Monroe's Brentwood Hacienda*. New York: Writers' Club, 1999.

Wolfe, Donald. *The Assassination of Marilyn Monroe*. New York: Little, Brown, 1998.

Notes

In the following notes, books are indicated by the author's name, or name and a short title if there is more than one book by the same author. All interviews are indicated by the abbreviation *int*. and were conducted by the author, unless otherwise designated.

Chapter 1

3 August 4, 1962, scene: int. Natalie Jacobs, 1985.
3 Coverage: *Hollywood Citizen-News*, Dec. 31, 1962.
3 District Attorney inquiry: int. Assistant District Attorney Ronald Carroll and Investigator Alan Tomich, 1983.
4 Mailer: int., 1985.
5 Last interview: Richard Meryman, *Life*, Aug. 3, 1962.
5 Geminis: Weatherby, 112.
6 Mother: Film Comment, Sept. 1982; *National Enquirer*, 1982; int. James Haspiel, 1983.
6 Gladys's birth: marriage certificate, in Slatzer, 351.
6 MM birth: certificate, in Slatzer, 347.
6 Mortenson: *Photoplay*, Dec. 1962; *Los Angeles Daily News* and *The Register*, Feb. 13, 1981 (on death of a Mortenson); corr. MM genealogist Roy Turner, 1983.
6 MM denies Mortenson: Hedda Hopper, int. transcript, March 10, 1953 (Zolotow collection). See also Dougherty, 73; Skolsky, *Don't Get Me Wrong*, 220.
6 Gifford: Guiles, *Norma Jean*, 7.
7 Gable: Guiles, *Norma Jean*, 38; int. Hildi Greenson, 1983; *Empire News* (London), May 9, 1954.
7 Official form: int. Marjorie Stengel, 1983.

7   Forebears: data supplied by Monroe genealogist Roy Turner; Guiles, *Norma Jean*, 16; *Empire News*, May 9, 1954.

7   Genetic risk from syphilis: int. Dr Burke Cunha, infectious disease specialist, and Dr Yehudi Fehnan, clinical professor of dermatology, both of New York City.

7   Delia 'smothered' MM: Arthur Miller, in Guiles, *Norma Jean*, 14.

8   Mother 'not mad': int. Inez Melson, 1983.

8   'Atheist Jew': int. Hildi and Joan Greenson, 1983.

10 Psychiatrists: corr. Dr Ruth Bruun, Dr Bertel Bruun, and Dr Valérie Shikhverg, all of New York, 1985.

10 Shikhverg: corr. and int. 1985.

Chapter 2

13 'Arrival at school': *Empire News*, May 16, 1954.

13 Hecht: *Empire News*, May 2–Aug. 1, 1954.

13 Controversy: George Carpozi, *New York Post*, June 21, 1974; *Los Angeles Herald-Examiner*, Sept. 1, 1954.

15 Dougherty marriage: Dougherty; Lytess; Wilkie, 126ff, 172ff; *Empire News*, May 16, 1954.

17 MM in factory: *Empire News*, May 16, 1954.

18 Conover: Conover, opening chapters; int. David Conover, 1983; *Modern Screen*, July 1954; Georges Belmont, int. Monroe, Jours de France, 1960.

18 Figure (fn.): Palmer 12; Donald Zec, London *Daily Express*, Aug. 6, 1962; int. Billy Travilla, 1983.

20 Acting: *Empire News*, May 23, 1954.

20 MM explores Hollywood: *Empire News*, May 23, 1954.

Chapter 3

21 MM on Norma Jean: *Empire News*, May 16, 1954.

21 'Faithful': *Empire News*, May 16, 1954.

21 Dougherty trust: Dougherty, 86.

22 MM in 1960: Jaik Rosenstein, *Hollywood Close-Up*, May 17, 1974.

22   De Dienes: Dougherty, 93–95; corr. André de Dienes, 1984; Jack Smith, *Los Angeles Times*, Aug. 8, 1962; Mailer, *Marilyn*, 76ff.; Hudson, 36.

24   Conover: int., 1983; int. Robert Markel, formerly of Grosset & Dunlap, 1984.

24   Lembourn: Lembourn; corr. Mrs Norman Nordstrand, 1984; *New York Times*, June 3, 1979; James Haspiel, Films in Review, Aug./Sept. 1979.

24   Jean-Louis: int., 1983.

25   MM on men in Hollywood: *Empire News*, May 16, 1954.

26   'Call-girl': Adams, *Imperfect Genius*, 253; Strasberg, in *Swank*, Aug. 1980; int. Cindy Adams, 1985.

26   Pepitone: int., 1984; Pepitone and Stadiem, 80.

26   Halsman: *Popular Photography*, June 1953 and Jan. 1956.

27   First sex: Skolsky, *Don't Get Me Wrong*, 222

27   Shearer: *Parade*, Aug. 5, 1973.

28   Rape (MM version): *Empire News*, May 9, 1954.

28   Feury: int., 1983.

29   Rosenstein: *Hollywood Close-Up*, May 17, 1974.

29   Greenson: corr. colleague, 1960.

30   Nightmare: Dougherty, 34.

30   Freud: *New York Times*, Science Supplement, Jan. 24, 1984.

30   'George': *Empire News*, May 9, 1954; Monroe, 19.

30   Greene: int., 1984.

31   Kinsey: Kinsey *et al.*, *Sexual Behavior in the Human Female*, Philadelphia: W. B. Saunders & Co., 1953, 282ff.

31   Dougherty: Dougherty, 37.

31   MM interest in sex: Monroe, 28.

31   'Something else': Wilkie, 127.

31   Mitchum: Wilson, *Show Business Nobody Knows*, 299; int. Wilson, 1984.

32   MM and babies: *Empire News*, May 16, 1954.

32   Diaphragm: Dougherty, 36.

33   Carmen: int., 1983.

33   Child?: Pepitone and Stadiem, 75; int., 1984; int. Amy Greene and Jeanne Carmen, 1983–84.

34   Leonardi: Wilson, *Show Business Laid Bare*, 61; int. James Haspiel, 1984.

35   Painkillers: Zolotow, *Marilyn Monroe*, 26.

35   Rosenfeld: int., 1984.

35   Monroe on future child: *Empire News*, May 16, 1955; Monroe, 31.

35   Suicide: *New York Post*, Aug. 7, 1962.

35   MM in Las Vegas: Dougherty, 99.

36   Dougherty (fn.): *Los Angeles Daily News*, July 15, 1984.

Chapter 4

37   Slatzer meeting: int., 1983; Slatzer, 86.

38   Slatzer *bona fides* (fn.): see chapter 11.

38   Zahn: corr. and int., 1983–84.

39   Hughes: *Los Angeles Times*, July 29, 1946; (fn.) Wilson, *Show Business Nobody Knows*, 308; Wilson, *Hot Times*, 72; int. Terry Moore, 1985.

39   Different names: int. James Haspiel, 1984.

40   Lyon: Parsons, 213; *Los Angeles Herald-Examiner*, Aug. 6, 1962; *Los Angeles Daily News*, June 13, 1953.

40   Screen test: Zolotow, *Marilyn Monroe*, 50.

40   MM on contract: *Empire News*, May 30, 1954.

40   Zahn: int., 1983.

40   Name: Wilson, *Los Angeles Daily News*, June 13, 1953.

41   Shawhan: int., 1983.

42   Skolsky: int., 1983; Skolsky, *Don't Get Me Wrong*, 213; Goodman, 53; John Sherwood, *Los Angeles Herald-Examiner*, Oct. 17, 1962.

43   Carnovsky: Zolotow, *Marilyn Monroe*, 61ff.

43   Burnside: London *Observer*, May 6, 1984.

44   School reports (for 1942): Los Angeles City High School District files, in Slatzer, 354.

44   Occult: *Los Angeles Daily News*, Aug. 18, 1962; int. Susan Strasberg and Kenny Kingston, 1983; David Robinson, Town, Nov. 1962; Joe Hyams, *New York Daily News*, Aug. 18, 1962; int. Gordon Heaver, Robert Slatzer, and Eli Wallach, 1983–84, int., 1985.

45   Literature: Zolotow, *Marilyn Monroe,* 66, 251; *Life,* April 7, 1952; Bill Burnside, London *Observer,* May 6, 1984; Knef, 256; Winters, 293.

45   Lincoln: int., Milton and Amy Greene, Joshua Logan, Brad Dexter, and James Haspiel, 1983–84.

45   Sandburg: int. Henry Weinstein, 1984; *Look,* Sept. 11, 1962; Weatherby, 141; int. Amy Greene, and Ted Strauss, 1983–84; Alan Levy, 'A Good Long Look at Myself,' *Redbook,* Aug. 1962; Winchell, *Los Angeles Herald-Examiner,* Aug. 6, 1962.

45   'The people': *Life,* Aug. 3, 1962.

45   Vesalius: in Rupert Allan, 1983; Zolotow, *Marilyn Monroe,* 46.

Chapter 5

47   Chaplin, Jr, affair: in Lita Grey, former wife Chaplin, Sr, 1983; int. Arthur James, 1983; int. Nan Morris, widow of Edward G. Robinson, Jr.

48   Slatzer: int. Robert Slatzer and Will Fowler, 1983.

48   Wohlander: Wilson, *Show Business Laid Bare,* 61, Int. Wilson, 1984.

48   Bodne: Theresa Garofalo, int. Mrs Bodne, 1984.

48   Nudity dream: *Empire News,* May 9, 1954; Monroe, 16.

49   Reading Freud: Zolotow, *Marilyn Monroe,* 10.

49   Policeman: *Parade,* Aug. 5, 1973; Monroe, 70; 'So Far to Go,' *Redbook,* June 1952; *Hollywood Citizen-News,* June 3, 1952; Graham, Confessions, 137.

49   Guardian's husband: Guiles, *Norma Jean,* 41.

50   Skolsky disbelief: Skolsky, *Don't Get Me Wrong,* 222.

50   Carroll meeting: int. May Mann, 1983; int. Robert Slatzer, 1983; Guiles, *Norma Jean,* 93.

51   MM on men in Hollywood: *Empire News,* May 30, 1954.

51   MM casting couch story: *Empire News,* May 23, 1954.

51   Churchill: corr. and int. Tommy Zahn, 1983.

51   Rosenstein: *Hollywood Close-Up,* May 17, 1974.

52   MM and Lyon: int. Sheilah Graham, 1985.

52   Schenck: int. Marion Marshall Wagner, 1983.

53 Taps: int., 1983.

54 Bacon: int., 1983; Bacon, *Hollywood Is a Four-Letter Town*, 125.

55 Chasin: int., 1983.

55 Minardos: int. 1983.

55 *Let's Make Love* party: int. Rupert Allan, 1983; Guiles, *Norma Jean*, 304.

55 Greene: int., 1984.

56 Romanoff: int., 1983.

56 Weatherby: Weatherby, 142.

56 Older men: Jaik Rosenstein, *Hollywood Close-Up*, May 17, 1974.

56 MM on Schenck: *Empire News*, June 6, 1954.

Chapter 6

58 Lytess: Lytess; Wilkie, 126ff., 172ff., Natasha Lytess, *Screen World*, Nov. 1953; Bill Tusher, *Movie Minor*, May 1957.

59 Pepitone: int., 1984; Pepitone and Stadiem, 192.

59 Muir: int. Robert Slatzer, 1983.

59 Skolsky: int. Steffi Skolsky, 1983.

59 MM on 'lesbian': Weatherby, 108; *Empire News*, June 13, 1954; Monroe, 76.

60 Lytess: Lytess, 4.

60 Karger affair: int. Anne Batté and Bennett Short, Patti Karger, Terry Melton, Elizabeth Karger, Vi Russell, and Richard Quine, 1983.

62 MM on affair: *Empire News*, June 13, 1954; Monroe, 78.

63 Watch: int. Elizabeth Karger, 1983; *Empire News*, June 20, 1954; Monroe, 83.

63 'Bitchy': Skolsky, *Don't Get Me Wrong*, 223.

64 Lytess: Lytess, 4.

65 Taps: int., 1983.

65 MM and Cohn: *Empire News*, June 6, 1954.

65 Variation on Cohn story: Hoyt, 54ff.

65 Krekes: Conway and Ricci, 29.

65 MM sees movie: int. Anne Batté, 1983.

Chapter 7

67   Lytess: Lytess, 6.

67   Starr: int., 1983.

68   *Photoplay* event: Adele Fletcher, *Photoplay*, Sept. 1965.

68   Wilson: int., 1984; Wilson, *Show Business Nobody Knows*, 306.

68   Rosenfeld: int., 1984.

69   Hyde (dentist and cosmetic surgery): int. Elizabeth Karger and James Haspiel, 1983.

70   Lytess and *Asphalt Jungle:* Lytess, 7.

70   Padded bosom: int. James Bacon, 1983.

70   Huston: int., 1983; Huston, 286.

70   Johnson: Johnson and Leventhal, 202.

71   Romanoff: int., 1983.

71   Wilder: int., 1983.

71   Kanin: Kanin, 355ff.

71   Bacon: int., 1983.

72   MM leaves Palm Springs: int. Patti Karger, 1983.

72   MM on Karger: Guiles, *Norma Jean,* 118.

72   Marry Hyde?: *Empire News,* June 27, 1954; Monroe, 104.

72   Craft: int., 1983.

72   Lytess on Hyde: Lytess, 12.

72   MM mourning Hyde: int. Amy Greene and Maureen Stapleton, 1983–84.

73   Johnson: Johnson and Leventhal, 210.

73   Suicide attempt: Lytess, 14.

73   Suicide Prevention Center: Report to Coroner, Aug. 1962, supplied by Dr Norman Farberow.

Chapter 8

74   Bernheim: int., 1983.

74   Knef: Knef, 255.

75   *Asphalt Jungle* reviews: Conway and Ricci, 40.

76   U.C.L.A.: Robert Cahn, *Collier's,* Sept. 8, 1951.

76   Paar: Paar, 85.

76 Lytess and studio joke: Lytess.

77 Chekhov: Weatherby, 41; Alan Levy, 'A Good Long Look at Myself,' *Redbook,* Aug. 1962; Monroe, 133.

77 Cahn: *Collier's,* Sept. 8, 1951.

78 *Look* and *Life:* int. Rupert Allan, Roy Craft, and Ted Strauss, 1983.

79 Winters: Winters, 98, 292; Adams, *Imperfect Genius,* 258; int. James Haspiel, 1985.

80 Einstein joke: int. Eli Wallach, 1984.

81 Howard: int., 1983.

81 Kazan declines interview: corr., 1984.

81 Kazan: int. Milton Greene, Eli Wallach, Alain Bernheim, and Milt Ebbins, 1983–84.

82 Kazan and Communist Party: *Current Biography,* 1972.

82 Allan: int., 1983.

84 Cameron Mitchell: Zolotow, *Marilyn Monroe,* 93.

84 'Weeping': Robert Levin, *Redbook,* Feb. 1958.

84 Lytess: Lytess, 14; Wilson, *Hot Times,* 73; int. Wilson, 1984.

84 Miller letter: Guiles, *Norma Jean,* 132.

84 MM on Miller: Parsons, 230.

85 Lytess: *New York Post,* July 8, 1956.

85 Stapleton: int., 1983.

85 Miller letter: Guiles, *Norma Jean,* 132.

85 Bacon call: Bacon, *Hollywood is a Four-Letter Town,* 129.

Chapter 9

87 Gardner: Hy Gardner, *New York Herald Tribune,* Aug. 8, 1962.

87 Nude calendar: Tom Kelley, *Man,* March 1955; Hedda Hopper, *Los Angeles Times,* Sept. 9, 1963; Natalie Kelley Grasco, *Movie Stars Parade,* July 1953; Tom Kelley, *Film-land,* Feb. 1954; Skolsky, *Don't Get Me Wrong,* 217; Aline Mosby, UPI, March 13, 1952; Aline Mosby, *Santa Monica Evening Outlook,* Aug. 6, 1962; int. Johnny Campbell, Sonia Wolfson, and Theo Wilson, 1983.

89 *Playboy:* Talese, 78ff.; *Playboy,* Dec. 1953.

89   MM and pornography: *Penthouse,* Oct. 1980; *Apple Knock-ers and the Coke Bottle* video; *Confidential,* March 1955; int. Steffi Skolsky, 1983.

90   MM and 'father': Dougherty, 73; int. Inez Melson, 1983; Skolsky, *Don't Get Me Wrong,* 220; int. Ralph Roberts and PatNewcomb,1985;corr.RalphRoberts,1984;Guiles,*Norma Jean,* 136; int. Amy Greene and Henry Rosenfeld, 1984.

92   Henaghan: *Redbook,* June 1962; Motion Picture, July 1955.

92   Johnson: *Los Angeles Daily News,* May 3, 1952.

93   Appendectomy: int. Dr Marcus Rabwin, 1984; corr. Mrs Rabwin, 1984; Graham, *Confessions,* 133.

94   DiMaggio call: Zolotow, *Marilyn Monroe,* 143.

Chapter 10

97   DiMaggio background: di Gregorio; Allen; Gay Talese, 'The Silent Season of a Hero,' *Esquire,* July 1966.

97   Reluctance on book: Melvin Durslag, *Los Angeles Times,* 1982.

98   DiMaggio sees picture: Carpozi, 73; Allen, 171; Spada, 36; int. Roy Craft, 1983.

98   MM and DiMaggio meet: *Empire News,* July 18, 1954; Allen, 173; Carpozi, 72.

101   Bragging: int. Wilson, 1984.

102   Williams: *Los Angeles Mirror,* March 10, 1953.

102   Minardos affair: int. Nico Minardos, 1983.

104   DiMaggio and press: Skolsky, *Marilyn,* 62.

105   Travilla: int., 1983.

105   'Act dumber': *New York Daily News,* in Conway and Ricci, 87.

Chapter 11

107   Slatzer: int., 1982–85.

109   Slatzer *bona fides:* Snyder, in Slatzer, xxi; int. Noble 'Kid' Chissell, Gordon Heaver, Dr Sanford Firestone, Lee Henry, Doral Chenoweth, and Ron Pataki, 1983–85.

110   Walking shot: int. James Haspiel, 1985.

110   Reporter on Toots Shor's: Carpozi, 81.

110   Neill: int., 1983.

111   Hairdresser: int. Gladys Whitten, 1983.

111   Snyder: int., 1983.

113   Male jealousy: *Hollywood Citizen-News,* Sept. 4, 1952.

113   Kilgallen: *New York Journal-American,* Aug. 28, 1952.

113   Slatzer and books: *New York Journal-American,* Sept. 17, 1952.

113   Firestone: int., 1985.

113   Moore: int., 1983–85; *Los Angeles Times,* Feb. 15, 1983.

114   Fowler: corr., 1985.

114   Chissell: int., 1982.

116   Russell: int., 1983.

117   Skolsky: Skolsky, *Marilyn,* 62; *Modern Screen,* Oct. 1953.

117   Progress as star: *Movieland,* Dec. 1952.

117   Ray Anthony: int. Lionel Newman and Leo Gill, 1983; *Movieland,* Dec. 1952; *Marilyn,* song by Starlight Songs Inc., 1952.

Chapter 12

119   Grauman's: int. Jane Russell, 1983; Spada, 74.

119   Whitten: int., 1983.

120   Noonan: int. Jane Russell, 1983.

121   Snyder and Plecher: int., 1983.

121   Lytess gifts: Lytess.

121   Travilla affair: int., 1983; Billy Travilla *bona fides* confirmed in int. Don Feld, 1985.

125   Robinson: int. Arthur James and Nan Morris, 1983.

126   Siegel: int., 1983.

126   Greene: int., 1984.

127   Gardel: int., 1983.

127   Death of McKee: death certificate, located by Roy Turner; Guiles, *Norma Jean,* 165.

127   *Photoplay* Award: int. Billy Travilla; Bacon, *Hollywood Is a Four-Letter Town,* 139.

128   *New York Times:* Barbara Jamison, July 12, 1953.

128   Negulesco: int., 1983; *Flashback,* Marbella Film Institute, 1983;CBSTV'Eye-witness,'Aug.10,1962;Negulesco,417ff.

128   Johnson: Pete Martin, 126.

128   Confused: Karlin, 358.

128   Bacall: Bacall, 208.

128   Johnson: Johnson and Leventhal, 106.

129   'Sloth': *Newsweek,* People section, Oct. 31, 1960.

129   Premiere: Johnson and Leventhal, 205ff.

130   Bacall: Bacall, 208.

Chapter 13

131   Apartment: Kendis Rochlen and Charles Park, *Los Angeles Mirror,* Jan. 19, 1954.

131   Skolsky: Skolsky, *Marilyn,* 65.

131   Mike DiMaggio: Carpozi, 91.

131   DiMaggio attitude: *Photoplay* Awards; Bacon, *Hollywood Is a Four-Letter Town,* 139; Zolotow, *Marilyn Monroe,* 172; Guiles, *Norma Jean,* 163.

132   Lytess: Lytess; int. George Masters and Henry Rosenfeld, 1983–84; & Wm. Burnside notes, 1985.

133   *River of No Return:* int. Whitey Snyder, 1983; *Collier's,* Oct. 16, 1953; Bacon, *Hollywood Is a Four-Letter Town,* p. 134.

133   Mitchum: int. Wilson, 1984; Goodman, 228; Barry Rehfeld int. Robert Mitchum, in *Esquire,* Feb. 1983.

134   Accidents: *Los Angeles Times,* Aug. 13 and 20, 1953; *Santa Monica Evening Outlook,* Aug. 9, 1962; int. Norman Bishop, 1984; Winters, 428ff.; Zolotow, *Marilyn Monroe,* 189.

136   Rettig: Guiles, *Norma Jean,* 168.

136   Intruding reporters: Kendis Rochlen, *Los Angeles Mirror,* Jan. 19, 1954.

136   Belser: int., 1984.

137   Wedding plans: *Los Angeles Times,* Jan. 5 and 6, 1954; *Los Angeles Daily News,* Jan. 5, 1954; *Hollywood Citizen-News,* Jan. 5, 1954; Monroe, 139.

Chapter 14

138   Wedding: *Los Angeles Mirror, Los Angeles Times, New York Times,* Jan. 15, 1954.

138   Phone calls: Skolsky, *Marilyn,* 80; Parsons, 228; int. Kendis Rochlen, 1983.

138   Ring: Sidney Skolsky, *New York Post,* March 9, 1954.

139   Nude pictures (fn.): Guiles, *Norma Jean,* 112.

140   Paso Robles: AP, Jan. 16, 1954.

140   Skolsky interview: Sidney Skolsky, *Hollywood Citizen-News,* Feb. 1, 1954.

141   Patterson: int., 1983.

141   Far East trip: Sidney Skolsky, *Photoplay,* May 1954; *Time,* Feb. 15, 1954; *Empire News,* Aug. 1, 1954; *Los Angeles Times,* Dec. 14, 1953; int. Amy Greene, 1984.

141   Size of crowd: Skolsky, *Don't Get Me Wrong,* 213.

144   Injury: *Los Angeles Times,* Jan. 30, 1954; int. Amy Greene and member of Karger family circle, 1983–84.

144   Weber: Allen, 198.

144   Rosenfeld: int., 1984.

144   Whitten: int., 1983.

144   Stapleton: int., 1983.

145   Miller: Skolsky, *Don't Get Me Wrong,* 213.

Chapter 15

146   DiMaggios in San Francisco: Gay Talese, 'Silent Season of a Hero,' *Esquire,* July 1966; *Movieland,* Aug. 1954.

146   MM at hotel: Skolsky, *Hollywood Citizen-News,* March 9, 1954.

146   DiMaggio and Oscar: Skolsky, *Marilyn,* 82.

147   *No Business Like Show Business:* Sidney Skolsky, *New York Post,* April–July, 1954; Lionel Newman int., 1983.

147   DiMaggio marriage: Aline Mosby, *Los Angeles Herald-Express,* Oct. 1954; Sidney Skolsky, *Photoplay,* Aug. 1954; Graham, *My Hollywood,* 113; int. Jet Fore and Amy Greene, 1983–84; Capote, *Chameleons,* 240.

148   Dexter: int., 1983.

149   Monroe testimony: *New York Daily News* and *Los Angeles Times,* Oct. 28, 1954.

149   Travilla: int., 1983.

150   Monroe nudity: Wilson, *Show Business Laid Bare,* 62; int. Wilson, 1984.

150   DiMaggio not on set: *Los Angeles Mirror,* Oct. 6, 1954.

150   Wilder: int., 1983.

151   Monroe and nude scene: int. Billy Wilder; Wilson, *Show Business Laid Bare,* 62.

151   Godiva: I.N.S., Sept. 15, 1954.

151   Brando: Sidney Skolsky, *New York Post,* Aug. 7, 1954.

152   Winchell: *Los Angeles Herald-Examiner,* Aug. 8, 1962.

152   Krasner: *Globe,* Dec. 22, 1981.

153   Whitten: int., 1983.

153   Amy Greene: int., 1984.

153   Snyder: int., 1983.

153   Monroe and sportswriters: *Life,* Sept. 27, 1954.

154   Monroe weeps and sequel: Zolotow, *Marilyn Monroe,* 214.

154   Separation: *Los Angeles Times, Los Angeles Mirror, Daily News, NANA, Houston Chronicle, Los Angeles Examiner, Hollywood Citizen-News,* Oct. 4–10, 1954.

154   Craft: int., 1983.

154   Whitten: int., 1983.

155   Travilla: int., 1983.

155   Hyams: Hyams, 141.

156   DiMaggio detectives: *Los Angeles Times,* Feb. 28, 1957; Irwin evidence; J. E. Leclair, *Confidential,* Sept. 1955.

156   Fox detectives: int. John Daley, former IRS agent, 1983.

156   Patti Karger: int., 1983.

157   Steffi Skolsky: int., 1983.

157   Dexter: int., 1983.

157   Sinatra: *Time,* Aug. 29, 1955; Gehman, Sciacca *(Sinatra),* Shaw, Wilson *(Sinatra).*

159   Divorce hearing: *New York Daily News, Los Angeles Times, Santa Monica Evening Outlook,* Oct. 27 and 28, 1954.

159   DiMaggio and reconciliation: *Los Angeles Herald-Express*, Oct. 28, 1954.

159   Monroe eve of divorce: *Los Angeles Herald-Express*, Oct. 26, 1954.

159   Refuge at Sinatra apartment: Jim Henaghan, *Motion Picture*, July 1955.

160   Winchell: *New York Mirror*, Aug. 8, 1962.

Chapter 16

161   Skolsky and DiMaggio meeting: Skolsky, *Don't Get Me Wrong*, 224.

161   Lesbian rumors: int. Steffi Skolsky, 1983.

161   Hal Schaefer: int., 1984; int. Lionel Newman, 1983.

164   Schaefer suicide attempt: int. Milt Ebbins and Sheila Stewart, 1983; *Los Angeles Herald-Examiner*, Oct. 6, 1954.

165   Press and Schaefer: Louella Parsons, *Los Angeles Herald-Examiner*, Oct. 6, 1954; Aline Mosby, *Hollywood Citizen-News*, Oct. 7, 1954; *Los Angeles Herald-Express*, Oct. 6, 1954.

166   DiMaggio reconciliation?: *Los Angeles Herald-Express*, Oct. 28, 1954; *Los Angeles Examiner*, Nov. 5, 1954.

167   Wrong Door Raid: *Confidential*, Sept. 1955; Report of the (California) State Interim Committee on Collection Agencies, Private Detectives and Debt Liquidators (Senate Resolution 21, 1957); *Los Angeles Times*, Feb. 17, 20, 27, 28, March 1, 2, 14, 21, and 27, 1957; *Beverly Hills Citizen*, Sept. 11, 1958; *Hollywood Citizen-News*, March 9, 1957; int. Hal Schaefer, Sheila Stewart, James Bacon, Brad Dexter, Fred Blasgen, Fred Otash, John Daley, Gloria Romanoff, 1983–84; Bacon, *Hollywood Is a Four-Letter Town*, 141; Otash, 73–84

170   Monroe condition: *Los Angeles Times*, Oct. 6, 1954; AP Oct. 4, 1954.

170   Krohn: int. Dr Lee Siegel and colleague's int. Dr Krohn, 1983.

170   Monroe operation: I.N.S. Nov. 4 and 8, 1954; *Los Angeles Daily News*, Nov. 8, 9, 1954; *Hollywood Citizen-News*, Nov.

8, 1954; *Los Angeles Examiner*, Nov. 9, 1954; Motion Picture
Editor, I.N.S., Nov. 13, 1954; *Los Angeles Times*, Dec. 13, 1954.

171   DiMaggio inquiries: int. Inez Melson, 1983.

172   *Itch* party: Sidney Skolsky column, *Hollywood Citizen-News*, Nov. 9, 1954; *Life*, Nov. 29, 1954.

172   Zonk alias: int. Milton Greene, 1983.

Chapter 17

176   Relationship with Greenes: int. Milton and Amy Greene, 1983–84; int. Rupert Allan, 1983.

176   Monroe's aspirations: *Los Angeles Mirror*, March 10, 1953.

177   Stay at Greenes: Helen Bolstad, *Photoplay*, Sept. 1955; Dorothy Manning, *Photoplay*, Oct. 1956.

178   Dumping of friends: int. Steffi Skolsky, 1983; Lytess.

179   Monroe's interests at Greenes's: Mailer, *Of Women and Their Elegance;* int. Milton and Amy Greene, 1983–84.

181   Endometriosis: int. Dr Lee Siegel, 1983; Robert Berkow, M.D., *The Merck Manual*, Merck Sharp Dohme Research Laboratories, N.J. 1977; Dr Michael Carrera, *Sex*, London: Mitchell Beazley, 1981.

181   WAIF: int. Jane Russell, 1983.

182   New York press conference: I.N.S., Jan. 1955; Louella Parsons, *Los Angeles Herald-Examiner*, Jan. 11, 1955; *New York Daily News*, Jan. 7, 1955; UPI, Jan. 6, 1955; Carpozi, 119.

183   Pink elephant: int. Milton Greene, 1983; *Photoplay*, Sept. 1955; Michael Todd, Jr., and Susan Todd, *A Valuable Property*, New York: Arbor House, 1983.

184   Berle as lover (fn.): Berle, 266.

184   'Person to Person': transcript of program, April 8, 1955; int. Amy and Milton Greene.

185   Haspiel: int., 1984–85.

185   Height: 1956 passport application, released under FOIA, 1984.

187   Monroe's 1955 reading: Zolotow, *Marilyn Monroe*, 251.

Chapter 18

188   Monroe and Collier: int. Amy Greene, 1984; Capote, *Music for Chameleons*, 227; *Time* and *Newsweek, May* 9, 1955.

189   Actors Studio and Strasberg: Adams, *Imperfect Genius*, 254–79; Strasberg, Zolotow, *Marilyn Monroe*, 236ff.; Lee Strasberg, *Swank*, Aug. 1980; Paula Strasberg, *Los Angeles Herald-Examiner*, Aug. 10, 1962; Parsons, 229; int. Kevin McCarthy and Maureen Stapleton, Eli Wallach, and Susan and John Strasberg, 1983–84. Monroe sketches: Zolotow, *Marilyn Monroe*, 265; W. J. Weatherby corr., 1984; int. Susan Strasberg, 1983. Monroe bequest: int. Jim Haspiel, 1984.

193   Monroe and Rostens: corr. and int. Norman Rosten, 1984; Norman Rosten, 1952. Sonnets: Slatzer, 136. Manhattan: Zolotow, *Marilyn Monroe*, 253. Yeats: *Selected Poetry*. Patricia Rosten: Peary, 321; Norman Rosten, *Newsday*, Aug. 1, 1982.

Chapter 19

202   Miller response: corr., 1982–84.

203   Miller background: Arthur Miller, 'A Boy Grew in Brooklyn,' *Holiday*, March 1955; Allan Seager, 'The Creative Agony of Arthur Miller,' *Esquire*, Oct. 1959; Samuel Freedman, *New York Times*, Oct. 23, 1983; Jim Cook, 'Inside Story of a Romance,' *New York Post* and *Los Angeles Mirror-News*, July 1956; Robert Martin; Tony Schwartz, 'Miller's Return to die "U",' *New York Times Magazine*, Dec. 2, 1973; Josh Greenfeld, 'Writing Plays Is Absolutely Senseless,' *New York Times Magazine*, Feb. 13, 1972; 'It's Miller Time —Again,' *Los Angeles Times* Calendar, June 10, 1984; Profile, London *Observer*, Oct. 14, 1956; Ira Wolfert, 'Arthur Miller, Playwright in Search of His Identity,' *New York Times*, 1953; Murray Schumach, 'Arthur Miller Grew in Brooklyn,' *New York Times*, 1949; Dan Sullivan, 'Arthur Miller, Harvest Time,' *Los Angeles Times*, Oct. 5, 1980.

203   *Time:* Robert Ajemian, int. Arthur Miller, April 1956.

204 'Triangle' in plays: Zolotow, *Marilyn*, 259.

204 Marilyn and Miller reunion: Zolotow, *Marilyn*, 263. April contact: Robert Ajemian, int. Arthur Miller.

205 Leonardi: *New York Post*, July 8, 1956.

205 Marilyn dinner parties: Robert Ajemian, int. Arthur Miller; int. Maureen Stapleton, 1983.

206 MM on political freedom: Alan Levy, 'A Good Long Look at Myself,' *Redbook*, Aug. 1962.

206 Close friend: Alan Levy, *Redbook*, Aug. 1962.

206 DiMaggio's reading: Meaker, 39.

206 Miller's intellect: Parsons, 232.

206 Rosten: Norman Rosten, 36.

206 *Time:* Robert Ajemian int. Arthur Miller.

208 Kargers in New Jersey: int. Bennett Short and Anne Batté, 1983.

208 DiMaggio pursuit: Wilson, *Show Business Nobody Knows*, 312; int. Wilson and Henry Rosenfeld, 1984. Row: Zolotow, *Marilyn*, 243; Haspiel: int., 1984.

209 Marilyn joke: int. Patti Karger and Bennett Short, 1983. Karger in New York: Guiles, *Norma Jean*, 202. Rosenfeld: int. Henry Rosenfeld and Norman Rosten, 1984.

210 Rainier scheme: int. Gardner and Fleur Cowles, and Milton and Amy Greene, 1983–84. Call to Kelly: Graham, *Confessions*, 135.

211 Brando: int. Milton and Amy Greene; *Movieland*, Dec. 1954; George Barris int. MM, *New York Daily News*, Aug. 17, 1962. Sex appeal: int. Pete Martin, *Saturday Evening Post*, May 5, 1956. Photograph: collection of Amy Greene. Phone calls in last days: corr. and int. Ralph Roberts, 1983–84.

212 Wilson interview: *New York Post*, Oct. 2, 1955; int. Wilson, 1984.

212 Marriage discussion: Jim Cook, *New York Post*, July 8, 1956.

212 *Anna Christie:* int. Maureen Stapleton, 1983. Lytess: Bill Tusher, *Movie Mirror*, May 1957. Kim Stanley: *American Film*, June 1983.

213 Strasberg praise: Logan, 43; int. Joshua Logan, 1984.

213 Dressing room: Dorothy Manning, *Photoplay,* Oct. 1956; Sidney Skolsky, *New York Post,* Aug. 2, 1955.

213 Contract: Zolotow, *Marilyn Monroe,* 266; int. Amy Greene, 1984.

214 Olivier press conference: *Time,* Feb. 20, 1956; Kiernan, *Sir Larry,* 257; Manning: *Photoplay,* Oct. 1956.

215 'Schizoid': Olivier, 205.

215 Psychiatric care (during 1954): Carpozi, 114; and Zolotow, *Marilyn Monroe,* 207.

215 Gottlieb: int., 1984.

215 Corday: int., 1983.

216 Drug equipment: Otash, 80; int. Fred Otash, 1983.

216 Psychiatric care: Stopped: Zolotow, *Marilyn Monroe,* 226. Greene: int., 1983. Haspiel: int., 1984.

216 Miller: Robert Ajemian int. Arthur Miller.

216 Wilder: Goodman, 227.

216 Rosenfeld: int., 1984.

216 Fletcher: *Photoplay,* Sept. 1965.

217 Leonardi: *New York Post,* July 15, 1956.

217 Notebook: Richard Gellman, *American Weekly,* May 1, 1960.

217 Pills: int. Milton and Amy Greene, 1983–84.

218 Strasberg help: Adams, *Imperfect Genius,* 263; Int. John Strasberg, 1984.

218 *Time*: May 14, 1956.

218 Goodman: Goodman, 231.

219 Rosten: int., 1984; Norman Rosten, *Newsday,* Aug. 1, 1962.

Chapter 20

220 Reception: *Time,* May 14, 1956.

220 *Bus Stop*: int. Joshua Logan and Milton Greene, 1983–84; Logan, 42.

221 Adler row: Robert Ajemian Int. Arthur Miller.

221 Lytess: Lytess, 27.

221 Paula Strasberg: int. Susan and John Strasberg; Adams, *Imperfect Genius;* Strasberg, 75.

222 'Iron fence': int. Rosie Steinberg, 1983.

222   Murray incident: Carpozi, 133.

223   Tranquilizers: Guiles, *Norma Jean*, 229.

223   Limousine: Adams, 269

223   Illness: *New York Times*, April 13, 1956.

224   Press: int. William R. Woodfield, 1984.

224   *Time* interview: int. Brad Darrach, 1984.

225   Newcomb: int. Pat Newcomb and Rupert Allan, 1983–84.

226   Lange: Hoyt, 176.

226   Psychiatrist: int. Milton Greene, 1983.

226   Reviews: *New York Times, New York Herald, New York Herald Tribune*, Sept. 1, 1956.

226   Award: Graham, *Confessions*, 114.

226   Logan: int., 1984; int. Wilson, *New York Post*, Sept. 1956.

Chapter 21

227   'Mr and Mrs Leslie': Goode, 17; Jim Cook, *New York Post*, July 8, 1956; Robert Ajemian Int. Arthur Miller, April 1956.

227   Mann: int. May Mann, 1983.

228   House Un-American Activities Committee: Transcript of proceedings for June 21, 1956, U.S. Government Printing Office, 1956; Feinman, 170ff.; Huston, chap. 11; Bentley; Cogley. McCarthy: Richard Rovere, 'The Frivolous Demagogue,' *Esquire*, Aug. 1958; George Will, *New York Times*, June 15, 1984. Miller session: Jim Cook, *New York Post*, July 13, 1956. Winchell: undated column, June 1956. Steinbeck: John Steinbeck, 'The Trial of Arthur Miller,' *Esquire*, June 1957; Weatherby, 125; *Los Angeles Times*, June 22 and July 1, 1956, June 1 and 19, 1957; *New York Daily News*, June 22 and July 26, 1956; *Los Angeles Herald-Examiner*, May 29, 1957; *Hollywood Citizen-News*, Feb. 18, 1957. Walter: Robert Martin, 291.

230   Marilyn on HUAC: *Newsweek*, July 2, 1956; *Los Angeles Times*, Aug. 8, 1958. In Washington: int. Eli Wallach, 1984; Guiles, *Norma Jean*, 247; Signoret, 290; int. Henry Rosenfeld, 1984. Skouras threat: Signoret, 290; *Life*, Aug. 3, 1962; Weatherby, 54.

230   Greenson: int. Danny Greenson, 1984.

231   Strasbergs and 'communism': Adams, *Imperfect Genius,* 172ff., 242; Capell, 43.

231   FBI releases: 1956 segment of Monroe documents released to author, 1983, and to Robert Slatzer, 1980.

231   Hoover: Wallace *et al.,* 628.

232   Rosten call: Norman Rosten, 34.

232   Repairman: *Newsweek,* July 2, 1956.

232   Wedding: *New York Daily News,* June 22 and 27, 1956; *Los Angeles Times,* July 2 and 3, 1956; *Los Angeles Herald-Express* June 28, 1956; *Los Angeles Herald-Examiner,* June 30, July 3 and 4, 1956; *Los Angeles Mirror-News,* June 30, 1956; Zolotow, *Marilyn Monroe,* 287ff.; *Westchester News,* July 3, 1956.

232   Miller's parents: Flora Rheta Schreiber, 'Remembrance of Marilyn,' *Good Housekeeping,* Jan. 1963; *Life,* July 16, 1956.

235   Jewish ceremony: Susan Wender, 'Marilyn Enters a Jewish Family,' *Modern Screen,* Nov. 1956.

235   Greene: int. 1983–84.

235   Rosten: Norman Rosten, 38.

235   Ring: Guiles, *Norma Jean,* 252.

235   'Hope': Wagenknecht, *Seven Daughters of the Theater,* 202.

Chapter 22

236   'Gershwin': Harris 186.

236   Press coverage: London *Daily Mail,* March 21, June 13, July 13, 14, 1956; London *Daily Herald,* April 27, 1956; London *Daily Mirror,* May 14, 1956. Bicycle: London *Daily Sketch,* July 16, 1956.

237   Millers at home: London *Daily Mail,* July 16 and 17, 1956; AP, July 14, 1956.

237   Coward: Payne and Morley, 308.

237   Olivier and Monroe meetings: Winters, 299; Harris, 183.

237   *The Prince and the Showgirl:* Olivier, chap. 10; Kiernan, Sir Larry, 257; *Time,* May 14, 1956; int. Joshua Logan, John Huston, Billy Wilder, 1983–84.

238   'Count?': Johnson and Leventhal, 206.

238   'Amateur': *Los Angeles Mirror,* Dec. 3, 1956.

238   Cardiff: London *Sunday Dispatch,* series in Nov. 1956.

239   Monroe on Olivier: Weatherby, 61.

239   Lateness: Harris, 188.

239   'Child': Parsons, 232.

239   Miller journey: McKnight notes (Zolotow collection); Maurice Zolotow, 'Who Runs Marilyn Monroe?' *Los Angeles Herald-Examiner,* Dec. 12, 1956.

239   Greene: London *Sunday Dispatch,* Nov. 8, 1956; Maurice Zolotow, *Los Angeles Herald-Examiner,* int. Milton Greene, 1983–84.

240   Greene ousted: *Los Angeles Times,* April 12 and 17, 1957; *New York Times,* April 12, 1957; Guiles, *Norma Jean,* 263–73; Zolotow, *Marilyn Monroe,* 303.

240   Coward: *Payne and Morley,* 358.

241   Queen: *Daily Sketch,* Oct. 30, 1956.

241   Apology: London *Daily Mail,* Nov. 17, 1956.

241   Definition of love: Zolotow, *Marilyn Monroe,* 265.

241   Note incident: Guiles, *Norma Jean,* 260; int. Bob Josephy and James Haspiel, 1984; Bigsby 589; Miller, *After the Fall,* 114.

243   Greene affair: Zolotow, *Marilyn Monroe,* 227; Davis, *Suitcase,* 238; int. Milton Greene, 1984.

243   Press and sleeping: *New York Daily News,* July 16, 1956; Guiles, *Norma Jean,* 259; int. Milton Greene, 1984.

244   Sitwell: London *Daily Mail,* July 16, 1956; *Newsweek,* Aug. 6, 1956; *Los Angeles Herald-Examiner,* Aug. 6, 1962.

244   Leigh miscarriage: Strasberg, 85.

244   Monroe pregnant?: Alan Arnold, publicity director of *Prince,* in *Sunday Dispatch,* Nov. 1956; Louella Parsons, *Los Angeles Herald-Examiner,* Aug. 2, 1957.

244   Tynan: Kiernan, *Sir Larry,* 259ff.

Chapter 23

246   Marilyn on marriage: int. Richard Meryman, *Life,* Nov. 4, 1966.

246 Jamaica: AP, Jan. 15, 1957; Carpozi, 145.

246 Apartment: Guiles, *Norma Jean,* 271; int. James Haspiel, 1984; Zolotow, *Marilyn Monroe,* 314.

246 Piano: Zolotow, *Marilyn Monroe,* 14.

246 Apartment: Elsa Maxwell, *American Weekly,* May 12, 1957.

247 Marilyn on marriage: *Movieland,* March 1957; *Redbook,* Feb. 1958; Parsons, 232; Alan Levy, 'A Good Long Look at Myself,' *Redbook,* Aug. 1962; Lester David int. June 1957, pub. This Week, *Los Angeles Times,* April 12, 1964; Adele Whitely Fletcher, *Photoplay,* Sept. 1965.

247 Nicknames: *Look,* Oct. 1, 1957.

247 Collected plays: Corrigan, 5.

247 Miller: *Redbook,* Feb. 1958.

248 NY activity: *Look,* Oct. 1, 1957.

248 Father: Flora R. Schreiber, *Good Housekeeping,* Jan. 1963.

248 Stepmother: Alan Levy, 'A Good Long Look at Myself,' *Redbook,* Aug. 1962; int. Lionel Newman and James Haspiel, 1983–84.

248 Domesticity: int. Maureen Stapleton and Norman Rosten, 1983–84; Norman Rosten, 54.

249 McCarthy: int., 1983.

249 Miller: 'Marilyn Stands by Her Man,' *Movieland,* July 1957.

249 Marilyn summoned: Carpozi, 146.

249 Slatzer: con. Slatzer; *Confidential,* May 1957.

249 DiMaggio: Roderick Man, London *Daily Express,* July 16, 1956.

250 Note: Norman Rosten, 50.

250 Amagansett: N. Polsky, 'And the Lord Taketh Away,' *Modern Screen,* Nov. 1957; Zolotow, *Marilyn Monroe,* 312; *Look,* Oct. 1, 1957.

251 Premiere: *Los Angeles Times,* This Week, Dec. 11, 1960.

251 Superintendents: Joe Hyams, *New York Herald Tribune,* July 3, 1957.

251 Baby: *Los Angeles Times,* This Week, April 12, 1964; int. Danny Greenson, 1984; Norman Rosten, 46; Wagenknecht, *Seven Daughters of the Theater,* 208, London *Observer,* Oct. 14, 1956.

252   Miscarriage: N. Polsky, 'And the Lord Taketh Away,' *Modern Screen*, Nov. 1957; 'Let My Baby Live,' *Movie Stars Parade*, Nov. 1957; Louella Parsons, *Los Angeles Herald-Examiner*, Aug. 2, 1957; UPI, Aug. 1, 1957; AP, Aug. 1, 1957; Zolotow, *Marilyn Monroe*, 316; Graham, *Confessions*, 141; Carpozi, 148; Norman Rosten, 72.

253   Pepitone: int. 1984; Pepitone and Stadiem, 27 and 48.

253   Estate: int. Bob Josephy, 1984; Hollis Alpert, *The Dreams and the Dreamers*, New York: Macmillan, 1962; *Look*, Oct. 1, 1957; Harris, 191; Norman Rosten, 66ff.; author's research on Diebolds, 1984; Patricia Rosten on Marilyn, Peary, 321.

254   Marilyn and nature: int. Inez Melson, 1983; Miller, 'Please Don't Kill Anything,' *Stories by Arthur Miller*, 1967.

255   Boys in park: int. James Haspiel, 1985.

255   Nasturtiums: int. Rupert Allan, 1983.

255   Rosten: corr. and int. Norman Rosten, 1984; Norman Rosten, 75 and 55; 'A Friend Remembers Marilyn,' *Newsday*, Aug. 1, 1982.

256   'Help': Norman Rosten, flyleaf.

Chapter 24

257   Beaton: Cecil Beaton, *The Face of the World*, New York: John Day, 1957.

257   *Life* issue: Arthur Miller, 'My Wife Marilyn,' *Life*, Dec. 22, 1958.

257   Clift: Bosworth, 297; LaGuardia, 191.

258   Arrival: *Los Angeles Times* and *Los Angeles Herald-Examiner*, July 9, 1958; This Week, *Los Angeles Times*, Oct. 5, 1958.

258   *Some Like It Hot*: Zolotow, *Marilyn Monroe*, 320; Guiles, *Norma Jean*, 285; LaGuardia, 192.

258   Obscenity: int. Billy Wilder, 1983; Guiles, *Norma Jean*, 287.

259   Champagne: *New York Daily News*, Feb. 3, 1960.

259   Arrogance: Carpozi, 152.

259   Shearer: *Parade*, Dec. 7, 1958.

259   Wilder: *Parade*, Dec. 7, 1958; int., 1983.

261   Rosten letter: Norman Rosten, 76.

261   Doctors: Carpozi, 150.

261   Wilder and Miller: int. Billy Wilder, 1983.

263   Rosten letter: Norman Rosten, 77.

263   Pregnancy ends: *Los Angeles Herald-Examiner*, Oct. 18 and Nov. 17, 1958; *Los Angeles Times*, Nov. 1 and Dec. 18, 1958; AP, Dec. 18, 1958; Carpozi, 153; Norman Rosten, 71.

263   Marriage founders: Norman Rosten, 79; Strasberg, 125; Adams, *Imperfect Genius*, 267; int. Maureen Stapleton and Martin Ritt, 1983.

264   Miller at work: Allan Seager, 'The Creative Agony of Arthur Miller,' *Esquire*, Oct. 1959.

264   British interview: David Lewin, London *Daily Express*, May 6, 1959.

265   Khrushchev: Fisher, 172; Guiles, *Norma Jean*, 292; int. Hildi Greenson, 1983.

265   Sukarno: int. Joshua Logan, 1984; AP and UPI, May 31, 1956; int. Gloria Romanoff and Robert Slatzer, 1983; Smith, chap. 14; Powers, 341; *Alleged Assassination Plots Involving Foreign Leaders;* in Marshall Noble, formerly U.S. State Dept., dealing with Far East Public Affairs, 1985; Adams, *Dictator*, 160; int. Joseph Shimon, 1985; Author's correspondence with Smith, 1984.

265   Monroe and Sukarno: Norman Rosten, 72; corr. Joseph B. Smith, 1984.

Chapter 25

267   Dressing room: Norman Rosten, 79.

267   Leading man: Joe Hyams, 'The Frenchman Who Rescued Marilyn,' *New York Herald Tribune*, This Week, Aug. 21, 1960.

267   Marilyn on Montand: Joe Hyams, *New York Herald Tribune;* Look, 1960.

268   Miller on Montand: Joe Hyams, *New York Herald Tribune;* Look, 1960.

268   Montand and Marilyn: Signoret, chap. 11.

269   Waiting: *Life*, Aug. 15, 1960.

269   Marilyn and doctors: int. with doctors and family of psychiatrist Dr Ralph Greenson, 1983–84.

270   Censor: int. Frank McCarthy, 1983.

270   Minardos: int. Nico Minardos.

270   List: Winters, 294.

270   Like DiMaggio: Bacon, *Hollywood Is a Four-Letter Town*, 142.

270   Affair begins: Graham, *Confessions*, 142; int. James Bacon and Wilson, 1983–84; Bacon, *Hollywood Is a Four-Letter Town*, 143.

271   Airport meeting: Graham, *Confessions*, 143; Skolsky, *Don't Get Me Wrong*, 229; Bacon, *Hollywood Is a Four-Letter Town*, 144; Guiles, *Norma Jean*, 324; Carpozi, 157.

271   Montand refuses calls: original wire service reports of Hedda Hopper int. with Montand, Aug. 31, 1960; *Los Angeles Times*, Sept. 1, 1960 and Aug. 7, 1962.

271   Buchwald: *Los Angeles Times*, Sept. 18, 1960.

271   Second reporter: Vernon Scott, UPI, Sept. 2, 1960.

272   Signoret on Marilyn: *Los Angeles Mirror-News*, Nov. 16, 1960; Signoret, 303.

Chapter 26

273   Greenson: Leo Rosten; notes of Dr Robert Litman, 1982; draft of Maurice Zolotow article from int. Dr Greenson, 1973; *Medical Tribune*, Oct. 24, 1973; Lloyd Shearer, 'Marilyn Monroe, Why Won't They Let Her Rest In Peace?' *Parade*, Aug. 5, 1973; Curriculum Vitae of Greenson; corr. and int. Dr Greenson's widow, Mrs Hildi Greenson, daughter Joan, son Danny, and secretary Susan Alexander, 1983–85; corr. with one of Dr Greenson's professional colleagues, who cannot be named here; int. Dr Robert Litman, Dr Norman Farberow, and Dr Norman Tabachnick, Los Angeles Suicide Prevention Center psychiatrists in Aug. 1962; conversations with Dr Maurice Lazarus and Paul Moor, 1983.

273   Greenson and Sinatra: int. Kitty Kelley, 1985.

274 'Best script': *New York Post,* Nov. 20, 1959.

276 Greenson interim opinion: int. and documents at Los Angeles Suicide Prevention Center, 1983–84; corr. Greenson.

Chapter 27

278 *Misfits,* Goode; Alan Levy, 'A Good Long Look at Myself,' *Redbook,* Aug. 1962.

278 Valentine: int. John Huston and Eli Wallach, 1983–84; Huston, 286ff.

279 Infidelity discussion: Weatherby, 13.

279 Dexter meeting: int. 1983.

280 Haspiel: int. 1985/6.

280 Cartier-Bresson: Goode, 101.

280 McIntyre: *Esquire,* March 1961.

280 Marilyn on Gable: *Cosmopolitan,* Dec. 1960.

281 Gable on Marilyn: int. George Chasin, 1983; Bacon, *Hollywood Is a Four-Letter Town,* 145.

281 Nembutal intake: draft of Maurice Zolotow article, 1973; int. John Huston and Whitey Snyder, 1983.

281 Row: *Los Angeles Examiner* and *Mirror,* Oct. 19, 1960.

282 Allan: int. Kathy Castle, 1984.

282 Makeup man's room: int. Whitey Snyder, 1983.

282 Lugging typewriter: Kathy Castle int. Mary Malone, 1984.

282 Strasberg: Adams, *Imperfect Genius,* 278.

282 Allan: int. Rupert Allan, 1983.

282 'Dyin'' speech: Goode, 122.

283 Suicide attempt?: int. Kendis Rochlen, reporter and friend of Gable, 1983; int. Eli Wallach, 1984.

283 Stomach pump: *Esquire,* March 1961.

283 Sheet: Strasberg, 135.

284 Brando and Sinatra calls: int. Rupert Allan, 1983.

284 Parsons: Carpozi, 163.

284 Suicide rumor: *Cosmopolitan,* Dec. 1960.

284 Ring into river: *Redbook,* 1962.

284 Wilson: int. Wilson, 1984.

284 Weatherby: Weatherby, 37–52.

285   Miller birthday: Goode, 245; Hamblett, 330.

285   Divorce: *Los Angeles Mirror and Examiner,* Nov. 11, 1960; *New York Times, New York Journal-American,* Nov. 12, 1960; *New York Post,* Nov. 14, 1960; *Los Angeles Herald-Examiner,* Dec. 26, 1960; *Time,* Nov. 21, 1960.

285   Chipped tooth: int. James Haspiel, 1985.

286   Gable death: *New York Journal-American,* Nov. 17, 1960; *New York Post,* Nov. 18, 1960.

286   Mrs Gable's reactions: int. Kendis Rochlen and Ross Acuna, 1983.

286   Marilyn reaction: Skolsky, *Don't Get Me Wrong,* 230.

286   *Misfits* reviews: Film Scripts No. 3, edited by George P. Garrett, O. B. Hardison, Jr, and Jane R. Gelfman, New Appleton Century-Crofts, 1972, p. 203; Conway and Ricci, 157.

286   Miller: LaGuardia, 220; Goode, 300.

286   Marilyn 'finding self': *Los Angeles Times,* Nov. 30, 1960.

287   Slatzer: picture in possession of Slatzer, seen 1983.

287   Minardos and Greene: int., 1983–84.

288   Montand: *Los Angeles Times,* London *Sunday Dispatch,* Nov. 13, 1960; *Los Angeles Mirror,* Nov. 16, 1960; *New York Journal-American,* Nov. 18, 1960; *Hollywood Citizen-News,* Dec. 14, 1960; int. Pat Newcomb, 1983–84; Pepitone and Stadiem, 163.

288   DiMaggio: Mailer, *Marilyn,* 290; int. Marjorie Stengel, 1983; Pepitone and Stadiem, 165.

289   Will: Guiles, *Norma Jean,* 342.

289   Capsules: Guiles, Norma Jean, 344.

289   Strasberg incidents: Adams, *Imperfect Genius,* 264; Strasberg, 156.

289   Divorce: *Hollywood Citizen-News,* Jan. 21, 1961; *El Correa-Ciudad Juarez, La Prensa, El Universal, Excelsior,* Jan. 22, 1961.

290   Haspiel: int., 1984.

290   *Misfits* review: Anderson, 178.

Chapter 28

291   Payne Whitney: Carpozi, 174ff.; *Life,* Aug. 1966; Strasberg, 156; int. Pat Newcomb, 1983; Norman Rosten, 92; int. Gloria Romanoff, 1983.

292   Kris Sessions: Monroe files in Melson archives.

292   Marilyn letter: *San Francisco Chronicle,* June 1, 1984; *Los Angeles Times,* Jan. 6, 1984; facsimile in Speriglio, 248; *Los Angeles Times, New York Post, New York Daily News,* Feb. 9, 1961; *New York Mirror,* Aug. 6, 1962.

293   Hospital change: *Hollywood Citizen-News, Los Angeles Times,* Feb. 2, 1961; *Los Angeles Herald-Examiner,* Feb. 12, 1961; *Los Angeles Herald-Examiner* and *New York Journal-American,* March 6, 1961; Norman Rosten, 93.

294   DiMaggio: *Santa Monica Evening Outlook,* Jan. 11, 1961; *Hollywood Citizen-News,* Apr. 1, 1961; *Newsweek,* April 4, 1961; *Los Angeles Mirror,* April 20, 1961; *Hollywood Citizen-News,* July 25, 1961; *Los Angeles Examiner,* Aug. 10, 1961.

294   Rain: *New York Post,* Feb. 9, 1961; Guiles, *Norma Jean,* 348ff.

294   Freud: *Los Angeles Mirror,* April 20, 1961; Huston, chap. 27; int. John Huston, 1983.

295   Gynecological operation: *Hollywood Citizen-News,* May 25, 1961; Richard Cottrell, 'I Was Marilyn Monroe's Doctor,' *Ladies Home Companion,* Jan. 1965.

295   Gall bladder: *New York Post,* June 29, 1961; *Los Angeles Herald-Examiner, Los Angeles Mirror, New York Times,* June 30, 1961; *Ladies Home Companion,* Jan. 1965.

296   Stengel: int., 1983.

296   Drugs: Marjorie Stengel, in LaGuardia, 197.

296   Masters: int. George Masters, 1983; and Masters and Browning, 75; Tierney, chap. 14; Bacon, *Hollywood Is a Four-Letter Town,* 259; Parmet, *Presidency,* 110.

297   Carmen: int., 1983; checks on Carmen's press file, and at Doheny apartment.

297   Apartment: int. Joan Greenson, 1983; Greenson, 12.

298   Bust enlargement: int. Jeanne Carmen and Jeanne Martin, 1983.

299 Relationship with Greensons: int. Greenson family, 1983–84; Greenson, II ff.

302 Telegram: courtesy of Hildi Greenson.

302 Heaver: corr. and int. Gordon Heaver, 1983–84.

Chapter 29

305 District Attorney's observation: int. Gary Wean, 1983.

305 Hronek: obituary, *Los Angeles Times,* Feb. 25, 1980; int. Frank Hronek's widow, son, and former colleagues, 1983.

306 Kennedys and sex: Ralph Martin, 34, 94; Blair, 145–54, 166–70, 435, 631ff., 641, 645, 666; Ralph Martin, 43, 50, 54, 55, 77, 199, 313ff., 491; Sciacca, *Kennedy and His Women,* 156; Dunleavy and Brennan, 76ff.; Bryant and Leighton, 24; int. Milton Ebbin, 1983.

307 JFK on RFK: Schlesinger, *Robert Kennedy,* 598.

307 Father of the Year: *Los Angeles Times,* Dec. 17, 1960.

307 Schlesinger: 1983.

308 Garbo: Michaelis, 177.

308 Dietrich: int. Joshua Logan, 1984.

308 Lawford background: Stephen Birmingham, *Cosmopolitan,* Oct. 1961; Helen Markel, *Good Housekeeping,* Feb. 1962; obituary of Lady Lawford, *Los Angeles Times,* Jan. 24, 1972; Twentieth Century-Fox publicity sheet, undated, early fifties. Spankings: Lady Lawford, *American Weekly; Los Angeles Herald-Examiner,* July 9, 1950.

308 Lawford home: *Los Angeles Times,* April 15 and June 8, 1978.

309 Lawfords and alcohol: *Los Angeles Times,* Jan. 9, 1984; *Herald Tribune,* Aug. 9, 1984; int. Deborah Gould and Peter Lawford, 1983. Pat L.: Saunders and Southwood, 118; int. Frank Saunders, 1984.

310 Jeanne Martin: int., 1984

Chapter 30

311 Kennedy surgery: Blair, 650ff.; Martin, 96.

311   Monroe poster: Priscilla McMillan, Collier and Horowitz, 204.

311   Feldman: Blair, 549; int. former Mrs Jean Feldman, 1983.

311   Dobish: int., 1983.

311   Bernheim: int., 1983.

312   Slatzer: int., 1983.

312   James: int., 1984.

313   Russell: int., 1983.

313   Gene Kelly: int. Alain Bernheim and Peter Lawford, 1983; Peary, 77.

313   Lawford denial of Kennedy affair: int., 1983; *Star*, Feb. 24, 1976; London *Observer*, July 15, 1973.

313   Monroe meets JFK 1961: int. District Attorney's office, 1983.

314   Summers: int., 1983.

314   Markel background: *New York Times*, Nov. 27, 1968.

316   Markel: int. 1984, Helen Markel, who provided copies of Monroe–Markel correspondence. (Monroe letter of March 29, 1960, enclosed a partial letter written first – both are quoted together here.)

317   Joan Greenson: Greenson, 17.

317   Nehru: Skolsky, *Marilyn*, 60.

317   Castro: Monroe–Markel correspondence.

317   SANE: *Valley Time*, March 22, 1960 (culled by FBI Los Angeles office and kept in their files).

318   Nightmare: *Redbook*, Aug. 1962.

318   Allan: int., 1983.

318   Marilyn delegate: UPI, April 13, 1960.

318   'Attend convention': *Hollywood Reporter* (undated), before convention.

Chapter 31

319   Joseph Kennedy: Schlesinger, *Robert Kennedy*, 205–11.

319   Karger: int. Patti Karger, 1983.

319   Roberts: int., 1983.

319   Coliseum speech: Ralph Martin, 335; Parmet, *Presidency*, 31.

320   Acuna: int., 1983.

320   Carmen: int., 1983.

320   Summers: int., 1983.

321   Seaton: int., 1985.

321   Weatherby: Weatherby, 53, 55; int. W. J. Weatherby, 1982.

322   Buchwald: *Los Angeles Times,* Nov. 9, 1960.

322   Weatherby meetings: Weatherby, 86; int. W. J. Weatherby, 1982.

323   Carlyle: Ralph Martin, 402.

324   Shalam: int., 1984.

324   Wilson: int. Wilson, 1984; *Show Business Laid Bare,* 65.

324   Ebbins: int., 1983.

324   Strasberg: Paula Strasberg, in int. James Haspiel, 1983.

325   Skolsky: in Skolsky, 1983; (on his death) int. Steffi Skolsky; Skolsky, *Don't Get Me Wrong,* 233.

325   Bacon and Starr: int., 1983.

325   Rosenfeld: int., 1984.

326   John Kennedy visit: *New York Times,* Nov. 17, 19, 20, 1961; *Los Angeles Times,* Nov. 19, 20, 1961; *Santa Monica Evening Outlook,* Nov. 20, 1961.

326   Watson: int., 1983; corroborated in details of Hilton reception in contemporary coverage.

327   Snyder (fn.): int., 1983.

327   Guthman: int. Edwin Guthman, 1985; Charles Casillo. *Marilyn Monroe: The Private Life of a Public Icon*, NY: St. Martin's Press, 2018, p. 213.

327   Tretick: int., 1985.

328   Smathers: int., 1983; Blair, 578–95; Schlesinger, *Robert Kennedy,* 493.

328   Newcomb: int., 1983–84.

328   Evans: int., 1984.

Chapter 32

330   Sinatra on Marilyn: *Redbook,* Aug. 1962.

330   First meeting?: int. Milton Greene, 1983.

330   *Misfits* company: Goode, 92; *Sierra,* 1960.

330 Cal-Neva: visit and int. Bethal van Tassell, local historian, and Wayne Ogle, former maintenance manager, 1983–84.

331 D'Amato: Exner and Demaris, 116 and 205; Blakey and Billings, 251–379.

331 Antoinette: Antoinette Giancana with Thomas C. Renner, *Mafia Princess*, NY: Morrow, 1984, p. 113.

331 Tina: Tina Sinatra with Jeff Coplon, *My Father's Daughter*, NY: Simon & Schuster, 2000, p. 73.

331 Lawford: *Star*, Feb. 17, 1976.

332 Giancana ownership?: Giancana and Renner, 113–225; review of Assassinations Committee, investigators' notes of FBI reports, 1982; *New York Times*, Feb. 2, 1984; *Dallas Morning News*, Feb. 20, 1981.

332 Sinatra withdrawal: Edward A. Olsen, official of Nevada Gaming Control Board, in Oral History contribution, 1967–69, held at University of Nevada; Arnold Shaw, 317ff.; Brashler, 261ff.; Gage, 86ff.

332 Kennedys and Cal-Neva: int. Wayne Ogle, maintenance manager, 1983–84.

332 Lawford and Cal-Neva: int. Peter Lawford, 1983; Lawford's interview with Los Angeles Police Department, Oct. 10, 1975.

332 Dog: Guiles, *Norma Jean*, 343; Pepitone and Stadiem, 171 and 183; int. Lena Pepitone, 1984.

332 Use of house: Guiles, *Norma Jean*, 353.

332 Masters: Masters and Browning, 52; int. George Masters, 1983.

333 Greenson: corr. with professional colleague, obtained by author, 1984.

333 Sands: wire story of June 7, 1961, in Wilson, *Show Business Laid Bare*, 63; Fisher, 203.

333 Greenson: corr. with a professional colleague, obtained by author, 1984.

334 Yacht: int. Jeanne Martin and Gloria Romanoff, 1983.

334 Pepitone: int., 1984; Pepitone and Stadiem, 199ff.; int. Marjorie Stengel and George Masters, 1983.

335 Prowse: Arnold Shaw, 297ff.

335   Sinatra sees Marilyn till death: int. Gloria Romanoff and Norman Rosten, 1983–84.

335   Photographs: Murray, 25; int. Eunice Murray, 1982.

Chapter 33

336   Cohen: background: Reid, *Mickey Cohen;* Cohen and Nugent; Martin and Lewis: Cohen and Nugent, 113. Sinatra: Gehman, 178; Cohen and Nugent, 228.

336   Villa Capri: Cohen and Nugent, 190; Reid, *Mickey Cohen,* 107.

337   District Attorney's surveillance: int. Gary Wean, 1983.

337   Recordings: int. Gary Wean, 1983; Morella and Epstein, *Lana,* 241.

337   Piscitelle and LoCigno (background): *Los Angeles Times,* Dec. 12, 1961 and later articles.

338   Corroboration: int. Jack Tobin, 1983; int. Virgil Crabtree, former Asst. Chief in California of Intelligence Division, U.S. Treasury Dept., 1983.

338   Cohen and Giancana: int. Jack Tobin; Blakey and Billings, 186ff., 195ff., 283, 303, 326ff., 377ff.; Cohen and Nugent, 39.

338   Cohn: Messick, 118.

338   Schenck: Messick, 120ff.

339   Karger: int., 1983.

339   Shimon: int., 1983.

339   Hall: int., 1983; checks on Hall's reliability with senior law enforcement official.

339   Campbell: Exner and Demaris. Exner is Campbell's married name today; *Alleged Assassination Plots,* 129; int. Prof. Robert Blakey, 1985.

340   Safire: *Dallas News* (New York Times News Service), Jan. 7, 1976.

340   Meredith: Exner and Demaris, 198; int. Fred Otash, 1982–83; Otash on 'Tomorrow Show,' NBC-TV, in *Los Angeles Herald-Examiner,* Nov. 25, 1976; Anthony Cook int. Peter Fairchild, 1983; Vicki Loewy int. Judy Meredith, 1983;

review of Assassinations Committee investigators' notes of FBI reports, 1982.

342 Smith: Edward Tivnan int. Sandy Smith, 1983.

342 Roselli: Exner and Demaris, 206; Blakey and Billings references; review of Assassinations Committee investigators' reports notes of FBI, 1982.

343 O'Hare: FBI report, July 18, 1961, files CG 139–105 & CG 92–349, released to Mark Allen, 1983; Brashler, 204; Giancana and Renner, 214; Blakey and Billings, 251.

343 McGuire: int., 1983.

344 Blakey: Blakey and Billings, 391.

345 Theodoracopulos: int. 1986; *Princes Playboys, & High-Class Tarts*, by Taki, Princeton: Kart-Cohl Publishing, 1984; *Spectator*, Oct. 19, 1985.

345 Smathers: int., 1983.

345 Kane: int., 1983.

345 Evans: int., 1984–85.

Chapter 34

347 Roselli and Giancana overheard: Blakey and Billings, 382; Giancana and Renner, 250; FBI surveillance document, Dec. 6, 1961, obtained through source, 1983.

348 Otash: ints. 1985 and briefing on colleagues interview 1985.

348 Spindel: Spindel, *Life*, May 20, 1966; *Collier's*, June 24, 1955; *Daily News*, July 1ff., 1968.

348 Wilson: ints., 1983–86.

349 Danoff: ints. 1983/85; John Daley, 1983.

Chapter 35

350 Clay: int., 1983.

351 Close calls: int. Gloria Romanoff, 1983.

351 Greenson: corr. with colleague, Aug. 20, 1962.

352 Newcomb: int., 1983.

352 MM promiscuity: int. Dr Norman Tabachnick, former member of Los Angeles Suicide Prevention Team, 1983;

Maurice Zolotow int. Dr Greenson. Agent: int. Marty Philpott, 1984.

352 Greenson: continuation of Aug. 20 corr.

353 Doctors/nurses: Monroe's address book, in Melson files.

353 DiMaggio visit: int. Mrs Greenson and daughter Joan, 1983; Greenson, 35.

353 House: Greenson manuscript, 44; Murray, 33ff.

354 House-hunting problem: Graham, *Confessions*, 148.

354 Purchase: Murray, 49; *Redbook*, Aug. 1962; int. Milton Greene and Henry Rosenfeld, 1983.

Chapter 36

355 Marilyn prepares for dinner: int. Danny Greenson, 1984.

355 Robert Kennedy visit: Murray, 85; Los Angeles visit confirmed by corr. John F. Kennedy Library, Oct. 17, 1984.

355 Habit of note-making: int. Billy Travilla, 1983.

357 Romanoff: int., 1983.

357 Melson: int., 1983–84; original document held by Melson, copied for author.

358 Kennedy Library: corr. of March 18, 1983, from William Johnson, Research Archivist, to Edward Tivnan.

358 Stephen Smith: int., 1984; corr., July 16, 1984.

358 Kennedy, Sr., stroke: *New York Times*, Dec. 20, 1961;

Chapter 37

361 Novello: int., 1983.

361 Guthman: Maurice Zolotow int. Edwin Guthman, & *Chicago Tribune*, Sept. 1973.

361 Evans: ints. 1984/5.

361 DeLoach: int., 1988.

362 Joan Greenson: int., 1983; Greenson, 78.

362 'General': *Life*, Jan. 26, 1962, 76.

363 Litman: int., 1983; original notes and subsequent reports filed at Los Angeles Suicide Prevention Center.

363 Tabachnick: int., 1983.

363 Farberow: int., 1983.

364 Sherman: int., 1983.

364 Mrs James: int., 1983.

365 Durgom: int., 1986.

365 Dye: int., 1983.

366 Carmen: int., 1983–1986, following up int. with Los Angeles District Attorney's Office, 1982.

366 Marilyn and Benny: *Los Angeles Daily News*, Sept. 20, 1953; int. Whitey Snyder, 1983.

367 Washington: int., 1983.

367 Murray: int., 1985.

367 Pepitone: int., 1984.

368 Murray: Murray, 86; ints., 1982/83/85.

368 'Two or three times': *Chicago Tribune*, Sept. 1973.

368 Jeffries: Ted Landreth int. Norman Jeffries, 1983.

368 Culver City: int. Robert Warner, 1983, Chief Special Agent, General Telephone Company in 1962; Ted Landreth, int. former Lt Ron Perkins and Bob Conlon, former head of detectives, both formerly with Culver City Police, 1983.

368 Anne Karger: int. Elizabeth Karger, Vi Russell, and Robert Slatzer (who had talked with the late Fred Karger), 1983.

368 Hall: int., 1984.

368 Rosenfeld: int., 1983.

368 Roberts: int., 1982–84.

369 Paul: reader's corr., 1985; int. members Paul family, 1986; *Current Biography*, 1957; *New York Times*, Nov. 26, 1967.

369 Skolsky: Skolsky, 234; int., 1983.

369 Moore: int., 1983/85.

369 Smathers: int., 1983.

370 McGuire: int., 1983.

Chapter 38

371 Miller, Sr.: Flora R. Schreiber, *Good Housekeeping*, Jan. 1963; & Miller letters in Monroe archives of Inez Mason.

371 Marilyn virtual collapse: Johnson and Leventhal, 201.

371　Miller remarriage and child: *Los Angeles Times*, Feb. 22, 1962. Child: *New York Times*, Sept. 29, 1962.

371　Weinstein: int., 1984.

372　Masters: int., 1983.

372　Mexico visit: *Excelsior*, Feb. 21, 23, 27, March 2 and 3, 1962; *La Prensa*, Feb. 22, 23, March 2, 3, Aug. 6, 9, 1962; *Novedades*, Feb. 22, 23, March 2, 3, Aug. 6, 7, 9, 12, 1962; Murray, chaps. 6 and 7; Field, 295ff.

373　One picture: eventually published in *Hustler*.

373　Field: int., 1983, Field, p.302.

374　Bolaños: int., 1983; cf. Mexico visit; Mary Powers, int. Jorge Barragan and Indio Fernandez, 1984; *San Francisco Chronicle*, Aug. 8, 1962; Florabel Muir, *New York Daily News*, Aug. 8, 9, 10, 1962.

375　Photographs of dancing: Camera Press Ltd., shot at Golden Globe Awards, March 5, 1962.

375　'Drunk': *Los Angeles Times*, Aug. 6, 1962; Hudson, 104.

375　Bolaños followed up: int. as indicated; Mary Powers int. Indio Fernandez, 1984.

375　Institute: *Novedades* and *La Prensa*, March 2, 1962.

375　New check: Louella Parsons, *Los Angeles Herald-Examiner*, Aug. 11, 1962.

375　Adoption?: Guiles, *Norma Jean*, 356; *Motion Picture*, Oct. 1963.

375　Yearning for babies: int. Whitey Snyder, Marjorie Plecher, and Arthur James, 1983; Murray, 40.

375　Departure: int. George Masters, 1983; *La Prensa* and *Excelsior*, March 3, 1962.

Chapter 39

377　Hoffa investigation: Kennedy, 161, 84ff.; Sheridan; Jack Tobin and Gene Blake, *Los Angeles Times*, May–Nov. 1962.

377　*The Enemy Within*: corr. Budd Schulberg, 1984; Schulberg introduction to Sheridan; Budd Schulberg, 'The Man,' *Playboy*, Jan. 1969; *Los Angeles Times*, Feb. 11, Sept. 23, 1961, Feb. 18, 1962.

377 Anonymous calls and letters: *Los Angeles Times;* FBI documents, Hoover's O. & C. files, March 23, 24, and 31, 1961, obtained under FOIA, 1984. See also FBI file 77-51387-90; FBI file 94-37374-61, obtained under FOIA by Prof. Herbert Parmet, 1978.

378 PT 109: FBI documents; Parmet, *Struggles,* 110.

378 Adulterer: corr. FBI on letter dated Nov. 12, 1961, file 94-39374-71, obtained under FOIA, 1983.

378 Marilyn seen by Wald: int. Curtis Harrington, Mrs Connie Wald's former assistant, 1983.

378 FBI surveillance: Blakey and Billings, 376, 383; Giancana and Renner, 247ff., citing verbatim FBI documents; unpublished notes and transcripts of FBI surveillance reports, obtained through source, 1983.

378 Lawyers complain: Gage, 83.

378 McMillan: int. Dougald McMillan, 1983; Howard Kohn, *Rolling Stone,* Mar. 19, 1981.

378 Campbell discoveries: Exner and Demaris, 379, 57, 251.

379 White House logs: JFK Library; *Sunday Times* [London], Oct. 6, 1991.

379 O'Donnell: Parmet, *Presidency,* 127.

379 Kennedys in California: *Los Angeles Times,* March 23–28, 1962.

379 Sinatra break: Peter Lawford, *Star,* Feb. 17, 1976; Schlesinger, *Robert Kennedy,* 496; But see *'Johnny, We Hardly Knew Ye': Memories of John Fitzgerald Kennedy,* Kenneth O'Donnell and David F. Powers, Boston: Little, Brown, 1970, 440.

379 MM on decision: int. Sidney Skolsky, 1983; Skolsky, *Don't Get Me Wrong,* 51ff.

379 Monroe at Palm Springs: int. Eunice Murray, 1982–83; Murray, 87; int.: Philip Watson and Ralph Roberts, 1983–85.

Chapter 40

383 James: int. 1983.

383 DeSapio links: Scheim, 381; Sheridan, 530; Shlesinger, *Robert Kennedy,* 199, 204, 370ff.

384 Remodeling: Murray, 68ff.; int. Ray Tolman, 1983.

384 Otash: ints. 1983–85.

384 Theodore: ints., 1985/6, introduction by Mark Monsky, then a Vice-President of NBC Television News.

385 Jaycox: ints. 1982–83

385 Bug in Justice Department: FBI memorandum, Evans to Belmont, Aug. 2, 1961, and March 13, 1962, from Hoover's O & C files.

386 Kelly: *People v. Spindel et al.*, Indictment No. 4817-1/2 1966, trans. Kelly testimony, 2379; int. John Constandy, Arnold Smith, Mrs Kelly, and William Kane, 1983; Kennedy, xiii, 321.

386 Kelly lunch: int. Dan Moldea, 1983.

387 Shimon: int., 1983.

387 Hoffa: *Playboy* int., Dec. 1975.

387 O'Brien: int., 1983.

387 Burns: int., 1983.

388 'Checked out': int. Eunice Murray, 1982–83; Murray, 49ff.

388 Slatzer: corr. and int., 1982–85.

388 Booth/James: *Redbook*, Aug. 1962; int., James 1983.

388 Rosten: int., 1984; Norman Rosten, 97.

390 Skolsky: int. Steffi Skolsky, 1983.

390 'Lost': Skolsky, *Don't Get Me Wrong*, 234.

Chapter 41

391 Polo Lounge: Stempel, *Screenwriter*, 171; Johnson and Leventhal, 207.

391 *Something's Got to Give:* int. Henry Weinstein and Ted Strauss, 1983–84.

392 Walter Bernstein, Esquire, July 1973; *Los Angeles Times* Calendar, July 22, 1973.

393 Absenteeism: *Los Angeles Herald-Examiner*, June 9, 1962.

393 Virus: Murray, chap. 12; int. Dr Lee Siegel, 1983; *Los Angeles Times*, May 10, 1962.

393 Masters: int., 1983.

393 Travilla: int., 1983.

394   Greenson visits: Greenson bill submitted to estate, in Slatzer, 369.

394   Greenson and Marilyn: Greenson corr. with colleague; Greenson, 67.

394   Jean-Louis: int., 1983.

394   Kennedy birthday: *New York Times*, May 19 and 20, 1962; int. Henry Weinstein, 1984.

395   Gould: int., 1986.

395   Rehearsals: Greenson, 68ff., int. Fred Field, Danny Greenson, Milt Ebbins, Peter Lawford, 1983–84.

396   Gala performance: as rendered in *The Legend of Marilyn Monroe*, TV documentary by Wolper Prod., 1967.

397   Activity after gala: Flora R. Schreiber int. Isadore Miller, *Good Housekeeping*, Jan. 1963; *Los Angeles Herald-Examiner*, Aug. 6, 1962; Schlesinger, *Robert Kennedy*, 590.

398   Nude swim: int. William Read Woodfield, 1984; *New York Herald Tribune*, May 25 and 27, 1962; *Los Angeles Herald-Examiner*, May 26, 1962; *Time*, June 1962; *Life*, June 22, 1962; int. Ed Wehl, 1983; *Sir*, Oct. 1962; int. Evelyn Moriarty, 1983; Evelyn Moriarty, *Motion Picture*, July 1963.

399   Playboy: *Playboy*, Jan. 1964, 190, and Jan. 1969, 164.

399   Calendar: *Modern Man*, March 1955; Hedda Hopper, *Los Angeles Times*, Sept. 9, 1953.

399   Marilyn birthday: *Motion Picture*, July 1963; *Los Angeles Times*, Aug. 6, 1962; int. Danny Greenson; Greenson, 71ff.; *New York Daily News*, Aug. 18, 1962.

400   Stand-in psychiatrist: Murray, 107.

401   'Questions': Murray, 107.

401   Nose: int. Dr Michael Gurdin and Dr Alfred Conti, 1983; Conti bill to estate, June 7, 1962.

401   Marilyn acting: Walter Bernstein, *Esquire*, July 1973.

401   Greenson returns: int. Hildi and Joan Greenson, 1983.

401   Firing: *Variety* and *Hollywood Citizen-News*, June 8, 1962; *Los Angeles Herald-Examiner* and *Los Angeles Times*, June 9, 1962; *New York Times* and *Los Angeles Times*, June 10, 1962; *Los Angeles Herald-Examiner*, June 12, 1962; *Variety*, June

20, 1962; *Time,* June 22, 1962; *New York Times,* Aug. 12, 1962; Gussow, 243.

402 Thirty-six: 'A Good Long Look at Myself,' Alan Levy, *Redbook,* Aug. 1962; Strasberg, 155.

402 *Life:* Aug. 3 and 17, 1962.

402 *Cosmopolitan* pictures: *New York Daily News,* Aug. 1962; estate papers, in Slatzer, 371.

402 *Vogue:* estate papers, in Slatzer; *Vogue,* Sept. 1982; Stern; int. Pat Newcomb, 1983; corr. Leif-Erik Nygirds, 1984.

403 *Life* interviews: corr. and int. Richard Meryman, 1984; *Life,* Aug. 3 and 17, 1962.

Chapter 42

407 'Two loves': *Vogue,* Sept. 1982.

407 *Something's Got to Give:* Murray, 90.

407 Marilyn and Kennedy party: int. Susan Strasberg, 1983; *New York Times,* May 20, 1962; Ralph Martin, 403; int. Ralph Roberts and James Haspiel, 1985.

408 Meyer: *Washington Post,* Feb. 23, 1976; Davies, 164, 230; *New York Times,* July 9, 1976; corr. Mrs Truitt, 1984.

408 MM and President and pills: int. Los Angeles law enforcement sources, 1983.

409 Leary: int. Timothy Leary, 1983; Leary, 128, 155, 179, 191.

410 Janiger: int., 1983.

411 MM in New York: Guiles, *Norma Jean,* 370.

411 Weatherby: int., 1983; Weatherby, 151ff.

411 Weinstein: int., 1984.

411 Murray: Murray, 107.

412 Jeffries: Ted Landreth int. Norman Jeffries, 1983.

412 Telegram: Western Union message, June 13, 1962, supplied by Kennedy Library, 1984.

412 Robert Kennedy in Los Angeles: itinerary and memoranda in FBI file 77-51387-260, obtained under FOIA, 1983; Murray, 86–112; int. Mrs Murray, 1982–83; Ted Landreth int. Norman Jeffries, 1983. 409 Lawford: int., 1983; Los Angeles law enforcement sources, 1983.

414   Doctors: bills, in Slatzer, 367–69.

414   Cal-Neva: int. Peter Lawford, George Jacobs, Julius Bengtsson, Joe and Ray Langford, Clarice Astle, Wayne Ogle, Gloria Romanoff, Mae Shoopman.

416   'Complete woman': *Novedades,* Feb. 23, 1962.

416   Barris: Theo Wilson, *New York Daily News,* Aug. 16, 1962 int. George Barris and Theo Wilson, 1983.

416   James: int., 1983.

416   Woodfield: int., 1984.

417   Otash: int., 1983.

417   Abortion and Sweden: *Los Angeles Times,* Aug. 6, 1962.

417   Phone records: retired law enforcement source, 1983.

417   Selsman: ints., 2012, 2019.

418   Jacobs: int., 1985.

418   Drugs & fantasy: correspondence of Dr Brian Wells, Maudsley Hospital Drug Dependence Unit, Beckenham, England, 1986; int. Dr Guy Neald, 1985.

Chapter 43

420   MM calls: Schlesinger, *Robert Kennedy,* 590.

420   Special number: int. with Murray, 1982.

420   Phone records: retired law enforcement source, 1983.

420   Kennedy itinerary: FBI file 77-51387-260, obtained under FOIA, 1983.

420   Slatzer: int., 1982–83; Slatzer, 1ff.

422   Threat (fn.): int. Thom Montgomery, 1985.

424   Diary: Goodman, 227; Bacon, *Hollywood Is a Four-Letter Town,* 137; int. Susan Strasberg and Amy Greene, 1983–84; *American Weekly,* May 1, 1960; int. Jeanne Carmen, 1983.

425   Chasin: int., 1983; *New York Times,* July 14, 1962.

425   Field: int., 1983.

425   Bolaños: int., 1983.

425   Wofford: Wofford, 405.

426   CIA briefs Robert Kennedy: *Alleged Assassination Plots,* 132.

426   Hoffa prosecution: Sheridan, 206; *New York Times,* May 19, 1962.

426   Hoffa murder plan: Sheridan, 217; Moldea, 148. Date: Sheridan, 210–17.

426   McGrath: *Fort Worth Star-Telegram*, Oct. 1, 1978. Abbreviated: Blakey and Billings, 382.

427   Sinatra reports: Messick, 198; int. Dougald McMillan, 1983.

427   No Giancana prosecution: *Alleged Assassination Plots Report*, 132 and 133n.2.

427   Delay movie?: FBI memorandum, Evans to Belmont, July 3, 1962, referring to discussion in Los Angeles, file 77-51387-274, obtained under FOIA, 1983.

427   Greenson birthday: Greenson, 81; Norman Rosten, 101.

428   Carmen: *Los Angeles Times*, Aug. 7, 1962.

428   Roberts: int., 1982.

428   Engelberg: doctor's bill, in Slatzer, 367; Ted Landreth conversation with Engelberg's son Michael, 1983.

428   Studio bosses: int. Pat Newcomb, 1983.

428   Strasberg: int. Steffi Skolsky, 1983; *Hollywood Citizen-News*, July 27, 1962; Monica Gruler int. Mrs Rand, of Rand Travel Agency, 1983; Weatherby, 120; int. Joan Greenson, 1983.

428   Jeffries: Ted Landreth int. Norman Jeffries, 1983.

428   Marilyn's insomnia: int. James Haspiel, 1983.

428   Pier: Monica Gruler int. Beryl Brunkow and George Gordon, 1984.

429   Tahoe: int. Eunice Murray, Joe and Ray Langford, Ed Pucci, Julius Bengtsson, 1983–84; Ted Landreth int. Dora Foley and Ken Rotkoph, 1983; Sidney Skolsky, *Hollywood Citizen-News*, Aug. 6, 1962; Robert Slatzer int. Jeron Criswell; int. Paul D'Amato, 1984.

429   Aircraft: *American Weekly*, Sept. 2, 1962.

429   Flight: int. the former Barbara Lieto and Dan Arney, 1983.

430   Firestone: int., 1983.

430   Woodfield photographs: ints., Woodfield, 1984, 2001, & (corroboration) conv. Ruth Shavelson, the ex-wife of Woodfield's then partner, 2002.

431   Marilyn by pool: Ted Landreth int. Ken Rotkoph, 1983.

431   Roberts: int., 1983.

431   Hall: int., 1984; corroborated by int. Paul Sann, formerly of *New York Post,* 1985.

432   Johnson: Johnson and Leventhal, 210.

432   Monette: *New York Daily News,* Aug. 14, 1962; Allen, 197.

432   Marilyn letter: Guiles, *Norma Jean,* 376, and *Legend,* 250.

433   Ries: Heidi Sorensen, int. Pamela Ries, 1983; *Los Angeles Times,* Aug. 8, 1962.

433   Roberts: int., 1985.

433   Slatzer: int., 1983., Slatzer, 228, 233, 241.

433   Wiretapping: int. John Dolan, 1983.

433   D'Amato: int., 1984.

434   Will: Wilson, *Show Business Nobody Knows,* 316.

434   Greenson: letter to Norman Rosten, Aug. 15, 1962.

434   *Life: Life,* Aug. 3, 1962.

434   Kennedy, July 26: FBI file 77-51387-284, obtained under FOIA 1983; *Los Angeles Times,* July 26, 1962; hotel bill, in Capell, 58; Conf. Kennedy Library, 1984.

434   Threat: FBI file 77-51387-285, memorandum from Hoover to Chief, U.S. Secret Service, July 26, 1962.

434   July 30 call: police log, obtained by author, 1983; Report to Los Angeles District Attorney, Dec. 1982, 17.

Chapter 44

437   Phone friend: Weatherby, 107.

437   Calls: int. Henry Rosenfeld, Maureen Stapleton, Bob Josephy, and Lena Pepitone, 1983–84.

437   Kelly: *Los Angeles Times* and *Los Angeles Herald-Examiner,* Aug. 6, 1962.

437   Skolsky: *Hollywood Citizen-News,* Aug. 6, 1962.

437   Sinatra dinner: int. Gloria Romanoff, 1983.

437   Thompson and Styne: int., 1983–84.

438   Snyder and Plecher: int., 1983.

438   Kingston: int., 1983.

438   Krohn: int., 1983.

438   Roberts: int., 1982–83.

439   James: int., 1983.

439   Rosten call: police log; int. Norman Rosten, who thought the call was Aug. 4; Rosten letter to Greenson, Aug. 11, 1962; Norman Rosten, 120.

439   Karger: int. Elizabeth Karger and Vi Russell, 1983.

439   Slatzer call; int. Robert Slatzer, Lee Henry, Doral Chenoweth, Dr Sanford Firestone, 1983.

440   Lawford confirms: Wilson, *Show Business Laid Bare*, 86.

440   Kennedy in California: FBI report, SAC to Hoover, Aug. 6, 1962; Evans to Belmont, Aug. 22, in FBI file 77-51387-274, obtained under FOIA; *San Francisco Chronicle*, Aug. 4, 1962.

441   Bates: int., 1983; Anthony Cook int. John Bates, 1983.

441   Muir: Ted Landreth int. Elizabeth Fancher, 1983.

441   White House announcement: *New York Times*, Aug. 4, 1962.

441   Marilyn on President's visit: int. Sidney Skolsky, 1983; Skolsky, *Don't Get Me Wrong*, 236.

441   Kilgallen: Israel, 327.

442   Nursery: int. Eunice Murray, 1982; John Goka of Frank's, 1983.

442   Visit north?: int. Ed Pucci and Barbara Lieto, 1983; Ted Landreth int. Dora Foley, 1983.

442   Newcomb dinner: Pat Newcomb, *Los Angeles Herald-Examiner*, Aug. 15, 1962; int., 1983; int. with District Attorney's team, 1983.

442   Liquor order: Don J. Briggs Inc. creditor's claim on estate, in Slatzer, 366.

442   Leon: int., 1983. Career: *Saturday Evening Post*, Aug. 11, 1962.

Chapter 45

443   Carmen: int., 1983.

443   James: int., 1983.

443   Weather: *Los Angeles Herald-Examiner*, Aug. 4, 1962.

443   Murray: int., 1982–84; Murray, 123.

444   Miller, Sr: *Good Housekeeping*, Jan. 1963.

444 Jeffries: Ted Landreth, int. Norman Jeffries, 1983; MM probate file, showing Jeffries paid Aug. 4.

444 Phones: *Life*, Nov. 4, 1966.

444 Roberts: int., 1983.

445 Skolsky: int. Steffi Skolsky, 1983.

445 Flanagan visit: int. Don Feld, 1985.

445 Tiger/RFK: Schlesinger, *RFK*, p. 239.

445 Greenson: two letters, to Norman Rosten, Aug. 15, 1962, and to colleague, Aug. 20, 1962.

445 Newcomb on rage: int., 1984.

446 Strasberg: Strasberg, 113.

447 Martin: int., 1984.

447 Suicide Prevention Team: int. Dr Robert Litman, Dr Norman Farberow, and Dr Norman Tabachnick, including access to original notes and files, 1983.

448 Greenson plans: int. Hildi Greenson, 1983.

448 Murray overnight: Murray, 129.

448 DiMaggio, Jr: police report of interview, Aug. 10, 1962, DR 62-509-463; *Los Angeles Times*, Aug. 8, 1962.

449 Music: *New York Daily News*, Aug. 6, 1962.

449 Dusk: *Los Angeles Herald-Examiner*, Aug. 4, 1962.

449 Question on Nembutal: Greenson corr. to colleague, Aug. 20, 1962.

449 Drugs: Toxicologist's list, Aug. 6, Coroner's file 81128. See also police Death Reports, containing confused information; District Attorney's Report, 1982, 25; int. Dr Lee Siegel, 1983; Engelberg bill, in Slatzer, 367; Mortuary Death Report, Aug. 5, 1962, in Coroner's file.

450 Oxygen: int. Eunice Murray, 1982–83; Murray, 127.

451 Carmen: int., 1983.

451 Rosenfeld: int., 1984.

451 Guilaroff: int., 1983; *New York Times*, June 1, 1997; Wilson *Show Business Laid Bare*, 84; Guilaroff, p. 165.

451 Bolaños: int., 1983.

451 Roberts: int., 1982.

Chapter 46

453   'secrets': Guilaroff, p. 167.

453   Bolaños: int., 1983.

453   DA unable to see FBI material: int. Assistant DA Ronald Carroll, 1983; 'The Death of Marilyn Monroe – Report to the DA,' Dec. 1982, p. 2.

453   105 file: FBI releases, revealing 1955 inception of file 105-40018 on Monroe, obtained by Robert Slatzer, 1980, and the author, 1983; (31 pages) letter of May 2, 1983, to attorney James Lesar from James K. Hall, Chief, FOI Privacy Acts Section, Records Management Division; report to author by attorney Lesar, Mar. 28, 1986; letter, David Flanders, Chief, Freedom of Information Division, Privacy Acts Branch, Records Management, to Robert Slatzer, May 29, 1980; (2012 release) www.fbi.gov.

454   March 6 document: 105-40018-2, to Director FBI, from LEGAT, MEXICO.

454   'blinding row': int., Bolaños, 1983.

454   July 13, 1962 document: 105-40018-3, to Director FBI, from LEGAT, MEXICO.

457   President's movements: research of Robert Ranftel in files of *New York Times, Washington Post,* and calls to John F. Kennedy Library, April 1986.

457   Robt. Kennedy travel: FBI file 77-51387, covering June/July 1962, and consultation with John F. Kennedy Library; itinerary and memoranda in FBI file 77-51387-260, obtained under FOIA, 1983; Murray, 86–112; int. Mrs Murray, 1982–83; Ted Landreth int. Norman Jeffries, 1983. 409 Lawford: int., 1983; Los Angeles law enforcement sources, 1983.

457   Atom tests & Cuba, 1962: research of Robert Ranftel in files of *New York Times, Washington Post,* and call to John F. Kennedy Library, April 1986; *Thirteen Days,* by Robert Kennedy, New York: W.W. Norton, 1969; *The Brink: Cuban Missile Crisis, 1962,* by David Detzer, New York: Thomas Y. Crowell, 1979.

458　Field/NY apartment/surveillance: ints., 1983–86; Frederick Field, *From Right to Left*, Westport, CT: Lawrence Hill, 1983, p. 304; FBI file 100-2278-418 to 436, on Frederick F. Field.

Chapter 47

459　Call to Greensons: Greenson corr.; Joan Greenson, 82ff.

459　Smashed pane: *Santa Monica Evening Outlook,* Aug. 6, 1962.

460　Photographs: obtained by author, 1983.

460　Call to police: police log, in Sgt. Byron's follow-up Report, Aug. 6, police file no. 62-509-463; int., Jack Clemmons 1982–85.

Chapter 48

462　Ramirez: int. 1983.

462　Woodfield and Hyams: int., 1983–84; Hyams, 138; *Show Business Illustrated,* Feb. 1962.

462　Bacon: int., 1983; *Los Angeles Herald-Examiner,* Oct. 9, 1979.

463　Hockett: int. 1982.

463　Gray: *Los Angeles Herald-Examiner,* Aug. 6, 1962; int. Harry Tessel, 1983.

463　Wiener: int., 1982; *Los Angeles Times* Calendar, Aug. 22, 1982.

464　Coverage of death: Unless otherwise identified, all news events and quotations following the death are taken from coverage, Aug. 6–19, 1962, in *New York Herald Tribune, Los Angeles Herald-Examiner, Los Angeles Times, San Francisco Chronicle, New York Daily News, Santa Monica Evening Outlook, Hollywood Citizen-News.*

464　Miller comment: *New York Post,* Aug. 7, 1962.

464　DiMaggio: int. Harry Hall, 1984; int. Inez Melson, 1983.

464　Butterfly: Strasberg, 157.

465　Greene: int. Amy and Milton Greene, 1983–84.

465　Wilder: int., 1983.

465 Greenson: int. Hildi and Joan Greenson, 1983; int. William R. Woodfield, 1964.

466 George Jacobs: int., 1983.

466 Sandals: int. Sherry Houser, 1983.

466 Zolotow: int., 1983.

467 Saunders: int., 1984; Saunders and Southwood, 130.

467 Kennedy at church: Anthony Cook int. Father John Dwyer, 1983.

467 Bates: int. 1983; Anthony Cook, int. John Bates, 1983.

467 RFK and CIA Director: FBI report 77-54397-30, Courtney Evans to J. Edgar Hoover, Aug. 22, 1962.

467 JFK and drugs: *New York Daily News,* Aug. 6, 1962.

468 Noguchi: int., 1984; Noguchi, chap. 3.

468 Brown: int. Virgil Crabtree, 1984.

468 Parker: int. Mrs Parker, 1983.

Chapter 49

470 Autopsy detail: Los Angeles Coroner's file 81128, especially Anatomical Summary; int. Dr Thomas Noguchi, John Miner, and Eddy Day, 1983–84.

470 Noguchi controversy: *New York Times,* Nov. 13, 1982; *New York Times,* June 23, 1984.

471 Marilyn in death: picture obtained from police file, 1983.

471 Toxicology: Reports of Dr Ralph Abernathy, Aug. 6 and 13, 1962, in Coroner's file 81128.

472 Foster: int. 1985 (pathologist at St Bartholomew's Hospital, London, M.D., Ph.D., M.R.C. Path.).

473 Curphey: text of statement to press, Aug. 17, 1962.

473 No glass: District Attorney's Report, 1982, p. 26; *San Francisco Chronicle,* Aug. 6, 1962.

473 House sealed: *New York Herald Tribune,* Aug. 6, 1962.

473 Melson: int., 1983.

474 Note on bottle picture (fn.): photograph in possession of Jame: Haspiel.

474 Medical examiners and coroners contacted: By DA, 1982: Dr Boyd G. Stephens (San Francisco) and Dr Kornblum.

For author: Prof Keith Simpson, senior Home Office forensic pathologist, Emeritus Prof Forensic Medicine, London University; Dr Christopher Foster, pathologist and biochemist, St Bartholomew's Hospital (London); Dr Henry Siegel (formerly New York City Dep. Chief. Med. Examiner); Dr Patrick Besant-Matthews (Dallas); Prof Earl Rose (Iowa); Dr Joseph Davis (Dade Co. Med. Examiner Florida); Dr Joseph Jachimczyk (Chief Med. Examiner Harris Co., Houston); Dr John Coe (Hennepin Co. Med Examiner, Minneapolis); Lee del Cortivo (Chief Toxicologist, Suffolk Co., NY.); Dr Bertram Fuchs (gastro-enterologist, Mineola, New York).

475   Breaking open capsules: Guiles, *Norma Jean,* 344.

475   Meal?: int. Eunice Murray and Pat Newcomb, 1983–84 Slatzer in Newcomb, 1973; Murray, 130.

475   Curphey press conference: *Los Angeles Herald-Examiner,* Aug 18, 1962.

477   Destruction of specimens: int. Dr Thomas Noguchi, 1984, Noguchi, 74.

477   Injection checks: int. Dr Thomas Noguchi, John Miner Eddy Day; District Attorney's Report, 1982, 4.

477   Marilyn and enemas: int. Amy Greene, 1984; int. Jeanne Carmen, 1983 (on constipation).

479   Right-wing tract: Capell.

480   Mailer: int., 1984; Mailer, *Marilyn,* 367.

480   Messick: int., 1983; Messick, 201, 207; FBI file 44-17593, on Ratterman, Kentucky sheriff candidate.

Chapter 50

482   Noguchi: int., 1984.

482   Bacon: int., 1983.

482   Hyams: *New York Herald Tribune,* Aug. 6, 1962.

483   Brown: int. Kenneth McCauley, 'Pete' Stenderup, 1983.

483   Phillips: int., 1983.

484   McCauley request: report to McCauley, Aug. 27, 1974, by Lt. Selby, Homicide Special Section, in recovered part of police file obtained by author.

484   1975 inquiry: commissioned by Police Chief Davis, report sent Oct. 14, 1975, by Daryl Gates, then Assistant Chief, Director of Operations; report obtained by author, 1983.

484   Finck: note found in police file, 1983.

485   Gates: corr. Dec. 20, 1984.

485   Reddin: int., 1986.

485   Phillips: int., 1983.

485   Yorty: int., 1983.

486   Carroll: 'The Death of Marilyn Monroe, Report to the District Attorney,' by Ronald H. Carroll, Assistant District Attorney, and Alan B. Tomich, Investigator, Dec. 1982.

486   Dickey: inquiry's existence discovered during research in District Attorney's office, 1982; Anthony Cook int. John Dickey, 1983.

486   Hronek: int. Gary Wean and Jack Egger, former colleagues, 1983; int. Mrs Hronek and Steve Hronek, 1983.

487   'Pressures': *New York Daily News* and *San Francisco Chronicle,* Aug. 12, 1962.

488   Danny and Hildi Greenson: ints. 1983 and 1984.

488   Greenson interview: taped in 1964, in files of William R. Woodfield.

Chapter 51

489   Farberow on phone: *San Francisco Chronicle,* Aug. 7, 1962.

489   Murray: *Los Angeles Herald-Examiner* (late edition), Aug. 6, 1962.

489   Light and door: WOR Radio broadcast (11:00 A.M. Sunday, New York time); Murray, 135; int. Eunice Murray, 1982–83.

490   Clayton: int. of Murray, 1982, witnessed by Marie Pollak, described in corr., 1985 & calls 1985, 2019.

490   Turner: corr. 1983/5/6; int. & corr. 2019.

490   'Sixth sense': Murray, 134; int. Eunice Murray, 1982–84.

490   'Mystery call': *Los Angeles Times* and *Los Angeles Herald-Examiner,* Aug. 7, 1962.

490   'Disturbed': *New York Daily News, Los Angeles Herald-Examiner,* Aug. 7, 1962; *San Francisco Chronicle,* Aug. 8, 1962.

490 Ebbins and Lawford: *Los Angeles Herald-Examiner*, Aug. 8, 1962.

490 Lawford statement: *New York Herald Tribune*, Aug. 8, 1962.

491 'End of mystery': *Hollywood Citizen-News*, Aug. 8, 1962.

491 'No calls received' (police): *Hollywood Citizen-News*, Aug. 10, 1962.

491 Byron report: Follow-up report, timed 4:15 P.M., Aug. 6, in surviving police file; int. Byron 1986.

491 General Telephone employees: John Gurak and Bob Warner of GTE Security, and a retired employee, 1983.

492 Two weeks later: see also District Attorney's Report, 1982, 17.

493 Muir: Hudson, 88.

493 Hyams discovery: Hyams, 142; int. Joe Hyams and former colleague, 1983.

494 DeLoach: int., 1988.

494 Funk: int., 1983, int. Mrs Tiarks, 1983.

494 FBI report: Document 66-1700-39, ADIC (LA) to Acting Director, July 6, 1973.

495 Doyle: ints., 1985, 2006.

495 Litman: int., 1983.

495 Brough: int., 1983.

496 Tobin: int., 1983–84.

496 Kennedy and Hamilton: Kennedy, 8, 264, xiii, xiv; int. Robert Hamilton, 1984.

496 Brown: int. Virgil Crabtree, 1983.

496 DeLoach: int., 1988.

497 Reddin: int., 1985.

497 Schiller: int., 1983.

Chapter 52

498 Lawford: int., 1983.

498 Police doubt Murray: Re-interview of Persons Known to Marilyn Monroe, police case 62-509-463, Sgt. Byron and Lt G. Armstrong reporting, Aug. 10, 1962, retrieved by author from police files, 1983, ints. and corr., Byron, 1982, 1986.

500   Lawford leaves: Police case 62-509-463 continuation sheet.

500   Kennedy compound: Lawford: *Los Angeles Herald-Examiner*, Aug 10, 1962, Newcomb; *Los Angeles Herald-Examiner*, Aug. 15 and 16, 1962 (by Dorothy Manners and Alfred Robbins).

500   Farberow: int., 1983.

501   Lawford guests: *Los Angeles Herald-Examiner*, Aug. 8, 1962.

501   Naar (Joe and former wife Dolores): int., 1983.

501   Wood: int. Robert Slatzer, 1983.

501   Friend of MM: int. Lana Wood, 1984, and James Haspiel, 1985.

501   Beatty: int., 1983.

501   Winther: int., 1986.

502   Durgom: int., 1983.

502   Lawford, 1975: police report of Lawford interview, Oct. 16, 1975.

503   Lawford, 1982: briefing by official sources, 1983.

503   Litman: int., 1983.

503   Ebbins: int., 1983.

503   Rudin, 1962: Continuation page of Re-interview of Persons Known to Marilyn Monroe, police case 62-509-463, Sgt. Byron & Lt. G. Armstrong reporting, Aug. 10, 1962, retrieved by author from police files, 1983.

504   Rudin declines interview: corr., 1983.

504   Murray on Rudin: Murray, 131; int. Eunice Murray, 1982–83.

504   Lawford's explanation: Wilson, *Show Business Nobody Knows*, 316.

506   Mrs Murray and 'midnight': *Los Angeles Herald-Examiner*, Aug. 6, 1962; *New York Daily News*, Aug. 6, 1962; Greenson corr. to friend Aug. 15, 1962, and to colleague; int. Eunice Murray, 1982.

Chapter 53

507   Jacobs: int. Natalie Jacobs, 1985.

508   Concert: *Los Angeles Times*, Aug. 4, 1962.

508   Roswell: int., 1985.

508 Simpson: int., 1985.

509 Ambulance: District Attorney's Report, 1982, 16; Hunter: int. Ken Hunter, 1985, 'comatose': Speriglio, *Conspiracy*, 59; Leib: int. Murray Leib, 1985; Schaefer: int. Walt Schaefer, 1985; seven employees: int. Joe Zilinski, Carl Bellonzi, Tom Fears, Sean O'Bligh, Joe Tamowski, Edgardo Villalobos, Murray Leib, 1985–6; Sherlock: int. John Sherlock. Former Schaefer employee James Hall claimed – initially in a paid newspaper interview – that he was on the ambulance crew that night. Neither the DA's staff nor this author, however, found his account credible. int. Hall, 1986; 'The Death of Marilyn Monroe – Report to the District Attorney,' Dec, 1982, 13 on.; Hall relatives: int., Dr George Hall (father), Lynn (sister), Kitty (ex-wife), 1986.

510 Landau: int. in 'The Reporters,' FoxTV, 1988 and see 'Marilyn: The Last Word,' syndicated TV program 1993, Slatzer, p. 183, Wolfe, p.3; but see Spoto, p. 642.

511 Ebbins on Rudin: int., 1983.

511 Newcomb: int., 1983–84; Robert Slatzer int. Pat Newcomb, 1973.

512 White House log: archived at Kennedy Library.

Chapter 54

513 Wilson: multiple ints., 1983–86.

513 Otash: int., 1983, 1985.

514 Lock company: estate papers, in Slatzer, 361–62.

514 Bates: Anthony Cook int. John Bates, 1983. Also int., 1983.

515 Kennedy at church: Anthony Cook int. Father John Dwyer, 1983.

515 Price: Anthony Cook int. Frank Price, 1983.

515 Lawford on Kennedy not in Los Angeles: London *Observer*, July 15, 1973, quoting Lawford as saying Kennedy had been on the East Coast.

515 Greene: int. Milton Greene, 1983–84.

515 Yorty: int., 1983.

515 Finis Brown: corr. and int., 1983.

516 McDonald: int., 1984.

516   Dickey: briefing on District Attorney's Report, 1983.

516   Gates: Daryl Gates, Chief: *My Life in the LAPD*. NY: Bantam, 1993, p. 165.

516   Landing at Fox: int. Frank Neill, 1983, and former policeman on pension, who requires anonymity.

516   Pollard: int., 1983.

516   Murray afternoon activity: int., 1983; Murray, 127ff.

517   Murray: int., 1985 (by author for BBC and separately); and by Sylvia Chase, 1985.

517   Newcomb: int. 2021.

517   D'Antonio (fn.): int., 1983.

517   Marilyn 'expecting to see V.I.P.': int. of Dr Norman Tabachnick, 1983.

518   Wood: int., 1983.

518   Hyams, Woodfield & Phillips: int., Hyams 1983–84; Woodfield re-int., 1985, int. Phillips, 1983; Hyams, 143ff.

518   Lawford and helicopters: int. Peter Lawford, Milt Ebbins, Lynn Sherman, Sherry Houser, and other neighbors. See also Ted Landreth int. James Gavin, pilot; files of *Santa Monica Evening Outlook, Time,* Aug. 12, 1966.

519   Woodfield's earlier article: traced to *American Weekly*, Sept. 2, 1962.

519   Conners: ints., Michael and Patricia Conners, 1985.

519   Zonlick: int., 1986, Rolling Stone, Dec. 5, 1985.

520   Connelly: int., 1986.

Chapter 55

521   Theodore: ints., 1985/6.

522   Phone 'clutched': Greenson corr., August 1962.

522   Pathologists: Prof. Gee, Home Office Pathologist (UK), int., 1986; and Dr Christopher Foster, St Bartholomew's Hospital (UK), on contraction of muscles, int. 1986.

523   Holt: int., 1983.

523   Morrissey: int., 1985.

523   Butterfields: int., 1983–86.

523   Kamin: int., 1986.

523 Jaycox: int., 1986.

525 Spindel raid: Spindel, 221; int. Mrs Spindel, 1982–86; *World Journal Tribune,* Dec. 18 & 20, 1966; Newark *Star-Ledger,* Dec. 21, 1966.

525 CIA and FBI: CIA memo, Feb. 20, 1967; two FBI documents, Mar. 13, 1967 (as well as Jan. 28, 1965), obtained under FOIA, 1985.

525 Suit: Court files: *New York Times,* Dec. 21, 1966.

525 Neary: int., 1983, drawing on notes of Jan. 1967 int. Spindel.

525 Court records: affidavit of Peter Andreoli, in *People of the State of New York v. George Varis, John Connors, Richard Rutherford, Bernard Spindel,* Indictment No. 4817-1/2 1966; inventory of Dec. 15, 1966.

525 Mrs Spindel: int., 1982–86; and by Frank Capell, July 20, 1973.

525 FBI destruction: letter, SAC Paul Daly to author's attorney, Feb. 8, 1984.

525 Stream: int., 1985.

Chapter 57

533 Globe Photos: int. former executive, who requested anonymity, 1986.

533 Evans briefing: FBI document 77-51387-310, Evans to Belmont, Aug. 20, 1962.

533 Kennedy/El Paso: FBI file 77-51387 & researcher Ranftel check with Henry J. Gwiazda II, Curator of Robert F. Kennedy Collection in John F. Kennedy Library, April 7, 1986; House Select Committee on Assassinations JFK Exhibit F-624, suppressed in HSCA press handout, Sept. 28, 1978, as described in *Fort Worth Star-Telegram,* Oct. 1, 1978.

533 Syndicate conversation: FBI surveillance documents, Aug. 20, 1962, for Vol. 7 of 13 files on organized crime. Vol. 7, which originated in LA, was obtained from a congressional source.

534 Hoover letter: FBI file 77-57387, letter of July 8, 1964, to Attorney General.

535 Clemmons: int., 1982–85; (Fi-Po) *Power on the Right,* by William Turner, Ramparts Press, 1971, 224.

536 Ries: int. Clemmons, 1982–85; *Toward Soviet America* (chapter notes: Maurice Ries), Elgin Publications, California; *New York Post,* Oct. 4, 1985.

536 Alliance: int., Helen Clay, 1983, and ints., Bobbie Butigan, 1983–86; Capell files, lodged with John Birch Society, Belmont, Mass.

536 Capell book: *The Strange Death of Marilyn Monroe,* by Frank A. Capell, Herald of Freedom, 1964.

536 Engelberg 'communist': Capell, *supra.* 33, citing Senate Fact Finding Committee of Un-American Activities of the State of California Report, 1948; & testimony of Dr Oner Barker and Dr Louise Light, in Report of same Committee, 1955; and of Elizabeth B. Cohen, in Hearings of U.S. House Committee on Un-American Activities, May 28, 1954.

536 Strasberg & Rosten: Capell, 43 & 44.

536 Hoffa-Otash contact: corr. of Sept. 15, 1964, Otash to Spindel, provided to author by Otash.

536 de Toledano: int., 1982–83–85; de Toledano, *Hoover,* 309.

537 *20/20* furore: ints., Ena Riisna, Stanhope Gould, Sylvia Chase, Av Westin, Robert Siegenthaler, 1986, int. and corr. William Haddad, 1986; *Datebook* (San Francisco), Dec. 22, 1985; Liz Smith columns, *New York Daily News,* Oct. 3, 4, 7, 1985; *New York Times,* Oct. 5, 1985; *Rolling Stone,* Dec. 5, 1985; *People,* Oct. 21, 1985; *New York Post,* Oct. 5, 1985.

538 Cukor: as reported to author, 1983, by Robin Thorne, who had taken notes.

Chapter 58

541 Snyder and Plecher: int., 1983.

541 'Doll': *New York Herald Tribune,* Aug. 9, 1962.

541 Melson: int., 1983.

541 Funeral: unless otherwise indicated, descriptions are from *New York Herald Tribune, Los Angeles Times, Santa Monica Evening Outlook, San Francisco Chronicle, New York Daily*

News, Aug. 8 and 9, 1962. See also printed *Services for Marilyn Monroe* (with guest list).

542 DiMaggio/'Damned' Kennedys: int., Emily Stevens, 1983.

542 Joan Greenson: Greenson, 86.

543 'Over the Rainbow': Monroe entry, Robert B. Dickerson, Jr, *Final Placement,* Guide to Deaths and Funerals of Notable Americans, Algonac, Mich.: Reference Books Inc., 1982.

544 Roses: int. Robert Slatzer, 1985; *Los Angeles Times,* Sept. 29, 1982; *Los Angeles Herald-Examiner,* Feb. 15, 1983; *Orange County Register,* Oct. 1, 1982.

544 Cukor: Lambert, *On Cukor,* 180.

544 Lawford and Wood remains: conversation, Patricia Seaton, 1985; *People,* Aug. 1982.

544 Winters: int., James Haspiel, 1985.

544 Hefner: NPR, 9/29/201 7 & see *Los Angeles Daily News,* Aug. 5, 1982.

545 DiMaggio and RFK: Gay Talese, 'Silent Season of a Hero,' *Esquire,* July 1966.

545 Mother's letter: sent to Inez Melson, Aug. 22, 1962, in Melson files.

545 Mother's escape: Whit Preston, *Photoplay,* Oct. 1963.

545 Levathes: int., 1985.

547 Meryman: *Life,* Aug. 17, 1962.

547 'Poster People': int. Jeanne Martin, 1984.

Acknowledgements

Four years in the making when I first wrote it, this book on the brilliant, sad creature named 'Marilyn Monroe' has had its hooks into me ever since.

The work began when, in the early 1980s, the Los Angeles District Attorney announced a review of the circumstances surrounding the actress's death. I was commissioned to write a short article on the case for a British newspaper, and traveled to California. I realized soon, though, that it would be pointless to tackle the death issue without lengthy research. I also discovered to my astonishment that not a single author had attempted an in-depth examination of the actress's personal life, coupled to serious inquiry into her death and the alleged connection with the Kennedys. In 1986, after publication of the hardback edition led to an international furore, I conducted further intensive research.

Some 650 people were interviewed. I thank them all – though many must have regretted ever having allowed me into their lives. A handful of interviewees asked to remain anonymous; I agreed in very few cases, when testimony was crucial to the story and when it withstood hard scrutiny. My publishers were briefed in each instance. Neither Joe DiMaggio nor Arthur Miller agreed to be interviewed. The late baseball star never did discuss his wife, and the playwright was busy writing his autobiography.

Of those who crossed paths with Marilyn Monroe, and who did talk to me, some were especially patient with my questions and frank in their answers. They included Rupert Allan, Marilyn's press aide, her New York hosts Amy Greene and her husband Milton, her psychiatrist's widow Hildi Greenson, and his children Danny and Joan. James Haspiel, once her teenage fan, still today perhaps the most informed person on the planet about Marilyn, generously gave me access to his knowledge and his archives.

Thanks are due to the family of Fred Karger, whom Marilyn once hoped to marry, and especially Anne Batté. Author Richard Meryman, a former *Life* reporter, proved that one writer's integrity can redeem a thousand column inches of the type of nonsense so often spewed out on Marilyn. Patricia Newcomb, the last close female intimate, granted me interviews where she rebuffed others. She tried to be honest without compromising old loyalties. In 2021, during preparation of this edition, she has again been courteous – and a little more open.

Gordon Heaver and Gloria Romanoff, who both knew Marilyn, offered insights into the Los Angeles of some sixty years ago. In New York, Ralph Roberts gave me his trust and a unique tape recording, and Norman Rosten opened up more than just the safe-deposit box in which he kept fragments of Marilyn's poetry. Hal Schaefer, the quiet musician who suffered for his relations with Marilyn during the DiMaggio marriage, impressed me with his courage. Lynn Sherman brought to life for me the social games once played by the wealthy beach dwellers of Santa Monica. Steffi Sidney, daughter of Marilyn's friend Sidney Skolsky, gave me first access to her father's papers, which are now lodged with the Academy of Motion Picture Arts and Sciences, where I was received with great courtesy. Thanks to the initiative of the author Lois Banner, who has herself written on Marilyn, the recordings of most of the interviews conducted for this book are also now lodged with the Academy.

Robert Slatzer, who claimed to have been briefly married to Marilyn, took my interrogations with good humor, even though seriously ill, and proved an invaluable source of vital documentation. Neil Spotts, one of the many former police-men interviewed, opened doors long tightly closed. Bobbette Butigan shared research done after Marilyn's death, and Nevada historian Bethel van Tassel told me about the Cal-Neva Lodge. Bill Woodfield shared rare knowledge of the aftermath of Marilyn's death and – together with his wife Lili – offered warm hospitality in what can be a chilly town.

The late Maurice Zolotow's book about Marilyn, written while she was still alive, still stands as one of the best overall works. He kindly allowed me access to the Zolotow Col-lection, housed at the Humanities Research Center of the University of Texas at Austin. I am grateful to Paul M. Bailey of the Theatre Arts Library there, and to Henry J. Gwiazda II, Curator of the Robert F. Kennedy Collection in the John F. Kennedy Library, who went out of his way to give honest answers to sensitive questions. Carl Rollyson allowed me to see parts of his manuscripts, *The Replicated Life of Marilyn Monroe.* Edward Wagenknecht, a veteran Marilyn scholar, gave me the benefit of his collection of rare articles. Roy Turner, an authority on Marilyn's ancestry, and – separately – Bud Clayton, generously shared the results of their exchanges with Marilyn's housekeeper Eunice Murray.

For the third time in my writing career, I turned for as-sistance to the late Professor Keith Simpson, who was one of Britain's most distinguished forensic pathologists. He pa-tiently analyzed the medical aspects of Marilyn's death along with Dr Christopher Foster, pathologist at St Bartholomew's Hospital in London. I am indebted to the psychiatrists of the Los Angeles Suicide Prevention Team, and especially Dr Robert Litman, who allowed me to see materials hitherto sealed. Former FBI Assistant Director Courtney Evans, who had the daunting job of acting as liaison between J. Edgar Hoover and Attorney General Robert Kennedy, more than lived up to his nickname, 'Courtly.' Assistant Los Angeles District Attorney 'Mike' Carroll, who conscientiously ran the limited 1982 review of Marilyn's death, trusted me to deal responsibly with a case that had left him troubled.

From its inception, this project included plans for a television documentary as well as a book. I joined forces with Ted Landreth, a former CBS executive who tried for three years to find an American television network with the guts and the will to bring the story of Marilyn's final tragedy to a national audience. Those in power in the networks in the 1980s were afraid to rock the historical boat. ABC TV's *20/20* producers did eventually make a breakthrough program, only to see it canceled by executives on the day of transmission.

Our efforts did bear fruit, however, thanks to the British Broadcasting Corporation and independent backers from several countries. Will Wyatt, George Carey, and producer Christopher Olgiati at the BBC were especially enthusiastic. The program they made, *Say Goodbye to the President,* was seen many times across the United States and around the world. It was the last film cut by a great BBC film editor, and faithful friend to many producers, the late Ian Callaway.

I came to respect Landreth and his investigative team, especially Ed Tivnan and Anthony Cook, for their tenacious journalism. When America is poorly served by a timid establishment media, there is honor in being freelance and determined.

Almost all important interviews were conducted by myself, even when witnesses had first been approached by colleagues. However, I am indebted to researchers Kathy Castle and Gay Watson in England, Theresa Garofalo and Charlie Holland in New York, Larry Harris and Robert Ranftel in Washington, Jack Crane, Monica Gruler and Paul Hoch in California, and Mary Powers in Mexico City.

I am indebted to Lori Winchester in Los Angeles, without whose expertise many witnesses could never have been traced, and to her partner Bill Jordan, a retired Los Angeles Police Department lieutenant. They offered, virtually free, the help of WCJ Inc., which provided investigative and protection services to clients as diverse as politicians, celebrities and – in 1984 – the organizers of the Olympic Games.

Kitty Kelley, who at the time was writing her Sinatra biography, generously exchanged information. Attorney James Lesar, a master of the labyrinth called the Freedom of Information Act, burned the midnight oil on my behalf. His work paid off handsomely. Mark Allen shared invaluable FBI documents.

Cynthia Rowan once again supplied wisdom and helped construct the chronology on which the book is based. Jean Manship and Joan Withington dug me out from under mountains of paper, and Angie Carpenter looked after logistics. Angela Curtin served as vital liaison in California. In Ireland, Joanne Kett, Lesley Morrisson, and Anne Stearn coped with me during the last stages of the hardback edition. Alma Clissman, Caroline Burrell, and Denise FitzGerald helped pull the first edition of the paperback together. Marathon runner Willie Henry was again a faithful friend.

I am grateful to my then agents at Curtis Brown, Anne McDermid and Peter Ginsberg, and – especially – to the company's present president Jonathan Lloyd, who has long since been a loyal friend. My publishers and editors, Hillel Black and Brenda O'Brien of Macmillan, Joanna Goldsworthy of Gollancz, Barbara Boote at Sphere and Gail Paten and Paul Murphy at Orion, were patient and enthusiastic. Juliet Ewers, Group Associate Publisher at Orion in London, and Mara Anastas, Vice President at Open Road Integrated Media in New York, have made this new edition possible. Jo Whitford, Orion's Managing Editor, shouldered the burden of bring *Goddess* up to date. Robbyn Swan, my wife of thirty years – and my co-author on several books – has as ever been indispensable.

Heartfelt thanks to all.

A.S.
March 2022

Index

Page numbers in *italic* refer to images.